Multi-Criteria Decision Making Methods and Sustainable Applications in the Digital Age

Serkan Derici
Nevşehir Hacı Bektaş Veli University, Turkey

Vice President of Editorial	Melissa Wagner
Director of Acquisitions	Mikaela Felty
Director of Book Development	Jocelynn Hessler
Production Manager	Mike Brehm
Cover Design	Jose Rosado

Published in the United States of America by
IGI Global Scientific Publishing
701 East Chocolate Avenue
Hershey, PA, 17033, USA
Tel: 717-533-8845
Fax: 717-533-7115
Website: https://www.igi-global.com E-mail: cust@igi-global.com

Library of Congress Cataloging-in-Publication Data

LCCN: 2024055913 (CIP Data Pending)
ISBN13: 9798369387894
Isbn13Softcover: 9798369387900
EISBN13: 9798369387917

British Cataloguing in Publication Data
A Cataloguing in Publication record for this book is available from the British Library.

Table of Contents

Detailed Table of Contents

Digitalization and sustainability are two major trends creating the current period, profoundly impacting societal, economic, and environmental landscapes. Multi-Criteria Decision Making (MCDM) emerges as a powerful framework to address the complexity and interconnection of these areas by providing organized approaches for analyzing and prioritizing diverse inputs. This chapter addresses the connection between digitization and sustainability, highlighting the crucial role of MCDM approaches in navigating this dynamic confluence. Through a comprehensive introduction of key MCDM approaches such as the Analytical Hierarchy Process (AHP) and TOPSIS, the chapter illustrates their applicability in encouraging sustainable digital transformation. By outlining significant trends, difficulties, and possibilities, this chapter seeks to serve as a foundational resource for academics, practitioners, and policymakers attempting to balance innovation with sustainability in the digital age.

Multi-Criteria Decision Making (MCDM) methods have become essential in the digital era, supporting sustainable decision-making across various sectors. These methods, including Analytic Hierarchy Process (AHP), TOPSIS, and ELECTRE, offer structured frameworks for evaluating diverse and often conflicting criteria, making them ideal for tackling sustainability challenges. In smart city development, MCDM helps optimize urban planning by balancing environmental, social, and economic factors. Similarly, in the energy sector, MCDM aids the transition to renewable energy by assessing projects based on cost, efficiency, and environmental impact. Companies use MCDM in sustainable supply chain management, evaluating suppliers on environmental and social criteria. Despite challenges like data quality and criteria subjectivity, advancements in digital technologies promise to enhance MCDM's role in fostering sustainable development globally.

The global food production system faces increasing challenges to meet rising demand while ensuring sustainable practices. Achieving this requires a careful balance of supply chain factors like environmental impact, cost, quality, and social responsibility. As these demands grow more complex, effective decision-making tools are essential. Sustainable food production hinges on strategic supply chain management not only optimizing production efficiency but also ensuring alignment with broader sustainability goals. The Analytic Hierarchy Process, a well-established MCDM method, offers a structured solution for managing these complexities in sustainable supply chains. This chapter explores AHP's application in optimizing sustainable food production, showcasing case studies that illustrate how AHP supports informed, balanced decisions in the face of diverse demands. This book is an essential resource for supply chain managers, sustainability professionals, and researchers focused on integrating sustainability into decision-making.

Technological advances after the Industrial Revolution led to increased production and the emergence of Industry 4.0, which introduced digitalization across all sectors. Technologies such as cyber-physical systems, IoT, and big data prioritized cost-efficiency and productivity. In logistics, this transformation gave rise to Logistics 4.0. However, rising production and mobility increased environmental harm, making sustainability a global concern. Logistics operations, with high carbon emissions, are critical in this context. Industry 4.0 has been criticized for overlooking human and environmental values. In response, Industry 5.0 emerged, focusing on human-centered and sustainable technologies. Accordingly, the logistics sector is transitioning toward Logistics 5.0. This study aims to identify key factors for Logistics 5.0 using the Analytic Network Process (ANP), based on expert evaluations of 18 criteria derived from a comprehensive literature review.

Airports, as vital nodes in the transportation network, contribute to environmental challenges such as carbon emissions, energy consumption, waste generation, and noise pollution. Addressing these challenges requires a comprehensive environmental management approach encompassing multiple criteria, including carbon footprint reduction, energy and water conservation, waste management, and biodiversity protection. This study aims to construct integrated environmental management criteria for airports and evaluate these criteria using the SWARA weighing method. As a result of the analysis, it is found that the most important criterion is carbon emission and energy management, while the least important criterion is biodiversity management. The remaining criteria are waste and water management, noise management, and green management from the most important to the least. Emission and energ-related activities such as building on-site renewable energy facilities, using electric vehicles, and adopting green building design will greatly improve the energy management performance of airports.

Digital applications have gained importance in the finance sector with digitalization. In addition, the importance given to sustainability within the scope of social responsibility by banks reaching many branches in the finance sector is obvious. In this respect, it is important to consider the factors affecting the success of sustainable policies of banks in a causality relationship and to address important factors with a scientific method in this direction. Therefore, within the scope of this chapter, the sustainable policies of banks operating in the digital age will be analysed with the DEMATEL method, one of the multi-criteria decision making methods.

Nowadays, due to the development of global and digital factors, the activities of businesses are affected by a large number of criteria. In this period of high uncertainty, businesses need to improve their digital capabilities and implement sustainable practices. In this direction, in this study, the digitalization and sustainability components that play a role in the activities of enterprises were identified through a literature review and a unique model was developed. In the study designed as a multi-criteria decision-making problem, the nine criteria in the model were ranked using the Analytic Hierarchy Process Method (AHP), and a holistic perspective was created by determining the relationships between the criteria with the DEMATEL Method. As a result of the study, which aims to contribute to the development of a systematic approach by determining the starting point, recommendations were developed.

This study aims to determine the importance ranking of healthcare quality standards in Türkiye. The latest version of the Healthcare Quality Standards-Hospital (Version 6.1) was used as the healthcare quality standards in Türkiye. The FUCOM method, one of the multi-criteria decision-making (MCDM) methods, was employed to rank the importance of these standards. To use this method, a questionnaire based on the healthcare quality standards was filled out by six experts. The data obtained from the questionnaire were transferred to Microsoft Excel Solver, and the FUCOM method was used with this program. Using the FUCOM method, the local importance weights of the main criteria and sub-criteria were initially determined. Then, the criteria were ranked based on these weights. Subsequently, after determining the global importance weights of the sub-criteria considering the local importance weights of both the main criteria and sub-criteria, their rankings were also established based on these weights.

Today, global problems such as climate change, resource depletion and social inequality motivate the need for tools that can be used to measure the sustainability performance of countries. In this section, a new MCDM approach, RATMI (Ranking by Alternatives Trace to Median Index), is proposed with this motivation. RATMI uses trace and median similarity techniques to provide a balanced and accurate ranking as the median minimises the effect of outliers. In this chapter, the RATMI method is used to assess the sustainability performance of 157 countries for the period 2016-2020 on the basis of economic, social and environmental dimensions. The contributions of this study include the potential to promote RATMI as an effective tool for sustainability assessment of countries, identify role models, and inform policymakers on the development of sustainability strategies at the global level. This practice not only advances the literature on MCDM in sustainability assessments, but also provides a practical framework to guide future policy and research aimed at promoting sustainable development

Digital technologies are increasing their importance day by day on a global scale. New concepts have emerged as digital technologies make their effects felt on both individuals and businesses. One of these concepts is digital intelligence. In this context, the main purpose of this study is to examine the digital intelligence performances of G7 countries. Within the framework of this main purpose, the digital intelligence performances of G7 countries were determined by using the 2020 Digital Intelligence Index (DII). The current index includes six criteria: state, momentum, environment, experience, behavior and attitudes. Within the scope of the analysis, the SD (Standard Deviation) method was used in weighting the criteria and the COCOSO (Combined Compromise Solution) method was used in ranking the alternatives/countries. According to the SD method results, it was seen that the criterion with the highest importance level was behavior, while state had the lowest importance level. After weighting the criteria, COCOSO analysis was conducted and as a result of the analysis, it was determined that the country with the highest digital intelligence performance was the USA; Germany followed the USA. The countries with the lowest performance were determined as France and Italy, respectively.

Sustainable development was defined in the Brundtland Report in 1987 as "the ability of humanity to meet its present needs without compromising the ability of future generations to meet their needs". Sustainability is addressed in four different dimensions: social, economic, environmental and governmental. These dimensions create value in an integrated manner and reveal the concept of sustainable development. This study aims to evaluate the sustainable development performances of G20 countries, which are among the world's largest economies. MEREC supported

Accurate prediction of molecular solubility is essential in fields such as drug discovery, environmental chemistry, and material science. This study investigates the effectiveness of Linear Regression for predicting solubility based on a large dataset of molecular structures and corresponding solubility values. By applying feature selection and data preprocessing techniques, we optimized the model to achieve strong performance, with a Mean Squared Error (MSE) of 0.00 and a perfect coefficient of determination (R^2) of 1.00. Linear Regression proved to be both accurate and interpretable, offering valuable insights into the molecular properties that influence solubility. When compared to other machine learning methods, it demonstrated competitive predictive power while maintaining simplicity and transparency. These findings highlight Linear Regression as a reliable and practical tool for solubility prediction, with broad applications across scientific and industrial domains.

This study explores the use of deep learning, particularly convolutional neural networks (CNNs), for breast cancer diagnosis through image analysis. It highlights the importance of early detection for improving survival rates and the limitations of traditional methods like mammography and ultrasound, which often lack sufficient sensitivity. Deep learning allows automatic feature extraction from medical images, improving accuracy. The paper reviews CNN architectures used for classification and detection, noting their advantages over conventional techniques. Challenges include the need for large annotated datasets, high computational power, and lack of standardized protocols for AI-based diagnostics. It also discusses model evaluation metrics such as AUC, precision, and recall, and the potential for integrating explainable AI to enhance interpretability and support personalized medicine.

Preface

In an era where digital transformation intersects with global sustainability challenges, decision-making has become more complex, interconnected, and consequential than ever before. The need to make informed, balanced, and data-driven decisions across multiple domains—ranging from environmental management and supply chain logistics to healthcare and finance—has elevated the relevance of Multi-Criteria Decision Making (MCDM) methods. This book, *Multi-Criteria Decision Making Methods and Sustainable Applications in the Digital Age*, was born from a desire to explore how MCDM techniques can serve as indispensable tools for guiding sustainable progress in a rapidly evolving digital landscape.

As editor of this volume, I have had the privilege of working with a distinguished and international group of scholars, researchers, and professionals who share a commitment to solving real-world problems through methodological innovation and interdisciplinary thinking. Each chapter presents a rigorous application of MCDM—whether AHP, TOPSIS, SWARA, DEMATEL, or newer hybrid approaches—integrated with current technological and societal demands. The chapters demonstrate not only the analytical strength of these methods but also their capacity to drive practical outcomes, such as improving urban development, optimizing healthcare systems, evaluating national sustainability performance, and combating food fraud.

What distinguishes this book is its breadth of application and commitment to bridging theory with implementation. By covering diverse sectors and geographies, it offers readers a panoramic view of how MCDM methods adapt to the digital age while staying anchored in sustainability principles. It is my hope that this collection will inspire both academic inquiry and operational innovation, equipping decision-makers with the frameworks they need to address today's multidimensional challenges.

CHAPTER OVERVIEW

Chapter 1: Digitalization and Sustainability: The Role of Multi-Criteria Decision Making

This introductory chapter explores the intersection of digital transformation and sustainability, emphasizing the value of Multi-Criteria Decision Making (MCDM) frameworks in managing complex, interrelated challenges. It introduces foundational MCDM techniques, including the Analytic Hierarchy Process (AHP) and TOPSIS, and examines how these tools support sustainable digital innovation. The chapter provides theoretical grounding, practical examples, and insights for researchers, decision-makers, and policymakers aiming to align technological advancement with environmental and social priorities.

Chapter 2: Sustainable Applications of MCDM in the Digital Age

This chapter delves into real-world applications of MCDM methods in advancing sustainability across sectors such as smart cities, renewable energy, and supply chain management. Using techniques like AHP, TOPSIS, and ELECTRE, the authors illustrate how these tools enable the evaluation of competing criteria—such as cost, environmental impact, and social responsibility. The chapter also addresses challenges like data reliability and subjective judgment, while highlighting how digital technologies are enhancing the capabilities and reach of MCDM frameworks globally.

Chapter 3: Supply Chain Management for Sustainable Food Production Using the Analytic Hierarchy Process

Focusing on the global imperative for sustainable food systems, this chapter demonstrates the use of AHP in optimizing supply chains for environmentally responsible and socially equitable food production. Through case studies, the authors showcase how AHP can balance multiple factors—including cost, quality, and environmental impact—to support informed decision-making. The chapter serves as a practical guide for sustainability professionals and researchers in agrifood industries seeking to integrate MCDM into strategic planning.

Chapter 4: Examining Logistics 5.0 Factors with ANP Method: An Application on the Turkish Logistics Sector

This chapter investigates the evolution of logistics from Industry 4.0 to Logistics 5.0, where sustainability and human-centric values are emphasized. Applying the

Analytic Network Process (ANP), the study identifies 18 key factors shaping the future of logistics in Turkey. Expert evaluations provide insights into the priorities and challenges of transitioning to greener, smarter logistics practices, making this chapter a relevant reference for logistics professionals and policymakers.

Chapter 5: An Expert-Based Evaluation of Airport Environmental Management Criteria Through the SWARA Method

Addressing the environmental impact of airports, this chapter applies the SWARA method to rank key management criteria such as carbon emissions, energy efficiency, waste reduction, and biodiversity. The results highlight carbon and energy management as the top priorities. The chapter proposes sustainable actions like electric vehicle use and renewable energy integration, offering strategic insights for airport authorities and environmental planners.

Chapter 6: Sustainability in the Banking Sector: Determination of Success Factors with the DEMATEL Method

In this chapter, the authors analyze the causal relationships among factors influencing sustainable banking practices in the digital era. Utilizing the DEMATEL method, they identify key drivers of successful sustainability policies within financial institutions. The findings support a structured approach to integrating sustainability into banking operations and corporate social responsibility agendas.

Chapter 7: The Determination of Criteria Affecting Digital and Sustainable Capabilities in Businesses with AHP and DEMATEL Methods

This chapter explores the interplay of digital transformation and sustainability in business strategy. A combined AHP-DEMATEL approach is used to prioritize and analyze nine critical criteria affecting enterprise performance. The study develops a decision-making model to guide businesses in systematically strengthening their digital and sustainability capabilities amid growing complexity and uncertainty.

Chapter 8: Assessment of Türkiye's Healthcare Quality Standards Using the FUCOM Method

Focusing on Türkiye's healthcare system, this chapter employs the FUCOM method to assess and rank the importance of hospital quality standards. Based on expert surveys and Version 6.1 of the national standards, the study identifies high-priority areas and offers data-driven insights to support policy development and institutional quality improvements in the healthcare sector.

Chapter 9: Applying RATMI for Ranking Countries Based on Sustainability Performance

This chapter introduces a novel MCDM method—RATMI—for evaluating the sustainability performance of 157 countries. By integrating trace and median similarity measures, RATMI offers a balanced approach to ranking based on economic, environmental, and social indicators. The chapter presents implications for global policy design, country benchmarking, and methodological advancement in sustainability assessment.

Chapter 10: Evaluation of G7 Countries in Terms of Their Digital Intelligence Performance with the CoCoSo Method

Using the Digital Intelligence Index and the CoCoSo method, this chapter assesses the digital intelligence performance of G7 nations. Criteria such as behavior, experience, and environment are weighted and analyzed. Results highlight the USA and Germany as top performers, offering valuable benchmarks and strategic insights for global digital competitiveness.

Chapter 11: Sustainable Development Performance Analysis of G20 Countries Using MEREC-Based MARCOS and CoCoSo Methods

This chapter evaluates sustainable development across G20 nations using a hybrid MCDM approach combining MEREC, MARCOS, and CoCoSo. Drawing from the 2022 Transaction Performance Index, it identifies social transition as the most influential factor. The findings contribute to global sustainability benchmarking and support informed policymaking.

Chapter 12: Integrating Spectroscopic and Isotopic Data with MCDM for Traceability and Fraud Detection in Edible Oils

Bridging analytical chemistry with decision science, this chapter proposes a hybrid methodology combining spectroscopic and isotopic data with MCDM for detecting fraud and ensuring traceability in edible oils. Case studies involving sesame oil highlight how PCA, PLS-DA, and MCDM frameworks can safeguard quality and sustainability in food supply chains.

Chapter 13: Industry 4.0 Analysis and Integration of Leading Technology Enterprises in Turkey

Through a SWOT analysis of leading Turkish tech enterprises, this chapter examines their awareness and adoption of Industry 4.0 technologies. While profitability remains a current priority, the study suggests a future shift toward broader integration of intelligent systems and sustainable innovation. The analysis offers a strategic outlook for technology-driven industrial development.

Chapter 14: Leveraging AI and Linear Regression for Advancements in Cheminformatics: A Focus on Predicting Molecular Solubility

This chapter presents a data science approach to cheminformatics, using linear regression to predict molecular solubility. With high accuracy and interpretability, the model aids drug discovery and materials science applications. The findings reinforce the role of simple yet powerful AI tools in advancing computational chemistry.

Chapter 15: Exploring the Role of Deep Learning in Image Analysis for Breast Cancer Diagnosis

Focusing on medical imaging, this chapter reviews the application of deep learning—especially CNNs—for early breast cancer diagnosis. It discusses accuracy, model evaluation, and the potential of explainable AI in enhancing trust and personalization in healthcare. The chapter offers both technical and clinical perspectives on AI-driven diagnostics.

Serkan Derici
Nevsehir Haci Bektas Veli University, Turkey

Chapter 1
Digitalization and Sustainability:
The Role of Multi-Criteria Decision Making

Mustafa Kayyali
https://orcid.org/0000-0003-3300-262X
Maaref University of Applied Sciences, Idlib, Syria

ABSTRACT

Digitalization and sustainability are two major trends creating the current period, profoundly impacting societal, economic, and environmental landscapes. Multi-Criteria Decision Making (MCDM) emerges as a powerful framework to address the complexity and interconnection of these areas by providing organized approaches for analyzing and prioritizing diverse inputs. This chapter addresses the connection between digitization and sustainability, highlighting the crucial role of MCDM approaches in navigating this dynamic confluence. Through a comprehensive introduction of key MCDM approaches such as the Analytical Hierarchy Process (AHP) and TOPSIS, the chapter illustrates their applicability in encouraging sustainable digital transformation. By outlining significant trends, difficulties, and possibilities, this chapter seeks to serve as a foundational resource for academics, practitioners, and policymakers attempting to balance innovation with sustainability in the digital age.

INTRODUCTION

The fast expansion of digital technologies is revolutionizing every area of modern life, ushering in an era frequently referred to as the "digital age." This transition, marked by the widespread adoption of modern technologies such as artificial

DOI: 10.4018/979-8-3693-8789-4.ch001

intelligence, big data analytics, blockchain, and the Internet of Things (IoT), has not only transformed how industries work but has also altered societal norms and global economic landscapes (Yu, & Jiang, 2024). Digitalization—the incorporation of digital technologies into everyday processes—has become a vital engine of innovation, efficiency, and competitiveness. Yet, as communities and enterprises increasingly embrace digital transformation, the imperative to ensure sustainable practices has become more pronounced. Sustainability, anchored in the principle of meeting present demands without compromising the ability of future generations to meet their own, is a major pillar of global growth. It comprises three interwoven dimensions: economic sustainability, environmental stewardship, and social equality. The United Nations Sustainable Development Goals (SDGs) have further formalized this vision, defining a comprehensive framework for addressing global concerns such as poverty, climate change, and inequality. While digitization has considerable promise to promote these goals by optimizing resource usage, decreasing waste, and enabling new solutions, it also poses hazards, including increased energy use, e-waste, and socioeconomic inequality.

Navigating the complex convergence of digitization and sustainability demands sophisticated frameworks that can address the inherent trade-offs and synergies between these disciplines. This is where Multi-Criteria Decision Making (MCDM) appears as a key tool (Sriram et al, 2022). MCDM comprises several approaches aimed at analyzing and prioritizing multiple, often conflicting criteria, enabling stakeholders to make educated and balanced decisions. In the context of digitalization and sustainability, MCDM provides a structured way to merge technical breakthroughs with sustainable practices, ensuring that digital transformation efforts match with broader social, economic, and environmental objectives. The relevance of MCDM in this confluence resides in its capacity to address the complexity and interconnection of modern decision-making settings. As organizations and policymakers grapple with decisions that involve multiple stakeholders, conflicting priorities, and uncertain outcomes, MCDM methodologies such as the Analytical Hierarchy Process (AHP), Technique for Order of Preference by Similarity to Ideal Solution (TOPSIS), and others offer a systematic framework for navigating these challenges (Asadabadi et al, 2019). By quantifying and comparing numerous elements, MCDM enables decision-makers to combine innovation with sustainability, ensuring that digitization initiatives contribute favorably to long-term development goals.

This chapter intends to explore the crucial role of MCDM in supporting sustainable digital transformation. It begins with an overview of the underlying concepts of digitization and sustainability, investigating their connectivity and reciprocal influence. The chapter then digs into the ideas and methodology of MCDM, demonstrating its application in addressing the difficulties and possibilities inherent in digitalization. Through the inclusion of case studies and real-world applications, this book highlights how MCDM may be leveraged to guide decision-making processes, ensuring that technological improvements are implemented ethically and equitably. By bringing light on the connection between digitization, sustainability, and decision-making, this chapter intends to add to the expanding discourse on sustainable innovation. It highlights the need to adopt holistic methods that include the varied implications of digital technology on society, the economy, and the environment. Ultimately, this chapter serves as a call to action for scholars, practitioners, and politicians to embrace MCDM as a strategic instrument in designing a future that is both digitally advanced and sustainably grounded.

UNDERSTANDING MULTI-CRITERIA DECISION MAKING (MCDM)

Decision-making has always been at the center of human progress (Duan et al, 2019). From simple everyday choices to complicated strategic decisions, the ability to weigh possibilities and select the best acceptable course of action is a key part of human behavior. However, as the globe grows more linked and dynamic, decision-making processes have grown increasingly convoluted. The complexities of modern decision-making generally stem from the need to weigh various considerations, often contradictory, and ensure that the outcomes correspond with greater objectives. In this environment, Multi-Criteria Decision Making (MCDM) has emerged as a useful tool, offering a methodical strategy for negotiating such complexity. At its foundation, MCDM is about making informed judgments in settings where numerous factors must be reviewed simultaneously (Sahoo & Goswami, 2023). These criteria might range from quantifiable variables like cost, efficiency, and resource allocation to intangible ones such as environmental effect, social equity, and long-term sustainability. Unlike traditional decision-making procedures that may focus on a single aim, MCDM emphasizes the complex nature of real-world difficulties. It lets decision-makers methodically examine various solutions based on their performance across all important criteria, providing a more comprehensive and balanced evaluation.

One of the fundamental qualities of MCDM is its versatility (Sahoo et al, 2024). It is not a one approach but rather a collection of methodologies, each designed to solve certain types of decision-making issues. Techniques like the Analytical Hierarchy Process (AHP) and the Technique for Order Preference by Similarity to Ideal Solution (TOPSIS) are among the most widely recognized within this subject. These methods give unambiguous frameworks for organizing and evaluating data, enabling decision-makers to assess alternatives and prioritize them efficiently. For instance, AHP entails arranging a decision problem into a hierarchy, evaluating criteria pairwise, and computing weighted scores to discover the most advantageous alternative. TOPSIS, on the other hand, examines possibilities by determining their proximity to an ideal solution while assessing their distance from the least favorable situation (Seyedmohammadi et al, 2018).

What makes MCDM particularly relevant in today's setting is its ability to handle complexity without losing sight of the broader goals. As technical improvements speed and societal needs evolve, decision-makers are frequently presented with trade-offs that require careful analysis. For example, a corporation engaging in digital transformation must evaluate not only the financial implications but also the possible impacts on employee well-being, customer happiness, and environmental sustainability. MCDM offers a formal study of such scenarios, enabling businesses to balance competing priorities and make decisions that line with their values and long-term aims (Acuña-Carvajal et al, 2019). The strength of MCDM resides not only in its technical rigor but also in its inclusion. Effective decision-making generally involves multiple stakeholders, each offering unique perspectives, goals, and concerns. MCDM frameworks are designed to include these various opinions, ensuring that decisions represent shared knowledge and consensus (Filatovas et al, 2022). By quantifying subjective preferences and integrating them into the analysis, MCDM bridges the gap between qualitative and quantitative concerns. This makes it a valuable tool for addressing complicated, multi-dimensional difficulties where standard approaches might fall short. MCDM is not bound to a certain topic or study; its applications span a wide range of domains. In environmental management, MCDM has been used to evaluate renewable energy projects, combine conservation efforts with economic development, and construct sustainable urban planning plans. In healthcare, it contributes to resource allocation, therapy selection, and policy formulation. Even in regular company operations, MCDM helps firms optimize supply chain management, product creation, and customer interaction. Its adaptability makes it a vital tool in decision-making processes across numerous sectors.

Despite its many virtues, applying MCDM is not without obstacles (Dhurkari, 2022). The quality of findings typically depends on the quality of the data and the assumptions made throughout the analysis. Decision-makers must be meticulous in creating criteria, acquiring correct data, and interpreting conclusions in context. The increased complexity of decision-making scenarios in the digital age needs ongoing refinement and innovation within MCDM techniques. The integration of developing technologies, such as artificial intelligence and machine learning, presents both opportunities and difficulties for expanding the scope and usefulness of MCDM frameworks. MCDM offers a way to navigate the complicated environment of modern decision-making by giving a systematic and inclusive approach. Its emphasis on analyzing numerous factors simultaneously and allowing varied opinions makes it ideally adapted to solve the issues of our times. As the world continues to evolve, the significance of solid, balanced decision-making will only rise, and MCDM will surely remain a cornerstone of efforts to attain this balance.

THE INTERCONNECTION BETWEEN DIGITALIZATION AND SUSTAINABLE DEVELOPMENT

The convergence of digitization with sustainable development constitutes one of the most significant and revolutionary forces of our time (Sparviero & Ragnedda, 2021). Both notions, while diverse in their origins and focus, share a profound and growing connection. Digitalization has altered the way industries, governments, and society operate by providing novel tools, processes, and systems that expedite operations and extend possibilities. Simultaneously, sustainable development, anchored in the ideals of environmental conservation, social equality, and economic stability, tries to ensure that human progress does not come at the price of future generations. Together, these two forces offer the potential to build a world that is not just technologically sophisticated but also socially inclusive and environmentally responsible. Digitalization serves as a facilitator for sustainable development by unlocking efficiency and bringing new approaches to handle long-standing difficulties. For instance, in the energy sector, digital technology has transformed how power is created, distributed, and consumed (Hossein Motlagh, 2020). Smart grids, backed by real-time data and advanced analytics, optimize energy distribution to reduce waste and incorporate renewable energy sources like solar and wind into national systems more effectively. Similarly, digital solutions in agriculture, such as precision farming, use sensors, drones, and data analytics to optimize water usage, reduce fertilizer application, and boost crop yields, all of which help to decrease the environmental impact of farming methods. The benefits of digitization in sustainable development are not restricted to environmental effects. Social and economic factors also stand to gain greatly. In the sphere of education, digital platforms have democratized access to knowledge, allowing students in remote or underserved places to benefit from the same resources available to their metropolitan counterparts. Online learning platforms, virtual classrooms, and free educational resources are tearing down barriers to excellent education, connecting directly with the ideals of sustainability (Chen, 2021). Economically, digitalization encourages innovation, creates jobs, and fosters entrepreneurship, particularly in emerging economies, where access to digital tools can empower individuals and small enterprises to engage in global markets.

However, the relationship between digitalization and sustainable development is not without its difficulties and challenges (Mondejar et al, 2021). While digital technologies can help sustainability goals, their fast proliferation has also generated new concerns. For instance, the manufacture and disposal of electronic gadgets lead to escalating volumes of e-waste, which, if correctly managed, offers substantial environmental and health dangers. Additionally, the increased energy consumption connected with data centers and blockchain technologies, among others, raises worries about the carbon footprint of the digital economy. These difficulties underline the necessity for a balanced approach to digitization, ensuring that its benefits are maximized while limiting any unfavorable repercussions. One of the most promising characteristics of the digitalization-sustainability center is its ability to stimulate collaboration and creativity. Digital tools provide unprecedented levels of communication and data exchange, facilitating global initiatives to solve urgent concerns such as climate change, poverty, and inequality (Stankovic et al, 2022). Platforms that aggregate and analyze environmental data, for example, offer policymakers with actionable insights to plan targeted solutions. Likewise, digitalization fosters the formation of circular economies by enabling more effective resource tracking, waste management, and recycling operations. Through such initiatives, digital technology boosts the effectiveness of sustainability policies, turning lofty aspirations into practical accomplishments.

Despite these developments, harnessing the full promise of digitalization for sustainable development requires deliberate and careful action (Sharma & Kohli, 2024). Policymakers, corporations, and communities must work together to establish an ecosystem where digital innovation aligns with sustainability values (Redman, 2018). This includes building legal frameworks that support green technologies, investing in education and digital literacy to ensure inclusivity, and fostering partnerships across sectors to scale beneficial solutions. Furthermore, a commitment to ethical and fair practices is vital to ensure that the advantages of digitalization are shared equitably and do not exacerbate existing inequities. The interconnection between digitalization and sustainable development is a story of possibilities and obligations. The digital age gives humanity tools that can expedite progress toward a more sustainable future, but it also challenges us to use them responsibly. By identifying the synergies and addressing the trade-offs inherent in this relationship, society may leverage the power of digitalization to advance sustainability in ways that were formerly imagined.

THE ROLE OF MCDM IN FACILITATING SUSTAINABILITY

Sustainability has emerged as one of the most important global concerns of the 21st century (Malik, 2018). As countries try to balance economic growth, environmental conservation, and social equality, decision-makers are increasingly presented with circumstances where trade-offs must be made between opposing agendas. Multi-criteria decision-making (MCDM) plays a critical role in managing this complexity by offering formal frameworks to evaluate possibilities, reconcile conflicting objectives, and guide decisions toward sustainable solutions. Its potential to methodically address varied and often contradictory criteria makes it a vital instrument for achieving sustainability in an interconnected society. At its foundation, sustainability is about making decisions today that do not undermine the ability of future generations to meet their requirements (Thiele, 2024). Converting this idea into meaningful tactics needs a comprehensive understanding of many elements that influence long-term outcomes. Environmental, social, and economic dimensions—often referred to as the three pillars of sustainability—are fundamentally interrelated, and decisions in one area frequently have rippling effects on the others. For example, boosting economic development might provide jobs and alleviate poverty, but it could also lead to greater resource use and environmental deterioration. MCDM helps decision-makers manage these complexities by presenting a systematic approach to analyzing the trade-offs and synergies among different factors.

One of the most significant contributions of MCDM to sustainability resides in its capacity to prioritize actions based on a comprehensive review of many criteria (Gyani et al, 2022). In many circumstances, sustainability-related decisions entail competing interests and values that are difficult to compare directly. For instance, a town contemplating whether to authorize a new infrastructure project would compare economic benefits, such as job creation and higher local revenue, against potential environmental impacts, such as habitat damage and pollution. MCDM approaches, such as the Analytical Hierarchy Process (AHP) or PROMETHEE, allow decision-makers to frame such situations, assign weights to distinct criteria based on their relative relevance, and evaluate the overall desirability of each alternative (Hodosi et al, 2023). This technique not only offers clarity to complex issues but also ensures that all important elements are evaluated systematically. Another essential role of MCDM in enabling sustainability is its potential to include stakeholder perspectives in decision-making processes (Chowdhury et al, 2020). Sustainability difficulties can involve multiple parties with varying priorities, from legislators and enterprises to local communities and environmental advocates. MCDM frameworks are meant to handle these discrepancies by integrating qualitative and quantitative information from all relevant stakeholders. For example, when developing a renewable energy project, decision-makers might utilize MCDM to balance technical issues, such as energy output and grid compatibility, with social concerns like community acceptance and land use consequences. By offering a transparent and interactive platform for evaluating possibilities, MCDM helps develop consensus and foster trust among stakeholders, which is vital for implementing sustainable solutions.

MCDM excels in handling the ambiguity and dynamic character of sustainability-related decisions (Bertoni, 2019). Sustainability concerns often unfold over extended time horizons, with outcomes that depend on complex interactions between environmental, social, and economic systems (Köhler et al, 2018). For instance, efforts to prevent climate change entail considering scenarios that contain unpredictable factors, such as technical improvements, governmental changes, and global economic trends. MCDM methodologies, such as fuzzy logic and scenario analysis, are particularly well-suited for handling these uncertainties. By allowing decision-makers to examine different possibilities and change their plans as new information becomes available, MCDM improves resilience and adaptability in sustainability planning. One area where MCDM has been particularly influential is environmental management. Governments, organizations, and people worldwide have challenging choices about how to exploit natural resources sustainably, maintain biodiversity, and decrease environmental impact. MCDM provides a robust framework for analyzing solutions that balance environmental conservation with economic and social goals (Kumar, 2020). For instance, in water resource management, decision-makers typically need to allocate limited supplies among competing users, such as agriculture, industry, and urban consumption, while guaranteeing ecological sustainability. MCDM technologies can help prioritize water consumption based on criteria including efficiency, equity, and environmental impact, enabling more effective and sustainable allocation strategies.

In addition to environmental applications, MCDM plays a significant role in fostering social sustainability (Rane et al, 2023). Issues such as poverty alleviation, equitable access to healthcare and education, and social inclusion require careful evaluation of many, often competing elements. For example, while planning urban development plans, decision-makers must analyze how proposed developments would affect housing affordability, transportation access, and community well-being, alongside financial and environmental issues. MCDM offers a holistic assessment of these factors, helping to identify solutions that maximize social benefits while minimizing negative repercussions. Economic sustainability is another arena where MCDM is beneficial. Businesses and governments have continual difficulties in managing resources efficiently, stimulating innovation, and ensuring financial stability. Decision-making in these domains typically requires considering trade-offs between short-term advantages and long-term resilience. For example, a corporation contemplating whether to invest in energy-efficient technologies must compare the initial expenses against possible savings and environmental benefits over time. MCDM methods give a formal means to assess these trade-offs, ensuring that economic decisions fit with broader sustainability goals (Akintayo et al, 2024). Beyond individual sectors, the adaptability of MCDM gives it a suitable framework for addressing cross-cutting sustainability concerns that span numerous disciplines. Climate change, for instance, demands integrated measures that include energy systems, land use, transportation, and social fairness simultaneously. MCDM approaches enable decision-makers to assess these interrelated elements, uncover synergies, and prioritize actions that have the greatest overall impact. By developing a systems-thinking approach, MCDM supports comprehensive and coordinated efforts to achieve sustainability on a global scale.

Despite its many virtues, employing MCDM for sustainability is not without hurdles. The efficiency of MCDM depends on the availability of precise, reliable data and the ability to set relevant criteria and weights. In some circumstances, the lack of facts or the subjective character of some criteria might add biases or uncertainties to the decision-making process. Additionally, adopting MCDM requires specific experience and resources, which may be limited in particular circumstances. Overcoming these issues calls for continual capacity-building, investment in data infrastructure, and collaboration among researchers, practitioners, and policymakers. MCDM serves as a valuable instrument for improving sustainability by helping decision-makers negotiate complexity, balance competing agendas, and achieve consensus among varied stakeholders. Its organized method of analyzing choices guarantees that decisions are informed, transparent, and linked with long-term goals. As the globe continues to battle with serious sustainability concerns, the role of MCDM in directing decisions toward more equitable, resilient, and sustainable outcomes will only grow in importance. By integrating MCDM into planning and policy processes, society can harness its full potential to build a better future for all.

MCDM TECHNIQUES: ANALYTICAL HIERARCHY PROCESS (AHP), TOPSIS, AND MORE

Multi-criteria decision-making (MCDM) has emerged as a cornerstone in tackling complex decision-making difficulties across numerous sectors, from sustainability and digital transformation to strategic planning and resource management (Hjort & De Souza Nazareth Giorgi, 2024). Central to the efficacy of MCDM are the approaches it employs—each geared to deliver systematic, clear, and robust evaluations of options based on various and frequently competing criteria. Among these strategies, some have achieved notoriety due to their diversity, ease of application, and capacity to tackle real-world difficulties. The Analytical Hierarchy Process (AHP) is likely one of the most extensively recognized and deployed MCDM methodologies (Dos Santos, 2019). Developed by Thomas Saaty in the 1970s, AHP provides a systematic framework for arranging complicated decision difficulties into a hierarchy of goals, criteria, sub-criteria, and options (Darms, 2023). At the core of AHP is the pairwise comparison approach, which enables decision-makers to assess the relative importance of criteria and the relative preference of alternatives against each criterion. The procedure entails assigning numerical values to these comparisons, generally using a specified scale, and later computing weights that reflect the priorities of the decision-maker.

One of the primary benefits of AHP resides in its capacity to simplify difficult situations without losing sight of the intricacies (Munier & Hontoria, 2021). For example, in the context of sustainability, a city looking to create a renewable energy project would utilize AHP to analyze choices such as solar, wind, and hydroelectric power. The factors for review could include environmental impact, cost, reliability, and societal acceptance. By splitting the problem into smaller, manageable sections and employing pairwise comparisons, decision-makers can arrive at a clear and sensible ranking of possibilities. AHP adds a consistency check to guarantee that the judgments made are logical and free from contradictions, providing a degree of reliability to the decision-making process (Petruni et al, 2019). Another strong MCDM technique is TOPSIS, which stands for the Technique for Order of Preference by Similarity to Ideal Solution. Introduced by Hwang and Yoon in the early 1980s, TOPSIS is based on the principle that the best alternative should have the shortest distance from the ideal solution (which maximizes benefit criteria and minimizes cost criteria) and the farthest distance from the negative ideal solution (which represents the worst possible outcomes). Unlike AHP, which depends mainly on pairwise comparisons, TOPSIS uses a clear mathematical approach to evaluate alternatives against several criteria (Durak et al, 2022).

The attractiveness of TOPSIS rests in its simplicity and computing efficiency (Duong et al, 2021). It is particularly well-suited for difficulties involving quantitative data, because the criteria may be measured directly. For instance, while examining supply chain choices for a corporation looking to promote sustainability, TOPSIS can be used to examine issues such as carbon footprint, transportation costs, delivery speed, and supplier reliability. The method comprises normalizing the choice matrix, computing the weighted normalized decision matrix depending on the importance of criteria, and determining the Euclidean distance of each alternative from the ideal and negative solutions. This systematic procedure concludes with a performance score for each choice, enabling decision-makers to determine the most suitable option. While AHP and TOPSIS are among the most often deployed techniques, the field of MCDM covers a diverse array of methodologies, each with its strengths and uses. One such method is ELECTRE (Elimination and Choice Translating Reality), a family of methodologies that focuses on discovering and rating alternatives through pairwise comparisons of criteria. ELECTRE is particularly useful in cases where qualitative data or ordinal preferences play a big role, making it well-suited for complex policy choices or urban planning endeavors.

Another noteworthy technique is PROMETHEE (Preference Ranking Organization Method for Enrichment Evaluations), which excels at solving challenges involving a large number of choices and criteria (Ragazzini, 2021). PROMETHEE allows for flexibility in designing preference functions for each criterion, enabling decision-makers to adjust the procedure to the specific characteristics of the problem at hand. While analyzing alternative sites for a new industrial facility, PROMETHEE might analyze criteria such as proximity to raw materials, environmental laws, labor availability, and community support, offering a thorough and nuanced evaluation of options. Additionally, the Weighted Sum Model (WSM) and Weighted Product Model (WPM) are simple yet efficient strategies that rely on straightforward mathematical calculations (Williams & Cai, 2024). In WSM, the performance of each alternative is calculated as the total of its weighted criteria scores, while WPM includes multiplying the weighted criteria scores. These methods are particularly appropriate for preliminary evaluations in circumstances when the number of criteria and choices is very small.

Fuzzy logic-based solutions have also gained popularity in recent years, notably for tackling uncertainty and imprecision in decision-making (Nalbant, 2024). Sustainability difficulties often require subjective judgments and inadequate information, making fuzzy logic an invaluable tool. By describing criteria and alternatives as fuzzy sets, these methods allow for a more flexible evaluation process that allows vagueness and ambiguity. For example, fuzzy TOPSIS extends the traditional TOPSIS approach by integrating fuzzy numbers to represent decision-maker's judgments, boosting its applicability to real-world difficulties. The choice of MCDM technique depends on various aspects, including the nature of the problem, the type and availability of data, the preferences of decision-makers, and the level of complexity involved. While AHP is frequently selected for its intuitive and hierarchical approach, TOPSIS is appreciated for its computing efficiency and uncomplicated implementation. Techniques like PROMETHEE and ELECTRE give additional flexibility and are particularly effective in scenarios involving qualitative criteria or a high degree of stakeholder involvement (Rane et al, 2023).

What links these various strategies is their fundamental commitment to creating transparency, consistency, and rigor in decision-making. By providing organized frameworks for evaluating options, MCDM approaches help decision-makers negotiate complexity with confidence and clarity. In the context of sustainability and digitization, where decisions can have far-reaching repercussions, these approaches are vital tools for balancing competing priorities, analyzing trade-offs, and identifying solutions that correspond with long-term goals. The continual progress of MCDM approaches reflects the dynamic and interdisciplinary nature of the discipline. Advances in computing technologies, data analytics, and artificial intelligence are paving the way for creative ways that augment the capabilities of existing methodologies. For instance, hybrid MCDM techniques that integrate the capabilities of different methodologies are becoming increasingly popular, providing more extensive and robust evaluations. Similarly, the integration of geographic information systems

(GIS) with MCDM is revolutionizing spatial decision-making, notably in fields like urban planning, disaster management, and environmental protection (Rezvani, 2023). As decision-makers cope with the complexities of the digital age and the requirement of sustainability, the importance of MCDM methodologies will only continue to expand. By harnessing the capabilities of approaches such as AHP, TOPSIS, PROMETHEE, and others, organizations and governments can navigate uncertainty, balance varied goals, and make informed choices that drive progress toward a more equitable and sustainable future. The adaptability and variety of these strategies ensure their lasting significance in addressing the challenges of our day.

APPLICATIONS OF MCDM IN DIGITAL TRANSFORMATION INITIATIVES

Digital transformation is a notion that beyond the mere adoption of modern technology, is primarily about transforming organizational processes, customer experiences, and operational models to meet the evolving demands of the digital world. It requires a fundamental rethink of how firms work and deliver value in an increasingly linked and data-driven environment. However, the complexities and uncertainties inherent in digital transformation programs demand structured and informed decision-making. Multi-criteria decision-making (MCDM) approaches play a significant role in directing these projects by enabling firms to analyze alternatives, prioritize investments, and handle trade-offs successfully (Thakkar, 2021). One of the most fundamental issues in digital transformation is selecting where to devote resources. Organizations are typically faced with a myriad of potential initiatives, from adopting cloud-based infrastructures and automating workflows to upgrading cybersecurity measures and establishing customer relationship management (CRM) systems. Each initiative entails variable degrees of investment, risk, and expected returns, making it necessary to analyze their feasibility and strategic alignment. MCDM techniques, such as the Analytical Hierarchy Process (AHP) or Technique for Order of Preference by Similarity to Ideal Solution (TOPSIS), provide a systematic framework to evaluate these options based on multiple criteria, including cost, scalability, alignment with organizational goals, and potential impact on stakeholders.

For instance, a retail organization planning to update its e-commerce platform could employ MCDM to prioritize between modernizing its website, incorporating artificial intelligence for tailored recommendations, or increasing its digital payment choices. By evaluating the advantages, risks, and costs associated with each alternative, decision-makers can pick the effort that gives the most value while aligning with long-term strategic goals. Another area where MCDM proved beneficial is in technology selection. The digital transformation path generally involves embracing new tools and platforms to increase productivity and foster creativity. However, with the multitude of technology solutions available in the market, picking the correct one can be a daunting endeavor. MCDM approaches provide a structured methodology to analyze options based on a range of characteristics, such as performance, ease of integration, vendor reputation, and total cost of ownership. Take the example of a healthcare organization planning to install an electronic health record (EHR) system. The decision-making process would require evaluating multiple suppliers and solutions against factors like data security, user-friendliness, compliance with legislation, and support services (Shanmuganathan, 2024). Using an MCDM technique such as PROMETHEE or ELECTRE, the business can systematically rank the different possibilities and select the one that best fulfills its needs, ensuring a successful and cost-effective deployment.

In addition to resource allocation and technology selection, MCDM plays a crucial role in risk management during digital transformation programs. The adoption of new technology and processes inherently implies a degree of uncertainty and risk, whether it is the potential for project delays, budget overruns, or resistance from staff and consumers. MCDM methodologies allow firms to identify and prioritize risks systematically, enabling proactive mitigation strategies.

For example, a firm shifting to a remote work paradigm can encounter risks relating to cybersecurity vulnerabilities, employee productivity, and data accessibility. By adopting MCDM, the firm can identify the most essential risks and deploy resources to address them effectively, whether through better cybersecurity measures, employee training programs, or investments in powerful collaboration technologies (Javaid et al, 2023). Digital transformation typically demands balancing opposing agendas. For instance, while a business may want to improve operational efficiency through automation, it must equally evaluate the possible impact on its personnel and organizational culture. MCDM provides a holistic review of such trade-offs, enabling businesses to establish a balance that matches their values and long-term aims. Sustainability considerations are increasingly becoming important to digital transformation efforts, thus underlining the necessity of MCDM. As organizations seek to adopt digital solutions that reduce environmental effects, they confront the problem of picking technologies and procedures that correspond with their sustainability goals. MCDM approaches enable firms to evaluate alternatives not just based on traditional criteria like cost and performance but also on their environmental and social effects.

For example, a manufacturing company wanting to adopt Industry 4.0 technologies may need to pick between investing in energy-efficient robotics, installing predictive maintenance systems, or boosting supply chain visibility using blockchain technology (Hasan & Trianni, 2023). By adding sustainability criteria into the decision-making process, the organization can develop solutions that not only improve operational efficiency but also contribute to its broader environmental and social objectives. The relevance of MCDM extends beyond individual enterprises, particularly in the context of digital transformation at a societal level. Governments and public sector organizations are rapidly leveraging digital technologies to enhance public services, improve infrastructure, and stimulate economic growth. However, the allocation of public resources involves careful consideration of various and frequently conflicting stakeholder interests. MCDM approaches provide a strong framework for analyzing and prioritizing digital transformation programs in the public sector, ensuring that resources are allocated in a manner that optimizes societal benefits.

Consider a government planning to develop smart city solutions. The decision-making process may involve examining alternatives like smart traffic management systems, energy-efficient lighting, and waste management technology. Using MCDM methodologies, policymakers can examine these possibilities based on criteria such as cost, environmental impact, social acceptance, and scalability, enabling a transparent and informed allocation of resources (Sahoo, 2024). MCDM methodologies improve stakeholder participation throughout digital transformation activities. By offering an organized and transparent decision-making process, these strategies enable firms to involve varied stakeholders, from employees and customers to suppliers and community members, in reviewing and prioritizing initiatives. This inclusive approach not only promotes the validity and acceptance of decisions but also encourages collaboration and trust among stakeholders.

For instance, a university planning to embrace digital learning platforms can use MCDM to involve professors, students, and administrators in the decision-making process (Al-Gerafi et al, 2024). By considering their viewpoints and preferences, the institution may propose solutions that address the needs of all stakeholders, guaranteeing a successful and inclusive transition. The implementation of MCDM in digital transformation initiatives is not confined to the first stages of planning and decision-making. These strategies are equally effective in monitoring and evaluating the development of efforts. By setting performance indicators and frequently analyzing them against predefined criteria, organizations can guarantee that their digital transformation activities remain on track and deliver the anticipated objectives. The function of MCDM in digital transformation initiatives is varied and vital. From resource allocation and technology selection to risk management and stakeholder engagement, these strategies give the structure and rigor needed to negotiate the complexity of the digital age. By helping companies analyze alternatives holistically, prioritize investments strategically, and handle trade-offs effectively, MCDM helps decision-makers generate revolutionary change that corresponds with their aims and values. As the digital revolution continues to impact companies and communities, the incorporation of MCDM methodologies will remain a cornerstone of informed, transparent, and sustainable decision-making.

CASE STUDIES: REAL-WORLD IMPLEMENTATION OF MCDM FOR SUSTAINABLE GOALS

The application of Multi-Criteria Decision Making (MCDM) methodologies in reaching sustainable goals has risen dramatically, confirming its worth across varied sectors. Real-world case studies emphasize the actual implementation of these methodologies, exhibiting their potential to address complex decision-making difficulties while balancing economic, environmental, and social considerations. Each scenario highlights how MCDM methodologies enable stakeholders to evaluate trade-offs, prioritize efforts, and match activities with long-term sustainability objectives.

Case Study 1: Renewable Energy Deployment in Urban Areas

One of the most serious global issues is switching to renewable energy sources to prevent climate change and reduce reliance on fossil fuels (Quaschning, 2019). A city authority in Europe faced the difficulty of finding acceptable areas for solar energy installations. The decision involved weighing various variables, including economic viability, societal acceptance, environmental impact, and technical feasibility. Using the Analytical Hierarchy Process (AHP), the city's decision-makers analyzed candidate sites based on characteristics such as sunshine availability, proximity to the electricity grid, land-use compatibility, and probable community resistance (Mensour et al, 2019). Each criterion was weighted according to its importance, with sunlight availability and grid closeness obtaining the greatest considerations. After selecting and scoring the sites, the decision-makers found optimal locations that maximized energy generation while minimizing interruption to nearby populations. The outcome was a successful deployment of solar panels that met energy production targets, lowered the city's carbon impact, and increased community engagement. This instance demonstrates how MCDM facilitated a transparent and inclusive process, ensuring that all important elements were considered in achieving sustainable energy targets.

Case Study 2: Sustainable Waste Management in Developing Regions

In a South Asian country, a local government confronted the problem of upgrading waste management techniques in a rapidly urbanizing region (Zhang et al, 2024). The municipality needed to pick among numerous measures, including recycling programs, waste-to-energy facilities, and landfill renovations. With limited resources and competing goals, decision-makers turned to the TOPSIS (Technique for Order of Preference by Similarity to Ideal Solution) method to evaluate alternatives. Key considerations included environmental impact, cost, scalability, and public health advantages. By assigning weights to these factors, the municipality examined the trade-offs between solutions. The analysis indicated that investing in waste-to-energy plants offered the greatest significant environmental and economic benefits while addressing public health issues (Yong et al, 2019). The implementation of the chosen program led to a 40% reduction in landfill garbage, improved air quality, and created renewable energy for local populations. This scenario demonstrates the power of MCDM in directing resource allocation and ensuring that decisions are consistent with sustainable development goals.

Case Study 3: Sustainable Agriculture Practices in Latin America

Agriculture is a crucial sector for food security, economic growth, and environmental protection (Pawlak & Kołodziejczak, 2018). A cooperative of farmers in Latin America wanted to implement sustainable practices to reduce pesticide use, preserve water, and improve soil health. They faced the issue of picking the most effective interventions from options such as precision farming, organic fertilizers, and drip irrigation systems. Using PROMETHEE (Preference Ranking Organization Method for Enrichment Evaluation), the cooperative analyzed the interventions against criteria like cost-effectiveness, environmental advantages, simplicity of adoption, and prospective yield improvements. Farmers participated in the decision-making process, ensuring their viewpoints were included. The analysis indicated that adopting drip irrigation delivered the highest return on investment while conserving water and boosting crop production. Supported by funding and training programs, the cooperative effectively adopted this technology, producing a 30% boost in output and a considerable reduction in water use. This case highlights how MCDM helps communities to make educated, participatory decisions that drive sustainability.

Case Study 4: Corporate Sustainability Strategy at a Global Retailer

A multinational retail corporation aimed to integrate sustainability into its supply chain operations (Naidoo & Gasparatos, 2018). The goal was to reduce carbon emissions, improve supplier compliance with environmental regulations, and boost resource efficiency. The organization employed a hybrid MCDM technique, incorporating AHP and fuzzy logic, to evaluate supplier performance and prioritize sustainability activities. Criteria for supplier evaluation included carbon footprint, waste management methods, labor standards, and cost efficiency. By adopting MCDM, the organization assessed suppliers based on their overall sustainability performance and identified areas for improvement. Simultaneously, it analyzed prospective initiatives, such as adopting circular supply chain models, investing in green logistics, and deploying renewable energy solutions in warehouses. The investigation led to a complete sustainability strategy that lowered supply chain emissions by 25%, boosted supplier compliance rates, and improved the company's brand reputation (Quintana-García et al, 2021). This instance shows how MCDM enables organizations to connect their operations with sustainability goals while preserving competitiveness.

Case Study 5: Urban Mobility Planning in a Growing Metropolis

Rapid urbanization has made efficient and sustainable transportation systems a priority for cities globally. A booming metropolis in Southeast Asia faced issues in managing traffic congestion, lowering greenhouse gas emissions, and boosting accessibility. The local government needed to select between extending public transit networks, adopting bike-sharing programs, or creating electric vehicle (EV) infrastructure. Using ELECTRE (Elimination and Choice Translating Reality), decision-makers analyzed the solutions against factors such as cost, environmental impact, practicality, and public approval. The analysis found that extending public transit networks offered the most substantial benefits in lowering congestion and pollution while addressing the requirements of a varied population. By promoting this effort, the city increased public transit ridership by 35%, lowered emissions by 20%, and enhanced the quality of life for inhabitants. This study highlights the crucial significance of MCDM in urban planning and the quest for sustainable mobility solutions.

Case Study 6: Renewable Energy Policy Development in a Nordic Country

A Nordic country intending to attain carbon neutrality by 2050 requires a comprehensive renewable energy program (Wråke et al, 2021). Policymakers faced considerations on financing allocations for wind energy, solar energy, and hydroelectric power. Each option presented unique advantages and challenges, needing a balanced approach to policy formation. Using MCDM methodologies, including AHP and Delphi methods, the government engaged experts and stakeholders to analyze the possibilities. Criteria included energy output potential, cost per megawatt-hour, environmental impact, and social acceptance. The analysis found that emphasizing wind and solar energy expenditures would give the most cost-effective and scalable strategies for reaching carbon neutrality. The ensuing policy led to expanded renewable energy capacity, reduced dependency on fossil fuels, and considerable progress toward national climate targets. This scenario demonstrates the significance of MCDM in designing policies that balance varied perspectives and produce sustainable outcomes.

Lessons from the Case Studies

Across these case studies, numerous common features appear. MCDM provides a formal and clear framework for tackling complicated decision-making difficulties (Sahoo et al, 2023). By embracing varied criteria and engaging stakeholders, it ensures that decisions are well-informed and aligned with sustainable goals. Second, the flexibility of MCDM approaches permits their application across sectors and scales, from local communities and organizations to national governments. Whether choosing technology, allocating resources, or formulating policies, MCDM promotes holistic evaluations and intelligent prioritizing. The combination of MCDM with participatory techniques promotes the validity and acceptance of judgments. By incorporating stakeholders in the decision-making process, MCDM builds collaboration and trust, supporting successful implementation and long-term sustainability. The real-world applications of MCDM for sustainable goals reveal its revolutionary potential in solving global concerns. As companies and governments navigate the complexity of the digital era, the continuous adoption of MCDM methodologies will be important for establishing a sustainable and inclusive future.

FUTURE TRENDS AND CHALLENGES IN DIGITALIZATION AND SUSTAINABILITY WITH MCDM

The convergence of digitization and sustainability is one of the most critical frontiers of innovation and advancement in the 21st century. As societies seek greener practices and harness digital technologies to address environmental, social, and economic challenges, Multi-Criteria Decision Making (MCDM) emerges as a vital tool for navigating this developing landscape. While MCDM techniques offer unique capabilities in balancing competing objectives, their application in future situations will be molded by new trends and ongoing obstacles.

Emerging Trends in Digitalization and Sustainability

The rapid speed of technological innovation is altering the way sustainability goals are tackled. Several significant themes are likely to influence the deployment of MCDM in this context:

1. Integration of Artificial Intelligence (AI) with MCDM: AI technologies are rapidly being linked with MCDM approaches to boost decision-making accuracy and efficiency (Nguyen et al, 2024). Machine learning algorithms can examine enormous information to adjust criteria weighting and simulate outcomes across various situations. For instance, AI can facilitate real-time revisions in criteria for sustainable urban planning, allowing stakeholders to adapt decisions to changing conditions. This combination of AI and MCDM is predicted to transform sectors such as energy management, disaster response, and resource allocation.
2. Blockchain for Transparency and Accountability: Blockchain technology is emerging as a method to enhance the transparency and accountability of decision-making processes (Theodorakopoulos et al, 2024). By storing criteria, weights, and results on an immutable ledger, stakeholders can ensure that MCDM applications in sustainability projects remain fair and transparent. This is particularly applicable in sectors such as carbon credit trading and supply chain management, where accountability is critical to achieving trust and compliance.
3. Focus on Circular Economies: The transition from linear to circular economic models is gaining popularity worldwide (Hopkinson et al, 2018). MCDM methodologies are well-suited for evaluating plans that prioritize resource efficiency, waste reduction, and product lifecycle management. For instance, firms can use MCDM to assess the environmental advantages of recycling activities against financial constraints, supporting more sustainable production and consumption patterns.
4. Global Collaboration through Digital Platforms: The rising reliance on digital platforms permits unprecedented levels of global collaboration (Gawer, 2022). Cloud-based MCDM solutions enhance cross-border engagement in sustainability projects, allowing experts and stakeholders from varied areas to provide insights. This trend fits with the United Nations' Sustainable Development Goals (SDGs), which encourage international cooperation to solve shared concerns such as climate change and biodiversity loss.
5. Decentralized Decision-Making Models: As businesses and communities embrace decentralized governance models, MCDM will play a vital role in guaranteeing inclusivity and fairness. By combining participatory methodologies, MCDM can assist balance varied stakeholder priorities, creating consensus and shared responsibility in sustainability programs.

Challenges in Applying MCDM to Future Scenarios

Despite its potential, the implementation of MCDM in digitization and sustainability is not without difficulties. These obstacles must be solved to fully utilize the benefits of MCDM in crafting a sustainable future.

1. Complexity of Criteria and Data Overload: The increased complexity of sustainability concerns means that decision-making criteria are becoming increasingly multidimensional (Carli et al, 2018). For example, reconciling biodiversity conservation with economic development includes analyzing multiple interdependent aspects. Furthermore, the volume of data generated by digital technology might overwhelm decision-makers, leading to analysis paralysis. Developing efficient methodologies for criterion selection and data synthesis will be vital.
2. Ethical and Social Considerations: Decisions in sustainability often have far-reaching social and ethical outcomes (Sheehy & Farneti, 2021). For instance, the preference for particular energy sources over others might affect minority groups disproportionately. MCDM approaches must grow to incorporate ethical issues openly, ensuring that decisions maintain values of equity and justice.
3. Dynamic and Uncertain Environments: Sustainability concerns are essentially dynamic, with factors such as climate change and technological changes generating significant unpredictability. Traditional MCDM approaches may struggle to adapt to quickly changing conditions (Alshamsi et al, 2023). Enhancing the flexibility and resilience of these methods will be crucial, potentially through scenario analysis and predictive modeling.
4. Digital Divide and Access Inequality: While digitalization offers various benefits, it also exacerbates disparities in access to technology and information. The digital divide can limit the effective deployment of MCDM in underrepresented or resource-constrained regions. Addressing these discrepancies would need investments in digital infrastructure, capacity building, and inclusive policies.
5. Resistance to Change: Implementing MCDM-driven methods frequently needs organizational and cultural transformations. Resistance to change, whether due to inertia or vested interests, can inhibit progress. Overcoming this obstacle will include establishing a culture of transparency, collaboration, and adaptability.
6. Balancing Local and Global Perspectives: Sustainability programs must reconcile local demands with global priorities. For example, measures to fight deforestation in one region may conflict with international trade aims. MCDM approaches must be modified to resolve these contradictions, ensuring that decisions accord with global sustainability goals while respecting local settings.

The Future Ahead

Looking to the future, the integration of MCDM with digitalization and sustainability will require a concerted effort by scholars, policymakers, and practitioners. Several ways can help overcome hurdles and magnify the influence of MCDM in attaining sustainable development:

1. Advancing Research and Innovation: Continued research into MCDM approaches will be vital for resolving rising difficulties (Sahoo & Goswami, 2023). This includes investigating hybrid approaches that incorporate various strategies, as well as building algorithms that account for uncertainty and interdependencies.
2. Strengthening Education and Capacity Building: Building awareness and expertise in MCDM techniques is vital for empowering decision-makers across industries. Educational programs, workshops, and online resources can increase capacity and ensure that stakeholders are equipped to utilize MCDM efficiently.
3. Promoting Collaboration and Knowledge Sharing: Collaboration between academics, industry, and government will encourage innovation and dissemination of best practices. Platforms for knowledge sharing can ease the exchange of thoughts and enhance collective problem-solving.
4. Prioritizing Ethics and Equity: Embedding ethical issues into MCDM frameworks will ensure that judgments support fairness and inclusivity. This entails involving different stakeholders and addressing the needs of vulnerable populations.
5. Leveraging Technology for Scalability: Digital technologies and platforms can enhance the scalability and accessibility of MCDM applications. For example, cloud-based systems and mobile apps can support decision-making in remote and resource-constrained contexts.

The future of digitalization and sustainability is intrinsically related to the ability to make educated and balanced decisions. MCDM offers a powerful framework for negotiating the intricacies of this shifting ecosystem, enabling stakeholders to prioritize activities that line with long-term sustainability goals (Collins, 2022). By addressing emerging trends and resolving difficulties, MCDM may play a revolutionary role in crafting a sustainable and equitable future for all. The journey ahead requires innovation, collaboration, and a persistent commitment to sustainable principles, ensuring that digitization becomes a driver for positive change rather than a hindrance to development.

CONCLUSION

The digital age has unmatched prospects to change businesses, improve quality of life, and drive economic growth. However, this transition must be led by principles of sustainability to guarantee that progress today does not undermine the well-being of future generations. Multi-criteria decision-making (MCDM) has shown to be a vital tool in tackling the complexity inherent in balancing digitization with sustainable growth. Through its organized approach, MCDM enables stakeholders to assess varied and often conflicting factors, enabling better informed and equitable decisions. Techniques such as the Analytical Hierarchy Process (AHP), TOPSIS, and others empower decision-makers to prioritize sustainability alongside innovation, linking digital transformation efforts with global Sustainable Development Goals (SDGs). The analysis of real-world case studies in this chapter underlines the practical relevance of MCDM in designing solutions that are not only technologically advanced but also environmentally responsible and socially inclusive. Despite its potential, obstacles exist in the use of MCDM in the quickly expanding digital context. The dynamic nature of technological breakthroughs, along with the complexity of sustainability criteria, needs continual refining and adaption of decision-making frameworks. Furthermore, the integration of MCDM with emerging technologies like as artificial intelligence, machine learning, and blockchain offers enormous potential for better decision-making processes but also involves rigorous ethical and practical considerations.

Looking ahead, the involvement of politicians, industry leaders, and academic researchers is important in establishing a culture where digital innovation is seamlessly integrated with sustainability. By embracing MCDM as a cornerstone of strategic planning, stakeholders can pass through the delicate junction of these two domains, paving the way for a future that is both digitally enabled and environmentally sustainable. This chapter contributes to the expanding discourse on using decision-making frameworks for sustainable digitalization and serves as a call to action for the global community to prioritize holistic, inclusive, and forward-thinking methods. Only by understanding and tackling the numerous difficulties of our period can we harness the full promise of digitalization as a driver for sustainable growth.

REFERENCES

Acuña-Carvajal, F., Pinto-Tarazona, L., López-Ospina, H., Barros-Castro, R., Quezada, L., & Palacio, K. (2019). An integrated method to plan, structure and validate a business strategy using fuzzy DEMATEL and the balanced scorecard. *Expert Systems with Applications*, *122*, 351–368. DOI: 10.1016/j.eswa.2019.01.030

Akintayo, B. D., Babatunde, O. M., & Olanrewaju, O. A. (2024). Comparative Analysis of Cement Production Methods Using a Life Cycle Assessment and a Multicriteria Decision-Making Approach. *Sustainability (Basel)*, *16*(2), 484. DOI: 10.3390/su16020484

Al-Gerafi, M. A., Goswami, S. S., Khan, M. A., Naveed, Q. N., Lasisi, A., AlMohimeed, A., & Elaraby, A. (2024). Designing of an effective e-learning website using inter-valued fuzzy hybrid MCDM concept: A pedagogical approach. *Alexandria Engineering Journal*, *97*, 61–87. DOI: 10.1016/j.aej.2024.04.012

Alshamsi, A. M., El-Kassabi, H., Serhani, M. A., & Bouhaddioui, C. (2023). A multi-criteria decision-making (MCDM) approach for data-driven distance learning recommendations. *Education and Information Technologies*, *28*(8), 10421–10458. DOI: 10.1007/s10639-023-11589-9 PMID: 36718426

Asadabadi, M. R., Chang, E., & Saberi, M. (2019). Are MCDM methods useful? A critical review of analytic hierarchy process (AHP) and analytic network process (ANP). *Cogent Engineering*, *6*(1), 1623153. DOI: 10.1080/23311916.2019.1623153

Bertoni, M. (2019). Multi-criteria decision making for sustainability and value assessment in early PSS design. *Sustainability (Basel)*, *11*(7), 1952. DOI: 10.3390/su11071952

Carli, R., Dotoli, M., & Pellegrino, R. (2018). Multi-criteria decision-making for sustainable metropolitan cities assessment. *Journal of Environmental Management*, *226*, 46–61. DOI: 10.1016/j.jenvman.2018.07.075 PMID: 30107310

Chen, F. H. (2021). Sustainable education through e-learning: The case study of ilearn2. 0. *Sustainability (Basel)*, *13*(18), 10186. DOI: 10.3390/su131810186

Chowdhury, P., & Paul, S. K. (2020). Applications of MCDM methods in research on corporate sustainability: A systematic literature review. *Management of Environmental Quality*, *31*(2), 385–405. DOI: 10.1108/MEQ-12-2019-0284

Collins, B. C. (2022). *Game Theory, Multiple-Criteria Decision Making, and Sustainability Focused Decisions for Mineral Development*. McGill University.

Darms, I. (2023). Fuzzy Analytic Hierarchy Process Utilization in Government Projects: A Systematic Review of Implementation Processes.

Dhurkari, R. K. (2022). MCDM methods: Practical difficulties and future directions for improvement. *Operations Research*, *56*(4), 2221–2233. DOI: 10.1051/ro/2022060

Dos Santos, P. H., Neves, S. M., Sant'Anna, D. O., De Oliveira, C. H., & Carvalho, H. D. (2019). The analytic hierarchy process supporting decision making for sustainable development: An overview of applications. *Journal of Cleaner Production*, *212*, 119–138. DOI: 10.1016/j.jclepro.2018.11.270

Duan, Y., Edwards, J. S., & Dwivedi, Y. K. (2019). Artificial intelligence for decision making in the era of Big Data–evolution, challenges and research agenda. *International Journal of Information Management*, *48*, 63–71. DOI: 10.1016/j.ijinfomgt.2019.01.021

Duong, T. T. T., & Thao, N. X. (2021). TOPSIS model based on entropy and similarity measure for market segment selection and evaluation. *Asian Journal of Economics and Banking*, *5*(2), 194–203. DOI: 10.1108/AJEB-12-2020-0106

Durak, İ., Arslan, H. M., & Özdemir, Y. (2022). Application of AHP–TOPSIS methods in technopark selection of technology companies: Turkish case. *Technology Analysis and Strategic Management*, *34*(10), 1109–1123. DOI: 10.1080/09537325.2021.1925242

Filatovas, E., Marcozzi, M., Mostarda, L., & Paulavičius, R. (2022). A MCDM-based framework for blockchain consensus protocol selection. *Expert Systems with Applications*, *204*, 117609. DOI: 10.1016/j.eswa.2022.117609

Gawer, A. (2022). Digital platforms and ecosystems: Remarks on the dominant organizational forms of the digital age. *Innovation (North Sydney, N.S.W.)*, *24*(1), 110–124. DOI: 10.1080/14479338.2021.1965888

Gyani, J., Ahmed, A., & Haq, M. A. (2022). MCDM and various prioritization methods in AHP for CSS: A comprehensive review. *IEEE Access : Practical Innovations, Open Solutions*, *10*, 33492–33511. DOI: 10.1109/ACCESS.2022.3161742

Hasan, A. M., & Trianni, A. (2023). Boosting the adoption of industrial energy efficiency measures through Industry 4.0 technologies to improve operational performance. *Journal of Cleaner Production*, *425*, 138597. DOI: 10.1016/j.jclepro.2023.138597

Hjort, J., & De Souza Nazareth Giorgi, R. (2024). Multi-Criteria Decision Analysis as a Supporting Tool for Decision-Making in Construction Projects.

Hodosi, G., Sule, E., & Bodis, T. (2023, November). MULTI-CRITERIA DECISION MAKING: A COMPARATIVE ANALYSIS. In Economic and Social Development (Book of Proceedings), 103rd International Scientific Conference on Economic and Social Development (p. 81).

Hopkinson, P., Zils, M., Hawkins, P., & Roper, S. (2018). Managing a complex global circular economy business model: Opportunities and challenges. *California Management Review*, *60*(3), 71–94. DOI: 10.1177/0008125618764692

Hossein Motlagh, N., Mohammadrezaei, M., Hunt, J., & Zakeri, B. (2020). Internet of Things (IoT) and the energy sector. *Energies*, *13*(2), 494. DOI: 10.3390/en13020494

Javaid, M., Khan, S., Haleem, A., & Rab, S. (2023). Adoption of modern technologies for implementing industry 4.0: An integrated MCDM approach. *Benchmarking*, *30*(10), 3753–3790. DOI: 10.1108/BIJ-01-2021-0017

Köhler, J., De Haan, F., Holtz, G., Kubeczko, K., Moallemi, E. A., Papachristos, G., & Chappin, E. (2018). Modelling sustainability transitions: an assessment of approaches and challenges.

Kumar, A., & A, R. (2020). An MCDM framework for assessment of social sustainability indicators of the freight transport industry under uncertainty. A multi-company perspective. *Journal of Enterprise Information Management*, *33*(5), 1023–1058. DOI: 10.1108/JEIM-09-2019-0272

Malik, R. S. (2018). Educational challenges in 21st century and sustainable development. *Journal of Sustainable Development Education and Research*, *2*(1), 9–20. DOI: 10.17509/jsder.v2i1.12266

Mensour, O. N., El Ghazzani, B., Hlimi, B., & Ihlal, A. (2019). A geographical information system-based multi-criteria method for the evaluation of solar farms locations: A case study in Souss-Massa area, southern Morocco. *Energy*, *182*, 900–919. DOI: 10.1016/j.energy.2019.06.063

Mondejar, M. E., Avtar, R., Diaz, H. L. B., Dubey, R. K., Esteban, J., Gómez-Morales, A., Hallam, B., Mbungu, N. T., Okolo, C. C., Prasad, K. A., She, Q., & Garcia-Segura, S. (2021). Digitalization to achieve sustainable development goals: Steps towards a Smart Green Planet. *The Science of the Total Environment*, *794*, 148539. DOI: 10.1016/j.scitotenv.2021.148539 PMID: 34323742

Munier, N., & Hontoria, E. (2021). *Uses and Limitations of the AHP Method*. Springer International Publishing. DOI: 10.1007/978-3-030-60392-2

Naidoo, M., & Gasparatos, A. (2018). Corporate environmental sustainability in the retail sector: Drivers, strategies and performance measurement. *Journal of Cleaner Production, 203*, 125–142. DOI: 10.1016/j.jclepro.2018.08.253

Nalbant, K. G. (2024). The interaction of fuzzy logic with machine learning and artificial intelligence in decision-making models. In *Decision-Making Models* (pp. 563–571). Academic Press. DOI: 10.1016/B978-0-443-16147-6.00006-2

Nguyen, T. M. H., Nguyen, V. P., & Nguyen, D. T. (2024). A new hybrid Pythagorean fuzzy AHP and COCOSO MCDM based approach by adopting artificial intelligence technologies. *Journal of Experimental & Theoretical Artificial Intelligence, 36*(7), 1279–1305. DOI: 10.1080/0952813X.2022.2143908

Pawlak, K., & Kołodziejczak, M. (2020). The role of agriculture in ensuring food security in developing countries: Considerations in the context of the problem of sustainable food production. *Sustainability (Basel), 12*(13), 5488. DOI: 10.3390/su12135488

Petruni, A., Giagloglou, E., Douglas, E., Geng, J., Leva, M. C., & Demichela, M. (2019). Applying Analytic Hierarchy Process (AHP) to choose a human factors technique: Choosing the suitable Human Reliability Analysis technique for the automotive industry. *Safety Science, 119*, 229–239. DOI: 10.1016/j.ssci.2017.05.007

Quaschning, V. V. (2019). *Renewable energy and climate change*. John Wiley & Sons.

Quintana-García, C., Benavides-Chicón, C. G., & Marchante-Lara, M. (2021). Does a green supply chain improve corporate reputation? Empirical evidence from European manufacturing sectors. *Industrial Marketing Management, 92*, 344–353. DOI: 10.1016/j.indmarman.2019.12.011

Ragazzini, A. (2021). R&D Project Selection Problem: An analysis and application of AHP and PROMETHEE (Doctoral dissertation, Politecnico di Torino).

Rane, N., Achari, A., & Choudhary, S. (2023). Multi-Criteria Decision-Making (MCDM) as a powerful tool for sustainable development: Effective applications of AHP, FAHP, TOPSIS, ELECTRE, and VIKOR in sustainability. *International Research Journal of Modernization in Engineering Technology and Science, 5*(4), 2654–2670.

Redman, A. (2018). Harnessing the Sustainable Development Goals for businesses: A progressive framework for action. *Business Strategy & Development, 1*(4), 230–243. DOI: 10.1002/bsd2.33

Rezvani, S. M., Falcão, M. J., Komljenovic, D., & de Almeida, N. M. (2023). A systematic literature review on urban resilience enabled with asset and disaster risk management approaches and GIS-based decision support tools. *Applied Sciences (Basel, Switzerland), 13*(4), 2223. DOI: 10.3390/app13042223

Sahoo, S. K., Choudhury, B. B., & Dhal, P. R. (2024). A bibliometric analysis of material selection using MCDM methods: Trends and insights. *Spectrum of Mechanical Engineering and Operational Research, 1*(1), 189–205. DOI: 10.31181/smeor11202417

Sahoo, S. K., & Goswami, S. S. (2023). A comprehensive review of multiple criteria decision-making (MCDM) Methods: Advancements, applications, and future directions. *Decision Making Advances, 1*(1), 25–48. DOI: 10.31181/dma1120237

Sahoo, S. K., & Goswami, S. S. (2024). Green supplier selection using MCDM: A comprehensive review of recent studies. *Spectrum of Engineering and Management Sciences, 2*(1), 1–16. DOI: 10.31181/sems1120241a

Seyedmohammadi, J., Sarmadian, F., Jafarzadeh, A. A., Ghorbani, M. A., & Shahbazi, F. (2018). Application of SAW, TOPSIS and fuzzy TOPSIS models in cultivation priority planning for maize, rapeseed and soybean crops. *Geoderma, 310*, 178–190. DOI: 10.1016/j.geoderma.2017.09.012

Shanmuganathan, M. P. (2024). A Strategic Decision Analysis Framework for Software-as-a-Service Selection: A Systematic Data-Driven Approach (Master's thesis, University of Twente).

Sharma, R. C., & Kohli, D. (2024). Embracing digital transformation for sustainable development: The synergy between learning organizations, human resource management, and service quality. *Journal of Chinese Human Resource Management, 14*(3), 3–17. DOI: 10.47297/wspchrmWSP2040-800501.20231403

Sheehy, B., & Farneti, F. (2021). Corporate social responsibility, sustainability, sustainable development and corporate sustainability: What is the difference, and does it matter? *Sustainability (Basel), 13*(11), 5965. DOI: 10.3390/su13115965

Sparviero, S., & Ragnedda, M. (2021). Towards digital sustainability: The long journey to the sustainable development goals 2030. Digital Policy. *Regulation & Governance, 23*(3), 216–228. DOI: 10.1108/DPRG-01-2021-0015

Sriram, S., Ramachandran, M., Chinnasamy, S., & Mathivanan, G. (2022). A review on multi-criteria decision-making and its application. REST Journal on Emerging trends in Modelling and Manufacturing, 7(4), 101-107.

Stankovic, M., Neftenov, N., & Gupta, R. (2022). Use of Digital Tools in Fighting Climate Change: A Review of Best Practices. Availabe online: https://bit. ly/3Gxodt6 (accessed on 21 October).

Thakkar, J. J. (2021). *Multi-criteria decision making* (Vol. 336). Springer. DOI: 10.1007/978-981-33-4745-8

Theodorakopoulos, L., Theodoropoulou, A., & Halkiopoulos, C. (2024). Enhancing Decentralized Decision-Making with Big Data and Blockchain Technology: A Comprehensive Review. *Applied Sciences (Basel, Switzerland)*, *14*(16), 7007. DOI: 10.3390/app14167007

Thiele, L. P. (2024). *Sustainability*. John Wiley & Sons.

Williams, A., & Cai, Y. (2024). Insights into Weighted Sum Sampling Approaches for Multi-Criteria Decision Making Problems. arXiv preprint arXiv:2410.03931.

Wråke, M., Karlsson, K., Kofoed-Wiuff, A., Folsland Bolkesjø, T., Lindroos, T. J., Hagberg, M., ... & Koljonen, T. (2021). Nordic clean energy scenarios: Solutions for carbon neutrality.

Yong, Z. J., Bashir, M. J., Ng, C. A., Sethupathi, S., Lim, J. W., & Show, P. L. (2019). Sustainable waste-to-energy development in Malaysia: Appraisal of environmental, financial, and public issues related with energy recovery from municipal solid waste. *Processes (Basel, Switzerland)*, *7*(10), 676. DOI: 10.3390/pr7100676

Yu, Y., & Jiang, Y. (2024). *Understanding the Digital Revolution and Its Influences*. Springer Books. DOI: 10.1007/978-981-97-4939-3

Zhang, Z., Chen, Z., Zhang, J., Liu, Y., Chen, L., Yang, M., Osman, A. I., Farghali, M., Liu, E., Hassan, D., Ihara, I., Lu, K., Rooney, D. W., & Yap, P. S. (2024). Municipal solid waste management challenges in developing regions: A comprehensive review and future perspectives for Asia and Africa. *The Science of the Total Environment*, *930*, 172794. DOI: 10.1016/j.scitotenv.2024.172794 PMID: 38677421

KEY TERMS AND DEFINITIONS

Digitalization: The integration of digital technologies into everyday processes to drive innovation, efficiency, and competitiveness, transforming industries and societal norms.

Sustainability: Meeting present needs without compromising future generations' ability to meet their own, encompassing economic viability, environmental stewardship, and social equity.

Multi-Criteria Decision Making (MCDM): A systematic approach for evaluating alternatives based on multiple, often conflicting criteria to facilitate informed and balanced decision-making.

Analytical Hierarchy Process (AHP): An MCDM technique that structures complex decisions into a hierarchy and uses pairwise comparisons to determine criteria weights and alternative priorities.

TOPSIS (Technique for Order Preference by Similarity to Ideal Solution): An MCDM method that ranks alternatives by their geometric distance from an ideal solution (maximizing benefits) and a negative-ideal solution (minimizing costs).

Trade-offs: The compromises required when choosing between alternatives, where improving one criterion (e.g., economic gain) may negatively impact another (e.g., environmental health).

Stakeholder Engagement: The process of involving diverse parties (e.g., policymakers, communities, businesses) in decision-making to incorporate their perspectives and build consensus.

Chapter 2
Sustainable Applications of MCDM in the Digital Age

Sundari M Shanmuga
https://orcid.org/0000-0001-5755-474X
BVRIT HYDERABAD College of Engineering for Women, India

M. A. Rithvik
https://orcid.org/0009-0003-3228-5186
Gokaraju Rangaraju Institute of Engineering and Technology, Hyderabad, India

ABSTRACT

Multi-Criteria Decision Making (MCDM) methods have become essential in the digital era, supporting sustainable decision-making across various sectors. These methods, including Analytic Hierarchy Process (AHP), TOPSIS, and ELECTRE, offer structured frameworks for evaluating diverse and often conflicting criteria, making them ideal for tackling sustainability challenges. In smart city development, MCDM helps optimize urban planning by balancing environmental, social, and economic factors. Similarly, in the energy sector, MCDM aids the transition to renewable energy by assessing projects based on cost, efficiency, and environmental impact. Companies use MCDM in sustainable supply chain management, evaluating suppliers on environmental and social criteria. Despite challenges like data quality and criteria subjectivity, advancements in digital technologies promise to enhance MCDM's role in fostering sustainable development globally.

DOI: 10.4018/979-8-3693-8789-4.ch002

INTRODUCTION

Background and Significance of MCDM

In today's rapidly evolving digital age, decision-making (Sahoo, Goswami, & Halder, 2024) has become increasingly complex, requiring advanced methodologies capable of navigating the intricate web of interconnected variables. Multi-Criteria Decision Making (MCDM) has emerged as an indispensable tool in addressing these complexities, particularly in the pursuit of sustainability across various sectors. The significance of MCDM is underscored by its capacity to systematically evaluate and integrate multiple, often conflicting criteria, thereby enabling decision-makers to manage complex problems with greater precision and foresight. As global challenges such as climate change, resource scarcity, and urbanization intensify, the ability to make informed, balanced decisions becomes critical. MCDM's structured approach facilitates this by providing a framework that not only considers the trade-offs between competing objectives but also aligns decisions with broader sustainability goals. For instance, in environmental planning, MCDM can assist in balancing economic development with ecological preservation, ensuring that both short-term and long-term impacts are considered. In corporate governance, MCDM supports the integration of social responsibility with profitability, helping businesses achieve sustainable growth.

Moreover, the adaptability of MCDM to various contexts—from urban planning to resource management—highlights its relevance in a world where decision-making environments are increasingly complex and dynamic. The use of MCDM encourages transparency and stakeholder involvement, as it allows for the explicit consideration of diverse perspectives and values in the decision-making process. This inclusivity is particularly important in achieving equitable outcomes, as it ensures that the voices of all affected parties are heard and integrated into the final decisions. As governments, businesses, and other stakeholders increasingly prioritize environmental, economic, and social sustainability in their decision-making processes, MCDM will continue to play a vital role. Its ability to structure and simplify complex decisions makes it an essential tool for navigating the challenges of the 21st century, helping to create a more sustainable and equitable world for future generations.

Definition of Multi-Criteria Decision Making (MCDM)

Multi-Criteria Decision Making (MCDM) encompasses a set of sophisticated methodologies designed to support decision-making processes that involve the consideration of multiple, often conflicting criteria. Unlike traditional decision-making methods that may focus on a single criterion, MCDM offers a more nuanced approach by accommodating the complexity inherent in real-world problems. This approach is particularly valuable when decisions have significant implications across various domains, such as economic viability, environmental sustainability, and social equity. MCDM methods provide structured frameworks that enable decision-makers to evaluate and prioritize alternatives based on a comprehensive set of criteria. Among the prominent MCDM methodologies are the Analytic Hierarchy Process (AHP), Technique for Order of Preference by Similarity to Ideal Solution (TOPSIS), Elimination and Choice Expressing Reality (ELECTRE), and Multi-Attribute Utility Theory (MAUT). Each of these methods has its unique approach to handling multiple criteria and making complex decisions more manageable.

The Analytic Hierarchy Process (AHP) decomposes a complex decision problem into a hierarchy of more manageable sub-problems, which can then be analysed individually. By comparing pairs of criteria and alternatives, AHP helps quantify their relative importance and performance (Stojčić, Zavadskas, Pamučar, Stević, & Mardani, 2019), providing a weighted score for each option. This method is widely used in scenarios where prioritization and ranking of alternatives are required, such as in urban planning and project selection. TOPSIS evaluates alternatives based on their distance from an ideal solution and a negative-ideal solution. The method ranks options by calculating their relative closeness to these ideal solutions, facilitating a comparison that accounts for both positive and negative aspects. TOPSIS is particularly useful in applications such as resource allocation and supplier selection, where it is essential to balance multiple competing factors.

ELECTRE is another MCDM method that addresses the problem of ranking and selecting from a set of alternatives by using a pairwise comparison approach. It establishes an outranking relationship among alternatives, considering both the advantages and disadvantages of each option. ELECTRE is well-suited for complex decision environments where trade-offs between competing criteria must be carefully managed, such as in policy-making and environmental management. Multi-Attribute Utility Theory (MAUT) evaluates alternatives based on a utility function that aggregates the performance scores across different criteria.

Purpose and Scope of the Paper

The primary purpose of this paper is to explore and elucidate the sustainable applications of Multi-Criteria Decision Making (MCDM) in the context of the digital era, with a particular focus on its critical role in advancing environmental, economic, and social sustainability. In an age where decision-making is increasingly complex and data-driven, MCDM offers a structured approach to evaluating and balancing multiple criteria, making it a valuable tool for sustainable development. This paper aims to provide a comprehensive examination of how MCDM methods are applied across various sectors that are pivotal for fostering sustainability. The scope of this paper is broad, encompassing a detailed analysis of MCDM applications in several key areas..

Another critical area is renewable energy, where MCDM aids in evaluating and selecting the most sustainable energy projects. The transition to renewable energy sources is essential for reducing greenhouse gas emissions and promoting environmental sustainability.

Environmental policy formulation is also a key area of focus. MCDM supports the development of policies that balance ecological, economic, and social goals. By providing a systematic way to weigh various policy options and their potential impacts, MCDM helps policymakers craft strategies that address environmental concerns while also considering economic and social factors. The process of MCDM can be illustrated as seen in the Fig.1.

Figure 1. A multi-criteria decision-making (MCDM) approach.

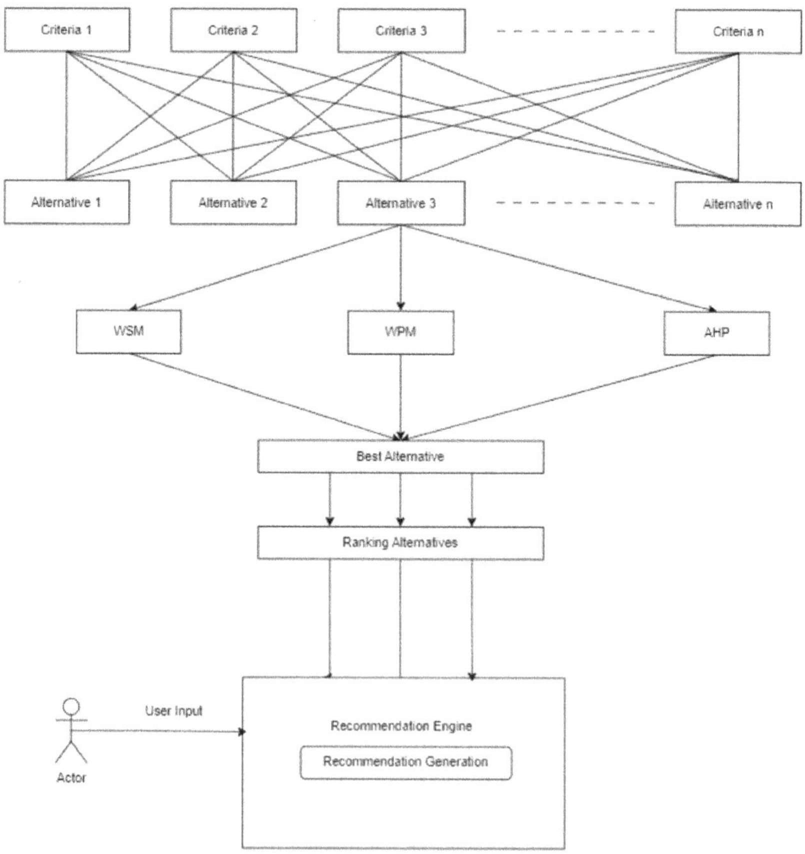

THEORETICAL FRAMEWORK

Fundamental Concepts of MCDM

Multi-Criteria Decision Making (MCDM) is grounded in the concept that real-world decisions often involve multiple, conflicting criteria that must be evaluated simultaneously. At its core, MCDM provides a structured approach to decision-making, where trade-offs between different criteria can be systematically analysed and balanced. This methodology is essential in scenarios where objectives often conflict with one another, necessitating a careful evaluation of priorities and outcomes. The fundamental concept of MCDM revolves around the need to make choices that best satisfy a set of objectives. For example, in urban planning, decision-makers might need to balance economic development (Ozkaya & Erdin, 2020) with environmental protection and social equity. These objectives often conflict, requiring a nuanced approach to identify the best possible outcome.

Criteria and Alternatives in Decision Making

In MCDM, the criteria represent the various factors or attributes that are considered important in the decision-making process, while the alternatives are the different options or courses of action that are being evaluated. The selection of criteria is a critical step in MCDM, as it defines the dimensions along which the alternatives will be judged. Criteria can be qualitative or quantitative and may cover a wide range of aspects such as cost, efficiency, environmental impact, social benefits, and risk. The challenge in MCDM is to accurately define and measure these criteria so that they can be meaningfully compared. Once the criteria are established, the next step involves evaluating the alternatives against these criteria.

Common MCDM Methods (e.g., AHP, TOPSIS, VIKOR, ELECTRE)

There are several well-established methods within the MCDM framework, each offering unique advantages depending on the specific decision-making context. The Analytic Hierarchy Process (AHP) is one of the most widely used MCDM methods. It involves breaking down a decision problem into a hierarchy of more easily comprehended sub-problems, each of which can be analysed independently. This hierarchical structure (Chowdhury & Paul, 2020) allows decision-makers to systematically evaluate the relative importance of each criterion and to prioritize alternatives based on these evaluations. TOPSIS (Technique for Order of Preference by Similarity to Ideal Solution) is another popular MCDM method. It is based on the concept that the best alternative should have the shortest distance from the ideal solution and the farthest distance from the worst-case scenario.

DIGITAL TOOLS FOR MCDM

Software and Platforms for MCDM

The digital transformation has significantly enhanced the capabilities of Multi-Criteria Decision Making (MCDM) through the development and availability of specialized software and platforms. These digital tools are designed to streamline the MCDM process, offering decision-makers user-friendly interfaces, powerful computational capabilities, and sophisticated analytical tools that simplify the evaluation of complex decision problems. By leveraging these tools, decision-makers can efficiently structure and analyse multi-criteria problems, improving both the quality and speed of decision-making.

Prominent examples of MCDM software include Expert Choice, which leverages the Analytic Hierarchy Process (AHP) to support decision-making by structuring problems into a hierarchy and facilitating pairwise comparisons between criteria and alternatives. This approach allows for a more intuitive and systematic evaluation, making it easier to identify the best options. Decision Lab and Visual PROMETHEE are other notable platforms that offer comprehensive support for a wide range of MCDM methods, including TOPSIS, VIKOR, and ELECTRE.

Integration of MCDM Tools with AI and Machine Learning

The integration of Multi-Criteria Decision Making (MCDM) tools with Artificial Intelligence (AI) and Machine Learning (ML) technologies (Sahoo & Goswami, 2023) represents a significant advancement in the decision-making landscape. AI and ML algorithms can process vast amounts of data more efficiently than traditional methods, enabling more precise and dynamic decision-making. When combined with MCDM methodologies, AI and ML can enhance the robustness of decision analyses by automatically identifying patterns, optimizing criteria weighting, and even predicting outcomes based on historical data.

Case Studies: Successful Implementation of Digital MCDM Tools

The successful implementation of digital MCDM tools in various real-world scenarios underscores their value in enhancing decision-making processes across different sectors. One notable case study involves the use of MCDM software in the planning and development of smart cities. For example, in Barcelona, the city government utilized MCDM tools to evaluate and prioritize urban development projects based on criteria such as environmental impact, cost efficiency, and social benefits.

Figure 2. MCDM methods comparison

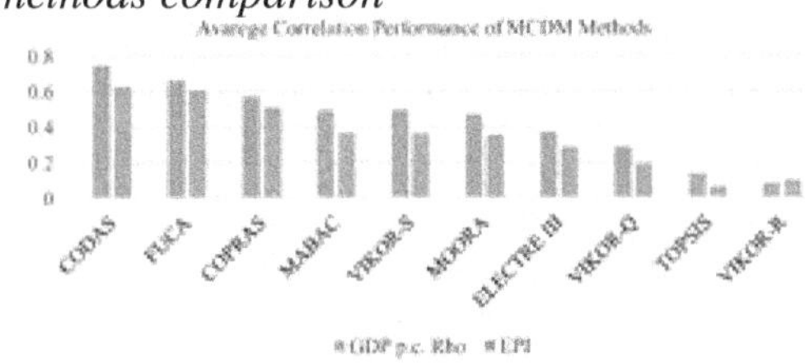

APPLICATIONS IN ENVIRONMENTAL MANAGEMENT

Sustainable Resource Allocation

Sustainable resource allocation is a critical challenge in environmental management, aiming to distribute resources in a way that meets current needs without compromising the ability of future generations to meet theirs. Multi-Criteria Decision Making (MCDM) methods (Sousa, Almeida, & Calili, 2021) are particularly valuable in this context because they allow decision-makers to evaluate and balance a wide range of economic, environmental, and social criteria. MCDM enables a holistic approach to resource management, ensuring that all relevant factors are considered in the decision-making process. For instance, when allocating water resources, decision-makers must consider a complex array of factors such as water availability, demand from agricultural, industrial, and residential sectors, environmental conservation needs, and the impact of water usage on local ecosystems.

Environmental Impact Assessment

Environmental Impact Assessment (EIA) is a crucial process in environmental management designed to evaluate the potential environmental consequences of proposed projects or policies before they are implemented. Traditional EIA methods often rely on single-criteria assessments, which may not fully capture the complexity of environmental issues. Multi-Criteria Decision Making (MCDM) methods enhance the EIA process by providing a structured, multi-dimensional approach to assessing and comparing the environmental impacts of various alternatives. MCDM methods offer a comprehensive framework (Mariyappan, Penthala, Nagaram, & Arisham, 2024) that takes into account a wide range of factors, including air and water quality, biodiversity, soil integrity, and socio-economic impacts on local communities. Unlike traditional methods that might focus narrowly on one aspect, MCDM enables a holistic evaluation by considering multiple criteria simultaneously. This approach ensures that all relevant factors are included in the decision-making process, leading to a more thorough understanding of potential environmental impacts.

By incorporating diverse criteria, MCDM tools facilitate a more nuanced analysis of the potential effects of different alternatives. This helps in identifying the most sustainable options and in mitigating negative impacts while enhancing positive outcomes. For example, when evaluating a new infrastructure project, MCDM can assess not only the environmental damage but also the potential benefits such as improved community infrastructure or economic development.

Renewable Energy Project Selection

The selection of renewable energy projects is a critical aspect of advancing towards a sustainable energy future, and Multi-Criteria Decision Making (MCDM) methods are increasingly being employed to optimize this process. The transition from conventional fossil fuels to renewable energy sources such as wind, solar, and hydroelectric power involves navigating a complex array of considerations. These include economic feasibility, environmental protection, and social acceptance. MCDM provides a structured framework that enables decision-makers to evaluate and prioritize renewable energy projects based on multiple, often conflicting criteria.

Complex Decision-Making in Renewable Energy

The shift to renewable energy requires careful planning and evaluation to ensure that new projects align with sustainability goals. Renewable energy projects are evaluated on various criteria that reflect their potential impact and benefits. For instance, in selecting a site for a new wind farm, decision-makers must consider several factors:

1. Wind Availability: The potential for energy production depends largely on wind availability. MCDM helps in assessing wind speed data and frequency to determine the most suitable locations for optimal energy generation.
2. Land Use: The choice of land for wind farms must consider current land use and potential conflicts with other uses. MCDM evaluates the impact of land use on the project's feasibility, including how the wind farm will affect agricultural activities, residential areas, and other land uses.
3. Proximity to the Grid: The integration of wind energy into the existing power grid is crucial for its effectiveness. MCDM allows decision-makers to weigh the costs and logistical aspects of connecting new wind farms to the grid, ensuring that energy generated can be efficiently distributed.
4. Environmental Impact: The environmental impact of renewable energy projects is a significant concern. MCDM provides a method for evaluating the effects on wildlife, local ecosystems, and natural resources. For wind farms, this includes assessing the potential impact on bird and bat populations and habitat disruption.
5. Public Opinion: Community support is essential for the successful implementation of renewable energy projects. MCDM incorporates public opinion and community acceptance into the decision-making process, helping to address concerns and build support for the project.

Benefits of Using MCDM in Renewable Energy Planning

MCDM offers several benefits in the selection and planning of renewable energy projects:

1. Holistic Evaluation: By considering multiple criteria simultaneously, MCDM provides a more comprehensive evaluation of potential projects. This multi-criteria approach ensures that decisions are not based solely on economic factors but also account for environmental and social impacts.
2. Informed Decision-Making: MCDM tools facilitate the comparison of different renewable energy options, helping decision-makers identify projects that offer the best overall balance of benefits and trade-offs. This structured approach supports more informed and balanced decisions.
3. Sustainability Focus: MCDM aids in prioritizing projects that align with long-term sustainability goals. For instance, it can help identify projects that offer

significant reductions in carbon emissions, contribute to biodiversity conservation, and provide economic benefits to local communities.

4. Enhanced Stakeholder Engagement: MCDM processes often involve engaging various stakeholders, including local communities, environmental groups, and industry experts. This engagement helps to address diverse perspectives and build consensus around project selection.
5. Accurate Trade-Off Analysis: MCDM methods provide tools for analysing trade-offs between different criteria, allowing decision-makers to weigh the relative importance of each factor and make choices that reflect the overall goals of sustainability and efficiency.

Case Example and Practical Application

In practice, MCDM has been successfully applied in several renewable energy projects. For example, in selecting a site for a new solar power plant, MCDM might be used to evaluate factors such as solar irradiance, land availability, environmental impact, and infrastructure requirements. By analysing these criteria, decision-makers can identify the site that offers the highest potential for energy production while minimizing negative impacts and aligning with community values.

Strategy for Implementation of MCDM in Environmental Management

To enhance the effectiveness of Multi-Criteria Decision Making (MCDM) in environmental management, several established strategies and models can be employed. For sustainable resource allocation, the Analytic Hierarchy Process (AHP) is useful for structuring complex decisions by breaking them down into manageable components and prioritizing them through pairwise comparisons. This approach helps balance economic, environmental, and social factors. In Environmental Impact Assessment (EIA), the ELECTRE method is valuable for ranking project alternatives based on their performance across multiple criteria, providing a nuanced view of trade-offs and helping identify the most acceptable options.

Conclusion

The application of MCDM in renewable energy project selection plays a crucial role in advancing sustainability goals. By providing a structured, multi-dimensional approach to evaluating projects, MCDM helps ensure that decisions are balanced, well-informed, and aligned with both environmental and social objectives. This approach not only enhances the effectiveness of renewable energy projects but also accelerates the transition to a low-carbon energy system, contributing to a more sustainable and resilient future.

Case Study: MCDM in Urban Green Space Planning

Urban green space planning is a critical aspect of sustainable urban development, offering significant benefits for environmental quality, public health, and social well-being. Effective planning (Kumar, Vrat, & Shankar, 2021) of green spaces ensures that cities can provide residents with accessible, well-maintained areas that enhance their quality of life while supporting broader sustainability goals. A notable example of applying Multi-Criteria Decision Making (MCDM) in this context is the planning of green spaces in Copenhagen, Denmark. This case study demonstrates how MCDM methods can be employed to optimize urban green space planning, contributing to the city's sustainability objectives which can be seen in Fig.3.

Figure 3. Urban green space planning

CONTEXT AND APPLICATION OF MCDM IN COPENHAGEN

Copenhagen, known for its commitment to sustainability, recognized the importance of integrating green spaces into its urban development strategy. To achieve this, the city employed MCDM methods to evaluate various locations and designs for new parks and green areas.

Criteria Considered in the MCDM Process

The MCDM process in Copenhagen involved a detailed evaluation of several key criteria:

1. Environmental Impact: The potential effects of green space development on local ecosystems were assessed. These included considerations of how new parks could enhance biodiversity, improve soil quality, and contribute to the reduction of urban heat islands. The goal was to ensure that green spaces provided environmental benefits and supported the city's climate adaptation strategies.
2. Accessibility: Accessibility was a crucial factor, as the aim was to ensure that new green spaces (Brodny & Tutak, 2021) were reachable to residents from various parts of the city. This included evaluating transportation options, pedestrian pathways, and the proximity of green spaces to residential areas. The MCDM process sought to enhance the inclusivity and usability of the green spaces for all community members.
3. Cost: The financial implications of developing and maintaining green spaces were carefully considered. This included initial construction costs, ongoing maintenance expenses, and potential funding sources. MCDM allowed for the comparison of different design options and their associated costs, helping the city to make cost-effective decisions that aligned with budget constraints.
4. Community Needs: Engaging local communities was integral to the MCDM process. The needs and preferences of residents were gathered through surveys, workshops, and consultations. This feedback helped ensure that the planned green spaces met the desires of the community, including recreational opportunities, social spaces, and areas for relaxation.

Stakeholder Engagement

An essential aspect of the MCDM process in Copenhagen was stakeholder engagement. The city involved a diverse group of stakeholders, including residents, urban planners, environmental experts, and local government officials. This inclusive approach ensured that the decision-making process considered various perspectives and interests, leading to more balanced and equitable outcomes.

Comparison of Scenarios and Decision-Making

Using MCDM tools, Copenhagen was able to compare different scenarios and designs for green spaces. Each option was evaluated against the criteria mentioned above, allowing for a systematic comparison of potential benefits and drawbacks.

This comparative analysis helped identify the options that offered the greatest overall benefit in terms of environmental impact, accessibility, cost-effectiveness, and community satisfaction.

Outcomes and Impact

The application of MCDM in Copenhagen's green space planning led to the successful creation of new parks and green areas that contributed significantly to the city's sustainability goals (Torkayesh & Torkayesh, 2021). The green spaces not only enhanced local biodiversity and provided recreational opportunities but also supported Copenhagen's broader objectives of reducing urban heat islands, improving air quality, and promoting social cohesion. The new parks served as valuable community assets, fostering social interaction and enhancing the quality of urban life.

Conclusion

The case study of Copenhagen illustrates the effective use of MCDM in urban green space planning. By incorporating a structured approach to evaluating various criteria, the city was able to make informed decisions that balanced environmental, economic, and social factors. The MCDM process facilitated stakeholder participation, ensuring that the needs and preferences of residents were addressed. As a result, Copenhagen successfully developed green spaces that contributed to its sustainability goals and improved the overall livability of the city. This case study highlights how MCDM can be a powerful tool in urban planning, supporting the creation of sustainable and vibrant urban environments.

APPLICATIONS IN BUSINESS AND INDUSTRY

Strategic Business Planning

Strategic business planning is a critical process for organizations aiming to achieve long-term goals and sustain competitive advantage. This process involves setting clear objectives and determining the best course of action to achieve them. Multi-Criteria Decision Making (MCDM) methods are invaluable in this context, as they provide a structured approach to evaluating multiple strategic options by balancing various criteria such as financial performance, market potential, competitive advantage, and risk management (Shanmuga Sundari, Sudha Rani, & Kranthi, 2022).

MCDM methods allow organizations to systematically assess different strategies, taking into account a wide range of factors that are crucial for long-term success. For instance, when a company is considering entering a new market, decision-makers must evaluate a complex set of criteria including market size, growth rate, regulatory environment, and competitive landscape. MCDM tools facilitate this process by enabling the comparison and prioritization of these criteria, helping organizations identify the most promising opportunities that align with their strategic objectives.

Supplier Selection and Supply Chain Management

Effective supplier selection and supply chain management are crucial for maintaining competitiveness and efficiency in business operations. MCDM methods aid in evaluating and choosing suppliers based on multiple criteria such as cost, quality, delivery performance, and sustainability practices. As shown in Fig.4, a company might use MCDM to assess potential suppliers for a new product line by weighing factors like price competitiveness, production capacity, reliability, and environmental impact.

Figure 4. Supply chain management lifecycle

Product Development and Innovation

In product development and innovation, MCDM methods support the evaluation and prioritization of new product ideas and development projects. Companies face numerous challenges in balancing factors such as market demand, technical feasibility, cost, and potential return on investment. MCDM provides a structured framework for analysing these criteria, helping organizations to select projects that offer the best potential for success. For example, when deciding which new product to develop, MCDM tools can be used to weigh criteria like customer needs, technological capabilities, production costs, and competitive positioning. This multi-criteria approach enables companies to focus on projects that align with their strategic goals, enhance innovation outcomes, and optimize resource allocation throughout the development process.

Case Study: MCDM in Lean Manufacturing Processes

Lean manufacturing aims to improve efficiency and reduce waste by optimizing production processes. A case study demonstrating the application of MCDM in lean manufacturing can be seen in Toyota's production system. Toyota employed MCDM methods to evaluate and implement various lean techniques, such as Just-In-Time (JIT) inventory, Kanban systems, and Total Productive Maintenance (TPM). The MCDM approach helped Toyota to systematically assess the benefits and trade-offs of different lean practices, considering factors like cost reduction, process improvement, and impact on production quality.

APPLICATIONS IN HEALTHCARE

Medical Diagnosis and Treatment Planning

In healthcare, accurate medical diagnosis and effective treatment planning are crucial for ensuring positive patient outcomes. The complexity of these processes often involves evaluating multiple diagnostic and treatment options, each with its own set of benefits and risks. Multi-Criteria Decision Making (MCDM) methods have become increasingly valuable in this context, as they allow healthcare providers to systematically assess various options based on a wide range of criteria, including clinical effectiveness, side effects, patient preferences, and costs.

When dealing with a patient who has a complex medical condition, healthcare providers face the challenge of selecting the most appropriate treatment plan. MCDM methods facilitate this decision-making process by enabling a comprehensive comparison of different therapies. For example, a treatment option may offer high clinical efficacy but come with significant side effects, while another option might be less effective but have a better safety profile. MCDM allows these factors to be weighed against each other, ensuring that the chosen treatment aligns with the patient's overall health goals and personal preferences.

Hospital Resource Management

Effective management of hospital resources is crucial for maintaining operational efficiency and ensuring high-quality patient care. Multi-Criteria Decision Making (MCDM) methods offer valuable tools for optimizing the allocation of resources such as staff, equipment, and facilities. By evaluating multiple factors simultaneously, MCDM helps hospitals make informed decisions that balance patient needs, resource availability, and operational efficiency.

Optimizing Resource Allocation with MCDM

One key application of MCDM in hospitals is the optimization of resource allocation during peak times. For example, the allocation of Intensive Care Unit (ICU) beds can be a challenging task, especially during high-demand periods. MCDM methods provide a structured approach to prioritize ICU beds based on various criteria:

1. Patient Acuity: Assessing the severity of patients' conditions is crucial in determining who should receive immediate care. MCDM can weigh factors such as the urgency of medical needs, likelihood of recovery, and potential for deterioration.
2. Bed Availability: The current availability of ICU beds is another critical factor. MCDM helps in evaluating how to best utilize the existing beds and when to consider transferring patients or managing temporary overflow situations.
3. Staff Capacity: The workload and availability of medical staff are important considerations. MCDM can analyze staff schedules, expertise, and current workloads to ensure that resources are allocated efficiently without overburdening the team.
4. Cost-Effectiveness: Evaluating the costs associated with different allocation strategies is essential. MCDM methods help in assessing not only the direct costs but also the potential impact on overall hospital operations and patient outcomes.

Investment and Expansion Decisions

MCDM is also valuable for decision-making related to investments in new technologies or the expansion of hospital services. When considering investments, hospitals need to weigh several factors:

1. Cost-Benefit Analysis: MCDM helps in comparing the costs of new technologies or service expansions with their potential benefits. This includes evaluating long-term financial returns, improvements in patient care, and operational efficiencies.
2. Strategic Alignment: It is important to ensure that new investments align with the hospital's strategic goals. MCDM methods can assess how well a proposed investment fits with the hospital's mission, vision, and strategic objectives.
3. Impact on Patient Care: Assessing how new technologies or expanded services will improve patient care is a key criterion. MCDM allows for the comparison of different options based on their potential to enhance patient outcomes and satisfaction.
4. Implementation Feasibility: MCDM can evaluate the practical aspects of implementing new technologies or services, including infrastructure requirements, training needs, and potential disruptions to existing operations.

Conclusion

In summary, MCDM methods are instrumental in managing hospital resources effectively. By providing a structured framework for evaluating multiple criteria, MCDM supports informed decision-making that optimizes resource allocation, enhances patient care, and aligns with strategic goals. Whether addressing immediate challenges like ICU bed allocation or making long-term investment decisions, MCDM ensures that hospitals can achieve operational efficiency while delivering high-quality care.

PUBLIC HEALTH POLICY DECISION MAKING

Public health policy decisions often require navigating complex trade-offs between health outcomes, economic costs, and social impacts. Multi-Criteria Decision Making (MCDM) methods offer a structured framework to evaluate and compare different policy options based on multiple criteria, facilitating more balanced and informed decision-making.

Application of MCDM in Public Health Policy

When addressing public health issues such as obesity, policymakers face a range of intervention options, including public education campaigns, dietary regulations, and community-based programs. MCDM methods help in systematically assessing these options by considering various criteria:

1. Effectiveness: MCDM evaluates the potential impact of each intervention on reducing obesity rates. This involves analysing evidence from studies or pilot programs to predict how well each option addresses the issue.
2. Equity: The fairness and inclusivity of each intervention are crucial. MCDM considers how different policies affect various demographic groups, ensuring that interventions do not disproportionately benefit or disadvantage specific populations.
3. Feasibility: Implementing new policies can be challenging. MCDM assesses the practicality of each option, including the required resources, infrastructure, and potential barriers to implementation.
4. Cost: Evaluating the cost-effectiveness of interventions is essential for budget-conscious decision-making. MCDM compares the costs of each policy option against their expected benefits, helping to identify the most economically viable solutions.

Benefits of Using MCDM in Public Health Policy

1. Structured Decision-Making: MCDM provides a clear framework for evaluating complex trade-offs, helping policymakers make decisions based on a comprehensive analysis of multiple factors.
2. Evidence-Based Choices: By incorporating data and stakeholder input, MCDM supports evidence-based decision-making, ensuring that chosen policies are grounded in solid analysis rather than anecdotal evidence.
3. Balanced Outcomes: MCDM facilitates the selection of policies that offer the best overall benefit to public health, considering effectiveness, equity, feasibility, and cost, leading to more balanced and equitable outcomes.
4. Stakeholder Engagement: MCDM allows for the inclusion of diverse perspectives, addressing the concerns of various stakeholders and enhancing the acceptability and support for chosen policies.

In summary, MCDM methods enhance public health policy decisions by providing a structured approach to evaluating and comparing interventions. This ensures that policies are effective, equitable, feasible, and cost-effective, ultimately supporting better health outcomes and more informed policymaking.

CASE STUDY: MCDM IN PANDEMIC RESPONSE STRATEGIES

The COVID-19 pandemic presented an unprecedented challenge to global public health systems, highlighting the critical need for effective response strategies to manage such crises. One notable application of Multi-Criteria Decision Making (MCDM) during the pandemic was in the strategic planning and prioritization of vaccine distribution. As the pandemic rapidly evolved, MCDM methods proved invaluable in assessing and ranking vaccination rollout, ensuring that vaccines were distributed efficiently and equitably.

Context of Vaccine Distribution During COVID-19

The arrival of COVID-19 vaccines marked a pivotal moment in the fight against the pandemic. However, the distribution of these vaccines posed significant challenges due to the limited initial supply, the need to prioritize certain populations, and the logistical complexities involved in reaching diverse groups. To navigate these challenges, decision-makers needed a systematic approach to prioritize vaccine distribution based on a range of factors.

Figure 5. Use of MCDM during Covid19

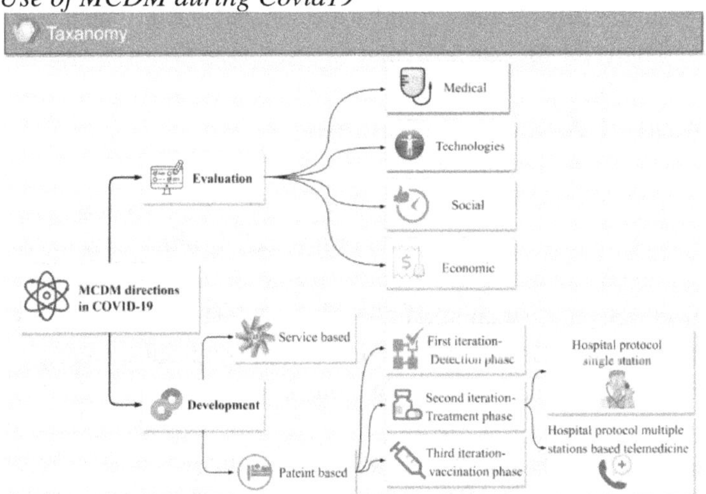

Application of MCDM in Vaccine Distribution

MCDM methods provided a structured framework for evaluating and prioritizing vaccine distribution by considering multiple criteria. Key factors included:

1. Infection Risk: One of the primary criteria was the level of infection risk among different population groups. MCDM methods helped assess the prevalence of

COVID-19 in various regions and the vulnerability of specific groups, such as those living in high-risk areas or with higher exposure rates.

2. Population Vulnerability: The vulnerability of different demographic groups was another critical factor. MCDM evaluated factors such as age, pre-existing health conditions, and socioeconomic status to prioritize those at greatest risk of severe illness or death from COVID-19. For example, the elderly and individuals with chronic health conditions were prioritized due to their higher risk of adverse outcomes.
3. Vaccine Availability: The availability of vaccines was a crucial consideration. MCDM methods assessed the supply chain constraints, including production rates, distribution capacities, and storage requirements. This helped in determining how to allocate limited vaccine doses effectively and prevent bottlenecks in the distribution process.
4. Logistical Challenges: The logistical aspects of vaccine distribution were complex, involving cold chain requirements, transportation infrastructure, and healthcare facilities' readiness. MCDM helped evaluate these logistical challenges, ensuring that vaccines could be distributed and administered efficiently without compromising safety or quality.

Prioritization of Vaccine Recipients

Using MCDM methods, decision-makers were able to establish prioritization frameworks that balanced these criteria. For instance, healthcare workers, who were at high risk of exposure and played a crucial role in treating COVID-19 patients, were prioritized for early vaccination. Similarly, vulnerable populations, including the elderly and individuals with underlying health conditions, were given priority to protect those most at risk of severe outcomes.

Balancing Factors for Effective Distribution

The MCDM approach facilitated a balanced evaluation of various factors to ensure a systematic and equitable distribution of vaccines. By integrating criteria such as disease prevalence, transmission rates, and healthcare capacity, decision-makers could create a prioritization strategy that maximized the impact of the vaccine rollout. This multi-criteria approach enabled a nuanced assessment of trade-offs and helped address the competing demands of different groups.

Impact and Effectiveness

The application of MCDM in vaccine distribution significantly enhanced the overall effectiveness of the pandemic response. By using a structured approach to prioritize vaccine allocation, MCDM ensured that vaccines reached those most in need and helped reduce the virus's impact on public health. The prioritization strategy not only improved the efficiency of the vaccine rollout but also contributed to achieving broader public health goals, such as reducing hospitalizations and deaths, controlling virus transmission, and eventually reaching herd immunity.

Challenges and Consideration

Despite its advantages, the use of MCDM in vaccine distribution also faced challenges. Ensuring that all relevant criteria were accurately assessed and weighted was complex, given the rapidly changing nature of the pandemic and the evolving data. Additionally, balancing equity with efficiency required careful consideration of ethical implications, as certain decisions could have significant social and political repercussions.

Conclusion

In summary, the COVID-19 pandemic underscored the importance of effective response strategies in managing public health crises. The application of MCDM methods in the strategic planning and prioritization of vaccine distribution demonstrated how structured decision-making frameworks can enhance the efficiency, equity, and overall effectiveness of pandemic responses.

Figure 6. MCDM in smart healthcare system

APPLICATIONS IN TRANSPORTATION AND LOGISTICS

Sustainable Transportation Planning

Sustainable transportation planning is critical in the development of systems that minimize environmental impact, reduce energy consumption, and promote social equity. In the face of growing urbanization and the pressing need to address climate change, cities and regions are increasingly focusing on creating transportation networks that are not only efficient but also sustainable. Multi-Criteria Decision Making (MCDM) methods have become essential tools in this context, as they allow planners to evaluate and balance a wide range of criteria, ensuring that transportation decisions align with broader sustainability goals.

Fleet Management and Route Optimization

Fleet management and route optimization are essential for boosting efficiency and cutting costs in transportation and logistics. MCDM methods play a key role in selecting the best routes and fleet configurations by evaluating criteria such as fuel consumption, travel time, vehicle maintenance, and operational costs. For example, MCDM can optimize delivery routes by weighing factors like traffic conditions, delivery windows, and fuel efficiency. Additionally, MCDM aids in deciding fleet composition, including the number and types of vehicles needed, by considering vehicle performance, maintenance costs, and environmental impact. This multi-criteria approach not only enhances fleet efficiency but also results in cost savings and a lower environmental footprint, supporting more sustainable and effective logistics operations.

Logistics and Supply Chain Sustainability

Sustainability in logistics and supply chain management focuses on reducing environmental impact, enhancing social responsibility, and improving economic efficiency. MCDM methods aid in this by assessing various sustainability criteria such as carbon footprint, resource use, cost-effectiveness, and supplier practices. For instance, MCDM helps in selecting suppliers by evaluating their sustainability performance, including environmental certifications, labour practices, and transportation emissions. It also supports the design of sustainable supply chain networks by comparing different logistics strategies and their effects on sustainability goals. By applying MCDM, decision-makers can ensure that supply chain choices meet broader sustainability objectives while still being operationally effective. This multi-criteria approach helps balance environmental, social, and economic factors to promote more sustainable supply chain practices.

Case Study: MCDM in Smart City Mobility Solutions

Smart city mobility solutions aim to enhance urban transportation systems to be more efficient, sustainable, and technologically advanced. A notable example of MCDM application in this field is the implementation of smart transportation systems in Barcelona, Spain. The city used MCDM methods to evaluate and prioritize various smart mobility initiatives, including intelligent traffic management, electric vehicle infrastructure, and shared mobility services.

As seen in Fig.7, This case study illustrates how MCDM can facilitate the development of innovative and sustainable transportation solutions in smart cities. The structured evaluation process led to more effective and balanced mobility planning, ultimately improving urban transportation systems and contributing to a higher quality of urban life.

Figure 7. MCDM in smart city transportation

APPLICATIONS IN ENERGY SECTOR

Renewable Energy Source Selection

Selecting the most suitable renewable energy sources is crucial for optimizing energy production and meeting sustainability goals, particularly in the face of increasing global energy demands and the urgent need to reduce greenhouse gas emissions. Multi-Criteria Decision Making (MCDM) methods have become invaluable in this process, as they allow decision-makers to systematically evaluate and compare various renewable energy options, ensuring that the chosen sources align with both economic and environmental objectives. Renewable energy sources such as solar, wind, hydro, and biomass each have distinct advantages and challenges. For example, solar energy is abundant and has low operational costs but requires significant initial investment and is dependent on geographic location and weather conditions. Wind energy is highly efficient in suitable areas but may face issues related to visual impact, noise, and intermittency. Hydropower is reliable and capable of providing large-scale energy but can have significant environmental and social impacts, particularly concerning water ecosystems and local communities. Biomass is versatile and can contribute to waste management, yet it may involve high costs and resource competition with food production.

Energy Policy and Planning

Energy policy and planning involve developing strategies to ensure a reliable, affordable, and sustainable energy supply. MCDM methods support this process by evaluating various policy options and planning scenarios based on criteria such as economic impact, environmental benefits, social acceptance, and feasibility. For example, when formulating energy policies to promote renewable energy adoption, MCDM can help compare different policy instruments—such as subsidies, tax incentives, and regulatory frameworks—by considering their effectiveness, cost implications, and impact on energy markets. This structured approach enables policymakers to design balanced and effective energy strategies that support overall energy goals while addressing diverse stakeholder interests.

Smart Grid and Energy Efficiency

Smart grids and energy efficiency initiatives focus on improving the reliability, efficiency, and sustainability of energy distribution and consumption. Multi-Criteria Decision Making (MCDM) methods play a crucial role in evaluating and prioritizing smart grid technologies and energy efficiency measures. MCDM helps assess various criteria such as implementation cost, technological compatibility, energy savings, and environmental impact.

Case Study: MCDM in Wind Farm Location Selection

Selecting optimal locations for wind farms requires a thorough assessment of various factors to ensure high energy production while minimizing environmental impact. A notable example of applying Multi-Criteria Decision Making (MCDM) in this context is the wind farm location selection process used by Ørsted, a leading energy company in Denmark. Ørsted employed MCDM methods to evaluate potential sites for new wind farms by considering multiple criteria such as wind resource availability, proximity to existing infrastructure, environmental impact, and socio-economic factors.

The MCDM approach enabled Ørsted to systematically compare and prioritize different sites as shown in Fig.8, based on a comprehensive assessment of these criteria. This process helped identify locations that provided the best balance between energy generation potential and environmental sustainability. By applying MCDM, Ørsted was able to make informed decisions that optimized both energy production and environmental stewardship. This case study highlights how MCDM can be instrumental in supporting decision-making in wind energy projects, ensuring that site selections contribute to more efficient and sustainable energy development while addressing key factors like resource availability and environmental considerations.

Figure 8. MCDM in wind farm location selection

APPLICATIONS IN EDUCATION

Curriculum Development and Evaluation

Curriculum development and evaluation are crucial processes in education, aimed at designing educational programs that meet the diverse needs of students while aligning with institutional and educational standards. Multi-Criteria Decision Making (MCDM) methods play a significant role in this process by enabling educators and curriculum developers to systematically assess various curriculum options against a range of relevant criteria. These criteria often include educational goals, student needs, resource requirements, learning outcomes, and alignment with broader educational standards.

E-learning and Educational Technology Integration

Integrating e-learning and educational technologies requires a thorough evaluation to ensure that chosen solutions are effective and accessible. Multi-Criteria Decision Making (MCDM) methods play a crucial role in this process by helping institutions assess various e-learning tools and technologies based on a range of criteria. These criteria typically include cost, ease of use, compatibility with existing systems, and educational effectiveness.

For example, As seen in Fig.8, when selecting a new e-learning platform, MCDM can be used to compare options by evaluating features such as user interface design, support services, and integration capabilities with other educational tools.

Figure 9. MCDM in E-Learning

Institutional Planning and Resource Allocation

Institutional planning and resource allocation involve making decisions about the strategic direction and efficient use of resources within educational institutions. MCDM methods aid in this process by evaluating various planning scenarios and resource allocation options based on criteria such as financial constraints, strategic priorities, and operational needs. For example, when planning for campus expansion or faculty hiring, MCDM can help institutions compare different scenarios by considering factors like cost, impact on educational quality, and alignment with institutional goals. This approach ensures that resources are allocated effectively and support long-term strategic objectives.

Case Study: MCDM in Higher Education Quality Assessment

A notable example of Multi-Criteria Decision Making (MCDM) in higher education quality assessment is the evaluation process implemented by the University of Melbourne. The university applied MCDM methods to comprehensively assess various dimensions of educational quality, including teaching effectiveness, student satisfaction, research output, and institutional facilities.

This case study demonstrates how MCDM can be a powerful tool for higher education institutions seeking to enhance their quality assessment processes. It supports data-driven decision-making by providing a clear framework for evaluating multiple quality dimensions, ultimately leading to informed decisions that improve educational outcomes and institutional performance.

APPLICATIONS IN SOCIAL SERVICES

Community Development Projects

Community development projects are crucial for enhancing the quality of life and fostering sustainable growth within communities. These initiatives can range from infrastructure improvements to educational and health programs, each with its own set of benefits and requirements. To effectively evaluate and prioritize these diverse projects, Multi-Criteria Decision-Making (MCDM) methods prove to be invaluable. MCDM helps decision-makers assess various development options by considering multiple criteria. For instance, when determining which community projects to pursue, MCDM evaluates factors such as community needs, project feasibility, cost, and potential impact. This structured approach allows for a comprehensive comparison of different initiatives, ensuring that resources are allocated efficiently and effectively.

Consider a scenario where a community is looking to decide between investing in new roads, launching educational programs, or enhancing local health services. MCDM methods would involve comparing these options based on several criteria: the social benefits each project would bring, the resources required, and how well each aligns with the community's overarching goals.

Social Welfare Program Evaluation

Evaluating social welfare programs involves assessing their effectiveness and impact on beneficiaries. MCDM methods support this by comparing different program options based on criteria such as program outcomes, cost-effectiveness, accessibility, and beneficiary satisfaction. For instance, when evaluating various welfare programs, MCDM can help policymakers assess options like income support, housing assistance, and job training by considering their impact on poverty reduction, program efficiency, and overall effectiveness. This approach facilitates evidence-based decision-making and helps in identifying programs that offer the greatest benefit to individuals and communities.

Policy Formulation for Social Equity

Formulating policies for social equity involves developing strategies to promote fairness and address societal disparities. Multi-Criteria Decision Making (MCDM) methods play a vital role in this process by providing a structured framework for evaluating various policy options against multiple criteria. These criteria often include equity, feasibility, cost, and social impact. For instance, when crafting policies to tackle income inequality, MCDM can be used to compare different approaches such as progressive taxation, social safety nets, and educational opportunities. Each approach is assessed based on its effectiveness in reducing income disparities, its implementation challenges, and its potential benefits for different segments of society.

Case Study: MCDM in Housing Allocation for Low-Income Families

A case study highlighting the application of Multi-Criteria Decision Making (MCDM) in housing allocation for low-income families can be observed in New York City's affordable housing program. Facing a complex challenge in distributing limited housing resources, the city implemented MCDM methods to prioritize and allocate housing applications in a fair and systematic manner. The MCDM approach involved evaluating various criteria such as income levels, family sizes, specific housing needs, and location preferences. The process began with defining a set of criteria essential for determining priority, which included not only economic factors but also social and logistical considerations. MCDM techniques enabled the city to assess each application based on these criteria, creating a comprehensive scoring system that ranked applicants accordingly.

CHALLENGES AND OPPORTUNITIES

Ethical Considerations in MCDM

Ethical considerations in Multi-Criteria Decision-Making (MCDM) are essential for ensuring that decision-making processes are fair, transparent, and uphold high ethical standards. Key challenges in this area include addressing biases in criteria selection, ensuring meaningful stakeholder participation, and maintaining transparency throughout the process. A significant issue is the potential for biases to affect how criteria are selected and weighted. Such biases can skew outcomes to favour specific interests, leading to decisions that do not accurately reflect the needs and values of all stakeholders.

Transparency is another critical aspect of ethical MCDM. Decision-makers must clearly document and communicate the process for selecting, weighting, and applying criteria. This transparency builds trust and allows all stakeholders to understand and scrutinize the rationale behind decisions. To enhance ethical practices in MCDM, developing robust frameworks and guidelines that integrate ethical principles is beneficial. Conducting ethical audits can help assess whether decision-making processes align with ethical standards.

Handling Subjectivity and Uncertainty

Subjectivity and uncertainty are inherent in Multi-Criteria Decision Making (MCDM) processes, as decisions often involve personal judgments and incomplete information. To manage subjectivity, it is crucial to employ structured methods that minimize individual biases, such as using consistent criteria and decision rules. This helps ensure that personal biases do not unduly influence outcomes. Uncertainty, on the other hand, can be addressed through techniques like sensitivity analysis and scenario planning.

Future Trends in MCDM Research and Application

Future trends in Multi-Criteria Decision Making (MCDM) research and application are set to leverage advanced technologies and methodologies to enhance decision-making processes. One prominent trend is the integration of artificial intelligence (AI) and machine learning, which can improve decision support by analysing complex data and identifying patterns that inform better decisions. Additionally, the development of hybrid MCDM approaches, which combine multiple techniques, aims to offer more nuanced and flexible decision-making frameworks.

Case Study: Addressing Bias in MCDM Processes

A notable case study of addressing bias in Multi-Criteria Decision Making (MCDM) processes is the city of Seattle's approach to selecting affordable housing projects. Initially, Seattle encountered challenges with biases in the criteria used to evaluate housing proposals, which risked disproportionately favouring certain types of projects or developers over others. Recognizing the need for fairness, the city revised its MCDM framework to better address these biases. To tackle this issue, Seattle adopted a comprehensive strategy that involved engaging diverse stakeholder groups in the decision-making process. This inclusive approach ensured that multiple perspectives were considered, which helped to identify and mitigate potential biases.

CONCLUSION

Summary of Key Insights

The application of Multi-Criteria Decision Making (MCDM) across various fields underscores its versatility and significance in managing complex decision-making processes. MCDM is particularly adept at handling multiple, often conflicting criteria in a structured manner, enabling more informed and balanced decisions. This capability proves beneficial across a range of domains including environmental management, healthcare, transportation, and social services. However, despite its advantages, MCDM faces challenges that need to be addressed to enhance its effectiveness. By navigating these challenges, MCDM can continue to support decision-making across various fields and ensure that decisions are well-rounded and aligned with strategic objectives.

Environmental Management

In environmental management, MCDM plays a critical role in evaluating the trade-offs between ecological preservation and economic development. This field often involves complex decisions where various factors must be weighed against each other. For instance, when assessing different land-use options, MCDM can be used to evaluate factors such as environmental impact, economic benefits, and social outcomes. By structuring the decision-making process, MCDM helps identify the most sustainable choice that balances ecological preservation with development goals.

Healthcare

In healthcare, MCDM assists in prioritizing treatment options and resource allocation by evaluating various criteria such as patient outcomes, cost-effectiveness, and accessibility. This application of MCDM is crucial in environments where resources are limited and decisions must be made to maximize health benefits across populations. For example, when deciding which new medical technology to adopt, MCDM can help weigh the benefits of improved patient outcomes against the costs of implementation and ongoing maintenance.

A practical application could involve evaluating different cancer treatments. MCDM can help in comparing treatment options based on effectiveness, side effects, cost, and patient quality of life. As expressed in Fig.10, this approach ensures that healthcare providers can make informed decisions that consider both clinical effectiveness and economic constraints, ultimately improving patient care and resource utilization.

Figure 10. Environmental management

Transportation Planning

In transportation planning, MCDM provides a structured framework for evaluating various infrastructure projects. Factors such as cost, traffic impact, and environmental effects are considered to ensure that projects align with strategic goals. For example, when planning a new highway, MCDM can help assess the trade-offs between construction costs, traffic congestion reduction, and environmental impact. This comprehensive evaluation helps decision-makers choose projects that best meet the transportation needs while minimizing negative impacts.

Social Services

Social services benefit from MCDM by aiding in the prioritization of programs and interventions. In this context, MCDM helps evaluate criteria such as community needs, program effectiveness, and cost. For example, when deciding which social programs to fund, MCDM can be used to assess various programs based on their potential impact, resource requirements, and alignment with community priorities.

Challenges and Opportunities

Despite its benefits, MCDM faces several challenges that need to be addressed to enhance its effectiveness. One major challenge is managing subjectivity in criteria selection and weighting. Personal biases can influence how criteria are chosen and how much weight is assigned to each, potentially skewing decision outcomes. To mitigate this issue, it is essential to involve diverse stakeholders in the decision-making process. This inclusion helps ensure that the criteria used are comprehensive and reflect a broad range of perspectives. Ensuring ethical practices and transparency is another critical challenge. Maintaining trust and fairness in decision-making requires clear documentation and communication of how criteria are selected, weighted, and applied. Developing robust frameworks and guidelines that integrate ethical principles can help address these concerns.

CONCLUSION

In summary, the application of Multi-Criteria Decision Making (MCDM) across various fields demonstrates its versatility and value in managing complex decision-making processes. MCDM excels in handling multiple, often conflicting criteria in a structured manner, which is particularly beneficial in areas such as environmental management, healthcare, transportation, and social services. By addressing challenges such as managing subjectivity, ensuring ethical practices, and improving accessibility, MCDM can continue to provide valuable support in making informed and balanced decisions. Embracing these challenges and opportunities will ensure that MCDM remains a powerful tool for decision-makers across diverse fields, helping them achieve well-rounded and strategically aligned outcomes.

Future Directions for MCDM in the Digital Age

As we look ahead, the future of Multi-Criteria Decision Making (MCDM) is poised to be significantly influenced by advancements in technology and the evolving landscape of decision-making needs. Several key directions are expected to shape the development and application of MCDM, ensuring its continued relevance and effectiveness in an increasingly complex and data-driven world.

Integration of Artificial Intelligence and Machine Learning

One of the most promising developments for MCDM is the integration of artificial intelligence (AI) and machine learning (ML) technologies. These advancements have the potential to revolutionize how MCDM methods are applied by enhancing decision support through more sophisticated data analysis and pattern recognition. AI and ML algorithms can process vast amounts of data more efficiently than traditional methods, providing more accurate and timely insights. For instance, AI can help in predicting future trends and outcomes based on historical data, while ML can refine decision models by learning from previous decisions and outcomes. This integration can lead to more dynamic and responsive MCDM tools, capable of handling complex and evolving criteria with greater precision.

Development of Adaptive and Scalable MCDM Methods

As decision-making environments become increasingly complex, there is a growing need for MCDM methods that are both adaptive and scalable. Traditional MCDM approaches may struggle to keep pace with rapid changes and growing amounts of data. Future advancements are likely to focus on developing methods that can adapt to changing criteria and decision contexts. Scalable MCDM techniques will be essential for applying these methods to large-scale problems, such as those encountered in global supply chains or large urban development projects. By enhancing the adaptability and scalability of MCDM methods, decision-makers will be better equipped to handle a wider range of scenarios and challenges. Table 1 explains the complete strategy of MCDM methods.

Table 1. Comparative table of MCDM methods

MCDM Method	Core Concept	Application	Strengths	Weaknesses
Analytic Hierarchy Process (AHP)	Decomposes decision problems, into a hierarchy of sub-problems, allowing pairwise comparison of criteria.	Urban planning, project selection	Intuitive, handles complex decisions well	Subjective weighting of criteria
TOPSIS	Evaluates alternatives based on their distance from an ideal and negative-ideal solution.	Resource allocation, supplier selection	Balances positive and negative aspects of alternatives	Sensitive to the relative importance of criteria
ELECTRE	Uses pairwise comparisons to establish an outranking relationship among alternatives.	Policy-making, environmental management	Effective for ranking and selecting from numerous alternatives	Complexity increases with more criteria and alternatives
Multi-Attribute Utility Theory (MAUT)	Aggregates performance scores across different criteria into a utility function for comparison.	Energy management, financial decision-making	Quantitative, provides a clear overall utility measure	Requires detailed utility functions for accurate results

MCDM Method	Core Concept	Application	Strengths	Weaknesses
VIKOR	Focuses on finding a compromise solution close to the ideal solution.	Conflict resolution, project prioritization	Effective in minimizing regret, good for scenarios with conflicting objectives	Can be sensitive to the selection of the ideal solution
PROMETHEE	Ranks alternatives based on preference flows, balancing pros and cons of each.	Environmental impact assessment, strategic planning	Simple, easy to apply, provides a clear ranking	Requires careful interpretation of preference flows

Application in New and Emerging Domains

The application of MCDM is expanding into new and emerging domains, driven by technological advancements and changing societal needs. One significant area is digital transformation, where MCDM can help organizations evaluate and prioritize technology investments, digital strategies, and innovation initiatives. In the realm of smart technologies, such as smart cities and the Internet of Things (IoT), MCDM can be used to assess the trade-offs between various technological solutions and their impacts on quality of life, sustainability, and economic development. By exploring these new domains, MCDM will continue to provide valuable insights into the complex interactions between technology and societal needs.

Improving Accessibility and Usability

Another important trend for the future of MCDM is the focus on improving the accessibility and usability of MCDM tools. As decision-making increasingly involves diverse stakeholders, it is crucial to develop tools that are user-friendly and accessible to a broader audience. This includes creating intuitive interfaces, providing clear explanations of decision models, and offering support for non-experts. By making MCDM tools more accessible, a wider range of users will be able to engage with and benefit from these methods, leading to more informed and collaborative decision-making processes.

Embracing Data-Driven Insights

In an era characterized by vast amounts of data, MCDM will increasingly rely on data-driven insights to support decision-making. Advanced data analytics and visualization techniques will play a key role in helping decision-makers understand complex data sets and make informed choices. By leveraging big data and analytics,

MCDM can provide more comprehensive evaluations of criteria and outcomes, leading to more nuanced and effective decisions.

Ensuring Ethical Considerations

As MCDM methods evolve, it will be important to continue addressing ethical considerations. This includes managing biases, ensuring transparency, and engaging diverse stakeholders in the decision-making process. Future developments in MCDM will need to incorporate robust ethical frameworks to maintain trust and fairness. This may involve implementing new standards for ethical decision-making and using technology to enhance transparency and accountability.

In summary, the future of MCDM will be shaped by technological advancements, the need for adaptive and scalable methods, and the expansion into new domains. By embracing these trends and focusing on accessibility, usability, and ethical considerations, MCDM will continue to provide valuable support and insights in a complex, data-driven world. The ongoing evolution of MCDM will ensure that it remains a powerful tool for making informed and balanced decisions across a wide range of applications.

REFERENCES

Brodny, J., & Tutak, M. (2021). Assessing the level of digital maturity of enterprises in the Central and Eastern European countries using the MCDM and Shannon's entropy methods. *PLoS One*, *16*(7), e0253965. DOI: 10.1371/journal.pone.0253965 PMID: 34228755

Chowdhury, P., & Paul, S. K. (2020). Applications of MCDM methods in research on corporate sustainability: A systematic literature review. *Management of Environmental Quality*, *31*(2), 385–405. DOI: 10.1108/MEQ-12-2019-0284

Kumar, V., Vrat, P., & Shankar, R. (2021). *Prioritization of strategies to overcome the barriers in Industry 4.0: a hybrid MCDM approach.* Opsearch, 1-40.

Mariyappan, S. S., Penthala, H. R., Nagaram, A., & Arisham, D. (2024, July). *Retina fundus disease gray scale image perception using semantic segmentation model.* In AIP Conference Proceedings (Vol. 3028, No. 1). AIP Publishing. DOI: 10.1063/5.0212988

Ozkaya, G., & Erdin, C. (2020). Evaluation of smart and sustainable cities through a hybrid MCDM approach based on ANP and TOPSIS technique. *Heliyon*, *6*(10), e05052. DOI: 10.1016/j.heliyon.2020.e05052 PMID: 33117896

Sahoo, S. K., & Goswami, S. S. (2023). A comprehensive review of multiple criteria decision-making (MCDM) Methods: Advancements, applications, and future directions. *Decision Making Advances*, *1*(1), 25–48. DOI: 10.31181/dma1120237

Sahoo, S. K., Goswami, S. S., & Halder, R. (2024). Supplier selection in the age of industry 4.0: A review on MCDM applications and trends. *Decision Making Advances*, *2*(1), 32–47. DOI: 10.31181/dma21202420

Shanmuga Sundari, M., Sudha Rani, M., & Kranthi, A. (2022). *Detect traffic lane image using geospatial LiDAR data point clouds with machine learning analysis.* In Intelligent System Design [Singapore: Springer Nature Singapore.]. *Proceedings of INDIA*, *2022*, 217–225.

Sousa, M., Almeida, M. F., & Calili, R. (2021). Multiple criteria decision making for the achievement of the UN sustainable development goals: A systematic literature review and a research agenda. *Sustainability (Basel)*, *13*(8), 4129. DOI: 10.3390/su13084129

Stojčić, M., Zavadskas, E. K., Pamučar, D., Stević, Ž., & Mardani, A. (2019). *Application of MCDM methods in sustainability engineering: A literature review* 2008–2018. *Symmetry*, *11*(3), 350. DOI: 10.3390/sym11030350

Torkayesh, A. E., & Torkayesh, S. E. (2021). *Evaluation of information and communication technology development in G7 countries:* An integrated MCDM approach. *Technology in Society*, *66*, 101670. DOI: 10.1016/j.techsoc.2021.101670

Chapter 3
Supply Chain Management for Sustainable Food Production Using the Analytic Hierarchy Process

Puppala Naga Sravanthi
https://orcid.org/0009-0006-3255-2194
SRM University, Mangalagiri, India

Kiran Kumar Meriga
Lakireddy Bali Reddy College of Engineering, Mylavaram, India

ABSTRACT

The global food production system faces increasing challenges to meet rising demand while ensuring sustainable practices. Achieving this requires a careful balance of supply chain factors like environmental impact, cost, quality, and social responsibility. As these demands grow more complex, effective decision-making tools are essential. Sustainable food production hinges on strategic supply chain management not only optimizing production efficiency but also ensuring alignment with broader sustainability goals. The Analytic Hierarchy Process, a well-established MCDM method, offers a structured solution for managing these complexities in sustainable supply chains. This chapter explores AHP's application in optimizing sustainable food production, showcasing case studies that illustrate how AHP supports informed,

DOI: 10.4018/979-8-3693-8789-4.ch003

balanced decisions in the face of diverse demands. This book is an essential resource for supply chain managers, sustainability professionals, and researchers focused on integrating sustainability into decision-making.

INTRODUCTION

The global food production system is increasingly challenged to meet the growing demand for food while ensuring that production practices remain sustainable. This task requires a delicate balance of numerous factors within the supply chain, including environmental impact, cost, quality, and social responsibility. As the world grapples with these complex and often competing demands, the need for effective decision-making tools becomes more critical. Sustainable food production cannot be achieved without careful and strategic management of the supply chain. This involves not only optimizing the efficiency of production processes but also ensuring that these processes align with broader sustainability goals. The Analytic Hierarchy Process (AHP), a widely recognized Multi-Criteria Decision-Making (MCDM) method, offers a powerful solution for addressing the multifaceted challenges of sustainable supply chain management. AHP provides a structured approach to decision-making by breaking down complex problems into a hierarchy of simpler, more manageable components. This hierarchical structure allows decision-makers to systematically evaluate and prioritize various criteria, such as environmental impact, cost, quality, and social responsibility. By comparing these criteria in pairs and assigning relative weights, AHP helps to ensure that decisions are made rationally, transparently, and in alignment with the overarching goal of sustainability.

This chapter aims to explore the application of AHP in optimizing supply chain management for sustainable food production. Through practical examples and case studies, it will demonstrate how AHP can be used to make informed decisions that balance the diverse and often competing demands of sustainability in food production. The book will serve as a valuable resource for supply chain managers, sustainability professionals, and researchers seeking to integrate sustainability into their decision-making processes.

Objectives

- To illustrate how the Analytic Hierarchy Process can be applied in various stages of the food production supply chain to enhance decision-making and ensure sustainable practices.

- To systematically assess and prioritize sustainability criteria such as environmental impact, cost, quality, and social responsibility within the context of food production.
- To offer step-by-step instructions on how supply chain managers can effectively implement AHP in their decision-making processes to achieve sustainable outcomes.
- To explore real-world case studies where AHP has been successfully used to optimize supply chain decisions.
- To ensure that decisions in sustainable food production are based on rational and structured evaluations of all relevant criteria, reducing bias and improving outcomes.
- To demonstrate how AHP can help align supply chain management strategies with the broader goals of sustainability, ensuring that economic, environmental, and social factors are balanced effectively.

Overview of the Global Food Supply Chain

The global food supply chain is a complex network linking agricultural producers, processors, distributors, retailers, and consumers. As globalization and consumer demands grow, the food supply chain faces several challenges that impact sustainability, efficiency, and security, creating opportunities for innovation and reform (Rajeev Bhat, 2019). Table 1 presents all key challenges in Global Food Supply chain.

Challenges in the Global Food Supply Chain

1. **Climate Change and Resource Scarcity**: Environmental factors like extreme weather, water scarcity, and declining arable land negatively affect crop yields and food production (Marija Jeremić).
2. **Food Waste and Losses**: Approximately one-third of all food produced is lost at different supply chain stages, from farms to retail, increasing global food insecurity. This waste often results from poor storage, transportation inefficiencies, and weak infrastructure, especially in developing countries (Shah, 2023).
3. **Technology Integration**: Although technologies like the Internet of Things (IoT) and blockchain can improve traceability and reduce food waste, their adoption remains slow due to financial, technical, and operational challenges (Osato Itohan Oriekhoe, 2023).

Opportunities for Sustainable Transformation

1. **Green Supply Chains**: Moving towards green procurement and sustainable logistics will minimize environmental footprints and align food production with global climate policies (Marija Jeremić).
2. **Technological Innovations**: Technologies such as AI, predictive analytics, and automated ordering systems can enhance efficiency and reduce spoilage by optimizing operations and forecasting demand (Shah, 2023).
3. **Government Policies and International Collaboration**: Policies fostering public-private partnerships, capacity building, and international cooperation can support supply chain resilience and technological adoption (Osato Itohan Oriekhoe, 2023).

Table 1. Key challenges and opportunities in global food supply chain

Aspect	Challenges	Opportunities
Environmental Impact	Climate change, water scarcity	Adoption of green wood supply chain models
Food Waste & Loss	Poor storage, transportation and processing	IoT-based monitoring and better infrastructure
Technology Adoption	High cost, lack of training, slow implementation	Use of blockchain, AI for predictive analytics
Global Trade & Policy	Supply chain disruptions, strict regulations	International collaboration, policy reforms

Hence, the global food supply chain is at a critical juncture, facing significant environmental, technological, and logistical challenges. However, these challenges present opportunities to build sustainable food systems that can better meet global demand through innovative practices and improved collaboration (Vinay Surendra Yadav, 2022).

DEFINING SUSTAINABILITY IN FOOD PRODUCTION

Sustainability in food production refers to practices that ensure the long-term availability of food while minimizing environmental harm, promoting economic viability, and fostering social well-being. Achieving sustainable food production involves balancing environmental conservation, economic benefits, and social equity. This balance is critical given the growing global population, the threat of climate change, and the need to address food insecurity.

1. Environmental Dimension of Sustainability

This dimension focuses on protecting ecosystems and minimizing the impact of agricultural activities. Sustainable food systems aim to reduce carbon emissions, conserve biodiversity, and ensure responsible use of water and soil resources. Practices such as regenerative agriculture, organic farming, and precision agriculture contribute to environmental sustainability by:

- **Reducing greenhouse gas emissions** through no-till farming or crop rotation.
- **Minimizing water usage** by employing drip irrigation systems and rainwater harvesting.
- **Preserving biodiversity** by reducing chemical fertilizers and pesticides (Marija Jeremić).

A shift towards plant-based diets and shorter food supply chains can also reduce the carbon footprint associated with food production. However, achieving environmental sustainability is complex, as it requires collaboration between policymakers, farmers, and industries to implement eco-friendly practices across the supply chain.

2. Economic Dimension of Sustainability

Economic sustainability ensures that food production systems remain financially viable over the long term while contributing to local economies. This involves optimizing productivity, reducing post-harvest losses, and promoting fair trade practices. Key aspects of economic sustainability in food production include:

- **Cost-efficient farming practices** that minimize waste while maximizing output.
- **Supply chain resilience** by diversifying markets and reducing dependency on imports.
- **Supporting smallholder farmers** through access to credit, subsidies, and modern technologies (Shah, 2023).

Additionally, integrating digital technologies such as blockchain for traceability or AI for demand forecasting can enhance supply chain efficiency, preventing both financial and food losses.

3. Social Dimension of Sustainability

The social pillar emphasizes fairness, community development, and human well-being. This dimension ensures that food production systems are equitable, providing access to nutritious food for all while supporting the livelihoods of farmers and workers. Social sustainability includes:

- **Ensuring food security** through inclusive policies that address hunger and malnutrition.
- **Promoting fair labour practices** and improving working conditions for farm labourers.
- **Engaging local communities** in food production to strengthen rural economies (Rajeev Bhat, 2019).

Fair trade initiatives and certifications, such as organic or Rainforest Alliance labels, also promote social sustainability by ensuring that consumers support ethical practices through their purchasing choices. Table 2 provides all dimensions of sustainability in food production.

Table 2. Dimensions of sustainability in food production

Dimension	Focus Areas	Example Practises
Environmental	Conservation of resources, biodiversity	Organic farming, drip irrigation and crop rotation
Economical	Financial Viability, market resilience	Fair trade, access to finance, use of technology
Social	Equity, food security and fair labour	Local food production, fair wages, community engagement

The Need for Multi-Criteria Decision-Making

Sustainable supply chain management (SSCM) requires balancing multiple, often conflicting goals, such as economic efficiency, environmental conservation, and social responsibility. In this context, Multi-Criteria Decision-Making (MCDM) methods are crucial tools that help decision-makers evaluate alternatives and address these complex trade-offs. MCDM offers a structured approach to incorporate quantitative and qualitative factors, enabling managers to assess competing priorities effectively. Table 3 presents common MCDM methods used in SSCM also Fig.1 depicts the same.

Why MCDM is Crucial for SSCM?

- **Complexity and Trade-offs**

Sustainability decisions often involve balancing competing objectives, such as reducing environmental impact while maintaining profitability. MCDM methods allow decision-makers to compare different alternatives using various criteria, ensuring a more informed and balanced decision. For example, reducing carbon emissions might increase costs, but MCDM helps identify solutions that strike an optimal balance.

- **Handling Uncertainty**

Supply chains are affected by uncertainties such as fluctuating demand, geopolitical risks, and environmental changes. MCDM tools, such as the Analytic Hierarchy Process (AHP) or TOPSIS (Technique for Order of Preference by Similarity to Ideal Solution), provide a framework to account for these uncertainties in evaluating sustainability strategies.

- **Stakeholder Involvement**

Sustainable decisions require inputs from multiple stakeholders, including suppliers, customers, and policymakers. MCDM allows for the integration of diverse stakeholder preferences, fostering collaboration and improving transparency.

Table 3. Common MCDM methods for SSCM

MCDM Method	Description	Application in SSCM
AHP	Breaks down complex decisions into a hierarchy	Supplier selection, risk assessment
TOPSIS	Ranks alternatives based on their proximity to an ideal solution	Evaluating sustainable practises
VIKOR	Focuses on finding a compromise solution	Balancing economic and environmental goals

Figure 1. Role of MCDM in SSCM decision-making

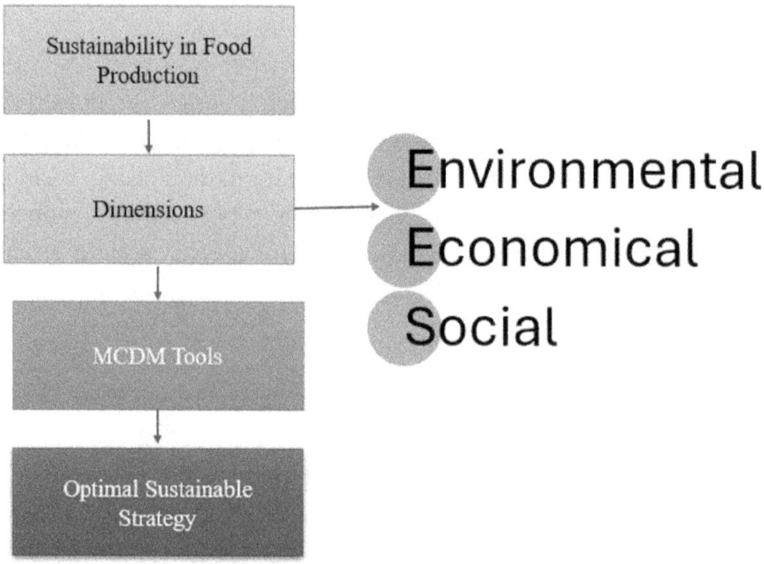

THE ANALYTIC HIERARCHY PROCESS

The Analytic Hierarchy Process (AHP) is a widely used decision-making tool developed by Saaty (1980). It helps structure complex problems into a hierarchy, breaking them into smaller, more manageable components. AHP allows decision-makers to evaluate alternatives based on multiple criteria by assigning weights through pairwise comparisons. This method is particularly useful in sustainable supply chain management for tasks like supplier selection, risk assessment, and resource allocation. By converting subjective judgments into numerical values, AHP improves decision quality and transparency, ensuring consistency across complex decision-making scenarios.

Introduction to AHP

The AHP is a decision-making framework. It is designed to help individuals and organizations deal with complex decisions by breaking them into smaller, hierarchical elements. AHP is particularly effective when decisions involve multiple, conflicting criteria, making it ideal for strategic management, project prioritization, and supplier selection.

Fundamental Principles of AHP

AHP operates based on the following key principles:

1. **Hierarchical Structuring**: The decision problem is divided into levels, usually starting with the main goal, followed by criteria, sub-criteria, and alternatives.
2. **Pairwise Comparison**: Decision-makers compare elements in pairs to determine their relative importance using a numerical scale (e.g., 1-9), where 1 indicates equal importance and 9 indicates extreme preference for one element.
3. **Weight Calculation**: Weights are assigned to criteria based on the comparisons. These weights are then aggregated to rank alternatives.
4. **Consistency Check**: AHP ensures that judgments remain consistent. A consistency ratio (CR) is calculated; if it exceeds a threshold (typically 0.1), the comparisons are re-evaluated.

Typical Applications of AHP

AHP is widely used in fields such as:

- **Sustainable Supply Chain Management**: To evaluate suppliers based on environmental, social, and economic criteria. Table 4 presents the pair-wise comparison matrix for SSCM criteria.
- **Project Management**: For prioritizing tasks and resources in large projects.
- **Urban Planning and Policy Making**: To assess multiple policy options or infrastructure investments.

Table 4. Pair-Wise comparison matrix for SSCM criteria

Criteria	Environmental (C1)	Economical (C2)	Social (C3)
Environmental (C1)	1	3	2
Economical (C2)	1/3	1	1/2
Social (C3)	½	2	1

- The matrix reflects the relative importance of **Environmental (C1)**, **Economical (C2)**, and **Social (C3)** criteria in SSCM.

- A higher score indicates greater importance (e.g., Environmental is more important than Economical, with a score of 3).

Figure 2. AHP hierarchy for SSCM

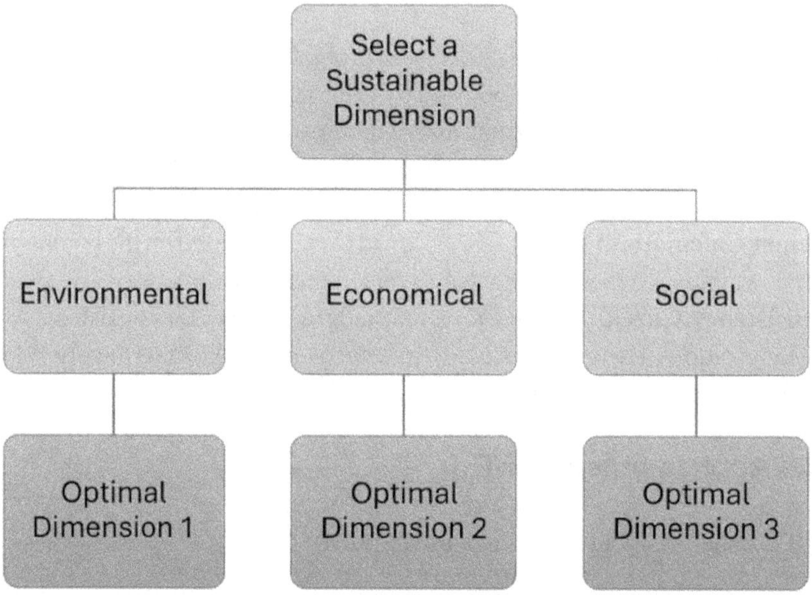

- The top-level goal is selecting the most sustainable dimension which provides optimal sustainable strategy.
- Criteria like Environmental, Economical, and Social are considered in evaluating optimal decision (1, 2, and 3).

AHP provides a structured and transparent decision-making process, helping decision-makers balance multiple factors effectively. It is especially beneficial in scenarios requiring both objective data and subjective judgments, such as sustainable supply chain management. By simplifying complex decisions into smaller comparisons, AHP ensures consistency and enhances decision quality. Fig.2 provides hierarchy for SSCM.

How AHP Works

The AHP simplifies complex decision-making by breaking down the decision problem into a structured hierarchy. This hierarchy typically consists of three levels: the goal, criteria and sub-criteria, and alternatives. Each element in the hierarchy is evaluated through pairwise comparisons, enabling a thorough assessment of trade-offs among criteria and alternatives.

Step-by-Step Process of AHP

1. Define the Goal

The first step is to clearly define the objective of the decision-making process. For example, in sustainable supply chain management, the goal might be to select the most sustainable supplier.

2. Develop the Hierarchy

The next step is to create a hierarchical structure. At the top of the hierarchy is the goal, followed by criteria (e.g., environmental, economic, social dimensions) and sub-criteria (e.g., carbon footprint, cost, labor practices). At the bottom are the alternatives, such as different suppliers or strategies.

3. Pairwise Comparisons

Decision-makers compare elements within the same level, such as evaluating two criteria (e.g., environmental vs. economic) or two suppliers based on one criterion. These comparisons are rated on a 1-9 scale, where 1 indicates equal importance and 9 indicates extreme preference for one element.

4. Calculate Weights and Priorities

AHP converts the comparisons into numerical weights that reflect the relative importance of each criterion. These weights are normalized and aggregated to rank the alternatives.

5. Check for Consistency

AHP includes a consistency ratio (CR) to ensure that the judgments are logical. If the CR exceeds 0.1, the comparisons must be reviewed to maintain consistency.

6. Select the Best Alternative

The final step is to aggregate the weights of all criteria and sub-criteria to determine the overall score for each alternative. The alternative with the highest score is the preferred choice.

By structuring complex decisions hierarchically, AHP enables organizations to compare subjective and objective criteria systematically. This method ensures that decisions are transparent, consistent, and well-informed. A crucial advantage in fields like SSCM, where multiple stakeholders and competing priorities must be considered.

Advantages of AHP in Supply Chain Management

AHP is a robust tool in supply chain management (SCM), particularly for complex decision-making within sustainable food supply chains. As these chains must balance environmental, economic, and social considerations, AHP enables structured and strategic choices by integrating various criteria and preferences.

Key Advantages of AHP in Sustainable Food Supply Chains

1. **Multi-Criteria Decision Making**

AHP excels in multi-criteria decision-making, which is vital for sustainable SCM, as it allows decision-makers to evaluate factors like environmental impact, cost-effectiveness, social impact, and risk. For instance, a study used AHP to weigh different Key Performance Indicators (KPIs) in food supply chains, identifying critical areas such as recycling costs and energy efficiency that impact overall sustainability (Danang Kumara Hadi, 2023).

2. **Risk Assessment and Mitigation**

Sustainable food supply chains often face risks related to product quality, transportation delays, and supplier reliability. AHP provides a quantitative way to assess these risks by assigning weights to each factor based on its potential impact. This helps in systematically prioritizing strategies to address critical risks and improves food safety and operational efficiency (Sinh, 2024).

3. **Stakeholder Preference Analysis**

Sustainable SCM requires alignment with diverse stakeholder interests—farmers, consumers, suppliers, and policymakers. AHP facilitates analysing and prioritizing these stakeholders' preferences for attributes like local production, environmental impact, and product quality, making it a valuable tool for engaging in a more inclusive and collaborative SCM strategy. In the tomato supply chain, for instance, AHP was used to evaluate stakeholders' priorities, enabling sustainable sourcing and shortened supply chains (Adrià Menéndez i Molist, 2024).

4. **Technology Selection and Implementation**

Sustainable food SCM increasingly relies on technologies like traceability systems to reduce waste and enhance transparency. A hybrid model using AHP has been effectively applied to optimize traceability technology selection, ensuring alignment with sustainability goals by balancing factors such as cost, technological benefits, and operational feasibility (by Samantha Islam, 2021).

5. **Long-Term Strategy Formulation**

AHP is also useful for formulating long-term strategies in sustainable SCM by helping organizations weigh success factors over time. For example, using AHP to analyse food safety and security within SCM has highlighted packaging and government policies as critical success factors for achieving sustainable goals (Y. Sharma, 2018). Table 5 presents AHP criteria and sub criteria for sustainable food SCM.

Table 5. AHP criteria and sub-criteria for substantial food SCM

Criteria	Sub-Criteria	Weightage
Environmental	Recycling, Green Labelling and Emissions Control	0.4
Economical	Cost Efficiency, Local Production and Profitability	0.3
Social	Stakeholder Engagement and Consumer Satisfaction	0.3

In conclusion, AHP's ability to integrate diverse criteria makes it well-suited for the multi-faceted decisions involved in sustainable food supply chains. By quantifying and prioritizing sustainability goals across stakeholders and resource constraints, AHP supports more informed, balanced, and strategic decision-making.

APPLYING AHP IN SUSTAINABLE SOURCING

Applying the AHP to sustainable sourcing in supply chains offers a structured way to make environmentally and socially responsible decisions. Sustainable sourcing requires companies to evaluate suppliers on numerous criteria beyond price, such as environmental practices, social responsibility, and long-term reliability. AHP simplifies this complexity by allowing decision-makers to prioritize these factors through a series of pairwise comparisons. This approach converts qualitative assessments into quantitative values, making it easier to rank and select suppliers based on their alignment with sustainability goals.

For example, in food supply chains, AHP can weigh factors like carbon footprint, water usage, local sourcing, and fair labor practices. By assigning a weight to each criterion, AHP helps companies balance trade-offs such as prioritizing lower emissions over minor cost savings. This method also allows businesses to integrate stakeholder values, ensuring decisions reflect consumer expectations for sustainable practices.

Ultimately, AHP not only facilitates more transparent and measurable sourcing choices but also supports companies in building resilient supply chains aligned with sustainability principles. This alignment can strengthen brand reputation, reduce environmental impact, and foster long-term supplier partnerships based on shared values.

Criteria for Sustainable Sourcing

Key criteria for sustainable sourcing typically focus on environmental impact, supplier reliability, cost, and ethical considerations, all which support building responsible, resilient supply chains. Here's a breakdown of each:

1. **Environmental Impact**

The environmental impact of sourcing decisions is pivotal, as organizations are increasingly accountable for their supply chain's carbon footprint, resource consumption, and waste production. Sustainable suppliers often prioritize renewable energy, water conservation, waste reduction, and efficient resource use, which can significantly reduce the overall environmental burden of production. For example, life cycle assessments (LCAs) are commonly used in evaluating a supplier's environmental performance, focusing on emissions, energy consumption, and waste generation. By partnering with suppliers committed to environmentally friendly practices, companies not only help meet global sustainability goals but also ensure compliance with environmental regulations, minimizing potential liabilities and enhancing brand reputation. Such efforts align companies with consumers who prioritize environmentally responsible products (Zenat Mohamed, 2024).

2. **Supplier Reliability**

Supplier reliability is essential in sustainable sourcing because it determines the continuity and stability of supply. Reliable suppliers provide high-quality products consistently and deliver them on time, which helps companies avoid disruptions that could lead to operational inefficiencies or missed opportunities. In the context of sustainable sourcing, reliability also means that suppliers can maintain their commitments to environmental and social standards, even under pressure. For instance, reliable suppliers are better able to handle fluctuations in demand and adapt to shifts in regulatory requirements, thereby supporting a more resilient supply chain. By selecting suppliers with proven reliability, organizations safeguard themselves against risks related to quality inconsistencies or delivery delays, ensuring a dependable supply for their operations (Cooper, 2024).

3. **Cost Efficiency**

Cost remains a key factor, but sustainable sourcing redefines it to account for long-term savings rather than immediate expense reductions. Although sustainable practices can incur initial higher costs, such as for eco-friendly materials or fair labor, they often lead to long-term savings through efficiencies and waste reduction. For example, sourcing from suppliers who use energy-efficient technologies or reduce material waste can translate into cost savings for both the supplier and the company over time. Sustainable cost management encourages organizations to view expenses in terms of life-cycle costs, considering factors such as durability and recyclability, which contribute to reduced costs across the supply chain's lifespan (Reynolds, 2024).

4. **Ethical Considerations**

Ethical considerations are central to sustainable sourcing, addressing social issues like fair wages, labor rights, and safe working conditions. This involves vetting suppliers for compliance with international labor standards, ensuring no child or forced labor is used, and verifying that work environments are safe and non-discriminatory. Suppliers with strong ethical practices foster better community relationships and provide a foundation for long-term partnerships based on shared values. Furthermore, ethical sourcing protects companies from potential reputational risks associated with poor labor practices in their supply chains. By holding suppliers to high ethical standards, companies can promote social responsibility and contribute to positive social impacts globally (Lidiia Savchenko, 2021).

Benefits of Integrating These Criteria

Together, these criteria help companies build resilient supply chains that are adaptable, responsible, and aligned with sustainability goals. They offer benefits like improved brand reputation, customer loyalty, risk mitigation, and operational efficiencies. For example, sustainable suppliers who use efficient practices or recycle materials often incur lower long-term costs, which can benefit all parties in the supply chain.

By embedding environmental, social, ethical, and economic criteria into sourcing practices, organizations can move beyond mere compliance and create a strategic advantage in the increasingly sustainability-focused market. This approach leads to more robust supply chain relationships and aligns businesses with growing global expectations for sustainability.

The Analytic Hierarchy Process (AHP) is a structured decision-making tool that can help companies prioritize and select suppliers based on sustainability criteria. Here is a step-by-step guide to applying AHP for sustainable supplier selection.

AHP in Action

- **Step 1: Define the Goal**

Start by clearly defining the goal of the decision-making process. In this case, the goal is to select a supplier who aligns best with the company's sustainability criteria. Sustainability criteria can vary, but typically include environmental impact, cost efficiency, supplier reliability, and ethical practices. Clarifying this goal is essential for organizing the rest of the AHP process.

- **Step 2: Identify Criteria and Sub-Criteria**

The next step is to identify key criteria and sub-criteria based on the sustainability objectives. Common primary criteria might include:

- o **Environmental impact** (e.g., energy use, waste reduction, and emissions),
- o **Supplier reliability** (e.g., delivery consistency and quality),
- o **Cost efficiency** (e.g., overall cost versus benefit), and
- o **Ethical practices** (e.g., labor conditions and fair-trade certifications).

Within each of these categories, you can add sub-criteria to capture specifics. For example, under environmental impact, you might consider carbon footprint, water usage, and recycling practices. The more precisely you define these criteria, the more targeted and meaningful the AHP analysis will be.

- **Step 3: Create a Hierarchical Structure**

Organize the goal, criteria, and sub-criteria in a hierarchy, with the goal at the top, followed by the main criteria, and then any sub-criteria. This hierarchical structure visually maps out the decision problem, making it easier to manage and analyse. Here, the top level is the goal (selecting a sustainable supplier), the second level consists of the main criteria, and the third level comprises the sub-criteria.

- **Step 4: Conduct Pairwise Comparisons**

In AHP, pairwise comparisons are used to quantify the relative importance of each criterion and sub-criterion. For each pair of criteria (e.g., environmental impact vs. cost), decision-makers assign a numerical value based on their relative importance on a scale from 1 to 9, where 1 means equal importance, and 9 means one is overwhelmingly more important than the other. For example, if environmental impact is twice as important as cost efficiency, you might assign it a value of 2 over cost.

- **Step 5: Calculate the Priority Weights**

After conducting all pairwise comparisons, calculate priority weights to reflect the relative importance of each criterion. To do this, you first sum each column in the comparison matrix, then normalize each entry by dividing it by the column total. Finally, average each row to produce the priority weights. These weights reflect the relative importance of each criterion, helping to determine which aspects should influence the final decision most heavily.

- **Step 6: Perform Consistency Check**

AHP includes a consistency check to ensure that the pairwise comparisons are logically consistent. Inconsistencies can occur if, for instance, you rated environmental impact as more important than cost, cost as more important than reliability, but then also rated reliability as more important than environmental impact. The consistency ratio (CR) is calculated, and a CR of 0.1 or below is generally acceptable. If the CR is too high, re-evaluate the pairwise comparisons.

- **Step 7: Score Each Supplier Against Criteria**

Now, evaluate each supplier against the criteria and sub-criteria using the same pairwise comparison process. Each supplier receives a score relative to each criterion based on how well they meet each sustainability goal. For example, if Supplier A has a strong environmental record but is less cost-efficient, the environmental score might be high but cost efficiency low.

- **Step 8: Aggregate Scores to Determine the Best Supplier**

Combine the weighted scores of each supplier across all criteria. Multiply each supplier's score by the priority weight of each criterion, and then sum the results to get a final score for each supplier. The supplier with the highest score is considered the best match for the sustainability criteria.

AHP offers a systematic way to prioritize and select suppliers that align with sustainability goals. By breaking down complex sustainability requirements into clear criteria and assigning priority weights, AHP helps companies make transparent, balanced decisions. This approach not only ensures that sustainability remains central to supplier selection but also promotes consistency, fairness, and accountability in decision-making.

Case Study: Real-world example of a company using AHP to improve sustainability in its sourcing strategy.

Green Foods Inc. is a mid-sized company in the organic packaged food industry, committed to environmental and social responsibility. As part of its sustainability goals, Green Foods aimed to revamp its supplier selection process to prioritize eco-friendly and ethical sourcing practices. Facing challenges with suppliers' varying degrees of sustainability, Green Foods implemented the Analytic Hierarchy Process (AHP) to ensure a structured, data-driven approach to selecting suppliers who met their stringent sustainability criteria.

Step 1: Define the Goal

The primary objective for Green Foods was to select suppliers that best aligned with its commitment to sustainability. To achieve this, Green Foods set specific criteria based on its sustainability goals, prioritizing low environmental impact, high supplier reliability, reasonable cost, and strong ethical practices.

Step 2: Identify Criteria and Sub-Criteria

Green Foods identified four main criteria:

1. **Environmental Impact** (carbon footprint, waste management, and energy efficiency),
2. **Supplier Reliability** (delivery punctuality and quality consistency),
3. **Cost Efficiency** (overall cost relative to benefits), and
4. **Ethical Practices** (fair labor practices and community support).

Step 3: Create the Hierarchical Structure

The hierarchy was created as follows:

1. **Goal**: Select a sustainable supplier.
2. **Criteria**: Environmental Impact, Supplier Reliability, Cost Efficiency, Ethical Practices.
3. **Sub-Criteria** for each primary criterion, ensuring each element contributing to Green Foods' sustainability goals was considered.

Step 4: Conduct Pairwise Comparisons

Green Foods' sustainability committee conducted pairwise comparisons of the criteria. Each pair was compared on a 1-9 scale, with the higher score indicating greater importance. The comparison was based on Green Foods' priorities, placing high emphasis on Environmental Impact and Ethical Practices. Table 6 provides sustainability in sourcing strategy.

Table 6. Sustainability in sourcing strategy

Criteria	Environmental Impact	Supplier Reliability	Cost Efficiency	Ethical Practices
Environmental Impact	1	3	5	2
Supplier Reliability	1/3	1	4	½
Supplier Reliability	1/5	1/4	1	1/3
Ethical Practices	1/2	2	3	1

Step 5: Calculate Priority Weights and Consistency Check

The comparison matrix was normalized, and each row was averaged to determine priority weights. After calculating, Green Foods conducted a consistency check, achieving a consistency ratio (CR) of 0.07, which was within acceptable limits, ensuring the comparisons were logically consistent.

The priority weights for each criterion were as follows:

- **Environmental Impact**: 0.40
- **Ethical Practices**: 0.30
- **Supplier Reliability**: 0.20
- **Cost Efficiency**: 0.10

Step 6: Score Each Supplier Against Criteria

Green Foods identified three potential suppliers: Supplier A, Supplier B, and Supplier C. Each supplier was scored based on the sub-criteria using the same pairwise method, ensuring each received a rating for their performance on carbon footprint, labor practices, etc. The scores were normalized and multiplied by the criteria weights. Table 7 provides supplier weightage against impact.

Table 7. Supplier weightage against impact

Supplier	Impact	Reliability	Efficiency	Practices	Score
Supplier A	0.35	0.15	0.05	0.25	0.80
Supplier B	0.25	0.20	0.10	0.30	0.85
Supplier C	0.30	0.25	0.08	0.20	0.83

Step 7: Aggregate Scores and Select the Supplier

With a final score of 0.85, Supplier B emerged as the best match for Green Foods' sustainability criteria. Despite being slightly higher in cost, Supplier B's strong environmental and ethical performance outweighed the minor cost difference, aligning best with Green Foods' sustainability goals.

Step 8: Implementation and Benefits

Green Foods established a partnership with Supplier B and noted several benefits. Not only did Supplier B's practices significantly reduce Green Foods' carbon footprint, but their ethical sourcing also enhanced the company's brand reputation. Additionally, the partnership helped Green Foods meet regulatory standards and consumer expectations for sustainability.

By applying AHP, Green Foods established a clear, quantifiable system for selecting suppliers that aligned with their sustainability goals. This structured approach not only optimized supplier selection but also fostered transparency, accountability, and brand integrity in Green Foods' supply chain strategy.

AHP IN PRODUCTION AND PROCESSING

The Analytic Hierarchy Process is widely used in production and processing to streamline decision-making, prioritize tasks, and evaluate alternatives. By breaking down complex problems into smaller, manageable parts, AHP helps managers weigh factors like cost, quality, time, and risk. In production, AHP can help select suppliers, choose materials, or decide on technology investments based on a structured comparison of criteria. In processing, it aids in optimizing workflows by assessing the most efficient methods or equipment. Overall, AHP fosters a systematic approach to making choices, ultimately improving efficiency and resource allocation in industrial operations.

Sustainable Production Practices

Sustainable production practices are essential for businesses aiming to minimize their environmental impact and contribute positively to society. With increasing concerns over climate change, resource scarcity, and environmental degradation, sustainable practices have shifted from being optional to vital. Core elements of sustainable production include energy use, waste management, and resource efficiency, each playing a significant role in reducing ecological footprints and fostering long-term economic resilience.

1. Energy Use

Energy use is one of the most impactful aspects of production. Conventional energy sources, like fossil fuels, contribute significantly to greenhouse gas emissions and are limited in supply, making them unsustainable in the long run. Transitioning to renewable energy sources—such as solar, wind, and hydroelectric power, allows companies to cut their carbon emissions and reduce their reliance on finite resources.

Energy efficiency measures also play a pivotal role. Using energy-efficient machinery, optimizing manufacturing processes, and adopting smart technologies help reduce energy consumption without compromising productivity. For example, installing smart sensors to monitor and control energy usage in real time enables companies to detect inefficiencies and make timely adjustments. Energy audits and assessments can further guide companies in identifying areas where improvements are possible, allowing them to prioritize high-impact actions.

2. Waste Management

Effective waste management is central to sustainable production. Industrial processes generate various types of waste, from raw material remnants to by-products and hazardous chemicals. Poor waste disposal practices can lead to soil, water, and air pollution, which have harmful consequences for ecosystems and human health. Sustainable waste management includes reducing, reusing, and recycling materials as much as possible to minimize waste sent to landfills.

Reducing waste starts with optimizing production processes to ensure that materials are used efficiently, and waste generation is minimized. For instance, lean manufacturing practices focus on eliminating non-value-adding activities and minimizing waste in every stage of production. When waste is unavoidable, reusing it within the process can often be a viable solution. For example, some manufacturing industries recycle scrap metal, plastics, and other materials back into production cycles, saving resources and energy.

Recycling is equally important and involves converting waste into reusable materials. Companies can implement closed-loop recycling systems to turn by-products into inputs, ensuring resources remain within the production cycle. Additionally, partnering with recycling companies allows for the proper disposal of materials that cannot be reused in-house. Hazardous waste, like certain chemicals and electronics, requires special handling to ensure environmental safety, making it essential to adhere to regulations and dispose of these materials responsibly.

3. Resource Efficiency

Resource efficiency focuses on maximizing output while minimizing resource input, including raw materials, water, and energy. By using fewer resources to produce goods, companies can reduce costs and lessen their environmental impact. Sustainable sourcing is one approach, where materials are obtained from renewable sources or suppliers with eco-friendly practices, like those certified for sustainable forestry or organic agriculture.

Process optimization is another way to improve resource efficiency. For example, using advanced manufacturing techniques, such as 3D printing, allows companies to produce parts with less material waste than traditional methods. Water conservation practices, like recycling and reusing water within the production cycle, also play a key role. In water-intensive industries, such as textiles and agriculture, employing closed-loop water systems significantly reduces water demand and wastewater generation.

Innovative technologies are driving resource efficiency further. Digitalization and automation enable precise control over production processes, minimizing resource waste. The Internet of Things (IoT), for instance, connects devices and systems to track material usage, allowing companies to identify inefficiencies and take corrective action. Additionally, incorporating artificial intelligence (AI) into production can improve planning and forecasting, ensuring that resources are allocated based on demand, preventing overproduction, and reducing resource waste.

Benefits of Sustainable Production

Adopting sustainable production practices benefits both companies and society. For companies, it reduces operational costs by cutting energy consumption, material waste, and resource usage. Sustainable practices can also enhance brand reputation, as consumers increasingly favor environmentally responsible businesses. This reputation can translate into stronger customer loyalty and, potentially, greater market share.

Sustainable production also has long-term societal benefits. By reducing pollution and conserving natural resources, it helps protect ecosystems and biodiversity. Cleaner air, soil, and water contribute to public health, while conservation efforts ensure that resources remain available for future generations. Furthermore, sustainable production often aligns with regulatory requirements, allowing companies to stay compliant and avoid penalties related to environmental standards.

Challenges in Implementing Sustainable Production

Despite its benefits, sustainable production faces challenges. Transitioning to sustainable energy sources or implementing new technologies can involve significant upfront costs, which may be prohibitive for smaller businesses. The need for skilled personnel to manage advanced systems and maintain sustainable practices can also be a barrier, particularly for companies in regions where technical expertise is scarce.

Additionally, while recycling and waste management are essential, they can be complex to execute. In some cases, recycling certain materials may be financially or technically unfeasible. For instance, certain plastics and hazardous materials require specialized treatment, which can be expensive or logistically challenging. Similarly, sourcing sustainable materials can be difficult, especially if demand for such resources surpasses supply, potentially driving up costs.

Hence, Sustainable production practices are increasingly necessary to address environmental and economic challenges in a rapidly changing world. By focusing on energy use, waste management, and resource efficiency, businesses can significantly reduce their environmental impact and contribute to a more sustainable future. Although obstacles exist, the benefits of sustainable production, both for the environment and companies make it a valuable pursuit. Embracing sustainable practices not only enhances operational efficiency and aligns with consumer expectations but also helps ensure a healthier planet for generations to come. Fig.3 provides sustainable production practices.

Figure 3. Sustainable production practices flowchart

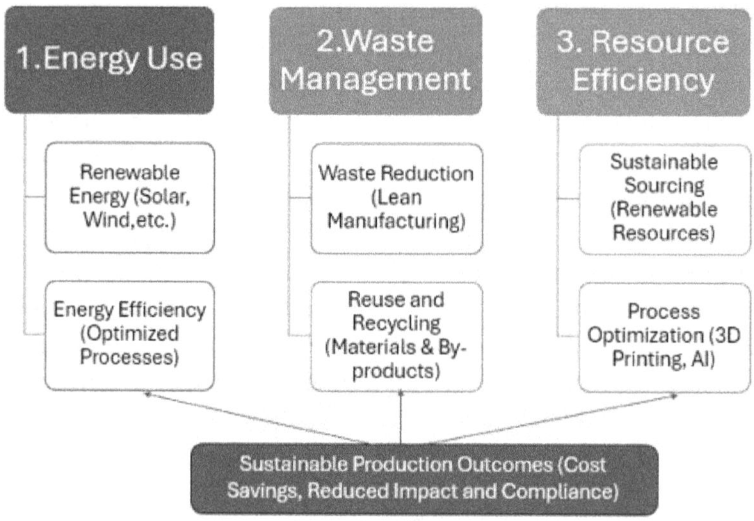

Optimizing Production Decisions with AHP

The AHP is a powerful tool for optimizing production decisions, particularly in complex scenarios where sustainability, efficiency, and cost-effectiveness must be balanced. AHP allows decision-makers to break down these goals into specific criteria, rank them in terms of importance, and evaluate production options in a structured, quantitative way.

Balancing Sustainability with Efficiency and Cost

In production, the balance between sustainability, efficiency, and cost-effectiveness is often challenging. Sustainability requires eco-friendly practices that can involve higher initial investments, such as using renewable energy sources or sustainable materials. Efficiency focuses on maximizing output with minimal resources, while cost-effectiveness demands careful management of expenses to remain competitive.

AHP is particularly valuable in this context because it enables decision-makers to compare these criteria systematically. For example, a company might want to implement a new manufacturing process and use AHP to evaluate each option's impact on sustainability, efficiency, and cost. By assigning weights to each factor based on their strategic priorities, the company can quantify how well each option aligns with its goals.

Using AHP to Evaluate and Prioritize Criteria

The first step in AHP is defining the primary goal and identifying relevant criteria and sub-criteria. For a production decision, the main goal might be "Select the Optimal Production Method." Criteria could include sustainability, production efficiency, and cost-effectiveness, each broken down into specific sub-criteria. For instance:

- Sustainability: could include resource conservation, waste reduction, and carbon footprint.
- Efficiency: might cover factors like time-to-output, energy consumption, and process reliability.
- Cost-effectiveness: could encompass initial investment, operational costs, and maintenance costs.

Once the criteria are defined, AHP helps prioritize them by using pairwise comparisons, allowing managers to indicate the relative importance of each criterion. This comparison creates a weighted matrix that quantifies how each factor should influence the final decision. For example, if sustainability is particularly important due to company goals or regulatory pressures, it might be weighted more heavily than initial investment cost.

Making a Balanced Production Decision

After setting criteria and weights, AHP allows managers to evaluate various production options against these criteria. Suppose there are three potential production methods: Traditional, Lean, and Sustainable. Each method can then be assessed in terms of how well it fulfils the criteria for sustainability, efficiency, and cost. The scores for each method are aggregated, producing an overall score that reveals the most balanced choice.

For example, while the sustainable method may have a higher upfront cost, AHP can reveal that its long-term benefits in resource savings and regulatory compliance outweigh the initial expense. Lean methods may rank high in efficiency but lower in sustainability, depending on the waste generated. AHP's structured comparison makes it possible to choose the option that aligns best with the organization's priorities, ensuring that the production decision is balanced, data-driven, and justifiable.

Advantages of AHP in Production Decision-Making

AHP's structured, transparent approach is a key advantage in production. Decisions that impact efficiency, sustainability, and cost are often complex and involve multiple stakeholders. AHP provides a transparent framework that allows everyone involved to understand the decision rationale, which can lead to better buy-in from team members and more consistency in long-term strategies.

Additionally, AHP's quantitative approach enables companies to assess trade-offs objectively. In production, this is valuable because it prevents personal biases from influencing critical choices. Decisions made using AHP are more likely to reflect organizational values, strategic goals, and environmental considerations.

Optimizing production decisions with AHP allows companies to balance sustainability, efficiency, and cost-effectiveness in a structured, data-driven way. By breaking down complex goals into specific, measurable criteria and assigning weights to reflect their priorities, companies can make decisions that are aligned with both short-term demands and long-term sustainability objectives. In today's competitive landscape, this approach can lead to more resilient production practices and a stronger commitment to sustainable growth.

Case Study: Enhancing Sustainability Practices in Green Sprout Foods Using the AHP

Green Sprout Foods, a mid-sized organic food processing company based in the Midwest, has been committed to sustainable practices since its founding. With increasing pressure from consumers, investors, and regulators to adopt more environmentally friendly processes, Green Sprout recognized the need to prioritize sustainability within its supply chain, production, and waste management practices. The challenge, however, was determining which sustainability initiatives would have the most significant impact, balancing environmental benefits with economic feasibility.

To address this, Green Sprout's management team chose to use the AHP to systematically evaluate and prioritize various sustainability projects. AHP was selected for its structured approach in breaking down complex decision-making into manageable parts, allowing Green Sprout to make informed, unbiased choices based on multiple criteria.

Objectives

1. Identify and evaluate key sustainability initiatives.
2. Prioritize these initiatives based on factors like environmental impact, cost-effectiveness, operational feasibility, and customer value.
3. Implement top-ranking initiatives within an 18-month timeline to align with Green Sprout's sustainability goals.

The AHP Approach: The first step was to create a cross-functional sustainability task force, consisting of managers from procurement, production, finance, and marketing. Together, they defined four main criteria for evaluating each potential sustainability project:

1. **Environmental Impact** - Assessing the positive effect on reducing carbon emissions, waste, or resource consumption.
2. **Economic Viability** - Evaluating the project's cost-effectiveness and potential for financial returns.
3. **Operational Feasibility** - Considering the ease and practicality of integrating the project within existing systems.
4. **Customer Perception** - Measuring how the initiative aligns with customer values and enhances brand loyalty.

Next, the team brainstormed several possible projects, including:

1. Transitioning to renewable energy for production facilities.
2. Implementing a zero-waste program.
3. Sourcing only from local, organic suppliers to reduce transportation emissions.
4. Reducing plastic in packaging by switching to biodegradable materials.
5. Investing in water recycling systems to minimize usage during production.

Using AHP, the team created a hierarchical structure with the main criteria as the top level and the projects as the alternatives. Each criterion was then given a weight based on Green Sprout's long-term goals, with environmental impact carrying the most weight (40%), followed by economic viability (30%), operational feasibility (20%), and customer perception (10%). Pairwise comparisons were conducted to rate each project against the criteria, yielding a final weighted score for each initiative. After completing the AHP calculations, the sustainability task force identified the following ranking:

1. **Renewable Energy Transition** – High environmental impact, significant customer perception benefits, and relatively high economic viability.
2. **Water Recycling Systems** – Reduced water consumption aligned with customer expectations, though the initial setup cost was high.
3. **Zero-Waste Program** – Operational feasibility and waste reduction were positive, but economic viability was moderate.
4. **Biodegradable Packaging** – Positive customer perception but lower feasibility due to increased production costs.
5. **Local Supplier Sourcing** – Lower ranking due to potential supply chain disruptions and limited impact on Green Sprout's overall sustainability footprint.

Implementation and Results

Based on the AHP results, Green Sprout Foods first invested in a renewable energy transition for its production facilities, installing solar panels and energy-efficient systems over a 12-month period. The transition led to a 35% reduction in carbon emissions, and the company received positive media coverage, which increased brand visibility. Customers noted the company's increased commitment to the environment, reinforcing Green Sprout's position as a trusted organic food brand. The next initiative, water recycling, was implemented within six months, leading to a 25% reduction in water usage, a notable achievement considering the water-intensive nature of food processing.

The AHP model allowed Green Sprout Foods to make informed, data-driven decisions in their journey toward sustainability. By identifying which initiatives would bring the highest value across environmental, economic, and operational dimensions, the company could focus its resources on projects that aligned with its long-term goals. This structured approach not only helped Green Sprout enhance its sustainability but also boosted its reputation, proving that sustainable practices could align well with financial growth and customer loyalty.

AHP IN DISTRIBUTION AND LOGISTICS

Distribution and logistics are crucial to the success of any business, especially as companies face complex challenges in a competitive global market. From choosing optimal warehouse locations to selecting the most cost-effective transportation routes, logistics decisions can significantly impact a company's efficiency and bottom line. One of the powerful decision-making tools that logistics managers often use to tackle these challenges is the AHP. AHP provides a structured framework for evaluating multiple alternatives based on defined criteria, helping logistics professionals make well-informed, balanced choices.

Challenges in Sustainable Distribution

In the journey from farm to fork, food products travel through a complex distribution network involving transportation, packaging, and storage. Each of these logistics elements has a significant impact on the environmental footprint of the food supply chain. As consumer awareness and demand for sustainability grow, food companies face the urgent challenge of rethinking traditional distribution methods to minimize environmental impacts without compromising efficiency or food quality. Let's delve into some of the major challenges in sustainable distribution and why logistics is central to creating a more sustainable food supply chain.

- **Transportation: Reducing Emissions and Fuel Dependency**

Transportation is one of the largest contributors to greenhouse gas emissions within the food supply chain. Moving food products, especially across long distances or international borders, requires significant fuel consumption, primarily from fossil fuels. This challenge is amplified by the perishability of food, which often demands faster (and therefore more fuel-intensive) transportation methods like air freight for fresh produce. Sustainable logistics solutions, like switching to electric or hybrid delivery vehicles, implementing more efficient routing software, and reducing the distance food travels from producer to consumer, are all ways to address this issue. However, the transition is not simple. Electric vehicle infrastructure is still limited, especially in rural or developing areas where many food producers operate. Additionally, integrating renewable energy sources and new technologies requires substantial upfront investment, which many companies especially smaller producers find challenging to afford.

- **Packaging: Balancing Durability with Eco-Friendly Materials**

Packaging plays a dual role in the food supply chain. It protects products during transportation and storage, reducing spoilage and waste, but it also often creates environmental challenges. Many packaging materials, like plastic, are durable and inexpensive but have a severe environmental impact. The food industry has traditionally relied on these materials because they extend shelf life and reduce the likelihood of damage in transit. However, non-biodegradable packaging contributes significantly to pollution, especially if it's not recyclable. Switching to sustainable packaging materials is increasingly seen as a priority, yet this shift comes with its own challenges. Eco-friendly packaging materials, such as biodegradable or compostable options, can be more expensive and sometimes lack the durability of traditional materials, increasing the risk of damage during transportation. Moreover, food safety regulations often restrict the types of packaging materials that can be used, especially for perishable items, limiting the options available to companies looking to "green" their packaging.

- **Storage: Energy Consumption and Waste Reduction**

Storage, particularly cold storage for perishable goods, is a major logistics element with sustainability challenges. Warehouses and refrigerated facilities consume large amounts of energy, often generated from non-renewable sources. Cold storage is necessary to maintain food quality and safety but can significantly increase a food product's overall carbon footprint. Optimizing energy usage in these facilities by implementing energy-efficient systems, using renewable energy, and improving insulation are essential steps for reducing environmental impact. Reducing waste during storage is also a crucial aspect of sustainable logistics. Food waste is a significant issue in the supply chain, with some products going bad before they even reach consumers due to poor inventory management or improper storage conditions. Advanced inventory tracking systems and real-time data analytics can help food companies manage their storage more efficiently, minimizing spoilage and ensuring that food is rotated and moved at the right times.

- **Balancing Costs with Sustainability Initiatives**

The economic aspect of sustainable distribution presents a major challenge. Adopting green logistics practices often requires considerable investment in technology, infrastructure, and training. Many small to medium-sized food producers and distributors operate on tight profit margins, making it difficult to afford these changes. Moreover, sustainable practices can sometimes result in higher operational costs. For instance, sustainable packaging is often more expensive than plastic, and renewable energy solutions might require significant initial investment before any cost savings are realized. Despite these costs, sustainable logistics can lead to long-term benefits for companies willing to invest. More sustainable practices can reduce overall waste, improve efficiency, and enhance brand reputation, attracting eco-conscious consumers. However, companies must find ways to balance immediate costs with long-term gains, which often requires careful planning, government incentives, or collaboration with other industry players.

- **The Complexity of Global Supply Chains and Localized Solutions**

The global nature of food supply chains adds layers of complexity to implementing sustainable logistics. Food distribution often involves multiple countries and regions, each with its own regulations, infrastructure capabilities, and environmental standards. While a country with developed infrastructure may offer green logistics options, others may lack facilities for sustainable packaging, renewable energy, or even efficient transportation routes. Localized solutions are emerging as one way to address these challenges, encouraging food companies to shorten supply chains by sourcing locally. However, local sourcing isn't always feasible for certain types of products or at scale. When possible, regionalizing production and distribution can reduce transportation emissions, improve responsiveness, and build resilience in the food supply chain by relying less on long-distance imports.

- **Why Sustainable Logistics is Essential to a Greener Food Supply Chain ?**

Sustainable distribution is not just about reducing environmental impact; it also contributes to the long-term resilience and efficiency of the food supply chain. As resources become scarcer and climate regulations more stringent, food companies that fail to invest in sustainable logistics may struggle to remain competitive. By addressing challenges in transportation, packaging, and storage, logistics can become a driver of positive environmental change rather than merely a source of emissions and waste. In the food industry, where consumer preferences are shifting towards eco-friendly options, logistics providers who prioritize sustainability will be better positioned to meet market demands. For this reason, integrating green logistics into the core of food distribution is no longer just an option, it's an essential step for companies committed to the sustainability of their operations and the health of the planet.

Using AHP for Logistics Optimization:

1. **Selecting Transportation Modes:** Transportation is a critical part of logistics, with multiple modes like road, rail, air, and sea, each having its pros and cons.

Logistics managers can use AHP to evaluate these modes based on factors such as cost, delivery speed, environmental impact, and reliability. For instance, air transport is fast but expensive and has a high carbon footprint, while sea transport is cost-effective and eco-friendly but slow. By assigning weights to each factor based on company priorities, AHP helps rank the transportation options, guiding managers to the most suitable choice.

2. **Warehouse Location Selection:** Choosing the right location for warehouses is a significant decision that affects delivery speed, cost, and customer satisfaction. Factors in this decision may include proximity to markets, transportation infrastructure, labor costs, and local taxes. AHP allows logistics teams to weigh each factor against their business goals, then compare potential locations through pairwise comparisons. By breaking down these complex criteria into manageable components, AHP aids in selecting a location that balances operational efficiency and cost-effectiveness.
3. **Inventory Management Strategies:** Inventory management involves balancing stock levels to ensure product availability while minimizing costs. Companies might consider options like Just-in-Time (JIT) inventory, Economic Order Quantity (EOQ), or safety stock strategies. With AHP, logistics teams can evaluate these inventory strategies based on factors like holding costs, lead times, demand fluctuations, and order frequency. By prioritizing these criteria, AHP helps managers select an inventory strategy that aligns with the company's goals, ensuring a stable supply chain while controlling costs.
4. **Supplier Selection:** Choosing reliable suppliers is essential for a smooth supply chain. However, the selection process involves evaluating each supplier's quality, reliability, pricing, and capacity. Using AHP, managers assign weights to each of these criteria, based on the company's requirements, and perform pairwise comparisons among suppliers. The final scores help determine which suppliers best match the business's needs, ensuring a dependable flow of materials.
5. **Route Optimization:** Efficient route planning is crucial for minimizing delivery times and fuel costs. Route optimization with AHP involves evaluating different routes based on traffic patterns, fuel efficiency, toll costs, and safety. Logistics managers can use AHP to prioritize these factors, analysing various routes to determine the optimal one. By balancing cost-effectiveness with delivery speed, AHP assists in creating routes that meet both customer expectations and budget constraints.

Case Study

Consider a logistics company, Trans Way Logistics, that operates a fleet of trucks across multiple states. As part of its expansion, the company faced challenges in selecting new warehouse locations and optimizing its delivery routes. Trans Way's management decided to apply AHP to make systematic, data-backed decisions on both fronts.

1. **Warehouse Location Selection:**

For new warehouses, the company evaluated potential sites based on proximity to customers, infrastructure quality, and labor costs. Using AHP, they determined the weights of these criteria, emphasizing customer proximity (40%), infrastructure quality (35%), and labor costs (25%). After performing pairwise comparisons, they chose a location that provided a good balance between accessibility and operational costs, allowing faster service to key markets.

2. **Route Optimization for Fuel Efficiency and Delivery Speed:**

Trans Way's fleet managers also used AHP to optimize routes based on fuel efficiency, traffic, and toll costs. Fuel efficiency was weighted highest due to rising fuel costs, followed by traffic avoidance for timely deliveries. The final AHP analysis highlighted the most efficient routes, reducing both fuel expenses and delivery times.

Benefits of AHP in Logistics

AHP brings several benefits to logistics and distribution, including:

- **Structured Decision-Making:** AHP helps organize complex logistics problems by breaking them down into criteria and alternatives, simplifying the decision process.
- **Transparency and Objectivity:** By assigning weights and evaluating criteria systematically, AHP reduces bias in decision-making, fostering transparency and objectivity.
- **Flexibility:** Logistics priorities can change based on economic conditions, customer demand, or environmental concerns. AHP's adaptable framework allows managers to adjust criteria weights as needed.

AHP provides distribution and logistics professionals with a powerful tool for making decisions across multiple facets, from transportation choices to supplier selection and route optimization. Its structured, step-by-step approach supports data-backed decision-making, leading to more efficient, cost-effective logistics operations. As companies continue to face growing demands for speed and sustainability in their supply chains, AHP can play a pivotal role in helping them make balanced, strategically sound logistics decisions.

INTEGRATING AHP ACROSS THE SUPPLY CHAIN

In today's global marketplace, supply chains are increasingly complex and require smart, data-driven decision-making at each stage. From supplier selection and inventory management to distribution and customer service, each link in the supply chain impacts the overall efficiency and sustainability of a company. Integrating the AHP across the supply chain can help companies make more structured and consistent decisions, prioritize objectives, and balance competing needs. By applying AHP at different points, organizations can improve coordination and align strategies for optimal performance.

Holistic Approach to Sustainability

Incorporating sustainability throughout the supply chain is no longer just a trend, it's essential for companies committed to reducing environmental impact while meeting consumer demand for responsible practices. Achieving sustainability across each stage of the supply chain, however, involves balancing diverse and sometimes competing priorities, from cost-effectiveness to product quality and speed of delivery. The AHP offers a powerful framework for aligning decisions across the supply chain with sustainability goals. Through AHP, companies can systematically prioritize sustainable choices and ensure they permeate each phase, fostering a holistic, integrated approach to sustainability.

Understanding AHP's Role in a Holistic Sustainability Strategy

AHP helps organizations break down complex, multi-criteria decisions into manageable steps, making it easier to weigh different sustainability factors against each other. By defining criteria at each stage, assigning weights to these criteria based on priorities, and performing pairwise comparisons, companies can ensure that sustainability is not just an afterthought but a guiding principle across sourcing, production, logistics, and customer service. Through AHP, companies can align each step in the supply chain with their overarching sustainability goals, creating a balanced approach that considers both environmental impact and operational efficiency.

1. Sourcing and Supplier Selection: Ensuring Ethical and Sustainable Inputs

Sourcing is the first step in most supply chains, and decisions made here significantly impact the sustainability of the entire chain. With AHP, companies can evaluate suppliers based on sustainability criteria such as environmental certifications, resource usage, waste management practices, and labor conditions. By assigning weights to each criterion, they can objectively select suppliers who align with their sustainability standards.

For example, a company might prioritize suppliers with eco-friendly practices, even if their materials are slightly more expensive, by assigning higher weights to criteria like carbon footprint and ethical sourcing. This approach ensures that sustainability is embedded from the beginning of the supply chain, setting a strong foundation for subsequent stages.

2. Manufacturing and Production: Minimizing Waste and Energy Use

Once materials are sourced, the focus shifts to manufacturing, where decisions around energy use, waste management, and production methods greatly influence a company's sustainability profile. AHP can assist in evaluating production processes based on criteria such as energy efficiency, emissions, water usage, and waste generated. For instance, if reducing carbon emissions is a top priority, AHP can help managers select production methods and equipment that optimize energy use, even if it requires an initial investment.

By aligning production practices with sustainable priorities through AHP, companies can make informed, data-backed decisions that reduce environmental impact while balancing cost and efficiency. This structured approach allows them to maintain a consistent commitment to sustainability even when faced with challenging trade-offs in production.

3. Packaging Decisions: Balancing Durability and Environmental Impact

Packaging presents a unique challenge in sustainable supply chains. While packaging needs to be durable enough to protect products, especially during long transit times, it also often contributes significantly to waste. AHP allows companies to weigh the environmental impact of different packaging materials against criteria such as durability, recyclability, cost, and customer perception.

For example, a company might face a choice between traditional plastic packaging and a biodegradable alternative that is more expensive but less harmful to the environment. By using AHP, they can objectively compare these options based on how well they align with their sustainability priorities. This approach allows the company to choose a solution that meets both its operational needs and environmental goals, ensuring a sustainable choice in a critical area.

4. Logistics and Distribution: Reducing Emissions and Improving Efficiency

Transportation is often one of the largest sources of emissions in the supply chain. AHP can play a key role in making logistics more sustainable by helping companies evaluate factors such as fuel efficiency, carbon footprint, cost, and delivery speed. By using AHP to weigh these criteria, companies can choose transportation modes and routes that minimize emissions without compromising timely delivery.

For example, if reducing carbon emissions is a high priority, AHP might guide the company toward more eco-friendly transportation methods, such as rail or electric vehicles, even if they have a higher upfront cost. Additionally, AHP can assist in optimizing distribution routes to further reduce fuel consumption, ensuring that sustainable logistics decisions are consistently integrated into the supply chain.

5. Inventory Management and Storage: Lowering Energy Use and Reducing Waste

Storage facilities, especially cold storage for perishable items, are significant energy consumers in the supply chain. AHP helps companies prioritize criteria such as energy efficiency, waste reduction, cost, and temperature control, enabling them to choose inventory practices and storage facilities that align with sustainability goals.

For instance, by using AHP, a company might prioritize energy-efficient refrigeration systems or implement a more flexible inventory management system that reduces waste due to spoilage. Through AHP, they can ensure that sustainability considerations inform their storage practices, resulting in a supply chain that's more energy-efficient and aligned with waste reduction goals.

6. Customer Service and Returns: Encouraging Sustainable Consumption

Customer service plays a crucial role in reinforcing sustainable supply chain practices, especially in managing returns and product end-of-life. AHP can be used to evaluate customer service practices based on sustainability criteria, such as minimizing returns, promoting responsible disposal, or incentivizing product reuse.

For instance, AHP can help companies design return policies that encourage customers to use products longer or offer incentives for returning products in a way that allows for recycling or refurbishment. By integrating AHP into these decisions, companies can extend sustainability to the end of the product lifecycle, aligning customer interactions with their environmental goals.

7. Coordinating Sustainability Across Departments and Teams

One of the strengths of AHP is its ability to provide a consistent, organization-wide decision-making framework. By using AHP to align sustainability criteria across different departments, companies ensure that every part of the supply chain adheres to the same principles. For instance, a company might establish shared sustainability criteria—such as carbon footprint, recyclability, and energy use, that are applied across sourcing, production, and distribution. Each department uses these criteria in their AHP models, ensuring that decisions align with overall sustainability objectives.

This coordinated approach helps prevent contradictory decisions between departments. For example, sourcing may select sustainable materials, but if distribution doesn't follow eco friendly practices, the company's overall sustainability efforts could be compromised. AHP helps avoid these inconsistencies by creating a shared framework that guides each stage toward a common sustainability goal.

Collaborative Decision-Making

The push for sustainability in supply chains requires more than just internal adjustments; it demands collaborative decision-making that includes input from all relevant stakeholders. From suppliers and manufacturers to logistics providers and customers, each participant in the supply chain has unique insights, priorities, and constraints that impact overall sustainability. In the AHP, stakeholder involvement is critical because it ensures that decisions reflect diverse perspectives, ultimately leading to more balanced and achievable sustainable outcomes.

- **The Importance of Stakeholder Involvement in AHP**

The AHP model involves identifying and weighting criteria based on organizational priorities, followed by pairwise comparisons to rank options. When it comes to sustainable supply chain decisions, the value of AHP is maximized by including stakeholders from different stages of the supply chain, each contributing their specific insights and priorities. For example:

- Suppliers: may have crucial input regarding the environmental impact of raw materials or processes.
- Manufacturers: can provide data on production efficiency, energy use, and waste management.
- Logistics providers: bring knowledge of transportation costs, carbon emissions, and route optimization.
- Customers and end-users: often expect transparency around sustainability practices, and their values can guide the weight given to criteria like ethical sourcing or carbon footprint reduction.

Involving stakeholders helps ensure that AHP decisions are grounded in practical realities and that sustainable practices are feasible across the supply chain. By collaborating on setting and weighing sustainability criteria, organizations can create a supply chain strategy that not only meets environmental goals but also aligns with the operational needs and values of all participants (Puppala NS, 2024).

- **Facilitating Collaboration for Sustainable Outcomes**

Facilitating effective collaboration in the AHP process requires clear communication, transparency, and a structured approach to gathering input. Here are some strategies for bringing stakeholders together in the AHP process:

- o **Identify Key Stakeholders and Their Roles:** First, outline who the critical decision-makers are at each stage of the supply chain. This list might include sourcing managers, production supervisors, logistics coordinators, and customer relations representatives, as well as external partners like suppliers and transportation providers (Manoharan, 2023).
- o **Establish Common Sustainability Goals:** Once stakeholders are identified, bring them together to discuss common sustainability objectives. This could involve reducing carbon emissions, minimizing waste, or sourcing materials responsibly. Clear goals help all parties understand the purpose behind the decisions and the criteria that will be prioritized in the AHP model (Manoharan, Cluster-based Trust Evaluation of Blockchain Miners in Pool Mining, 2023).

- **Collaborative Criteria Setting:** In the AHP process, sustainability criteria should reflect the priorities of all participants. For example, suppliers might emphasize renewable materials, while logistics teams may prioritize efficient fuel use. By collectively setting criteria, stakeholders can ensure that all aspects of sustainability are accounted for, creating a shared commitment to the final decisions.
- **Pairwise Comparisons and Weighting with Stakeholder Input:** Each criterion must be weighted, and decisions made through pairwise comparisons to rank options. Involving stakeholders in this process—either by directly participating or by providing input that informs decision-makers—ensures that criteria like cost, environmental impact, and operational efficiency are properly balanced.
- **Regular Review and Feedback Loops:** Sustainability goals evolve, so regular check-ins with stakeholders are essential to assess progress and adjust criteria or priorities as needed. Keeping lines of communication open for feedback ensures continuous improvement and alignment with shifting supply chain dynamics.

By fostering a collaborative AHP process, organizations can make supply chain decisions that are both sustainable and supported by all key players. This alignment strengthens commitment to sustainability goals and enhances the resilience and flexibility of the supply chain.

Case Study: Applying AHP for Sustainability from Farm to Table

Consider a food company focused on creating a fully sustainable supply chain, from sourcing raw ingredients on farms to delivering finished products to consumers. This case study illustrates how AHP can guide sustainable decision-making across the entire farm-to-table process, ensuring that every link in the chain supports the company's environmental goals.

Step 1: Sustainable Sourcing at the Farm Level

The journey begins at the farm, where the company sources ingredients. For instance, if the company is producing organic snack bars, it needs high-quality, sustainably farmed fruits and grains. AHP is used to evaluate potential farms based on several sustainability criteria, such as:

- Environmental impact of farming practices (e.g., pesticide use, water conservation)
- Certifications (such as organic or fair-trade labels)
- Carbon footprint of transportation from farm to production facilities
- Cost of raw materials and overall affordability

By assigning weights to these criteria, the company determines which farms align best with their sustainability values. For example, they might prioritize farms with organic certification and responsible water use, even if transportation costs are higher due to distance.

Step 2: Manufacturing Decisions Focused on Resource Efficiency

Once raw materials are sourced, they move to the manufacturing stage. Here, AHP helps in selecting production practices and equipment that align with sustainability goals. Criteria in the AHP model for this stage include:

- Energy efficiency of equipment
- Waste management capabilities
- Environmental compliance of the facility
- Production costs and operational feasibility

Using AHP, the company might prioritize energy-efficient machinery and waste reduction systems. Even if these options come with higher upfront costs, they align with the company's commitment to reducing its environmental footprint. This ensures that sustainability is built into the manufacturing process itself.

Step 3: Eco-Friendly Packaging Decisions

Packaging is a critical part of sustainability in the food supply chain. AHP is applied to select packaging materials that balance durability and environmental impact. The decision criteria might include:

- Recyclability or biodegradability of materials
- Cost of materials
- Customer expectations around eco-friendly packaging
- Protection and shelf life of the product

Through AHP, the company might determine that biodegradable packaging aligns best with their values, despite a slightly shorter shelf life. By prioritizing recyclability and customer expectations of eco-friendliness, the company ensures that packaging reflects its sustainability commitments.

Step 4: Sustainable Logistics and Transportation

Transporting goods from the production facility to distribution centres and retail locations is another area where sustainability is key. AHP helps the company make eco-friendly logistics choices by weighing criteria such as:

- Fuel efficiency of transportation options
- Carbon emissions and environmental impact
- Cost of transportation
- Delivery speed and reliability

AHP might guide the company to choose a mix of electric vehicles for short-distance routes and fuel-efficient trucks for long-haul shipments. By factoring in both emissions and cost, the company creates a logistics plan that reduces environmental impact without compromising operational efficiency.

Step 5: Customer Service and Product Returns

In the final stage, the company uses AHP to develop customer service and return policies that are sustainable. Criteria for AHP here might include:

- Ease of product recycling for customers
- Costs associated with returns and replacements
- Sustainability of return logistics (e.g., consolidating returns to minimize trips)
- Customer satisfaction and ease of use

The AHP results might indicate that incentivizing recycling (for instance, by offering discounts for product returns) is the best approach. This not only supports sustainability but also strengthens customer loyalty by showing a commitment to eco-friendly practices.

Integrating AHP across the supply chain provides companies with a structured, consistent approach to embedding sustainability into every decision, from sourcing and production to logistics and customer service. By using AHP to weigh and prioritize sustainability criteria at each stage, companies can align their actions with a holistic, end-to-end sustainability strategy. This approach not only reduces environmental impact but also enhances operational resilience, brand reputation, and customer loyalty, positioning the company as a responsible leader in the market.

CHALLENGES AND FUTURE DIRECTIONS

Limitations of AHP in Complex, Dynamic Supply Chains

The Analytic Hierarchy Process (AHP) is a valuable tool for decision-making, particularly when evaluating criteria across different dimensions. However, when applied to complex and dynamic supply chains, AHP faces several limitations. First, it relies heavily on pairwise comparisons, which can become cumbersome and impractical as the number of criteria and alternatives increases. In large-scale supply chains, this can lead to decision fatigue and increased cognitive load on the decision-makers. Additionally, AHP requires consistency in judgments, which is challenging in dynamic environments where supply chain variables like demand, costs, and resource availability frequently change. Moreover, AHP assumes that criteria are independent of each other, but in real-world supply chains, factors are often interdependent, making it hard for AHP to capture the full scope of these relationships. These limitations highlight the need to supplement AHP with other decision-making tools in complex, evolving supply chains.

Combining AHP with Other MCDM Methods for Robust Sustainability Assessments

To address some of these limitations, AHP can be combined with other multi-criteria decision-making (MCDM) methods, creating a hybrid approach for a more robust sustainability assessment. For instance, combining AHP with the Technique for Order Preference by Similarity to Ideal Solution (TOPSIS) can help rank alternatives more effectively, as TOPSIS accounts for both the ideal and the worst-case scenarios. Another popular combination is AHP with the Delphi method, which incorporates expert consensus and refines subjective judgments, reducing potential bias and improving decision accuracy. By integrating AHP with other MCDM tools, decision-makers can create a more comprehensive evaluation framework, balancing qualitative insights with quantitative analysis. These hybrid models are increasingly popular in sustainability assessments, as they offer a more nuanced and adaptable approach to complex issues like resource management, waste reduction, and eco-friendly logistics.

Future Trends in Sustainable Food Production and the Role of MCDM Methods

The field of sustainable food production is rapidly evolving, with trends focusing on resilience, circular economy principles, and low-impact agriculture. As consumer demand for transparency and environmentally friendly practices grows, so does the need for sophisticated tools to assess sustainability efforts comprehensively. Emerging technologies like blockchain and IoT are expected to play a pivotal role in real-time data collection, which, when integrated with MCDM methods like AHP, can significantly improve decision accuracy and responsiveness. In the future, MCDM methods are likely to incorporate more advanced analytics and artificial intelligence, enabling dynamic re-evaluation of criteria as supply chain conditions shift. This evolution will allow AHP and similar tools to become more flexible, data-driven, and suited to the increasingly complex needs of sustainable food systems.

CONCLUSION

This chapter fills an important gap in the existing literature by providing a comprehensive analysis of how the AHP can be effectively applied to improve sustainable supply chain management in the food production industry. By focusing on the practical implementation of AHP, the chapter offers detailed insights into how this Multi-Criteria Decision-Making method can address the unique challenges of balancing environmental, economic, and social factors in food production. Through the inclusion of real-world case studies, it demonstrates the practical benefits and potential of AHP in making more informed, rational decisions that align with sustainability goals. This chapter is designed to serve as a crucial resource for professionals, researchers, and students, equipping them with the knowledge and tools necessary to navigate the complexities of sustainable supply chain management. Ultimately, it aims to contribute to more responsible and effective strategies in the evolving landscape of the global food production system.

REFERENCES

Adrià Menéndez i Molist, Z. K. (2024). Assessing the Downstream and Upstream Preferences of Stakeholders for Sustainability Attributes in the Tomato Value Chain. *Sustainability (Basel)*, *16*(6), 1–24. DOI: 10.3390/su16062505

Islam, L. M. (2021). A Hybrid Traceability Technology Selection Approach for Sustainable Food Supply Chains. *Sustainability*, 1–23.

Cooper, M. (2024). Understanding Supplier Selection Criteria: Perspectives from Procurement Professionals in Diverse Industries.

Danang Kumara Hadi, A. P. (2023). Evaluation of Sustainability Supply Chain Performance in the Food Industry: A Case Study. *Journal Teknik Industri*, 1-11.

Lidiia Savchenko, S. S. (2021). *ENVIRONMENTAL AND SOCIAL RESPONSIBILITY IN SUPPLY CHAINS.* Izdevniecība "Baltija Publishing".

Manoharan, N. S. (2023). Cluster-based Trust Evaluation of Blockchain Miners in Pool Mining. *2023 Second International Conference on Advances in Computational Intelligence and Communication (ICACIC),* Puducherry, India, 2023 (pp. 1-6). Puducherry: IEEE Publisher.

Manoharan, N. S. (2023). Trust Model to Identify Reputed Miners in Blockchain Pool Mining. *International Conference on Signal Processing, Computation, Electronics, Power and Telecommunication (IConSCEPT), Karaikal, India, 2023* (pp. 1-6). Karikal: IEEE.

Marija Jeremić, B. M. (n.d.). The Green Food Supply Chain Concept. *29th International Scientific Conference Strategic Management and Decision Support Systems in Strategic Management.*

Naga Sravanthi Puppala, R. M. (2023). "Cluster-based Trust Evaluation of Blockchain Miners in Pool Mining". *Second International Conference on Advances in Computational Intelligence and Communication (ICACIC),* 1-6.

Osato Itohan Oriekhoe, B. A. (2023). Review of technological advancement in food supply chain management: Comparison between USA and Africa. *World Journal of Advanced Research and Reviews*, 1681-1693.

Puppala, N. S., & Manoharan, R. (2024). Optimizing pool mining performance: A VIKOR-based model for identifying reputed miners in blockchain networks. *Concurrency and Computation*, *36*(21), 1–30. DOI: 10.1002/cpe.8211

Rajeev Bhat, I. J. (2019). *Emerging issues and challenges in agri-food supply chain.* Academic Press.

Reynolds, S. (2024). Exploring Sustainable Procurement Practices: A Qualitative Study of Supplier Selection Criteria.

Shah, N. (2023). Technology Adoption in Food Supply Chain Management in Developing Countries: A Review. *International Journal of Engineering and Advanced Technology*, *12*(3), 11–18. DOI: 10.35940/ijeat.C3961.0212323

Sharma, Y., Yadav, A. K., Mangla, S. K., & Patil, P. P. (2018). Ranking the Success Factors to Improve Safety and Security in Sustainable Food Supply Chain Management Using Fuzzy AHP. *Materials Today: Proceedings*, *5*(5), 12187–12196. DOI: 10.1016/j.matpr.2018.02.196

Sinh, U. (2024). IDENTIFICATION AND EVALUATION OF DISTRIBUTION RISK IN FOOD SUPPLY CHAIN USING AHP METHOD. *INTERANTIONAL JOURNAL OF SCIENTIFIC RESEARCH IN ENGINEERING AND MANAGEMENT*, 1-5.

Vinay Surendra Yadav, B. E. (2022). A systematic literature review of the agro-food supply chain: Challenges, network design, and performance measurement perspectives. *Sustainable Production and Consumption*, *29*, 685–704. DOI: 10.1016/j.spc.2021.11.019

Zenat Mohamed, M. I.-G. (2024). Sustainable Supplier Selection using Neutrosophic Multi-Criteria Decision Making Methodology. *Sustainable Machine Intelligence Journal* .

Chapter 4
Examining Logistics 5.0 Factors with ANP Method, an Application on Turkish Logistics Sector

Bayram Şirin
https://orcid.org/0000-0003-3357-9138
Istanbul Ticaret University, Turkey

ABSTRACT

Technological advances after the Industrial Revolution led to increased production and the emergence of Industry 4.0, which introduced digitalization across all sectors. Technologies such as cyber-physical systems, IoT, and big data prioritized cost-efficiency and productivity. In logistics, this transformation gave rise to Logistics 4.0. However, rising production and mobility increased environmental harm, making sustainability a global concern. Logistics operations, with high carbon emissions, are critical in this context. Industry 4.0 has been criticized for overlooking human and environmental values. In response, Industry 5.0 emerged, focusing on human-centered and sustainable technologies. Accordingly, the logistics sector is transitioning toward Logistics 5.0. This study aims to identify key factors for Logistics 5.0 using the Analytic Network Process (ANP), based on expert evaluations of 18 criteria derived from a comprehensive literature review.

INTRODUCTION

Following the advancement of electronic and automation processes, the concept of Industry 4.0 has emerged as a new industrial revolution. The term Industry 4.0

DOI: 10.4018/979-8-3693-8789-4.ch004

originated in Germany and was first introduced in 2011 in an article that addressed the country's high-tech initiatives. Subsequently, in 2013, the concept was presented at an industrial fair held in Hannover, Germany, and was rapidly adopted as a national strategy (K. Zhou et al., 2015). Industry 4.0, driven by digital technologies, initially had a significant impact on the manufacturing sector, leading to rapid changes in industrial environments. Over time, this new industrial revolution fueled by the adoption of digital technologies expanded its influence across all sectors and played a major role in transforming both products and processes. Consequently, Industry 4.0 has substantially reshaped supply chains, business models, and operational processes. In the face of these developments and the transition to the digital age, companies have encountered numerous challenges (Schmidt et al., 2015).

As in all other sectors, the logistics industry has also entered a process of digital transformation to meet emerging needs related to personalized products, respond to global competitive pressures, and ensure sustainability (Hofmann & Rüsch, 2017). However, managing today's global logistics systems, which involve a vast variety of products, is becoming increasingly difficult. Although various strategies—such as postponement—have been developed to address these challenges, it remains questionable whether such approaches can effectively cope with increasingly complex and customized logistics systems (e.g., one-off or highly individualized products) while simultaneously ensuring low costs and high quality (Windt et al., 2008). Therefore, in order to logistical objectives to be successfully achieved, the sector requires a more dynamic and customer-oriented approach. To this end, real-time visibility in logistics has become increasingly important. From this perspective, Logistics 4.0 has been defined as follows: "A logistics system that enables the sustainable fulfillment of personalized customer demands without increasing costs, and that supports this advancement in industry and commerce through the use of digital Technologies" (Winkelhaus & Grosse, 2020b). Some of the technologies used in this system to meet emerging needs include the Internet of Things (IoT), big data, and cyber-physical systems (CPS) (Lu, 2017b).

Although the digitalization brought by Industry 4.0 has provided numerous benefits in terms of speed, efficiency, and profitability, it has also led to significant negative consequences. One of the most prominent concerns is its impact on the human labor force. The implementation of digital technologies and the resulting development of unmanned systems are often cited as contributing factors to rising unemployment. In addition, the rapid pace of technological change and the widespread use of new devices have led to an increase in digital waste and energy consumption, causing serious environmental concerns. Another major drawback is the growing risk of cybersecurity threats, due to the high level of connectivity across systems and devices. Moreover, considering obstacles such as limited operational resources and a lack of specialized expertise, it becomes increasingly difficult for logistics companies in developing economies to make effective investments in critical and strategic areas with their constrained capital. In light of all these developments, it has become evident that the human factor and sustainability have been overlooked in Industry 4.0. As a result of ongoing discussions and criticisms, the concept of Industry 5.0 has emerged. Industry 5.0 places the human factor at its core and advocates for the implementation of sustainable technological systems (Grosse et al., 2023).

As a result of successive industrial revolutions, the acceleration of global-scale production has led to an increase in environmental degradation. Since the late 1990s, the reduction of environmental harm and the preservation of natural resources have begun to be implemented as international policy priorities. Various national and international summits have been held to promote sustainable practices, set targets, and develop and implement strategies accordingly. These efforts began with the 1992 Rio Summit, followed by the 1997 Kyoto Protocol, the 2015 Paris Agreement, and most recently, the 2019 European Green Deal. One of the most critical issues addressed in discussions on environmental damage has been the reduction of carbon emissions. In this context, the logistics sector stands out as a major contributor. According to a report published in 2024 by the United Nations Environment Programme (UNEP), the transportation sector accounts for 15% of global carbon emissions (United Nations Environment Programme, 2024). Therefore, ensuring sustainability in logistics has become critically important. In this regard, various sustainable practices have begun to be implemented within the logistics sector. Examples include the use of electric and hybrid vehicles, the adoption of recyclable packaging materials, the implementation of loading and route optimization, the deployment of smart warehouse systems and vehicle tracking technologies, as well as the application of reverse logistics operations. The implementation of these practices requires the use of digital technologies such as Radio Frequency Identification (RFID), artificial intelligence (AI), machine learning, and the Internet of Things (IoT). Therefore, the use of digitalization technologies is essential for achieving sustainability. In this context, sustainability and digitalization emerge as interconnected and jointly addressed concepts.

1. DIGITALIZATION IN LOGISTICS PROCESSES (LOGISTICS 4.0)

All industries and sectors are compelled to adapt to the technological advancements, transformations, innovations, and evolving demands of the era. In this context, major developments and shifts throughout history are referred to as industrial revolutions. This process, which began with the mechanical revolution known as Industry 1.0, continued with the electrical revolution (Industry 2.0) and the electronics and automation revolution (Industry 3.0) (Özdemir & Özgüner, 2018). In recent years, significant advancements in production processes and technology have led to profound transformations in industry, giving rise to Industry 4.0, a concept widely recognized as the industrial revolution of our time (Pereira & Romero, 2017). This revolution, fundamentally driven by digitalization and digital transformation, encompasses a process shaped around concepts such as artificial intelligence, smart products, big data, the Internet of Things (IoT), and intelligent automation systems. Industry 4.0, along with the closely associated notions of digitalization and digital transformation, has become a widely discussed topic both in the industrial sector and in the academic literature.

Logistics is one of the most critical processes for a company, encompassing the management, control, and integration of products, as well as operations such as transportation, warehousing, handling, and packaging (Antoniuk et al., 2021). From a cost perspective, studies have shown that logistics costs can account for up to 20% of the total product price (Gümüş, 2009; Tanyaş, 2015). Moreover, logistics holds critical importance for national economies as well. When examining the share of logistics costs within a country's Gross Domestic Product (GDP), it is observed to range between 8% and 20%. Even in developed countries, this share hovers around 10%, clearly demonstrating the strategic significance of the logistics sector (Bayraktutan & Özbilgin, 2015; Yapraklı & Ünalan, 2017). Therefore, considering the critical importance of logistics for both companies and national economies, it is inconceivable for the logistics sector to remain unaffected by digitalization and Industry 4.0, or not to undergo a transformation in parallel with them.

The logistics sector has undergone a significant transformation alongside rapid technological advancements. This transformation has reached its peak with digitalization, introduced by Industry 4.0, which is regarded as the most recent industrial revolution. Digitalization first emerged on the production side, where it brought numerous advantages that led to substantial improvements in production processes. Existing practices were enhanced through the integration of new technologies, resulting in a dramatic increase in global-scale production (Kayikci, 2018). At the core of Industry 4.0 lies the implementation of digital technologies such as the Internet of Things (IoT), Big Data (BD), and Cyber-Physical Systems (CPS), with the aim of establishing a flexible, efficient, and sustainable production process that ensures high quality and low cost simultaneously (E. A. Lee, 2008; Rajkumar et al., 2010; Wang et al., 2016). Indeed, with the onset of the digital age, one of the first concepts to emerge was that of the "Smart Factory." However, the successful implementation of a smart factory also depends on ensuring real-time transparency across the entire value chain—from suppliers to end customers. Therefore, it is not only the production processes that need to be "smart," but also the logistics activities throughout the entire supply chain must be transformed into intelligent systems

(Henning Kagermann, 2015). In production engineering, Cyber-Physical Systems (CPS) are defined as integrated systems that improve bidirectional information flow between execution and decision-making layers. CPS incorporate computing, data storage, mechanical, and electronic components, and they require the Internet as a communication medium. At this very point, another technological advancement—namely the Internet of Things (IoT)—comes into play (Ashton, 2010). These systems have also needed to be considered within the field of logistics. Since the early 2000s, digitalization and the concept of the digital supply chain have emerged as prominent trends in logistics and supply chain management worldwide, gradually becoming central focus areas across the industry (Özdemir & Özgüner, 2018). Logistics 4.0 has been defined in various ways in the literature, with scholars approaching the concept from different perspectives. For instance, (Strandhagen et al., 2017)describe Logistics 4.0 based on five key characteristics:

1. Real-time big data analytics (e.g., optimized routing)
2. Reduced storage requirements due to new production techniques
3. Autonomous robots equipped with tracking and decision-making systems that enable optimized inventory control
4. Real-time information exchange
5. The prevention of information overload through the use of smart devices and technologies

These features collectively emphasize the transformation of traditional logistics into a more intelligent, connected, and adaptive system. (Barreto et al., 2017), on the other hand, define Logistics 4.0 as the combination of logistics processes with the applications and innovations enabled by Cyber-Physical Systems (CPS). In addition, (Timm & Lorig, 2015) characterize Logistics 4.0 as a transformation from hardware-focused logistics to software-focused logistics, highlighting the increasing role of digital technologies and intelligent systems in modern logistics operations. Logistics 4.0 emerged as a result of digitalization, characterized by the development of real-time, internet-based communication between machines and humans (Barreto et al., 2017). In other words, the concept is considered a direct outcome of digital transformation. According to (Lin & Jones, 2008) and (Gulledge & Chavusholu, 2008), the successful implementation of this concept depends on several key factors:

- The impact of the new digital logistics system on daily operations must be accurately anticipated and understood.
- Management must appoint qualified and competent personnel to lead the digital supply chain/logistics project from the outset.

- Success is enhanced through supplier network design, effective information sharing, visibility, and proactive measurement and monitoring.
- Process designs and complete enterprise process documentation must be finalized before initiating solution design.
- The organization's future state must be clearly defined, well-documented, and properly communicated to employees.
- The project team must maintain strong collaboration with software vendors and consultants.

These factors emphasize that successful digital logistics transformation requires not only technological integration but also strategic planning, cross-functional coordination, and organizational readiness. The conceptual framework of Logistics 4.0 consists of three dimensions (Winkelhaus & Grosse, 2020a).

The first dimension refers to external factors and includes the changes resulting from customers' growing demand for high-quality and personalized products, the developments within the Industry 4.0 process, as well as the effects of globalization and sustainability. In addition to these, this dimension also encompasses broader societal transformations (Hofmann & Rüsch, 2017; Lasi et al., 2014).

The second dimension is shaped by technology. This dimension includes the technological building blocks that enable the paradigmatic shift from traditional logistics systems to Logistics 4.0. While it primarily consists of the core technological drivers of Industry 4.0, it is not limited to them. It also covers key complementary technologies introduced by digital transformation, such as big data analytics, cloud computing, and social media applications (Lasi et al., 2014).

The third dimension focuses specifically on logistics. This dimension is addressed in three respects: tasks, areas, and the human factor. Tasks refer to both management and operational activities, which—by following the direction of material flow—can be divided into four main areas: procurement logistics, production logistics, distribution logistics, and reverse logistics. Lastly, logistics is also influenced by people—their knowledge and skills (Gudehus & Kotzab, 2012; Islam et al., 2013). Human factors such as physical limitations, psycho-social interactions, decision-making, and motivation have a significant impact on the overall quality and efficiency of logistics operations. Logistics 4.0 is the result of the interaction among these three dimensions, and it ensures the realization and integration of all related components.

1.1. Cyber Physical Systems (CPS)

Cyber-Physical Systems (CPS) form the foundation of Industry 4.0. When examining digital applications such as smart manufacturing and autonomous systems introduced by Industry 4.0, it becomes evident that these innovations are not feasible without CPS. These systems are responsible for managing the physical systems within industrial operations. In simple terms, CPS can be defined as systems in which information technologies (cyber components) and physical processes (physical components) operate interactively and are fully integrated. Therefore, CPS consist of two core structures: the cyber and the physical components. These two layers continuously exchange data in real time. Based on the transmitted data, CPS are capable of making decisions and executing operations autonomously (Alguliyev et al., 2025).

Thanks to CPS, higher levels of efficiency can be achieved, real-time data exchange enables faster decision-making, and error rates are significantly reduced. However, despite these advantages, CPS also come with certain risks—most notably, the high implementation costs and the presence of cybersecurity threats due to increased connectivity and system complexity (Lu, 2017a).

From the perspective of the logistics sector, CPS are among the most critical technologies for enabling the digitalization of supply chains. Applications such as smart warehouse management systems, autonomous vehicles, and real-time tracking serve as examples of CPS integration in logistics. CPS enhance the speed and efficiency of key logistics operations such as transportation, storage, and inventory management, while also contributing to a significant reduction in error rates (N. Zhang, 2018).

1.2. Internet of Things (IoT)

The Internet of Things (IoT), alongside CPS, is one of the most essential technologies introduced by Industry 4.0. For CPS to function effectively, continuous data exchange is required. Since this data is transmitted between systems and devices, internet connectivity becomes a fundamental necessity—this is precisely where IoT comes into play. IoT is a technological system that enables physical objects within a system to exchange data with one another by utilizing sensors and network connectivity. Through this technology, objects can communicate both with each other and with the systems they are integrated into. IoT facilitates real-time data exchange within the system; the collected data is then analyzed, and appropriate responses are generated accordingly. Beyond industrial systems, many everyday machines and devices have also evolved into smart, internet-connected tools. Thus, IoT can be defined as a network of interconnected systems and smart devices, enabling seamless communication and interaction across both industrial and consumer environments (Gubbi et al., 2013).

IoT technology operates as a system that begins with sensors collecting data such as temperature, speed, and location. The data gathered by these sensors is then transmitted to other components of the system through network connections. Once transmitted, the relevant data is analyzed on designated servers or cloud platforms, and based on the results of this analysis, the system generates an appropriate response or action (Tran-Dang et al., 2022).

IoT has become a critically important technology in the logistics sector. By integrating IoT into logistics operations, processes can be automated, enabling them to be carried out more quickly, transparently, and efficiently. Vehicles used in transportation can be monitored in real time through sensors such as GPS and RFID. Factors such as vehicle speed, location, and the temperature and humidity conditions of transported goods can be continuously monitored, allowing for timely interventions when necessary. The ability to track products in real time during transit is highly valuable—both in terms of transparency for businesses and customer satisfaction. Moreover, IoT plays a critical role in maintaining cold chains, ensuring that perishable goods remain within required environmental conditions. In warehouse and inventory management, IoT also enables real-time monitoring of product locations, stock levels, and movements within storage facilities, enhancing operational control and responsiveness across the supply chain (I. Lee & Lee, 2015; Tran-Dang et al., 2022).

1.3. Big Data (BD)

With Industry 4.0 and the rise of digitalization, the use of advanced technologies has led to an explosive increase in data generation. As a result, managing and processing this massive volume of data has become increasingly complex and challenging (K. Zhou et al., 2015). This is precisely where the concept of Big Data (BD) emerges. Big Data does not refer solely to the volume of data produced; rather, it encompasses five key dimensions (Winkelhaus & Grosse, 2020a):

1. Volume – the sheer amount of data
2. Velocity – the speed at which data is generated and processed
3. Variety – the different types and formats of data
4. Value – the potential insights and benefits that can be extracted from the data
5. Veracity – the accuracy, reliability, and trustworthiness of the data

Thus, BD represents a comprehensive concept that is central to unlocking the full potential of digital technologies in Industry 4.0 BD, by integrating large volumes of data with varying dimensions, not only serves as a technology that supports informed decision-making, but also provides significant advantages in terms of cost reduction and operational efficiency (K. Zhou et al., 2015). Moreover, by analyzing the collected data, it contributes to understanding customer demands, thereby playing a key role in enhancing customer satisfaction levels (Ndiango et al., 2025).

BD also plays a significant role in the logistics sector. By utilizing historical sales data, customer behavior, and societal trends, it enables highly accurate demand forecasting, which in turn helps reduce inventory costs (Chong et al., 2016). Moreover, BD is extensively used in route optimization. The data collected through BD technologies allows for the identification of the most reliable and fuel-efficient routes, thereby contributing to energy savings and overall operational efficiency (Remondino & Zanin, 2022).

1.4. Cloud Computing

In today's era of digitalization, accessing information technologies requires various software and hardware resources. At this point, cloud computing technology offers significant convenience to users. Without the need for dedicated software or hardware infrastructure, users can access the computing resources they require through various service providers. As a result, data and services become accessible from anywhere, enhancing flexibility, mobility, and operational continuity (Xie & Liang, 2014). Cloud computing offers users flexibility, scalability, and resource optimization with low investment costs (Subramanian & Abdulrahman, 2017).

Cloud computing technology is also utilized in logistics and supply chain management. As is well known, logistics activities are of critical importance to all stakeholders throughout the supply chain. During the execution of these activities, real-time data sharing and traceability are essential. To ensure that operations are carried out effectively and efficiently, there must be strong coordination and collaboration among all parties involved in the supply chain—something that can only be achieved through transparent data sharing. Cloud computing enables all stakeholders within the supply chain to be interconnected, thereby facilitating collaboration and enhancing overall system performance (Pagano & Liotine, 2020).

1.5. Autonomous Vehicles (AV)

One of the most important technologies in digital transformation processes is automation. With the widespread adoption of automation technology—particularly over the past decade—vehicles that do not require human intervention, can perceive their surroundings through sensors, and are capable of determining their own direction and movement to perform specific tasks have begun to be developed. These vehicles are referred to as Autonomous Vehicles (AVs). AVs are equipped with integrated sensors, cameras, and radars, which allow them to perceive their environment and generate a map of their surroundings. Using this map, they can determine how to move and respond through the use of advanced algorithms (Katrakazas et al., 2015).

In the logistics sector, autonomous vehicles (AVs) are increasingly utilized in various areas, particularly in road transportation, in-warehouse operations, last-mile delivery, and cargo handling at ports. In road transportation, autonomous trucks capable of long-distance freight movement are being developed (e.g., Tesla Semi). These vehicles enable continuous operations without the need for a driver or mandatory rest periods, significantly enhancing efficiency. Within warehouses, Autonomous Mobile Robots (AMRs) are used to reduce order picking times and allow for the more efficient use of storage space. These technologies not only improve operational speed but also contribute to better space optimization and cost savings (Yılmaz & Duman, 2019). With the advancement of automation, drones have begun to be used in last-mile delivery operations, particularly for short-distance deliveries in crowded urban areas with heavy traffic. Drone deliveries significantly reduce delivery times and also contribute to energy savings by minimizing fuel consumption, making them an efficient and environmentally friendly solution for modern logistics challenges (Niu et al., 2024). AVs are also used in loading and unloading operations at ports. Their integration into port logistics allows handling processes to be completed in a shorter time, enhancing operational efficiency and reducing turnaround times.

2. SUSTAINABILITY IN LOGISTICS (GREEN LOGISTICS) AND LOGISTICS 5.0

The increasing environmental damage observed worldwide has led to growing concern over ecological issues. These concerns have significantly influenced corporate management practices, social initiatives, and national policies. In response to mounting pressures to minimize environmental harms such as climate change, air pollution, and the rapid depletion of natural resources, there has been a strong push toward sustainable development and a transition to a circular economy. This pressure serves as a driving force for the adoption of green logistics and green supply chain management practices (Bressanelli et al., 2020; Korhonen et al., 2018). Companies are increasingly facing pressures—both internal and external—to implement green innovation practices. As a result, initiatives related to sustainability and green practices have become a central focus of the global community, driving efforts across industries to align with environmentally responsible strategies (El-kassar & Kumar, 2019). Therefore, in both developing and developed countries, companies are increasingly striving to enhance their efficiency by utilizing sustainable resources, with the goal of reducing environmental damage while also maintaining operational effectiveness (Simão et al., 2016). Environmental problems are also encountered during the execution of logistics activities. In particular, carbon emissions generated during transportation processes have significant negative impacts not only environmentally, but also socially and economically. In addition to carbon emissions, the environmental impact of logistics operations in terms of noise and pollution is undeniable. As a result, the concept of sustainable logistics has gained increasing importance and has become a key factor in competitiveness. Moreover, regulatory measures implemented by governments and international bodies have begun to exert pressure on logistics companies to adopt and implement sustainable strategies in their operations (Murphy & Poist, 2000).

The sustainable implementation of logistics activities is referred to as green logistics. At its core, green logistics focuses on the sustainable production and distribution of goods in light of social and environmental concerns. In other words, it involves minimizing the environmental impact of logistics operations. The goal is not only to address the economic implications for organizations applying logistics policies, but also to consider the broader societal consequences, such as the effects of environmental pollution. Green logistics encompasses the assessment of the environmental impact of various distribution strategies, the reduction of energy consumption resulting from logistics activities, and the improvement of waste management practices (Sbihi & Eglese, 2010). Ensuring sustainability in logistics is not solely limited to carbon emissions and energy consumption. Therefore, sustainability cannot be addressed purely from an environmental perspective; it must also take into account economic and social objectives. In fact, many practices aimed at reducing the environmental impact of logistics activities also lead to cost savings from an economic standpoint, highlighting the interconnected nature of environmental responsibility and operational efficiency (Mckinnon et al., 2010). From this perspective, green logistics can be defined as a set of environmentally friendly practices in areas such as freight and material transportation, packaging, warehousing, and waste management—all carried out to meet customer needs and create added value, while minimizing environmental and energy footprints, and positively contributing to environmental, social, and economic performance (Akandere, 2021). When discussing green logistics, it is essential to consider all stakeholders involved, including suppliers, manufacturers, distribution centers, and customers. This indicates that green logistics encompasses the entire supply chain, thereby emphasizing the importance of coordination among all parties to achieve truly sustainable outcomes.

Green logistics encompasses a wide range of activities and can be examined under three main categories: green performance measurement, green operations, and green strategy management (S. Zhang et al., 2015). Green performance measurement involves the monitoring, tracking, and reporting of logistics sustainability indicators, often referred to as Key Performance Indicators (KPIs). These indicators are typically grouped into environmental, economic, and social dimensions.

- Environmental indicators include factors such as carbon emissions (carbon footprint), fuel consumption, energy usage across all logistics processes, recycling rates, and levels of noise and air pollution.
- Economic indicators refer to costs incurred throughout logistics operations.
- Social indicators address the health and safety of workers, employee satisfaction, and the impact of logistics activities on local communities.

Green operations focus on the application of environmentally friendly practices in core logistics functions such as transportation, warehousing, packaging, and handling. This category also includes reverse logistics, which deals with the return, recycling, and proper disposal of products and materials. Different green practices are employed for each type of logistics activity. In transportation, green applications include the use of alternative-fuel vehicles, the implementation of route optimization techniques (Dewi & Utama, 2021), the adoption of intermodal transportation systems, and freight consolidation to reduce the number of shipments. In warehousing, green practices involve improving energy efficiency in lighting systems, adopting solar-powered technologies, and obtaining environmentally friendly building certifications. In packaging and labeling, green approaches include the use of recyclable materials and the application of ecological designs aimed at minimizing material usage, thereby achieving green packaging and packing standards (McKinnon et al., 2015). One of the most critical components within the scope of green logistics is reverse logistics operations. Reverse logistics begins with the collection of products from customers. Once collected, the condition of these products is evaluated to determine whether they can be repaired and reused from an economic and technological standpoint. Products that cannot be reused are discarded, while those that still hold potential value are restored and reintegrated into the supply chain. These recovered products then re-enter the forward distribution process, contributing to sustainability by reducing waste and conserving resources (Eskandarpour et al., 2014).

With the rise of digitalization through Industry 4.0 and the growing environmental concerns resulting from increased production supply, the concept of Industry 5.0 has emerged, driven by the need for a more sustainable and human-centered approach. Prior to this, the term "Society 5.0" was first introduced in Japan in 2016 as part of the country's 5th Science and Technology Basic Plan. Society 5.0 refers to a social structure in which digital transformation is achieved while placing humans at the center. This concept later served as the inspiration for Industry 5.0, combining advanced technology with human values to create a more balanced and sustainable industrial model (Yukihide, 2019). The term "Industry 5.0" was first officially introduced in 2021 in a report published by the European Commission. The report emphasized that, alongside the automation and efficiency brought by Industry 4.0, it is also essential to place a stronger focus on human well-being and environmental sustainability. While Industry 4.0 largely prioritized performance and profit, often at the expense of humans, society, and the environment, the European Commission argued that such an approach would not be sufficient to ensure prosperity for all stakeholders. As a response, the concept of Industry 5.0 was proposed. At its core, Industry 5.0 envisions a model of sustainable and resilient production, where humans and machines collaborate, and social and ethical values are fully integrated into industrial systems. It marks a shift toward a human-centric, value-driven, and inclusive industrial paradigm (Breque et al., 2021). The process that began with automation continued through digitalization, and with the subsequent inclusion of the human factor, the era of Industry 5.0 has emerged. The key differences between these industrial revolutions are illustrated in Figure 1 (Raja Santhi & Muthuswamy, 2023). With this new phase, the goal is to create sustainable, resilient, and flexible systems that place humans at the center and consider their role within industrial processes. Industry 5.0 makes it possible to develop systems that generate value not only for companies, but also for society as a whole, aligning technological advancement with human and environmental well-being (Grosse et al., 2023). Industry 5.0 has recently begun to create a significant impact in both industrial domains and society at large, and it has become a focal point of interest in the business world, the academic community, and even within political discourse (Hsu et al., 2024).

Figure 1. Main differences between Industry 3.0, Industry 4.0 and Industry 5.0

With the emergence of the Industry 5.0 era, the aim in logistics and supply chain management is to establish a strong integration and collaboration between humans and machines (Akundi et al., 2022a). Developing systems in which human-machine cooperation functions as seamlessly as a single organism enables unprecedented flexibility and resilience in logistics operations. This, in turn, facilitates the ability to meet customers' increasingly personalized, diverse, and complex demands. As a more advanced and comprehensive evolution of Industry 4.0, Industry 5.0 enhances logistics operations by making them smarter and more efficient, while also introducing innovative solutions that contribute to a sustainable economy (Raja Santhi & Muthuswamy, 2023). Moreover, through intelligent transformation and improved efficiency, Industry 5.0 has become a crucial factor for success in the highly competitive and dynamic environment of the logistics sector (Leng et al., 2022).

2.1. Human-Machine Collaboration (HRC)

Smart machines and robots are increasingly being adopted in today's world. These technologies are not only used in industrial settings, such as flexible manufacturing systems, but also in everyday life—for instance, in the form of assistive robots and smart home appliances. As a result, robotic technology is becoming a part of many people's daily lives, with individuals utilizing these machines as tools that simplify and enhance their routines (Semeraro et al., 2023). Human-Robot Collaboration (HRC) is defined as a system in which human intelligence and capabilities interact with the processing power and speed of machines equipped with automation and artificial intelligence (Gervasi et al., 2020). The primary goal of HRC is to enhance the performance of both the systems being used and the human operators involved. While humans possess creative and intuitive thinking, they lack the speed and precision inherent to machines. Collaboration between the two creates a balance, leveraging the strengths of both parties. Although collaborative robots (cobots) offer several advantages, they also come with certain disadvantages that must be considered in their implementation and operation. The main advantages of HRC include the improvement of operator working conditions, more efficient use of workspace, enhanced quality in production processes, and greater flexibility in operations. However, the fact that operators and machines share the same physical space and move simultaneously can pose significant safety risks. Additionally, it is essential for operators to adapt to the working conditions introduced by these collaborative systems, which may require new skills, awareness, and training to ensure safe and effective interaction (Valentina et al., 2022).

Human-machine collaboration also plays a significant role in the logistics sector. In activities such as transportation, warehousing, and distribution, the coordination between humans and machines allows workers to delegate physically demanding tasks to machines. This not only reduces physical fatigue among logistics employees but also lowers the risk of workplace accidents, thereby improving overall safety and operational efficiency within the sector.

2.2. Digital Twins

Digital twins are defined as functioning digital replicas of physically existing entities such as a machine, factory, or logistics system, which are modeled and operated in a virtual environment. Through digital twin models, simulations are conducted using real-time data collected from the original physical system replicated in the digital space. This allows for the prediction of system behavior, enabling the prevention of potential failures and contributing to the extension of the system's operational lifespan (Raja Santhi & Muthuswamy, 2023). The digital twin technology is built upon three fundamental components: mirroring, shadowing, and threading. Mirroring refers to the capability of accurately reflecting the physical system in a virtual environment, in line with the intended purpose of the digital twin. Shadowing denotes the synchronization and alignment between the physical system and its digital counterpart, ensuring that changes in the physical system are reflected in real time in the digital model (Y. Jiang et al., 2021). Threading involves the storage of data collected from the physical system within the digital model as a record or digital thread. To store and manage these data streams, cloud computing technology is commonly utilized. Together, these elements enable digital twins to function as dynamic, real-time models that support decision-making, predictive maintenance, and system optimization.

Digital twin technology is also utilized in the simulation of logistics processes. It enables the analysis and optimization of various logistics activities by creating virtual models of physical systems. For example, fuel consumption of transportation vehicles can be analyzed, maintenance schedules can be planned proactively, and simulations of supply chains can be conducted using their virtual twins to identify performance improvements. These applications enhance decision-making, reduce operational costs, and contribute to more sustainable and efficient logistics operations.

2.3. Smart Sensors

Sensors are devices capable of detecting physical changes in their environment and transmitting the corresponding measurements as output. In contrast, smart sensors not only perceive their surroundings but also have the ability to process and analyze the data they collect, and, when necessary, make decisions based on that data. While traditional sensors contain only a sensing unit, smart sensors are equipped with a sensing unit, a microcontroller unit (MCU), and a communication module. This allows them to collect data, process information, and communicate with external systems, such as a cloud server or a centralized monitoring platform (Raja Santhi & Muthuswamy, 2023).

From a logistics sector perspective, smart sensors are especially critical in cold chain logistics, where maintaining precise environmental conditions is essential. For instance, smart sensors placed inside a container carrying food products continuously monitor temperature and humidity levels in real time during transportation. If environmental conditions deviate from the required range, the sensors immediately trigger an alert and transmit the data to a cloud-based system. The system then notifies the operator, prompting actions such as activating the container's cooling system or making necessary adjustments. As a result, the quality of the products is preserved, and potential financial losses due to spoilage or non-compliance with safety standards are effectively prevented (Luo et al., 2016).

2.4. Blockchain

Blockchain fundamentally refers to a data structure designed to store information in a transparent, immutable, and decentralized manner—meaning the data is not held in a single location, but is distributed across all participants in the system. The system operates like a digital ledger, recording every transaction or action into blocks. These blocks are arranged chronologically and are securely linked to one another using cryptographic methods. When a transaction—such as sending money or validating a contract—is initiated, it is first verified by the system. Once confirmed, it is grouped with other validated transactions into a new block, which is then added to the chain. Each block contains a cryptographic hash (digital fingerprint) of the previous block, ensuring continuity and integrity. After blocks containing data sets are added, the chain is updated and permanently locked, making the data irreversible. Since all data is distributed and visible to every participant in the system, blockchain enables trust among participants without the need for a central authority. Additionally, the inability to delete or alter data once it has been added to the chain significantly enhances security. Because blockchain eliminates the need for intermediaries, it also offers cost-saving advantages, making it a transformative technology in various sectors, including finance, logistics, and supply chain management (Fu & Zhu, 2019).

Although blockchain technology first emerged in 2008 with the introduction of Bitcoin, it has since been adopted across various industries due to the advantages mentioned above. In logistics and supply chain management, blockchain enables the transparent tracking of a product throughout its entire lifecycle—from the raw material stage all the way to the end consumer. Thanks to blockchain's decentralized and immutable structure, every step in the supply chain can be recorded, verified, and viewed by authorized stakeholders. This enhances traceability, accountability, and trust among participants, while also helping to prevent fraud, improve compliance, and optimize operational efficiency across the entire supply chain network (Fu & Zhu, 2019).

2.5. Quantum Technologies

Quantum technology can be defined as a type of technology based on the principles of quantum physics, which operates at the subatomic level where classical physics laws are no longer sufficient to explain phenomena. In this context, these principles are utilized within information technologies to develop new and advanced applications. The influence of quantum physics on technology is examined under four key principles: superposition, quantum entanglement, quantum interference, and quantum tunneling.

Superposition refers to the ability of a quantum particle to exist in multiple states simultaneously. In classical computers, the basic unit of information is called a bit, which can exist in one of two states: "0" or "1". In contrast, quantum computers use quantum bits (qubits) as the basic unit of information. While classical systems are limited to one state at a time ("0" or "1"), qubits can exist in both states simultaneously due to superposition. This allows quantum computers to process extremely large datasets in parallel. Quantum interference is the principle that allows the qubit to be directed toward a desired state or set of states by manipulating probability amplitudes. The third fundamental principle, quantum entanglement, describes a condition in which particles that are spatially separated become interconnected, such that the state of one particle instantly influences the state of the other, regardless of the distance between them. Therefore, any operation performed on one of the entangled qubits is inherently linked to the others, meaning that the state of one qubit can be predicted by measuring the state of another. The fourth and final principle, quantum tunneling, refers to the phenomenon in which a particle is able to pass through a potential barrier even when it does not possess sufficient energy to overcome it according to classical physics. In quantum mechanics, particles behave like waves, allowing them to extend into and even beyond potential barriers. Considering all these principles together, quantum technology enables the analysis and resolution of highly complex scenarios involving numerous combinations of states, offering powerful computational capabilities far beyond those of classical systems (Gachnang et al., 2022).

In logistics and supply chain management, quantum technologies have increasingly been applied, particularly in route optimization and inventory forecasting. Through quantum computing, complex route planning problems can be addressed by evaluating multiple routes simultaneously, allowing for the identification of shortest and most cost-effective routes (Masuda et al., 2023). Moreover, quantum technologies have proven to be particularly useful in optimizing inventory levels under uncertainty. By leveraging quantum-based models, it becomes possible to minimize the costs associated with overstocking or stockouts, while simultaneously enhancing customer satisfaction (H. Jiang et al., 2022).

3. ANALYTIC HIERARCHY PROCESS (ANP) APPLICATION

In the transition that began with Logistics 4.0 and continues with Logistics 5.0, a shift from a purely efficiency-, speed-, and cost-oriented approach toward a more human-centered perspective has taken place. The business world has responded to this change by developing new applications alongside emerging technologies. This section evaluates Logistics 5.0 practices in the Turkish logistics sector. The aim of the study is to assess the key factors for the applicability of Industry 5.0 within the sector. The Analytic Network Process (ANP), one of the multi-criteria decision-making (MCDM) methods, was employed in the study. Factors that are currently implemented in the logistics sector and are considered components of the Logistics 5.0 framework were identified through a comprehensive literature review. These factors were then weighted and ranked based on their relative importance using the expert opinions of professionals working in the logistics industry.

3.1. Analytic Network Process (ANP)

As the number of criteria and alternatives in decision-making processes increases, traditional methods have become insufficient for handling the growing complexity. In 1977, Thomas L. Saaty developed the Analytic Hierarchy Process (AHP), which emerged as a highly influential method in the field of multi-criteria decision making (MCDM). However, AHP presents certain limitations, primarily due to its requirement to structure the decision problem in a strictly top-down, non-interacting hierarchical format, and its inability to account for interdependencies among criteria. To overcome these limitations, Saaty further developed the method and introduced the Analytic Network Process (ANP) in 1996. ANP is a more advanced approach than AHP, as it allows for the inclusion of interrelationships and feedback among all criteria. Additionally, ANP enables the evaluation of not only quantitative data but also qualitative judgments, making it a more flexible and comprehensive tool for complex decision-making scenarios (Saaty, 1996).

Unlike the Analytic Hierarchy Process (AHP), which is based on a hierarchical structure, the Analytic Network Process (ANP) represents the interdependencies among criteria in the form of a network that aligns with the objective of the decision problem. While ANP adopts many of the fundamental principles used in AHP such as the pairwise comparison scale (as shown in Table 1) it goes beyond AHP by allowing for mutual influences among elements. In ANP, the concept of dependency is classified into two types. When the relationship exists among elements within the same cluster, it is called inner dependence. On the other hand, if the relationship is between elements in different clusters, it is termed outer dependence. These dependencies allow ANP to capture complex feedback loops and interrelations that are often present in real-world decision-making scenarios but are ignored in strictly hierarchical models like AHP (Ömürbek & Tunca, 2013). Because ANP considers these interrelationships, it enables more effective problem-solving than traditional hierarchical models. Figure 2 presents an example of an ANP network structure. In this figure, the circles represent clusters in which the criteria are grouped.

Figure 2. Network structure

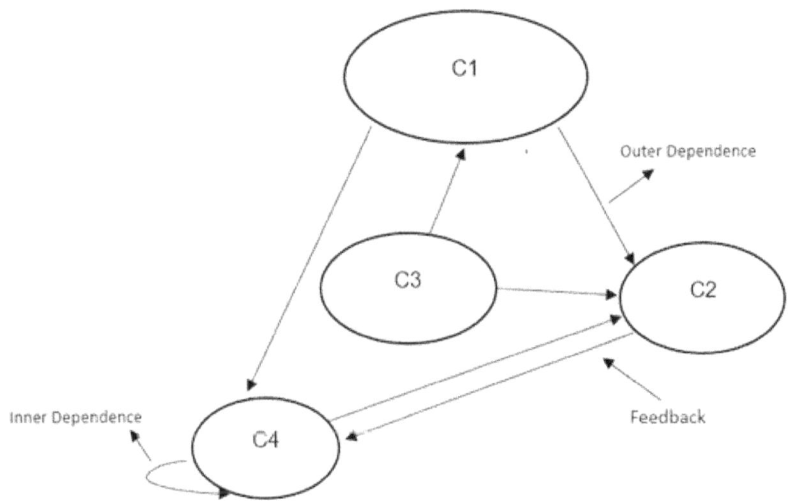

Table 1. The fundamental scale of absolute numbers (Saaty & Vargas, 2006)

	Intensity of Definition Importance	**Explanation**
1	Equal Importance	Two activities contribute equally to the objective
3	Moderate importance	Experience and judgment slightly favor one activity over another
5	Strong importance	Experience and judgment strongly favor one activity over another

continued on following page

Table 1. Continued

	Intensity of Definition Importance	Explanation
7	Very strong demonstrated importance	An activity is favored very strongly over another; its dominance demonstrated in practice
9	Extreme importance	The evidence favoring one activity over another is of the highest possible order of affirmation
2,4,6,8	Consensus (average) values	

ANP is fundamentally implemented in five main steps:

1. Problem Definition: The problem must be clearly defined. Clusters and their respective elements (i.e., sub-criteria and alternatives) should be identified.
2. Constructing the Decision Network: A decision network is constructed using the identified clusters and elements. The overall goal of the decision problem is positioned at the top of this network. Finally, the interconnections among clusters and their internal elements are determined.
3. Preparing the Pairwise Comparison Matrices and Priority Vectors: Pairwise comparisons are conducted among clusters and elements within clusters. These comparisons are made based on a fundamental scale (as shown in Table 1). All elements that are linked within the network are subjected to pairwise comparisons. The matrix formulation for these comparisons is presented in Equation (1). In these comparisons, the value a_{ij} represents the relative importance of element i with respect to element j. As in the Analytic Hierarchy Process (AHP), priority vectors are derived from these comparisons.

$$A = \begin{bmatrix} a_{11} & a_{12} & \cdots & a_{1n} \\ a_{21} & a_{22} & \cdots & a_{2n} \\ \cdots & \cdots & \cdots & \cdots \\ a_{i1} & a_{i2} & \cdots & a_{in} \\ \cdots & \cdots & \cdots & \cdots \\ a_{n1} & a_{n2} & \cdots & a_{nn} \end{bmatrix} \tag{1}$$

4. Construction of the Supermatrix and the Limit Supermatrix: A supermatrix is developed to represent the interactions among clusters and elements in the decision network. The priority vectors obtained from the pairwise comparisons are used to populate the supermatrix. The structure of the supermatrix is illustrated in Equation (2) (Özbek, 2019). To obtain the limit supermatrix, the supermatrix is raised to a sufficiently large power until it converges and reaches a steady state.

$$W_{i,j} = \begin{bmatrix} W_{i_1 j_1} & W_{i_1 j_2} & \cdots & W_{i_1 j_{sj}} \\ W_{i_2 j_1} & W_{i_2 j_2} & \cdots & W_{i_2 j_{sj}} \\ \cdots & \cdots & \cdots & \cdots \\ W_{i_{si} j_1} & W_{i_{si} j_2} & \cdots & W_{i_{si} j_{sj}} \end{bmatrix} \quad (2)$$

5. Selecting the best alternetive: Once the limit supermatrix is obtained, the final priority values are examined. The alternative with the highest priority value is selected as the optimal decision (Özbek, 2019).

4. APPLICATION

The transition initiated by Logistics 4.0 and further advanced through Logistics 5.0 has marked a shift from a focus on efficiency, speed, and cost toward a more human-centered approach. In response to this transformation, the business world has begun to implement new practices alongside emerging technologies. This section evaluates the implementation of Logistics 5.0 practices in the Turkish logistics sector. The primary objective of the study is to identify the key factors for Logistics 5.0. For this purpose, ANP, a widely used multi-criteria decision-making (MCDM) method, has been employed.

To identify the key Logistics 5.0 factors for the logistics sector in Türkiye, an extensive literature review was conducted. As a result, three main criteria and a total of eighteen sub-criteria were identified. In addition, two key factors influencing the implementation of Logistics 5.0 also derived from the literatüre were included in the study, and their impact on the main criteria was taken into account. All identified criteria are presented in Table 2. The ANP-based model developed for this purpose is illustrated in Figure 2.

Figure 3. Decision model

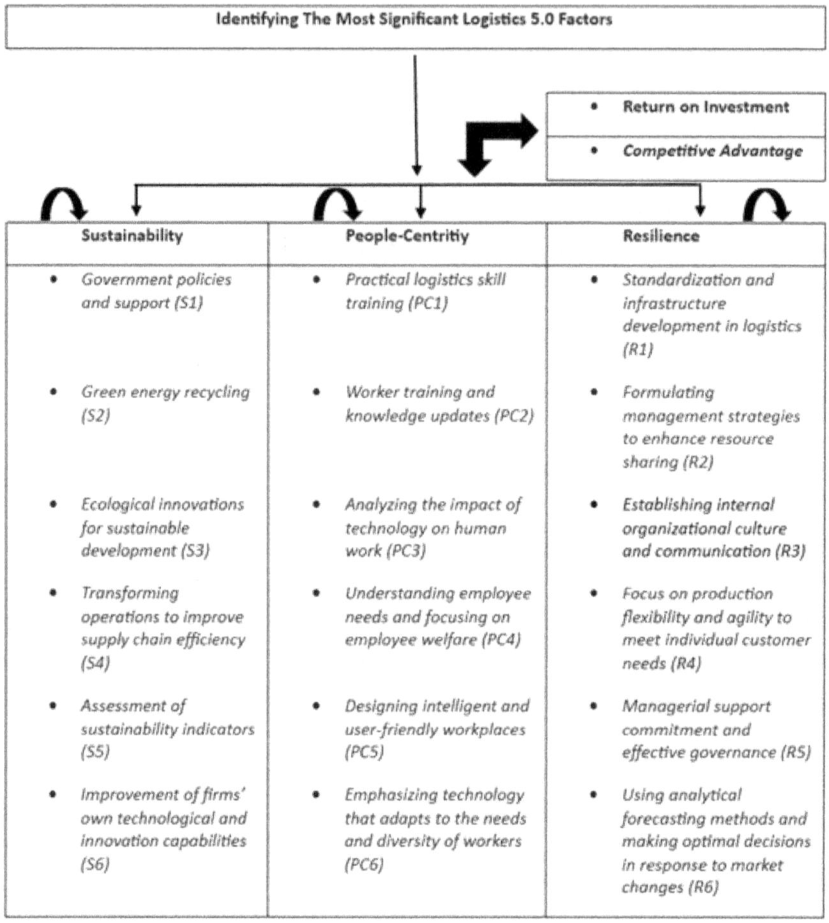

Table 2. Logistics 5.0 factors

Main Criteria	Sub-Criteria (Logistics 5.0 Factors)	References
Return on Investment (ROI)	-	(Leng et al., 2022; Murphy & Poist, 2000)
Competitive Advantage (CA)	-	(Grosse et al., 2023; Subramanian & Abdulrahman, 2017)
Sustainability (S)	Government policies and support (S1)	(Grosse et al., 2023; Raja Santhi & Muthuswamy, 2023)
	Green energy recycling (S2)	(Carayannis & Morawska-Jancelewicz, 2022; McFarlane et al., 2016)
	Ecological innovations for sustainable development (S3)	(Akundi et al., 2022b; F. Zhou et al., 2024)
	Transforming operations to improve supply chain efficiency (S4)	(Grosse et al., 2023; Raja Santhi & Muthuswamy, 2023)
	Assessment of sustainability indicators (S5)	(Akundi et al., 2022b; Xu et al., 2021)
	Improvement of firms' own technological and innovation capabilities (S6)	(Zhao et al., 2023)
People-Centricity (PC)	Practical logistics skill training (PC1)	(Akundi et al., 2022b; Grosse et al., 2023; F. Zhou et al., 2024)
	Worker training and knowledge updates (PC2)	(Liu et al., 2022; F. Zhou et al., 2024)
	Analyzing the impact of technology on human work (PC3)	(Grosse et al., 2023; F. Zhou et al., 2024)
	Understanding employee needs and focusing on employee welfare (PC4)	(Liu et al., 2022; Raja Santhi & Muthuswamy, 2023)
	Designing intelligent and user-friendly workplaces (PC5)	(Maddikunta et al., 2022)
	Emphasizing technology that adapts to the needs and diversity of workers (PC6)	(Akundi et al., 2022b; Liu et al., 2022)
Resilience (R)	Standardization and infrastructure development in logistics (R1)	(Akundi et al., 2022b; F. Zhou et al., 2024)
	Formulating management strategies to enhance resource sharing (R2)	(Hsu, Wu, et al., 2024)
	Establishing internal organizational culture and communication (R3)	(Akundi et al., 2022b; Raja Santhi & Muthuswamy, 2023)
	Focus on production flexibility and agility to meet individual customer needs (R4)	(Grosse et al., 2023)
	Managerial support commitment and effective governance (R5)	(Akundi et al., 2022b; Raja Santhi & Muthuswamy, 2023)
	Using analytical forecasting methods and making optimal decisions in response to market changes (R6)	(Grosse et al., 2023; Maddikunta et al., 2022)

Pairwise comparison matrices were constructed based on the criteria identified through the literature review. In developing these matrices, expert opinions from professionals working in Turkey's logistics sector were utilized. The pairwise comparison matrices and priority vectors (PV) created for both the main criteria and all sub-criteria are presented in Table 3, Table 4, Table 5, Table 6, Table 7, Table 8, and Table 9.

Table 3. The relative importance levels among the main criteria (CR=0,043).

	S	PC	R	PV
S	1	2	0.5	0,311905
PC	0.5	1	0.5	0,197619
R	2	2	1	0,490476

According to the pairwise comparisons of the main criteria—sustainability, people-centricity, and resilience—the most important criterion is resilience, with a priority weight of 0.4904.

Table 4. The relative importance levels among the sub-criteria of sustainability (CR=0.098).

S	S1	S2	S3	S4	S5	S6	PV
S1	1	3	3	2	5	5	0.3303
S2	0.333333	1	5	3	7	7	0.299631
S3	0.333333	0.2	1	3	5	5	0.173167
S4	0.5	0.333333	0.333333	1	3	3	0.1124
S5	0.2	0.142857	0.2	0.333333	1	1	0.042251
S6	0.2	0.142857	0.2	0.333333	1	1	0.042251

According to the pairwise comparisons of the sub-criteria under the sustainability dimension, the most important sub-criterion is Government Policies and Support (S1), with a priority weight of 0.3303.

Table 5. The relative importance levels among the sub-criteria of people-centricity (CR=0.065)

PC	PC1	PC2	PC3	PC4	PC5	PC6	PV
PC1	1	2	9	4	3	5	0.36171
PC2	0.5	1	8	6	4	5	0.319525
PC3	0.111111	0.125	1	0.25	0.333333	0.5	0.032677
PC4	0.25	0.166667	4	1	2	3	0.121833
PC5	0.333333	0.25	3	0.5	1	4	0.111537
PC6	0.2	0.2	2	0.333333	0.25	1	0.052719

According to the pairwise comparisons of the sub-criteria under the people-centricity dimension, the most important sub-criterion is Practical Logistics Skill Training (PC1), with a priority weight of 0.36171.

Table 6. The relative importance levels among the sub-criteria of resilience (CR=0.042)

R	R1	R2	R3	R4	R5	R6	PV
R1	1	5	6	4	0.5	7	0.288092
R2	0.2	1	2	0.5	0.142857	5	0.084476
R3	0.166667	0.5	1	0.333333	0.125	2	0.047765
R4	0.25	2	3	1	0.2	4	0.111585
R5	2	7	8	5	1	9	0.436942
R6	0.142857	0.2	0.5	0.25	0.111111	1	0.031141

According to the pairwise comparisons of the sub-criteria under the resilience dimension, the most important sub-criterion is Managerial Support, Commitment, and Effective Governance (R5), with a priority weight of 0.436942.

Table 7. The relative importance levels among the three main criteria in terms of return on investment

ROI	S	PC	R	PV
S	1	0,5	0,5	0.2
PC	2	1	1	0.4
R	2	1	1	0.4

According to the pairwise comparisons of the three main criteria in terms of return on investment, people-centricity and resilience are found to be equally important, each with a priority weight of 0.4.

Table 8. The relative importance levels among the three main criteria in terms of competitive advantage

RA	S	PC	R	PV
S	1	3	0.5	0.320238
PC	0.333333	1	0,25	0.122619
R	2	4	1	0.557143

According to the pairwise comparisons of the three main criteria in terms of competitive advantage, the most important criterion is resilience, with a priority weight of 0.557143.

Table 9. The relative importance levels of return on investment and competitive advantage in terms of the three main criteria

S	ROI	CA	PV
ROI	1	2	0.666667
CA	0.5	1	0.333333
PC	ROI	CA	PV
ROI	1	0.5	0.333333
CA	2	1	0.666667
R	ROI	CA	PV
ROI	1	3	0.75
CA	0.333333	1	0.25

From the perspective of the three main criteria, return on investment is found to be more important for sustainability and resilience, whereas competitive advantage appears to be more significant for human-centricity.

Following the construction of the pairwise comparison matrices, the next step involves generating the supermatrix and the limit supermatrix. This process enables the calculation of final priority weights, through which the key factors are identified. The limit supermatrix was derived by exponentiating the supermatrix to the 32nd power, allowing the system to reach a steady state of priority weights. The resulting supermatrices are presented in Table 10, Table 11, and Table 12.

Table 10. Supermatrix for the main criteria

	Goal	S	PC	R	ROI	CA
Goal	0	0	0	0	0	0
S	0.311905	0	0	0	0.2	0.320238
PC	0.197619	0	0	0	0.4	0.122619
R	0.490476	0	0	0	0.4	0.557143
ROI	0	0.666667	0.333333	0,75	0	0
CA	0	0.333333	0.666667	0,25	0	0

Table 11. Supermatrix for the sub-criteria

	S	PC	R
S1	0.3303	0	0
S2	0.299631	0	0
S3	0.173167	0	0
S4	0.1124	0	0
S5	0.042251	0	0
S6	0.042251	0	0
PC1	0	0.36171	0
PC2	0	0.319525	0
PC3	0	0.032677	0
PC4	0	0.121833	0
PC5	0	0.111537	0
PC6	0	0.052719	0
R1	0	0	0.288092
R2	0	0	0.084476
R3	0	0	0.047765
R4	0	0	0.111585
R5	0	0	0.436942
R6	0	0	0.031141

Table 12. Limit supermatrix

	Goal	S	PC	R	ROI	CA
Goal	0	0	0	0	0	0
S	0	0,247128	0,247128	0,247128	0	0
PC	0	0,291278	0,291278	0,291278	0	0
R	0	0,461594	0,461594	0,461594	0	0
ROI	0,60804	0	0	0	0,60804	0,60804
CA	0,39196	0	0	0	0,39196	0,39196

As a result of the constructed supermatrices, the normalized values of the three main criteria were calculated as 0.247128 for sustainability, 0.291278 for human-centricity, and 0.461594 for resilience. When these normalized values were multiplied with the supermatrix values of the sub-criteria through matrix multiplication, the final priority weights for each criterion were obtained. The final priority weights are presented in Table 13.

Table 13. Final priority weights

Criteria	PV
S1	0,081627
S2	0,074047
S3	0,042795
S4	0,027777
S5	0,010441
S6	0,010441
PC1	0,105358
PC2	0,09307
PC3	0,009518
PC4	0,035487
PC5	0,032488
PC6	0,015356
R1	0,132981
R2	0,038993
R3	0,022048
R4	0,051507
R5	0,20169
R6	0,014374

An examination of the final priority weights presented in Table 13 reveals that the most important sub-criterion is Managerial Support, Commitment, and Effective Governance (R5), while the least important one is Analyzing the Impact of Technology on Human Work (PC3).

5. CONCLUSION

In order to identify the key Logistics 5.0 factors, a study was conducted on the Turkish logistics sector, in which a total of three main criteria and eighteen sub-criteria were defined. These criteria were evaluated based on expert opinions from professionals working in the logistics industry. The analysis was carried out using the Analytic Network Process (ANP) method. According to the results, resilience (R) was identified as the most important main criterion for Logistics 5.0. Resilience (R) was followed by people-centricity (PC), while sustainability (S) ranked last among the main criteria. When evaluated in terms of the two additional criteria identified through the literature review—Return on Investment (ROI) and Competitive Advantage (CA)—resilience (R) again emerged as the most prominent factor. ROI was found to be more important in relation to both sustainability and resilience, whereas CA appeared to be more significant for people-centricity.

Among the sub-criteria under the resilience dimension, the most important factors were identified as Managerial Support, Commitment, and Effective Governance (R5), followed by Standardization and Infrastructure Development in Logistics (R1), and Focus on Production Flexibility and Agility to Meet Individual Customer Needs (R4), respectively.

Among the sub-criteria under the people-centricity dimension, the most important factors were identified as Practical Logistics Skill Training (PC1), followed by Worker Training and Knowledge Updates (PC2) and Understanding Employee Needs and Focusing on Employee Welfare (PC4), respectively.

Among the sub-criteria under the sustainability dimension, the most important factors were identified as Government Policies and Support (S1), followed by Green Energy Recycling (S2) and Ecological Innovations for Sustainable Development (S3), respectively.

When all criteria are taken into account, the top five key factors for Logistics 5.0 are identified as follows:

1. Managerial Support, Commitment, and Effective Governance (R5)
2. Standardization and Infrastructure Development in Logistics (R1)
3. Practical Logistics Skill Training (PC1)
4. Worker Training and Knowledge Updates (PC2)

5. Government Policies and Support (S1)

Considering the identified key factors, it is evident that management, standardization and infrastructure, training, and government policies hold critical importance. The overall ranking of all criteria along with their final priority weights is presented in Table 14. This study was conducted specifically within the context of the logistics sector; therefore, analyses conducted in other sectors using different criteria and methodologies may yield different results.

Table 14. Ranking of the criteria based on their final priority weights

Criteria	PV
R5	0,20169
R1	0,132981
PC1	0,105358
PC2	0,09307
S1	0,081627
S2	0,074047
R4	0,051507
S3	0,042795
R2	0,038993
PC4	0,035487
PC5	0,032488
S4	0,027777
R3	0,022048
PC6	0,015356
R6	0,014374
S5	0,010441
S6	0,010441
PC3	0,009518

REFERENCES

Akandere, G. (2021). DİJİTALLEŞME DÜZEYİ VE YEŞİL LOJİSTİK UYGULAMALARIN LOJİSTİK PERFORMANSA ETKİSİ. *Nevşehir Hacı Bektaş Veli Üniversitesi SBE Dergisi*, *11*(4), 1979–2000. DOI: 10.30783/nevsosbilen.1022778

Akundi, A., Euresti, D., Luna, S., Ankobiah, W., Lopes, A., & Edinbarough, I. (2022a). State of Industry 5.0—Analysis and Identification of Current Research Trends. *Applied System Innovation*, *5*(1), 27. DOI: 10.3390/asi5010027

Akundi, A., Euresti, D., Luna, S., Ankobiah, W., Lopes, A., & Edinbarough, I. (2022b). State of Industry 5.0—Analysis and Identification of Current Research Trends. *Applied System Innovation 2022, Vol. 5, Page 27, 5*(1), 27. DOI: 10.3390/asi5010027

Alguliyev, R., Aliguliyev, R., & Sukhostat, L. (2025). An approach for assessing the functional vulnerabilities criticality of CPS components. *Cyber Security and Applications*, *3*, 100058. DOI: 10.1016/j.csa.2024.100058

Antoniuk, I., Svitek, R., Krajcovic, M., & Furmannová, B. (2021). Methodology of design and optimization of internal logistics in the concept of Industry 4.0. *Transportation Research Procedia*, *55*, 503–509. DOI: 10.1016/j.trpro.2021.07.093

Ashton, K. (2010). That "internet of things" Thing. In *RFID Journal*.

Barreto, L., Amaral, A., & Pereira, T. (2017). Industry 4.0 implications in logistics: An overview. *Procedia Manufacturing*, *13*, 1245–1252. DOI: 10.1016/j.promfg.2017.09.045

Bayraktutan, Y., & Özbilgin, M. (2015). Lojistik Maliyetler ve Lojistik Performans Ölçütleri. *Maliye Araştırmaları Dergisi*, *1*(2), 95–112.

Breque, M., De Nul, L., & Petridis, A. (2021). *Industry 5.0: towards a sustainable, human-centric and resilient European industry.*

Bressanelli, G., Saccani, N., Pigosso, D. C. A., & Perona, M. (2020). Circular Economy in the WEEE industry : A systematic literature review and a research agenda. *Sustainable Production and Consumption*, *23*, 174–188. DOI: 10.1016/j.spc.2020.05.007

Carayannis, E. G., & Morawska-Jancelewicz, J. (2022). The Futures of Europe: Society 5.0 and Industry 5.0 as Driving Forces of Future Universities. *Journal of the Knowledge Economy*, *13*(4), 3445–3471. DOI: 10.1007/s13132-021-00854-2 PMID: 40477679

Chong, A. Y. L., Li, B., Ngai, E. W. T., Ch'ng, E., & Lee, F. (2016). Predicting online product sales via online reviews, sentiments, and promotion strategies. *International Journal of Operations & Production Management*, *36*(4), 358–383. DOI: 10.1108/IJOPM-03-2015-0151

Dewi, S. K., & Utama, D. M. (2021). A New Hybrid Whale Optimization Algorithm for Green Vehicle Routing Problem. *Systems Science & Control Engineering*, *9*(1), 61–72. DOI: 10.1080/21642583.2020.1863276

El-kassar, A., & Kumar, S. (2019). Social Change Green innovation and organizational performance : The in fl uence of big data and the moderating role of management commitment and HR practices. *Technological Forecasting and Social Change*, *144*, 483–498. DOI: 10.1016/j.techfore.2017.12.016

Eskandarpour, M., Masehian, E., Soltani, R., & Khosrojerdi, A. (2014). A reverse logistics network for recovery systems and a robust metaheuristic solution approach. *International Journal of Advanced Manufacturing Technology*, *74*(9–12), 1393–1406. DOI: 10.1007/s00170-014-6045-7

Fu, Y., & Zhu, J. (2019). Operation Mechanisms for Intelligent Logistics System: A Blockchain Perspective. *IEEE Access : Practical Innovations, Open Solutions*, *7*, 144202–144213. DOI: 10.1109/ACCESS.2019.2945078

Gachnang, P., Ehrenthal, J. C. F., Hanne, T., & Dornberger, R. (2022). Quantum Computing in Supply Chain Management State of the Art and Research Directions. *Asian Journal of Logistics Management*, *1*(1), 57–73. DOI: 10.14710/ajlm.2022.14325

Gervasi, R., Mastrogiacomo, L., & Franceschini, F. (2020). A conceptual framework to evaluate human-robot collaboration. *International Journal of Advanced Manufacturing Technology*, *108*(3), 841–865. DOI: 10.1007/s00170-020-05363-1

Grosse, E. H., Sgarbossa, F., Berlin, C., & Neumann, W. P. (2023). Human-centric production and logistics system design and management: transitioning from Industry 4.0 to Industry 5.0. In *International Journal of Production Research* (Vol. 61, Issue 22, pp. 7749–7759). Taylor and Francis Ltd. DOI: 10.1080/00207543.2023.2246783

Gubbi, J., Buyya, R., Marusic, S., & Palaniswami, M. (2013). Internet of Things (IoT): A vision, architectural elements, and future directions. *Future Generation Computer Systems*, *29*(7), 1645–1660. DOI: 10.1016/j.future.2013.01.010

Gudehus, T., & Kotzab, H. (2012). *Comprehensive Logistics* (2nd ed.). Springer. DOI: 10.1007/978-3-642-24367-7

Gulledge, T., & Chavusholu, T. (2008). Automating the construction of supply chain key performance indicators. *Industrial Management & Data Systems*, *108*(6), 750–774. DOI: 10.1108/02635570810883996

Gümüş, Y. (2009). Lojistik Faaliyetlerin Rekabet Stratejileri ve İşletme Kârı İle Olan İlişkisi. *Muhasebe ve Finansman Dergisi*, 97–114.

Henning Kagermann. (2015). Change Through Digitization - Value Creation in the Age of Industry 4.0. In Albach, H., Pinkwart, A., Meffert, H., & Reichwald, R. (Eds.), *Management of Permanent Change* (1st ed., pp. 23–45). Springer Gabler. DOI: 10.1007/978-3-658-05014-6_2

Hofmann, E., & Rüsch, M. (2017). Industry 4.0 and the current status as well as future prospects on logistics. *Computers in Industry*, *89*, 23–34. DOI: 10.1016/j.compind.2017.04.002

Hsu, C. H., Chen, S. J., Huang, M. Q., & Le, Q. (2024). Industry 5.0 Drivers Analysis Using Grey-DEMATEL: A Logistics Case in Emerging Economies. *Mathematics*, *12*(22), 3588. DOI: 10.3390/math12223588

Hsu, C. H., Wu, J. Z., Zhang, T. Y., & Chen, J. Y. (2024). Deploying Industry 5.0 drivers to enhance sustainable supply chain risk resilience. *International Journal of Sustainable Engineering*, *17*(1), 1–28. DOI: 10.1080/19397038.2024.2327381

Islam, D. M. Z., Fabian Meier, J., Aditjandra, P. T., Zunder, T. H., & Pace, G. (2013). Logistics and supply chain management. *Research in Transportation Economics*, *41*(1), 3–16. DOI: 10.1016/j.retrec.2012.10.006

Jiang, H., Shen, Z. J. M., & Liu, J. (2022). Quantum Computing Methods for Supply Chain Management. *Proceedings - 2022 IEEE/ACM 7th Symposium on Edge Computing, SEC 2022*, 400–405. DOI: 10.1109/SEC54971.2022.00059

Jiang, Y., Yin, S., Li, K., Luo, H., & Kaynak, O. (2021). Industrial applications of digital twins. *Philosophical Transactions. Series A, Mathematical, Physical, and Engineering Sciences*, *379*(2207), 20200360. DOI: 10.1098/rsta.2020.0360 PMID: 34398651

Katrakazas, C., Quddus, M., Chen, W. H., & Deka, L. (2015). Real-time motion planning methods for autonomous on-road driving: State-of-the-art and future research directions. *Transportation Research Part C, Emerging Technologies*, *60*, 416–442. DOI: 10.1016/j.trc.2015.09.011

Kayikci, Y. (2018). Sustainability impact of digitization in logistics. *Procedia Manufacturing*, *21*, 782–789. DOI: 10.1016/j.promfg.2018.02.184

Korhonen, J., Honkasalo, A., & Seppälä, J. (2018). Circular Economy : The Concept and its Limitations. *Ecological Economics*, *143*, 37–46. DOI: 10.1016/j.ecolecon.2017.06.041

Lasi, H., Fettke, P., Kemper, H. G., Feld, T., & Hoffmann, M. (2014). Industry 4.0. *Business & Information Systems Engineering*, *6*(4), 239–242. DOI: 10.1007/s12599-014-0334-4

Lee, E. A. (2008). Cyber Physical Systems: Design Challenges. *11th IEEE Symposium on Object/Component/Service-Oriented Real-Time Distributed Computing, ISORC*, 363–369. DOI: 10.1109/ISORC.2008.25

Lee, I., & Lee, K. (2015). The Internet of Things (IoT): Applications, investments, and challenges for enterprises. *Business Horizons*, *58*(4), 431–440. DOI: 10.1016/j.bushor.2015.03.008

Leng, J., Sha, W., Wang, B., Zheng, P., Zhuang, C., Liu, Q., Wuest, T., Mourtzis, D., & Wang, L. (2022). Industry 5.0: Prospect and retrospect. *Journal of Manufacturing Systems*, *65*, 279–295. DOI: 10.1016/j.jmsy.2022.09.017

Lin, B., & Jones, C. (2008). Digital Supply Chain Management and Implementation: A Research Review. *Southwest Decision Sciences Institute*, 589–592. http://swdsi.org/swdsi2009/Papers/9Q02.pdf

Liu, W., Zhang, J., Shi, Y., Lee, P. T. W., & Liang, Y. (2022). Intelligent logistics transformation problems in efficient commodity distribution. *Transportation Research Part E, Logistics and Transportation Review*, *163*, 102735. DOI: 10.1016/j.tre.2022.102735

Lu, Y. (2017a). Cyber Physical System (CPS)-Based Industry 4.0: A Survey. *Journal of Industrial Integration and Management*, *02*(03), 1750014. DOI: 10.1142/S2424862217500142

Lu, Y. (2017b). Industry 4.0: A survey on technologies, applications and open research issues. *Journal of Industrial Information Integration*, *6*, 1–10. DOI: 10.1016/j.jii.2017.04.005

Luo, J., Yi, J., Zhu, X., & Xu, J. (2016). A Smart Sensors-based real-time decision making system for the Cold Supply Chain. In Yarlagadda, P. (Ed.), *Proceedings of the 2016 3rd International Conference on Mechatronics and Information Technology* (pp. 714–719). ICMIT., DOI: 10.2991/icmit-16.2016.128

Maddikunta, P. K. R., Pham, Q. V., B, P., Deepa, N., Dev, K., Gadekallu, T. R., Ruby, R., & Liyanage, M. (2022). Industry 5.0: A survey on enabling technologies and potential applications. *Journal of Industrial Information Integration*, *26*, 100257. DOI: 10.1016/j.jii.2021.100257

Masuda, K., Tsuyumine, Y., Kitada, T., Hachikawa, T., & Haga, T. (2023). Optimization of Delivery Plan by Quantum Computing. *SEI Technical Review*, *96*, 85–88.

McFarlane, D., Giannikas, V., & Lu, W. (2016). Intelligent logistics: Involving the customer. *Computers in Industry*, *81*, 105–115. DOI: 10.1016/j.compind.2015.10.002

McKinnon, A., Browne, M., Whiteing, A., & Piecyk, M. (2015). *Green Logistics: Improving The Environmental Sustainability of Logistics* (3rd ed.). KoganPage.

Mckinnon, A., Cullinane, S., Browne, M., & Whiteing, A. (2010). Greenn Logistics: Improving the environmental sustaintability of logistics. In *The Chartered Institute of Logistics and Transport (UK)*. Kogan Page.

Murphy, P. R., & Poist, R. F. (2000). Green Logistics Strategies: An Analysis of Usage Patterns. *Transportation Journal*, *40*(2), .

Ndiango, S., Mwagike, L. R., & Changalima, I. A. (2025). Mapping the conceptual structure of green and sustainable human resource management in supply chain management research. *Discover Sustainability*, *6*(1), 348. DOI: 10.1007/s43621-025-00952-0

Niu, B., Zhang, J., & Xie, F. (2024). Drone logistics' resilient development: Impacts of consumer choice, competition, and regulation. *Transportation Research Part A, Policy and Practice*, *185*, 104126. DOI: 10.1016/j.tra.2024.104126

Ömürbek, N., & Tunca, M. Z. (2013). ANALİTİK HİYERARŞİ SÜRECİ VE ANALİTİK AĞ SÜRECİ YÖNTEMLERİNDE GRUP KARARI VERİLMESİ AŞAMASINA İLİŞKİN BİR ÖRNEK UYGULAMA. *Süleyman Demirel Üniversitesi İktisadi ve İdari Bilimler Fakültesi Dergisi, 18*(3), 47–70. https://dergipark.org.tr/tr/pub/sduiibfd/issue/20817/222729

Özbek, A. (2019). *Çok Kriterli Karar Verme Yöntemleri ve Excel İle Problem Çözümü: Kavram - Teori - Uygulama* (2nd ed.). Seçkin Yayıncılık.

Özdemir, A., & Özgüner, M. (2018). Endüstri 4.0 ve Lojistik Sektörüne Etkileri: Lojistik 4.0. *İsletme Ve İktisat Çalışmaları Dergisi, 6*(4), 39–47. https://dergipark.org.tr/en/pub/iicder/issue/49884/639432

Pagano, A. M., & Liotine, M. (2020). *Technology in Supply Chain Management and Logistics: Current Practice and Future Applications*. Elsevier.

Pereira, A. C., & Romero, F. (2017). A review of the meanings and the implications of the Industry 4.0 concept. *Procedia Manufacturing*, *13*, 1206–1214. DOI: 10.1016/j.promfg.2017.09.032

Raja Santhi, A., & Muthuswamy, P. (2023). Industry 5.0 or industry 4.0S? Introduction to industry 4.0 and a peek into the prospective industry 5.0 technologies. *International Journal on Interactive Design and Manufacturing*, *17*(2), 947–979. DOI: 10.1007/s12008-023-01217-8 PMID: 40478102

Rajkumar, R., Lee, I., Sha, L., & Stankovic, J. (2010). Cyber-physical systems: The next computing revolution. *Design Automation Conference*, 731–736. DOI: 10.1145/1837274.1837461

Remondino, M., & Zanin, A. (2022). Logistics and Agri-Food: Digitization to Increase Competitive Advantage and Sustainability. Literature Review and the Case of Italy. *Sustainability (Basel)*, *14*(2), 787. DOI: 10.3390/su14020787

Saaty, T. L. (1996). *Decision making with dependence and feedback: The analytic network process*. RWS Publications. https://scholar.archive.org/work/bmi3dl3urnhn3kx6x5cauuyyz4/access/wayback/http://www.cs.put.poznan.pl/ewgmcda/pdf/SaatyBook.pdf

Saaty, T. L., & Vargas, L. G. (2006). *DECISION MAKING WITH THE ANALYTIC NETWORK PROCESS Economic, Political, Social and Technological Applications with Benefits, Opportunities, Costs and Risks*. Springer.

Sbihi, A., & Eglese, R. W. (2010). Combinatorial optimization and Green Logistics. *Annals of Operations Research*, *175*(1), 159–175. DOI: 10.1007/s10479-009-0651-z

Schmidt, R., Möhring, M., Härting, R. C., Reichstein, C., Neumaier, P., & Jozinović, P. (2015). Industry 4.0 - Potentials for Creating Smart Products: Empirical Research Results. *18th International Conference on Business Information Systems, LNBIP*, 16–27. DOI: 10.1007/978-3-319-19027-3_2

Semeraro, F., Griffiths, A., & Cangelosi, A. (2023). Human–robot collaboration and machine learning: A systematic review of recent research. *Robotics and Computer-integrated Manufacturing*, *79*, 102432. DOI: 10.1016/j.rcim.2022.102432

Simão, L. E., Gonc, M. B., Manuel, C., & Rodriguez, T. (2016). *An approach to assess logistics and ecological supply chain performance using postponement strategies*. *63*, 398–408. DOI: 10.1016/j.ecolind.2015.10.048

Strandhagen, J. O., Vallandingham, L. R., Fragapane, G., Strandhagen, J. W., Stangeland, A. B. H., & Sharma, N. (2017). Logistics 4.0 and emerging sustainable business models. *Advances in Manufacturing*, *5*(4), 359–369. DOI: 10.1007/s40436-017-0198-1

Subramanian, N., & Abdulrahman, M. D. (2017). Logistics and cloud computing service providers' cooperation: A resilience perspective. *Production Planning and Control*, *28*(11–12), 919–928. DOI: 10.1080/09537287.2017.1336793

Tanyaş, M. (2015). *İstanbul Loji sti k Sektör Anali zi Raporu*. Mavi Ofset. www.musiad.org.tr

Timm, I. J., & Lorig, F. (2015). Logistics 4.0 - A challenge for simulattion. *Winter Simulation Conference*, 3118–3119. DOI: 10.1109/WSC.2015.7408428

Tran-Dang, H., Nicolas, K., Patrick, C., & Kim, D.-S. (2022). The Internet of Things for Logistics: Perspectives, Application Review, and Challenges. *IETE Technical Review*, *39*(1), 93–121. DOI: 10.1080/02564602.2020.1827308

United Nations Environment Programme. (2024). *Emissions Gap Report 2024: No more hot air ... please! With a massive gap between rhetoric and reality, countries draft new climate commitments*. United Nations Environment Programme., DOI: 10.59117/20.500.11822/46404

Valentina, D. S., Di Pasquale, V., Giubileo, V., & Miranda, S. (2022). Human-Robot Collaboration: An analysis of worker's performance. *Procedia Computer Science*, *200*, 1540–1549. DOI: 10.1016/j.procs.2022.01.355

Wang, S., Wan, J., Li, D., & Zhang, C. (2016). Implementing Smart Factory of Industrie 4.0: An Outlook. *International Journal of Distributed Sensor Networks*, *2016*(1), 3159805. DOI: 10.1155/2016/3159805

Windt, K., Böse, F., & Philipp, T. (2008). Autonomy in production logistics: Identification, characterisation and application. *Robotics and Computer-integrated Manufacturing*, *24*(4), 572–578. DOI: 10.1016/j.rcim.2007.07.008

Winkelhaus, S., & Grosse, E. H. (2020a). Logistics 4.0: A systematic review towards a new logistics system. *International Journal of Production Research*, *58*(1), 18–43. DOI: 10.1080/00207543.2019.1612964

Winkelhaus, S., & Grosse, E. H. (2020b). Work characteristics in logistics 4.0: Conceptualization of a qualitative assessment in order picking. *IFAC-PapersOnLine*, *53*(2), 10609–10614. DOI: 10.1016/j.ifacol.2020.12.2816

Xie, F., & Liang, C. Z. (2014). Research of internet of things based on cloud computing. *Applied Mechanics and Materials*, *443*, 589–593. . DOI: 10.4028/www.scientific.net/AMM.443.589

Xu, X., Lu, Y., Vogel-Heuser, B., & Wang, L. (2021). Industry 4.0 and Industry 5.0—Inception, conception and perception. *Journal of Manufacturing Systems*, *61*, 530–535. DOI: 10.1016/j.jmsy.2021.10.006

Yapraklı, T. Ş., & Ünalan, M. (2017). Küresel lojistik performans endeksi ve Türkiye'deki son 10 yıllık lojistik performans analizi. *Atatürk Üniversitesi İktisadi ve İdari Bilimler Dergisi*, *31*(3), 589–606.

Yılmaz, Ü., & Duman, B. (2019). Lojistik 4.0 Kavramına Genel Bir Bakış: Geçmişten Bugüne Gelişim ve Değişimi. *Bilecik Şeyh Edebali Üniversitesi Sosyal Bilimler Enstitüsü Dergisi*, 186–200. DOI: 10.33905/bseusbed.465962

Yukihide, H. (2019). Japanese Science and Technology Basic Plan: A Perspective of Policy Process. *Xinli Kexue Jinzhan*, *1*(1), 24. DOI: 10.3724/SP.J.2096-5141.2019.0003

Zhang, N. (2018). Smart Logistics Path for Cyber-Physical Systems With Internet of Things. *IEEE Access: Practical Innovations, Open Solutions*, *6*, 70808–70819. DOI: 10.1109/ACCESS.2018.2879966

Zhang, S., Lee, C. K. M., Chan, H. K., Choy, K. L., & Wu, Z. (2015). Swarm intelligence applied in green logistics: A literature review. *Engineering Applications of Artificial Intelligence*, *37*, 154–169. DOI: 10.1016/j.engappai.2014.09.007

Zhao, N., Hong, J., & Lau, K. H. (2023). Impact of supply chain digitalization on supply chain resilience and performance: A multi-mediation model. *International Journal of Production Economics*, *259*, 108817. DOI: 10.1016/j.ijpe.2023.108817 PMID: 36852136

Zhou, F., Yu, K., Xie, W., Lyu, J., Zheng, Z., & Zhou, S. (2024). Digital Twin-Enabled Smart Maritime Logistics Management in the Context of Industry 5.0. *IEEE Access: Practical Innovations, Open Solutions*, *12*, 10920–10931. DOI: 10.1109/ACCESS.2024.3354838

Zhou, K., Liu, T., & Zhou, L. (2015). Industry 4.0: Towards Future Industrial Opportunities and Challenges. *12th International Conference on Fuzzy Systems and Knowledge Discovery (FSKD)*, 2147–2152. DOI: 10.1109/FSKD.2015.7382284

Chapter 5 An Expert-Based Evaluation of Airport Environmental Management Criteria Through the SWARA Method

Mustafa Uzgör
https://orcid.org/0000-0002-8804-0343
Muğla Sıtkı Koçman University, Turkey

Savaş Selahattin Ateş
Eskişehir Technical University, Turkey

ABSTRACT

Airports, as vital nodes in the transportation network, contribute to environmental challenges such as carbon emissions, energy consumption, waste generation, and noise pollution. Addressing these challenges requires a comprehensive environmental management approach encompassing multiple criteria, including carbon footprint reduction, energy and water conservation, waste management, and biodiversity protection. This study aims to construct integrated environmental management criteria for airports and evaluate these criteria using the SWARA weighing method. As a result of the analysis, it is found that the most important criterion is carbon emission and energy management, while the least important criterion is biodiversity management. The remaining criteria are waste and water management, noise management, and green management from the most important to the least. Emission

DOI: 10.4018/979-8-3693-8789-4.ch005

and energ-related activities such as building on-site renewable energy facilities, using electric vehicles, and adopting green building design will greatly improve the energy management performance of airports.

1. INTRODUCTION

The industrial environmental impacts, such as climate change caused primarily by fossil fuel use, have been a global concern for years, especially in terms of government policies, business strategies, and ecological effects. Although technological and industrial advancements facilitate human life, they are at the core of these issues (Rajan, 2006). The air transportation industry, as one of the leading industries in terms of technological accumulation, provides social and economic benefits while also drawing attention due to its environmental impacts. This environmental footprint is particularly significant in the context of the industry's rapid and continuous growth. While air transportation has been affected by crises such as the oil crisis, the 9/11 attacks, the SARS virus, and the 2008 economic crisis, it has shown a consistent upward trend (Pearce, 2012; Tanrıverdi et al., 2020). Although the COVID-19 pandemic had a greater impact than previous crises, post-pandemic data indicates that growth will likely continue as it did after past crises (EUROCONTROL, 2021). However, environmental impacts of aviation operations have become a growing concern in recent years. The aviation industry consumes large amounts of fuel, making aviation greenhouse gas emissions (GHG) a primary contributor to climate change. Globally, the aviation industry is responsible for about 2% of total human-induced CO_2 emissions, and within the entire transportation industry, aviation's share is approximately 12% (ATAG, 2020). Current projections estimate that demand for air passenger travel could exceed 10 billion by 2050. The projected carbon emissions from 2021 to 2050 under normal conditions are around 21.2 gigatons of CO_2 (IATA, 2021). This indicates that the growth in air transportation will only be meaningful if the environmental impact is minimized and managed effectively.

Airports, as central hubs for air transportation, not only contribute significantly to local and national economies but also serve as clustering points for aircrafts and the people. However, airports induce substantial environmental impacts, particularly in terms of air pollution, noise, and soil/water contamination (Budd, 2017; Uzgör et al., 2024). While much of the focus on environmental sustainability in aviation has been directed at reducing aircraft emissions, airports are also under increasing pressure to support the green transformation vision of the aviation industry (Ryley et al., 2013). Although emissions from aircraft dominate aviation emissions, airport operations and the movement of employees, passengers, cargo, goods, and waste across airport sites also release gases and particles into the atmosphere (Daley,

2010). These emissions typically result from any fossil fuel combustion process. Therefore, airports with their operating vehicles potentially emit CO_2, H_2O, NO_x, SO_x, HC, CO, and particulates.

Another significant environmental and social impact is noise pollution around airports. Noise is a major source of complaints related to airport aircraft operations and is one of the main concerns expressed by local residents and neighboring communities when an airport expansion is proposed (Antoine & Kroo, 2004). Furthermore, noise is one of the primary constraints to airport growth (Gasco et al., 2017). Additional environmental impacts include interactions with surrounding plant and animal species (Altuntaş, 2019), and the effects of solid/liquid waste on water and soil contamination (Pitt et al., 2002).

In summary, airport operations carry a pollution potential at every stage. To mitigate these impacts, the International Civil Aviation Organization (ICAO) is implementing new regulations and setting environmental targets at general assemblies, while the Airports Council International (ACI), through its environmental committee, provides policy recommendations on carbon accreditation, local air quality, and noise (ACI, 2023; ICAO, 2019). Although aircraft emissions are not included in the Kyoto Protocol, emissions directly controlled by airport operators are ground-based and therefore subject to national emissions targets. Adapting to updated environmental regulations and controlling environmental impacts are critical for continuing international aviation activities in the future. Therefore, effective environmental management at airports is not only essential for regulatory compliance, but also for ensuring the long-term sustainability and social acceptance of air transportation activities. In this context, this research aims to identify the criteria (green criteria) that determine the environmental management performance of airports and to evaluate the importance of these criteria, contributing to airports' capacity to manage their environmental impacts.

In a similar vein to this study, Kılkış and Kılkış (2016) evaluated the sustainability performance of airports by combining environmental criteria with service quality criteria. Kumar et al. (2020) focused solely on qualitative criteria to assess the green performance of Indian airports. Chao et al. (2017) used the Delphi method to establish environmental performance indicators and assessed five unnamed international airports, with all indicators in this study being qualitative. Lu et al. (2018) measured the sustainability levels of three airports in Taiwan using a balanced scorecard. Sreenath et al. (2021) examined the sustainability practices of high-traffic airports in developing countries, highlighting the link between these practices and sustainable development goals, and presented innovative technologies supporting sustainability initiatives.

As a contribution to the previous work, this study has uniquely developed both qualitative and quantitative criteria to obtain more comprehensive and holistic results.

This allows for a broader environmental criteria evaluation than seen in previous literature. While existing environmental criteria were utilized, original criteria not previously encountered in the literature were developed through semi-structured interviews with experts. Moreover, the study focused exclusively on environmental sustainability performance indicators, excluding social and economic sustainability aspects.

2. ENVIRONMENTAL IMPACTS OF AIRPORTS

Although air transportation generates significant economic and social benefits, it also brings various and increasingly severe negative environmental impacts. Some of these environmental impacts from air transportation activities are local to the airport area, while others are of global concern (Daley, 2010). This study focuses on airport-related impacts, primarily assessed within the context of local effects.

Airports pose noise issues for those residing nearby and along flight paths. Globally, aircraft and airport operations contribute to air pollution through emissions of CO_2, NO_x, and other harmful particulates. Additionally, airports create further local problems, such as influencing surrounding land development, causing loss or damage to natural habitats, generating waste, and polluting water sources. These issues are particularly prominent for large airports often situated near population centers, meaning a significant portion of society can be affected by airport operations (Graham, 2023).

On the other hand, implementing necessary measures to balance the economic and social benefits of airport operations with the potential costs arising from environmental impacts is key to effective planning and management (Dimitriou et al., 2014). On a global scale, environmental concerns related to aviation are intensely focused on issues like climate change and ozone layer depletion. However, among these impacts, local effects are primarily relevant to airports (Postorino & Mantecchini, 2014). The environmental impacts occurring at airports are listed in Figure 1.

Figure 1. Environmental impacts of airports (Budd, 2017, p.284).

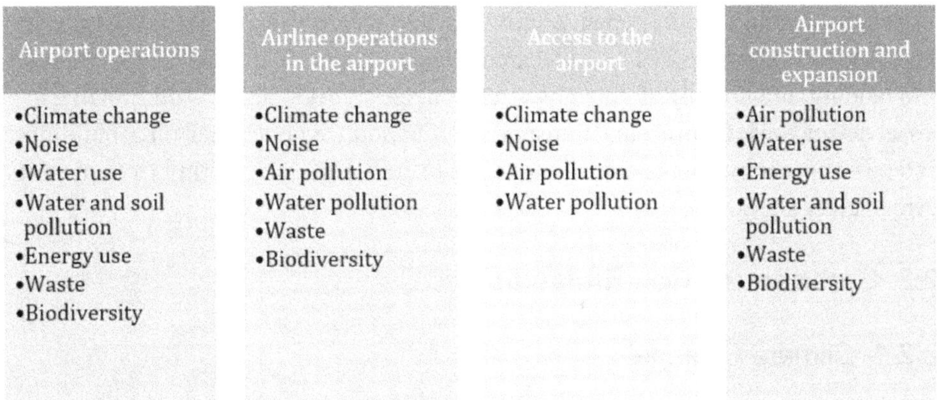

2.1. Noise

Aircraft noise is traditionally considered the most significant environmental issue at airports, often leading to operational restrictions and denial of planning permits (Paling & Thomas, 2018). With the continuous growth of air traffic, aircraft noise has become an increasingly severe problem for people living near airports. Noise has various sources, with departure and approach noise being the primary reasons for community complaints. Taxiing and engine start-up noise also contribute to these complaints. In quiet areas, such as national parks and nature reserves, overflight noise from aircraft at cruising altitudes can be disturbing and may lead to noise complaints (Marais et al., 2016). Although air transportation has global environmental impacts in various dimensions, noise is primarily a local concern.

Despite the development of quieter aircraft and stricter noise certification requirements, noise remains a persistent issue today (Graham, 2023). Noise impact, the first environmental area regulated by ICAO through Annex 16, became a concern in the U.S. in the 1950s with the introduction of jet-engine aircraft. The subsequent rise in air traffic made it challenging to manage, leading to various measures like source reduction, restrictions, and bans to control noise impacts (Mahashabde et al., 2011). Technological and operational developments aimed at reducing aircraft noise have been offset by increases in traffic, changes in flight paths, and the encroachment of urban areas on airports (Thomas et al., 2010). Among the major reasons for the increase in the population exposed to noise are the shift of residential areas toward airports and the growing urban population.

Primary sources of noise at airports include construction activities, aircraft noise and engine testing, ground service activities, and road traffic noise from airport access vehicles (Durmaz, 2018). Land areas closer to aircraft approach paths (takeoff and landing) are notably affected by aircraft noise (ICAO, 2023). Additionally, to a lesser extent, noise from ground transportation, announcements in terminal buildings, and passenger movements contribute to the overall noise originating from airports (Sreenath et al., 2021).

2.2. Greenhouse Gas Emissions

2.2.1. Climate Change

Greenhouse gas emissions around airports have significant environmental impacts, contributing to climate change and air pollution (Postorino & Mantecchini, 2014). Airports produce emissions from various sources, including construction, aircraft operations, management and maintenance activities, ground support equipment, energy use, and on-site transportation. While these emissions are smaller in scale compared to total aircraft emissions, they still represent a substantial portion of the carbon footprint directly attributable to airports (Daley, 2010).

The main sources of greenhouse gas emissions at airports are as follows (Budd, 2017; Graham, 2023; Uzgör, 2024):

- Aircraft movements
- Passenger transport to the airport
- Employee commuting
- Ground service vehicles
- Cargo operations
- Direct energy consumption (gas and electricity)
- Waste production and processing
- Food and water consumption

Aircraft movements are the primary source of greenhouse gas emissions from airports, accounting for a significant portion of total emissions (Masiol & Harrison, 2014). These emissions, which are largely the result of fossil fuel combustion, include carbon dioxide (CO_2), carbon monoxide (CO), nitrogen oxides (NO_X), water vapor (H_2O), sulfur oxides (SO_X), particulate matter (PM), volatile organic compounds (VOC), and other pollutants. Among these, CO_2 is the most significant contributor to climate change, with a long atmospheric lifetime, although it does not pose direct health risks (Budd, 2017; Kazda & Caves, 2015). CO_2 emissions are associated with severe weather events, rising sea levels, and other environmental disasters that are outcomes of climate change. Meanwhile, NO_X emissions from aircraft engines contribute to air pollution, which can lead to respiratory health issues, though they do not present global-scale problems.

Surface transport vehicles operating within airports—particularly those powered by diesel or gasoline—also have a notable impact on greenhouse gas and aerosol emissions within and around the airport area. Ground support equipment, like baggage carts and service vehicles, also contribute to emissions due to fuel consumption. Furthermore, energy consumption in airport facilities for lighting, heating, and cooling adds to greenhouse gas emissions. Terminal facilities (check-in and security counters, ticket booths, baggage facilities, as well as restaurants and retail areas) also require energy, which, depending on the source, can be considered a contributor to carbon emissions (Postorino & Mantecchini, 2014). Transportation to and from airports, including private and public transit, is another factor contributing to greenhouse gas emissions.

Xiong et al. (2023) categorize airport emissions into two phases: construction and operational processes. Thus, emissions from airport expansion and construction phases are not to be overlooked. Major concerns during construction include soil erosion, water and air quality, noise from equipment and construction methods, and issues related to material sourcing and quantity, as well as disruptions or relocations affecting workplaces and residential areas (Horonjeff et al., 2010).

2.2.2. Air Pollution

While the atmospheric impacts of air transportation are generally considered in terms of global effects, local air pollution and air quality issues around airports are also significant concerns. Emissions of CO_2, NO_X, CO, HC, SO_X, and other particulates from aircraft, road traffic to airports, energy production, and on-site ground transport negatively affect local air quality (Budd, 2017). Those contributing to local air pollution are specified in ICAO's air quality guidance manual as NO_X, CO, HC, particulate matter ($PM_{2,5}$ and PM_{10}), and SO_X (ICAO, 2015). Some of these pollutants are primary, as they are directly released into the air from pollution sources, while secondary pollutants result from the reactions of these primary substances with other compounds in the atmosphere (Müezzinoğlu, 2000). Poor air quality from these pollutants poses potential health risks for people living and working around airports, including an increased risk of heart and lung diseases or aggravation of existing conditions (Li & Loo, 2016). Consequently, ICAO has introduced increasingly strict limitations on some of these emissions in new aircraft engines, with tighter regulatory controls on local air quality standards being applied in Europe and North America.

The World Business Council for Sustainable Development (WBCSD) and the World Resources Institute (WRI) have prepared a guide titled Corporate Accounting and Reporting Standards for CO_2 (Ashford et al., 2013). Here, direct emissions are defined as those from sources owned or controlled by the reporting organization (the airport operator). Indirect emissions result from the reporting organization's activities but occur at sources owned or controlled by another entity (airport service partners). Although air quality regulations vary by country, an increasing number of airport operators are recording and reporting emissions as Scope 1, 2, and 3. Table 1 displays these emission types for airports. Scope 3 emissions represent the largest share of emissions at an airport but are also the ones over which the airport operator typically has the least control. This complexity arises due to the numerous tenants, government agencies, ground access transportation operators, and other stakeholders involved in airport operations, making the reduction of airport emissions challenging.

Table 1. Airport emission scopes

Scope	Description
Scope 1	Direct emissions from sources owned and/or controlled by the airport, including airside vehicles or airport buildings.
Scope 2	Indirect emissions, primarily from the purchase of electricity generated elsewhere for use at the airport.
Scope 3	Indirect and/or optional emissions resulting from airport operations, including aircraft and ground maneuvering activities.

2.3. Energy and Water Consumption

Although the atmospheric effects of air transportation are generally considered from a global perspective, local air pollution and air quality issues around airports are also significant concerns. Airports require a continuous and secure supply of energy to meet the intense demand from service partners and passengers, ensuring operational capacity at maximum levels, as well as large quantities of available water to maintain essential services (Ashford et al., 2013). The energy and water consumption of a busy airport is approximately equal to that of a large city (Sreenath et al., 2021). Therefore, implementing energy and water consumption practices in an environmentally friendly, efficient, and effective manner is essential for sustainable airport management.

The energy consumption of the air transport industry is increasing faster than that of other polluting industries (Kazda & Caves, 2015). Despite improvements in energy efficiency, increasing passenger numbers are causing energy consumption and costs to rise at many airports, which in turn can lead to potential power outages and grid failures. The main energy consumers at airports are heating and cooling systems to maintain indoor air temperature and quality within terminal buildings for the comfort of passengers and staff, followed by terminal and airport lighting (Budd, 2017). Although these are directly controlled by airport operators, careful management is required given airports' growing reliance on retail and commercial activities. Retailers often demand bright lighting to make products appealing to potential customers, which not only raises energy demand for lighting but also increases air conditioning needs to offset the additional heat generated by these lights (Ashford et al., 2013). Besides heating, ventilation, air conditioning, and lighting, energy management related to the operation of computers, equipment, and automation systems is crucial. Addressing these issues is financially viable for airports since environmental improvements in energy savings can lead to significant cost reductions (Graham, 2023). To reduce long-term operating costs and ensure that energy demands are met, airports are increasingly prioritizing energy-saving measures in the design of new terminal buildings. Many new airport facilities are being designed or renovated to make the most of natural light and ventilation, minimizing energy needs (Marais et al., 2016).

A significant portion of the electricity used in airports is supplied externally rather than generated on-site. This factor drives airports to reduce their energy consumption and/or increase the share of on-site generated electricity from renewable sources such as solar, biomass, and wind energy. In recent years, a trend has emerged where airports are increasingly focused on reducing CO_2 impacts by using cleaner electricity sources or producing renewable energy within the facility through solar, wind, hydro, and geothermal options (ICAO, 2022). A growing number of airports are adopting carbon-neutral strategies by integrating renewable energy systems, such as on-site solar and wind power, and participating in international carbon accreditation programs like ACI's Airport Carbon Accreditation program.

Large amounts of water are used in airport terminals for drinking, food preparation, medical purposes, and cleaning. Airside, water is also used for aircraft cleaning, firefighting activities, and de-icing, supporting various airport operations and maintenance needs (Graham, 2023). An airport's operational capacity and the quality of service provided to customers and service partners can be severely limited if it fails to guarantee a safe, adequate, and cost-effective water supply to meet peak demand. However, meeting the growing water demand for airports is increasingly challenging, especially in areas where water resources are under pressure from factors like excessive extraction, high surface runoff, or decreased rainfall due to climate change. (Ashford et al., 2013; Daley, 2010). Additionally, the rising competition from other industries for water resources further complicates this situation. Sustainable water management practices, such as rainwater harvesting and recycling, reusing water in vehicle washing and toilet systems, using smart water systems, and dry washing methods, can reduce the high-water demand and usage at airports. The most sustainable approach to water management is for airports to strive for self-sufficiency in water supply by maximizing opportunities for water harvesting, recycling, and minimizing consumption (Marais et al., 2016).

2.4. Waste

According to ICAO, waste is defined as any "unwanted or unused" products/materials/substances generated and/or arriving at the airport site that must undergo proper treatment (ICAO, 2017). Within the airport context, waste is generally given less emphasis in environmental management plans compared to issues like noise and aircraft emissions (Pitt et al., 2002). However, waste disposal can be a significant cost for airports and, due to its environmental impact, requires proper management. Increased passenger traffic and expanded airport activities have significantly raised both the types and volumes of waste produced at airports. It has been reported that some airports generate waste volumes comparable to those of a small city, highlighting the considerable environmental impact involved (Sebastian & Louis, 2021). Since its opening, İstanbul Airport, with its steadily increasing passenger traffic, generated over 120 tons of waste daily on average by 2022 (İGA, 2023). The amount of waste generated is generally positively correlated with air traffic volumes (Janić, 2011). Waste from stakeholders operating within airports can primarily be grouped into municipal solid waste, construction and demolition waste, hazardous waste, waste from aircraft operations, and wastewater from sources such as lavatories and toilets (Budd, 2017; Sebastian & Louis, 2021). Municipal waste is the most varied of these types, resulting from the activities of various stakeholders. Typically, municipal waste at airports is generated from terminal areas, tenants occupying airport spaces, airlines, and cargo operations (Greer et al., 2020a; Sebastian & Louis, 2021). Terminal waste includes waste from public areas, office spaces, etc. Airport operators generally have greater control over waste from office administration, engineering, and security operations, as well as green waste from airport maintenance, such as grass clippings. In contrast, airlines and other service providers are responsible for waste resulting from in-flight catering, cleaning, and retail activities (Budd, 2017; Paling & Thomas, 2018).

Airports also produce biodegradable and green organic waste from food service operations and landscaping activities. Food preparation at restaurants and other dining facilities at airports, as well as discarded food waste, contribute significantly to food waste volumes. Landscaping activities around airports produce debris such as leaves, branches, soil, and dirt. This waste can be composted on-site or in collaboration with regional facilities (Greer et al., 2020a; Winter et al., 2021).

Waste at airports is generated by airport operators, airlines, ground service providers, concessionaires, and other companies. Although most waste comes from airlines, airport operators are typically the primary stakeholders responsible for overall waste management across all airport activities (S. Gössling & Upham, 2009). As local entities, airports are subject to regional policies and regulations regarding waste management. However, due to the nature of aviation operations, airports also face specific operational constraints. For instance, airports are required to incinerate or send all international food waste from aircraft to controlled landfill sites. Additionally, the transfer of waste from airside to landside at airports is complicated due to security, customs, and insurance restrictions (Graham, 2023).

According to Pitt and Smith (2003), waste-related pollution, although having social and economic impacts, is essentially an environmental issue. In line with the polluter-pays principle, airports must develop a comprehensive waste management system, including sorting and recycling waste at the source along with other subsystems (dos Santos et al., 2020).

2.5. Water and Soil Pollution

Another environmental impact arising from airport operations is water and soil pollution. Many studies have highlighted water and soil pollution as primary pollution factors at airports, and their management is considered among the key performance indicators (Upham & Mills, 2005). Polluted or contaminated runoff water within an airport's operational area poses significant environmental threats, as these waters contain relatively high levels of pollutants that can contaminate groundwater (Greer et al., 2020a). Soil pollution at airports, on the other hand, occurs when harmful substances released into the ground alter its natural properties. Sources contributing to water and soil pollution at airports include the following (Durmaz, 2018; Paling & Thomas, 2018):

- Construction activities
- Anti-icing and de-icing operations
- Terminal building waste
- Maintenance and washing of vehicles
- Oil and fuel spills from storage tanks
- Firefighting training
- Pesticides and emergency services

Polluted waters from aircraft refueling, aircraft operations, maintenance of aircraft and ground support equipment, and facility cleaning can potentially enter nearby lakes and streams via stormwater drainage systems (Baxter, 2022). Similarly, airport construction—especially runway construction—can disrupt groundwater systems not only within the airport site but also in the wider surrounding area. Rainwater quickly flows from paved surfaces, causing flooding in waterways fed by rain drains (Kazda & Caves, 2015). Repairing damage to surface water or river systems can take many years and be very costly (Ashford et al., 2011). Surface water discharge or runoff to local water bodies from runways, aprons, parking lots, and other surface structures may be contaminated by anti-icing and de-icing fluids used during winter. Large amounts of propylene glycol (PG) and ethylene glycol (EG) based products are used to prevent and remove ice on aircraft during winter for flight safety. Glycol, used in these fluids, is the highest volume water pollutant discharged from airports (Franchuk et al., 2005). Chemicals used for maintenance and cleaning of aircraft and vehicles, as well as firefighting activities and fuel spills, also contribute to this pollution. Leakage of fuel and oil from underground tanks and pipes installed in airport infrastructure and fertilizers used in landscaping activities pollute both groundwater and soil. Additionally, routine wastewater from buildings and facilities, including domestic sewage, is another source of water pollution (Baxter et al., 2014; Graham, 2023).

Potentially toxic elements (mercury, zinc, lead, nickel, etc.) that may result from airport operations can contaminate soil due to their persistence and biological accumulation, thereby threatening the health of all living systems (Brtnický et al., 2020). In this context, fueling and storage activities at airports are of critical importance. Petroleum products are among the main soil pollutants at aviation facilities. Being mixtures of various carbon-containing substances, they are referred to as petroleum hydrocarbons (Radomska et al., 2020). Once these substances seep into the soil, they can persist for extended periods, damaging the ecosystem. Additionally, fossil fuel derivatives at airports pose an additional threat by contaminating soil with heavy metals, making it unsuitable for plant growth. Moreover, natural renewal processes in soil contaminated with heavy metals are slow, and ecosystem restoration can take 10-15 years (Lim et al., 2016). Similarly, the use of de-icing and anti-icing fluids during winter operations or chemical materials used in emergency response and rescue drills can have environmental effects when they mix into the soil. Airports can minimize these effects through effective environmental management systems.

2.6. Biodiversity

Biodiversity is generally defined as the diversity of living organisms on Earth (Altuntaş, 2019). In terms of airport environmental management, protecting the local environment and wildlife is a crucial issue. Air traffic continues to increase steadily, and aircraft speeds are rising, with numerous low-altitude flights by general aviation, military aviation, and commercial aircraft during takeoffs and landings. This situation thus raises the potential for conflicts between air transport operations and surrounding wildlife (Kazda & Caves, 2015). Airports are often located among fields, forests, and other natural habitats, making it impossible to imagine these vast areas without fauna. Many airports near large urban settlements are located in greenbelt areas, which are ecologically significant or recreationally valuable to local residents. The expansion of an airport or construction on part of its land may be restricted due to ecological habitats threatened by development (Paling & Thomas, 2018).

The construction phase of an airport is one of the most impactful stages concerning biodiversity around the airport (Zhao et al., 2019). Issues such as the destruction of surrounding trees, endemic plant species (flora), the alteration of habitats and behaviors of animal communities (fauna), and changes to the ecosystem and natural landforms are likely to arise during airport construction. During the construction and expansion of airports, farmland occupation and the reduction of forests, grasslands, and water sources inevitably destroy habitats for wild animals and plants (Niu et al., 2021). This is because airport development requires extensive infrastructure and superstructure projects that will affect the surrounding area, including the conversion of large tracts of land into runways, taxiways, aprons, and terminal buildings, as well as road and railway connections (Daley et al., 2008).

The occupation of various types of land cover by wildlife can significantly increase the risk of wildlife collisions with aircraft (Martin et al., 2013). Additionally, climate change may lead to changes in wildlife, such as increases in wildlife hazard incidents, shifts in migration patterns, and effects on local biodiversity (ICAO, 2018). For example, the diversity of bird species at an airport might change, or certain regions might see an increase in large migratory bird populations. With the increase in bird strikes involving jet-engine aircraft, each airport faces unique challenges. If an airport lies along a bird migration route, numerous birds will be seen around the airport during the migration season. Moreover, if the runway orientation is perpendicular to the bird migration path, the likelihood of bird strikes increases significantly, and airport lighting and noise may also impact migratory birds (Zhao et al., 2019). Each airport operator is responsible for developing, implementing, and demonstrating an effective bird/wildlife strike and wildlife control program. ICAO (2018) has detailed land uses that may contribute to wildlife hazards at or near airports and has rated these uses within radii of 3 and 8 kilometers from the airport center according to their acceptability. Therefore, airport planners should consider biodiversity and species conservation related to wildlife safety threats (Blackwell et al., 2009).

In the context of sustainable development, airports must manage their existing land to promote biodiversity and protect habitats, while also facing constraints on new infrastructure development due to sensitive areas and species in the surrounding rural areas that are protected by international and national regulations (Ashford et al., 2013).

Cultural heritage may also be affected by airport development. For instance, historical buildings may be located within areas designated for airport expansion. In such cases, as seen at Manchester and Copenhagen airports, these historic buildings have been relocated using special techniques (Graham, 2023). Additionally, airport developments and landscapes that may disrupt the ecosystem or fail to be visually pleasing may face opposition from local communities and authorities.

3. METHODOLOGY

3.1. Determination of the Criteria

One of the original contributions of this study to the literature is the evaluation of the criteria that are important in determining the environmental management performance of airports. To determine the evaluation criteria, a comprehensive literature review was initially conducted. The "green airport" criteria derived from this review were then refined with insights from interviews with field experts, resulting in a finalized list. To reveal these unique criteria, semi-structured interviews, a qualitative data collection technique, were conducted.

Semi-structured interviews are one of the qualitative data collection techniques primarily used in qualitative research methodologies and represent a hybrid approach between informal, unstructured conversational interviews and formal, structured interviews (Patton, 2002). In semi-structured interviews, questions that have been systematically and consistently prepared in advance are asked to the participant, while the researcher also has the flexibility to ask probing questions to delve deeper into the responses.

The following criteria were sought in the experts interviewed:

- Experience working in the airport industry
- Middle to upper management experience
- Specialization in airport and environmental issues through education and/or industry experience

In such interviews, it is accepted that the number of interviews is sufficient when the researcher is no longer able to obtain new information (Creswell, 2013;

Malterud et al., 2016). Accordingly, in this study, semi-structured interviews were conducted with a total of five experts until the point where no new criteria were proposed and redundancy was reached.

The final environmental management performance evaluation criteria, resulting from the literature review and expert interviews, are presented in Table 2. Description of the criteria are also based on the interviews.

Table 2. Airport environmental management criteria

Criteria Code	Criteria Name	Description
C1	Carbon and energy management	Carbon emissions from aircraft and ground sources, energy consumption, renewable energy opportunities, airport public transport facilities.
C2	Noise management	Noise levels from aircraft and ground vehicles, noise exposure of the surrounding community, proximity to the center, noise mitigation measures.
C3	Water and waste management	Water usage, wastewater treatment, waste quantity and rate, waste segregation, waste reduction.
C4	Biodiversity management	Protection of local wildlife, the number of bird strike incidents, afforestation, monitoring of local wildlife.
C5	Green management	Management's commitment and support, green certification, environmental training, stakeholder interaction.

3.2. Weighing the Criteria With SWARA

In this study, the SWARA (Step-Wise Weight Assessment Ratio Analysis) method, which gives a critical role to experts in determining the weights of environmental performance evaluation criteria for airports, was chosen. The SWARA method, developed by Keršuliene et al. (2010), is also referred to as an expert-oriented method, where the importance levels of the criteria are determined based on the knowledge, expertise, and experience of the experts (Bardakçı, 2020).

The SWARA method stands out compared to other methods due to its features, such as allowing decision-makers to evaluate without difficulty, being simple to apply, assisting in coordinating and collecting data from experts, and providing consistent results with a small number of pairwise comparisons (Keršuliene et al., 2010). For (n) number of criteria, only ($n-1$) number of comparisons are needed.

When determining the weights of the criteria, the standard weighting form of the SWARA method was used. This form includes a definition and example application to help expert decision-makers understand the scoring system. Accordingly, the expert decision-makers first ranked the criteria from most important to least important. Then, the most important criterion received a score of 1, and each criterion was scored based on how much more important it was compared to the one below it in a pairwise comparison.

The information regarding the importance weights evaluated by the expert decision-makers is presented in Table 3.

Table 3. The information regarding the decision-makers weighing the criteria

Expert decision makers	Position	Tenure
DM1	Environmental engineer	4 years
DM2	Environmental department director	8 years
DM3	Deputy director of environmental management	14 years
DM4	Sustainability director	10 years
DM5	Environmental engineer	12 years

The SWARA method is executed in five fundamental application steps (Keršuliene et al., 2010):

Step 1: Expert decision-makers determine the order of importance of the criteria according to their own perspectives. Decision-makers assign a value score between 0.00 and 1.00 to these criteria based on their importance ranking. The level of importance is the primary basis for scoring the criteria, where the most important criterion is assigned a score of 1.00. After scoring, the arithmetic average of each criterion's score is calculated, resulting in the average value score (pj), and the criteria are ranked according to their importance.

Step 2: A relative importance weight is determined for each criterion. This is done by identifying the difference between the (j+1) criterion and the j-th criterion, where the j-th criterion is the first criterion in the ranking. This difference is expressed as sj (the comparative importance of the average score).

Step 3: A coefficient (kj) for each criterion is determined according to Equation (1).

$$k_j = \begin{cases} 1 & , \ j = 1 \\ s_j + 1 & , \ j > 1 \end{cases} \tag{1}$$

Step 4: The importance vector (qj) of the criteria is determined according to Equation (2).

$$q_j = \begin{cases} 1 & , \ j = 1 \\ \dfrac{q_{j-1}}{k_j} & , \ j > 1 \end{cases} \tag{2}$$

Step 5: The final importance weights (wj) for each criterion are calculated using Equation (3). This value represents the relative importance of the j-th criterion.

$$W_j = \frac{q_j}{\sum_{k=1}^{n} q_j} \quad (3)$$

4. RESULTS

The importance rankings and scores given by the decision-makers for the airport environmental management criteria are shown in Table 4 and 5. The decision-makers ranked the criteria from most important to least important based on their knowledge and perceptions.

Table 4. Decision makers' ranking of importance for the criteria

Criteria		Decision Makers				
		DM1	DM2	DM3	DM4	DM5
C1	Carbon emission and energy management	1	1	1	1	1
C2	Noise management	2	3	5	2	3
C3	Water and waste management	3	2	2	3	2
C4	Biodiversity management	4	4	4	4	5
C5	Green management	5	5	3	5	4

Table 5. Weighting scores of decision makers for the criteria

Criteria		Decision Makers					Mean Importance Score (pj)
		DM1	DM2	DM3	DM4	DM5	
C1	Carbon emission and energy management	1,00	1,00	1,00	1,00	1,00	1,00
C2	Noise management	0,9	0,75	0,5	0,5	0,68	0,666
C3	Water and waste management	0,8	0,9	0,85	0,95	0,78	0,856
C4	Biodiversity management	0,75	0,5	0,52	0,55	0,4	0,544
C5	Green management	0,7	0,45	0,7	0,9	0,55	0,66

When examining the criteria, it is observed that all decision-makers consider the reduction of carbon emissions and energy management (C1) as the most important criterion. When calculating the arithmetic means (pj) of the importance scores, the criteria are ranked from most important to least important as follows: water and waste management (C3), noise management (C2), green management (C5), and biodiversity management (C4). The criteria with the closest importance levels are green management and biodiversity management, with a difference of 0.006 points.

In calculating the criterion weights, the criteria were ranked and scored by decision-makers, and then the average importance scores (pj) were calculated. Subsequently, the sj value, indicating the importance of each criterion compared to the next, was computed according to the ranking. The sj value represents the percentage difference between the pj values. The coefficient values for all criteria were calculated using Equation (1), and the adjusted weight values were calculated using Equation (2). Here, the qj value for the most important criterion is 1. The final weight values for the criteria were calculated using Equation (3). The final weight values were obtained by dividing the adjusted weight values of each criterion by the total of the adjusted weight values. All these values are presented in Table 6. Accordingly, the importance level of the most important criterion, carbon emissions reduction and energy management, is 25%. The criteria are ranked from most to least important as follows: water and waste management at 21.9%, noise management at 18.4%, green management at 18.3%, and biodiversity management at 16.4%.

Table 6. Average and comparative importance ratings, coefficients, adjusted and final weights for the criteria

Criteria	pj	sj	kj	qj	wj
C1	1,00	-	1,000	1,00	0,250
C3	0,86	0,144	1,144	0,87	0,219
C2	0,67	0,190	1,190	0,73	0,184
C5	0,66	0,006	1,006	0,73	0,183
C4	0,54	0,116	1,116	0,65	0,164

Note: The criteria weights are highlighted in green in the far-right column.

The weights of the criteria provided in Table 6 are illustrated in Figure 2.

Figure 2. The final importance levels of the criteria

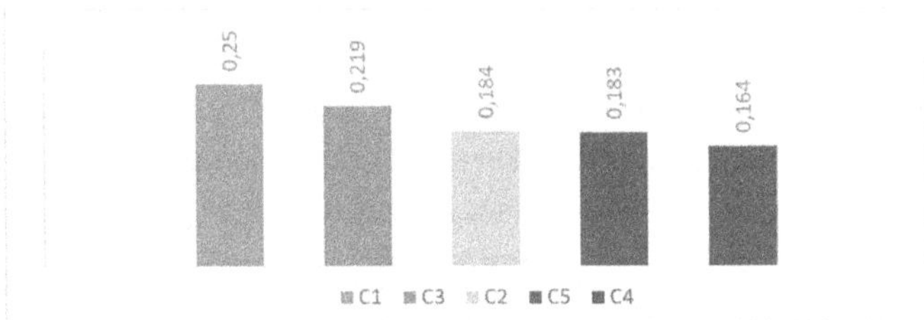

5. DISCUSSION AND CONCLUSION

In this research, evaluations conducted by experts revealed that the carbon emission and energy management criterion is ranked first among the most critical factors influencing airport environmental performance, carrying a weight of 25%. This conclusion is corroborated by a variety of studies found in the literature (Chao et al., 2017; Lu et al., 2018; Monsalud et al., 2015). Furthermore, the significance of criteria associated with carbon emissions consistently remains above 20% across various studies. This suggests that carbon emissions represent a crucial and influential factor in the assessment of airport environmental performance. The rationale behind this observation lies in the direct correlation between greenhouse gas emissions from aircraft and those stemming from energy consumption, both of which contribute significantly to global warming and climate change.

Water and waste management emerged as the second most significant criterion in the ranking of environmental factors. This observation can be attributed to the potential environmental challenges arising from waste incineration or landfill disposal, including the formation of large garbage piles, foul odors, harm to biodiversity, visual pollution, and increased greenhouse gas emissions. Furthermore, the diminishing availability of water resources, exacerbated by global warming, highlights the growing significance of effective and efficient water management practices. Although waste and water management are among the important criteria, Uzgör et al. (2024) has indicated through his bibliometric analysis that studies on waste and water management are significantly limited in the literature. On the other hand, the results of this study suggest that waste and water management activities at airports are indeed effective criteria in environmental management performance and should be more widely covered in the literature. A similar conclusion has also been drawn by Greer et al. (2020b) and Sebastian & Louis (2021).

Noise is a frequently utilized environmental performance criterion in the literature, with numerous researchers examining the impacts of airport noise from diverse angles and investigating potential mitigation strategies (Josimović et al., 2016; Lijesen et al., 2010; Ozkurt, 2014). Due to its social implications, noise adversely affects various aspects of life, including community well-being, health, stress levels, and sleep quality, particularly in modern airports that are integrated with urban areas. Consequently, experts included noise as one of the evaluation criteria in this study. However, in this assessment, noise management was ranked third in importance among the five primary criteria, with a weight score closely aligned with that of the fourth-ranked criterion, green management.

The green management criterion was identified as the fourth most important factor in the ranking. Its relatively lower significance is attributed to the tendency for environmental considerations to be overshadowed by financial priorities in management decisions. Nonetheless, managerial support for environmental management remains a crucial element in achieving the environmental objectives of airports.

Biodiversity management was positioned as the fifth and final criterion, with an importance level of 16.9%. The criteria associated with biodiversity encompass extensive and long-term practices such as wildlife monitoring and management, along with the conservation of flora and fauna. Experts regard these criteria as less critical compared to those focusing on emissions, energy, noise, and water and waste management in terms of enhancing overall environmental management performance. For instance, large-scale greening initiatives can impose substantial financial burdens on airports. In contrast, reducing taxiway maneuver times by five minutes—considering the thousands of flights that occur daily—can lead to a much more immediate impact on emission reductions than planting hundreds of trees or safeguarding particular species. Comendador et al. (2019) highlighted that biodiversity receives considerably less focus from ACI compared to emission-related criteria, with environmental programs primarily concentrating on emission control. Their findings align with the results of this study.

These findings highlight the importance of various criteria necessary for improving the environmental management performance of airports. In particular, areas such as carbon emissions, water, and waste management are critical for ensuring the sustainability of airport operations. However, the integration of digital solutions today plays a revolutionary role in managing and implementing these criteria. Air traffic management, energy monitoring systems, and smart waste management applications help airports minimize their environmental impacts. The management of carbon and energy emissions at airports can be significantly enhanced through the implementation of various technologies and systems. Electric vehicle technologies, smart building applications, on-site renewable energy production facilities, and the seamless integration of public transportation systems are among the strategies that will improve overall environmental management performance. For waste management, establishing comprehensive recycling programs and promoting waste reduction strategies, such as minimizing single-use plastics in catering services, can significantly reduce landfill contributions. Additionally, composting organic waste can transform food scraps into valuable fertilizers. In terms of water management, airports can harness rainwater harvesting systems for non-potable uses and implement water-saving fixtures to reduce consumption. Sustainable landscaping with native plants can further minimize irrigation needs. Regarding noise management, installing continuous noise monitoring systems and adjusting flight paths to avoid densely populated areas can mitigate the impact on local communities. Implementing soundproofing initiatives for nearby residential areas can also enhance community relations. Lastly, for biodiversity management, protecting and restoring natural habitats around the airport is crucial. This can be achieved through wildlife monitoring programs and the promotion of local flora. Educational initiatives aimed at employees and visitors can raise awareness about the importance of biodiversity conservation, ensuring a holistic approach to environmental stewardship at airports.

Finally, this study has certain limitations. We aim to identify and prioritize environmental management performance criteria for airports through expert opinions, without focusing on a specific type of airport such as international hubs or regional airports. However, it is acknowledged that the importance and applicability of certain criteria may vary depending on airport size, capacity, and operational complexity. Likewise, differences in geographic context, such as climate conditions and regional environmental challenges, were not explicitly addressed in the analysis. Furthermore, the influence of regulatory environments—such as the stringency of national environmental laws or participation in international initiatives—was not a direct focus of this study, although it is recognized as a critical factor shaping environmental sustainability strategies of airports. These dimensions represent important areas for future research to ensure broader applicability and contextual sensitivity of environmental management performance assessments.

REFERENCES

ACI. (2023). *Environment*. https://aci.aero/advocacy/environment/

Altuntaş, H. (2019). Biodiversity Management. In *Sustainable Aviation* (pp. 81–95). Springer.

Antoine, N. E., & Kroo, I. M. (2004). Aircraft optimization for minimal environmental impact. *Journal of Aircraft*, *41*(4), 790–797. DOI: 10.2514/1.71

Ashford, N., Mumayiz, S., & Wright, P. (2011). *Airport Engineering: Planning, Design, and Development of 21st Century Airports* (4. baskı). John Wiley & Sons.

Ashford, N. J., Stanton, H. P. M., Moore, C. A., Coutu, P., & Beasley, J. R. (2013). *Airport Operations* (3.baskı). McGraw-Hill.

ATAG. (2020). *Aviation: Benefits Beyond Borders*. https://aviationbenefits.org/media/167517/aw-oct-final-atag_abbb-2020-publication-digital.pdf

Bardakçı, S. (2020). SWARA Yöntemi. In Bircan, H. (Ed.), *Çok kriterli karar verme problemlerinde kriter ağırlıklandırma yöntemleri* (1st ed.). Nobel Akademik Yayıncılık.

Baxter, G. (2022). An assessment of water management at a major global hub airport: A case study of Frankfurt Airport. *International Journal of Environment, Agriculture and Biotechnology*, *7*(1), 1–13. DOI: 10.22161/ijeab.71.1

Baxter, G., Wild, G., & Sabatini, R. (2014). A sustainable approach to airport design and operations: Case study of Munich airport. In Arora, M. (Ed.), *Proceedings of Practical Responses to Climate Change 2014*.

Blackwell, B. F., DeVault, T. L., Fernández-Juricic, E., & Dolbeer, R. A. (2009). Wildlife collisions with aircraft: A missing component of land-use planning for airports. *Landscape and Urban Planning*, *93*(1), 1–9. DOI: 10.1016/j.landurbplan.2009.07.005

Brtnický, M., Pecina, V., Baltazár, T., Vašinová Galiová, M., Baláková, L., Bęś, A., & Radziemska, M. (2020). Environmental Impact Assessment of Potentially Toxic Elements in Soils Near the Runway at the International Airport in Central Europe. *Sustainability (Basel)*, *12*(17), 7224. DOI: 10.3390/su12177224

Budd, T. (2017). Environmental impacts and mitigation. In L. Budd & S. Ison (Eds.), *Air transport management: an international perspective* (1. baskı). Routledge.

Chao, C. C., Lirn, T. C., & Lin, H. C. (2017). Indicators and evaluation model for analyzing environmental protection performance of airports. *Journal of Air Transport Management, 63*, 61–70. DOI: 10.1016/j.jairtraman.2017.05.007

Comendador, V. F. G., Valdés, R. M. A., & Lisker, B. (2019). A holistic approach to the environmental certification of green airports. *Sustainability (Basel), 11*(15), 4043. DOI: 10.3390/su11154043

Creswell, J. W. (2013). *Research Design: Qualitative, Quantitative and Mixed Method Approaches* (4th Editio). *Sage (Atlanta, Ga.).*

Daley, B. (2010). *Air Transport and the Environment* (1. baskı). Ashgate.

Daley, B., Dimitriou, D., & Thomas, C. (2008). The environmental sustainability of aviation and tourism. In Anne Graham & P. Forsyth (Eds.), *Aviation and Tourism* (1. baskı, pp. 239–253). Routledge.

Dimitriou, D., Voskaki, A., & Sartzetaki, M. (2014). Airports environmental management: Results from the evaluation of European airports environmental plans. [IJISSCM]. *International Journal of Information Systems and Supply Chain Management, 7*(1), 1–14. DOI: 10.4018/IJISSCM.2014010101

dos Santos, A. J., Mancini, S. D., Frutuoso Roveda, J. A., Ewbank, H., & Roveda, S. R. M. M. (2020). A fuzzy assessment method to airport waste management: A case study of Congonhas Airport, Brazil. *Journal of Air Transport Management, 87*(January), 101838. DOI: 10.1016/j.jairtraman.2020.101838

Durmaz, V. (2018). Havaalanı Çevre Etkileşimi. In Oktal, H. (Ed.), *Havaalanı Sistemi*. Anadolu Üniversitesi Açıköğretim Yayınları.

EUROCONTROL. (2021). *EUROCONTROL Comprehensive Assessment for Thursday, 25 November 2021.* https://www.eurocontrol.int/sites/default/files/2021-11/covid19-eurocontrol-comprehensive-air-traffic-assessment-25112021.pdf

Franchuk, G. M., Antonov, A. M., Madzhd, S. M., & Zagoruy, Y. V. (2005). Analysis of pollution of ground waters in the airport zone. *Proceedings of the National Aviation University*. DOI: 10.18372/2306-1472.24.1159

Gasco, L., Asensio, C., & de Arcas, G. (2017). Communicating airport noise emission data to the general public. *The Science of the Total Environment, 586*, 836–848. DOI: 10.1016/j.scitotenv.2017.02.063 PMID: 28214112

Gössling, S., & Upham, P. (2009). Introduction: Aviation and Climate Change in Context. In Gössling, S., & Upham, P. (Eds.), *Climate Change and Aviation: Issues, Challenges and Solutions*. Springer.

Graham, A. (2023). *Managing Airports: An International Perspective* (6th ed.). Routledge.

Greer, F., Rakas, J., & Horvath, A. (2020a). Airports and environmental sustainability: A comprehensive review. *Environmental Research Letters, 15*(10), 103007. DOI: 10.1088/1748-9326/abb42a

Greer, F., Rakas, J., & Horvath, A. (2020b). Airports and environmental sustainability: A comprehensive review. *Environmental Research Letters, 15*(10), 103007. DOI: 10.1088/1748-9326/abb42a

Horonjeff, R., McKelvey, F. X., Sproule, W. J., & Young, S. B. (2010). *Planning and Design of Airports* (5th ed.). McGraw-Hill.

IATA. (2021). *Net-Zero Carbon Emissions by 2050.* https://www.iata.org/en/pressroom/pressroom-archive/2021-releases/2021-10-04-03/

ICAO. (2015). *Airport Local Air Quality Guidance Manual Doc 9889.*

ICAO. (2017). *Waste Management at Airports.* https://www.icao.int/environmental-protection/Documents/ecoairports/Final Waste_Management_Case_Studies.pdf

ICAO. (2018). *Airport Planning Manual 9184 Part 2 - Land use and environmental management.*

ICAO. (2019). *Consolidated statement of continuing ICAO policies and practices related to environmental protection - Climate change.* https://www.icao.int/environmental-protection/Documents/Assembly/Resolution_A40-18_Climate_Change.pdf

ICAO. (2022). *A Focus on the Production of Renewable Energy at the Airport Site.*

ICAO. (2023). *Aircraft Noise.* https://www.icao.int/environmental-protection/Pages/noise.aspx

İGA. (2023). *İGA Sustainability Report 2021-2022.* https://www.igairport.aero/umbraco/surface/download/DownloadReport?filePath=/media/ioze1im2/2021-22-sustainability-report-1.pdf&fileName=2021 22 Sustainability Report (1)&type=pdf

Janić, M. (2011). *Greening airports: Advanced technology and operations.* Springer Science & Business Media. DOI: 10.1007/978-0-85729-658-0

Josimović, B., Krunić, N., & Nenković-Riznić, M. (2016). The impact of airport noise as part of a Strategic Environmental Assessment, case study: The Tivat (Montenegro) Airport expansion plan. *Transportation Research Part D, Transport and Environment, 49*, 271–279. DOI: 10.1016/j.trd.2016.10.005

Kazda, A., & Caves, R. E. (2015). *Airport Design and Operation* (3rd ed.). Emerald.

Keršuliene, V., Zavadskas, E. K., & Turskis, Z. (2010). Selection of rational dispute resolution method by applying new step-wise weight assessment ratio analysis (Swara). *Journal of Business Economics and Management, 11*(2), 243–258. DOI: 10.3846/jbem.2010.12

Kılkış, Ş., & Kılkış, Ş. (2016). Benchmarking airports based on a sustainability ranking index. *Journal of Cleaner Production, 130*, 248–259. DOI: 10.1016/j.jclepro.2015.09.031

Kumar, A., Aswin, A., & Gupta, H. (2020). Evaluating green performance of the airports using hybrid BWM and VIKOR methodology. *Tourism Management, 76*(July 2019), 103941. DOI: 10.1016/j.tourman.2019.06.016

Li, L., & Loo, B. P. Y. (2016). Impact analysis of airport infrastructure within a sustainability framework: Case studies on Hong Kong International Airport. *International Journal of Sustainable Transportation, 10*(9), 781–793. DOI: 10.1080/15568318.2016.1149647

Lijesen, M., van der Straaten, W., Dekkers, J., van Elk, R., & Blokdijk, J. (2010). How much noise reduction at airports? *Transportation Research Part D, Transport and Environment, 15*(1), 51–59. DOI: 10.1016/j.trd.2009.07.006

Lim, M. W., Von Lau, E., & Poh, P. E. (2016). A comprehensive guide of remediation technologies for oil contaminated soil — Present works and future directions. *Marine Pollution Bulletin, 109*(1), 14–45. DOI: 10.1016/j.marpolbul.2016.04.023 PMID: 27267117

Lu, M., Hsu, C., Liou, J. J. H., & Lo, H. (2018). A hybrid MCDM and sustainability-balanced scorecard model to establish sustainable performance evaluation for international airports. *Journal of Air Transport Management, 71*, 9–19. DOI: 10.1016/j.jairtraman.2018.05.008

Mahashabde, A., Wolfe, P., Ashok, A., Dorbian, C., He, Q., Fan, A., Lukachko, S., Mozdzanowska, A., Wollersheim, C., Barrett, S. R. H., Locke, M., & Waitz, I. A. (2011). Assessing the environmental impacts of aircraft noise and emissions. *Progress in Aerospace Sciences, 47*(1), 15–52. DOI: 10.1016/j.paerosci.2010.04.003

Malterud, K., Siersma, V. D., & Guassora, A. D. (2016). Sample Size in Qualitative Interview Studies: Guided by Information Power. *Qualitative Health Research, 26*(13), 1753–1760. DOI: 10.1177/1049732315617444 PMID: 26613970

Marais, K., Wolfe, P. J., & Waitz, I. A. (2016). Air Transport and the Environment. In Belobaba, P., Odoni, A., & Barnhart, C. (Eds.), *The Global Airline Industry*. Wiley.

Martin, J. A., Conkling, T. J., Belant, J. L., Biondi, K. M., Blackwell, B. F., DeVault, T. L., Fernández-Juricic, E., Schmidt, P. M., & Seamans, T. W. (2013). Wildlife conservation and alternative land uses at airports. In DeVault, T. L., Blackwell, B. F., & Belant, J. L. (Eds.), *Wildlife in airport environments: preventing animal-aircraft collisions through science-based management*. Johns Hopkins University Press.

Masiol, M., & Harrison, R. M. (2014). Aircraft engine exhaust emissions and other airport-related contributions to ambient air pollution: A review. *Atmospheric Environment*, *95*, 409–455. DOI: 10.1016/j.atmosenv.2014.05.070 PMID: 32288558

Monsalud, A., Ho, D., & Rakas, J. (2015). Greenhouse gas emissions mitigation strategies within the airport sustainability evaluation process. *Sustainable Cities and Society*, *14*, 414–424. DOI: 10.1016/j.scs.2014.08.003

Müezzinoğlu, A. (2000). *Hava Kirliliği ve Kontrolünün Esasları*. Dokuz Eylül Yayınları.

Niu, Y., Xie, G., Xiao, Y., Qin, K., Gan, S., & Liu, J. (2021). Spatial and temporal changes of ecosystem service value in airport economic zones in China. *Land (Basel)*, *10*(1054), 1–16. DOI: 10.3390/land10101054

Ozkurt, N. (2014). Current assessment and future projections of noise pollution at Ankara Esenbo a Airport, Turkey. *Transportation Research Part D, Transport and Environment*, *32*, 120–128. DOI: 10.1016/j.trd.2014.07.011

Paling, C., & Thomas, C. (2018). Airport sustainability and corporate social responsibility. In Halpern, N., & Graham, A. (Eds.), *The Routledge Companion to Air Transport Management*. Routledge. DOI: 10.4324/9781315630540-19

Patton, M. Q. (2002). Qualitative research and evaluation methods. In *Sage* (3rd ed.). Sage., DOI: 10.2307/330063

Pearce, B. (2012). The state of air transport markets and the airline industry after the great recession. *Journal of Air Transport Management*, *21*, 3–9. DOI: 10.1016/j.jairtraman.2011.12.011

Pitt, M., Brown, A., & Smith, A. (2002). Waste management at airports. *Facilities*, *20*(5/6), 198–207. DOI: 10.1108/02632770210426684

Pitt, M., & Smith, A. (2003). Waste management efficiency at UK airports. *Journal of Air Transport Management*, *9*(2), 103–111. DOI: 10.1016/S0969-6997(02)00063-7

Postorino, M. N., & Mantecchini, L. (2014). A transport carbon footprint methodology to assess airport carbon emissions. *Journal of Air Transport Management*, *37*, 76–86. DOI: 10.1016/j.jairtraman.2014.03.001

Radomska, M., Cherniak, L., Madzhd, S., & Mikhyeyev, O. (2020). Environmental pollution in the airport impact area–case study of the Boryspil. *Environmental Problems*, *5*(2), 76–82. DOI: 10.23939/ep2020.02.076

Rajan, S. C. (2006). Climate change dilemma: technology, social change or both?: An examination of long-term transport policy choices in the United States. *Energy Policy*, *34*(6), 664–679. DOI: 10.1016/j.enpol.2004.07.002

Ryley, T., Elmirghani, J., Budd, T., Miyoshi, C., Mason, K., Moxon, R., Ahmed, I., Qazi, B., & Zanni, A. (2013). Sustainable development and airport surface access: The role of technological innovation and behavioral change. *Sustainability (Basel)*, *5*(4), 1617–1631. DOI: 10.3390/su5041617

Sebastian, R. M., & Louis, J. (2021). Understanding waste management at airports: A study on current practices and challenges based on literature review. *Renewable & Sustainable Energy Reviews*, *147*(May), 111229. DOI: 10.1016/j.rser.2021.111229

Sreenath, S., Sudhakar, K., & Yusop, A. F. (2021). Sustainability at airports: Technologies and best practices from ASEAN countries. *Journal of Environmental Management*, *299*(August), 113639. DOI: 10.1016/j.jenvman.2021.113639 PMID: 34479146

Tanrıverdi, G., Bakır, M., & Merkert, R. (2020). What can we learn from the JATM literature for the future of aviation post Covid-19? - A bibliometric and visualization analysis. *Journal of Air Transport Management*, *89*(June), 101916. DOI: 10.1016/j.jairtraman.2020.101916 PMID: 32901183

Thomas, C. S., Maughan, J. A., Hooper, P. D., & Hume, K. I. (2010). Aircraft noise and community impacts. In R. Blockley & W. Shyy (Eds.), *Encyclopaedia of Aerospace Engineering: Volume 6 Environmental Impact, Manufacturing and Operations*. John Wiley & Sons. DOI: 10.1002/9780470686652.eae343

Upham, P. J., & Mills, J. N. (2005). Environmental and operational sustainability of airports: Core indicators and stakeholder communication. *Benchmarking*, *12*(2), 166–179. DOI: 10.1108/14635770510593103

Uzgör, M. (2024). *Evaluation of airport environmental management performance with multi criteria decision making methods: An application at five major airports in Türkiye.* (Publication No. 843343) [Doctoral dissertation, Anadolu University] YÖK Ulusal Tez Merkezi.

Uzgör, M., Selahattin Ateş, S., & Kafalı, H. (2024). Bibliometric Analysis of Environmental Management Literature in Aviation. *Transportation Research Record*, *2678*(8), 374-395. DOI: 10.1177/03611981231216981

Winter, S. R., Crouse, S. R., & Rice, S. (2021). The development of 'green' airports: Which factors influence willingness to pay for sustainability and intention to act? A structural and mediation model analysis. *Technology in Society*, *65*(March), 101576. DOI: 10.1016/j.techsoc.2021.101576

Xiong, X., Song, X., Kaygorodova, A., Ding, X., Guo, L., & Huang, J. (2023). Aviation and carbon emissions: Evidence from airport operations. *Journal of Air Transport Management, 109*(August 2022), 102383. DOI: 10.1016/j.jairtraman.2023.102383

Zhao, B., Wang, N., Fu, Q., Yan, H. K., & Wu, N. (2019). Searching a site for a civil airport based on bird ecological conservation: An expert-based selection (Dalian, China). *Global Ecology and Conservation*, *20*, e00729. DOI: 10.1016/j.gecco.2019.e00729

Chapter 6
Sustainability in the Banking Sector Determination of Success Factors with DEMATEL Method:
Determination of Success Factors with DEMATEL Method on Sustainability in the Banking Sector

Bedirhan Elden
https://orcid.org/0000-0001-5955-1606
Kayseri University, Turkey

ABSTRACT

Digital applications have gained importance in the finance sector with digitalization. In addition, the importance given to sustainability within the scope of social responsibility by banks reaching many branches in the finance sector is obvious. In this respect, it is important to consider the factors affecting the success of sustainable policies of banks in a causality relationship and to address important factors with a scientific method in this direction. Therefore, within the scope of this chapter, the sustainable policies of banks operating in the digital age will be analysed with the DEMATEL method, one of the multi-criteria decision making methods.

DOI: 10.4018/979-8-3693-8789-4.ch006

1 INTRODUCTION

Nowadays, the concept of sustainability has expanded to include not only environmental concerns but also economic and social dimensions. The interaction between individuals' consumption preferences and ecological balance is frightening when the world is considered in general. The world population is increasing rapidly, but natural resources are not increasing at the same rate and are gradually decreasing (Altın, 2023). As a key sector supporting economic growth and financial stability, the banking sector faces the need to integrate sustainability principles into its business processes. Increasing regulations, investor expectations and social awareness are causing banks to reshape their sustainability strategies. This situation necessitates that sustainability efforts in the banking sector should not only be an environmental policy but also a fundamental component of corporate strategy.

This transformation in sustainability requires banks to consider not only their economic earnings but also their social responsibilities and environmental impact. In this context, it is crucial for banks to identify critical success factors to ensure sustainability. Although various methods are used to analyse these factors, DEMATEL (Decision Making Trial and Evaluation Laboratory) method stands out in this study. DEMATEL analyses the interactions between factors in complex systems, allowing the identification of the most influential and influencable factors.

The purpose of this study is to identify the key success factors that drive sustainability practices in the banking sector and to reveal the relationship between these factors. The results obtained aim to help banks plan and manage their sustainability strategies more effectively. In this context, the DEMATEL method will be used to determine the priority factors in the sector and their effects on each other.

Sustainability requires both digital transformation through the use of technology and environmentally compatible production by reducing unnecessary consumption. The socio-economic structures shaping the economy have revealed the necessity of new economic models in which environmental factors are at the forefront. Organisations have changed their management processes thanks to corporate sustainability and started to report their corporate footprints in this context. Financial sustainability investments have led companies to allocate more resources to green investments (such as green bonds and clean energy projects).

The banks affect the economy and environment of the society both directly and indirectly through the loans, investments and financial products they offer. Therefore, it is of great importance to analyse and evaluate the sustainability performance of banks in order to finance sustainable investments and raise awareness of target audiences (Aras et al., 2018). The examination of these processes within the framework of sustainability criteria brings along certain standards. With the development of sustainability understanding, it is concluded that non-financial values should also be considered within this framework.

The banks are responsible for attracting funds to the financial system in order to provide resources to the sectors that can make the most progress in development. Moreover, the implementation of an effective monetary policy can only be possible with a strong and developed banking sector, which in turn can strengthen the country's international economic relations and integration with the world (Savram and Karakoç, 2012). The main dimensions to be considered in sustainability assessments are economic, social and environmental factors. The banks should meet the needs of their stakeholders and customers without jeopardising potential future customer requirements (Onay, 2015). Banks' lending and investment processes, by their nature, create both direct and indirect impacts on environmental and social structures. In this context, analyzing sustainability performance in the banking sector not only contributes to more conscious investment decisions, but also plays a decisive role in shaping public perception. As a matter of fact, as shown by recent studies that use multi-criteria decision-making methods such as AHP and TOPSIS together for financial and strategic purposes in different sectors (Soydaş, 2024), adapting similar analyses to the banking sector allows for more effective management of sustainability efforts.

In this study, it is aimed to contribute to the literature by analysing the sustainability and success factors of banks, which are indispensable for the continuity of the economic system, with the DEMATEL method. On the other hand, it is also aimed to determine the potential status of companies in the banking sector that receive investment consultancy for corporate sustainability in line with the relevant criteria. In addition, the study is considered important in terms of analysing the actual situation of the enterprises in this transformation and change process. As a result of the literature research, the factors that have an impact on sustainability in banking have been identified. Then, by applying DEMATEL methodology, mutual influence matrices were determined for all pairs of criteria.

2 LITERATURE REVIEW

2.1 Sustainability in the Banking Sector and Determination of Success Factors with DEMATEL Method

2.1.1 DEMATEL Method

The DEMATEL method was first used in 1973 by the Battelle Memorial Institute through the Geneva Research Centre. This method, which aims to create a structural model by analysing the relationships between complex criteria and their degree of influence, is based on graph theory (Chang et al., 2011). DEMATEL allows decision makers to analyse and solve apparent problems. In this process, decision makers can identify cause-effect relationships and categorise them into cause and effect groups in order to better express various measurement criteria (Huang et al., 2007). In other words, criteria are categorised as influencing or being influenced by others.

The DEMATEL method was developed to enhance the understanding of specific problems, analyze problem sets, and identify feasible solutions within a hierarchical structure. Based on graph theory, this method categorizes factors as causes and effects, facilitating the planning and resolution of problems (Li and Tzeng, 2009).

The main advantage of the DEMATEL method is the creation of a cause-effect model showing the indirect relationships between decision components. This method is an effective tool that analyses the structure and connections between system components in an alternative approach. DEMATEL can prioritise decision criteria according to the nature of their interrelationships and the importance of these relationships. In this method, the criteria that have more influence on other criteria and have a high priority are called 'cause criteria', while the criteria that are under more influence and have a lower priority are defined as 'result criteria' (Gabus et al., 1973).

The researches on the application areas of DEMATEL method show that this method has successful applications in various subjects such as supplier selection, strategy determination, determination of critical success factors, solution of facility layout problems, creation of marketing strategies, control systems, social security problems, evaluation of managerial skills and solution of group decision-making processes (Fontela et al., 1974).

The DEMATEL method analyzes the structure, relationships, and alternatives among components and provides a reconciliatory cause-effect model. This method also considers indirect relationships and prioritizes criteria based on the type of their relationships and the significance of their impacts on one another. Cause criteria are those that have a greater influence on other criteria and are assigned higher priority, while effect criteria are more influenced by other criteria and are given lower priority (Tseng and Lin, 2009).

The DEMATEL method categorizes criteria affecting decision-making problems into two groups: *cause group* and *effect group*. This method is frequently preferred in decision-making processes as it enables the analysis of complex problems by grouping criteria. DEMATEL is a powerful tool that facilitates the creation of a structural model and the visualization of causal relationships between subsystems. One of its key advantages is its ability to include indirect relationships, providing a consensus-based cause-and-effect model. The method is an effective tool for analyzing relationships among system components and evaluating the impacts of a limited number of alternatives. It ranks criteria based on the type of relationships and their influence on each other. Criteria with a greater impact and considered of higher priority are classified as cause criteria, while those predominantly influenced by others and deemed lower priority are referred to as effect criteria (Organ, 2013). Developed by the Geneva Research Center, DEMATEL is a comprehensive approach used to analyze, visualize, and weight causal relationships between criteria. It allows for the transformation of the relationships between the causes and effects of criteria into a clear and understandable model. The importance levels of criteria are determined, and their rankings are calculated using mathematical modeling and graphical techniques (Dumlu, 2022).

The DEMATEL method is utilized in solving complex problems and finds applications in fields such as technology and the environment. It is particularly effective in analyzing complex issues that involve causal relationships. By employing matrix methods and mathematical techniques, it analyzes and interprets the strength of dependencies and relationships between factors (Lee, Huang, Chang, and Cheng, 2011).

2.1.2 Sustainability in the Banking Sector and Determination of Success

A bank is an institution that acts as an intermediary between individuals with excess capital and individuals in need of capital. The main activities of banks within the framework of this intermediary function include lending and receiving loans, making investments, counselling, mediation services, payment transactions, providing guarantees, property-related transactions and providing property security. The main sources of income of the banking sector are divided into two: interest income, which is generated by the bank taking risks on its own behalf; and transaction income, which is generated from the risks assumed on behalf of both the bank and its customers (Jeucken and Bouma, 1999).

In the 1980s, the banking sector started to integrate environmental and social issues into its operations on a global scale. The first steps focused on internal environmental management, which resulted in saving environmental resources, reducing emissions and improving reputation (Babiak and Trendafilova, 2011). In the next stage, banks incorporated environmental considerations into areas such as lending, investing, asset management and project finance (Scholtens, 2008). Environmental risks such as climate change are important factors that can affect the financial risk of loan and investment portfolios. Therefore, it is necessary to manage these risks effectively (Weber et al., 2015). In this context, many banks have implemented environmental credit risk assessment procedures (Weber, 2012). In addition, the financial sector has developed strategies to manage investment risks and capitalise on SRI opportunities by adopting socially responsible investment (SRI) processes (Cerin and Scholtens, 2011).

The integration of sustainability into banking activities is a complex process that is increasingly required by financial institutions (Carlucci, 2018). This integration basically takes two forms: (i) initiatives based on social and environmental responsibility (e.g., support for cultural events, charitable giving, recycling programmes and efforts to improve energy efficiency); and (ii) integrating environmental and social considerations into product design, corporate mission and business strategies (e.g., incorporating environmental criteria into investment and lending strategies) (Jeucken, 1999).

In the 20th century, one of the most remarkable developments in world banking was the rapid growth of US banks. One of the main reasons for this was the Federal Reserve Act of 1913, which allowed US national banks to open branches abroad. Moreover, the UK's inability to collect its debts before the First World War and the difficulties in financing the war reduced the influence of the British economy in global banking. These developments weakened the reputation of the pound sterling as an international means of payment and caused the dollar to fill the gap. Despite the efforts of European countries, New York became an international financial centre, while capital flows from Europe to the US accelerated. As a result of all these processes, the USA, which was one of the most indebted countries in the world before the First World War, became an important lender country in the post-war period (Erol, 2006).

The financial crisis and the social problems caused by banks lacking credit and investment discipline and excessive indebtedness in asset-backed securities have clearly demonstrated the importance of sustainability in the financial sector. This process became more evident when banks investing in sectors associated with climate change and environmental degradation were subjected to intense criticism by environmental groups and other stakeholders. These criticisms and pressures on the finance and banking sector have emphasised the importance of regulatory frameworks and highlighted the need for banks to build trust (Stephens and Skinner, 2013). In these developments, banks in advanced economies, recognising the regulatory shortcomings and the potential impact on the safety of bank funds, started to take voluntary steps to develop policies on environmental and social issues. These voluntary arrangements, which were initially made between individual banks or a few banks, were implemented with the aim of harmonising and strengthening environmental and social responsibility.

Sustainability aims to ensure the transfer of resources to future generations and to protect these resources while realising economic growth. Sustainability provides resources for future generations by establishing the interaction between the environment, human and nature. Sustainability, which is also known as a concept that combines different fields such as economics, social justice, environmental science, business and law, is important in terms of human future (Tıraş, 2012). In addition to these, it has also found its place in definitions as a building block that includes elements such as democracy, rights and honesty, which are considered important by society. The concept of sustainability, which also appears as development when evaluated within the framework of economic science, ensures environmentally responsible behaviour by recording the inputs used during production together with all activity processes until they reach the consumer (Wilson, 2003).

Corporate sustainability is defined as 'the endeavour to ensure the continuity of enterprises, to carry out activities that will enable the protection and development of resources that can be used in the future as well as meeting today's needs by turning to social and environmental activities as well as purely economic profit, and to continue the profitability of the enterprise as a living entity' (Hillman and Keim, 2001).

Corporate sustainability can be defined as taking into account economic, environmental and social factors in decision-making and execution processes and managing risks effectively in order to create long-term value by addressing them in line with management principles and values. This approach, which combines financial, environmental and social sustainability, emphasises that businesses should adopt a long-term profit-oriented strategy instead of short-term goals. In this respect, it is not sufficient for enterprises to create economic value only through production. They need to carry out various studies in order to minimise or completely eliminate the negative impacts that arise while continuing their activities. It is an important requirement for businesses to have a transparent, fair and accountable structure. For this reason, businesses act with a sense of social responsibility, use environmentally sensitive technologies and try to integrate environmental awareness into all levels of the organisation. Thus, they strive to ensure corporate sustainability (Dinica, 2019).

The economic role of banks differs from that of other enterprises. Their main functions are to provide access to financial services and to enable participation in the economic system. In this context, banks assume a special responsibility within the economic structure (Bai, 2011). Money can be considered as the main means of entry into this system. While every business has the potential to influence social welfare and the future, banks have a unique influence in this regard. Every decision they make plays a decisive role on social welfare and our future. Banks and financial institutions have the power to shape the social and economic structure when deciding which projects, initiatives and enterprises they will or will not finance. Therefore, the criteria used by banks in their decision-making processes are of great importance. Banks are considered as one of the key elements of social transformation towards building a more just and equitable society.

Jeucken identified four stages of actions taken by banks for sustainability: defensive banking, preventive banking, offensive banking, and sustainable banking.

In the first stage, defensive banking, banks remain inactive or resist environmental regulations, as their interests may be directly or indirectly harmed through their customers. In this phase, environmental management costs can be avoided, as banks opt to remain passive despite the risks. In the preventive banking stage, banks integrate environmental risk management into their daily operations, driven by factors such as reputational risk or pressure from governments and NGOs. This stage reflects an approach where environmental concerns are addressed to minimize risks rather than fully adopting them. Offensive banking takes a more proactive approach, viewing environmental concerns not as burdens but as competitive opportunities. At this stage, banks develop and market products and services designed to address environmental issues. The ideal stage for banks, sustainable banking, shifts the focus from financial returns to sustainable returns. This approach emphasizes the long-term profitability of sustainable banking, even though it may initially conflict with the traditional profit-maximization mindset of businesses. In the short term, sustainable banking might reduce profits or contradict the interests of some stakeholders. However, by integrating sustainability into core strategies and practices, banks can achieve their financial and environmental goals in the long run (Jeucken, 2001).

Banks are considered to be among the environmentally favourable sectors; however, due to their size, they have direct impacts on the environment through the use of natural resources and energy they demand. In addition, since they meet the capital needs of the private sector, they are indirectly responsible for the environmental and social impacts that arise in production processes. This situation shows that the banking sector has environmental, social and economic impacts. The impact of the banking sector on the environment is directly related to the size of the sector. Especially the high amount of energy demanded by the sector is an important factor in terms of environmental impacts. For example, widespread use of credit cards is one of the main factors that increase energy consumption. When the banking sector is compared to sectors such as chemicals, mining, pharmaceuticals, petroleum and textiles, it is observed that its environmental impacts are relatively lower. However, direct impacts (e.g. use of paper, electricity and fuel) arising from the activities of banks are less important than indirect impacts (Tandoğan and Özyurt, 2013).

Banks have not paid enough attention to proactive strategies on environmental and sustainability issues because they believe that they are in a more favourable position in terms of the environment compared to other sectors (Jo, Kim, and Park, 2014). However, in the aftermath of the financial crisis, the global environment has revealed the importance of the financial sector's impact on the economy and society. At the same time, it has also drawn attention that an increasing number of financial products do not serve the real economy. These developments are pushing the financial sector to take more steps towards implementing environmental policies and supporting sustainable societies and businesses. This is mainly because sustainability principles are a vital requirement for the growth and success of both individuals and organisations (Oyegunle, 2016).

Studies on sustainable banking worldwide have been addressed and developed since the 1900s. This section includes works conducted by various researchers. In this context, the number of studies on the subject is quite extensive, and their content varies significantly from one another.

Aras and Crowther (2009), in their study covering publicly traded firms outside the financial sector in Turkey, found that sustainability performance is directly related to firm size. According to the results of the study, the increase in firm size increases the level of disclosure and the effectiveness of sustainability practices.

Khan et al. (2011) analysed the sustainability practices of 12 banks listed on the Dhaka Stock Exchange between 2008 and 2009 and reporting in accordance with GRI G3 guidelines by content analysis method. In this study, it was determined that the banks made the most disclosures in the field of social sustainability within the scope of corporate sustainability indicators. On the other hand, it was observed that the disclosures made in the dimensions of human rights and product responsibility were quite limited.

The environmental and social impacts of financial institutions arise in two ways: internal (direct) and external (indirect) (Pinter, Nikolett and Zoltan, 2006). The environmental impact of the internal activities of financial institutions is quite low compared to other sectors. However, considering the size of the financial system, the amount of waste generated by the consumption of energy, water, paper, etc. reaches non-negligible dimensions. It would not be wrong to say that the external activities of financial institutions do not affect the environment at first glance. This is because the products offered by financial institutions do not have a direct impact on the environment. However, the users of these financial products may affect the environment or people through their activities. Therefore, investments made by banks, loans and other financial products may indirectly cause the environment or people to be negatively affected. The direct impact of banks on the environment arising from the consumption of electricity, paper, etc. is quite insignificant compared to the indirect impact.

Sobhani et al. (2009) content analysed the annual reports of 100 companies listed on both Dhaka Stock Exchange and Chittagong Stock Exchange for corporate, social and environmental disclosures. The results of the study showed that the sustainability disclosures of these companies were generally inadequate. In a later study, Sobhani et al. (2012) analysed corporate sustainability indicators of 29 Bangladeshi banks. In the study, criteria were evaluated using GRI reports and survey results on environmental, economic and social sustainability dimensions. It was determined that the banks made disclosures on the social dimension the most.

Rebai et al. (2012) aimed to evaluate the concept of sustainable bank among different stakeholders and to compare the degree of sustainability. This study was conducted on 5 French banks. In the study, the ranking process was carried out with the multi-attribute utility method.

Nobanee and Ellili (2016), in their study comparing conventional and Islamic banking practices, analysed the sustainability reports of 16 banks listed on the Dubai and Abu Dhabi stock exchanges between 2003 and 2013. The findings showed that conventional banks made more disclosures than Islamic banks during this period.

Hussain, Rigoni and Orij (2016) evaluated the sustainability performance of US companies in the context of corporate governance and conducted content analyses within the framework of triple bottom line reporting focusing on economic, social and environmental dimensions.

The 'Corporate Governance Principles' published by the Capital Markets Board (CMB) is a legal document on corporate social responsibility (CSR) practices, which are of great importance in the process of ensuring sustainable development. The principles of corporate governance, which were developed by taking into consideration the principles published by the OECD and Turkey's specific conditions, were published by the CMB in July 2003 (SPK, 2005). Later, the principles were revised and published again in February 2005 under four headings: shareholders, public disclosure and transparency, stakeholders, and board of directors. In addition, the implementation of corporate governance principles is optional. However, the implementation of the principles should be disclosed to the public. In other words, the principles adopt the 'apply, if not, disclose' approach.

Nowadays, especially in developed countries, the understanding of sustainable finance is becoming more and more widespread. Some international organisations, such as the United Nations Environment Programme Finance Initiative (UNEP FI, 2008), are making serious efforts to increase the environmental awareness of financial institutions and many internationally large financial institutions are responding positively to these efforts. The most important indicator of this is the fact that 177 financial institutions have signed the United Nations Environment Programme Finance Initiative Commitments by the end of 2008. 59% of these institutions are banks, 18% are insurance companies and 23% are other financial institutions (UNEP FI, 2008). The fact that financial institutions have signed this commitment means that they accept the role of the financial sector in the sustainable development process and that they will take into account the environmental factor in all their activities.

Weber (2016) analysed the sustainability performance of banks in China and examined the relationship between this performance and financial indicators. As a result of the study, it was found that sustainability performance has a strong relationship with financial indicators such as total assets and net profit.

Raut et al. (2017), the study was addressed on the grounds that most of the studies on the service sector are at the point of improving service quality and delivery time and that the issue of sustainability is not sufficiently addressed. The study emphasised the improvement of sustainable banking performances. It is also concluded that corporate social responsibility is misunderstood in relation to environmental issues (Raut et al., 2017).

Şendurur and Temelli (2018) determined the sustainability scores of traditional and participation banks in Turkey regarding their annual reports on social and environmental issues. The variables determined with sustainability scores were analysed with the help of multiple regression analysis and the relationship between them was examined. In addition, the differences between the groups of the variables determined by t-test and the adopted groups according to the types of banks were analysed. In the study, while no statistically significant relationship was found between dummy variables and sustainability scores, according to the regression results, only ownership structure, leverage ratio, liquidity and profitability variables could be included in the model. According to the t-test results of the study, there is a significant relationship between size, liquidity, profitability, age, environmental score and sustainability scores and bank types.

Lin and Chang (2019) study is addressed to address the attitude of the Taiwanese government in increasing sustainability activities in the field of banking and to contribute to the literature on business sustainability. In this context, data on a total of 18 financial criteria for the years 2012-2016 were obtained and analysed. Analyses were made with Dematel, Saw and Danp methods. The conclusion of the article is that private banks are ahead of public banks in terms of sustainability performance. At this point, it is suggested that banks should take risks and diversify their financial products. In addition, it is concluded that the government's steps to privatise the banks are positive and they should continue to privatise them.

Scholtens and Klooster (2019) tried to analyse the relationship between sustainability activities and risk concept on bank, market and country basis. In this context, a significant risk was found between banks' sustainability scores and low default risk. In other words, it is understood that sustainability performance exhibits a negative attitude towards the systematic risk of banks.

Yang and Stohl (2020) examine the degree of alignment between the most popular CSR performance indicators and corporate reputation indicators. In the study, two different factors consisting of social factors, environmental factors and corporate governance factors were identified through multivariate analysis. Future research should tailor analyses by industry to understand how different business sectors affect changes in CSR expectations, incentives and outcomes, and how plans should change accordingly.

Brotons and Sansalvador (2020) used the Fuzzy method to create variables and explain the relationship between Spanish companies with IQNet SR10 certification and their financial performance and used statistical analysis to try to explain the binary relationship. The findings show that IQNet SR10 certification increases company value, but neither the development of the company nor the economic sector in which they are located significantly affect this relationship.

Belas et al. (2021) conducted a survey study on 1,585 Small and Medium Enterprises (SMEs) operating in four Central European countries. Using linear regression analysis, this study analysed the impact of corporate sustainability indicators on SMEs. The questionnaire consists of four main sections. The first section focuses on identifying the basic characteristics of companies. The second section focuses on corporate governance, corporate social responsibility (CSR), social media, marketing and internationalisation. In the third section, evaluations on business risks were included, and in the last section, the attitudes and behaviours of the participants towards corporate bankruptcy were examined. The findings of the study revealed that entrepreneurs' understanding of the concept of CSR and realising it in business management positively affected the awareness of SMEs towards sustainable development.

Companies have to share their activities with the public within the scope of sustainability. This should also be seen as an obligation within the sustainability paradigm. As well as informing them by sharing their sustainability-related activities with the public, organisations must also show that their actions are not isolated activities, but an approach that involves the public in decision-making mechanisms (Kuhn and Deetz, 2009). Because for many organisations, corporate sustainability has gradually become not only a corporate value but also a business strategy (Signitzer et al., 2007). Therefore, in order for corporate sustainability activities to achieve their true character, the form and quality of their communication with the society is also very important.

Jeucken identified four stages of action taken by banks for sustainability as defensive banking, preventive banking, offensive banking and sustainable banking. In this respect, in defensive banking, the bank remains inactive or resists environmental regulations as the interests of the bank may be directly or indirectly harmed through its customers. At this stage, the cost of environmental management can be avoided. In preventive banking, banks prefer to integrate environmental risk management only into their day-to-day business due to reputational risk, governmental or NGO pushback. In the conservative banking concept, banks will recognise environmental concerns as a competitive opportunity in the market and will develop and market products and services to address environmental concerns. When banks reach the stage of sustainable banking, which is ideal for banks, banks focus on sustainable returns rather than financial high returns because it is sustainable banking that will be profitable in the long run. The concept of sustainable banking, which contradicts the idea of maximising profit, may cost the bank's profit in the short term and go against the interests of stakeholders, but businesses will achieve their goals in terms of both profit and environment in the long term with sustainability incorporated into their core practices and strategies (Jeucken, 2001).

The financial sector, although heavily regulated compared to other industries, is largely unaffected by institutional pressure or regulations related to society, labour issues and the environment (Helleiner and Thistlethwaite, 2009). Regulations in the financial sector generally focus on the provision of risk-adjusted financial capital and the management of financial risks to ensure the stability of the sector. Therefore, for a long time, the financial sector has been under pressure to perform on the sustainability impacts of its main products and services - lending and investing - compared to many other sectors (Weber et al., 2014). However, research shows that environmental and sustainability reporting has a positive relationship with the size and profitability of financial institutions and that environmental and sustainability issues have become more integrated into the products and services of the financial sector over time (Scholtens, 2008).

Some research emphasises the importance of addressing sustainability reporting in three main dimensions - environmental, social and corporate governance (ESG). Sobhani et al. (2012) found that the disclosure rate of the social dimension is higher than the economic and environmental dimensions. However, the reporting of environmental issues is often neglected by listed banks. A similar investigation was conducted by Nobanee and Ellili (2016) and measured corporate sustainability reporting using annual data of banks in the UAE financial markets. The results show that sustainability reporting in UAE banks is generally low. Furthermore, while many studies confirm that Islamic finance principles promote socially inclusive, environmentally friendly and developmental activities, in practice, the contribution to these goals remains below potential (Akhtar, 2008).

In the literature, it is determined that the basic elements required for corporate sustainability are economic, environmental and social dimensions. These elements are necessary for sustainability. In this framework, if organisations continue their activities by taking these main elements into consideration, they will also contribute to the field of sustainability. Considering the relevant studies in the literature, a total of 14 criteria, 6 for the economic dimension, 4 for the social dimension and 4 for the environmental dimension, which are used to evaluate the corporate sustainability performance of banks, were determined to be evaluated in the analyses of the study. The basic characteristics of these criteria are presented in Table 1 (Yarlikaş and Öztürk);

Table 1. Sustainability success criteria

Criterion Code	Criterion Name	Criterion Category
K1	Total number of branches	Social
K2	Total number of employees	Social
K3	Total number of customers	Social
K4	Total number of ATMs	Social
K5	Average training duration	Social
K6	Staff turnover rate	Social
K7	Capital adequacy ratio	Economic
K8	Return on equity	Economic
K9	Total assets	Economic
K10	Net profit	Economic
K11	Per capita direct greenhouse gas emissions	Environmental
K12	Per capita water consumption	Environmental
K13	Per capita paper consumption	Environmental
K14	Per capita fuel consumption	Environmental

3 DESIGN AND METHODOLOGY

The DEMATEL (Decision Making Trial and Evaluation Laboratory Method) method was used to evaluate the success factors detailed in the previous section. While the DEMATEL method was initially used to provide an understanding of complex and contradictory problems, it was later widely applied to visualise complex causal structures and to analyse interactions and evaluations between factors (Zhou et al., 2011). DEMATEL is considered to be one of the most effective methods for analysing direct and indirect relationships between components of a system according to their type and importance (Li et al., 2014). In addition, DEMATEL is a method that analyses the relationships between complex structures and builds a structural model based on them (Wu, 2008).

Multi-Criteria Decision Making (MCDM) studies do not aim to generalise, as a framework is usually created based on the opinions of decision makers. MCDM methods are methods used to make the most appropriate decision by evaluating a large number of qualitative and/or quantitative criteria together. These methods analyse different qualitative and quantitative criteria that contradict each other and select the most appropriate one among the alternatives (Eğilmez and Savaş, 2021).

Multi-Criteria Decision Making (MCDM) methods refer to the selection of the most appropriate one according to certain criteria among alternatives with different characteristics. In this process, decision makers objectively determine the importance levels of the criteria and as a result of the evaluation, the performance values of the alternatives are multiplied by the criteria weights and the scores of the alternatives are calculated (Aytekin and Sakarya, 2013).

Multi-Criteria Decision Making Techniques are used in the evaluation of concepts formed by a large number of criteria based on expert opinions. A policy maker (manager, practitioner, etc.) with decision-making authority determines and ranks alternatives in line with his/her own and other experts' opinions. In real life decisions, results are obtained by taking into account the opinions of a few experts with sufficient knowledge and experience on the subject. However, with the increase in the number of experts, the fact that experts with different perspectives may also be involved in the decision process should be taken into consideration. Therefore, each expert may offer a different perspective that may affect the decision (Toktaş and Can, 2020).

The main stages of the DEMATEL method and the methodology of the study are shown below. (Wu, 2008, Nilashi et al., 2015):

Stage 1: Creation of the Direct Relationship Matrix

In this stage, a scale is determined for the experts to evaluate the factors in pairs. Although this scale, which will help to construct the direct relationship matrix, can be applied in different ways, the five-stage binary evaluation scale presented below in linguistic expressions is preferred in this study.

Table 2. DEMATEL method evaluation scale

Numerical Value	Definition
0	No Effect
1	Low Effect
2	Moderate Effect
3	High Effect

The direct relationship matrix has an nxn structure and is formed after the experts evaluate the level of influence of the factors on each other in pairs using the scale in Table 2.

Stage 2: Creation of the Normalised Direct Relationship Matrix

At this stage, normalisation is performed in order to minimise the distortion of the integrated decision structure. The normalised direct relationship matrix (X) is obtained by using the direct relationship matrix (A) and using the following formulas. In this process, each value in the direct relationship matrix is normalised by dividing by the maximum value of the row sums of this matrix.

Stage 3: Creation of the Total Relationship Matrix

After the normalised relationship matrix (X) is formed, the total relationship matrix (T) is calculated with the help of the following formula. Here, I represents the unit matrix.

Stage 4: Determination of D and R Values

At this stage, by utilising the total relationship matrix, i d values expressing the influencing power of the factors and j r values expressing the level of influence are calculated through the following formulae. The sum of the row values of the total relationship matrix expresses the D value and the sum of the column values expresses the R value.

Stage 5: Determination of D+R, D-R and Factor Weights and Creation of the Effect Graph

At this stage, D+R values indicating the level of relationship for each factor and D-R values determining the influence levels of the factors are calculated. The D+R value on the horizontal axis in the influence graph expresses the interaction level of a factor. In other words, the higher the D+R value of a factor, the higher the interaction of this factor with other factors. On the vertical axis of the influence graph, there are D-R values indicating the influence power of a factor. If the D-R value of a factor is positive, it means that it is in the influencing group, and if it is negative, it means that it is in the influenced group.

Stage 6: Creation of the Impact Relationship Map

At this stage, a threshold value is calculated by averaging all total relationship matrix values to determine the direction and strength of influence between factors and an influence relationship map is created. The influence relationship map provides a visual tool to understand the level and direction of influence of factors on each other.

4 RESULTS

The application of this study was carried out in an international bank organisation operating in Turkey. The business managers evaluated fourteen success factors and the results were analysed by DEMATEL method. The application part was carried out with the stages explained in detail in the previous section as shown below.

Stage 1. Development of the Direct Relationship Matrix

At this stage, the opinions of six experts who are in decision-making positions among the bank managers were taken. The experts preferred to evaluate the success factors by brainstorming together instead of evaluating them separately. As a result, the direct relationship matrix shown in Table 4 was obtained by translating the evaluation results obtained with linguistic expressions into numerical scale using the scale in Table 2.

Table 3. Direct relationship matrix

	K1	K2	K3	K4	K5	K6	K7	K8	K9	K10	K11	K12	K13	K14
K1	0	2	3	3	1	1	2	1	2	1	0	0	0	0
K2	2	0	3	2	2	2	1	1	2	1	0	0	0	0
K3	3	3	0	3	2	1	2	2	3	2	0	0	0	0
K4	3	2	3	0	1	1	2	1	2	1	0	0	0	0
K5	1	2	2	1	0	2	1	1	2	1	0	0	0	0
K6	1	2	1	1	2	0	1	1	1	1	0	0	0	0
K7	2	1	2	2	1	1	0	2	3	3	0	0	0	0
K8	1	1	2	1	1	1	2	0	3	3	0	0	0	0
K9	2	2	3	2	2	1	3	3	0	4	1	1	1	1
K10	1	1	2	1	1	1	3	3	4	0	1	1	1	1
K11	0	0	0	0	0	0	1	1	1	1	0	2	2	2
K12	0	0	0	0	0	0	1	1	1	1	2	0	2	2
K13	0	0	0	0	0	0	1	1	1	1	2	2	0	2
K14	0	0	0	0	0	0	1	1	1	1	2	2	2	0

K1:Total number of branches, K2:Total number of employees, K3:Total number of customers, K4:Total number of ATMs, K5:Average training duration, K6:Staff turnover rate, K7:Capital adequacy ratio, K8:Return on equity, K9:Total assets, K10:Net profit, K11: Per capita direct greenhouse gas emissions, K12:Per capita water consumption, K13: Per capita paper consumption, K14: Per capita fuel consumption

Stage 2. Development of a Normalised Direct Relationship Matrix

The normalised direct relationship matrix in Table 6 was created by using the direct relationship matrix obtained at this stage by using formulas 1 and 2.

Table 4. Normalised direct relationship matrix

	K1	K2	K3	K4	K5	K6	K7	K8	K9	K10	K11	K12	K13	K14
K1	0.0	0.0769	0.1154	0.1154	0.0385	0.0385	0.0769	0.0385	0.0769	0.0385	0.0	0.0	0.0	0.0
K2	0.0769	0.0	0.1154	0.0769	0.0769	0.0769	0.0385	0.0385	0.0769	0.0385	0.0	0.0	0.0	0.0
K3	0.1154	0.1154	0.0	0.1154	0.0769	0.0385	0.0769	0.0769	0.1154	0.0769	0.0	0.0	0.0	0.0
K4	0.1154	0.0769	0.1154	0.0	0.0385	0.0385	0.0769	0.0385	0.0769	0.0385	0.0	0.0	0.0	0.0
K5	0.0385	0.0769	0.0769	0.0385	0.0	0.0769	0.0385	0.0385	0.0769	0.0385	0.0	0.0	0.0	0.0
K6	0.0385	0.0769	0.0385	0.0385	0.0769	0.0	0.0385	0.0385	0.0385	0.0385	0.0	0.0	0.0	0.0
K7	0.0769	0.0385	0.0769	0.0769	0.0385	0.0385	0.0	0.0769	0.1154	0.1154	0.0	0.0	0.0	0.0
K8	0.0385	0.0385	0.0769	0.0385	0.0385	0.0385	0.0769	0.0	0.1154	0.1154	0.0	0.0	0.0	0.0
K9	0.0769	0.0769	0.1154	0.0769	0.0769	0.0385	0.1154	0.1154	0.0	0.1538	0.0385	0.0385	0.0385	0.0385
K10	0.0385	0.0385	0.0769	0.0385	0.0385	0.0385	0.1154	0.1154	0.1538	0.0	0.0385	0.0385	0.0385	0.0385
K11	0.0	0.0	0.0	0.0	0.0	0.0	0.0385	0.0385	0.0385	0.0385	0.0	0.0769	0.0769	0.0769
K12	0.0	0.0	0.0	0.0	0.0	0.0	0.0385	0.0385	0.0385	0.0385	0.0769	0.0	0.0769	0.0769
K13	0.0	0.0	0.0	0.0	0.0	0.0	0.0385	0.0385	0.0385	0.0385	0.0769	0.0769	0.0	0.0769
K14	0.0	0.0	0.0	0.0	0.0	0.0	0.0385	0.0385	0.0385	0.0385	0.0769	0.0769	0.0769	0.0

K1:Total number of branches, K2:Total number of employees, K3:Total number of customers, K4:Total number of ATMs, K5:Average training duration, K6:Staff turnover rate, K7:Capital adequacy ratio, K8:Return on equity, K9:Total assets, K10:Net profit, K11: Per capita direct greenhouse gas emissions, K12:Per capita water consumption, K13: Per capita paper consumption, K14: Per capita fuel consumption

Stage 3: Development of the Total Relationship Matrix

The total relationship matrix in Table 5 is obtained by using the normalised direct relationship matrix obtained by using the formula number 3.

Table 5. Total relationship matrix

	K1	K2	K3	K4	K5	K6	K7	K8	K9	K10	K11	K12	K13	K14
K1	0.0	0.0769	0.1154	0.1154	0.0385	0.0385	0.0769	0.0385	0.0769	0.0385	0.0	0.0	0.0	0.0
K2	0.0769	0.0	0.1154	0.0769	0.0769	0.0769	0.0385	0.0385	0.0769	0.0385	0.0	0.0	0.0	0.0
K3	0.1154	0.1154	0.0	0.1154	0.0769	0.0385	0.0769	0.0769	0.1154	0.0769	0.0	0.0	0.0	0.0
K4	0.1154	0.0769	0.1154	0.0	0.0385	0.0385	0.0769	0.0385	0.0769	0.0385	0.0	0.0	0.0	0.0
K5	0.0385	0.0769	0.0769	0.0385	0.0	0.0769	0.0385	0.0385	0.0769	0.0385	0.0	0.0	0.0	0.0
K6	0.0385	0.0769	0.0385	0.0385	0.0769	0.0	0.0385	0.0385	0.0385	0.0385	0.0	0.0	0.0	0.0
K7	0.0769	0.0385	0.0769	0.0769	0.0385	0.0385	0.0	0.0769	0.1154	0.1154	0.0	0.0	0.0	0.0
K8	0.0385	0.0385	0.0769	0.0385	0.0385	0.0385	0.0769	0.0	0.1154	0.1154	0.0	0.0	0.0	0.0
K9	0.0769	0.0769	0.1154	0.0769	0.0769	0.0385	0.1154	0.1154	0.0	0.1538	0.0385	0.0385	0.0385	0.0385
K10	0.0385	0.0385	0.0769	0.0385	0.0385	0.0385	0.1154	0.1154	0.1538	0.0	0.0385	0.0385	0.0385	0.0385
K11	0.0	0.0	0.0	0.0	0.0	0.0	0.0385	0.0385	0.0385	0.0385	0.0	0.0769	0.0769	0.0769
K12	0.0	0.0	0.0	0.0	0.0	0.0	0.0385	0.0385	0.0385	0.0385	0.0769	0.0	0.0769	0.0769
K13	0.0	0.0	0.0	0.0	0.0	0.0	0.0385	0.0385	0.0385	0.0385	0.0769	0.0769	0.0	0.0769
K14	0.0	0.0	0.0	0.0	0.0	0.0	0.0385	0.0385	0.0385	0.0385	0.0769	0.0769	0.0769	0.0

K1:Total number of branches, K2:Total number of employees, K3:Total number of customers, K4:Total number of ATMs, K5:Average training duration, K6:Staff turnover rate, K7:Capital adequacy ratio, K8:Return on equity, K9:Total assets, K10:Net profit, K11: Per capita direct greenhouse gas emissions, K12:Per capita water consumption, K13: Per capita paper consumption, K14: Per capita fuel consumption

Stage 4: Determination of D and R Values

The row (D) and column (R) totals in the total relationship matrix are formed using formulae 4, 5 and 6 and shown in Table 6.

Stage 5: Determination of D+R, D-R and Factor Weights and Creation of the Effect Graph

At this stage, D+R and D-R values and the importance levels of the factors were calculated using formulae 7 and 8 and shown in Table 6.

Table 6. D, R, D+R, D+R, D-R values and importance degrees of factors

Factor	D (Impact)	R (Influence)	D+R (Importance)	D-R (Direction)
K1	1.9090	1.9806	3.8896	-0.0716
K2	1.8676	1.9288	3.7964	-0.0612
K3	2.4420	2.5327	4.9748	-0.0907
K4	1.9090	1.9806	3.8896	-0.0716
K5	1.5371	1.5899	3.1270	-0.0528
K6	1.2771	1.3243	2.6014	-0.0471
K7	2.0588	2.3787	4.4376	-0.3198
K8	1.8514	2.1661	4.0175	-0.3147
K9	2.8479	2.9176	5.7655	-0.0696
K10	2.3595	2.4176	4.7772	-0.0580
K11	0.9563	0.6669	1.6233	0.28938
K12	0.9563	0.6669	1.6233	0.28938
K13	0.9563	0.6669	1.6233	0.28938
K14	0.9563	0.6668	1.6233	0.28938

K1:Total number of branches, K2:Total number of employees, K3:Total number of customers, K4:Total number of ATMs, K5:Average training duration, K6:Staff turnover rate, K7:Capital adequacy ratio, K8:Return on equity, K9:Total assets, K10:Net profit, K11: Per capita direct greenhouse gas emissions, K12:Per capita water consumption, K13: Per capita paper consumption, K14: Per capita fuel consumption

The effect graph according to all these data is shown in Figure 1.

Figure 1. Impact graph

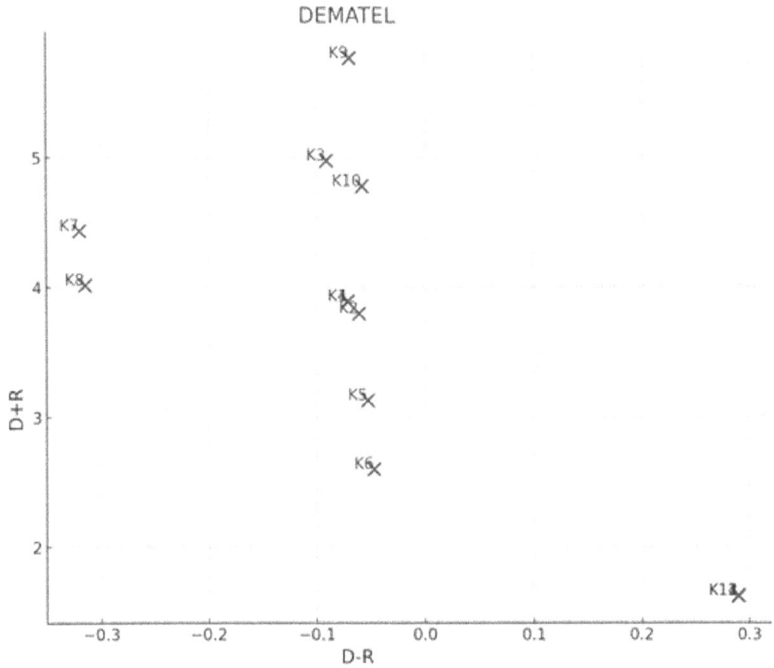

Analyses Results Evaluation

- ✓ Total Relationship Matrix: The analysis shows the interaction of each factor with other factors. For example, K3 (Total number of customers) has a strong relationship with many other factors (D: 2.44, R: 2.53), indicating that K3 is both an influencing and an influenced factor in the system.
- ✓ Degrees of Influence and Importance (D+R and D-R Values): K9 (Total assets) has the highest importance (D+R: 5.77) and strong influence-direction balance (D-R: -0.07). K3 (Total number of customers) is also of high importance (D+R: 4.97) and plays an influential role. Factors K7 (Capital adequacy ratio) and K8 (Return on equity) also play important roles in the system (D+R: 4.44 for K7, D+R: 4.02 for K8), but both have a negative D-R, indicating that they are more influential.
- ✓ Environmental Factors (K11-K14): Direct greenhouse gas emissions per capita (K11), water consumption (K12), paper consumption (K13) and fuel con-

sumption (K14) have low impact values, indicating that these factors are less determinant in the analysis (D+R $\approx$ 1.62, D-R positive).

5 CONCLUSION AND DISCUSSION

DEMATEL analysis reveals how factors in a system interact with each other and the degree of importance and influence of each factor within the system. The data in your analysis can be used to identify how 14 key factors of the banking sector are interrelated and to determine their strategic priorities. Detailed assessment and developed recommendations are as follows:

1. Critical and Influencing Factors (High D+R and D-R Values):
   - ✓ Total Assets (K9): It stands out as one of the most important factors in the system with the highest D+R (5.77). This indicates that the bank's assets have a major impact on its financial health and also have the potential to be influenced by other factors. Effective management of total assets and optimisation of credit and investment strategies can increase the financial resilience of the bank. Diversification of the asset portfolio and risk management strategies will have a positive impact on this factor.
   - ✓ Total Number of Customers (P3): It has a high importance and impact value (D+R: 4.97). This factor indicates that the size of the customer base directly affects the bank's overall performance. Investing in customer acquisition and loyalty programmes, improving customer experience and service quality can increase the positive impact of K3. Moreover, the development of digital banking services and personalisation of customer service can make this factor stronger.
2. Highly Affected Factors (Negative D-R Values):
   - ✓ Capital Adequacy Ratio (K7) and Return on Equity (K8): These factors are among the more influenced factors in the system with high importance (D+R: 4.44 and 4.02) and negative D-R values. This indicates that these factors are more vulnerable to external factors and the influence of other factors. Strengthening the bank capital structure can stabilise these factors. The capital adequacy ratio is an important indicator of a bank's ability to withstand potential economic fluctuations. Return on equity should be monitored to enhance the bank's sustainable growth and investment attractiveness. In this context, operational efficiency and cost optimisation projects can be initiated.
3. Environmental and Sustainability Factors (K11-K14):

- ✓ Per Capita Direct Greenhouse Gas Emissions (K11), Water Consumption (K12), Paper Consumption (K13), Fuel Consumption (K14): These factors have a low D+R (around 1.62) and positive D-R values, making them relatively less influential but more influential in the system. Environmental sustainability is an important area of social responsibility for the financial sector today. To maximise the impact of these factors, banks should invest in projects that reduce their environmental impact. For example, paperless banking practices, energy efficiency projects, green building certificates, etc. can emphasise these factors and strengthen the bank's corporate reputation.

4. Human Resources and Operational Factors:
   - ✓ Total Number of Employees (K2) and Average Training Duration (K5): They have a direct impact on operational efficiency with moderate importance (D+R: 3.79 and 3.13) and impact levels. Talent management and personnel development programmes should be prioritised in human resources strategies. Increasing the duration of training can improve the bank's overall performance and customer satisfaction by improving employees' competences. Career development and motivational programmes should be implemented to keep employee turnover rate (P6) low.
5. Risk Management and Strategic Planning:
   - ✓ Net profit (K10) and other financial indicators are directly linked to risk management strategies. It has a high impact and absorptive capacity (D+R: 4.78). Strengthening the bank's risk management systems can have a positive impact on financial performance. In this context, advanced analysis techniques and artificial intelligence supported solutions can be used to effectively manage market risks, credit risks and operational risks.

When the results of the analyses are summarised, they serve as a guide in determining the areas that should be prioritised in the bank's strategic planning. In particular, investments in areas such as financial soundness, customer base management, sustainability, and employee management can ensure the bank's long-term success. Environmental sustainability factors, although currently of low importance, may gain strategic value in the future due to increasing regulatory pressures and societal expectations.

Ensuring sustainability in banks is crucial for long-term success and societal benefit. In this context, banks need to integrate sustainability principles into their corporate policies. Adopting an environmentally sustainable approach, banks can reduce their carbon footprint by utilizing renewable energy sources, increasing energy efficiency, and improving waste management systems. Additionally, they can play an active role in social responsibility by supporting projects that benefit society. Transparency, ethical governance, and accountability also stand out as fundamental elements of a sustainable banking structure.

Restructuring financial products and services with a focus on sustainability is another significant step in this process. Banks can mitigate the environmental impact of economic growth by offering green loans and sustainable bonds for environmentally friendly projects. Furthermore, through social impact investments, they can contribute to the development of education, healthcare, or support for low-income individuals. Such financial instruments not only ensure the responsible growth of banks but also support the sustainable development of society.

Incorporating a sustainability perspective into risk management processes is also a critical necessity. Environmental risks such as climate change, depletion of natural resources, or loss of biodiversity can have long-term impacts on banks' business models. Therefore, banks should include these risks in their financial decision-making processes to build a more resilient structure against potential threats. Moreover, these analyses can encourage a stronger focus on sustainability-oriented investments.

Technological innovations and digitalization provide significant tools to support banks' sustainability goals. Digital banking applications can minimize environmental impact by reducing paper usage. Additionally, technologies like blockchain and data analytics can help better measure and report the impact of sustainable projects. Technology also enhances financial inclusion by reaching individuals without access to banking services, thereby contributing to societal development.

Employee training and awareness-raising activities are also essential for achieving sustainability goals. Raising awareness among bank employees and executives about sustainability plays a critical role in adopting and implementing these objectives. Similarly, offering sustainability-focused financial products to customers and promoting this understanding across society can strengthen banks' environmental and social impact.

Finally, international collaborations and compliance with global standards can enhance banks' effectiveness in sustainability efforts. For instance, setting goals aligned with the United Nations Sustainable Development Goals (SDGs) and participating in global initiatives to achieve these targets enable banks to implement a more effective sustainability strategy both locally and internationally. Such approaches enhance banks' societal and environmental contributions while also strengthening their competitive advantages.

REFERENCES

Akhtar, S. (2008). Islamic Finance: Sustainability and Challenges. *NBR Anal.*, *18*, 15–24.

Altın, S. (2023). Sürdürülebilir Tüketimi Sağlamak İçin Çevresel Duyarlilik Etkili Bir Faktör Müdür? *Erciyes Akademi*, *37*(3), 1062–1083. DOI: 10.48070/erciyesakademi.1343768

Aras, G., & Crowther, D. (2009). Corporate Sustainability Reporting: A Study in Disingenuity? *Journal of Business Ethics*, *87*(S1), 279–288. DOI: 10.1007/s10551-008-9806-0

Aras, G., Tezcan, N. ve Kutlu Furtuna, Ö. (2018). Çok Boyutlu Kurumsal Sürdürülebilirlik Yaklaşımı ile Türk Bankacılık Sektörünün Değerlemesi: Kamu-Özel Banka Farklılaşması, Ege Akademik Bakış. Cilt 18 · Sayı 1 · SS. 47 / 62.

Aytekin, S., ve Sakarya, Ş. (2013). Bist de işlem gören gıda işletmelerinin topsis yöntemi ile finansal performanslarının değerlendirilmesi,1. *Yönetim ve Ekonomi Araştırmaları Dergisi*, (21), 30–47.

Babiak, K., & Trendafilova, S. (2011). CSR and environmental responsibility: Motives and pressures to adopt green management practices. *Corporate Social Responsibility and Environmental Management*, *18*(1), 11–24. DOI: 10.1002/csr.229

Bai, Y. (2011), Financing A Green Future An Examination Of China's Banking Sector For Green Finance, Master Thesis, Beijing, Lund University, Master of Science in Environmental Sciences Policy & Management.

Belas, J., Çera, G., Dvorský, J., & Čepel, M. (2021). Corporate social responsibility and sustainability issues of small-and medium-sized enterprises. *Corporate Social Responsibility and Environmental Management*, *28*(2), 721–730. DOI: 10.1002/csr.2083

Brotons, J. M., & Sansalvador, M. E. (2020). The relation between corporate social responsibility certification and financial performance: An empirical study in Spain. *Corporate Social Responsibility and Environmental Management*, *27*(3), 1465–1477. DOI: 10.1002/csr.1899

Carlucci, D., Ferreira, F. A. F., Schiuma, G., Jalali, M. S., & António, N. J. S. (2018). A Holistic Conception of Sustainable Banking: Adding Value with Fuzzy Cognitive Mapping. *Technological and Economic Development of Economy*, *24*(4), 1303–1322. DOI: 10.3846/20294913.2016.1266412

Cerin, P., & Scholtens, B. (2011). Linking responsible investments to societal influence: Motives, assessments and risks. *Sustainable Development (Bradford), 19*(2), 71–76. DOI: 10.1002/sd.508

Chang, B., Chang, C. W., & Wu, C. H. (2011). Fuzzy DEMATEL method for developing supplier selection criteria. *Expert Systems with Applications, 38*(3), 1850–1858. DOI: 10.1016/j.eswa.2010.07.114

Dinica, V., Lund-Durlachery, D., & Reiser, D. (2019). *Challenges for tourism-transitioning to corporate sustainability and responsibility.* Springer International Publishing.

Eğilmez, Ö, Savaş, B . (2021). İş Etiği Dinamiklerinin Dematel Yöntemi ile İncelenmesi . İnsan ve Toplum Bilimleri Araştırmaları Dergisi, 10 (2), 1580-1600 .

Erol, H. M. (2006). *Dünyada ve Türkiye'de bankacılık sektörünün gelişimi ve Türkiye'de kamu bankalarının yeniden yapılandırılması.* Marmara Üniversitesi Sosyal Bilimler Enstitüsü.

Fontela, E. ve Gabus, A., (1974). "DEMATEL, innovative methods, Technical Report no. 2, Structural analysis of the world problematique". Battelle Geneva Research Institute

Gabus, A. ve Fontela, E., (1973). "Perceptions of the world problematique: Communication procedure, communicating with those bearing collective responsibility (DEMATEL Report no. 1)". Battelle Geneva Research Centre.

Helleiner, E., & Thistlethwaite, J. (2009). The greening of international financial regulation. In Clapp, J. (Ed.), *Environmental Sustainability and the Financial Crisis: Linkages and Policy Recommendations* (pp. 10–12). CIGI Working Group on Environment and Resources.

Hillman, J., & Keim, G. (2001). Shareholder value, stakeholder management, and social issues: What's the bottom line? *Strategic Management Journal, 22*(2), 125–139. DOI: 10.1002/1097-0266(200101)22:2<125::AID-SMJ150>3.0.CO;2-H

Hussain, N, Ugo R ve Rene´ P. Orij. (2016). Corporate Governance and Sustainability Performance: Analysis of Triple Bottom Line Performance. *Journal of Business Ethics, 25*, 1–22.

Jeucken, M. (2001). *Sustainable Finance And Banking, The Finance Sector And The Future Of The Planet, (1.Baskı).* Earthscan.

Jeucken, M. (2001). *Sustainable Finance And Banking, The Finance Sector And The Future Of The Planet, (1.Baskı).* Earthscan.

Jeucken, M.H.A. & Bouma, J. J. (1999). The Changing Environment of Banks, GMI Theme Issue: Sustainable Banking: The Greening of Finance, 21-35.

Jeucken, M. H. A., & Bouma, J. J. (1999). The Changing Environment of Banks. *Greener Manag. Int.*, *27*, 21–35.

Jo, H., Kim, H., & Park, K. (2014). Corporate Environmental Responsibility And Firm Performance İn The Financial Services Sector. *SSRN*, *131*, 1–28. DOI: 10.2139/ssrn.2470872

Khan, M., Azizul Islam, M., Kayeser Fatima, J., & Ahmed, K. (2011). Corporate Sustainability Reporting of Major Commercial Banks in line with GRI: Bangladesh Evidence. *Social Responsibility Journal*, *7*(3), 347–352. DOI: 10.1108/17471111111154509

Kuhn, T., & Deetz, S. (2009). Critical theory and corporate social responsibility: Can/Should we get beyond cynical reasoning? In Crane, A., McWilliams, A., Matten, D., Moon, J., & Siegel, D. S. (Eds.), *The Oxford handbook of social responsibility, (ss* (pp. 1–29). Oxford University Press. DOI: 10.1093/oxfordhb/9780199211593.003.0008

Li, C. W., & Tzeng, G. H. (2009). Identification of a threshold value for the DEMATEL method using the maximum mean de-entropy algorithm to find critical services provided by a semiconductor intellectual property mall. *Expert Systems with Applications*, *36*(6), 9891–9898. DOI: 10.1016/j.eswa.2009.01.073

Li, Y., Hu, Y., Zhang, X., Deng, Y., & Mahadevan, S. (2014). An Evidential DEMATEL Method to Identify Critical Success Factors in Emergency Management. *Applied Soft Computing*, *22*, 504–510. DOI: 10.1016/j.asoc.2014.03.042

Lin, A. J., & Chang, H. Y. (2019). Business Sustainability Performance Evaluation For Taiwanese Banks—A Hybrid Multiple-Criteria Decision-Making Approach. *Sustainability (Basel)*, *11*(8), 2236. DOI: 10.3390/su11082236

Nilashi, M., Zakaria, R., Ibrahim, O., Majid, M., Zin, R., & Farahmand, M. (2015). MCPCM: A DEMATEL-ANPBased Multi-Criteria Decision-Making Approach to Evaluate the Critical Success Factors in Construction Projects. *Arabian Journal for Science and Engineering*, *40*(2), 343–361. DOI: 10.1007/s13369-014-1529-1

Nobanee, H., & Ellili, N. (2016). Corporate Sustainability Disclosure in Annual Reports: Evidence from UAE Banks: Islamic versus Conventional. *Renewable & Sustainable Energy Reviews*, *55*, 1336–1341. DOI: 10.1016/j.rser.2015.07.084

Nobanee, H., & Ellili, N. (2016). Corporate Sustainability Disclosure in Annual Reports: Evidence from UAE banks: Islamic versus Conventional. *Renewable & Sustainable Energy Reviews*, *55*, 1336–1341. DOI: 10.1016/j.rser.2015.07.084

ONAY, A. (2015). Sürdürülebilir Kalkınma, Kurumsal Sürdürülebilirlik ve Sürdürülebilirlik Raporlaması. *Elektronik Mesleki Gelişim ve Araştırma Dergisi, 3*, 104–118.

Oyegunle, A. (2016), An Assessment of Sustainable Banking Regulations in Emerging Economies, Watrerloo, Yüksek Lisans Tezi, University of Waterloo, Sustainability Management.

Pinter, É., Nikolett, D., & Zoltán, O. 2006. New Direction Line of Sustainable Development and Marketing in Green Banking. 22nd IMP-Conference in Milan. Italy.

Raut, R., Naoufel, C., & Kharat, M. (2017). Sustainability in The Banking Industry: A Strategic Multi-Criteria Analysis. *Business Strategy and the Environment, 26*(4), 550–568. DOI: 10.1002/bse.1946

Rebai, S., Azaiez, M., & Saidane, D. (2012). Sustainable Performance Evaluation of Banks Using A Multi-Attribute Utility Model: An Application to French Banks. *Procedia Economics and Finance, 2*, 363–372. DOI: 10.1016/S2212-5671(12)00098-6

SAVRAM. M. ve KARAKOÇ, A. (2012). Bankacılık Sektöründe İtibar Riskinin Önemi. International Conference on Euroasian Economies (ss. 328-332). Almaata: Kazakistan.

Scholtens, B. (2008). Corporate social responsibility in the international banking industry. *Journal of Business Ethics, 86*(2), 159–175. DOI: 10.1007/s10551-008-9841-x

Scholtens, B., & Van't Klooster, S. (2019). Sustainability and Bank Risk. *Palgrave Communications, 5*(1), 1–8. DOI: 10.1057/s41599-019-0315-9

Şendurur, U., & Temelli, F. (2018). Türkiye'de Faaliyet Gösteren Geleneksel Bankalar ve Katılım Bankalarının Sürdürülebilirlik Açısından Karşılaştırılması. *Muhasebe Bilim Dünyası Dergisi, 20*(2), 330–346. DOI: 10.31460/mbdd.344785

Signitzer, B., & Prexl, A. (2007). Corporate sustainability communications: Aspects of theory and professionalization. *Journal of Public Relations Research, 20*(1), 1–19. DOI: 10.1080/10627260701726996

Sobhani, F. A., Amran, A., & Zainuddin, Y. (2009). Revisiting the Practices of Corporate Social and Environmental Disclosure in Bangladesh. *Corporate Social Responsibility and Environmental Management, 16*(3), 167–183. DOI: 10.1002/csr.193

Sobhani, F. A., Amran, A., & Zainuddin, Y. (2012). Sustainability Disclosure in Annual Reports and Websites: A Study of Banking Industry in Bangladesh. *Journal of Cleaner Production, 23*(1), 75–85. DOI: 10.1016/j.jclepro.2011.09.023

Sobhani, F. A., Amran, A., & Zainuddin, Y. (2012). Sustainability Disclosure in Annual Reports and Websites: A Study of the Banking Industry in Bangladesh. *Journal of Cleaner Production*, *23*(1), 75–85. DOI: 10.1016/j.jclepro.2011.09.023

Soydaş, Ş. S. (2024). Portfolio selection with AHP and TOPSIS methods: An application in BIST. *Trends in Business and Economics*, *39*(2), 181–194. DOI: 10.16951/trendbusecon.1580489

SPK. (2005). *Kurumsal Yönetim İlkeleri.*

Stephens, C., Skinner, C. (2013), " Banks For A Better PLlanet? The Challenge of Sustainable Social and Environmental Development and the Emerging Response of the Banking Sector" Environmental Development, 5-1, 175-179, DOI: 10.1016/j.envdev.2012.11.011

Tandoğan, D., & Özyurt, H. (2013). Bankacılık sektörünün ekonomik büyüme ve sürdürülebilir ekonomik kalkınma üzerine etkisi: Türkiye ekonomisi üzerine nedensellik testleri (1981-2009). *Marmara Üniversitesi İktisadi İdari Bilimler Dergisi*, *35*(2), 49–80. DOI: 10.14780/iibdergi.201324459

Tıraş, H. H. (2012). Sürdürülebilir kalkınma ve çevre: Teorik bir inceleme. *Kahramanmaraş Sütçü İmam Üniversitesi İktisadi ve İdari Bilimler Fakültesi Dergisi*, *2*(2), 57–73.

Toktaş, P., & Can, G. (2020). Görev Temelli Yeni Bir Stokastik Çok Kriterli Karar Verme Yaklaşımı Önerisi. *Avrupa Bilim ve Teknoloji Dergisi*, (18), 61–75. DOI: 10.31590/ejosat.657719

Tseng, M. L., & Lin, Y. H. (2009). Application of fuzzy DEMATEL to develop a cause and effect model of municipal solid waste management in Metro Manila. *Environmental Monitoring and Assessment*, *158*(1-4), 519–533. DOI: 10.1007/s10661-008-0601-2 PMID: 18951134

Tzeng, G. H., & Huang, J. J. (2011). *Multiple attribute decision making: methods and applications*. Chapman and Hall/CRC. DOI: 10.1201/b11032

UNEP FI. 2008 Overview, https://www.unepfi.org/fileadmin/documents/unepfi_overview_2008.pdf

Weber, O. (2012). Environmental credit risk management in banks and financial service institutions. *Business Strategy and the Environment*, *21*(4), 248–263. DOI: 10.1002/bse.737

Weber, O., Diaz, M., & Schwegler, R. (2014). Corporate social responsibility of the financial sector – strengths, weaknesses and the impact on sustainable development. *Sustainable Development (Bradford)*, *22*(5), 321–335. DOI: 10.1002/sd.1543

Weber, R. P. (1990). *Basic Content Analysis*. Sage. DOI: 10.4135/9781412983488

Wilson, M. (2003). Corporate sustainability: what is it and where does it come from? *Ivey Business Journal*, *1*(2), 1–5.

Wu, W. W. (2008). Choosing Knowledge Management Strategies By Using A Combined ANP and DEMATEL Approach. *Expert Systems with Applications*, *35*(3), 828–835. DOI: 10.1016/j.eswa.2007.07.025

Yang, Y., & Stohl, C. (2020). The (in) congruence of measures of corporate social responsibility performance and stakeholder measures of corporate social responsibility reputation. *Corporate Social Responsibility and Environmental Management*, *27*(2), 969–981. DOI: 10.1002/csr.1859

Yarlıkaş, S., & Öztürk, C. (2021). Bankacılık sektöründe kurumsal sürdürülebilirlik performansının Critic-Moora önem katsayısı yaklaşımı ile değerlendirilmesi. *Journal of Social and Humanities Sciences Research*, *8*(77), 3124–3136.

Zhou, Q., Huang, W., & Zhang, Y. (2011). Identifying Critical Success Factors in Emergency Management Using A Fuzzy DEMATEL method. *Safety Science*, *49*(2), 243–252. DOI: 10.1016/j.ssci.2010.08.005

Chapter 7
The Determination of Criteria Affecting Digital and Sustainable Capabilities in Businesses with AHP and DEMATEL Methods

Serkan Derici
https://orcid.org/0000-0003-2581-6770
Nevşehir Hacı Bektaş Veli University, Turkey

ABSTRACT

Nowadays, due to the development of global and digital factors, the activities of businesses are affected by a large number of criteria. In this period of high uncertainty, businesses need to improve their digital capabilities and implement sustainable practices. In this direction, in this study, the digitalization and sustainability components that play a role in the activities of enterprises were identified through a literature review and a unique model was developed. In the study designed as a multi-criteria decision-making problem, the nine criteria in the model were ranked using the Analytic Hierarchy Process Method (AHP), and a holistic perspective was created by determining the relationships between the criteria with the DEMATEL Method. As a result of the study, which aims to contribute to the development of a systematic approach by determining the starting point, recommendations were developed.

DOI: 10.4018/979-8-3693-8789-4.ch007

INTRODUCTION

Human beings have constantly invented and developed new things from the past to the present. As each invention has led to a new invention, today's advanced technology has been reached and this level of technology is gradually increasing. In order to understand the phenomenon called digitalization today, it is necessary to know the past and to examine the developments in the past periods. In this direction, it is necessary to examine the situations that have a widespread impact throughout the world and change the era. It is known that the main of these developments are known to be with the industrial revolutions. On the other hand, due to factors such as the rapid increase in the world population, the diversification of human needs and preferences, and the increase in the level of education, the use of the scarce resources of our world is increasing. Agricultural production is insufficient with this increase, and countries and companies are working under the obligation to carry out production and activities considering the future. The increase in human population, the development of production and industry has revealed the problem of environmental pollution and scarce resource management. In this direction, activities such as increasing carbon emissions, lack of green transformation in industrial production, unconscious agriculture cause global warming. Today, these studies are carried out intensively under the name of sustainability throughout the world and the future of the world is tried to be saved (Dubey & Lal, 2009; Seidel et. al., 2013).

A rapid transformation is being carried out worldwide depending on two basic philosophies under sustainability and digital transformation, while businesses operate under intense competition conditions with the increase in internet usage and globalisation. This transformation is carried out by adding digital technologies to classical business processes, while on the other hand, the development in any part of the world affects business processes. In this case, it reveals the necessity of not only digital transformation but also agile and resilient structures (Grover & Malhotra, 1997; Parviainen et. al., 2017; Rachmad, 2003.

In this period of changing conditions and uncertainties called the VUCA era, it is necessary to know the concepts of digitalization and sustainability together with past events in order to understand the era. For this reason, the aforementioned information is included under this heading. In addition to the necessity of these concepts, classical decision-making methods are insufficient as many different criteria affect business processes. Nowadays, managers cannot directly choose an alternative, nor can they directly say which criterion to give importance to in creating a digital and sustainable structure. Because activities are carried out under many conditions and are affected by many factors. This situation, that is, the fact that many criteria or factors affect business processes, transforms the decisions to be taken into a multi-dimensional situation. This transformation makes it more accurate to make analyses with multi-criteria decision making methods. In these analyses using multi-criteria decision-making methods, an objective approach is put forward in which all criteria affecting the activities will be included. According to the results obtained, inferences can be made such as which criterion and which alternative is more important, which criterion is more effective on other criteria. Naturally, this situation directly affects the effectiveness of the decisions to be taken (Wang et. al., 2009; Aruldoss et. al., 2013; Kaivo-Oja & Lauraeus, 2018).

This study is based on the theme of digital transformation and sustainability in enterprises due to the importance and situation mentioned in the previous sections. In accordance with this theme, a literature review was conducted, and in the light of those studies, a set of criteria was determined and a unique model was created. The model developed consists of criteria related to sustainability and digitalization. The analyses of this model are considered as a multi-criteria decision making problem since there are many criteria. In this direction, the ranking of the criteria according to the level of importance of the criteria that informs managers where to start in order to create a digital and sustainable structure has been done with the Analytical Hierarchy Process (AHP) Method. Again, in order to determine the starting point and to provide a holistic perspective to the problem, the effect of the criteria on other criteria was determined by DEMATEL Method.

In the scope of this study, digitalization is one of the main issues addressed. The phenomenon of digitalization has entered our lives with Industry 4.0. However, it is necessary to know the past industrial revolutions since the developments in the past periods constitute the basis for digitalization. We can see the four industrial revolutions that have been experienced so far together with the last industrial revolution through Figure 1. In this direction, firstly, the first industrial revolution appears in the historical process. In the 18th century, with the invention of steam engines in the first industrial revolution, which was announced in England, mechanical production was switched from workshop-type production based on manual labour. By the end of the 19th century, the second industrial revolution was announced in Germany. The second industrial revolution led to the use of electrical energy in industry and this innovation led to the start of mass production. The best example of mass production that started in this period is the Ford Model T produced by Henry Ford. Ford produced these vehicles, which were quite troublesome and costly, in the same colour and type. A century after the second industrial revolution, that is, at the end of the 20th century, the third industrial revolution was declared in England. In the third industrial revolution, information technologies started to be used in industry and automation started. So far, there has been an announcement in every industrial revolution, and then innovation has entered our lives. However, the innovations that entered our lives in the last industrial revolution (Industry 4.0), which was announced at the fair held in Hannover, Germany in 2011 at the beginning of the 21st century, had entered our lives in the previous three industrial revolutions. Innovations such as cloud computing, internet of things, big data, smart devices were already in our lives. However, it was only in 2011 that these were announced as Industry 4.0 as a whole. The world has entered the digital age with the announcement of Industry 4.0. The question of how we can use technology in the business world has now been replaced by the question of how we can use the available technology more effectively. After this date, a new technological innovation has started to enter our lives every passing moment. In this process where digital components rapidly enter our lives, the situation of accessing a livable world by using resources effectively is called sustainability (De Vries, 1994; Alizon et. al., 2008; Xu et. al., 2018; Stearns, 2020).

Figure 1. Illustration of the four industrial revolutions

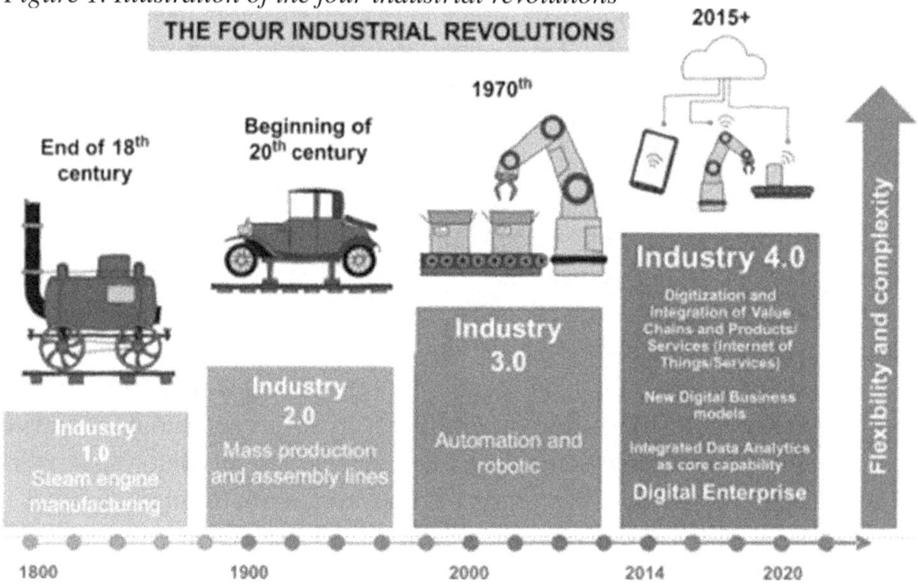

Resource: Munirathinam, S. (2020)

Worldwide today, both businesses and individuals are exploring how to achieve sustainable performance when using digital innovations. So what is the concept of sustainability? Sustainability is basically defined as the ability to meet the needs of the present without restricting the ability of future generations to meet their own needs (Marmara, 2006). Sustainability As can be understood from the basic definition of the concept of sustainability, businesses now have to think about the future while carrying out their current activities. Because it is a necessity to protect the environment for a livable world, to use resources effectively and to meet today's human needs while doing these. However, as a result of the studies carried out by considering the environment today, we can leave a livable world to future generations.

Sustainability has three main components: economic, social and environmental. The economic component from a sustainable point of view is not the income generation of the enterprise as we think. It is the savings that businesses will make thanks to the technology and works they use while carrying out their activities. These savings, that is, environmentalist activities, create economic advantage by saving raw materials and energy over time. In the meantime, businesses carry out environmentally friendly practices, whether within the scope of legal regulations or social responsibility. In this respect, activities such as recycling activities and the use of electric vehicles to reduce carbon emissions are examples of environmental practices. On the other hand, processes such as not polluting the environment, using renewable resources, recycling activities are considered within the scope of social responsibility. In short, businesses should now operate by considering economic, social and environmental factors (Basiago, 1998; Rondinelli & Berry, 2000; Doane & MacGillivray, 2001; Nordelöf et. al., 2014; Shrivastava, 2018).

Global warming has increased the importance of sustainable activities around the world. The Paris Agreement, which was established by the United Nations in 2015 and signed by 197 countries in order to combat climate change, is one of the most important of these. The Paris Agreement aims to limit the global temperature increase to 1.5 degrees Celsius and to create a carbon-neutral world by reducing greenhouse gas emissions. In addition, with this agreement, it is aimed to adapt to climate change and to create societies that are resistant to this change. In addition to the Paris agreement, another important work is carried out by the European Commission. In the framework of the European Green Deal announced by the European Commission in 2019, it is aimed that the European continent will be a climate-neutral continent by 2050. There are also objectives such as reaching zero greenhouse gas emission level by 2050, reducing greenhouse gas emissions by 55% by 2030, supporting the use of clean energy, and ensuring green transformation by sustainable agriculture and transport. Furthermore, within the scope of the European Green Deal, an obligation is created with practices such as taxation of carbon-intensive products. These two agreements show that international organisations play an active role by creating policies in order to create a sustainable world (Savaresi, 2016; Fetting, 2020; Tolliver et. al., 2020).

This study provides information about digital transformation and sustainability in enterprises that constitute the application area of this study. In addition to this information, the methods used in the analysis of the model created within the scope of the study are not given in this section since they will be explained in the application section. The concepts of digitalization and sustainability are extremely important in the field of business administration, while the creation of the model of this research and the examination of past research is important in terms of understanding the subject.

This study consists of three chapters following the introduction. These chapters start with a literature review where past studies on digitalization, sustainability and multi-criteria decision making methods are presented. According to the literature review, the application model of this study has been created uniquely and digital and sustainable components have been included in this model. The application model in question is created and presented as a result of the literature review, and it is given in the application section. After the literature review, Analytical Hierarchy Process (AHP) method and DEMATEL Method, which are among the multi-criteria decision making methods used in this study, are briefly explained and presented with their mathematical formulations. The model developed with these methods is analysed and the results are interpreted.

1. LITERATURE REVIEW

Nowadays, businesses operate under very different situations. These different situations are mainly due to high communication, competition and accessibility. Digitalization is the main cause of these. Businesses therefore operate in an era called the digital age. Since these activities are influenced by many criteria, uncertainties prevail, which is referred to as the VUCA era. While businesses operate in the digital age under VUCA, i.e. uncertainties, sustainable practices have gained importance due to the rapid depletion of scarce resources and the increase in environmental awareness worldwide.

The ability to compete with competitors and to use digital capabilities under uncertainty depends on effective situation analyses. On the other hand, businesses should know what to emphasise in the theme of sustainability. In the determination of these, classical methods are insufficient due to the complex structure of the business world. Therefore, using improved multi-criteria decision-making methods will give more accurate results. Within the scope of this study, a literature-supported model has been developed by considering digital and sustainable factors together. In this way, these criteria will be determined by applying a modern and effective multi-criteria decision making method and a road map will be presented to managers.

In this section, the factors affecting digital and sustainability capability in enterprises will first be determined using the Analytical Hierarchy Process (AHP) Method and ranked according to their importance levels. Then, the relationships between these criteria, whose importance levels are determined, will be determined by using the DEMATEL Method, one of the subjective criteria weighting methods. For this reason, the model to be applied in these methods, which will be used as an application methodology in this chapter, should be determined through a literature review.

In the literature, in accordance with the theme of the book and our purpose, first of all, studies that include criteria related to digitalization and sustainability are discussed. In this way, the criteria affecting digitalization and sustainability in enterprises were determined reliably. Subsequently, studies on digitalization and sustainability with multi-criteria decision-making methods are examined. The literature review including all these issues is presented in Table 1.

Table 1. The studies on digitalization, sustainability and multi-criteria decision making methods

Concept	Author(s)	Year	
Sustainability	Weber et. al.	2010	Credit Risk Management
	Markevičius et. al.	2010	Liquid Biofuels
	Hallstedt	2017	Product Development
	Breuer et. al.	2018	Business Model Development
Digitalization	Brodovskaya et.al.	2020	Educational Process in Universities
	Stankovic et. al.	2021	Digital Competitiveness
	Singh et. al.	2022	Significant Enablers
	Salimian & Mousavi	2023	Evaluating Digital Technology Strategies
MCDM - Sustainability	Cinelli et. al.	2014	Sustainability Assessment
	Wang et. al.	2009	Sustainable Energy
	Jamwal et. al.	2021	Sustainable Manufacturing
	Khalili & Duecker	2013	Sustainable Environmental Management System
MCDM - Digitalization	Mian & Al-Ahmari	2019	Comparative analysis of different digitization systems and selection of best alternative
	Deepu & Ravi	2021	Inter-Organizational Information Systems Selection
	Sergi & Ucal Sari	2021	Prioritization Of Public Services
	Maretto et. al.	2022	Selection Of Digital Technologies

The table shows that the literature review includes sustainability, digitalization and multi-criteria decision making methods. As a result of this literature review, the criteria in the application model of this study were determined. These criteria are as follows:

1. Legal Regulations
2. Environmental Factors
3. Use of Technology

4. Senior Management
5. Financial Structure
6. Data Management and Analytics
7. Technological Infrastructure
8. Corporate Culture
9. Supply Chain Management and Logistics

A model to be used as a basis for applications has been developed based on the scientific studies in the literature examined to include digitalization, sustainability and multi-criteria decision-making methods. This model, which includes digital and sustainable perspectives, consists of nine criteria. This model, which consists of the nine criteria given above, is unique as it reflects two different perspectives. The most important criteria will be determined by using this model by first ranking these criteria according to their importance with the AHP Method. In this way, managers will learn which criteria they should focus on first. This is also important for determining the starting point. Subsequently, the relationships between these criteria will be determined by using DEMATEL Method. Thus, the managers will know which criterion to start from and which criterion is important and will provide a holistic perspective to the problem.

In this study, the criteria affecting digitalization and sustainability capabilities in enterprises were determined with the support of the literature and a unique model consisting of nine criteria was created as given above. Multi-criteria decision-making analysis was applied to help managers determine which of these capabilities, which are important in creating a digital and sustainable structure, are prioritised and to provide a holistic perspective on these criteria. In this context, the nine criteria determined in the model will first be ranked with the Analytic Hierarchy Process Method, one of the multi-criteria decision-making methods, and then the DEMATEL Method was applied to provide a holistic perspective on the criteria and to determine the relationships between the criteria. For this reason, the Analytic Hierarchy Process Method and DEMATEL Method, which constitute the application methodology of this study, are explained respectively in the next section.

2. METHODOLOGY

The application methodology of this study has been determined as Analytic Hierarchy Process Method and DEMATEL Method among the multi-criteria decision making methods. Therefore, under this heading, these methods are explained in order to understand the applications.

2.1. Analytic Hierarchy Process (AHP) Method

Multi-criteria decision making methods are the methods used to select, rank and classify alternatives by evaluating these criteria within themselves in the face of a problem or objective affected by more than one criterion. These methods consist of objective methods using numerical data and subjective methods using expert opinions. The subjective methods are analysed by converting the opinions of the experts whose opinions are consulted into numerical values with developed scales. The selection of experts is very important for the success of subjective methods. Because personal judgements of individuals should not affect the decision. For this reason, more than one experienced and knowledgeable expert working in that field is consulted for the solution of the problem. Afterwards, these expert opinions are converted into a single value with the group average technique and analyses are performed. In the literature, the group average techniques to be used are arithmetic mean and geometric mean (Yang & Tzeng, 2011; Aruldoss et. al., 2013; Mardani et. al., 2017).

Analytic Hierarchy Process (AHP) Method is one of the methods used when there are subjective evaluations among multi-criteria decision making methods. The Analytical Hierarchy Process Method, developed by Thomas Saaty in 1980s, is a linear programming based multi-criteria decision making method in which the criteria affecting a problem or objective are expressed hierarchically depending on this objective, experts make pairwise comparisons at each stage and these comparisons are analysed to enable ranking, classification and selection (Özdağoğlu & Özdağoğlu, 2007; Sipahi & Timor, 2010; Saaty & Vargas, 2012).

The criteria at a stage in the hierarchy are compared pairwise by using the pairwise comparison scale shown in Table 2 and the subjective opinions of the experts are converted into numerical values by means of this scale. The subjective and verbal opinions of the experts are converted into numerical values in this way and the pairwise comparison matrices in Table 3 are formed. These matrices are different for each level in the hierarchy. In other words, they are created separately. If more than one expert opinion is used, pairwise comparison matrices are created separately for each expert. Then, the arithmetic or geometric mean of each element of each pairwise comparison matrix is taken and converted into a single value. In this way, each pairwise comparison matrix is converted into a single matrix containing the opinions of all experts and analyses are performed. In the matrices created in this way, the personal judgements of an expert are prevented from affecting the problem and the decisions to be taken are ensured to be objective and rational (Saaty, 2001; Saaty, 2008).

As shown in Table 2, each criterion in the hierarchy is compared with the others. In the pairwise comparisons to be made, which criterion is more important than the other criterion is found on the scale in Table 2 and its numerical value is written in the pairwise comparison matrix. While creating this matrix, the intersection of the row and column of the same criterion is expressed as 1 since a criterion has no superiority over itself. If we talk about Table 3; the comparisons of criterion 1 with criterion 1, criterion 2 with criterion 2 and criterion 3 with criterion 3 are with themselves and these values are 1. In Analytic Hierarchy Process Method applications, these values form a diagonal and this diagonal consists of 1 values. When making pairwise comparisons, it is sufficient to have the experts compare the cells at the top of the diagonal. This is because the diagonal diagonal acts as a mirror and its lower part is the inverse of its upper part according to the multiplication operation. For example, if criterion 1 is 3 times more important than criterion 2, criterion 2 will be one third more important than criterion 1. Since we can already determine this logically, there is no need to ask the experts again (Zeshui & Cuiping, 1999; Saaty, 2004).

Table 2. Basic scale used in pairwise comparisons (Saaty, 1980)

Importance Level	Description	Explanation
1	Equally important	Both criteria contribute equally to the objective.
3	Moderately important	Experience and judgement favour one criterion slightly over the other.
5	Strongly important	Experience and judgement make one criterion significantly superior to the other.
7	Very strongly important	One criterion is superior to the other and this superiority is evident in practice.
9	Extremely important	The evidence for the superiority of one criterion over the other has great reliability.
2, 4, 6, 8	Intermediate values	It is the values between two consecutive judgements that are used when compromise is required.

Analytic Hierarchy Process Method applications are based on the pairwise comparison scale in Table 2 and the pairwise comparison matrices in Table 3, which are created using this scale (Saaty, 1980).

Table 3. Creation of the pairwise comparisons matrix for criteria 5.

	Criteria 1	Criteria 2	Criteria n
Criteria 1	w_1/w_1	w_1/w_2	w_1/w_n
Criteria 2	w_2/w_1	w_2/w_2	w_2/w_n
Criteria n	w_n/w_1	w_n/w_2	w_n/w_n

The analyses are then performed by applying these pairwise comparison matrices to each stage of the hierarchy. In the applications of the Analytic Hierarchy Process Method, the operations to be performed using this basis are carried out in six steps and these steps are called the steps of the Analytic Hierarchy Process Method. These steps are as follows (Al-Harbi, 2001; Saaty, 2004):

- Defining the Problem
- Observing the System
- Establishing the Hierarchical Structure
- Determining the Priorities
- Synthesising
- Calculating the Consistency Ratio and Evaluation

Analytical Hierarchy Process Method applications start with the determination of the problem or objective as in all other scientific methods. Then the observation of the system, in which the criteria affecting the problem or objective are determined, is started. All the factors affecting the problem or objective are determined here. These criteria are then ranked one below the objective depending on the objective. If only criteria are included in this ranking, these criteria are included. However, if one of the alternatives is to be selected among certain alternatives based on these criteria, alternatives are listed under all criteria. After the model is expressed hierarchically in this way, the pairwise comparison matrices in Table 3 are created in line with the expert opinions by using the pairwise comparison scale given in Table 2. In this way, priorities are determined. At this point, it should be reminded again that more than one expert opinion should be consulted and these opinions are converted into a single data by group averaging technique. Then, in the synthesis phase, the importance levels of the criteria are determined by using the synthesis steps given below. These importance levels are called the priorities vector and indicate which of the criteria is the most important. The criteria are ranked from the most important to the least important using this vector. The last stage of the Analytic Hierarchy Process Method is the consistency calculation. As the Analytical Hierarchy Process Method is based on the personal judgements of experts, it is desired to be consistent in the comparisons made. That is why the consistency ratio is determined. If it is determined that a matrix is not consistent, these matrices must be reconstructed by eliminating the inconsistencies. Otherwise, the analyses will not be realistic and erroneous decisions will be made (Vargas, 1990; Zeshui & Cuiping, 1999; Bhushan & Rai, 2004).

These are the general steps of the Analytical Hierarchy Process Method. Generally, after the steps of the method are expressed, the step of determining the priorities, which is the main purpose of the method, should be known with its mathematical formulation according to the process steps. In this context, the steps of the synthesis stage, which is used to rank the criteria by finding the priority values of the criteria in Analytic Hierarchy Process Method applications, should be known. The synthesis process is performed in three steps and these steps are expressed as follows (Vargas, 1990; Saaty, 2004):

- Step 1. The sum of the values in each column is taken.
- Step 2. Normalisation is performed by dividing each element by the sum of the column to which it belongs.
- Step 3. The average of the elements in each row of the normalised pairwise comparisons matrix is taken. These averages express the relative priorities of the compared items quite close to reality.

The priorities vector is calculated by following the three steps of the synthesis process mentioned above. Each value in this vector indicates the level of importance of the relevant criterion and according to these values, the criteria are ranked according to their importance. Analytic Hierarchy Process Method is a subjective multi-criteria decision-making method based on expert opinion, so the comparisons made by the experts must be made consistently. The consistency of the experts is checked by calculating the consistency ratios of the pairwise comparison matrices. While calculating the consistency ratio, the random index values given in Table 4 are used according to the number of criteria. When the calculated consistency ratio is equal to or less than 0.10, the pairwise comparison matrix is said to be consistent. If a consistency ratio higher than 0.10 is calculated, the pairwise comparison matrix is said to be inconsistent and needs to be reconstructed. In general, the five steps used in the calculation of the consistency ratio of pairwise comparison matrices in Analytic Hierarchy Process Method applications and the mathematical formulations of these steps are as follows (Srdjevic, 2005; Saaty, 2013; Kou et. al., 2016):

- Step 1. The values in the columns of the pairwise comparisons matrix are multiplied by the priority value of the relevant decision alternative and the values obtained are summed to obtain the total weight vector.
- Step 2. The elements in the weighted sum vector are divided by the corresponding priority values.
- Step 3. The values calculated in Step 2 are averaged and this average is denoted by the symbol λ_{max}.
- Step 4. Consistency Index (CI) is calculated. In the calculation of CI, n is the number of decision alternatives.

$$CI = \frac{\lambda_{max} - n}{n - 1}$$

- Step 5. Consistency Ratio (CR) is calculated. In the CR calculation, RI stands for the Random Index value.

$$CR = CI/RI$$

Table 4. Random index values (RI) (Saaty, 1980)

n	3	4	5	6	7	8
RI	0,58	0,90	1,12	1,24	1,32	1,41

In this study, after the Analytic Hierarchy Process Method is applied, the relationships between the criteria in the original model developed will be revealed by DEMATEL Method. For this reason, DEMATEL Method is explained and its mathematical formulation is given in the next section.

2.2. DEMATEL Method

The DEMATEL Method, which is a subjective multi-criteria decision-making method like the Analytic Hierarchy Process Method, was first developed by the Battelle Memorial Institute in Geneva in 1972. In DEMATEL Method applications, just like in the Analytic Hierarchy Process Method, expert opinions are consulted and multiple expert opinions are reduced to a single data by group averaging technique. In this method, in addition to the other method, the relationships between the criteria are revealed and the criteria are expressed as affected and influencing criteria. Thus, a general view of the problem is provided. For this reason, DEMATEL Method differs from other methods and becomes important. This method, first introduced by Fontela and Gabus in 1972, visualises the results obtained by giving a relationship graph as well as priority relationships and relationships between criteria (Kobryń, 2017; Si et. al., 2018; Bircan, 2020).

DEMATEL Method applications, the verbal opinions of the decision makers whose expert opinions are consulted are quantified with a linguistic scale between 0-4. This scale is shown in Table 5 (Ismail et. al., 2023).

Table 5. Linguistic scale used in DEMATEL method

Score	Variable
0	No Effect
1	Low Effect
2	Medium Effect
3	High Effect
4	Very High Effect

DEMATEL Method is applied and the experts express how one criterion has an effect on another criterion with the linguistic scale given in Table 5 (Ismail et. al., 2023). In the following, a direct relationship matrix is formed by taking the numerical value corresponding to this expressed effect in the linguistic scale. Analyses are made on the created direct relationship matrix. DEMATEL Method applications using the direct relationship matrix are expressed in six steps in the literature. These steps are as follows respectively (Chang et. Al., 2011):

- Determination of Direct Relationship Matrix
- Creation of Normalised Direct Relationship Matrix
- Creating the Total Relationship Matrix
- Identification of Affecting and Affected Criteria Groups
- Drawing Relationship Map and Influence Diagram
- Calculation of Criterion Weights

In the applications of the DEMATEL Method applied in six steps, after the direct relationship matrix is obtained, the weights of the criteria and the rankings among these criteria are determined by the mathematical method of the method. The mathematical formulation of the DEMATEL Method consisting of ten steps is as follows (Si et. Al. 2018; Bircan, 2020):

$$X = k.A$$

$$k = \frac{1}{\underset{1 \leq i \leq n}{max} \sum_{j=1}^{n} a_{ij}}, \; i,j = 1,2,\ldots,n$$

$$T = X + X^2 + \ldots + X^k$$

$$T = X(I + X + X^2 + \ldots + X^{k-1}$$

$$T = X(I + X + X^2 + \ldots + X^{k-1}).(I - X)(I - X)^{-1}$$

$$T = X.(I - X)^{-1}, \text{ when } h \rightarrow \infty$$

$$c = [c_i]_{1xn} = \left[\sum_{j=1}^{n} t_{ij}\right]_{1xn}$$

$$r = [r_j]_{nx1} = \left[\sum_{i=1}^{n} t_{ij}\right]_{nx1}$$

$$S_i = \sqrt{(D_i + R_i)^2 + (D_i - R_i)^2}\ ,\ i = 1,2,\ldots,n$$

$$w_i = \frac{s_i}{\sum_{i=1}^{n} s_i}$$

DEMATEL Method is applied by using ten mathematical formulations in six steps. While applying the DEMATEL Method, firstly a direct relationship matrix is created. The values of the criteria in each row of the direct relationship matrix in that row show its effect on the criteria in the columns. In multi-criteria decision making methods, raw data are usually normalised to eliminate extreme values. For this reason, in DEMATEL Method, direct relationship matrices are normalised and normalised direct relationship matrix is obtained. In the normalisation process, rows and columns of the direct relationship matrix are summed. Taking the highest total value, each value in the direct relationship matrix is divided by this degree. As a result, the direct relationship matrix is normalised. Then, as seen in the mathematical formulation, the total relationship matrix is obtained by applying the four formulas used for T value calculation respectively. After the total relationship matrix is obtained, D and R values are calculated to determine whether a criterion is an influencing criterion or an influenced criterion by using c and r formulae as shown in the mathematical formulation. In the last step, the weights of the criteria are determined by using the formula w (Chang et. al., 2011; Jassbi et. al., 2011; Chen & Huang, 2022).

In this study, it is aimed to determine the factors affecting the ability of digitalization and sustainability in enterprises. The subject is considered as a multi-criteria decision making problem. In this direction, the criteria were ranked with the Analytical Hierarchy Process Method, one of the multi-criteria decision making methods, and the relationships between these criteria were revealed with the DEMATEL Method. Since these two methods are used, only these two methods and application steps are explained among the multi-criteria decision making methods. In the next section, analyses are made using these two methods.

3. APPLICATIONS OF ANALYTICAL HIERARCHY PROCESS METHOD AND DEMATEL METHOD

Nowadays, digitalization and sustainability are among the issues that businesses face and deal with the most. In order for businesses to continue their activities by gaining competitive power, to meet the expectations of consumers, to comply with legal regulations, to fulfil their social responsibilities and to make a profit, they must successfully integrate digital transformation and sustainable activities into their business processes. This study therefore analyses which criteria should be considered when creating a digitalization and sustainable structure in enterprises and where to start the transformation process. In this direction, a unique model consisting of nine criteria was developed by making use of the literature on digitalization and sustainability. This model was used to rank the criteria using the Analytic Hierarchy Process Method and the relationships between these criteria were analysed using the DEMATEL Method. Two sector employees and three academicians were included in the study as experts. The opinions of these five experts were quantified with the relevant scales and analyses were made by taking their geometric averages. In this part of the study, these analyses made on Microsoft Excel are included.

Before proceeding with the method applications, the original model developed with the support of the literature for the Analytic Hierarchy Process Method and DEMATEL Method applications is shown in Figure 2. Firstly, Analytic Hierarchy Process Method and then DEMATEL Method were applied by using the mentioned criteria.

Figure 2. The model developed for the application of analytical hierarchy process method and DEMATEL method

3.1. Application With Analytical Hierarchy Process Method

In this study, the model developed as a result of the literature review and given in Figure 2 was used. In this context, firstly, the nine criteria in the model developed by the Analytic Hierarchy Process Method were compared. The opinions of five experts were quantified using the scale developed by Saaty.

Table 6. Pairwise comparison matrix in terms of criteria

	C1	C2	C3	C4	C5	C6	C7	C8	C9
C1	1,00	1,00	1/2	1/4	2,00	1/2	1/4	1/6	1,00
C2		1,00	1/2	1/3	2,00	1,00	1/2	1/5	1/2
C3			1,00	1/2	3,00	1,00	1,00	1/4	2,00

continued on following page

Table 6. Continued

	C1	C2	C3	C4	C5	C6	C7	C8	C9
C4				1,00	3,00	3,00	1,00	1/2	1/4
C5					1,00	1/3	1/4	1/7	1/2
C6						1,00	1/2	1/3	2,00
C7							1,00	1/2	3,00
C8								1,00	6,00
C9									1,00

The opinions of these five experts were converted into a single data by taking the geometric mean of each cell in the pairwise comparison matrix. The pairwise comparison matrix obtained as a result of the process is given in Table 6. In Table 6, the diagonal diagonal is shown in gray. The bottom of this diagonal is the inverse of the top with respect to the multiplication operation. In this way, the pairwise comparison matrix is completed and given in Table 7.

Table 7. Completed pairwise comparison matrix

	C1	C2	C3	C4	C5	C6	C7	C8	C9
C1	1,00	1,00	0,50	0,25	2,00	0,50	0,25	0,17	1,00
C2	1,00	1,00	0,50	0,33	2,00	1,00	0,50	0,20	0,50
C3	2,00	2,00	1,00	0,50	3,00	1,00	1,00	0,25	2,00
C4	4,00	3,00	2,00	1,00	3,00	3,00	1,00	0,50	0,25
C5	0,50	0,50	0,33	0,33	1,00	0,33	0,25	0,14	0,50
C6	2,00	1,00	1,00	0,33	3,00	1,00	0,50	0,33	2,00
C7	4,00	2,00	1,00	1,00	4,00	2,00	1,00	0,50	3,00
C8	6,00	5,00	4,00	2,00	7,00	3,00	2,00	1,00	6,00
C9	1,00	2,00	0,50	4,00	2,00	0,50	0,50	0,17	1,00
T	21,50	17,50	10,83	9,75	27,00	12,33	7,00	3,26	16,25

After creating two comparison matrices, each cell value is divided by the sum of the column in which it is located. By this way, a normalized pairwise comparison matrix is found. This matrix is calculated and presented in Table 8.

Table 8. Normalized pairwise comparison matrix

	C1	C2	C3	C4	C5	C6	C7	C8	C9
C1	0,05	0,06	0,05	0,03	0,07	0,04	0,04	0,05	0,06
C2	0,05	0,06	0,05	0,03	0,07	0,08	0,07	0,06	0,03
C3	0,09	0,11	0,09	0,05	0,11	0,08	0,14	0,08	0,12
C4	0,19	0,17	0,18	0,10	0,11	0,24	0,14	0,15	0,02
C5	0,02	0,03	0,03	0,03	0,04	0,03	0,04	0,04	0,03
C6	0,09	0,06	0,09	0,03	0,11	0,08	0,07	0,10	0,12
C7	0,19	0,11	0,09	0,10	0,15	0,16	0,14	0,15	0,18
C8	0,28	0,29	0,37	0,21	0,26	0,24	0,29	0,31	0,37
C9	0,05	0,11	0,05	0,41	0,07	0,04	0,07	0,05	0,06

Then, by taking the row averages of the normalized binary comparison matrix, the priorities vector is obtained. In the obtained priorities vector, each value is the priority of that criterion. These results obtained are given in Table 9.

Table 9. Analytical hierarchy process method analysis results

	Priority Value	Criteria Order
C1	0,049	8
C2	0,056	7
C3	0,098	5
C4	0,146	2
C5	0,032	9
C6	0,085	6
C7	0,143	3
C8	0,289	1
C9	0,102	4

As a result of the analyses conducted using the Analytical Hierarchy Process Method, the most important criterion was determined as the Corporate Culture (C1) criterion with a weight of 0.289. The other criteria are Senior Management with a criterion weight of 0.146 (C4), Technological Infrastructure with a criterion weight of 0.143 (C7), Supply Chain Management and Logistics with a criterion weight of 0.102 (C9), Technology Use with a criterion weight of 0.098 (C3), Data Management and Logistics with a criterion weight of 0.085 (C6), Environmental Factors with a criterion weight of 0.056 (C2), Legal Regulations with a criterion weight of 0.049 (C1) and at the least importance level, respectively the Financial Structure is in the form of (C5) with a criterion weight of 0.032. In other words, according to the results of the analysis, when businesses want to improve their capabilities for digitalization and sustainability, the main things they need to do are to develop corporate culture in this direction, support senior management by making strategic plans in this direction, develop technological infrastructure and use them.

By applying the Analytical Hierarchy Process Method in this way, the DEMATEL Method was applied to determine the relationships of these criteria to each other after the criteria were sorted.

3.2. Application With DEMATEL Method

Analytical Hierarchy Process Method DEMATEL Method starts with the creation of a direct relationship matrix where the criteria are in the row and column. While creating this matrix, each expert says how much a criterion in the row affects the criteria in the column. The same criteria have zero effect on each other. The direct relationship matrix is given in Table 10.

Table 10. Direct relationship matrix

	C1	C2	C3	C4	C5	C6	C7	C8	C9	Σ
C1	0,000	3,000	1,000	1,000	1,000	1,000	1,000	1,000	2,000	11,00
C2	1,000	0,000	1,000	1,000	1,000	1,000	2,000	1,000	2,000	10,00
C3	2,000	1,000	0,000	1,000	2,000	3,000	1,000	0,000	2,000	12,00
C4	0,000	1,000	3,000	0,000	3,000	2,000	2,000	3,000	3,000	17,00
C5	0,000	1,000	3,000	2,000	0,000	2,000	3,000	1,000	2,000	14,00
C6	1,000	1,000	4,000	1,000	1,000	0,000	1,000	0,000	3,000	12,00
C7	1,000	1,000	4,000	1,000	1,000	4,000	0,000	1,000	3,000	16,00
C8	0,000	1,000	2,000	3,000	0,000	1,000	1,000	0,000	1,000	9,00
C9	0,000	2,000	3,000	1,000	2,000	2,000	0,000	0,000	0,000	10,00
Σ	5,00	11,00	21,00	11,00	11,00	16,00	11,00	7,00	18,00	

After the direct relationship matrix is created, this matrix is normalized to remove extreme values. When creating this matrix, the rows and columns are totaled. Then each element is divided by its largest total value. The normalized direct relationship matrix is given in Table 11.

Table 11. Normalized direct relationship matrix (M)

	C1	C2	C3	C4	C5	C6	C7	C8	C9
C1	0,000	0,176	0,059	0,059	0,059	0,059	0,059	0,059	0,118
C2	0,059	0,000	0,059	0,059	0,059	0,059	0,118	0,059	0,118
C3	0,118	0,059	0,000	0,059	0,118	0,176	0,059	0,000	0,118
C4	0,000	0,059	0,176	0,000	0,176	0,118	0,118	0,176	0,176
C5	0,000	0,059	0,176	0,118	0,000	0,118	0,176	0,059	0,118
C6	0,059	0,059	0,235	0,059	0,059	0,000	0,059	0,000	0,176
C7	0,059	0,059	0,235	0,059	0,059	0,235	0,000	0,059	0,176
C8	0,000	0,059	0,118	0,176	0,000	0,059	0,059	0,000	0,059
C9	0,000	0,118	0,176	0,059	0,118	0,118	0,000	0,000	0,000

The normalized direct relationship matrix is subtracted from the identity matrix, then its inverse is taken. Then this value is multiplied by the normalized direct relationship matrix. The matrix obtained in this way is called the total relation matrix.

Table 12. Total relation matrix (T)

	C1	C2	C3	C4	C5	C6	C7	C8	C9	D
C1	0,094	0,326	0,371	0,213	0,240	0,307	0,219	0,148	0,378	2,295
C2	0,145	0,158	0,368	0,205	0,233	0,305	0,258	0,142	0,368	2,181
C3	0,216	0,246	0,369	0,227	0,318	0,444	0,237	0,100	0,419	2,575
C4	0,148	0,302	0,668	0,255	0,446	0,514	0,357	0,295	0,577	3,562
C5	0,137	0,269	0,605	0,316	0,257	0,470	0,372	0,176	0,482	3,084
C6	0,170	0,241	0,562	0,222	0,273	0,295	0,227	0,093	0,460	2,543
C7	0,203	0,292	0,678	0,276	0,329	0,582	0,221	0,169	0,554	3,304
C8	0,088	0,197	0,401	0,302	0,182	0,292	0,201	0,092	0,307	2,061
C9	0,100	0,257	0,462	0,201	0,290	0,352	0,164	0,083	0,262	2,171
R	1,298	2,288	4,484	2,219	2,567	3,561	2,256	1,298	3,805	

The sum of the rows of the total relation matrix is called D, and the sum of the columns is called R. D is the effect of the relevant criterion on other criteria. R is the effect of the relevant criterion from other criteria. These values are presented in Table 13.

Table 13. Influencing and influenced criteria

Criteria	D	R	D+R	D-R	Impact Status
C1	2,295	1,298	3,593	0,996	Influencing
C2	2,181	2,288	4,468	-0,107	Influenced
C3	2,575	4,484	7,059	-1,909	Influenced
C4	3,562	2,219	5,780	1,343	Influencing
C5	3,084	2,567	5,651	0,517	Influencing
C6	2,543	3,561	6,105	-1,018	Influenced
C7	3,304	2,256	5,560	1,048	Influencing
C8	2,061	1,298	3,359	0,763	Influencing
C9	2,171	3,805	5,975	-1,634	Influenced

*D+R: high or close, indicating that the criteria are related to each other.
**D-R: positives are affecting criteria, negatives are affected

As a result of the analysis made with DEMATEL Method, it was determined that C1, C4, C5, C7 and C8 criteria are affecting criteria and other criteria are affected criteria. In other words, legal regulations, Senor Manegement, Financial Structure, Technological Infrastructure and Corporate Culture criteria affect other criteria. On the other hand, Environmental Factors, Use of Technology, Data Mangement and Analysis, Supply Chain Management and Logistics criteria are affected by other criteria.

RESULTS AND CONCLUSION

The world has entered the digital age with the announcement of the last industrial revolution. As digital components have started to be used in the business world, businesses have started to operate in an intense competitive environment. This situation has brought many uncertainties. The ability of businesses to combat these uncertainties depends on how they integrate digital technologies into their business processes. In other words, businesses must ensure digital transformation within their operational network. Its success at this point directly affects the success of the business.

In this period of intense digitalization and the introduction of new technologies into our lives, another important phenomenon is sustainability. The concept of sustainability is important for businesses with its three dimensions: environmental, social and economic. Businesses operate under the constraints of legal regulations, social responsibilities of businesses and the responsibility to pollute the world less. Businesses need to implement environmentally friendly practices for a more livable world. This is an important area of work worldwide, as seen in the Paris Agreement and the European Green Deal.

Digitalization and the integration of sustainability perspectives into the business processes of businesses play a key role in the success of businesses in today's conditions. This study was therefore designed to help managers identify which criteria are important in these transformations and their starting points. Since the problem consists of many criteria, multi-criteria decision-making methods were used in this study. A model consisting of nine criteria was developed by conducting research on digitalization, sustainability and multi-criteria decision-making methods in the literature. Digital and sustainable criteria were included in the developed model. These criteria were then evaluated by five experts. As a result of these evaluations, which were converted into single data using the group average technique, the degree of importance of the criteria was determined by the Analytic Hierarchy Process Method and the relationships between the criteria were determined by the DEMATEL Method.

As a result of the Analytic Hierarchy Process Method analysis, the criteria were ranked in order of importance as follows: Corporate Culture (C1), Senior Management (C4), Technological Infrastructure (C7), Supply Chain Management and Logistics (C9), Technology Use (C3), Data Management and Logistics (C6), Environmental Factors (C2), Legal Regulations (C1) and Financial Structure (C5). As it is understood from this, what is important in evaluating the digital and sustainable capabilities of enterprises is the development of the corporate culture in this direction, the support of the top management to the transformation process, the creation of the vision and mission in this way, and the development of the technological infrastructure.

As a result of the analysis made with the DEMATEL Method, the affected and influencing criteria were determined. In this way, it is aimed to provide managers with a holistic perspective on the problem. Legal regulations, Senior Management, Financial Structure, Technological Infrastructure and Corporate Culture criteria affect other criteria. It is revealed that when Senior Management and Technological Infrastructure criteria, which have a high level of influence on other criteria, are prioritized; Technology Use, Data Management and Logistics, Supply Chain Management and Logistics and Corporate Culture will directly improve.

This study focuses on the criteria that determine the digital and sustainable capabilities of businesses in general. In this direction, Analytic Hierarchy Process Method and DEMATEL Method were used. Similar studies can be sector-specific, applied with a wider set of criteria including sub-criteria and other MCDM methods can be used.

REFERENCES

Al-Harbi, K. M. A. S. (2001). Application of the AHP in project management. *International Journal of Project Management, 19*(1), 19–27. DOI: 10.1016/S0263-7863(99)00038-1

Alizon, F., Shooter, S. B., & Simpson, T. W. (2008, January). Henry Ford and the Model T: lessons for product platforming and mass customization. In International Design Engineering Technical Conferences and Computers and Information in Engineering Conference (Vol. 43291, pp. 59-66).

Aruldoss, M., Lakshmi, T. M., & Venkatesan, V. P. (2013). A survey on multi criteria decision making methods and its applications. *American Journal of Information Systems, 1*(1), 31–43.

Basiago, A. D. (1998). Economic, social, and environmental sustainability in development theory and urban planning practice. *The Environmentalist, 19*(2), 145–161. DOI: 10.1023/A:1006697118620

Bhushan, N., & Rai, K. (2004). The analytic hierarchy process. In *Strategic decision making: applying the analytic hierarchy process* (pp. 11–21). Springer London. DOI: 10.1007/978-1-85233-864-0_2

Breuer, H., Fichter, K., Lüdeke-Freund, F., & Tiemann, I. (2018). Sustainability-oriented business model development: Principles, criteria and tools. *International Journal of Entrepreneurial Venturing, 10*(2), 256–286. DOI: 10.1504/IJEV.2018.092715

Brodovskaya, E. V., Dombrovskaya, A. Y., Pyrma, R. V., & Azarov, A. A. (2020). Criteria for rating the level and quality of digitalization of the educational process in universities of the Russian Federation. *Vestnik Volgogradskogo Gosudarstvennogo Universiteta. Serii a 4, Istorii a , Regionovedenie, Mezhdunarodnye Otnoshenii a , 25*(2), 268-283.

Chang, B., Chang, C. W., & Wu, C. H. (2011). Fuzzy DEMATEL method for developing supplier selection criteria. *Expert Systems with Applications, 38*(3), 1850–1858. DOI: 10.1016/j.eswa.2010.07.114

Chen, C. Y., & Huang, J. J. (2022). A novel DEMATEL approach by considering normalization and invertibility. *Symmetry, 14*(6), 1109. DOI: 10.3390/sym14061109

Cinelli, M., Coles, S. R., & Kirwan, K. (2014). Analysis of the potentials of multi criteria decision analysis methods to conduct sustainability assessment. *Ecological Indicators, 46*, 138–148. DOI: 10.1016/j.ecolind.2014.06.011

De Vries, J. (1994). The industrial revolution and the industrious revolution. *The Journal of Economic History*, *54*(2), 249–270. DOI: 10.1017/S0022050700014467

Deepu, T. S., & Ravi, V. (2021). Supply chain digitalization: An integrated MCDM approach for inter-organizational information systems selection in an electronic supply chain. *International Journal of Information Management Data Insights*, *1*(2), 100038. DOI: 10.1016/j.jjimei.2021.100038

Doane, D., & MacGillivray, A. (2001). Economic sustainability: The business of staying in business. *New Economics Foundation*, *1*, 52.

Dubey, A., & Lal, R. (2009). Carbon footprint and sustainability of agricultural production systems in Punjab, India, and Ohio, USA. *Journal of Crop Improvement*, *23*(4), 332–350. DOI: 10.1080/15427520902969906

Fetting, C. (2020). The European green deal. ESDN Report, December, 2(9), 53.

Grover, V., & Malhotra, M. K. (1997). Business process reengineering: A tutorial on the concept, evolution, method, technology and application. *Journal of Operations Management*, *15*(3), 193–213. DOI: 10.1016/S0272-6963(96)00104-0

Hallstedt, S. I. (2017). Sustainability criteria and sustainability compliance index for decision support in product development. *Journal of Cleaner Production*, *140*, 251–266. DOI: 10.1016/j.jclepro.2015.06.068

Ismail, J. N., Rodzi, Z., Al-Sharqi, F., Hashim, H., & Sulaiman, N. H. (2023). The Integrated Novel Framework: Linguistic Variables in Pythagorean Neutrosophic Set with DEMATEL for Enhanced Decision Support. [IJNS]. *International Journal of Neutrosophic Science*, *21*(2), 129–141. DOI: 10.54216/IJNS.210212

Jamwal, A., Agrawal, R., Sharma, M., & Kumar, V. (2021). Review on multi-criteria decision analysis in sustainable manufacturing decision making. *International Journal of Sustainable Engineering*, *14*(3), 202–225. DOI: 10.1080/19397038.2020.1866708

Jassbi, J., Mohamadnejad, F., & Nasrollahzadeh, H. (2011). A Fuzzy DEMATEL framework for modeling cause and effect relationships of strategy map. *Expert Systems with Applications*, *38*(5), 5967–5973. DOI: 10.1016/j.eswa.2010.11.026

Kaivo-Oja, J. R. L., & Lauraeus, I. T. (2018). The VUCA approach as a solution concept to corporate foresight challenges and global technological disruption. foresight, 20(1), 27-49.

Khalili, N. R., & Duecker, S. (2013). Application of multi-criteria decision analysis in design of sustainable environmental management system framework. *Journal of Cleaner Production*, *47*, 188–198. DOI: 10.1016/j.jclepro.2012.10.044

Kobryń, A. (2017). DEMATEL as a weighting method in multi-criteria decision analysis. *Multiple Criteria Decision Making, 12*(12), 153–167. DOI: 10.22367/mcdm.2017.12.11

Kou, G., Ergu, D., Lin, C., & Chen, Y. (2016). Pairwise comparison matrix in multiple criteria decision making. *Technological and Economic Development of Economy, 22*(5), 738–765. DOI: 10.3846/20294913.2016.1210694

Mardani, A., Zavadskas, E. K., Khalifah, Z., Zakuan, N., Jusoh, A., Nor, K. M., & Khoshnoudi, M. (2017). A review of multi-criteria decision-making applications to solve energy management problems: Two decades from 1995 to 2015. *Renewable & Sustainable Energy Reviews, 71*, 216–256. DOI: 10.1016/j.rser.2016.12.053

Maretto, L., Faccio, M., & Battini, D. (2022). A multi-criteria decision-making model based on fuzzy logic and AHP for the selection of digital technologies. *IFAC-PapersOnLine, 55*(2), 319–324. DOI: 10.1016/j.ifacol.2022.04.213

Markevičius, A., Katinas, V., Perednis, E., & Tamašauskienė, M. (2010). Trends and sustainability criteria of the production and use of liquid biofuels. *Renewable & Sustainable Energy Reviews, 14*(9), 3226–3231. DOI: 10.1016/j.rser.2010.07.015

Marmara, A. (2006). *Sürdürülebilir Kalkınma Çerçevesinde İşletmelerin Sosyal Sorumluluğu* (Master's thesis, Sakarya Universitesi (Turkey)).

Mian, S. H., & Al-Ahmari, A. (2019). Comparative analysis of different digitization systems and selection of best alternative. *Journal of Intelligent Manufacturing, 30*(5), 2039–2067. DOI: 10.1007/s10845-017-1371-x

Munirathinam, S. (2020). Industry 4.0: Industrial internet of things (IIOT). [). Elsevier.]. *Advances in Computers, 117*(1), 129–164. DOI: 10.1016/bs.adcom.2019.10.010

Nordelöf, A., Messagie, M., Tillman, A. M., Ljunggren Söderman, M., & Van Mierlo, J. (2014). Environmental impacts of hybrid, plug-in hybrid, and battery electric vehicles—What can we learn from life cycle assessment? *The International Journal of Life Cycle Assessment, 19*(11), 1866–1890. DOI: 10.1007/s11367-014-0788-0

Özdağoğlu, A., & Özdağoğlu, G. (2007). Comparison of AHP and fuzzy AHP for the multi-criteria decision making processes with linguistic evaluations. İstanbul Ticaret Üniversitesi. *Fen Bilimleri Dergisi, 6*(11), 65–85.

Parviainen, P., Tihinen, M., Kääriäinen, J., & Teppola, S. (2017). Tackling the digitalization challenge: how to benefit from digitalization in practice. International journal of information systems and project management, 5(1), 63-77.

Rachmad, Y. E. (2003). *Digital Ecological Transformation Philosophy Theory*. Education Training Centre.

Rondinelli, D. A., & Berry, M. A. (2000). Environmental citizenship in multinational corporations: Social responsibility and sustainable development. *European Management Journal*, *18*(1), 70–84. DOI: 10.1016/S0263-2373(99)00070-5

Saaty, T. (1980, November). The analytic hierarchy process (AHP) for decision making. In Kobe, Japan (Vol. 1, p. 69).

Saaty, T. L. (2001). Fundamentals of the analytic hierarchy process. The analytic hierarchy process in natural resource and environmental decision making, 15-35.

Saaty, T. L. (2004). Decision making—The analytic hierarchy and network processes (AHP/ANP). *Journal of Systems Science and Systems Engineering*, *13*(1), 1–35. DOI: 10.1007/s11518-006-0151-5

Saaty, T. L. (2008). Relative measurement and its generalization in decision making why pairwise comparisons are central in mathematics for the measurement of intangible factors the analytic hierarchy/network process. RACSAM-Revista de la Real Academia de Ciencias Exactas, Fisicas y Naturales. Serie A. *Matematicas*, *102*, 251–318.

Saaty, T. L. (2013). Analytic hierarchy process. In *Encyclopedia of operations research and management science* (pp. 52–64). Springer. DOI: 10.1007/978-1-4419-1153-7_31

Saaty, T. L., & Vargas, L. G. (2012). *Models, methods, concepts & applications of the analytic hierarchy process* (Vol. 175). Springer Science & Business Media. DOI: 10.1007/978-1-4614-3597-6

Salimian, S., & Mousavi, S. M. (2023). A multi-criteria decision-making model with interval-valued intuitionistic fuzzy sets for evaluating digital technology strategies in COVID-19 pandemic under uncertainty. *Arabian Journal for Science and Engineering*, *48*(5), 7005–7017. DOI: 10.1007/s13369-022-07168-8 PMID: 36090763

Savaresi, A. (2016). The Paris Agreement: A new beginning? *Journal of Energy & Natural Resources Law*, *34*(1), 16–26. DOI: 10.1080/02646811.2016.1133983

Seidel, S., Recker, J., & Vom Brocke, J. (2013). Sensemaking and sustainable practicing: Functional affordances of information systems in green transformations. *Management Information Systems Quarterly*, *37*(4), 1275–1299. DOI: 10.25300/MISQ/2013/37.4.13

Sergi, D., & Ucal Sari, I. (2021). Prioritization of public services for digitalization using fuzzy Z-AHP and fuzzy Z-WASPAS. *Complex & Intelligent Systems*, *7*(2), 841–856. DOI: 10.1007/s40747-020-00239-z

Shrivastava, P. (2018). Environmental technologies and competitive advantage. In *Business Ethics and Strategy* (Vol. I and II, pp. 317–334). Routledge.

Si, S. L., You, X. Y., Liu, H. C., & Zhang, P. (2018). DEMATEL technique: A systematic review of the state-of-the-art literature on methodologies and applications. *Mathematical Problems in Engineering*, *2018*(1), 3696457. DOI: 10.1155/2018/3696457

Singh, S., Agrawal, V., & Mohanty, R. P. (2022). Multi-criteria decision analysis of significant enablers for a competitive supply chain. *Journal of Advances in Management Research*, *19*(3), 414–442. DOI: 10.1108/JAMR-09-2021-0322

Sipahi, S., & Timor, M. (2010). The analytic hierarchy process and analytic network process: An overview of applications. *Management Decision*, *48*(5), 775–808. DOI: 10.1108/00251741011043920

Srdjevic, B. (2005). Combining different prioritization methods in the analytic hierarchy process synthesis. *Computers & Operations Research*, *32*(7), 1897–1919. DOI: 10.1016/j.cor.2003.12.005

Stankovic, J. J., Marjanovic, I., Drezgic, S., & Popovic, Z. (2021). The digital competitiveness of European countries: A multiple-criteria approach. *Journal of Competitiveness*, *13*(2), 117–134. DOI: 10.7441/joc.2021.02.07

Stearns, P. N. (2020). *The industrial revolution in world history*. Routledge. DOI: 10.4324/9781003050186

Tolliver, C., Keeley, A. R., & Managi, S. (2020). Drivers of green bond market growth: The importance of Nationally Determined Contributions to the Paris Agreement and implications for sustainability. *Journal of Cleaner Production*, *244*, 118643. DOI: 10.1016/j.jclepro.2019.118643

Vargas, L. G. (1990). An overview of the analytic hierarchy process and its applications. *European Journal of Operational Research*, *48*(1), 2–8. DOI: 10.1016/0377-2217(90)90056-H

Wang, J. J., Jing, Y. Y., Zhang, C. F., & Zhao, J. H. (2009). Review on multi-criteria decision analysis aid in sustainable energy decision-making. *Renewable & Sustainable Energy Reviews*, *13*(9), 2263–2278. DOI: 10.1016/j.rser.2009.06.021

Weber, O., Scholz, R. W., & Michalik, G. (2010). Incorporating sustainability criteria into credit risk management. *Business Strategy and the Environment, 19*(1), 39–50. DOI: 10.1002/bse.636

Xu, M., David, J. M., & Kim, S. H. (2018). The fourth industrial revolution: Opportunities and challenges. International journal of financial research, 9(2), 90-95.

Yang, J. L., & Tzeng, G. H. (2011). An integrated MCDM technique combined with DEMATEL for a novel cluster-weighted with ANP method. *Expert Systems with Applications, 38*(3), 1417–1424. DOI: 10.1016/j.eswa.2010.07.048

Zeshui, X., & Cuiping, W. (1999). A consistency improving method in the analytic hierarchy process. *European Journal of Operational Research, 116*(2), 443–449. DOI: 10.1016/S0377-2217(98)00109-X

KEY TERMS AND DEFINITIONS

Digitalization: It is the execution of activities in a digital environment by integrating digital components such as the Internet, IoT, cloud computing, sensors and big data analytics into business processes.

Sustainability: It is the ability to meet the needs of the present without compromising the ability of future generations to meet their own needs.

Analytical Hierarchy Process Method: It is a subjective MCDM method based on linear programming developed to make a selection or sorting.

DEMATEL Method: It is a subjective MCDM method that reveals the relationships between the criteria in addition to the ranking of the criteria in the process of solving a problem or examining the criteria for a purpose.

Chapter 8

Assessment of Türkiye's Healthcare Quality Standards Using the FUCOM Method:

FUCOM Method

Banu Bolayır
Gümüşhane University, Turkey

ABSTRACT

This study aims to determine the importance ranking of healthcare quality standards in Türkiye. The latest version of the Healthcare Quality Standards-Hospital (Version 6.1) was used as the healthcare quality standards in Türkiye. The FUCOM method, one of the multi-criteria decision-making (MCDM) methods, was employed to rank the importance of these standards. To use this method, a questionnaire based on the healthcare quality standards was filled out by six experts. The data obtained from the questionnaire were transferred to Microsoft Excel Solver, and the FUCOM method was used with this program. Using the FUCOM method, the local importance weights of the main criteria and sub-criteria were initially determined. Then, the criteria were ranked based on these weights. Subsequently, after determining the global importance weights of the sub-criteria considering the local importance weights of both the main criteria and sub-criteria, their rankings were also established based on these weights.

DOI: 10.4018/979-8-3693-8789-4.ch008

INTRODUCTION

To achieve the highest level of service in the service industry, it is necessary to establish quality standards suitable for that industry. Considering the importance of human life, the most significant one among service industries is the healthcare sector. Establishing quality standards to provide individuals with the best service and adhering to these standards in the healthcare sector will facilitate operations for both the healthcare industry and society, as well as benefit the national economy. Moreover, evaluating these quality standards, addressing deficiencies, and/or making necessary changes will contribute to improvements in the healthcare sector. Utilizing digitalization to make prompt corrections will also save time. All these actions will contribute to the economic and social dimensions of sustainable development.

Studies addressing the quality in healthcare were brought to the agenda in Türkiye with the "Health Transformation Program" in 2003, and the General Directorate of Health Services initiated these studies. Accordingly, a quality system was defined to establish, enhance, and improve the quality objectives regarding health services by considering the World Health Organization's (WHO) goals, international developments, and Türkiye's priorities and needs, to establish common quality standards in the healthcare field in Türkiye, and to make evaluations according to these standards. Standard sets were created for the service areas in this system, and evaluations were conducted based on these sets (General Directorate of Health Services, 2020).

The healthcare quality standards prepared by the Ministry of Health in Türkiye underwent revisions in 2005, 2007, 2008, 2009, 2011, 2016, and 2020, and the current standards used for hospitals were achieved (General Directorate of Health Services, n.d.; General Directorate of Health Services, 2016).

The versions prepared related to healthcare quality standards include the "Service Quality Standards Guide (Version 2.0)" in 2008, "Service Quality Standards for Private Hospitals (Version 3)" in 2009, "Hospital Service Quality Standards (Version 4)" in 2011, "Healthcare Quality Standards-Hospital (Version 5)" in 2016, and both "Healthcare Quality Standards-Hospital (Version 6.0)" and "Healthcare Quality Standards-Hospital (Version 6.1)" in 2020 (General Directorate of Health Services, n.d.). Moreover, the Healthcare Quality Standards-Hospital was prepared for all public and private hospitals providing healthcare services in Türkiye (General Directorate of Health Services, 2020).

In this study, the FUCOM method, one of the MCDM methods, was applied by using Microsoft Excel Solver to determine the importance ranking of the standards in the latest version of the Healthcare Quality Standards-Hospital (Version 6.1) prepared for healthcare quality standards in Türkiye. In the present study, the standards in the Healthcare Quality Standards-Hospital (Version 6.1) and their sub-standards were taken as main criteria and sub-criteria. An FUCOM survey was prepared based on five main criteria and a total of forty-five sub-criteria, and the opinions of six experts were gathered. As a result of the FUCOM method application, the local importance weights of the main and sub-criteria, their rankings according to these weights, and the global importance weights of the sub-criteria, derived from the local importance weights of the main and sub-criteria, and their rankings were found. This study is expected to contribute to the literature in healthcare and MCDM fields by using the FUCOM method in healthcare quality evaluation and to serve as a resource for future studies in determining the importance rankings of healthcare quality standards in Türkiye.

The present study was organized as follows. The introduction section provides information on healthcare quality standards in Türkiye. The first section presents a literature review on MCDM methods in healthcare quality evaluation and studies specifically using the FUCOM method. The second section, the methodology, explains the theoretical structure of the FUCOM method. The third section includes the FUCOM method application, where the importance weights and rankings of the standards in the Healthcare Quality Standards-Hospital (Version 6.1) according to expert opinions were determined using Microsoft Excel Solver. The final section, the fourth, contains the conclusion and suggestions of the application findings.

LITERATURE REVIEW

In the literature, there are many studies and practices involving multicriteria decision-making (MCDM) methods. Some of these studies carried out in the health sector that evaluate quality using MCDM methods related to this research are provided below.

In the study carried out by Herrera et al. (2008), the Analytic Hierarchy Process (AHP), one of the MCDM methods, was used to analyze the service quality of an information and communication technology network system in healthcare services. Their study involved a pilot survey based on user perception, encompassing three hospital categories in Chile. Data collection was conducted by considering various representatives from the health sector. In the AHP method used in their study, three criteria were established: clinical care, medical research, and management, with five sub-criteria identified for each criterion: reliability, functionality, usability, service convenience, and efficiency. The implementation of the method revealed that, in terms of importance ranking, the most critical criterion was clinical care, with usability as the key sub-criterion under clinical care, functionality under medical research, and efficiency under management. Their study offers insights into making decisions related to a system linked to an information technology network, characterizing end-users and their needs, and ensuring their alignment with institutional goals.

Shieh et al. (2010) aimed to identify the key determinants of success regarding hospital service quality. For this purpose, they conducted a survey at a hospital in Taiwan by using the SERVQUAL model to determine seven main criteria considering the perspectives of patients or their relatives. After establishing the main criteria, they developed a second survey to assess the importance of these criteria by making use of the DEMATEL (Decision Making Trial and Evaluation Laboratory) method.

In their study, Büyüközkan et al. (2011) aimed to evaluate service quality in the healthcare sector. For this purpose, they utilized the fuzzy AHP method to examine the service quality of some leading hospitals in Türkiye. Given the literature review conducted in their study, six main criteria - empathy, physical structure, assurance, reliability, professionalism, and responsiveness - and a total of nineteen sub-criteria were identified, with four hospitals considered as alternatives. The study emphasized the need for greater emphasis on empathy, reliability, and professionalism for hospitals to provide satisfactory and high-quality service according to the importance ranking of the fuzzy AHP method. Additionally, the study ranked the hospitals based on their service quality.

In their study carried out by using AHP, fuzzy decision-making, SERVQUAL, and TOPSIS (Technique for Order Preference by Similarity to Ideal Solution) methods to assess and compare the service quality of four hospitals in Iran, Afkham et al. (2012) highlighted the importance of hospitals, which are responsible for human lives, from the aspect of service quality in the health sector. They noted that service quality, typically consisting of abstract concepts, is difficult to measure, and therefore, proposed a fuzzy method to eliminate the uncertainty in these measurements. The SERVQUAL model was utilized to assess the service quality assessments of survey participants. For comparing the hospitals, they utilized the fuzzy AHP method to reveal the importance weights and the TOPSIS method to rank the hospitals.

In their study, Büyüközkan and Çifçi (2012) measured the service quality of the websites of private hospitals in Türkiye by using fuzzy AHP and fuzzy TOPSIS methods. Given the literature review conducted in their study, six main criteria - information quality, empathy, physical structure, assurance, reliability, and responsiveness - and a total of twenty sub-criteria were identified, with thirteen hospitals in Türkiye considered as alternatives. They concluded that reliability and responsiveness were the most critical criteria in terms of importance ranking, and they ranked the websites of the thirteen hospitals based on their service quality.

Khan et al. (2012) aimed to assess the service quality of corporate hospitals in their study. For this purpose, they chose five corporate hospitals in Tamil Nadu, India. The service quality in these hospitals was determined based on the five dimensions of the SERVQUAL model - empathy, physical structure, assurance, reliability, and responsiveness. These dimensions were taken as the main criteria, and a total of ten sub-criteria were identified to evaluate the service quality of the five hospitals using the AHP method. The results obtained from the AHP method were used in ranking the criteria, sub-criteria, and the five hospitals selected as alternatives.

In a previous study, Akdag et al. (2014) used four MCDM methods to assess the service quality of Turkish hospitals: AHP, TOPSIS, Ordered Weighted Averaging (OWA), and Yager's min-max approach. Their study was carried out in four B-class hospitals (private hospitals in Türkiye are divided into different classes.) affiliated with the Social Security Institution (SGK) in Istanbul. An expert panel consisting of three medical doctors and three academics was assembled to determine the importance weights of the forty-six criteria identified in this study by using the AHP method. The implementation of these methods revealed that the ranking of hospitals in terms of quality remained consistent across the different methods.

In a study, Chang (2014) used the fuzzy VIKOR (VlseKriterijumska Optimizacija I Kompromisno Resenje) method to evaluate the service quality of hospitals. This study involved two public and three private hospitals in Taiwan, which were assessed by eighteen evaluators by considering thirty-three criteria. The analysis revealed that private hospitals provided better service quality compared to public hospitals.

In their study, Alimohammadzadeh et al. (2016) utilized the AHP method to assess the service quality of radiology departments in six teaching hospitals in Tehran, Iran, in 2015. Using the standards of the Joint Commission International (JCI), four criteria were established: requirements and facilities, safety, quality improvement and data collection, and human resources management and empowerment. Expert Choice 10.0 software was utilized for the AHP analysis. The results they achieved indicated that "human resources management and empowerment" was the most important criterion, whereas the "requirements and opportunities" criterion was considered the least important.

In their study, Jiang et al. (2017) developed a model to measure the quality of public health service organizations using the fuzzy Delphi and weighted TOPSIS methods.

Yüksel and Arıkan (2019) collected the opinions of service users through surveys to assess the service quality of different types of hospitals in Ankara. The AHP method was used to calculate the weights of the survey criteria, and the fuzzy TOPSIS method, based on a two-element linguistic representation model, was used to assess the service quality of hospital types by considering these weights. The survey was designed according to the dimensions of empathy, physical conditions, assurance, reliability, and responsiveness from the SERVQUAL model. These dimensions were considered as the main criteria, and their forty-two sub-criteria were identified, with four types of hospitals - public, private, university, and research and training - used as alternatives. The study concluded that, in terms of service quality, private hospitals in Ankara offered superior services.

In the study carried out by Kar and Özer (2020), the VIKOR method was utilized to evaluate the necessary resources, the total services provided with these resources, and the health outcomes achieved in Türkiye's twelve Nomenclature of Territorial Units for Statistics (NUTS)-1 regions. Using data from these statistical regions, three different rankings were established: healthcare infrastructure, healthcare utilization, and health outcomes. Their study identified eight criteria for healthcare infrastructure, nine criteria for healthcare utilization, and five criteria for health outcomes. The results showed that the Eastern Black Sea region ranked highest for healthcare infrastructure, while the Southeastern Anatolia region ranked lowest. For healthcare utilization, Western Anatolia ranked highest, and Middle Eastern Anatolia ranked lowest. In terms of health outcomes, Central Anatolia ranked highest, and Southeastern Anatolia ranked lowest.

Yucesan and Gul (2020) developed a model based on Pythagorean fuzzy AHP and fuzzy TOPSIS methods to assess hospital service quality. The authors identified six criteria—hospital equipment, service attitude, pharmacy and medical treatment, professional competence, management policies, and hospital cleanliness - and a total of thirty-two sub-criteria, with three hospitals (two public and one private) used as alternatives. The developed model produced meaningful and reliable results that better represented uncertainty in the decision-making process.

In a study, Derici and Doğan (2021) used fuzzy AHP to assess the service quality of hospitals from the perspective of patients, emphasizing the importance of service quality in the healthcare sector for meeting community and individual health needs. The hierarchy of criteria affecting hospital service quality was established by adding a professionalism dimension to the SERVQUAL model's five dimensions: empathy, tangibles, assurance, reliability, and responsiveness. Their study included six main criteria and eighteen sub-criteria, with twenty-three patients interviewed. The group average of the data obtained from these patients was used for the fuzzy AHP analysis. The authors concluded that reliability was the most important criterion, while tangibles were the least important. Among the sub-criteria, staff expertise was found to be the most significant, while compensation was the least significant.

Examining the studies carried out using the FUCOM method in the literature, it can be seen that despite its recent introduction, this method was used in various fields. These studies include those carried out by Durmić (2019), Durmić et al. (2020), and Ecer (2021a) on sustainable supplier selection, those carried out by Fazlollahtabar et al. (2019) on forklift selection; Pamucar et al. (2020) on transportation demand management, the one carried out by Stević and Brković (2020) on human resources management, the one carried out by Ayçin and Aşan (2021) on the selection of business intelligence applications, the one carried out by Ecer (2021b) on wind farm site selection, the one carried out by Abdullah et al. (2022) on healthcare performance management, the one carried out by Badi et al. (2022)

on sustainable performance indicators, those carried out by Everest et al. (2022) and Roosta et al. (2024) on agricultural land management, the one carried out by Arman and Kundakcı (2023) on cloud service provider selection, the one carried out by Çilek and Şeyranlıoğlu (2023) on mobile banking usage, the one carried out by Duško and Bozanic (2023) on optimizing military decision-making processes, the one carried out by Mercan and Can (2023) on employee selection, the one carried out by Badi et al. (2024) on parallel machine scheduling, the one carried out by Kaya et al. (2024) on financial performance determination, the one carried out by Radenović et al. (2024) on waste management for solid waste landfill sites, and the one carried out by Rakhmangulov et al. (2024) on selecting dump truck models for transportation in mining operations.

Upon conducting a literature review regarding the subject examined in the present study, no study utilizing the FUCOM method in the evaluation of healthcare quality through MCDM methods could be found. The reason for choosing the FUCOM method in this study is that it offers the potential for more consistent solutions using fewer pairwise comparisons, and it facilitates easy resolution through a linear programming-based model. Therefore, this study aims to contribute to the literature by determining the prioritization of healthcare quality standards using the FUCOM method, one of the newer MCDM methods in the literature.

FUCOM METHOD

MCDM methods are analytical techniques that enable the simultaneous evaluation of numerous functional and strategic factors, both measurable and non-measurable, by incorporating multiple individuals into the decision-making process. These methods allow for the assessment of criteria and alternatives in the decision-making process, thereby ensuring the more efficient use of resources (Dağdeviren et al., 2005).

One of the fundamental challenges in MCDM problems is determining the weights of the criteria, and selecting the appropriate method for assigning these weights is the most critical phase that complicates the decision-making process. Since the determination of criteria weights can affect the results of the decision-making process, particular attention should be given to the objectivity of these weights (Pamucar et al., 2018). There are many objective and subjective methods for determining the weights of criteria in MCDM problems.

The FUCOM method (Full Consistency Method), a novel approach in the field of MCDM, was developed by Pamucar et al. in 2018 as a subjective method for weighting criteria. Based on the linear programming method, the FUCOM method offers several advantages: it evaluates criteria through pairwise comparisons of one less criterion than the total number, allowing for consistent and reliable calculation of criteria weights with fewer comparisons compared to methods like AHP, ANP (Analytic Network Process), and BWM (Best-Worst Method). It also features a simpler structure and can be utilized in group decision-making processes (Ayçin and Aşan, 2021; Ecer, 2021b; Pamucar et al., 2018). Additional advantages of the FUCOM method include the establishment of an objective function to minimize deviation values and the indication of accurate expert assessment when the objective function value is close to zero (Özdağoğlu et al., 2021). The preference for the FUCOM method over AHP and BWM in studies determining subjective criteria weights in MCDM is due to its elimination of unnecessary repetition in pairwise comparisons of criteria found in AHP and BWM models (Mercan and Can, 2023).

The steps utilized in the FUCOM method are presented below (Ayçin and Aşan, 2021; Ecer, 2021b; Pamucar et al., 2018):

Step 1. Ranking the Criteria by Importance by Decision-makers: Decision-makers rank the set of criteria $\boldsymbol{C} = \{\boldsymbol{C}_1, \boldsymbol{C}_2, \ldots, \boldsymbol{C}_n\}$, defined for the decision problem, from the criterion expected to have the highest weight coefficient to the criterion with the least importance. The criteria are then ranked by considering the expected values of the weight coefficients, as shown in formula (1). If two or more criteria hold equal importance, the ">" symbol in formula (1) is replaced with the "=" symbol to denote their ranking by equal importance.

$$\boldsymbol{C}_{j(1)} > \boldsymbol{C}_{j(2)} > \ldots > \boldsymbol{C}_{j(k)},\ \boldsymbol{k\ criterion\ degree} \tag{1}$$

Step 2. Determining the Mutual Priorities of the Ranked Criteria: The ranked criteria are compared by decision-makers, and the comparative priorities denoted by $\boldsymbol{\varphi}_{k/(k+1)}$ are determined, where k refers to the degree to which the ranking of criterion $\boldsymbol{C}_{j(k)}$ to advantageous in comparison to criterion $\boldsymbol{C}_{j(k+1)}$. The vectors of the comparative priorities of the evaluation criteria are thus obtained as shown in formula (2).

$$\boldsymbol{\Phi} = \left(\boldsymbol{\varphi}_{1/2}, \boldsymbol{\varphi}_{2/3}, \ldots, \boldsymbol{\varphi}_{k/(k+1)}\right) \tag{2}$$

Moreover, the FUCOM model permits the use of integer, decimal, or predefined scale values in the pairwise comparison of criteria within the decision problem.

Step 3. Calculating the Importance Weights of the Criteria with Determined Priorities: The final importance weights of the weight coefficients of the criteria $(\boldsymbol{w}_1, \boldsymbol{w}_2, \ldots, \boldsymbol{w}_n)^T$ are calculated. To compute the final importance weights of weight coefficients, conditions 1 and 2 must be met.

Condition 1: The ratio of the weight coefficients must equal the observed comparative priority between the criteria in Step 2, as shown in formula (3).

$$\varphi_{k/(k+1)} = \frac{w_k}{w_{k+1}} \tag{3}$$

Condition 2: In addition to formula (3), the final values of the weight coefficients must also satisfy the transitivity condition, where $\varphi_{k/(k+1)} \otimes \varphi_{(k+1)/(k+2)} = \varphi_{k/(k+2)}$. From formula (3), since $\varphi_{k/(k+1)} = \frac{w_k}{w_{k+1}}$ and $\varphi_{(k+1)/(k+2)} = \frac{w_{k+1}}{w_{k+2}}$, it yields $\frac{w_k}{w_{k+1}} \otimes \frac{w_{k+1}}{w_{k+2}} = \frac{w_k}{w_{k+2}}$. Thus, another condition that the final values of the weight coefficients must meet, as represented by formula (4), is obtained.

$$\frac{w_k}{w_{k+2}} = \varphi_{k/(k+1)} \otimes \varphi_{(k+1)/(k+2)} \tag{4}$$

If the conditions represented by formulas (3) and (4) are satisfied, full consistency, i.e., minimum Full Consistency Deviation (FCD), denoted by χ, is achieved. Thus, the maximum consistency requirement is met so that the FCD value for the obtained values of the weight coefficients will be χ=0. In other words, to meet the maximum consistency requirement, the values of the weight coefficients $(w_1, w_2, \ldots, w_n)^T$ must satisfy the conditions $\left|\frac{w_k}{w_{k+1}} - \varphi_{k/(k+1)}\right| \leq \chi$ and $\left|\frac{w_k}{w_{k+2}} - \varphi_{k/(k+1)} \otimes \varphi_{(k+1)/(k+2)}\right| \leq \chi$ by minimizing the value of χ. To clarify further, full consistency deviation represents the deviation of the calculated weight coefficients from the estimated comparative priorities of the criteria, and this value is calculated to test the reliability of the estimated weight coefficients. A value close to zero indicates that the weight coefficients are reliable.

Based on the definitions above, the linear programming model for determining the final values of the weight coefficients of the evaluation criteria is defined in formula (5).

Objective function: $min\chi$

Con traints:

$$\left|\frac{w_{j(k)}}{w_{j(k+1)}} - \varphi_{k/(k+1)}\right| \leq \chi, \forall j$$

$$\left|\frac{w_{j(k)}}{w_{j(k+2)}} - \varphi_{k/(k+1)} \otimes \varphi_{(k+1)/(k+2)}\right| \leq \chi, \forall j$$

$$\textstyle\sum_{j=1}^{n} w_j = 1$$

$$w_j \geq 0, \forall j \tag{5}$$

As a result of solving the linear programming model represented by formula (5), the final importance weights of the weight coefficients of the criteria $(w_1, w_2, \ldots, w_n)^T$ and the FCD(χ) value are obtained.

APPLICATION

In this study, the FUCOM method, which is one of the MCDM methods, was used due to its mathematical structure and implementation stages to determine the ranking and importance weights of healthcare quality standards in Türkiye. The main criteria and their sub-criteria, defined according to the standards outlined in the Turkish Healthcare Quality Standards-Hospital (Version 6.1), are presented in Table 1.

Table 1. Main and Sub-Criteria for Türkiye's Healthcare Quality Standards

Main Criteria	Sub-Criteria
A-Institutional Services	A1-Institutional Structure
	A2-Quality Management
	A3-Document Management
	A4-Risk Management
	A5-Institutional Efficiency
	A6-Incident Reporting System
	A7-Disaster and Emergency Management
	A8-Chemical, Biological, Radiological, and Nuclear (CBRN) Hazard Management
	A9-Education Management
	A10-Social Responsibility
B-Patient - and Employee - Centered Services	B1-Patient Experience
	B2-Service Accessibility
	B3-End-of-Life Services
	B4-Healthy Work Environment

continued on following page

Table 1. Continued

Main Criteria	Sub-Criteria
C-Healthcare Services	C1-Patient Care
	C2-Medication Management
	C3-Infection Prevention and Control
	C4-Cleaning, Disinfection, and Sterilization Services
	C5-Transfusion Services
	C6-Therapeutic Apheresis Services
	C7-Radiation Safety
	C8-Emergency Department
	C9-Operating Room
	C10-Intensive Care Unit
	C11-Neonatal Intensive Care Unit
	C12-Maternity Services
	C13-Dialysis Unit
	C14-Psychiatry Services
	C15-Community Mental Health Services
	C16-Biochemistry Laboratory
	C17-Microbiology Laboratory
	C18-Pathology Laboratory
	C19-Tissue Typing Laboratory
	C20-Chemotherapy Services
	C21-Organ and Tissue Transplantation Services
	C22-Physical Medicine and Rehabilitation Services
	C23-Palliative Care Clinic
	C24-Home Healthcare Services
D-Support Services	D1-Facility Management
	D2-Hospitality Services
	D3-Information Management System
	D4-Material and Equipment Management
	D5-Medical Records and Archive Services

Table 2. Cont.

Main Criteria	Sub-Criteria
D-Support Services	D6-Waste Management
	D7-Outsourcing
E- Indicator Management	

Source: (General Directorate of Health Services, 2020).

The FUCOM questionnaire, based on the main and sub-criteria presented in Table 1, was filled in by six expert decision-makers who are responsible for inspecting healthcare quality standards within the Provincial Health Directorate and the hospital's quality department. These experts included one deputy director of health services, one deputy director of support services, one provincial quality coordinator, one director of healthcare services, one quality director, and one quality unit supervisor. Furthermore, these six experts, five women and one man aged between 30 and 45, each have 5 to 15 years of experience working in the quality departments of the Provincial Health Directorate and the hospital. The experts evaluated both the main criteria and their sub-criteria in the FUCOM questionnaire using the 1-9 pairwise comparison scale developed by Saaty (2008), as presented in Table 2.

Table 3. Pairwise Comparison Scale

Importance Level	Definition
1	Equally important
2	Slightly important
3	Moderately important
4	Moderately more important
5	Important
6	More important
7	Very important
8	Extremely important
9	Absolutely important

Source: (Saaty, 2008).

The data obtained from the questionnaires were subjected to the application stages of the FUCOM method by using Microsoft Excel Solver software. Initially, the experts ranked the importance of the main and sub-criteria, and these rankings are presented in Table 3. After ranking the main and sub-criteria, the experts determined the pairwise priorities for both, according to the 1-9 scale shown in Table 2. In this evaluation, the experts assigned a value of "1" to the most important criterion and compared all other criteria to it, assigning scale values relative to the most important criterion. A crucial point to emphasize here is that the most important criterion was given a value of 1, and progressively larger values (e.g., 2) were assigned to slightly less important criteria. The pairwise priorities for the main and sub-criteria, as determined by the experts, are also presented in Table 3. In Table 3, the ">" symbol indicates that the criterion on the left is more important than the criterion on the right, while the "=" symbol signifies that the criteria are of equal importance.

Table 4. Experts' Importance Rankings and Reciprocal Priorities for Main and Sub-Criteria

<table>
<tr><th colspan="20">Expert 1</th></tr>
<tr><td rowspan="2">Importance Rankings for Main Criteria
Reciprocal Priorities for Main Criteria</td><td colspan="3">C</td><td>></td><td colspan="3">B</td><td>></td><td colspan="3">A</td><td>></td><td colspan="3">D</td><td>></td><td colspan="3">E</td></tr>
<tr><td colspan="3">1</td><td></td><td colspan="3">3</td><td></td><td colspan="3">5</td><td></td><td colspan="3">6</td><td></td><td colspan="3">9</td></tr>
<tr><td rowspan="2">Importance Rankings for Sub-Criteria under Institutional Services (A)
Reciprocal Priorities for Sub-Criteria under Institutional Services (A)</td><td>A4</td><td>=</td><td>A7</td><td>></td><td>A1</td><td>=</td><td>A5</td><td>></td><td>A2</td><td>=</td><td>A3</td><td>=</td><td>A6</td><td>=</td><td>A9</td><td>></td><td>A10</td><td>></td><td>A8</td></tr>
<tr><td>1</td><td></td><td>1</td><td></td><td>2</td><td></td><td>2</td><td></td><td>4</td><td></td><td>4</td><td></td><td>4</td><td></td><td>4</td><td></td><td>6</td><td></td><td>7</td></tr>
<tr><td rowspan="2">Importance Rankings for Sub-Criteria under Patient - and Employee - Oriented Services (B)
Reciprocal Priorities for Sub-Criteria under Patient - and Employee - Oriented Services (B)</td><td colspan="4">B2</td><td>></td><td colspan="4">B4</td><td>></td><td colspan="4">B1</td><td>></td><td colspan="4">B3</td></tr>
<tr><td colspan="4">1</td><td></td><td colspan="4">2</td><td></td><td colspan="4">4</td><td></td><td colspan="4">5</td></tr>
<tr><td>Importance Rankings for Sub-Criteria under Healthcare Services (C)
Reciprocal Priorities for Sub-Criteria under Healthcare Services (C)</td><td colspan="19">C3 = C4 > C1 = C2 > C8 = C9 = C10 = C11 = C12 = C20 = C21 = C22 = C23 = C24 > C5 = C7 = C16 > C13 > C14 = C15 > C17 > C18 > C19 = C6
1 1 2 2 3 3 3 3 3 3 3 3 3 3 4 4 4 5 6 6 7 8 9 9</td></tr>
</table>

continued on following page

Table 4. Continued

Expert 1

Importance Rankings for Sub-Criteria under Support Services (D) Reciprocal Priorities for Sub-Criteria under Support Services (D)	D2	>	D1	>	D3	=	D4	>	D6	>	D7	>	D5
	1		3		4		4		5		6		7

Expert 2

Importance Rankings for Main Criteria Reciprocal Priorities for Main Criteria	C	>	A	>	B	=	D	>	E
	1		3		5		5		9

Importance Rankings for Sub-Criteria under Institutional Services (A) Reciprocal Priorities for Sub-Criteria under Institutional Services (A)	A1	=	A2	>	A4	=	A7	=	A8	>	A3	=	A5	=	A6	=	A9	>	A10
	1		1		3		3		3		5		5		5		5		7

Importance Rankings for Sub-Criteria under Patient - and Employee - Oriented Services (B) Reciprocal Priorities for Sub-Criteria under Patient - and Employee - Oriented Services (B)	B4	>	B2	>	B1	>	B3
	1		3		4		6

Importance Rankings for Sub-Criteria under Healthcare Services (C) Reciprocal Priorities for Sub-Criteria under Healthcare Services (C)	C1 = C2 > C3 = C4 > C5 = C7 = C8 = C9 = C10 = C11 = C12 = C20 = C21 = C22 = C23 > C16 > C24 > C17 > C13= C14 = C15 = C18 > C6 > C19 1 1 2 2 3 3 3 3 3 3 3 3 3 3 3 4 5 6 7 7 7 7 8 9

Importance Rankings for Sub-Criteria under Support Services (D) Reciprocal Priorities for Sub-Criteria under Support Services (D)	D3	=	D4	>	D2	>	D1	>	D6	>	D7	>	D5
	1		1		3		4		5		6		7

Table 5. Cont.

Expert 3	
Importance Rankings for Main Criteria Reciprocal Priorities for Main Criteria	C > B > A = D > E 1 2 5 5 8
Importance Rankings for Sub-Criteria under Institutional Services (A) Reciprocal Priorities for Sub-Criteria under Institutional Services (A)	A4 = A7 > A5 > A2 > A1 > A9 > A3 > A8 > A6 > A10 1 1 2 3 4 5 6 7 8 9
Importance Rankings for Sub-Criteria under Patient - and Employee - Oriented Services (B) Reciprocal Priorities for Sub-Criteria under Patient - and Employee - Oriented Services (B)	B4 > B2 > B1 > B3 1 2 3 4
Importance Rankings for Sub-Criteria under Healthcare Services (C) Reciprocal Priorities for Sub-Criteria under Healthcare Services (C)	C1 = C2 > C3 = C4 > C5 = C7 = C8 = C9 > C16 > C17 > C18 > C19 > C10 = C11 = C12 = C13 = C14 = C15 = C20 = C21 = C22 = C23 = C24 > C6 1 1 2 2 3 3 3 3 4 5 6 7 8 8 8 8 8 8 8 8 8 8 8 9
Importance Rankings for Sub-Criteria under Support Services (D) Reciprocal Priorities for Sub-Criteria under Support Services (D)	D2 > D1 > D4 > D3 > D7 > D6 > D5 1 2 3 4 5 6 7
Expert 4	
Importance Rankings for Main Criteria Reciprocal Priorities for Main Criteria	A = C > B = D > E 1 1 3 3 9

continued on following page

Table 5. Continued

	Expert 3
Importance Rankings for Sub-Criteria under Institutional Services (A) Reciprocal Priorities for Sub-Criteria under Institutional Services (A)	A1 = A2 = A3 = A4 = A5 = A6 = A7 = A8 > A9 > A10 1 1 1 1 1 1 1 1 3 5
Importance Rankings for Sub-Criteria under Patient - and Employee - Oriented Services (B) Reciprocal Priorities for Sub-Criteria under Patient - and Employee - Oriented Services (B)	B1 = B4 > B2 > B3 1 1 3 5
Importance Rankings for Sub-Criteria under Healthcare Services (C) Reciprocal Priorities for Sub-Criteria under Healthcare Services (C)	C1 > C2 > C3 = C4 > C5 = C8 = C9 = C10 = C11 = C12 = C13 = C14 = C15 = C18 = C20 = C21 = C22 = C23 > C16 > C7 > C24 > C17 = C19 > C6 1 2 3 3 4 4 4 4 4 4 4 4 4 4 4 4 4 4 5 6 7 8 8 9
Importance Rankings for Sub-Criteria under Support Services (D) Reciprocal Priorities for Sub-Criteria under Support Services (D)	D6 = D7 > D1 = D2 = D3 = D4 = D5 1 1 3 3 3 3 3

Table 6. Cont.

	Expert 5
Importance Rankings for Main Criteria	C > A > B > E > D
Reciprocal Priorities for Main Criteria	1 3 4 5 6
Importance Rankings for Sub-Criteria under Institutional Services (A)	A1 = A2 > A4 > A7 > A9 > A3 > A8 > A6 > A5 > A10
Reciprocal Priorities for Sub-Criteria under Institutional Services (A)	1 1 2 3 4 5 6 7 8 9
Importance Rankings for Sub-Criteria under Patient - and Employee - Oriented Services (B)	B4 > B1 > B2 > B3
Reciprocal Priorities for Sub-Criteria under Patient - and Employee - Oriented Services (B)	1 2 3 4
Importance Rankings for Sub-Criteria under Healthcare Services (C)	C1 > C3 = C4 > C2 > C8 = C9 = C10 = C11 = C12 = C13 > C7 = C16 = C17 = C18 = C19 > C5 = C6 > C21 = C22 = C23 = C24 > C20 > C14 = C15
Reciprocal Priorities for Sub-Criteria under Healthcare Services (C)	1 2 2 3 4 4 4 4 4 4 5 5 5 5 5 6 6 7 7 7 7 8 9 9
Importance Rankings for Sub-Criteria under Support Services (D)	D1 = D3 > D2 > D6 > D4 > D5 > D7
Reciprocal Priorities for Sub-Criteria under Support Services (D)	1 1 3 4 5 6 7
Expert 6	
Importance Rankings for Main Criteria	A > C > D > B > E
Reciprocal Priorities for Main Criteria	1 2 4 5 7

continued on following page

Table 6. Continued

Expert 5	
Importance Rankings for Sub-Criteria under Institutional Services (A) Reciprocal Priorities for Sub-Criteria under Institutional Services (A)	A4 = A7 = A8 > A1 = A5 > A2 > A9 > A3 > A6 > A10 1 1 1 2 2 4 5 6 7 8
Importance Rankings for Sub-Criteria under Patient - and Employee - Oriented Services (B) Reciprocal Priorities for Sub-Criteria under Patient - and Employee - Oriented Services (B)	B1 = B2 > B4 > B3 1 1 5 7
Importance Rankings for Sub-Criteria under Healthcare Services (C) Reciprocal Priorities for Sub-Criteria under Healthcare Services (C)	C1 > C2 > C3 = C4 > C8 = C9 = C10 = C11 = C12 = C13 > C7 = C16 = C17 = C18 = C19 = C20 = C21 = C22 > C5 > C14 = C15 > C23 = C24 > C6 1 2 3 3 4 4 4 4 4 4 5 5 5 5 5 5 5 5 6 7 7 8 8 9
Importance Rankings for Sub-Criteria under Support Services (D) Reciprocal Priorities for Sub-Criteria under Support Services (D)	D2 > D1 > D3 > D4 > D7 > D6 > D5 1 2 3 4 5 6 7

Separate linear programming models were established for each expert's evaluations on main and sub-criteria, and their solutions were computed using Microsoft Excel Solver. The weights for the main and sub-criteria were found by using the calculations made, and the local importance weights were obtained by taking the arithmetic average of these weights. The values obtained are presented in Table 4. The deviation values from perfect consistency in the solutions of all linear programming models were found to be "χ=0." This indicates that the estimated weight coefficients are reliable. Additionally, the rankings of both main and sub-criteria according to local importance weights, from most to least important, are also provided in Table 4. Furthermore, no calculations were made for sub-criteria under the indicator management criterion (E) in Türkiye's healthcare quality standards (Table 1), as this criterion does not have sub-criteria.

Table 7. Local Importance Weights of the Main Criteria and Sub-Criteria and Their Rankings by These Local Importance Weights

Main Criteria	**Expert 1**	**Expert 2**	**Expert 3**	**Expert 4**	**Expert 3**	**Expert 6**	**Local Importance Weights**	**Rankings By Local Importance Weights**
A	0,110	0,181	0,099	0,360	0,171	0,478	0,233	2
B	0,184	0,108	0,247	0,120	0,128	0,096	0,147	3
C	0,552	0,542	0,494	0,360	0,513	0,239	0,450	1
D	0,092	0,108	0,099	0,120	0,103	0,119	0,107	4
E	0,061	0,060	0,062	0,040	0,085	0,068	0,063	5
Sub-Criteria under Institutional Services (A)	Expert 1	Expert 2	Expert 3	Expert 4	Expert 3	Expert 6	Local Importance Weights	Rankings By Local Importance Weights
A1	0,116	0,254	0,065	0,117	0,261	0,102	0,153	3
A2	0,058	0,254	0,087	0,117	0,261	0,051	0,138	4
A3	0,058	0,051	0,044	0,117	0,052	0,034	0,059	7
A4	0,232	0,085	0,261	0,117	0,131	0,205	0,172	1
A5	0,116	0,051	0,131	0,117	0,033	0,102	0,092	5
A6	0,058	0,051	0,033	0,117	0,037	0,029	0,054	8
A7	0,232	0,085	0,261	0,117	0,087	0,205	0,164	2
A8	0,033	0,085	0,037	0,117	0,044	0,205	0,087	6
A9	0,058	0,051	0,052	0,039	0,065	0,041	0,051	9
A10	0,039	0,036	0,029	0,023	0,029	0,026	0,030	10
Sub-Criteria under Patient - and Employee - Oriented Services (B)	Expert 1	Expert 2	Expert 3	Expert 4	Expert 3	Expert 6	Local Importance Weights	Rankings By Local Importance Weights
B1	0,128	0,143	0,160	0,395	0,240	0,427	0,249	3
B2	0,513	0,190	0,240	0,132	0,160	0,427	0,277	2
B3	0,103	0,095	0,120	0,079	0,120	0,061	0,096	4
B4	0,256	0,571	0,480	0,395	0,480	0,085	0,378	1

Table 8. Cont.

Sub-Criteria under Healthcare Services (C)	**Expert 1**	**Expert 2**	**Expert 3**	**Expert 4**	**Expert 3**	**Expert 6**	**Local Importance Weights**	**Rankings By Local Importance Weights**
C1	0,062	0,124	0,152	0,153	0,164	0,164	0,136	1
C2	0,062	0,124	0,152	0,076	0,055	0,082	0,092	2
C3	0,123	0,062	0,076	0,051	0,082	0,055	0,075	3
C4	0,123	0,062	0,076	0,051	0,082	0,055	0,075	3
C5	0,031	0,041	0,051	0,038	0,027	0,027	0,036	6
C6	0,014	0,015	0,017	0,017	0,027	0,018	0,018	16
C7	0,031	0,041	0,051	0,025	0,033	0,033	0,036	6
C8	0,041	0,041	0,051	0,038	0,041	0,041	0,042	4
C9	0,041	0,041	0,051	0,038	0,041	0,041	0,042	4
C10	0,041	0,041	0,019	0,038	0,041	0,041	0,037	5
C11	0,041	0,041	0,019	0,038	0,041	0,041	0,037	5
C12	0,041	0,041	0,019	0,038	0,041	0,041	0,037	5
C13	0,025	0,018	0,019	0,038	0,041	0,041	0,030	10
C14	0,021	0,018	0,019	0,038	0,020	0,023	0,023	14
C15	0,021	0,018	0,019	0,038	0,020	0,023	0,023	14
C16	0,031	0,031	0,038	0,031	0,033	0,033	0,033	7
C17	0,018	0,021	0,030	0,019	0,033	0,033	0,026	12
C18	0,015	0,018	0,025	0,038	0,033	0,033	0,027	11
C19	0,014	0,014	0,022	0,019	0,033	0,033	0,022	15
C20	0,041	0,041	0,019	0,038	0,020	0,033	0,032	8
C21	0,041	0,041	0,019	0,038	0,023	0,033	0,033	7
C22	0,041	0,041	0,019	0,038	0,023	0,033	0,033	7
C23	0,041	0,041	0,019	0,038	0,023	0,021	0,031	9
C24	0,041	0,025	0,019	0,022	0,023	0,021	0,025	13
Sub-Criteria under Support Services (D)	Expert 1	Expert 2	Expert 3	Expert 4	Expert 3	Expert 6	Local Importance Weights	Rankings By Local Importance Weights
D1	0,142	0,081	0,193	0,091	0,323	0,193	0,171	3
D2	0,427	0,108	0,386	0,091	0,108	0,386	0,251	1
D3	0,107	0,323	0,096	0,091	0,323	0,129	0,178	2
D4	0,107	0,323	0,129	0,091	0,065	0,096	0,135	4
D5	0,061	0,046	0,055	0,091	0,054	0,055	0,060	7
D6	0,085	0,065	0,064	0,273	0,081	0,064	0,105	5
D7	0,071	0,054	0,077	0,273	0,046	0,077	0,100	6

Examining Table 4, it can be seen that the most important main criterion for Türkiye's healthcare quality standards is the Healthcare Services criterion (C) with 45%, whereas the least important main criterion is Indicator Management (E) with 6.3%. The most important sub-criterion for the Institutional Services criterion (A) is Risk Management (A4) with 17.2%, and the least important is Social Responsibility (A10) with 3%. For the Patient and Employee-Oriented Services criterion (B), the most important sub-criterion is Healthy Work Life (B4) with 37.8%, and the least important one is End-of-Life Services (B3) with 9.6%. For the Healthcare Services criterion (C), the most important sub-criterion is Patient Care (C1) with 13.6%, and the least important one is Therapeutic Apheresis Services (C6) with 1.8%. For the Support Services criterion (D), however, the most important sub-criterion is Hospitality Services (D2) with 25.1%, and the least important one is Medical Records and Archiving Services (D5) with 6%.

In the final stage of the application, global weights were obtained by multiplying the local weights of the main criteria in Table 4 by the local weights of their sub-criteria. The global weights and the rankings of all sub-criteria according to these weights, listed from most to least important, are presented as global rankings in Table 5.

Table 9. Global Importance Weights of Sub-Criteria and Rankings Based on Global Importance Weights

Main Criteria	Sub-Criteria	Global Importance Weights	Rankings By Global Importance Weights
A (0,233)	A1 (0,153)	0,036	7
	A2 (0,138)	0,032	9
	A3 (0,059)	0,014	18
	A4 (0,172)	0,040	4
	A5 (0,092)	0,021	11
	A6 (0,054)	0,013	19
	A7 (0,164)	0,038	5
	A8 (0,087)	0,020	12
	A9 (0,051)	0,012	20
	A10 (0,030)	0,007	24
B (0,147)	B1 (0,249)	0,037	6
	B2 (0,277)	0,041	3
	B3 (0,096)	0,014	18
	B4 (0,378)	0,056	2

continued on following page

Table 9. Continued

Main Criteria	Sub-Criteria	Global Importance Weights	Rankings By Global Importance Weights
C (0,450)	C1 (0,136)	0,061	1
	C2 (0,092)	0,041	3
	C3 (0,075)	0,034	8
	C4 (0,075)	0,034	8
	C5 (0,036)	0,016	16
	C6 (0,018)	0,008	23
	C7 (0,036)	0,016	16
	C8 (0,042)	0,019	13
	C9 (0,042)	0,019	13
	C10 (0,037)	0,017	15
	C11 (0,037)	0,017	15
	C12 (0,037)	0,017	15
	C13 (0,030)	0,014	18
	C14 (0,023)	0,010	22
	C15 (0,023)	0,010	22
	C16 (0,033)	0,015	17
	C17 (0,026)	0,012	20
	C18 (0,027)	0,012	20
	C19 (0,022)	0,010	22
	C20 (0,032)	0,014	18
	C21 (0,033)	0,015	17
	C22 (0,033)	0,015	17
	C23 (0,031)	0,014	18
	C24 (0,025)	0,011	21

Table 10. Cont.

Main Criteria	Sub-Criteria	Global Importance Weights	Rankings By Global Importance Weights
D (0,107)	D1 (0,171)	0,018	14
	D2 (0,251)	0,027	10
	D3 (0,178)	0,019	13
	D4 (0,135)	0,014	18
	D5 (0,060)	0,006	25
	D6 (0,105)	0,011	21
	D7 (0,100)	0,011	21

Examining the global rankings, determined based on the global importance weights in Table 5, which collectively evaluate all sub-criteria for Türkiye's healthcare quality standards, the most important sub-criterion is found to be Patient Care (C1) with 6.1%, and the least important one is Medical Records and Archiving Services (D5) with 0.6%.

CONCLUSION

Determining quality standards in the healthcare sector not only ensures that services in hospitals are established following a scientific standard but also facilitates the delivery of these services. Implementing quality standards in line with the established criteria enables the measurement and evaluation of hospital services, as well as the efficient and effective use of resources. Moreover, with the advancement of digitalization, adjustments to these standards are expected to contribute positively to the healthcare sector and the national economy in terms of time savings. Because the development of information technologies, innovations brought by Industry 4.0 such as sensors, cloud computing and big data contribute to the more efficient and effective operation of the health sector (Derici, 2024). These factors will economically and socially benefit both society and the country, thereby contributing to sustainable development.

This study aims to rank the importance of healthcare quality standards in Türkiye. For this purpose, the quality standards from the currently used "Healthcare Quality Standards-Hospital (Version 6.1)" were utilized. The FUCOM method was employed to achieve the importance ranking of these healthcare quality standards. To implement the method, a FUCOM survey form was prepared based on the five main criteria and the forty-five sub-criteria within the "Healthcare Quality Standards-Hospital (Version 6.1)". The prepared survey form was then administered to six expert decision-makers working in the Provincial Health Directorate and the hospital quality unit who oversee the quality standards. The FUCOM method was applied to the data obtained from the survey. The implementation of the method was carried out using Microsoft Excel Solver.

By making use of the FUCOM method, the importance ranking of the main criteria (Table 4) was found to be as follows: health services (C) - 45%, institutional services (A) - 23.3%, patient and employee-focused services (B) - 14.7%, support services (D) - 10.7%, and indicator management (E) - 6.3%. Among the sub-criteria of the main criteria, the most significant sub-criteria were identified as (Table 4): risk management (A4) under institutional services (A) - 17.2%, healthy working life (B4) under patient and employee-focused services (B) - 37.8%, patient care (C1) under health services (C) - 13.6%, and hospitality services (D2) under support services (D) - 25.1%. Furthermore, since there was no sub-criterion for the indicator management (E) main criterion in Türkiye's healthcare quality standards (Table 1), no calculation was made for this criterion's sub-criteria. When evaluating all sub-criteria of the main criteria globally, the top three most significant sub-criteria were found to be: patient care (C1) at 6.1%, healthy working life (B4) at 5.6%, and medication management (C2) at 4.1%, while the three least significant sub-criteria were found to be: therapeutic apheresis services (C6) at 0.8%, social responsibility (A10) at 0.7%, and medical records and archiving services (D5) at 0.6%.

When the importance rankings were shared with experts, they stated that the importance ranking of healthcare quality standards in Türkiye generally aligned with the study's results. Experts highlighted that the primary objective of a healthcare institution is to provide healthcare services, and thus, they expected health services (C) to be the most important main criterion. Although the ranking of the main criteria from most to least important was anticipated to be health services (C), institutional services (A), patient and employee-focused services (B), support services (D), and indicator management (E), they emphasized that each main criterion should not be overlooked. They also noted that the ultimate outcome of all standards is to maintain high levels of patient and employee safety. Furthermore, they pointed out that while there are no sub-criteria for the indicator management (E) criterion in Türkiye's healthcare quality standards, there is a guideline for indicator management, which is used in hospital assessments.

In this study, which underscores the importance of quality standards in the healthcare sector, different MCDM or fuzzy MCDM methods could be used in future studies to rank the importance of healthcare quality standards in Türkiye. The results to be obtained in future studies could then be compared with those achieved in this study for further evaluation. Additionally, in future studies, instead of using Microsoft Excel Solver for the FUCOM method application, a specialized software could be developed for the implementation of the chosen method. Moreover, future research could focus on each sub-criterion's own sub-criteria rather than using the main and sub-criteria of Türkiye's healthcare quality standards as in this study.

REFERENCES

Abdullah, A., Ahmad, S., Athar, M. A., Rajpoot, N., & Talib, F. (2022). Healthcare performance management using integrated FUCOM-MARCOS approach: The case of India. *The International Journal of Health Planning and Management*, *37*(5), 2635–2668. DOI: 10.1002/hpm.3488 PMID: 35484727

Afkham, L., Abdi, F., & Komijan, A. R. (2012). Evaluation of service quality by using fuzzy MCDM: A case study in Iranian health-care centers. *Management Science Letters*, *2*(1), 291–300. DOI: 10.5267/j.msl.2011.08.009

Akdag, H., Kalaycı, T., Karagöz, S., Zülfikar, H., & Giz, D. (2014). The evaluation of hospital service quality by fuzzy MCDM. *Applied Soft Computing*, *23*, 239–248. DOI: 10.1016/j.asoc.2014.06.033

Alimohammadzadeh, K., Bahadori, M., & Hassani, F. (2016). Application of analytical hierarchy process approach for service quality evaluation in radiology departments: A cross-sectional study. *Iranian Journal of Radiology : a Quarterly Journal published by the Iranian Radiological Society*, *13*(1). DOI: 10.5812/iranjradiol.29424 PMID: 27127577

Arman, K., & Kundakcı, N. (2023). Yeni bütünleşik FUCOM-WEDBA yaklaşımı ile bir işletme için bulut hizmet sağlayıcısı seçimi. *Pamukkale Üniversitesi Sosyal Bilimler Enstitüsü Dergisi*, (56), 281–295. DOI: 10.30794/pausbed.1212975

Ayçin, E., & Aşan, H. (2021). İş zekası uygulamaları seçimindeki kriterlerin önem ağırlıklarının FUCOM yöntemi ile belirlenmesi. *KOCATEPEİİBFD*, *23*(2), 195–208. DOI: 10.33707/akuiibfd.903563

Badi, I., Bouraima, M. B., Qiu, Y., & Stević, Ž. (2024). Optimizing priority sequencing rules in parallel machine scheduling: An evaluation and selection approach using hybrid MCDM techniques. *Decision Making Advances*, *2*(1), 22–31. DOI: 10.31181/dma21202422

Badi, I., Muhammad, L. J., Abubakar, M., & Bakır, M. (2022). Measuring sustainability performance indicators using FUCOM-MARCOS methods. *Operational Research in Engineering Sciences: Theory and Applications*, *5*(2), 99–116. DOI: 10.31181/oresta040722060b

Büyüközkan, G., & Çifçi, G. (2012). A combined fuzzy AHP and fuzzy TOPSIS based strategic analysis of electronic service quality in healthcare industry. *Expert Systems with Applications*, *39*(3), 2341–2354. DOI: 10.1016/j.eswa.2011.08.061

Büyüközkan, G., Çifçi, G., & Güleryüz, S. (2011). Strategic analysis of healthcare service quality using fuzzy AHP methodology. *Expert Systems with Applications, 38*(8), 9407–9424. DOI: 10.1016/j.eswa.2011.01.103

Chang, T. H. (2014). Fuzzy VIKOR method: A case study of the hospital service evaluation in Taiwan. *Information Sciences, 271*, 196–212. DOI: 10.1016/j.ins.2014.02.118

Çilek, A., & Şeyranlıoğlu, O. (2023). Mobil bankacılık kullanımını etkileyen faktörlerin BWM ve FUCOM yöntemiyle analizi. Bal, H., Kandır, S. Y., & Ülbeği, İ. D. (Ed.), *Ekonomi ve Yönetim Bilimlerinde Güncel Akademik Araştırmalar II* (pp. 131-155). Ankara: Akademisyen Publishing.

Dağdeviren, M., Eraslan, E., Kurt, M., & Dizdar, E. N. (2005). Tedarikçi seçimi problemine analitik ağ süreci ile alternatif bir yaklaşım. *Teknoloji, 8*(2), 115-122. https://eds.p.ebscohost.com/eds/pdfviewer/pdfviewer?vid=0&sid=9071ff55-b7c3-41a3-8be6-7e9fa7c72714%40redis

Derici, S. (2024). Digitalization Concept and the Historical Evolution of Digitalization. Ahmed, E. M. (Ed.), *Developing Digital Inclusion Through Globalization and Digitalization* (pp. 93-110). USA: IGI Global. DOI: 10.4018/979-8-3693-4111-7.ch006

Derici, S., & Doğan, N. Ö. (2021). Hasta perspektifinden hastanelerde hizmet kalitesi: Bulanık AHP ile bir uygulama. *Nevşehir Hacı Bektaş Veli Üniversitesi SBE Dergisi, 11*(3), 1155–1177. DOI: 10.30783/nevsosbilen.994496

Durmić, E. (2019). The evaluation of the criteria for sustainable supplier selection by using the FUCOM method. *Operational Research in Engineering Sciences: Theory and Applications, 2*(1), 91–107. DOI: 10.31181/oresta1901085d

Durmić, E., Stević, Ž., Chatterjee, P., Vasiljević, M., & Tomašević, M. (2020). Sustainable supplier selection using combined FUCOM–Rough SAW model. *Reports in Mechanical Engineering, 1*(1), 34–43. DOI: 10.31181/rme200101034c

Duško, T., & Bozanic, D. (2023). Optimizing military decision-making: Application of the FUCOM–EWAA–COPRAS-G MCDM model. *Acadlore Transactions on Applied Mathematics and Statistics, 1*(3), 148–160. DOI: 10.56578/atams010303

Ecer, F. (2021a). Sürdürülebilir tedarikçi seçimi: FUCOM sübjektif ağırlıklandırma yöntemi temelli MAIRCA yaklaşımı. *Mehmet Akif Ersoy Üniversitesi İktisadi ve İdari Bilimler Fakültesi Dergisi, 8*(1), 26–48. DOI: 10.30798/makuiibf.691693

Ecer, F. (2021b). FUCOM sübjektif ağırlıklandırma yöntemi ile rüzgâr çiftliği yer seçimini etkileyen faktörlerin analizi. *Pamukkale Üniversitesi Mühendislik Bilimleri Dergisi, 27*(1), 24–34. DOI: 10.5505/pajes.2020.93271

Everest, T., Savaşkan, G. S., Or, A., & Özcan, H. (2022). Suitable site selection by using full consistency method (FUCOM): A case study for maize cultivation in northwest Turkey. *Environment, Development and Sustainability*, *26*(1), 1831–1850. DOI: 10.1007/s10668-022-02787-5 PMID: 36506642

Fazlollahtabar, H., Smailbašić, A., & Stević, Ž. (2019). FUCOM method in group decision-making: Selection of forklift in a warehouse. *Decision Making: Applications in Management and Engineering*, *2*(1), 49–65. DOI: 10.31181/dmame1901065f

General Directorate of Health Services. (2016). *Healthcare quality standards-hospital (version-5, revision-01)*. Ankara: Ministry of Health of the Republic of Turkey, General Directorate of Health Services, Department of Quality and Accreditation in Health. Accessed at: https://dosyamerkez.saglik.gov.tr/Eklenti/3460/0/skshastanesetiv5r1pdf.pdf Access Date: 12.04.2024.

General Directorate of Health Services. (2020). *Healthcare quality standards-hospital (version 6.1)*. Ankara: Ministry of Health of the Republic of Turkey, General Directorate of Health Services, Department of Quality and Accreditation in Health. Accessed at: https://www.saglikpersoneli.com.tr/images/upload/Ek-2._SKS_Hastane_Surum_6_pdf_tYklayYnYz.pdf Access Date: 12.04.2024.

General Directorate of Health Services. (n.d.). *SKS kospitals (versions)*. Ministry of Health of the Republic of Turkey, General Directorate of Health Services, Department of Quality and Accreditation in Health and Employee Rights. Accessed at: https://shgmkalitedb.saglik.gov.tr/TR,9064/sks-hastaneversiyonlar.html Access Date: 12.04.2024.

Herrera, A. O., González, R. C., & Abu-Muhor, E. B. (2008). Multi-criteria decision model for assessing health service information technology network support using the analytic hierarchy process. *Computación y Sistemas*, *12*(2), 173–182. https://www.redalyc.org/articulo.oa?id=61513251003

Jiang, S., Li, Y., Jiang, P., & Gan, L. (2017). Evaluating the quality performance of reconstructive community public health service based on weighted TOPSIS method. *Proceedings of the Tenth International Conference on Management Science and Engineering Management* (pp. 113-123). Singapore: Springer. DOI: 10.1007/978-981-10-1837-4_10

Kar, A., & Özer, Ö. (2020). Türkiye'de sağlık hizmetleri altyapı kaynaklarının, hizmet kullanım düzeylerinin ve sağlık sonuçlarının bölgesel düzeyde karşılaştırılması. *Dicle Üniversitesi İktisadi ve İdari Bilimler Fakültesi Dergisi*, *10*(20), 331–350.

Kaya, A., Pamucar, D., Gürler, H. E., & Ozcalici, M. (2024). Determining the financial performance of the firms in the Borsa Istanbul sustainability index: Integrating multi criteria decision making methods with simulation. *Financial Innovation*, *10*(1), 21. DOI: 10.1186/s40854-023-00512-3

Khan, A. M. R., Prasad, P. N., & Rajamanoharane, S. (2012). Service quality performance measurement management in corporate hospitals using analytical hierarchy process. *International Journal of Manufacturing Technology and Management*, *26*(1-4), 196–212. DOI: 10.1504/IJMTM.2012.051434

Mercan, T., & Can, A. (2023). İşgören seçiminde etkili olan faktörlerin FUCOM yöntemi ile değerlendirilmesi: Bir havayolu işletmesinde uygulama. *Süleyman Demirel Üniversitesi Vizyoner Dergisi*, *14*(40), 1311–1329. DOI: 10.21076/vizyoner.1271318

Özdağoğlu, A., Keleş, M. K., & Genç, V. (2021). FUCOM ve PROMETHEE yöntemleri ile ticari araç seçimi: Peyzaj firmasında bir uygulama. *Atatürk Üniversitesi Sosyal Bilimler Enstitüsü Dergisi, 25*(Özel Sayı), 231-253. DOI: 10.53487/ataunisosbil.825910

Pamucar, D., Deveci, M., Canıtez, F., & Bozanic, D. (2020). A fuzzy full consistency method-Dombi-Bonferroni model for prioritizing transportation demand management measures. *Applied Soft Computing*, *87*, 105952. DOI: 10.1016/j.asoc.2019.105952

Pamucar, D., Stević, Ž., & Sremac, S. (2018). A new model for determining weight coefficients of criteria in MCDM models: Full consistency method (FUCOM). *Symmetry*, *10*(9), 393. DOI: 10.3390/sym10090393

Radenović, M., Tenodi, S., Krčmar, D., Zrnić Tenodi, K., Rončević, S., Radjenovic, D., & Dalmacija, B. (2024). Navigating the transition: An in-depth analysis of a non-sanitary landfill and a novel approach to selecting future sanitary landfill sites. *SSRN*. DOI: 10.2139/ssrn.4719592

Rakhmangulov, A., Burmistrov, K., & Osintsev, N. (2024). Multi-criteria system's design methodology for selecting open pits dump trucks. *Sustainability (Basel)*, *16*(2), 863. DOI: 10.3390/su16020863

Roosta, M., Javadpoor, M., & Ebadi, M. (2024). Operationalizing urban cooling; a framework for heat-resilient spaces in Iran's dry climates. *SSRN*. DOI: 10.2139/ssrn.4733169

Saaty, T. L. (2008). Relative measurement and its generalization in decision making why pairwise comparisons are central in mathematics for the measurement of intangible factors the analytic hierarchy/network process. *RACSAM-Revista de la Real Academia de Ciencias Exactas Fisicas y Naturales. Serie A. Revista de la Real Academia de Ciencias Exactas, Físicas y Naturales. Serie A, Matemáticas*, *102*(2), 251–318. DOI: 10.1007/BF03191825

Shieh, J. I., Wu, H. H., & Huang, K. K. (2010). A DEMATEL method in identifying key success factors of hospital service quality. *Knowledge-Based Systems*, *23*(3), 277–282. DOI: 10.1016/j.knosys.2010.01.013

Stević, Ž., & Brković, N. (2020). A novel integrated FUCOM-MARCOS model for evaluation of human resources in a transport company. *Logistics (Basel)*, *4*(1), 4–14. DOI: 10.3390/logistics4010004

Yucesan, M., & Gul, M. (2020). Hospital service quality evaluation: An integrated model based on pythagorean fuzzy AHP and fuzzy TOPSIS. *Soft Computing*, *24*(5), 3237–3255. DOI: 10.1007/s00500-019-04084-2

Yüksel, L. İ. Ç., & Arıkan, M. (2019). Sağlık sektöründe hizmet kalitesinin çok ölçütlü karar verme yöntemleri ile değerlendirilmesi: Ankara'da bir uygulama. *Uludağ Üniversitesi Mühendislik Fakültesi Dergisi*, *24*(3), 13–30. DOI: 10.17482/uumfd.450667

KEY TERMS AND DEFINITIONS

FUCOM Method: One of the MCDM methods used to determine the criteria weights.

Healthcare Quality Standards: A set of standards developed to provide implementation guidance in line with prioritized needs and goals, aiming to improve the quality level across all healthcare institutions in Türkiye. These healthcare quality standards are structured into five dimensions: Institutional Services, Patient- and Employee-Centered Services, Healthcare Services, Support Services, and Indicator Management.

Healthcare Services Dimension: This dimension consists of standards designed to ensure that all medical service processes provided in hospitals are delivered in accordance with the goals set by the Healthcare Quality Standards-Hospital.

Indicator Management Dimension: This dimension consists of section prepared to ensure the sustainability of quality improvement processes by continuously monitoring service delivery performance.

Institutional Services Dimension: This dimension consists of standards developed to establish an effective quality management structure involving all hospital staff, enabling the systematic execution of activities related to the delivery of quality services.

Patient - and Employee - Centered Services Dimension: This dimension consists of standards developed to safeguard patients' fundamental rights, ensure their safety and satisfaction, and promote a healthy working environment for employees, emphasizing a dual perspective that considers both patient and employee viewpoints in evaluating services.

Support Services Dimension: This dimension consists of standards aiming to establish the necessary infrastructure to ensure the safety and continuity of medical service processes.

Chapter 9
Applying RATMI (Ranking by Alternatives Trace to Median Index) for Ranking Countries Based on Sustainability Performance

Ahmet Bahadır Şimşek
https://orcid.org/0000-0002-7276-2376
Gumushane University, Gümüşhane, Turkey

Aybala Şimşek
https://orcid.org/0000-0002-2202-9889
Burdur Mehmet Akif Ersoy University, Turkey

ABSTRACT

Today, global problems such as climate change, resource depletion and social inequality motivate the need for tools that can be used to measure the sustainability performance of countries. In this section, a new MCDM approach, RATMI (Ranking by Alternatives Trace to Median Index), is proposed with this motivation. RATMI uses trace and median similarity techniques to provide a balanced and accurate ranking as the median minimises the effect of outliers. In this chapter, the RATMI method is used to assess the sustainability performance of 157 countries for the period 2016-2020 on the basis of economic, social and environmental dimensions. The contributions of this study include the potential to promote RATMI as an effective tool for sustainability assessment of countries, identify role models, and inform

DOI: 10.4018/979-8-3693-8789-4.ch009

policymakers on the development of sustainability strategies at the global level. This practice not only advances the literature on MCDM in sustainability assessments, but also provides a practical framework to guide future policy and research aimed at promoting sustainable development

INTRODUCTION

Growing numbers of people, less access to resources and worsening climate change are putting great stress on the Earth, lowering its ability to support life. Carrying capacity is the highest amount of human activity Earth's resources can support; current signs indicate that we have already surpassed this limit, mainly in industrial countries (Binder et al., 2020; Cohen, 2017; Tucker, 2020). Expanding use of groundwater for farming is making water more rare and also poses a risk to the clean water needed by millions (Foster et al., 2024). Similarly, burning large amounts of fossil fuels puts more carbon into the atmosphere which speeds up the climate crisis and causes chain reactions such as sea levels rising, more extreme weather and losses in ecosystems (Nyambuu and Semmler, 2023). Because of these environmental changes, nature is threatened and society faces food shortages, more people must leave their homes and the economy weakens.

Due to these many problems, nations are coming up with intervention plans that focus on sustainable development. Denmark and Germany are both focusing on switching to renewables by changing their energy sectors and Japan is doing so by improving its recycling and waste management (Ravan Ramzani et al., 2024, Hu et al., 2024). Sustainable forestry in Sweden helps preserve biodiversity and China and India are making efforts to protect the environment as they grow their economies by encouraging green technologies (Angelstam et al., 2023; Sanjay Narang et al., 2024). They prove that countries are becoming more aware of the environment and are also including sustainability in their main development strategies. Consequently, developing countries are using social measures such as poverty, inequality and access to education guided by the United Nations' Sustainable Development Goals to promote both environmental sustainability and the well-being of their people (Sain et al., 2024).

However, the real impact of these policies depends not only on their feasibility but also on their effective monitoring and evaluation. Empirical evaluation models are needed to ensure that sustainability does not remain a mere concept but is supported by concrete outputs. Comparative analyses between countries are critical in this regard. Such evaluations enable the replication of successful practices, understanding the reasons behind delayed strategies, and transferring solutions that work in different contexts to policymakers (Arbolino et al., 2022; Bhatia & Tuli, 2018;

Bin, 2023). Sustainability is thus not only a universal goal but also a governance issue that needs to be continuously measured and adapted.

In this context, measuring sustainability requires methods that can analyse data structures containing multidimensional and heterogeneous indicators. To overcome the limitations of traditional average-focused analyses, multi-criteria decision-making (MCDM) methods are emerging. The RATMI (Ranking of Alternatives by Tracing to Median Index) method used in this study allows decision-makers to reduce performance indicators from different dimensions to a single ranking while representing the central tendency more accurately by using the median as a reference (Abdulaal and Bafail, 2022). The median-based ranking structure makes evaluation results more balanced, especially in large-scale data sets where outliers are frequently observed, and increases statistical reliability in issues with a high normative dimension, such as sustainability.

Within the scope of this study, the RATMI method was used to evaluate the performance of 157 countries based on sustainable development indicators between 2016 and 2020, and the efforts of countries to achieve the SDGs were analysed through objective and comparable criteria. The research offers two main contributions. First, by addressing sustainability performance at both theoretical and practical levels, a conceptual model has been developed that enables policy learning across countries. This model allows the experiences of high-performing countries to be transferred to low-performing countries in a way that provides guidance. Second, the RATMI method contributes to the multi-criteria decision-making literature by providing statistical robustness and normative balance, particularly in multi-dimensional policy areas such as sustainability, offering decision-makers objective, balanced, and centrally biased ranking outputs.

The rest of the study is as follows: Section 2 presents a literature review on sustainability and multi-criteria decision making techniques. Section 3 provides an overview and the procedure of the RATMI method. Section 4 evaluates the countries' sustainability performance using RATMI based on the selected indicators. It also discusses the implications of the findings for policy makers, researchers and sustainable development strategies. The conclusions of the chapter are presented in Section 5.

BACKGROUND

Concept and Criteria of Sustainability

Sustainability, initially regarded as environmental awareness limited to the conservation of natural resources, has evolved over time into a multidimensional and dynamic conceptual framework encompassing concepts such as social equity and economic continuity. This transformation gained an institutional foundation with the definition provided by the World Commission on Environment and Development in 1987; sustainability was defined as 'meeting the needs of the present without compromising the ability of future generations to meet their own needs' (Labuschagne and Brent, 2005). Within this framework, it has been emphasised that sustainability is not merely a technical application but also a normative framework that redefines the concept of development. Today, the three core components of sustainability—economic, environmental, and social costs—play a decisive role in all stages of policy-making and implementation across various sectors (Ahmad and Anwar, 2023; Murphy, 2012).

The first of these dimensions, economic sustainability, refers to the creation of structures that enable economic growth without consuming resources. However, in practice, economic interests often take precedence over environmental and social concerns, particularly in areas requiring high infrastructure, such as urban transport and health services (Sekasi and Martens, 2021). This priority is clearly observed in the literature; economic sustainability emerges as a theme that is more frequently referenced and addressed more prominently than other dimensions. This situation demonstrates how sustainability is intertwined with neoliberal development models and how market logic often relegates environmental and social goals to a secondary position.

Environmental sustainability, by contrast, tries to use environmental resources efficiently and without harming the environment's ability to support life. It includes efforts to stop pollution and to maintain both the health of ecosystems and the variety of living things (Padilla-Rivera et al., 2019). Due to sustainability indices and environmental performance indicators, it is now easier to add environmental concerns to agriculture, urbanisation and industry, allowing environmental policies to be tracked and compared (Aragão et al., 2022).

Nevertheless, it should be understood that environmental sustainability is linked to social and cultural values as well as being a management style. Social sustainability covers principles such as equality, social support, participation and cultural preservation, but frequently goes unseen when compared to the noticeable economic and environmental areas (Murphy, 2012).

This is particularly evident in contexts such as sustainable tourism, where contextual sensitivity is high, as social sustainability relies more on local value systems, subjective perceptions, and cultural norms than on universal norms (Ardaniah, 2022; Jasrotia et al., 2023). As a result, the social dimension is often relegated to a secondary role in decision-making processes and marginalised in sustainability practices on the grounds that it is difficult to measure and govern. However, neglecting social sustainability creates vulnerabilities that threaten the systemic integrity of the system in the long term.

These three dimensions of sustainability have been reshaped over time, not as separate areas but as increasingly intertwined ones. This convergence reflects not only the evolution of the concept of sustainable development but also the transformation of development paradigms at the global level. Indeed, the United Nations Sustainable Development Goals (SDGs) bring together economic growth, social inclusion, and environmental integrity within the same framework, transforming sustainability from a purely environmental policy issue into a multi-actor vision of transformation (Tuazon et al., 2013; Bali Swain and Yang-Wallentin, 2020). In this context, sustainability has evolved from a technical goal to a values-based governance pursuit, bringing not only the sustainability of resources but also that of systems, institutions, and relationships to the forefront.

Use of MCDM Methods in Sustainability

Sustainability assessments are difficult for decision-makers because they cover many areas and have competing requirements. In this situation, MCDM methods have become vital for sustainability analysis because they help structure and organise decisions that depend on various criteria. People most often use the Analytic Hierarchy Process (AHP), the Technique for Order of Preference by Similarity to Ideal Solution (TOPSIS) and the Preference Ranking Organisation and Enrichment Evaluation Method (PROMETHEE). Every approach has its own strengths and weaknesses which depend on the nature of the environmental decision being made.

AHP makes the decision problem simpler by dividing it into smaller parts, so that criteria can be compared in pairs and the process is organised by importance. With this method, decision-makers can be flexible and gain a better understanding, especially when decisions depend on uncertain judgements about sustainability (Agusti et al., 2022; Shaktawat and Vadhera, 2021). With a larger set of criteria or participants, it is harder to keep judgements consistent which weakens the method's reliability (Ogrodnik, 2023). Besides, when the information is unclear or decision-makers have limited mental capacity, AHP will likely be less useful and the process can take a lot of time (Navarro et al., 2020).

TOPSIS makes it easy to understand by comparing alternatives using their distance from the best and worst solutions. This approach works well in sustainability analyses because it relies heavily on cost-benefit data (Dobrovolskienė and Pozniak, 2021; Mulliner et al., 2013). Even so, the idea that perfect solutions can be set in advance is not always correct in practise, as sustainability decisions are often uncertain, have conflicting values and involve several actors (Mulliner et al., 2013).

Because the ranking is strongly affected by how the data is normalised, the scaling method used can directly change the structure of the ranking (Navarro et al., 2020).

Unlike other methods, PROMETHEE can handle both quantitative and qualitative criteria in the same way by using a dominance relationship approach. This feature is especially useful when multiple, hard-to-compare and subjective criteria are involved, as in the case of sustainability (Talukder and Hipel, 2018; Wulf et al., 2021). PROMETHEE is flexible in representing what decision-makers prefer, handles uncertain information well and has enough parameters to model multi-criteria situations. Still, this approach has its drawbacks; choosing the preference functions is crucial, as it greatly affects the results, so the model's reliability depends a lot on how the decision-maker intervenes and the method used (Corrente et al., 2021). If the number of options is very high or the preferences are complicated, the method's computational effort and interpretation may be questioned (Della Spina and Lanteri, 2024).

When comparing these three approaches; AHP is strong in logically constructing the decision structure but is limited by consistency issues and implementation burden; TOPSIS provides an intuitively easy-to-understand ranking but the stability of results may be questioned due to its sensitivity to data normalisation; PROMETHEE offers flexibility in managing multidimensional structures but involves methodological complexity due to its dependence on preference functions. Therefore, in decision-making environments with high normative intensity, such as sustainability, high data diversity, and multiple actors, the selection of an appropriate MCDM method should not be based solely on technical performance criteria but should also consider the decision context, stakeholder structure, data qualities, and value orientations.

METHODOLOGY

RATMI (Ranking by Alternatives Trace to Median Index) developed by Abdulaal and Bafail (2022) is a technique that addresses the challenges associated with the conventional MCDM approaches such as sensitivity to outliers and the problem of assigning weights to the criteria. RATMI is the integration of RAMS which is Ranking by Alternatives Median Similarity and MCRAT which is Multiple Criteria Ranking by Alternative Trace. RAMS reduces the influence of extreme values by focusing on the averages while MCRAT assesses other performance in terms of criteria and interaction.

Incorporating all these methods, RATMI sorts out the options depending on a median index but with an understanding of the interactions between the criteria. This approach is impartial, balanced and comprehensive to provide a solution in complex and cross-sectoral challenges like sustainability.

Steps of the RATMI method

Step 1: Construction of the decision matrix

In the presence of m alternatives and n criteria, the sets of alternatives and criteria are respectively shown as follows $i \in A = [A_1, A_2, \ldots, A_m], j \in C = [C_1, C_2, \ldots, C_n]$. X_{ij} shows the performance of alternative i on criterion j.

Step 2: Normalisation of the decision matrix

Uniformisation is ensured by eliminating unit and scale differences in the criteria.
For the benefit orientated criterion (max) $r_{ij} = \frac{x_{ij}}{\max_i(x_{ij})}, \forall i \in A$
For the cost orientated criterion (min) $r_{ij} = \frac{\min_i(x_{ij})}{x_{ij}}, \forall i \in A$

Step 3: Weighting of the normalised decision matrix

The normalised decision matrix is weighted to reflect the influence of each criterion on the decision process.

$$u_{ij} = w_j r_{ij}, \forall i \in A, j \in C$$

Where w_j indicates the importance of criterion j. Subject to $\sum_{j=1}^{n} w_j = 1$

Step 4: Determination of the optimum alternative

The optimum alternative Q is determined by identifying the best performance in each criterion.

$$q_j = \max\left(u_{ij} 1 \leq j \leq n\right), \forall i \in A$$

$$Q = \left\{q_1, q_2, \ldots, q_j\right\}, j = 1, 2, \ldots, n$$

Step 5: Decomposition of the optimum alternative

The optimum alternative is separated into two components, each with different characteristics: Q^{max} and Q^{min}. This separation allows to distinguish between criteria that should be maximised and minimised. The aim is to evaluate each set of criteria separately, enabling a more precise evaluation of alternatives by providing a better understanding of their interactions.

$$Q = Q^{max} \cup Q^{min}$$

$$Q = \{q_1, q_2, \ldots, q_k\} \cup \{q_1, q_2, \ldots, q_h\}; k + h = j$$

Where k and h denote the total number of benefit-oriented and cost-oriented criteria, respectively.

Step 6: Decomposition of alternatives

As with the optimal alternative, each alternative is separated into two components: U_i^{max} and U_i^{min}. The aim is to analyse in more detail how each alternative performs in terms of the criteria to be optimised.

$$U_i = U_i^{max} \cup U_i^{min}, \forall i \in A$$

$$U_i = \{u_{i1}, u_{i2}, \ldots, u_{ik}\} \cup \{u_{i1}, u_{i2}, \ldots, u_{ih}\}, \forall i \in A$$

Step 7: Magnitude of component

The magnitudes of the components U_i^{max}, U_i^{min}, Q^{max}, Q^{min} of each alternative and optimum are calculated. This magnitude refers to the vectorial lengths of the components and is calculated by the formula:

$$Q_k = \sqrt{q_1^2 + q_2^2 + \ldots + q_k^2} \; Q_h = \sqrt{q_1^2 + q_2^2 + \ldots + q_h^2}$$

$$U_{ik} = \sqrt{u_{i1}^2 + u_{i2}^2 + \ldots + u_{ik}^2} \; U_{ih} = \sqrt{u_{i1}^2 + u_{i2}^2 + \ldots + u_{ih}^2}$$

From this point on, two different methods (MCRAT and RAPS) are used for ranking the alternatives.

Step 7.1: Ranking by alternatives trace (MCRAT)

In the MCRAT, the performance of each alternative is evaluated together in terms of benefit and cost orientated criteria. The calculated trace value (tr) expresses the overall performance of the alternatives in a single number and enables the alternatives to be compared and ranked.

Construct the F matrix of the optimum alternative components $F = \begin{bmatrix} Q_k & 0 \\ 0 & Q_h \end{bmatrix}$

Create the matrix G_j consisting of alternative components $G_j = \begin{bmatrix} U_{ik} & 0 \\ 0 & U_{ih} \end{bmatrix}$

Create the T_i matrix $T_i = FxG_j = \begin{bmatrix} t_{11i} & 0 \\ 0 & t_{22i} \end{bmatrix}$

The trace of the matrix T_i $tr(T_i) = t_{11i} + t_{22i}$

The trace of this matrix is defined as the sum of the elements on the diagonal. Alternatives are ranked in descending order of $tr(T_i)$.

Step 7.2: Ranking by alternatives perimeter similarity (RAPS)

In this method, the extent of the distance of the alternatives to the best or the optimal one is determined. Perimeter similarity takes into account the performance of the alternatives in an integrated manner and develops a rank of the alternatives by comparing with the best alternative.

Using the Q^{max} and Q^{min} components of the optimal alternative, the perimeter (P) is calculated. This perimeter is treated as the perimeter of a right triangle formed by these two components. For each alternative, a similar perimeter (P_i) is calculated using the U_i^{max} and U_i^{min} components of the relevant alternative.

$$P = Q_k + Q_h + \sqrt{Q_k^2 + Q_h^2}$$

$$P_i = U_{ik} + U_{ih} + \sqrt{U_{ik}^2 + U_{ih}^2}$$

The perimeter similarity of each alternative to the optimal alternative is calculated as the ratio of the perimeter of the relevant alternative to the perimeter of the optimal alternative.

$$PS_i = \frac{P_i}{P}, \forall i \in A$$

The PS_i indicates how similar each alternative is to the optimal alternative. Alternatives are ranked in descending order of PS_i.

Step 8: Ranking by alternatives median similarity (RAMS)

The RAMS evaluates the similarity of each alternative with the optimal alternative through median similarity.

The median value (M) of the optimal alternative is calculated. This median is defined as half of the hypotenuse length of a right triangle formed by the components Q^{max} and Q^{min}.

$$M = \frac{\sqrt{Q_k^2 + Q_h^2}}{2}$$

Similarly, a median value (M_i) is calculated for each alternative.

$$M_i = \frac{\sqrt{U_{ik}^2 + U_{ih}^2}}{2}$$

The median similarity of each alternative to the optimum is calculated as the ratio of the median of the relevant alternative to the median of the optimal alternative.

$$MS_i = \frac{M_i}{M}, \forall i \in A$$

Alternatives are ranked in descending order of MS_i.

Step 9: Ranking the alternatives using the trace to median index (RATMI)

The trace value (tr) obtained from the MCRAT method is combined with the median similarity (MS) obtained from the RAMS method. This merging is done in order to express the results of both methods in a single index (E).

In this process, the trace value and median similarity are combined using a certain weighting parameter (v). v value determines how much importance to give to the results of both methods. For example, when $v = 0.5$, both methods are evaluated with equal weight.

$$E_i = v\frac{(tr_i - tr^*)}{(tr^- - tr^*)} + \left(1 - v\right)\frac{(MS_i - MS^*)}{(MS^- - MS^*)}$$

Here;

$$tr_i = tr\left(T_i\right), \forall i \in A$$

$$tr^* = \min\left(tr_i, \forall i \in A\right)$$

$$tr^- = \max\left(tr_i, \forall i \in A\right)$$

$$MS^{*} = \min\left(MS_i, \forall i \in A\right)$$

$$MS^{-} = \max\left(MS_i, \forall i \in A\right)$$

v: Weighting parameter (between 0 and 1)

Alternatives are ranked with decreasing E_i value.

Combining both methods, RATMI offers a more reliable ranking by combining different assessment dimensions.

APPLICATION: ASSESSMENT OF SUSTAINABILITY PERFORMANCE OF COUNTRIES BY RATMI

Sustainable development is one of the biggest goals in the current development agenda that has emerged in the last few years with the aim of developing an economy, enhancing the quality of people, and preserving the resources. Nevertheless, the problem of environment degradation and social inequality does not disappear even if the economy is highly developed. The UN in 2015 came up with the SDGs which was meant to assist countries in the improvement of sustainable development and also in the assessment of the progress across nations.

In this research, the RATMI approach is applied in evaluating the countries' performance in the attainment of the SDGs in the three sustainability dimensions; economic, social and environmental. The purpose is to provide an impartial decision and indicate who the leaders are and what the recommendations for the countries with a low sustainability index are.

Data Set and Criteria Selection

While selecting the indicators for the RATMI methodology for the evaluation of the countries' sustainability performance, the indicators were selected in the economic, social, and environmental dimensions. These indicators are aligned with the SDGs and the data obtained from these indicators is relevant to understand the status of sustainable development in various countries. The following are the selected indicators for each dimension and the rationale behind them as presented in Table 1.

Table 1. Indicators

	Indicator	Dimension	Motivation	Orientation
I1	Access to electricity (% of population)	Economic	Electricity is a basic necessity in the economic development of any country as it supports industries, education and health sectors. Higher access rates are an indication of infrastructure development of a country and its capacity to support economic activities in all sectors leading to productivity and economic growth.	Benefit (Max)
I2	Foreign direct investment, net inflows (BoP, current US$)	Economic	FDI is an important factor in economic development particularly in the developing nations. FDI brings technology, generates employment and assists in the absorption of countries into the global value system. The nations receiving more FDI flows are considered to be more appealing to the foreign investors, suggesting better economic regulation and stability.	Benefit (Max)
I3	GDP per capita (current US$)	Economic	GDP per capita is one of the most common indicators of a country's economic performance, which shows the gross domestic product per capita, and indicates the level of development and well-being of the population. Higher values of the GDP per capita mean that the country is more developed and has more resources to tackle social and environmental problems.	Benefit (Max)
I4	GNI per capita (US$)	Economic	GNI per capita is the total income of a country's residents including income earned from abroad. It is a sign of how well the country's economy is doing and how much it can afford to spend on social capital which include health, education, and shelter that are basic necessities for man.	Benefit (Max)
I5	Merchandise trade (% of GDP)	Economic	Merchandise trade as a ratio of GDP shows the importance of trade in a country's economy. It shows the extent of globalization and how trade impacts on the economy as a whole. Increased trade means that the economy of the two countries is growing and the industries are competitive.	Benefit (Max)
I6	Total natural resources rents (% of GDP)	Economic	This indicator is defined as the percentage of a country's Gross Domestic Product that is earned from the sale of natural resources such as oil and gas and minerals. Dependence on natural resource rents is regarded as one of the indicators of economic openness since it indicates that the economy is not diversified and depends on the non-renewable sources. The use of natural resources is not sustainable in the long run though it is important to exploit them, there is need to balance.	Cost (Min)
I7	Unemployment, total (% of total labor force)	Economic	The unemployment rates provide information concerning the status of the labour market in a specific country. High unemployment rate is associated with high social problems and economic challenges while low unemployment rate is associated with good economic status and people have chances to be useful in society.	Cost (Min)

continued on following page

Table 1. Continued

	Indicator	Dimension	Motivation	Orientation
I8	Access to clean fuels and technologies for cooking (% of population)	Environmental	This indicator measures access to clean energy which is useful in preventing indoor pollution and environmental degradation. The countries with higher access rates are likely to be in harmony with the objectives of environmental conservation particularly in the utilization of non-renewable and environmentally unfriendly fuels such as coal or wood.	Benefit (Max)
I9	Forest area (% of land area)	Environmental	The proportion of the land area that is covered by forests is one of the significant predictors of the biological richness, the preservation of ecosystems and carbon stocks. The findings also indicated that countries with more forest area are likely to have more effective policies on environmental conservation and are therefore well placed to combat climate change and support ecosystems.	Benefit (Max)
I10	Terrestrial and marine protected areas (% of total territorial area)	Environmental	Conservation areas are very essential in the protection of biological diversity, the environment and natural resources. The higher percentage of protected land and marine areas is often an implication of the country's willingness to protect the environment and sustainable use of land hence minimizing on deforestation, pollution and loss of habitats.	Benefit (Max)
I11	Adolescent fertility rate (births per 1,000 women ages 15-19)	Social	Adolescent fertility rate is a gender, reproductive health and social status index of the youths. Low adolescent fertility is linked to higher education and health care and better gender equality. These co-high fertility rates may be an indication of social problems in these areas.	Cost (Min)
I12	Incidence of tuberculosis (per 100,000 people)	Social	Tuberculosis prevalence rate is one of the most important indicators of health as it shows how well the population's health needs are met by the public health services. This is as a result of the fact that countries with low TB prevalence usually have better public health measures and health care systems that are likely to improve the health of the population.	Cost (Min)
I13	Mortality rate, under-5 (per 1,000 live births)	Social	Under five mortality is one of the simplest indicators of child well-being and the effectiveness of the health care system. Hypothesis: under-5 mortality rate is a good measure of health care, nutrition and good health policies in a given country and this is an aspect of social development.	Cost (Min)
I14	Proportion of seats held by women in national parliaments (%)	Social	The concern of the gender balance in leadership is crucial in the governance processes, and this is why political leadership is crucial. That is why it is possible to conclude that more women in parliaments mean that there are changes in gender equality for the better, which is one of the social sustainability. This is an indication of a country's preparedness to ensure that there is integration of the minority in the decision making process.	Benefit (Max)

The selected indicators give a clear picture of the sustainability performance of the countries in terms of economic, social and environmental aspects. This approach makes it possible to capture all the aspects of sustainable development in equal measure. The data for this study was obtained from the World Bank Data Bank to enhance reliability and coverage of the study. The countries under consideration are 157 with the data available for all the 14 chosen indicators, which allows providing a comprehensive assessment of both developed and developing countries.

To evaluate the changes in sustainability, percentage variations of the indicators in the period of 2016 and 2020 were calculated. This period provides the snapshot of the economic, social and environmental status and the progress or otherwise of each country towards the realization of the SDGs.

RATMI Implementation

The RATMI approach used in the analysis of countries' sustainability performance is a structured approach that ensures the analysis of economic, social, and environmental aspects. Due to the large number of countries included in the study, which is 157, results are presented with examples while the full data is presented in the appendix.

The process involves three key steps:

Step 1: Constructing the Decision Matrix

A matrix is created with countries as rows and sustainability indicators across economic, social, and environmental dimensions as columns. Table 2 shows raw data for a subset of countries.

Step 2: Normalization of the Decision Matrix

To enable comparability, data is normalized, ensuring consistent evaluation across indicators and countries. Table 3 presents the normalized matrix for selected indicators.

Step 3: Weighting the Normalized Matrix

Weights are applied to reflect each indicator's importance in the sustainability assessment. Table 4 shows the weighted normalized matrix.

For brevity, Table 2 displays data for a subset of the 157 countries.

Table 2. Decision matrix

Criteria	I1	I2	I3	I4	I5	I6	I7	I8	I9	I10	I11	I12	I13	I14
Orientation	Max	Max	Max	Max	Max	Min	Min	Max	Max	Max	Min	Min	Min	Max
Weight	7.14%	7.14%	7.14%	7.14%	7.14%	7.14%	7.14%	7.14%	7.14%	7.14%	7.14%	7.14%	7.14%	7.14%
AFG	0.0000	-0.8614	0.0092	0.0087	-2.9924	0.0259	0.5520	4.6000	0.0000	3.5325	-0.2365	0.0212	-0.1407	-0.6947
ALB	0.1100	0.0243	0.2929	0.2512	-2.0367	-0.0098	-2.0910	3.5000	-0.0102	1.0262	-0.0215	-0.1176	0.0426	6.6511
DZA	0.4539	-0.3123	-0.1621	-0.1710	-8.0588	-0.0673	2.3500	0.1000	-0.0029	-2.7055	-0.0973	-0.1571	-0.0847	-5.8442
⋮	⋮	⋮	⋮	⋮	⋮	⋮	⋮	⋮	⋮	⋮	⋮	⋮	⋮	⋮
VNM	0.8000	0.2540	0.2844	0.2973	22.2013	-0.7027	0.5400	4.3000	0.8560	0.0001	-0.1990	-0.0881	-0.0324	0.0000
ZMB	9.0990	-1.2606	-0.2308	-0.2286	7.3899	5.7888	1.9760	-3.0000	-1.0126	3.2103	-0.0708	-0.1516	-0.0597	-1.1976
ZWE	10.1859	-0.5617	-0.1708	-0.1827	9.8657	7.3795	0.5630	0.6000	-0.4764	0.0002	-0.1456	-0.1717	-0.0818	0.3704

Table 3. Normalized decision matrix

	I1	I2	I3	I4	I5	I6	I7	I8	I9	I10	I11	I12	I13	I14
AFG	0.0000	-0.0080	0.0091	0.0087	-0.0647	-1349.7818	-18.3786	0.2788	0.0000	0.1459	1.9796	-31.3250	3.2593	-0.0253
ALB	0.0054	0.0002	0.2886	0.2529	-0.0440	3581.4672	4.8517	0.2121	-0.0070	0.0424	21.8075	5.6352	-10.7798	0.2419
DZA	0.0224	-0.0029	-0.1597	-0.1721	-0.1742	519.4183	-4.3170	0.0061	-0.0020	-0.1117	4.8131	4.2189	5.4172	-0.2125
⋮	⋮	⋮	⋮	⋮	⋮	⋮	⋮	⋮	⋮	⋮	⋮	⋮	⋮	⋮
VNM	0.0394	0.0023	0.2802	0.2993	0.4799	49.7564	-18.7870	0.2606	0.5853	0.0000	2.3533	7.5266	14.1547	0.0000
ZMB	0.4487	-0.0116	-0.2274	-0.2302	0.1597	-6.0401	-5.1341	-0.1818	-0.6924	0.1326	6.6136	4.3732	7.6805	-0.0435
ZWE	0.5023	-0.0052	-0.1682	-0.1840	0.2132	-4.7381	-18.0195	0.0364	-0.3257	0.0000	3.2162	3.8618	5.6097	0.0135

Table 4. Weighted normalized decision matrix

	I1	I2	I3	I4	I5	I6	I7	I8	I9	I10	I11	I12	I13	I14
AFG	0.0000	-0.0006	0.0007	0.0006	-0.0046	-96.4130	-1.3128	0.0199	0.0000	0.0104	0.1414	-2.2375	0.2328	-0.0018
ALB	0.0004	0.0000	0.0206	0.0181	-0.0031	255.8191	0.3466	0.0152	-0.0005	0.0030	1.5577	0.4025	-0.7700	0.0173
DZA	0.0016	-0.0002	-0.0114	-0.0123	-0.0124	37.1013	-0.3084	0.0004	-0.0001	-0.0080	0.3438	0.3013	0.3869	-0.0152
⋮	⋮	⋮	⋮	⋮	⋮	⋮	⋮	⋮	⋮	⋮	⋮	⋮	⋮	⋮
VNM	0.0028	0.0002	0.0200	0.0214	0.0343	3.5540	-1.3419	0.0186	0.0418	0.0000	0.1681	0.5376	1.0110	0.0000
ZMB	0.0320	-0.0008	-0.0162	-0.0164	0.0114	-0.4314	-0.3667	-0.0130	-0.0495	0.0095	0.4724	0.3124	0.5486	-0.0031
ZWE	0.0359	-0.0004	-0.0120	-0.0131	0.0152	-0.3384	-1.2871	0.0026	-0.0233	0.0000	0.2297	0.2758	0.4007	0.0010

The initial three steps—constructing the decision matrix, normalizing data, and applying weights—are foundational in any MCDM process, ensuring indicator comparability and relevance across sustainability dimensions. Building on these steps, RATMI introduces its unique methodology.

RATMI then decomposes alternatives relative to the optimal alternative, which is benchmarked by calculating component scores across all criteria, as shown in Table 5. This optimal alternative serves as a reference point for evaluating the performance of other alternatives.

Table 5. Decomposition of the optimal alternative

	I1	I2	I3	I4	I5	I6	I7	I8	I9	I10	I11	I12	I13	I14
	Max	Max	Max	Max	Max	Min	Min	Max	Max	Max	Min	Min	Min	Max
	q1	q2	q3	q4	q5	q6	q7	q8	q9	q10	q11	q12	q13	q14
Q^{max}	0.0714	0.0714	0.0714	0.0714	0.0714			0.0714	0.0714	0.0714				0.0714
Q^{min}						-3461.7818	-36.2322				-30.8240	-17.9000	-1.3434	

Table 6 presents the decomposition of the remaining alternatives, comparing each country's performance to the optimal benchmark. This breakdown provides a detailed analysis of strengths and weaknesses, highlighting areas for potential improvement.

Table 6. Decomposition of alternatives

	I1	I2	I3	I4	I5	I6	I7	I8	I9	I10	I11	I12	I13	I14
	Max	**Max**	**Max**	**Max**	**Max**	**Min**	**Min**	**Max**	**Max**	**Max**	**Min**	**Min**	**Min**	**Max**
	u1	**u2**	**u3**	**u4**	**u5**	**u6**	**u7**	**u8**	**u9**	**u10**	**u11**	**u12**	**u13**	**u14**
AFG U^{max}	0.0000	-0.0006	0.0007	0.0006	-0.0046			0.0199	0.0000	0.0104				-0.0018
AFG U^{min}						-96.4130	-1.3128				0.1414	-2.2375	0.2328	
ALB U^{max}	0.0004	0.0000	0.0206	0.0181	-0.0031			0.0152	-0.0005	0.0030				0.0173
ALB U^{min}						255.8191	0.3466				1.5577	0.4025	-0.7700	
⋮	⋮	⋮	⋮	⋮	⋮	⋮	⋮	⋮	⋮	⋮	⋮	⋮	⋮	⋮
ZMB U^{max}	0.0320	-0.0008	-0.0162	-0.0164	0.0114			-0.0130	-0.0495	0.0095				-0.0031
ZMB U^{min}						-0.4314	-0.3667				0.4724	0.3124	0.5486	
ZWE U^{max}	0.0359	-0.0004	-0.0120	-0.0131	0.0152			0.0026	-0.0233	0.0000				0.0010
ZWE U^{min}						-0.3384	-1.2871				0.2297	0.2758	0.4007	

Table 7 shows the magnitude of both the optimal alternative and the other alternatives, offering a clear view of how far each country deviates from the optimal solution. This provides a comprehensive comparison of countries' relative performance in the sustainability assessment.

Table 7. Magnitude of optimal alternative and alternatives

	Qk	**Qh**
	0.0459	11986518.3165
	Uk	Uh
AFG	0.0005	9302.2676
ALB	0.0013	65446.7068
DZA	0.0007	1376.9609
⋮	⋮	⋮
VNM	0.0041	15.7714
ZMB	0.0044	0.9423
ZWE	0.0024	2.0606

Table 8 presents the ranking results using the MCRAT (Multi-Criteria Ranking by Alternative Trace) method, a key element of RATMI. MCRAT ranks alternatives based on their proximity to the optimal benchmark across all criteria. This ranking reflects each country's overall sustainability performance. Higher-ranked countries show stronger alignment with sustainable development goals, vice versa.

Table 8. Alternatives ranked according to MCRAT method

	tr	**Rank**
ISL	4.69E+15	1
SGP	1.84E+15	2
BHS	1.44E+14	3
⋮	⋮	⋮
KGZ	5763868	155
GUY	4988835	156
ARM	4290971	157

After evaluating alternatives using the MCRAT method, the RATMI process continues with the RAPS (Ranking by Alternatives' Performance Similarity) method. Table 9 presents this ranking, which offers a different perspective on sustainability performance. Unlike MCRAT, RAPS ranks countries based on the similarity of their performance to one another, rather than solely against the optimal benchmark. This method highlights countries with similar sustainability profiles, providing insights into shared strengths and weaknesses, and offering a more nuanced understanding of how countries compare in their sustainability efforts.

Table 9. Alternatives ranked according to RAPS method

	Max	Min					
	Qk	Qh	P				
	0.0459	11986518.3165	23973036.6789				
	Uik	Uih	Pi	PSi		PSi	Rank
AFG	5.3E-04	9.3E+03	1.9E+04	7.8E-04	ISL	3.27E+01	1
ALB	1.3E-03	6.5E+04	1.3E+05	5.5E-03	SGP	1.28E+01	2
DZA	7.3E-04	1.4E+03	2.8E+03	1.1E-04	BHS	1.00E+00	3
⋮	⋮	⋮	⋮	⋮	⋮	⋮	⋮
VNM	4.1E-03	1.6E+01	3.2E+01	1.3E-06	KGZ	4.01E-08	155
ZMB	4.4E-03	9.4E-01	1.9E+00	7.9E-08	GUY	3.48E-08	156
ZWE	2.4E-03	2.1E+00	4.1E+00	1.7E-07	ARM	2.99E-08	157

Table 10 presents the ranking of alternatives using the RAMS method, which focuses on the median performance across all criteria. Unlike methods that emphasize extremes, RAMS evaluates each alternative based on its median values, providing a balanced ranking by reducing the impact of outliers. This approach offers a robust assessment of sustainability performance, highlighting consistency across indicators rather than exceptional results in specific areas.

Table 10. Alternatives ranked according to RAMS method

	Max	Min					
	Qk	Qh	M				
	0.0459	11986518.3165	5993259.1583				
	Uik	Uih	Mi	MSi		MSi	Rank
AFG	5.3E-04	9.3E+03	4.7E+03	7.8E-04	ISL	3.27E+01	1
ALB	1.3E-03	6.5E+04	3.3E+04	5.5E-03	SGP	1.28E+01	2
DZA	7.3E-04	1.4E+03	6.9E+02	1.1E-04	BHS	1.00E+00	3
⋮	⋮	⋮	⋮	⋮	⋮	⋮	⋮
VNM	4.1E-03	1.6E+01	7.9E+00	1.3E-06	KGZ	4.01E-08	155
ZMB	4.4E-03	9.4E-01	4.7E-01	7.9E-08	GUY	3.47E-08	156
ZWE	2.4E-03	2.1E+00	1.0E+00	1.7E-07	ARM	2.99E-08	157

The structure of the RATMI method, which is not limited to ranking algorithms, also offers the opportunity to measure countries' overall compliance levels with sustainability norms through derivative indicators such as the Majority Index (E). This index, presented in Table 11, is constructed by considering both the proximity of each alternative to ideal performance and its similarity to the central tendency of the data set. A high E value indicates that the country is strongly aligned with global sustainability norms, while a low value indicates either the existence of contextually unique strategies or the need for serious improvements at the structural level. This indicator enables the tracking of alignment or deviation patterns, serving as an important decision-support function for targeted policy development and strategic direction.

Table 11. Calculation majority index (E) of RATMI

	MCRAT	**RAMS**	
tr*=	4.29E+06	MS*=	0.0000
tr-=	4.69E+15	MS-=	32.6551
	tri	MSi	Ei
AFG	1.12E+11	7.76E-04	2.38E-05
ALB	7.84E+11	5.46E-03	1.67E-04
DZA	1.65E+10	1.15E-04	3.52E-06
⋮	⋮	⋮	⋮
VNM	1.89E+08	1.32E-06	3.94E-08
ZMB	1.13E+07	7.86E-08	1.49E-09
ZWE	2.47E+07	1.72E-07	4.35E-09

Table 12 ranks countries' sustainability performance based on the Majority Index (E) values calculated using the RATMI method. This index serves as a composite indicator summarising each country's overall level of alignment with sustainability norms based on all evaluated criteria. Thus, it objectively and comparably reveals the extent to which countries are aligned with sustainable development goals.

Table 12. Alternatives ranked according to majority index (E) of RATMI method

	Country Name	Ei	Rank			Country Name	Ei	Rank			Country Name	Ei	Rank
ISL	Iceland	1.0000	1		**JPN**	Japan	0.0000	54		**UKR**	Ukraine	0.0000	106
SGP	Singapore	0.3919	2		**BWA**	Botswana	0.0000	55		**TGO**	Togo	0.0000	107
BHS	Bahamas, The	0.0306	3		**USA**	United States	0.0000	56		**BEN**	Benin	0.0000	108
MUS	Mauritius	0.0204	4		**PRY**	Paraguay	0.0000	57		**MOZ**	Mozambique	0.0000	109
CHE	Switzerland	0.0111	5		**DJI**	Djibouti	0.0000	58		**ARG**	Argentina	0.0000	110
MDV	Maldives	0.0059	6		**KOR**	Korea, Rep.	0.0000	59		**NOR**	Norway	0.0000	111
LUX	Luxembourg	0.0033	7		**VUT**	Vanuatu	0.0000	60		**GIN**	Guinea	0.0000	112
BEL	Belgium	0.0024	8		**IND**	India	0.0000	61		**RWA**	Rwanda	0.0000	113
HRV	Croatia	0.0009	9		**BLZ**	Belize	0.0000	62		**JOR**	Jordan	0.0000	114
TON	Tonga	0.0004	10		**QAT**	Qatar	0.0000	63		**SLE**	Sierra Leone	0.0000	115
LCA	St. Lucia	0.0004	11		**LSO**	Lesotho	0.0000	64		**MLT**	Malta	0.0000	116
PAN	Panama	0.0004	12		**KAZ**	Kazakhstan	0.0000	65		**ECU**	Ecuador	0.0000	117
CYP	Cyprus	0.0003	13		**BGD**	Bangladesh	0.0000	66		**DOM**	Dominican Republic	0.0000	118
FRA	France	0.0002	14		**BIH**	Bosnia & Herzegovina	0.0000	67		**ZAF**	South Africa	0.0000	119
GRC	Greece	0.0002	15		**SLV**	El Salvador	0.0000	68		**JAM**	Jamaica	0.0000	120
ALB	Albania	0.0002	16		**THA**	Thailand	0.0000	69		**SEN**	Senegal	0.0000	121
VCT	St. Vincent & Grenadines	0.0001	17		**CRI**	Costa Rica	0.0000	70		**POL**	Poland	0.0000	122
PER	Peru	0.0000	18		**LVA**	Latvia	0.0000	71		**TTO**	Trinidad and Tobago	0.0000	123

continued on following page

Table 12. Continued

	Country Name	Ei	Rank			Country Name	Ei	Rank			Country Name	Ei	Rank
AUT	Austria	0.0000	19		**TUR**	Turkey	0.0000	72		**UGA**	Uganda	0.0000	124
AFG	Afghanistan	0.0000	20		**NER**	Niger	0.0000	73		**STP**	Sao Tome and Principe	0.0000	125
ITA	Italy	0.0000	21		**CHN**	China	0.0000	74		**CAN**	Canada	0.0000	126
HUN	Hungary	0.0000	22		**GTM**	Guatemala	0.0000	75		**COL**	Colombia	0.0000	127
EST	Estonia	0.0000	23		**EGY**	Egypt, Arab Rep.	0.0000	76		**IRN**	Iran, Islamic Rep.	0.0000	128
LTU	Lithuania	0.0000	24		**TZA**	Tanzania	0.0000	77		**CPV**	Cabo Verde	0.0000	129
MDA	Moldova	0.0000	25		**PNG**	Papua New Guinea	0.0000	78		**KEN**	Kenya	0.0000	130
SVK	Slovak Republic	0.0000	26		**MMR**	Myanmar	0.0000	79		**NGA**	Nigeria	0.0000	131
IRL	Ireland	0.0000	27		**BDI**	Burundi	0.0000	80		**BTN**	Bhutan	0.0000	132
LKA	Sri Lanka	0.0000	28		**BLR**	Belarus	0.0000	81		**AUS**	Australia	0.0000	133
ESP	Spain	0.0000	29		**TUN**	Tunisia	0.0000	82		**TCD**	Chad	0.0000	134
SVN	Slovenia	0.0000	30		**MLI**	Mali	0.0000	83		**BRN**	Brunei Darussalam	0.0000	135
PAK	Pakistan	0.0000	31		**PHL**	Philippines	0.0000	84		**MAR**	Morocco	0.0000	136
ROU	Romania	0.0000	32		**IRQ**	Iraq	0.0000	85		**NIC**	Nicaragua	0.0000	137
ISR	Israel	0.0000	33		**CIV**	Cote d'Ivoire	0.0000	86		**MWI**	Malawi	0.0000	138
PRT	Portugal	0.0000	34		**NZL**	New Zealand	0.0000	87		**SAU**	Saudi Arabia	0.0000	139
SRB	Serbia	0.0000	35		**HND**	Honduras	0.0000	88		**ZWE**	Zimbabwe	0.0000	140

continued on following page

Table 12. Continued

	Country Name	Ei	Rank			Country Name	Ei	Rank			Country Name	Ei	Rank
DZA	Algeria	0.0000	36		**NPL**	Nepal	0.0000	89		**CAF**	Central African Republic	0.0000	141
IDN	Indonesia	0.0000	37		**URY**	Uruguay	0.0000	90		**BRA**	Brazil	0.0000	142
DEU	Germany	0.0000	38		**SWZ**	Eswatini	0.0000	91		**GNQ**	Equatorial Guinea	0.0000	143
BRB	Barbados	0.0000	39		**GAB**	Gabon	0.0000	92		**NAM**	Namibia	0.0000	144
FJI	Fiji	0.0000	40		**TJK**	Tajikistan	0.0000	93		**GHA**	Ghana	0.0000	145
BHR	Bahrain	0.0000	41		**CMR**	Cameroon	0.0000	94		**GNB**	Guinea-Bissau	0.0000	146
NLD	Netherlands	0.0000	42		**ARE**	United Arab Emirates	0.0000	95		**CHL**	Chile	0.0000	147
RUS	Russian Federation	0.0000	43		**COD**	Congo, Dem. Rep.	0.0000	96		**AZE**	Azerbaijan	0.0000	148
FIN	Finland	0.0000	44		**SLB**	Solomon Islands	0.0000	97		**GMB**	Gambia, The	0.0000	149
GBR	United Kingdom	0.0000	45		**VNM**	Vietnam	0.0000	98		**ZMB**	Zambia	0.0000	150
MNE	Montenegro	0.0000	46		**MNG**	Mongolia	0.0000	99		**ETH**	Ethiopia	0.0000	151
CZE	Czech Republic	0.0000	47		**TLS**	Timor-Leste	0.0000	100		**UZB**	Uzbekistan	0.0000	152
MKD	North Macedonia	0.0000	48		**MEX**	Mexico	0.0000	101		**BOL**	Bolivia	0.0000	153
COG	Congo, Rep.	0.0000	49		**LBR**	Liberia	0.0000	102		**SUR**	Suriname	0.0000	154
DNK	Denmark	0.0000	50		**KHM**	Cambodia	0.0000	103		**KGZ**	Kyrgyz Republic	0.0000	155
MYS	Malaysia	0.0000	51		**GEO**	Georgia	0.0000	104		**GUY**	Guyana	0.0000	156

continued on following page

Table 12. Continued

	Country Name	Ei	Rank			Country Name	Ei	Rank			Country Name	Ei	Rank
SWE	Sweden	0.0000	52		**OMN**	Oman	0.0000	105		**ARM**	Armenia	0.0000	157
WSM	Samoa	0.0000	53										

The ranking results obtained based on country performance for the 2016–2020 period using the RATMI method provide decision-makers with the opportunity to assess policy success at both the macro and micro levels and identify areas for improvement. This assessment does not merely capture the current state of affairs; it also enables a comparative analysis of the effectiveness of sustainable development policies.

Macro-Level Findings

Iceland, Singapore and Switzerland are some of the countries that have implemented sustainable development in tandem with economic growth and social development. Iceland has embraced renewable energy sources such as geothermal and hydropower hence cutting down on energy expenses and attaining energy self sufficiency. Singapore being a highly urbanized country has recorded a great improvement in waste management, water recycling and sustainable urban development. Switzerland has been able to embrace green technologies through its large investment in research and development. These nations use their good education systems and economic power to support innovation, put in place policies that are sustainable and can be used as benchmarks by other nations, especially the developing ones. Their success proves that the long-term economic development and sustainability goals are not incompatible and need to be pursued in order to address climate issues around the world.

Micro-Level Findings

On a more specific level, the ranking shows the advantages and the disadvantages of particular countries. Although Luxembourg has a strong financial industry, it has also spent much of its resources in energy efficiency programs to support its environmental initiatives. Likewise, the Maldives, which relies on tourism, has put measures in place for the protection of coastal and marine environments, which means that the two objectives do not have to be mutually exclusive. These examples show how the countries with the resource-based economy can develop their economy without compromising the environment.

On the other hand, emerging nations like Zambia and Zimbabwe have issues like dependence on the natural resources, volatility and poor infrastructure. These are some of the factors that slow down their development towards sustainable development. To sustain such levels in the long-run, these nations need to invest in education, infrastructure and economic diversification.

Policy Implications

The ranking can be very useful for policy makers as it provides information about the state of the country. The developed nations can offer their experience and extend their help in the form of technical support for the sustainability processes worldwide. It means that the countries such as Bangladesh can implement the concept of green economy and put sustainability as one of the priorities in the development of industrial growth. Educational reforms, environmental consciousness, and green technologies shall be some of the key areas that these nations will have to invest in.

France and Belgium are the best examples of how to decrease energy dependence and create effective and sustainable urban development strategies based on energy and urban planning policies. The experiences of these countries can help others in the process of changing the urban planning and energy policies towards the carbon neutrality objectives.

CONCLUSION

Sustainability is a major issue that is of paramount importance when countries are trying to achieve economic development, social justice and environmental conservation. Evaluation of countries' sustainability is crucial to track the progress in solving such issues as climate change and resource scarcity. This evaluation helps in determining the national policies and also help the countries to compare their achievements. Nevertheless, because sustainability is a complex concept with many aspects, these evaluations must be systematic and include a range of factors.

AHP, TOPSIS, and PROMETHEE are the most common methods used in MCDA for sustainability assessment; however, they fail to handle extreme values and criterion interactions. The above limitations are eliminated in RATMI since it aims at central tendencies and balances benefit- and cost-oriented criteria, which makes it suitable for sustainability assessments. The use of RATMI has the following benefits: minimisation of the impact of outliers and a more objective evaluation, which is essential when the decision-makers are in need of accurate rankings to compare countries' sustainability performance.

In this study, RATMI was used to analyze the shifts in the performance of countries from 2016 to 2020 with regard to different sustainability indices. The method offered a more complex view of the situation, which allowed to distinguish leaders and countries with sustainability issues. This application helps to extend the literature by presenting RATMI as a viable approach to sustainability assessment. Thus, by providing a more reasonable and fair ranking, RATMI contributes to the development of the future research and policy, allowing countries to compare their progress and improve the strategies for achieving sustainable development worldwide.

REFERENCES

Abdulaal, R. M. S., & Bafail, O. A. (2022). Two New Approaches (RAMS-RATMI) in Multi-Criteria Decision-Making Tactics. *Journal of Mathematics, 2022*(1). DOI: 10.1155/2022/6725318

Angelstam, P., Bush, T., & Manton, M. (2023). Challenges and Solutions for Forest Biodiversity Conservation in Sweden: Assessment of Policy, Implementation Outputs, and Consequences. *Land (Basel)*, *12*(5), 1098. DOI: 10.3390/land12051098

Arbolino, R., Boffardi, R., Ioppolo, G., Lantz, T. L., & Rosa, P. (2022). Evaluating industrial sustainability in OECD countries: A cross-country comparison. *Journal of Cleaner Production*, *331*, 129773. DOI: 10.1016/j.jclepro.2021.129773

Bhatia, A., & Tuli, S. (2018). Sustainability reporting practices in US and UK: An empirical comparison. *International Journal of Law and Management*, *60*(4), 1034–1056. DOI: 10.1108/IJLMA-04-2017-0102

Bin, A. (2023). Assessing the Role of Sustainable Construction Practices in the One Belt One Road Initiative: A Comparative Analysis of China and Southeast Asian Countries. *Journal of Digitainability* [DREAM]. *Realism & Mastery*, *2*(02), 39–44. DOI: 10.56982/dream.v2i02.86

Binder, S., Holdahl, E., Trinh, L., & Smith, J. H. (2020). Humanity's Fundamental Environmental Limits. *Human Ecology: an Interdisciplinary Journal*, *48*(2), 235–244. DOI: 10.1007/s10745-020-00140-w

Cohen, J. (2017). How many people can the Earth support? *The Journal of Population and Sustainability*, *2*(1). DOI: 10.3197/jps.2017.2.1.37

Foster, T., Pérez-Blanco, C. D., & Schmidt, G. (2024). *Monitoring agricultural water use: challenges and solutions for sustainable water management.*, DOI: 10.19103/AS.2023.0123.26

Hu, J., Miao, L., Han, J., Zhou, W., & Qian, X. (2024). Waste separation behavior with a new plastic category for the plastic resource circulation: Survey in Kansai, Japan. *Journal of Environmental Management*, *349*, 119370. DOI: 10.1016/j.jenvman.2023.119370 PMID: 37879224

Nyambuu, U., & Semmler, W. (2023). *Fossil Fuel Resources*. Environment, and Climate Change., DOI: 10.1007/978-3-031-27982-9_4

Ravan Ramzani, S., Konhaeusner, P., Olaniregun, O. A., Abu-Alkheil, A., & Alsharari, N. (2024). Integrating AI-Driven Green Finance Strategies for Sustainable Development: A Comparative Analysis of Renewable Energy Investments in Germany and Denmark. *European Journal of Business and Management Research*, *9*(2), 43–55. DOI: 10.24018/ejbmr.2024.9.2.2277

Sain, Z. H., Nurtina, S., Agoi, M. A., & Thelma, C. C. (2024). Sustainable Development. *Journal of Information Systems and Technology Research*, *3*(2), 80–85. DOI: 10.55537/jistr.v3i2.830

Sanjay Narang, D., Monika Panchani, D., Kiran Chauhan, D., Manoj Thakur, D., & Radhika Jamwal, D. (2024). ENVIRONMENTAL INNOVATION AND SUSTAINABLE DEVELOPMENT THROUGH GREEN TECHNOLOGYs. In *Futuristic Trends in Renewable & Sustainable Energy Volume 3 Book 3* (pp. 285–291). Iterative International Publishers, Selfypage Developers Pvt Ltd. DOI: 10.58532/V3BIRS3P12CH1

Tucker, C. (2020). We know how many people the earth can support. *The Journal of Population and Sustainability*, *5*(1). DOI: 10.3197/jps.2020.5.1.77

KEY TERMS AND DEFINITIONS

Sustainability: An integrated concept encompassing economic, environmental and social issues. It refers to meeting current needs without compromising the ability of future generations to meet their needs.

Sustainable Development Goals: A globally recognised framework consisting of 17 interconnected goals launched by the United Nations to address important global issues such as poverty, inequality, climate change and ecological degradation.

Multi-Criteria Decision Making (MCDM): It is a systematic set of methods that enables the simultaneous consideration of multiple and often conflicting criteria in decision-making processes. Especially in areas such as sustainability, where balancing economic efficiency, environmental integrity, and social justice is required, MCDM methods provide decision-makers with the ability to make structured comparisons among complex variables and establish preference rankings.

RATMI (Ranking Alternatives by Trace to Median Index): RATMI is a ranking approach that contributes uniquely to the MCDM field by analysing both the proximity of decision alternatives to an idealised reference point and their similarity to the central tendency of the data set, i.e. the median. This dual evaluation ensures both statistical balance and normative soundness in the ranking results, producing more reliable and balanced results, especially in contexts such as sustainability where outliers are frequently encountered.

Benefit-oriented and cost-oriented criteria: Benefit-oriented criteria contribute positively to sustainable development when maximised (e.g., electricity access rate). In contrast, cost-oriented criteria represent improvement when minimised (e.g., unemployment rate). The correct classification of these two types of criteria serves as a guiding function in decision models and increases the interpretability of analysis results.

Normalisation: It is the standardisation process used to make meaningful comparisons between criteria with different measurement units and scales. Normalisation preserves the structural integrity of the data, making the weighting and combined analysis processes between criteria methodologically valid.

Optimal Alternative: In the RATMI approach, the optimal alternative is a reference structure created by theoretically combining the best values observed in each criterion. This structure serves as a benchmark for comparing the performance of real alternatives. This allows the sustainability levels of countries or options to be evaluated in terms of consistency with a normative ideal.

Majority Index (E): The Majority Index combines the two core components of RATMI—trace-based proximity and median similarity—into a comprehensive index. This index reveals the extent to which an alternative aligns with sustainable development priorities. High E values indicate that the alternative is strongly aligned with the normative ideal and serve as a strong indicator for prioritisation by decision-makers.

Chapter 10
Evaluation of G7 Countries in Terms of Their Digital Intelligence Performance With the Cocoso Method

Hande Eren
https://orcid.org/0000-0002-9166-5037
Kapadokya University, Nevşehir, Turkey

Emel Gelmez
https://orcid.org/0000-0002-8774-607X
Selçuk University, Konya, Turkey

ABSTRACT

Digital technologies are increasing their importance day by day on a global scale. New concepts have emerged as digital technologies make their effects felt on both individuals and businesses. One of these concepts is digital intelligence. In this context, the main purpose of this study is to examine the digital intelligence performances of G7 countries. Within the framework of this main purpose, the digital intelligence performances of G7 countries were determined by using the 2020 Digital Intelligence Index (DII). The current index includes six criteria: state, momentum, environment, experience, behavior and attitudes. Within the scope of the analysis, the SD (Standard Deviation) method was used in weighting the criteria and the COCOSO (Combined Compromise Solution) method was used in ranking the alternatives/countries. According to the SD method results, it was seen that the criterion with the highest importance level was behavior, while state had the lowest

DOI: 10.4018/979-8-3693-8789-4.ch010

importance level. After weighting the criteria, COCOSO analysis was conducted and as a result of the analysis, it was determined that the country with the highest digital intelligence performance was the USA; Germany followed the USA. The countries with the lowest performance were determined as France and Italy, respectively.

1. INTRODUCTION

In recent years, there has been an increase in the use of advanced technology, innovations and artificial intelligence initiatives in countries. In order to survive in a competitive environment and meet the expectations of citizens and businesses, countries should constantly analyze their strategies to choose the right technology (Mittal, 2020). In this context, the G7 group countries, the seven largest economies in the world, are countries that have made significant progress in digitalization performance. These countries can also guide the strategies and policies of other countries in terms of digitalization. Digital intelligence performance is an important concept in digitalization and refers to the effective, efficient and environmentally sensitive operation of digital systems and artificial intelligence applications over time (Cismaru et al., 2018). At the same time, this performance is also important for countries to adopt a long-term sustainability goal in terms of technology, environment, economy and society. Multi-Criteria Decision Making (MCDM) methods can help countries manage the complexity they face in the digitalization process.

MCDM are mathematical models that help make decisions in scenarios where possible alternatives are evaluated according to multiple conflicting criteria (Ceballos et al., 2016). In our daily lives, many decisions are made according to various criteria. Therefore, decisions can be made by giving weights to different criteria and obtaining all weights from expert groups. It is important to determine the structure of the problem and evaluate multiple criteria clearly. For example, when building a nuclear power plant, certain decisions were made according to different criteria. It is not only about very complex issues that include multiple criteria. Some criteria can be effective on some problems. However, in order to have an optimum solution in general, all alternatives must have common criteria that lead to more informed and better decisions (Aruldoss et al., 2013).

MCDM is a useful tool in solving various problems such as economics, production, material selection, military, construction. It plays an important role especially in investment decisions, project evaluation, economic benefit evaluation, personnel evaluation. It has already been proposed for solving many technical and multi-attribute decision-making problems (Gavade, 2014).

Various ranking methods are widely used in the literature for MCDM problems. Among these methods, VIKOR (Vise Kriterijumska Optimizacija I Kompromisno

Resenje) stands out with its compromise-based structure, especially when there is a conflict between criteria, by offering balanced solutions to decision makers (Opricovic & Tzeng, 2004). EDAS (Evaluation based on Distance from Average Solution) method brings a different approach to the decision process by evaluating alternatives according to their positive and negative distances to the average solution (Ghorabaee et al., 2015). TOPSIS (Technique for Order Preference by Similarity to Ideal Solution) is a method that has been preferred for a long time with its ranking structure based on the principle of proximity to the ideal solution and distance to the anti-ideal solution (Hwang & Yoon, 1981). In addition to these methods, the CoCoSo (Combined Compromise Solution) method attracts attention especially for decision makers in terms of both ease of calculation and methodological flexibility. The most obvious advantage of CoCoSo is that it combines the simple weighted sum model and the exponential weighted multiplication model in the same structure through three different integration strategies. In addition, the ability to calculate in decision matrices containing negative values without the need for a special transformation process significantly increases the practicality and applicability of the method (Yazdani et al., 2019). In this respect, CoCoSo stands out as a strong alternative in both theoretical and applied contexts compared to classical methods in the literature.

The data used in the study was obtained from the Digital Intelligence Index (DII) Report published by Tufts University in 2020. DII reports have been published three times in total, in 2014, 2017 and 2020. DII is a research platform created to provide evidence-based, actionable insights on increasing digital competitiveness, trust in the digital economy and productivity, and encouraging the use of data, artificial intelligence and other advanced technologies. DII is also important in terms of drawing an overall picture of global digital development. This index also provides insights into the key factors driving change and momentum, and reveals the impact of digital trust and digital evolution on a country's digital competitiveness (DII, 2020).

DII is a data-driven holistic assessment of the progress of the digital economy in 90 countries. Digital intelligence is expressed by two basic criteria: Digital Evolution and Digital Trust. These two basic criteria are explained by six sub-dimensions: state, momentum, environment, experience, behavior, and attitudes. These criteria and dimensions are important in terms of considering the reliability of the digital ecosystem in each economy, digital experiences, the depth of interaction between internet users, and the level of trust citizens have in the digital ecosystem (DII, 2020). No study has been found in the literature using DII data. In this regard, it is thought that the study will contribute to the literature.

The technological solutions offered by digital intelligence play a critical role in achieving environmental, economic and social sustainability goals by increasing the efficiency of digitalization. In this context, the concepts of digitalization and sustainability in digitalization are explained in detail in the study. Then, information on the methods used in the study is explained and the findings of the research are included.

1.1. Digitalization

The concept of "digitalization", which is at the focal point of the academy and the business world, is expressed as the future of everything. Therefore, it is of vital importance for countries to realize their digital transformation, to catch up with and manage change for their future. Countries that cannot keep up with the digital world will be doomed to extinction. Businesses are important actors that encourage and sustain economic development. The development of a country is usually directly related to the existence of strong and efficient businesses. In this context, the concept of digitalization is also important for businesses. Businesses should use digital technologies effectively and efficiently to change a business model and provide new income and value-generating opportunities (Gray & Rumpe, 2015).

Digitalization, also referred to as digitization, can provide businesses with significant operational efficiencies and significantly reduce errors at every stage. However, the business itself does not change with digitalization. The creation of new business models and the change of basic business strategies are the areas of digitalization. Digitized data form the basis of the information to be used to take action and create change in the digitalization process. The digital transformation of institutions is actually their digitalization. In other words, it is the restructuring of the business around the new opportunities and new demands offered by digital technology (Gobble, 2018).

With the digital revolution, technological innovations used in every area of life have created application areas in homes through electronic devices, and in industrial kitchens with developments such as big data, smart products and the internet of things (Baker & Evans, 2015). Digitalization has integrated into many areas of daily life such as entertainment, security, smart cities, childcare and smart homes. Digital technologies are considered as a multifaceted concept that enables businesses to make correct and strategic decisions by affecting the ability of inputs such as information, machines and data to work in harmony with individuals and organizations in the formation of new business models. Digitalization has a widespread use opportunity in many areas, from relationships carried out through social media applications to e-services offered by public institutions (Kreiss & Brennen, 2016).

Digital transformation is defined as the deep and accelerating transformation of commercial activities, processes, competencies and models in order to take full advantage of the changes and opportunities brought by digital technologies, as well as their impacts on society, in a strategic and prioritized manner (Haffke et al., 2016). Businesses and organizations create new business models by taking advantage of technological developments in order to increase profitability, gain competitive advantage and workforce efficiency, and personalize customer experiences (Gray & Rumpe, 2015).

The change in consumer behavior that has emerged with digital transformation has led to the emergence of new solutions in customer experience applications. Technological applications that provide competitive advantage to the service sector make it very important to develop long-term digital strategies and use technology to create digital value for businesses (Styvén & Wallström, 2019).

In the era of the Fourth Industrial Revolution, Artificial Intelligence and Digital Transformation, digitalization has emerged as a major concern for both economists and policymakers. In particular, the changes that emerge with digitalization are expected to affect the pace of economic development, employment rates and labor productivity. While digitalization makes things easier for some, it can make life difficult for others. Although it is seen as an effective concept for accelerating economic growth, if there is no appropriate framework and ground, this concept can also be seen as a growth hindering function. Digitalization depends on a number of different factors, including the level of development, the level of permanent unemployment, population size and the quality of human and physical capital (Aly, 2019).

Today, economic growth is impossible without the use of information and communication technologies. Because they cover more and more diverse areas of economic activity and create new opportunities for socio-economic development. Globalization, transformation of consumer behavior, mobility, accessibility of information have become important concepts of our day. Digital technologies are reshaping the global economic system. The formation of an effective digital economy will provide significant opportunities for the emergence and development of businesses, will help increase investment flows and accumulate financial resources in the world (Jorgenson, 2001).

The digital economy is growing rapidly on a global scale. The foundations of innovation, competitiveness and economic growth in the world are laid by the digital economy. The main products of the digital economy consist of the same goods and services as the traditional economy, provided by digital systems such as computer equipment and the global internet. The advantages of this situation include increasing users' access to certain markets (goods or services), reducing transaction costs, and increasing efficiency and competitiveness (Kravchenko et al., 2019).

1.2. Sustainability in Digitalization

The transition from the analog world to the digital world in the twenty-first century has brought with it increased processing power and communication speed, which facilitates the sharing of information and data. The increased availability of information helps individuals not only to learn about current product features and service offerings in the market, but also to share goods and services. While it was once common to share things among friends and family, with the emergence of the concept of digitalization, efficient use of resources with lower consumption is possible as a community. Thus, this concept has become a profitable business model that has led to increased flexibility and therefore a more sustainable society (Aksin-Sivrikaya & Bhattacharya, 2017).

The three main areas of digitalization affecting the sustainability of societies are specified as follows (Osburg, 2017):

- *Data:* Sustainable data is generally considered the "oxygen" of sustainable policy. Regional, national and global sustainable data provide a basis for companies to take action. Sustainable data of businesses can be values related to energy, water, wastewater, waste, emissions, hazardous substances (Kreeb & Haasis, 2017).
- *Algorithms:* Algorithms, which used to be a more technical term, have now become a critical concept in today's information society. Recently, decisions taken at every level are determined by algorithms, which are self-organizing and a series of operational steps.
- *Bots:* In a world where digital processes are more dominant, machines and robots are becoming increasingly capable of replacing the tasks that people perform today. The issue of whether robots will significantly reduce employment is also of equal importance. For now, uncertainties continue about whether there will be positive or negative effects and in what time frame these effects will occur.

The concept of sustainability, which requires a systemic transformation, has become a structure that provides multidimensional gains for institutions, societies and the world in the medium and long term (Börü, 2022). Digitalization, on the other hand, provides access to an integrated network of unprocessed big data with potential benefits for society and the environment. Digitalization creates significant opportunities for the development of smart systems connected to the Internet of Things and the creation of a fair, environmentally sustainable and healthy society. If technology and processes are designed according to appropriate criteria, digitalization will support the transition to a more sustainable society. This is only possible by systematically focusing on the risks and benefits of digital technologies in environmental, social and economic terms. From this perspective, digitalization is thought to be an important tool for creating a sustainable society of the future (Mondejar et al., 2021).

2. METHODOLOGY

2.1. SD (Standard Deviation) Method

SD method was developed by Diakoulaki et al. (1995). In this method, weights are determined according to the standard deviations of the criteria (Türkoğlu & Tuzcu, 2021). This weighting method is generally used to solve complex and uncertain problems in MCDM studies (Baydaş & Pamučar, 2022). The method consists of three stages. These stages are listed below (Diakoulaki et al. 1995):

Step 1. The decision matrix $X=\left[x_{ij}\right]_{m*n}$ is created as shown in Equation (1) below.

$$X = \left[x_{ij}\right]_{m*n} = \begin{bmatrix} x_{11} & \cdots & x_{12} & \cdots & x_{1n} \\ \vdots & \ddots & \vdots & \ddots & \vdots \\ x_{21} & \cdots & x_{22} & \cdots & x_{2n} \\ \vdots & \ddots & \vdots & \ddots & \vdots \\ x_{m1} & \cdots & x_{m2} & \cdots & x_{mn} \end{bmatrix} \tag{1}$$

x_{ij}, represents the value of alternative *i.* in criterion *j.*

Step 2. In the normalization process of the criteria in the decision matrix, if the criterion has the benefit feature, Equality (2) is used, if it has the cost feature, Equality (3) is used.

x_j^{max} = *j.* maximum value of the criterion among the alternatives
x_j^{min} = *j.* minumum value of the criterion among the alternatives
$i = 1,2, \ldots, m$ (alternatives)
$j = 1,2, \ldots, n$ (criteria);

$$x_{ij}^{*} = \frac{x_{ij} - x_j^{min}}{x_j^{max} - x_j^{min}} \tag{2}$$

$$x_{ij}^{*} = \frac{x_j^{max} - x_{ij}}{x_j^{max} - x_j^{min}} \tag{3}$$

x_{ij}^{*}, represents the normalized value of alternative *i.* in criterion *j.*

Step 3. In the last step of the SD method, the weight of each criterion is calculated with Equation (4).

$$w_j = \frac{\sigma_j}{\sum_{j=1}^{n} \sigma_j}, \text{j} = 1,2, \ldots \text{m} \tag{4}$$

The σ_j value in Equation 4 is the standard deviation value of the criterion j.

2.2. CoCoSo (Combined Compromise Solution) Method

CoCoSo, one of the MCDM methods, is a method introduced to the literature by Yazdani et al. (2019) in 2019 and is based on the combined consensus algorithm. This method is based on the mathematical combination of SAW (Simple Additive Weighing) and EWP (Exponentially Weighted Product) methods (Yazdani et al., 2019). The basis of this method is the combination of consensus perspectives. And ultimately, it reconciles evaluation criteria that often conflict with each other. In this context, the CoCoSo method provides an overview of the possible consensus solutions offered to the decision maker (Popović, 2021).

The optimum solution screened by the CoCoSo method is not easily affected by changes in the weight distribution of the criteria or the deletion/addition of alternatives. These mean that the CoCoSo method is a robust method with advantages in terms of reliability and stability of decision-making results. In addition, the CoCoSo method is an easy-to-understand method. This method has wide applicability and therefore has been extended to different conditions to solve decision-making problems in various fields (Lai et al., 2020). Indeed, although the CoCoSo method is a new method, it has been applied to cloud service provider selection (Lai et al., 2020); selection of the most appropriate engineering sustainability components (Dwivedi & Sharma, 2022); circular economy practices (Khan & Haleem, 2021); advancing global innovation metrics (Nişel & Nişel, 2024); supply chain anti-fragility (Hadizadeh et al., 2023); evaluation of healthcare sectors (Torkayesh et al., 2021); It is a method that has been used and accepted in various decision-making problems such as knowledge adoption solutions (Jafari & Khanachah, 2024); supplier selection (Yazdani et al., 2019); optimizing personnel selection (Andrejić & Pajić, 2023); university ranking (Ozdagoglu et al., 2020); spray painting robot selection (Kumar et al., 2022); selection of medical best bearing ring (Nabeeh & Sallam, 2024); logistics performance (Arman & Organ, 2023). Studies conducted with the CoCoSo method in these areas are summarized as follows.

Lai et al. (2020) proposed the (CoCoSo) method to determine the ranking of cloud service providers in their study. In order to demonstrate the applicability of the proposed method in the study, a numerical example was given for the trust assessment of cloud service providers. In addition, sensitivity analysis and comparative analysis were performed to determine the accuracy of the decision outputs derived with the proposed method. As a result of the study, it was concluded that the CoCoSo method is a feasible and reliable method.

Dwivedi and Sharma (2022) used the CoCoSo method for the best material selection in their study. The study presents an integrated strategy that includes an engineering design to select the most sustainable material that provides the best performance at the lowest cost. As a result of the study, it was concluded that the CoCoSo method is a powerful decision-making tool for selecting the best target.

Khan and Haleem (2021) aimed to investigate circular economy practices in their study to transform an existing linear model into a circular economy model. In order to achieve this goal, fifteen circular economy practices were identified in the study through literature review and expert input. These circular economy practices were evaluated using the CoCoSo method and circular economy practices were prioritized according to their importance. As a result of the study, it was seen that important circular practices were consumer awareness, legislation and policies, developing the circular culture, awareness among the supply chain partners and designing products for circularity.

Nisel and Nisel (2024) aimed to examine various aspects of innovation such as research and development, collaboration and the economic impact of innovative efforts using various indicators in the OECD guidelines. The criteria in the study were weighted with the LOPCOW method and the CoCoSo method was used to systematically classify countries. The methodology used covers certain criteria, including not only the development of new technologies, but also the improvement of the production process and innovations in services and policies. This comprehensive analysis is important in terms of highlighting the capabilities of global innovation. The study concluded that traditionally innovative countries continue to be ahead.

Hadizadeh et al. (2023) tried to determine the fragility factors of textile industries in the supply chain in their study. In the study, fragility factors were first determined and these factors were analyzed using the BWM (Best-Worst Method) method. Then, the literature on the textile industry was reviewed and experts in this industry were interviewed to rank and evaluate the fragility factors. In the study where the CoCoSo method was used, it was concluded that lack of investment in the (clothing) industry, saturation of the market with counterfeit brands due to the structural weakness of the distribution and smuggling network and undeveloped distribution alternatives were the best alternatives.

Torkayesh et al. (2021) developed an integrated multi-criteria decision-making analysis in their study to evaluate the health sector, which is one of the basic infrastructures for countries. For this purpose, a hybrid weight determination model including BWM and LBWA (Level Based Weight Assessment) methods was applied to determine the weights of health indicators. After determining the criteria weights, countries were evaluated in terms of their health performance with the CoCoSo method. As a result of the study, it was determined that Lithuania and Slovakia had the best health systems compared to countries such as Poland and Estonia.

Yazdani et al. (2019) aimed to propose a hybrid MCDM methodology in their study and discuss the advantages of this proposed methodology. In the study where the best logistics and transportation companies in France were selected with the CoCoSo method from the MCDM methods, sensitivity analysis was also performed and it was determined that the results obtained as a result of the study were consistent.

Andrejić and Pajić (2023) proposed a hybrid MCDM approach using the CoCoSo and BWM method in their study. This proposed approach is important in that it was used for the first time to improve the recruitment process in the transportation sector. The criteria were weighted with BWM and the candidates were ranked with the CoCoSo method. It was determined that an effective approach that increased reliability in various problems and various hierarchical layers emerged with the use of these methods together. It is also anticipated that the study will provide an effective tool for decision makers in the sector in personnel selection.

Ozdagoglu et al. (2020) aimed to evaluate the performance of 166 universities according to 5 criteria in their study. The data used in the study were obtained from the URAP (University Ranking by Academic Performance) Report published in 2019. CoCoSo and MARCOS (Measurement of Alternatives and Ranking according to Compromise Solution) methods were used in the ranking of universities. According to the results of the analyzes, it was seen that Hacettepe University, Middle East Technical University and Istanbul Technical University were in the top three places. However, it was determined that there was a great similarity between the ranking results in the URAP report and the ranking results made with the methods used in the study. It was suggested that this study would contribute to the literature because the CoCoSo and MARCOS methods have been used in several studies in the literature. It is also thought that this study will contribute to university administrations, academicians and students.

Kumar et al. (2022) aimed to determine the most suitable spray painting robot for an automobile industry based on seven evaluation criteria (payload, mass, speed, repeatability, reach, cost and power consumption). For this purpose, SWARA (Step-Wise Weight Assessment Ratio Analysis) method was used in weighting the criteria and the alternatives were evaluated with the CoCoSo method. While the SWARA method determined the cost criterion as the most important criterion in a certain order of preference, Fanuc P-350iA/45 was selected as the best spray painting robot with the CoCoSo method.

Nabeeh and Sallam (2024) investigated the criteria and difficulties of selecting the ideal medical bearing ring for medical devices and equipment. The criteria investigated include material compatibility, biocompatibility, lubrication requirements, precision, cleanliness, durability, noise and vibration control, size and dimension, load capacity, temperature and environmental conditions, regulatory compliance, manufacturing considerations, compatibility with adjacent components, maintenance and serviceability. The best medical bearing ring was selected with the CoCoSo method in line with the criteria considered and the purpose in question. As a result of the analysis, alternative 10 emerged as the best alternative, while alternative 7 ranked last.

Arman and Organ (2023) analyzed the logistics performance of 27 EU member countries and 8 candidate countries including Turkey using MEREC (Method Based on the Removal Effects of Criteria) and CoCoSo methods. According to the MEREC method results, the criteria are infrastructure, customs management, tracking-tracing, logistics service quality, delivery of shipments within the planned or expected periods and ease of shipment arrangement, respectively, according to their weight levels. According to the CoCoSo method application results, Finland, Germany, Denmark and the Netherlands are among the first five countries with the highest LPI for 2023. Among the EU candidate countries, Turkey was found to have the highest and Albania the lowest logistics performance. In addition, it was determined that Turkey showed higher logistics performance than the 9 EU member countries for 2023. It is thought that the results obtained from this study will contribute to the literature in terms of revealing the advantages and deficiencies of countries in terms of logistics performance and implementing logistics policies accordingly.

After the relevant literature review, the application steps of the CoCoSo method are as follows. With the CoCoSo method, firstly, alternatives and criteria are determined in solving the decision problem (Yazdani et al., 2019).

Step 1: Determining the decision-making matrix

$$X = \left[x_{ij}\right]_{m*n} = \begin{bmatrix} x_{11} & \cdots & x_{12} & \cdots & x_{1n} \\ \vdots & \ddots & \vdots & \ddots & \vdots \\ x_{21} & \cdots & x_{22} & \cdots & x_{2n} \\ \vdots & \ddots & \vdots & \ddots & \vdots \\ x_{m1} & \cdots & x_{m2} & \cdots & x_{mn} \end{bmatrix} \tag{5}$$

x_{ij}, represents the value of alternative *i.* in criterion *j.*

Step 2: Normalize the benefit and cost criteria

$$r_{ij} = \frac{x_{ij} - \min_i x_{ij}}{\max_i x_{ij} - \min_i x_{ij}} \text{ ; for benefit criterion} \tag{6}$$

$$r_{ij} = \frac{\max_i x_{ij} - x_{ij}}{\min_i x_{ij} - \min_i x_{ij}} \text{ ; for cost criterion} \tag{7}$$

Step 3: Calculating S_i and P_i values

Equality (8) is used to find the sum of the weighted comparability series, and Equality (9) is used to calculate the sum of the comparability series for each of the alternatives.

$$S_i = \sum_{j=1}^{n} \left(w_j r_{ij} \right) \tag{8}$$

$$P_i = \sum_{j=1}^{n} \left(r_{ij} \right)^{w_j} \tag{9}$$

Step 4: Calculating the relative performance of alternatives

To calculate the relative performance of alternatives, three evaluation score strategies are calculated using Equations (10), (11). The value of λ (usually λ=0.5) shown in Equation (12) is left to the decision maker.

$$k_{ia} = \frac{S_i + P_i}{\sum_{i=1}^{m} \left(S_i + P_i \right)} \tag{10}$$

$$k_{ib} = \frac{S_i}{\min_i S_i} + \frac{P_i}{\min_i P_i} \tag{11}$$

$$k_{ic} = \frac{\lambda S_i + (1-\lambda) P_i}{\lambda \max_i S_i + (1-\lambda) \max_i P_i} ; 0 \leq \lambda \leq 1 \tag{12}$$

Step 5: Final ranking of alternatives

The final ranking of alternatives is determined by the k_i values and is given in Equation (13).

$$k_i = \left(k_{ia} k_{ib} k_{ic} \right)^{1/3} + \frac{1}{3} \left(k_{ia} + k_{ib} + k_{ic} \right) \tag{13}$$

3. FINDINGS

In the study, G7 countries were evaluated in terms of digital intelligence index using the CoCoSo method from the MCDM methods. The criteria and the values belonging to the criteria used in the study were obtained from the Digital Intelligence Index Report (2020) published by Tufts University. All of the criteria were determined as benefit-oriented and 6 criteria, namely state (C1), momentum (C2), environment (C3), experience (C4), behavior (C5), attitudes (C6), were first weighted with the SD (Standard Deviation) method. G7 countries United States

(A1), Germany (A2), United Kingdom (A3), France (A4), Italy (A5), Canada (A6), Japan (A7) were ranked and evaluated in terms of digital intelligence performance using the CoCoSo method. First, the application steps of the SD method will be included and then the application steps of the CoCoSo method will be moved on.

3.1. Application of SD Method

Step 1: Creating the decision matrix

The decision matrix consisting of 6 criteria and 7 alternatives, using data obtained from the Digital Intelligence Index Report, is as shown in Table 1.

Table 1. Decision Making Matrix

	C1	C2	C3	C4	C5	C6
A1	89.82	49.34	58.41	78.16	72.16	33.03
A2	79.27	48.28	64.96	55.99	32.46	64.23
A3	81.48	44.81	65	55.33	55.68	46.74
A4	72.99	43.37	54.05	54.39	35.78	41.17
A5	61.27	47.27	60.4	48.14	38.45	58.47
A6	80.24	38.12	62.24	57.17	51.5	46.82
A7	77.76	44.96	58.67	60.37	31.12	49.16

Step 2: Normalizing the decision matrix

The normalization process of the decision matrix was calculated using Equation (2).

Table 2. Normalized decision matrix

	C1	C2	C3	C4	C5	C6
A1	1.0000	1.0000	0.3982	1.0000	1.0000	0.0000
A2	0.6305	0.9055	0.9963	0.2615	0.0327	1.0000
A3	0.7079	0.5963	1.0000	0.2395	0.5984	0.4394
A4	0.4105	0.4679	0.0000	0.2082	0.1135	0.2609
A5	0.0000	0.8155	0.5799	0.0000	0.1786	0.8154
A6	0.6644	0.0000	0.7479	0.3008	0.4966	0.4420
A7	0.5776	0.6096	0.4219	0.4074	0.0000	0.5170

Step 3: Calculating criterion weights

In the last step, the criterion weights were calculated with the SD method. Equation (4) was used in the calculation of the criterion weights.

Table 3. Criteria Weights

	C1	C2	C3	C4	C5	C6
w_j	0.1525	0.1660	0.1779	0.1557	0.1828	0.1651

According to the results of the SD method, the criterion with the highest importance was behavior (C5), followed by environment (C3).

3.2. Application of the CoCoSo Method

Step 1: Determining the decision matrix

The decision matrix is not included in this step as it is included in Table 1.

Step 2: Normalizing the benefit and cost criteria

Since all criteria are benefit-oriented, the normalized decision matrix is calculated with Equation (7). The normalized decision matrix is as shown in Table 4.

Table 4. Normalized decision matrix

	C1	C2	C3	C4	C5	C6
A1	1.0000	1.0000	0.3982	1.0000	1.0000	0.0000
A2	0.6305	0.9055	0.9963	0.2615	0.0327	1.0000
A3	0.7079	0.5963	1.0000	0.2395	0.5984	0.4394
A4	0.4105	0.4679	0.0000	0.2082	0.1135	0.2609
A5	0.0000	0.8155	0.5799	0.0000	0.1786	0.8154
A6	0.6644	0.0000	0.7479	0.3008	0.4966	0.4420
A7	0.5776	0.6096	0.4219	0.4074	0.0000	0.5170

Step 3: Calculation of S_i and P_i values

In the third step, the S_i and P_i values of the countries were calculated with Equality (9) and Equality (10). The calculated values are shown in Table 5 and Table 6.

Table 5. S_i values of the countries

	C1	C2	C3	C4	C5	C6	S_i
A1	0.1525	0.1660	0.0708	0.1557	0.1828	0.0000	0.7279
A2	0.0962	0.1504	0.1773	0.0407	0.0060	0.1651	0.6355
A3	0.1080	0.0990	0.1779	0.0373	0.1094	0.0725	0.6041
A4	0.0626	0.0777	0.0000	0.0324	0.0208	0.0431	0.2365

continued on following page

Table 5. Continued

A5	0.0000	0.1354	0.1032	0.0000	0.0326	0.1346	0.4058
A6	0.1013	0.0000	0.1331	0.0468	0.0908	0.0730	0.4450
A7	0.0881	0.1012	0.0751	0.0634	0.0000	0.0853	0.4131

Table 6. P_i values of countries

	C1	C2	C3	C4	C5	C6	S_i
A1	1.0000	1.0000	0.8489	1.0000	1.0000	0.0000	4.8489
A2	0.9321	0.9837	0.9993	0.8115	0.5350	1.0000	5.2616
A3	0.9487	0.9177	1.0000	0.8005	0.9104	0.8731	5.4504
A4	0.8730	0.8815	0.0000	0.7832	0.6719	0.8011	4.0108
A5	0.0000	0.9667	0.9076	0.0000	0.7299	0.9669	3.5711
A6	0.9396	0.0000	0.9496	0.8294	0.8799	0.8739	4.4724
A7	0.9197	0.9273	0.8767	0.8720	0.0000	0.9043	4.4999

Step 4: Calculating the Relative Performance of Alternatives

The relative performance values of the alternatives are calculated with Equality (11), Equality (12) and Equality (13) and are shown in Table 7.

Table 7. Relative performance values of countries

	k_{ia}	k_{ib}	k_{ic}
A1	0.1567	4.4350	0.9026
A2	0.1657	4.1602	0.9545
A3	0.1702	4.0801	0.9800
A4	0.1194	2.1231	0.6875
A5	0.1118	2.7157	0.6437
A6	0.1382	3.1335	0.7959
A7	0.1381	3.0067	0.7952

Step 5: Final Ranking of Alternatives

k_i values are calculated with Equation (10) and the ranking results of these values are shown in Table 8.

Table 8. k_i values and ranking results

	k_i	Rank
A1	2.6875	1
A2	2.6299	2
A3	2.6229	3
A4	1.5352	7
A5	1.7373	6
A6	2.0570	4
A7	2.0045	5

According to the results of the CoCoSo method, the country that ranks first in terms of digital intelligence performance is the United States (A1), followed by Germany (A2). The countries with the lowest performance are France (A4) and Italy (A5), respectively.

4. CONCLUSION AND EVALUATION

Developments in digital technologies have made it important for individuals to gain skills, abilities and usage qualities in the face of digital technologies. However, what is more important than this is the concept of digital intelligence, which can be developed with various tendencies or awareness. In our age, where digitalization dominates every field, digital intelligence also emerges as an important concept. In this direction, this concept should be one of the priorities in terms of developing the competencies to use digital technologies and reducing the digital divide within society, far beyond using smartphones (Gür et al., 2019).

In this study, G7 countries were evaluated in terms of their artificial intelligence performance. First, the criteria (state, momentum, environment, experience, behavior, attitudes) were weighted with the SD method. According to the results obtained with this method, the criterion with the highest importance was behavior (C5). Behavior examines the interaction of consumers in various parameters such as technology use, social media, e-commerce and mobile payments (DII, 2020). After the criteria were weighted, G7 countries were ranked and evaluated in terms of their artificial intelligence performance with the CoCoSo method. According to the results of the analysis, the country that ranked first in terms of digital intelligence performance was the United States (A1), while the country that ranked last was France (A4).

When the United States is evaluated in the context of the current criteria, it is seen that it is the country with the highest values in all criteria except the environment criterion. The reasons why the United States is also the best in terms of digital intelligence compared to other countries can be shown as being good in technological infrastructure and innovation, making high investments, having the capacity to have big data, advanced education and strong human resources, and having an effective digital ecosystem. The United States is one of the leading global technological countries. At the same time, this success of the United States is closely related to its comprehensive artificial intelligence policies, supported by advanced digital infrastructure and strategic legislation such as the National AI Initiative Act of 2020. Such strategies increase public-private partnerships, direct research investments, and develop human resources that support digital intelligence (Zhang & Dafoe, 2019). France, on the other hand, ranked last among the G7 countries in terms of digital intelligence performance. When evaluated in line with the current criteria, it was seen that this country received the lowest scores in most criteria. France is a country that has developed in the field of digital intelligence, but has fallen behind in this area compared to technology giants such as the United States. This country will be able to advance to higher levels in the digital intelligence ecosystem if it solves the problems of investment and financing deficiencies, digital literacy, education and limited data infrastructure.

Increasing the digital intelligence level of countries requires much more than technological infrastructure. Effective administrative policy frameworks, sustainable investment models, a strong digital education infrastructure and human-centered artificial intelligence strategies are the key factors that increase digital intelligence. In this context, countries should not only follow good practices, but also develop national strategies that are appropriate for their local contexts, reducing the digital divide and achieving sustainable development goals with a digital intelligence-based approach. Countries also need to improve their digital intelligence performance by following the policies and strategies of countries such as the United States, China, South Korea, and Japan. With the right investments and research, it is possible for countries to take themselves to higher levels in terms of digital intelligence. In this way, their prosperity levels will increase and they will continue to show continuous development.

Based on the explanations, in future studies, analyses can be performed using various MCDM methods using the DII. A more comprehensive performance evaluation can be made by increasing the number of alternatives (countries). The studies to be conducted on this subject can be compared with this study and the literature can be enriched in this context.

REFERENCES

Aksin-Sivrikaya, S., & Bhattacharya, C. B. (2017). Where digitalization meets sustainability: opportunities and challenges. *Sustainability In a Digital World: New Opportunities Through New Technologies*, 37-49. DOI: 10.1007/978-3-319-54603-2_3

Aly, H. (2020). Digital transformation, development and productivity in developing countries: Is artificial intelligence a curse or a blessing? *Review of Economics and Political Science*, *7*(4), 238–256. DOI: 10.1108/REPS-11-2019-0145

Andrejić, M., & Pajić, V. (2023). Optimizing personnel selection in transportation: An application of the BWM-CoCoSo decision-support model. *Journal of Organizations. Technology and Entrepreneurship*, *1*(1), 35–46. DOI: 10.56578/jote010103

Arman, K., & Organ, A. (2023). AB'ye üye ve aday ülkelerin lojistik performanslarının MEREC ve COCOSO yöntemleri ile değerlendirilmesi. *Uluslararası Ticaret ve Ekonomi Araştırmaları Dergisi*, *7*(2), 36–46. DOI: 10.30711/utead.1360959

Aruldoss, M., Lakshmi, T. M., & Venkatesan, V. P. (2013). A survey on multi criteria decision making methods and its applications. *American Journal of Information Systems*, *1*(1), 31–43. DOI: 10.12691/ajis-1-1-5

Baker, D., & Evans, W. (2015). *Digital information strategies: From applications and content to libraries and people.* Chandos Publishing.

Baydaş, M., & Pamučar, D. (2022). Determining objective characteristics of MCDM methods under uncertainty: An exploration study with financial data. *Mathematics*, *10*(7), 1115. DOI: 10.3390/math10071115

Börü, E. (2022). *Sürdürülebilirlik en iyi yatırım aracı. Fast Company, 13.* Şubat-Mart.

Ceballos, B., Lamata, M. T., & Pelta, D. A. (2016). A comparative analysis of multi-criteria decision-making methods. *Progress in Artificial Intelligence*, *5*(4), 315–322. DOI: 10.1007/s13748-016-0093-1

Cismaru, D. M., Gazzola, P., Ciochina, R. S., & Leovaridis, C. (2018). The rise of digital intelligence: Challenges for public relations education and practices. *Kybernetes*, *47*(10), 1924–1940. DOI: 10.1108/K-03-2018-0145

Diakoulaki, D., Mavrotas, G., & Papayannakis, L. (1995). Determining Objective Weights in Multiple Criteria Problems: The CRITIC Method. *Computers & Operations Research*, *22*(7), 763–770. DOI: 10.1016/0305-0548(94)00059-H

Digital Intelligenge Index. (2020). Digital in the time of covid trust in the digital economy and Its evolution across 90 economies as the planet paused for a pandemic, https://digitalplanet.tufts.edu/wp-content/uploads/2022/09/digital-intelligence-index .pdf, (accessed on 01 September 2024).

Dwivedi, P. P., & Sharma, D. K. (2022). Application of Shannon entropy and CoCoSo methods in selection of the most appropriate engineering sustainability components. *Cleaner Materials*, *5*, 100118. DOI: 10.1016/j.clema.2022.100118

Gavade, R. K. (2014). Multi-Criteria Decision Making: An overview of different selection problems and methods. *International Journal of Computer Science and Information Technologies*, *5*(4), 5643–5646.

Ghorabaee, M. K., Zavadskas, E. K., Amiri, M., & Turskis, Z. (2016). Extended EDAS method for fuzzy multi-criteria decision-making: An application to supplier selection. *International Journal of Computers, Communications & Control*, *11*(3), 358–371. DOI: 10.15837/ijccc.2016.3.2557

Gobble, M. M. (2018). Digitalization, digitization, and innovation. *Research Technology Management*, *61*(4), 56–59. DOI: 10.1080/08956308.2018.1471280

Gray, J., & Rumpe, B. (2015). Models for digitalization. *Software & Systems Modeling*, *14*(4), 1319–1320. DOI: 10.1007/s10270-015-0494-9

Gür, E. D., Canan, G. O., Hamutoğlu, N. B., Kaya, U. G., & Demirtaş, T. T. (2019). The relation of lifelong learning trends, digital literacy levels and usage of web 2.0 tools, with social entrepreneurship characteristics. *Croation Journal of Education*, *21*(1), 45–76. DOI: 10.15516/cje.v21i1.2989

Hadizadeh, M., Khodaparast, P., Ghasemi, A., & Fakhrzad, M. B. (2023). Analysis of supply chain anti-fragility in the textile industry using the Best-Worst method and CoCoSo. *Journal of Advertising and Sales Management, 4*(3), 426-440. DOI: JABM.3.2.15564.0954

Hwang, C. L., & Yoon, K. (1981). Methods for multiple attribute decision making. In *Multiple attribute decision making: methods and applications a state-of-the-art survey* (pp. 58-191). Springer Berlin Heidelberg.

Jafari, M., & Khanachah, S. N. (2024). Integrated knowledge management in the supply chain: Assessment of knowledge adoption solutions through a comprehensive CoCoSo method under uncertainty. *Journal of Industrial Information Integration*, *39*, 100581. DOI: 10.1016/j.jii.2024.100581

Jorgenson, D. W. (2001). Information technology and the US economy. *The American Economic Review*, *91*(1), 1–32. DOI: 10.1257/aer.91.1.1

Khan, S., & Haleem, A. (2021). Investigation of circular economy practices in the context of emerging economies: A CoCoSo approach. *International Journal of Sustainable Engineering, 14*(3), 357–367. DOI: 10.1080/19397038.2020.1871442

Kravchenko, O., Leshchenko, M., Marushchak, D., Vdovychenko, Y., & Boguslavska, S. (2019). The digitalization as a global trend and growth factor of the modern economy. In SHS Web of Conferences (Vol. 65, p. 07004). EDP Sciences. DOI: 10.1051/shsconf/20196507004

Kreeb, M., & Haasis, H. D. (2017). Sustainable cooperate information portals: Digital knowledge communities for SME. *Sustainability in a digital world: New opportunities through new technologies,* 145-158.

Kreiss, D., & Brennen, J. S. (2016). Normative models of digital journalism. *The Sage Handbook of Digital Journalism*, 299-314.

Kumar, V., Kalita, K., Chatterjee, P., Zavadskas, E. K., & Chakraborty, S. (2022). A SWARA-CoCoSo-based approach for spray painting robot selection. *Informatica (Vilnius), 33*(1), 35–54. DOI: 10.15388/21-INFOR466

Lai, H., Liao, H., Wen, Z., Zavadskas, E. K., & Al-Barakati, A. (2020). An improved CoCoSo method with a maximum variance optimization model for cloud service provider selection. *The Engineering Economist, 31*(4), 411–424. DOI: 10.5755/j01.ee.31.4.24990

Mittal, P. (2020, November). A multi-criterion decision analysis based on PCA for analyzing the digital technology skills in the effectiveness of government services. In *2020 International Conference on Decision Aid Sciences and Application (DASA)* (pp. 490-494). IEEE. DOI: DOI: 10.1109/DASA51403.2020.9317241

Mondejar, M. E., Avtar, R., Diaz, H. L. B., Dubey, R. K., Esteban, J., Gómez-Morales, A., Hallam, B., Mbungu, N. T., Okolo, C. C., Prasad, K. A., She, Q., & Garcia-Segura, S. (2021). Digitalization to achieve sustainable development goals: Steps towards a Smart Green Planet. *The Science of the Total Environment, 794*, 148539. DOI: 10.1016/j.scitotenv.2021.148539 PMID: 34323742

Nabeeh, N. A., & Sallam, K. M. (2024). A Combined Compromise Solution (CoCoSo) of MCDM Problems for Selection of Medical Best Bearing Ring. *Neutrosophic Optimization and Intelligent Systems, 1*, 1-13. https://orcid.org/0000-0003-3214-1556

Nişel, R., & Nişel, S. (2024). Advancing Global Innovation Metrics: A Comprehensive Country Ranking Using the Novel LOPCOW-CoCoSo Model. In *Ethics and Sustainability in Accounting and Finance* (Vol. IV, pp. 99–118). Springer Nature Singapore.

Opricovic, S., & Tzeng, G. H. (2004). Compromise solution by MCDM methods: A comparative analysis of VIKOR and TOPSIS. *European Journal of Operational Research, 156*(2), 445–455. DOI: 10.1016/S0377-2217(03)00020-1

Osburg, T. (2017). Sustainability in a digital world. T. Osburg & C. Lohrmann (Eds.), *Sustainability in a Digital World Needs Trust* (pp. 3-19). Springer International Publishing.

Ozdagoglu, A., Ulutas, A., & Keles, M. K. (2020). The ranking of Turkish universities with COCOSO and MARCOS. *Journal of Economic Behavior & Organization,* •••, 374–392.

Popović, M. (2021). An MCDM approach for personnel selection using the CoCoSo method. *Journal of process management and new technologies, 9*(3-4), 78-88. DOI:DOI: 10.5937/jouproman2103078P

Styvén, M. E., & Wallström, Å. (2019). Benefits and barriers for the use of digital channels among small tourism companies. *Scandinavian Journal of Hospitality and Tourism, 19*(1), 27–46. DOI: 10.1080/15022250.2017.1379434

Torkayesh, A. E., Pamucar, D., Ecer, F., & Chatterjee, P. (2021). An integrated BWM-LBWA-CoCoSo framework for evaluation of healthcare sectors in Eastern Europe. *Socio-Economic Planning Sciences, 78*, 101052. DOI: 10.1016/j.seps.2021.101052

Türkoğlu, S. P., & Tuzcu, S. E. (2021). Assessing country performances during the COVID-19 pandemic: A standard deviation based range of value method. *Operational Research in Engineering Sciences: Theory and Applications, 4*(3), 59–81. DOI: 10.31181/oresta081221059t

Vartolomei, V. C., & Avasilcai, S. (2019, August). Challenges of digitalization process in different industries. Before and after. In *IOP Conference Series: Materials Science and Engineering, 568* (Vol. 1). IOP Publishing.

Yazdani, M., Wen, Z., Liao, H., Banaitis, A., & Turskis, Z. (2019). A grey combined compromise solution (CoCoSo-G) method for supplier selection in construction management. *Journal of Civil Engineering and Management, 25*(8), 858–874. DOI: 10.3846/jcem.2019.11309

Yazdani, M., Zarate, P., Kazimieras Zavadskas, E., & Turskis, Z. (2019). A combined compromise solution (CoCoSo) method for multi-criteria decision-making problems. *Management Decision, 57*(9), 2501–2519. DOI: 10.1108/MD-05-2017-0458

Zhang, B., & Dafoe, A. (2019, January 9). Artificial intelligence: American attitudes and trends. *SSRN*. DOI: 10.2139/ssrn.3312874

Chapter 11
Sustainable Development Performance Analysis of G20 Countries Using Merec Based Marcos and Cocoso Methods

Eda Çinaroğlu
https://orcid.org/0000-0002-2904-3376
Erciyes University, Kayseri, Turkey

ABSTRACT

Sustainable development was defined in the Brundtland Report in 1987 as "the ability of humanity to meet its present needs without compromising the ability of future generations to meet their needs". Sustainability is addressed in four different dimensions: social, economic, environmental and governmental. These dimensions create value in an integrated manner and reveal the concept of sustainable development. This study aims to evaluate the sustainable development performances of G20 countries, which are among the world's largest economies. MEREC supported MARCOS and CoCoSo methods are employed during the analysis using component values of the 2022 Transaction Performance Index (TPI). According to the results, It has been determined that the most important factor in analyzing the G20 countries' sustainable development performance is social transition. Germany has the highest sustainable development performance among G20 countries. United Kingdom ranks second with France coming in third. South Africa has the lowest sustainable development performance.

DOI: 10.4018/979-8-3693-8789-4.ch011

INTRODUCTION

Sustainability is defined as a strategy to maintaining the balance between the environment, society and economy. In this context, it is intended to ensure the proper utilization of natural resources, the minimization of environmental damage and social fairness in the process of serving human needs optimally in societies. Most definitions of sustainable development (SD) include elements of economy, environment and society (Parris and Kates, 2003). It necessitates strong scholarship and evidence-based decision-making that takes into consideration present conditions and trends while demonstrating how lifestyles, economies, technology and social practices may be effectively modified to reduce risks, minimize harm and provide long-term benefits (Portney, 2015).

Hans Carl von Carlowitz used the word term sustainability for the first time in his book work Sylvicultura Oeconomica in 1713. The term became popular after the Brundtland Report of the United Nations' World Commission on Environment and Development described SD as "meeting the needs of the present generation without compromising the ability of future generations to meet their own needs" (Heinberg and Lerch, 2010).

SD might be seen as an intersection between the economic development and the protection of the environment. The goal of SD is to enhance the quantity and quality of products and services while minimizing environmental impact. That highlights the issues of population growth and environmental problem avoidance. It combines balanced ecology and economic expansion to ensure efficient use of earth's resources, prioritize environmental quality and fulfill future needs (Ecer et al., 2019).

SD has economic, social, environmental and governmental components. The economic dimension seeks to carry out economic operations that will meet the requirements of individuals in a sustainable manner. For this goal, it is intended to raise national revenue while maintaining or increasing capital stock (Rogers et al., 2012). The environmental dimension seeks to encourage the sustainable usage of natural resources while minimizing environmental consequences in order to meet human needs (Morelli, 2011). This preference allows for the consideration of reducing environmental damage in manufacturing processes as well as encouraging renewable energy sources. The social dimension seeks to promote social fairness while dealing with people's needs. Social sustainability is associated with necessities such as health, nutrition, shelter, education, gender equality and inclusion (Moldan et., 2012). The governance dimension relates to the systems, processes, norms and habits that govern how individuals in communities take decisions, share authority, perform responsibility and assure transparency (Patterson et al., 2017; Cundill and Fabricius, 2010).

The G20 countries, including Turkey, represent nearly two thirds of the worldwide population and 85% of the global GDP. This platform, established by EU members and the world's leading economies, focuses on topics such as energy, climate change, development, employment and the fight against corruption, as well as guaranteeing global financial stability. The goal is for member countries to create and execute common policies concerning these issues.

In this study, the performance of SD in G20 countries is analyzed in terms of economic, social, environmental and governmental aspects applying the multi-criteria decision making (MCDM) methodologies MEREC, MARCOS and CoCoSo. In this context, it will be possible to understand the effects of the G20 countries' efforts to promote social welfare through increased production on aspects of the environment and society. The goal is to compare the SD policies and so add valuable information to the literature by allowing for the comparative assessment of the efficiency of SD policies in G20 countries. This approach is meant to objectively investigate various aspects of SD, allowing for the future formulation of more effective and complete policies.

The study's following five sections are as follows. The definition, scope and development processes of the idea of SD are explored in the first section. The literature review is provided in the second section. The study's methodology is explained in detail in the third section. The fourth section presents the analysis process and results. The conclusion and related recommendations for the future are included in the last section.

1. SUSTAINABLE DEVELOPMENT

Human activity has increased to the point where it has the potential to change the planet's temperature and biological composition for the first time in history. The driving force is economics. Carbon emissions are produced when fossil fuels are burned to obtain energy for production. The earth's climate was altered by the emissions produced since World War II. This excessive use of resources, which has its roots mostly in industrialized nations, has led to a widening gap between industrial and emerging nations' resource consumption and welfare (Chichilinisk, 1999).

One of the most urgent concerns for world policy during the 1992 United Nations Earth Summit in Rio de Janeiro was SD. UN Agenda 21 was approved by 150 participating countries, which included SD on meeting the fundamental needs of developing countries as part of its policy agenda. Members to this agreement commit to provide financial and technological resources to developing countries and reducing their emissions of greenhouse gases to 1990 levels through national programs. The Bariloche Model first proposed this development criterion in 1976 and the Brundtland Commission's 1987 proposal that "sustainable development is development that satisfies the needs of the present without compromising the needs of the future" gave it an additional effect (Chichilinisk, 1999).

As part of this framework agreement, the Kyoto Protocol was signed in 1977 requiring the developed countries to decrease the emissions of their greenhouse gases by 5.2% from 1990 values. The protocol's primary goal was to lower the average emission levels of greenhouse gases over a five-year period from 2008 to 2012 (Böhringer, 2003).

The Millennium Declaration was released in 2000, following the United Nations Millennium Summit. The declaration established several development goals that are expected to be achieved by 2015. These aims included eliminating hunger and poverty, providing elementary school education to all citizens, promoting equal rights for women and men, improving the health of women and children and combating AIDS, HIV, AIDS and numerious other illnesses (Ecer et al., 2019).

The United Nations Conference on Sustainable Development (Rio+20 Summit) took place in Brazil, from June 20 to 22, 2012. At the Rio+20 Summit, world leaders aimed to achieve a common definition in the global arena for the purpose of "green growth," which has been reshaped according to today's requirements (battling climate change, surviving economic crises, low-carbon emission improvement, etc.) of the SD goal, which has been widely used around the world since the 1992 Rio Summit 20 years ago. The summit covered the following topics: "Institutional Framework for SD, Climate Change, Sustainable Production and Consumption, Disaster Risk Reduction, Chemicals and Waste, Sustainable Transport and Cities, Health and Population, Sustainable Tourism, Oceans and Seas, Water and Sanitation, Food Security and Sustainable Agriculture, Employment, Forests, Biodiversity, Desertification, Land Degradation and Famine, Mining, Gender Equity and Empowerment of Women, Poverty Reduction" (Sánchez and Croal, 2012; Barrutia et al., 2015).

In 2015, the United Nations Sustainable Development Summit established the 2030 Sustainable Development Goals (SDGs). The 17 SDGs that UN member countries intend to attain by 2030 have been agreed within the framework of 169 sub-goals. These SDGs aim to eliminate inequalities, boost economic growth and employment, improve cities and settlements, ensure industrialization, protect oceans and ecosystems, produce and consume energy more sustainably, combat climate change, develop sustainable production and consumption and strengthen human rights. The 2030 Agenda aims to integrate all societies in attempts for reducing poverty and improve global wellbeing, conserve cultural and social values and minimize the destruction of the environment. Gender equality, addressing the demands of disadvantaged groups, minimizing wasted food, preventing desertification and drought and protecting the environment, as well as economic issues such as growth in the economy, advences in technology, employment and growth in industrialization have all been added to the sustainable development agenda (Brodny and Tutak, 2023; Pradhan et al., 2017).

SD seeks to maintain the well-being of both present and future generations by striking a balance between economic, social and environmental sustainability (Hall et al., 2010). SD has three key dimensions: economic, social and environmental.

The economic dimension is based on avoiding and protecting capital (Goodland, 1995). It is concerned with the utilization of capital without degradation. This dimension is reflected by data such as GDP, inflation, unemployment rate, purchasing power parity and export/import.

The social dimension entails enhancing working and living conditions for employees, customers, society and future generations. It demands the maintenance of society's integrity and ability to collaborate toward common goals. It addresses issues such as health, nutrition, housing, education, diversity, quality of life, democracy, data privacy, gender equality, human rights and safe working conditions. This dimension is demonstrated in selected variables such as education level, infant mortality rate, healthcare professionals, number of hospital beds, poverty rate and female parliamentary representation (Moldan et al., 2012).

The environmental dimension is concerned with removing or reducing the harmful effects of production operations carried out using environmental techniques, as well as maintaining the continuity and transfer of limited resources to future generations. It is defined as “the ability to maintain qualities that are valued in the physical environment” (Sutton, 2004). This dimension covers issues such as climate change and carbon dioxide emissions, efficinet use of water, energy and air pollution, drought and biodiversity. The indicators used to assess environmental effectiveness include CO2 emissions, population use of drinking water services, the consumption of natural resources, freshwater withdrawal from available sources, CO2 emissions from the combustion of fuel per total electricity output, renewable energy share in total primary energy supply and production-based nitrogen emissions (Alpdoğan, 2023).

The governance dimension is a later addition to the SD framework. The concept of governance, whose association with SD dates back to the 1980s, expresses the common mind of planning and organization required to realize the goal of development sustainability (Keefer, 2004). The concept has come to be considered as the traditions and institutional structures that govern how a country's resources are employed for economic and social development. The quality of governance depends on the decision-making procedures, wielding authority and the participation of the public in this process (Özer, 2006). It includes indicators such as bureaucratic quality, transparency, rule of law, participation, anti-corruption efforts, human rights protection, accountability and political stability (Güney, 2016).

The Transition Performance Index (TPI), produced by the EU Commission, is one of the metrics used to evaluate countries global sustainability performances.

The TPI is a scoreboard that evaluates and rates countries based on their four steps toward balanced and prosperous sustainability. The index is based on a comprehensive conceptual framework developed in consultation with many stakeholders and experts, as well as 29 internationally available indicators. This index assesses the SD performance of all EU members, as well as 45 other countries. This measurement is addressed in four fundamental dimensions. The first fundamental dimension, economic transformation, expresses the welfare-oriented work of the economy. This dimension includes four sub-dimensions: wealth, education, labor productivity and research and development intensity and industrial base. The second basic dimension is the social transformation dimension, which emphasizes fairness and inclusivity. This dimension encompasses the sub-dimensions of work and inclusion, free or non-remunerated time, health and equality. The third dimension is environmental transformation, which aligns with the European Green Deal goals. This dimension encompasses the sub-dimensions of greenhouse gas emissions reduction, biodiversity, material utilization and energy productivity. The final dimension, governance transformation, expresses democratic progress and is divided into four sub-dimensions: fundamental rights, transparency, security and sound public finances. These metrics concentrate on resilience, inclusiveness, sustainability and prosperity. They complement the EU's 2022 Annual Sustainable Growth Strategy. The TPI is an effective communication tool for tracking progress over a span of a decade and evaluating countries to identify strengths and areas for improvements (European Commission, Transitions Performance Index 2021, p.39).

2. LITERATURE REVIEW

This section includes two subsections. The first subsection comprises studies that use MCDM approaches to analyze countries SD performance. The second subsection summarizes studies on different topics conducted using the MEREC supported MARCOS and CoCoSo techniques.

Altıntaş (2024) evaluated EU countries' SD performance with the MEREC based WEBDA approach. The study assessed the Transaction Performance Index (TPI) components of EU countries in 2022. According to the study's findings, where the environmental dimension was given highest importance in sustainability measurement, Denmark, Ireland and Malta were identified as the top three countries with the highest SD performance. The GKRK, Finland, and Estonia were the EU countries with the lowest SD performance.

Alpdoğan's (2023) study was aimed at evaluating OECD countries SD policy performance. In this context, an ARAS methodology was used based on five economic (GDP, unemployment rate, inflation, export/import and purchasing power parity

(PPP)), six social (education level, number of hospital beds, number of healthcare professionals, infant mortality rate, poverty and number of female parliamentarians rate) and eight environmental criteria (CO2 emission, population using at least basic drinking water services, natural resource consumption, freshwater withdrawal % of available freshwater resources, CO2 emissions from fuel combustion per total electricity output, share of renewable energy in total primary energy supply, production-based nitrogen emissions and unrecycled municipal solid waste). The results indicate that New Zealand, Korea and Iceland have the most effective SD policies. According to the study's findings, Turkey, Canada and the United States had the lowest SD performance among OECD countries.

In their study, Ateş and Usman (2021) examined the SD of 25 countries from the Morgan Stanley Capital International Emerging Markets Index. In this context, 37 criteria were used in five sub-dimensions: economic, financial, social, environmental and governance. The gray relational analysis method was applied during the analytical procedure. According to the analysis' findings, the countries with the highest SD were South Korea, the Czech Republic and Greece, whereas Pakistan, India and the Philippines had the worst rankings.

Alkan and Merdivenci (2021) assessed the SD performance of the top five countries (Germany, Sweden, Belgium, Austria and Japan) based on the rankings of 2018 logistics performance index. Within the scope of the three dimensions of SD, the study was based on 20 criteria of economic (LPE scores, sustainability economic development score, GDP growth rate, GDP per capita, high-tech exports and Gini index), social (population internet usage rate, life expectancy, secondary education enrollment rate, state education expenditures, highly educated workforce, health expenditures per capita) and environmental (surface area, agricultural area, food production index, forest area, alternative and nuclear energy, renewable energy consumption, renewable fuel and waste, electricity produced from renewable resources). The entropy-supported EDAS approach was employed in this research. As stated in the study's findings, Sweden ranks the first in terms of SD.

To assess the SD performance of Latin American countries, Goker et al. (2021) proposed a fuzzy MCDM approach that combines data envelopment analysis (DEA) and quality function deployment (QFD). Peru came in first place, following Chile and Costa Rica, based on the results.

Resce and Schiltz (2021) introduced a new method using Hierarchical Stochastic Multicriteria Acceptability Analysis (HSMAA) to assess European nations on the SDGs. Regardless of the weights assigned to certain indicators and objectives, the results demonstrated that Denmark ranks as the first. Bulgaria and Romania showed lower performance levels.

Stanujkic et al. (2020) assessed EU countries' SD performance using the Entropy-supported CoCoSo technique. 17 SDG components were used as criteria in the study.

The final results reveal Sweden as the country that best performed the stated SD goals and had the best outcomes in contrast to them, with Romania in last position.

Kaya (2020) investigated how the COVID-19 epidemic affected the SD of countries in OECD. The countries' SD performance were evaluated using the MAIRCA, MABAC and WASPAS techniques. According to MAIRCA research, the United States had the best sustainability performance among OECD countries. Japan and Germany followed this country. The results obtained using MAIRCA, MABAC and WASPAS techniques were relatively similar. The United States performed the best in terms of SD within all three methods.

Oliveira et al. (2019) combined two fuzzy MCDM approaches (fuzzy AHP and fuzzy TOPSIS), prospective structural analysis (PSA) and network theory tools to provide a contextual and systemic basis framework for choosing SDG targets for the Brazilian 2030 Agenda.

Ecer et al. (2019) evaluated the SD performance of the OPEC countries employing 41 SD indicators across 10 dimensions using the Combined Compromise Solution (CoCoSo) approach. The results show that the United Arab Emirates is the most sustainable OPEC participant with the highest performance score, followed by Qatar, Kuwait and Iran.

Karaşan and Kahraman (2018) developed an IVN EDAS method to apply for prioritizing the United Nations' national SDGFs. According to the results of the proposed method, the most significiant United Nations' national SDGs for Turkey are poverty, unemployment, promoting societies that are inclusive and peaceful, good health and sustainable agriculture.

Megyesiova and Lieskovska (2018) carried out another study assessing the OECD countries performance in SD. Cluster analysis was used to identify similarities and contrasts within the 15 SD indicators of the OECD countries on topics such economic growth, environmental performance, social inequality, health and education.

Mateusz et al. (2018) assessed the EU countries' SD performance using TPI component values. The TOPSIS method's ranking results show that Austria, Belgium and Germany have the highest SD performance, while Romania, Poland and Latvia have the lowest. According to the VIKOR approach, Austria, France and Germany have the highest SD performance. Romania, Estonia and the Cyprus have the lowest levels of SD performance.

Antanasijevic et al. (2017) conducted an empirical study to analyze European countries' SD performance using the PROMETHEE (Preference Ranking Organization MeTHod for Enrichment Evaluations) methodology. The analysis was conducted over a 10-year period in 30 European nations to identify both theme-specific and general sustainability progress. The findings found that a great deal of European countries have achieved progress in sustainability over the study period, with the

Czech Republic, Germany, Hungary and Sweden improving their SD performance across every dimension.

Balcerzak and Pietrzak (2016) conducted a study on the SD of EU countries. The study used Eurostat data from 2004 to 2013 and analyzed it using the TOPSIS approach. Sweden, Denmark, Netherlands, United Kingdom and Ireland were identified as the countries with the greatest SD levels.

Santana et al. (2014) used data envelopment analysis (DEA) to assess the SD performance of the BRICS (Brazil, India, Russia, South Africa and China) countries. According to the findings, Brazil was the country with the greatest economic and social performance.

Table 1 provides some recent research using the MEREC-based MARCOS technique in the analytical process, including selection, ranking and performance evaluation, whereas Table 2 indicates some recent studies using the MEREC-based CoCoSo approach.

Table 1. Review of studies on MEREC based MARCOS approach

Subject	Researcher (Year)
Sustainability performance analysis	Rao&Shukla (2024)
Sustainable forest resources management modelling	Mondal et al. (2024)
Financial performance evaluation	Mastilo et al. (2024), Sezgin et al. (2024)
Material selection	Kumar et al. (2024), Das&Sarkar (2024)
Travel and tourism development ranking	Štilić et al. (2024)
Food security characteristics evaluation	Tang et al. (2024)
Pedestrian crossings evaluation	Ristik et al. (2024)
Macroeconomic performance analysis	Yalman et al. (2023)
Circular economy indicators evaluation	Seyhan (2023), Kaya et al. (2023)
Smart city evaluation	Taş&Alptekin (2023)
Supply chain resilience evaluation	Duran (2023)
Project evaluation	Mahmoudian & Mousavi (2023)
Personnel selection	Noyan (2023)
Welding robot selection	Hong Son & Hieu (2023)
Logistics center location selection	Şahin (2023)
Innovation performance evaluation	Meral (2023), Ersoy (2022)
Policy selection for minimizing the climate change impacts of urban transportation	Simic et al. (2022)
Sustainable material selection	Haq et al. (2022)
Efficiency and productivity analysis	Ünlü et al. (2022)
Scissors mechanism best schema selection	Huy et al. (2022)

Table 2. Review of studies on MEREC based CoCoSo approach

Subject	Researcher (Year)
Supplier selection	Sönmez and Toktaş (2024)
Green university ranking	Abacıoğlu et al. (2024), Yaşar&Ünlü (2023)
Information Communication Technology Level Assessment	Ecer&Güneş (2024)
Regional agricultural E-commerce development evaluation	Huang et al. (2024)
Copper electrical wire selection	Thinh et al. (2024)
Location selection of special economic zone	Ghosh et al. (2024)
Financial performance evaluation	Sezgin&Aytekin (2024), Yürüyen et al. (2023), Ghosh&Bhattacharya (2022)
Assessing airlines' operational, financial and environmental sustainability	Tanrıverdi et al. (2023)
Assessment of the digital transformation in universities	Wang et al. (2023)
Sustainability performance evaluation	Arsu&Arsu (2023)
Selection of the optimal autonomous vehicle	Gamal et al. (2023)
Innovation performance evaluation	Ecer&Ayçin (2023)
Logistics performance evaluation	Arman&Organ (2023)
Forklift selection	Van Dua (2023)
Aircraft selection	Özdağoğlu et al. (2022)
Insurance sector evaluation	Bektaş (2022)
Urban transport planning	Simić et al. (2022)
Wind turbines selection	Yu et al. (2022)

3. RESEARCH METHODOLOGY

This section provides an explanation of the MCDM approaches used in the study as well as an extensive overview of the methodologies' analysis procedures.

3.1. MEREC Method

MEREC (Method based on the Removal Effects of Criteria) is a new objective criterion weighting method developed by Keshavarz-Ghorabaee et al. (2021). It calculates criteria weights by taking into account the consequences of each criterion's removal on the overall performance of alternatives. In other words, the criterion gains greater importance when its removal has greater impact on the overall performance of the alternatives. In other words, the criterion is given more weight when its removal "has a greater impact on the overall performance of the alternatives. The MEREC approach employs a logarithmic function to assess the total performance of alternatives. The method's main advantage is its flexibility, which allows decision makers to calculate performance using a variety of functions. The method analysis process steps are listed below (Keshavarz-Ghorabaee et al., 2021).

Step 1. An initial decision matrix showing the values of each alternative for each criterion is constructed in the first stage. This matrix's elements, denoted by the symbol x_{ij}, must all be bigger than zero. In the event that the decision matrix contains negative values, such values must be changed from negative to positive by applying the appropriate technique for negative values. Equation-1 establishes this matrix, which has n alternatives and m criteria.

$$X = \begin{bmatrix} x_{11} & x_{12} & \dots x_{1j} & \dots & x_{1m} \\ x_{21} & x_{22} & \dots x_{2j} & \dots & x_{2m} \\ \vdots & \vdots & \ddots \vdots & \ddots & \vdots \\ x_{i1} & x_{i2} & \dots x_{ij} & \dots & x_{im} \\ \vdots & \vdots & \ddots \vdots & \ddots & \vdots \\ x_{n1} & x_{n2} & \dots x_{nj} & \dots & x_{nm} \end{bmatrix} \quad (1)$$

Step 2. In this step, the decision matrix's elements are scaled using a basic linear normalization. The normalized matrix elements are indicated as n^x_{ij}. Equation (2) is used to normalize the set of beneficial criteria (J^+) and the set of non-beneficial criteria (J^-).

$$n^x_{ij} = \begin{cases} \dfrac{\min_j x_{ij}}{x_{ij}} j J^+ \\ \dfrac{x_{ij}}{\max_j x_{ij}} j J^- \end{cases} \quad (2)$$

Step 3. In this stage, a logarithmic metric with equal weights for criteria is applied to reach the overall performance values of the alternatives. Equation (3) is used to calculate these general performance values (S_i).

$$S_i = ln\left(1 + \left(\frac{1}{m}\sum_j \left|ln\left(n_{ij}^x\right)\right|\right)\right) \tag{3}$$

Step 4. In this step, the alternatives' performances are calculated by eliminating each criterion individually. Let S'_{ij} represent the overall performance of i th alternative after removing j th criterion. Equation (4) is used to calculate the changes in the alternatives' performance values.

$$S'_{ij} = ln\left(1 + \left(\frac{1}{m}\sum_{k,\, k\neq j} \left|ln\left(n_{ik}^x\right)\right|\right)\right) \tag{4}$$

Step 5. The sum of absolute deviations $\left(E_j\right)$ is calculated in this step. The removal effect of each criterion on the alternatives' overall performance is computed based on the values obtained in steps 3 and 4. This step is calculated via Equation (5).

$$E_j = \sum_i \left|S'_{ij} - S_i\right| \tag{5}$$

Step 6. In this step, the objective weight of each critarion is determined using the removal effects $\left(E_j\right)$ from step 5. $\left(w_j\right)$ represents the weight of the j th criterion. Equation (6) is used for calculating w_j.

$$w_j = \frac{E_j}{\sum_k E_k} \tag{6}$$

3.2. MARCOS Method

MARCOS (Measurement Alternatives and Ranking according to COmpromise Solution) method involves describing the relationship between alternatives and reference values (ideal and anti-ideal alternatives). The utility functions of the alternatives are determined using the established relationships and a compromise ranking is created based on ideal and anti-ideal solutions. Utility functions provide the foundation for defining decision preferences. Utility functions describe an alternative's position relative to the ideal and anti-ideal solutions. The optimal alternative is the one that is closest to the ideal while also being the farthest from the anti-ideal reference point. The approach consists of the following application steps (Stević et al., 2020).

Step 1. The decision matrix containing m alternatives and n criteria is created as in Equation (7).

$$X_{ij} = \begin{bmatrix} x_{11} & x_{12} & \cdots & x_{1n} \\ x_{21} & x_{22} & \cdots & x_{2n} \\ \vdots & \vdots & \ddots & \vdots \\ x_{m1} & x_{m2} & \cdots & x_{mn} \end{bmatrix}; i = 1,2,\ldots,m; j = 1,2,\ldots,n. \quad (7)$$

Step 2. In this step, the expanded initial matrix is created as in Equation (8). The expansion of the initial matrix involves defining the ideal (AI) and anti-ideal (AAI) solutions.

$$X = [X_{ij}]_{m*n} = \begin{matrix} AAI \\ A_1 \\ A_2 \\ \cdot \\ A_m \\ AI \end{matrix} \begin{bmatrix} X_{aa1} & X_{aa2} & \cdots & X_{aan} \\ X_{11} & X_{12} & \cdots & X_{1n} \\ X_{21} & X_{22} & \cdot & X_{2n} \\ & \cdot & \cdot & \\ X_{m1} & X_{m2} & \cdot & X_{mn} \\ X_{ai1} & X_{ai2} & \cdots & X_{ain} \end{bmatrix} \quad (8)$$

The ideal solution (AI) is the best alternative, whereas the anti-ideal solution (AAI) is the worst. Depending on the nature of the criterion, AAI and AI are defined using Equations (9 and 10))):

$$AAI = \min_i X_{ij} \ if\, j\epsilon\, B \ and \max_i X_{ij} \ if\, j\epsilon\, C \quad (9)$$

$$AI = \max_i X_{ij} \ if\, j\epsilon\, B \ and \ \min_i X_{ij} \ if\, j\epsilon\, C \quad (10)$$

Here, B represents the benefit criteria group, while C represents the cost criteria group.

Step 3. This step is the normalization step of the expanded initial matrix. The normalized matrix $N = \left[n_{ij}\right]_{m*n}$ is established using the Equations (11) and (12).

$$n_{ij} = \frac{X_{ai}}{X_{ij}} \ if\, j\epsilon\, C \quad (11)$$

$$n_{ij} = \frac{X_{ij}}{X_{ai}} \ if\, j\epsilon\, B \quad (12)$$

Step 4. This step is the step of creating the weighted matrix $V = \left[v_{ij}\right]_{m*n}$. The weighted matrix is obtained by multiplying the normalized matrix with the criterion weight values as shown in Equation (13).

$$v_{ij} = n_{ij} * w_j \quad (13)$$

Step 5. This is the calculation step of the utility degrees of the options K_i. Equations (14) and (15) are used to calculate an alternative's utility degree based on its anti-ideal and ideal solutions.

$$K_i^- = \frac{S_i}{S_{aai}} \tag{14}$$

$$K_i^+ = \frac{S_i}{S_{ai}} \tag{15}$$

$S_i (i = 1, 2, \ldots m)$ is the sum of weighted matrix elements for each choice, as stated in Equation (16).

$$S_i = \sum_{i=1}^{m} v_{ij} \tag{16}$$

Step 6. At this step, the alternatives' utility functions $f(K_i)$ are calculated. The compromise of the observed alternative in relation to the ideal and anti-ideal solutions is known as the utility function. Equation (17) defines the alternatives' utility function.

$$f(K_i) = \frac{K_i^+ + K_i^-}{1 + \frac{1 - f(K_i^+)}{f(K_i^+)} + \frac{1 - f(K_i^-)}{f(K_i^-)}} \tag{17}$$

In this equation, the utility function according to the ideal solution is denoted by $f(K_i^+)$, whereas the utility function according to the non-ideal solution is denoted by $f(K_i^-)$.

The utility functions according to the ideal and non-ideal solutions are calculated using Equations (18) and (19).

$$f(K_i^-) = \frac{K_i^+}{K_i^+ + K_i^-} \tag{18}$$

$$f(K_i^+) = \frac{K_i^-}{K_i^+ + K_i^-} \tag{19}$$

Step 7. The ranking of alternatives is obtained based on the final values of the utility functions. The utility function values are sorted in decreasing order and the alternative with the highest utility function value is determined as the best alternative.

3.3. CoCoSo Method

Yazdani et al. (2018) introduced the CoCoSo (Combined COmpromise SOlution) technique, which relies the compromise decision-making algorithm on the integrated SAW (Simple Additive Weighting) and EWP (Exponentially Weighted Product) models (Qiyas et al, 2022). The basic idea behind it is to employ three separate measures to determine the relative value of each alternative and rank them accordingly. By merging these three aggregation strategies, the final evaluation results are made more superior and reasonable. This approach effectively incorporates multiple aggregation ideas to create internal balance, decreases decision result variability and eliminates the issue of biased outcomes caused by a single decision procedure (Zhu et al., 2023). This method also allows operations on a decision matrix with negative valued input without the requirement for a particular transformation, such as a positive transformation. The steps within the CoCoSo technique solution process are as follows (Yazdani et al, 2019):

Step 1. The first step involves creating the initial decision matrix. This matrix is given in Equation (20).

$$X_{ij} = \begin{bmatrix} x_{11} & x_{12} & \cdots & x_{1n} \\ x_{21} & x_{22} & \cdots & x_{2n} \\ \vdots & \vdots & \ddots & \vdots \\ x_{m1} & x_{m2} & \cdots & x_{mn} \end{bmatrix}; i = 1,2,\ldots,m; j = 1,2,\ldots,n. \tag{20}$$

Step 2. At this stage, the benefit and cost criteria are normalized. The normalization process is carried out using Equation (21) and Equation (22), depending on the criteria types.

$$r_{ij} = \frac{x_{ij} - \min_i x_{ij}}{\max_i x_{ij} - \min_i x_{ij}}; \textit{ for benefit criterion} \tag{21}$$

$$r_{ij} = \frac{\max_i x_{ij} - x_{ij}}{\max_i x_{ij} - \min_i x_{ij}}; \textit{ for cost criterion} \tag{22}$$

Step 3. In this step, the total weighted comparability sequence (S_i) of every alternative is calculated using Equation (23). For the sum of the power weighted of comparability sequence of every alternative (P_i), Equation (24) is used.

(S_i) value is generated through a gray relational generating approach.

$$S_i = \sum_{j=1}^{n} (w_j r_{ij}) \tag{23}$$

The (P_i) value is determined employing the WPM (Weighted Product Model) which is also utilized in the WASPAS (Weighted Aggregated Sum Product Assessment) approach.

$$P_i = \sum_{j=1}^{n} (r_{ij})^{w_j} \tag{24}$$

Step 4. The options' relative weights of the options are calculated applying the aggregation algorithms described below. In this stage, three evaluation score procedures are employed to establish relative weights of alternatives, which are generated by Equations (25)-(27).

$$k_{ia} = \frac{P_i + S_i}{\sum_{i=1}^{m} (P + S_i)} \tag{25}$$

$$k_{ib} = \frac{S_i}{\min_i S_i} + \frac{P_i}{\min_i P_i} \tag{26}$$

$$k_{ic} = \frac{\lambda(S_i) + (1-\lambda)(P_i)}{\left(\lambda \max_i S_i + (1-\lambda)\max_i P_i\right)}; \; 0 \leq \lambda \leq 1. \tag{27}$$

Equation (25) is interpreted as the arithmetic mean of the sums of WSM and WPM scores, whereas Equation (26) indicates the total of relative WSM and WPM scores compared to the ideal. Equation (27) yields a balanced compromise of WSM and WPM model scores. In this equation, decision-makers select λ (typically λ ¼ 0.5).

Step 5. At this stage, the integrated scores of the alternatives are generated. The relative assessments achieved with Equations (25)-(27) are incorporated into Equation (28).

$$k_i = \left(k_{ia} k_{ib} k_{ic}\right)^{\frac{1}{3}} + \frac{1}{3}\left(k_{ia} + k_{ib} + k_{ic}\right). \tag{28}$$

Equation (28) yields the k_i values, which are then sorted in decreasing order to determine the overall ranking of alternatives and complete the problem's solution.

4. APPLICATION

Analysis of G20 countries' SD performance using MCDM techniques will be included in this section of the study. The MEREC method, one of the objective criteria weighting techniques and the MARCOS and CoCoSo approaches, recent ranking methods, are employed in this assesment process. Using the MARCOS-CoCoSo methods and the weight data from the MEREC method, the study's evaluation of SD performance of countries is determined. There are two parts in the study's application section. In the first part, the objective criterion weighting approach MEREC is performed to weight the collected data. The second part includes the analysis of the G20 countries' sustainability performance using the MARCOS and CoCoSo evaluation techniques.

The countries included in the analysis are as follows: Argentina, Australia, Brazil, Canada, China, France, Germany, India, Indonesia, Italy, Japan, Mexico, Russia, Saudi Arabia, South Africa, South Korea, Turkey, United Kingdom, United States and the European Union.

Countries' SD development performance is measured based on the 2022 Transaction Performance Index (TPI) component values. Table 3 shows the abbreviations for the TPI components that are used as criteria in the analysis.

Table 3. TPI components and criteria codes

TPI component	Codes
Economic transition	TPI1
Social transition	TPI2
Environmental transition	TPI3
Governance transition	TPI4

The MEREC approach, an objective weighting method, is employed in this research. MEREC has considerable advantages over other objective weighting algorithms, including a strong mathematical basis, fast computation and simplicity of comprehension (Ristono et al, 2024; Ecer and Zolfani, 2022). MARCOS and CoCoSo techniques are preferred in the evaluation. Among the benefits of the MARCOS technique are its flexibility, ability to evaluate multiple criteria with a compromise solution and simplicity of solution algorithm that may be applied to difficult issues (Ayçin and Arsu, 2021). Applying the concepts of SAW, WASPAS and MEW techniques, CoCoSo yields more reliable findings than these methods. Applying this method into practice improves the decision-making system's accuracy (Ecer et al., 2019; Yazdani et al., 2018).

The 2022 TPI report is used to evaluate the SD performances. This can be described as a research limitation. After a more recent TPI report is released, the research can be resurrected. It can also be stated that adding TPI values from various years to the study could improve its ability to assess the stability of countries' SD over a certain time frame.

4.1. Calculating Criteria Weights with the MEREC Method

In the study, the significance levels of the countries' TPI components are initially assessed using the MEREC approach. The first stage of the MEREC approach is to generate the initial decision matrix, as shown in Table 4.

Table 4. Initial decision matrix

	TPI1	TPI2	TPI3	TPI4
Argentina	39,8	57,9	51,2	49,3
Australia	55,6	77,9	28,1	80,9
Brazil	33	48,3	52,6	36,5
Canada	60,9	77,1	26,4	72,7
China	52,1	68,2	34,9	52,7
France	58,9	81	66,8	73,2
Germany	70,7	82	65	79,1
India	27,4	47,7	58,1	54,1
Indonesia	29,5	60,6	64,3	63,9
Italy	56,7	70,2	73,8	65,7
Japan	62,2	81,4	58,8	72,6
Mexico	36,2	55,9	61,7	33
Russia	41	66,8	35,5	38,7
Saudi Arabia	57	39,8	36,1	57,6
South Africa	36,5	30	46,4	39,6
South Korea	75,4	75,4	37,6	76,7
Turkey	47,1	53,5	55,6	49,3
United Kingdom	58,2	77,1	78	75,7
United States	68,2	62,5	36,1	61,7
EU 27	61,1	77,5	65	74

Equation 2 is used to normalize the initial decision matrix in the method's second stage. The benefit-oriented nature of the criteria is considered in this normalization process. The normalized decision matrix is presented in Table 5.

Table 5. Normalized decision matrix (MEREC)

	TPI1	TPI2	TPI3	TPI4
Argentina	0,6884	0,5181	0,5156	0,6694
Australia	0,4928	0,3851	0,9395	0,4079
Brazil	0,8303	0,6211	0,5019	0,9041
Canada	0,4499	0,3891	1,0000	0,4539
China	0,5259	0,4399	0,7564	0,6262
France	0,4652	0,3704	0,3952	0,4508
Germany	0,3876	0,3659	0,4062	0,4172
India	1,0000	0,6289	0,4544	0,6100
Indonesia	0,9288	0,4950	0,4106	0,5164
Italy	0,4832	0,4274	0,3577	0,5023
Japan	0,4405	0,3686	0,4490	0,4545
Mexico	0,7569	0,5367	0,4279	1,0000
Russia	0,6683	0,4491	0,7437	0,8527
Saudi Arabia	0,4807	0,7538	0,7313	0,5729
South Africa	0,7507	1,0000	0,5690	0,8333
South Korea	0,3634	0,3979	0,7021	0,4302
Turkey	0,5817	0,5607	0,4748	0,6694
United Kingdom	0,4708	0,3891	0,3385	0,4359
United States	0,4018	0,4800	0,7313	0,5348
EU 27	0,4484	0,3871	0,4062	0,4459

In the third step of the MEREC approach, the general performance values (S_i) of the countries (decision alternatives) are measured using Equation (3). The countries' performance changes (S'_{ij}) are then determined by removing all component values (criteria) individually using Equation (4) in step 4. Table 6 provides an explanation of these S_i and S'_{ij} values.

Table 6. S_i and S'_{ij} values

	S_i	S'_{ij}			
		TPI1	TPI2	TPI3	TPI4
Argentina	0,4211	0,3579	0,3070	0,3061	0,3530
Australia	0,5039	0,3909	0,3483	0,4945	0,3584
Brazil	0,3098	0,2751	0,2184	0,1746	0,2911

continued on following page

Table 6. Continued

	S_i	S'_{ij}			
		TPI1	**TPI2**	**TPI3**	**TPI4**
Canada	0,4905	0,3601	0,3344	0,4905	0,3616
China	0,4400	0,3308	0,2982	0,3941	0,3617
France	0,6264	0,5185	0,4840	0,4940	0,5139
Germany	0,6586	0,5278	0,5193	0,5347	0,5386
India	0,3624	0,3624	0,2782	0,2147	0,2724
Indonesia	0,4587	0,4469	0,3409	0,3071	0,3484
Italy	0,6008	0,4957	0,4768	0,4488	0,5016
Japan	0,6162	0,4989	0,4714	0,5018	0,5036
Mexico	0,3629	0,3132	0,2483	0,2031	0,3629
Russia	0,3470	0,2731	0,1944	0,2932	0,3184
Saudi Arabia	0,3861	0,2532	0,3369	0,3315	0,2867
South Africa	0,2297	0,1711	0,2297	0,1109	0,1928
South Korea	0,5781	0,4250	0,4398	0,5273	0,4523
Turkey	0,4489	0,3585	0,3521	0,3224	0,3827
United Kingdom	0,6433	0,5391	0,5109	0,4897	0,5278
United States	0,4984	0,3494	0,3803	0,4497	0,3986
EU 27	0,6232	0,5095	0,4871	0,4945	0,5086

The calculation of the sum of absolute deviations $\left(E_j\right)$ is performed in the fifth step. In the last step, the importance levels of the TPI components (w_j) are determined with Equation (6). In this context, Table 7 depicts E_j and w_j values .

Table 7. E_j and w_j values

	TPI1	**TPI2**	**TPI3**	**TPI4**
E_j	1,8490	2,3497	2,0230	1,7710
w_j	0,2313	0,2940	0,2531	0,2216

Table 7 shows the importance levels of TPI components as social transition (w_2=0,2940), environmental transition (w_3=0,2531), economic transition (w_1=0,2313) and governance transition (w_4=0,2216). It has been determined that the most important factor in analyzing the G20 countries' SD performance is social transition, whereas the least important criterion is governance transition.

4.2. Analysis of G20 Countries' SD Performance with the MARCOS Method

The MARCOS approach is initially used to rank G20 countries based on their success in SD. Table 4's initial decision matrix is enlarged by adding ideal (*AI*) and anti-ideal (*AAI*) values from Table 8.

Table 8. Ideal (AI)and Anti-ideal (AAI) values

	TPI1	TPI2	TPI3	TPI4
AI	75,4	82	78	80,9
AAI	27,4	30	26,4	33

The weighted normalized decision matrix shown in Table 9 has been generated by multiplying the extended decision matrix with the criterion weight values obtained through the MEREC approach.

Table 9. Weighted normalized decision matrix (MARCOS)**Error! Not a valid link.**The next step of the method includes establishing the utility degrees and utility functions of the alternatives in comparison to the anti-ideal solution, as well as the utility degrees and utility functions of the alternatives in comparison to the ideal solution. Table 10 provides these values.

In the final step, the utility functions of the options are calculated and ranked in descending order to determine the G20 countries' SD performance rankings. These results are also included in the Table 10.

Table 10. K_i^-, K_i^+, $f(K_i^-)$, $f(K_i^+)$, $f(K_i)$ values and ranking of the alternatives

	K_i^-	K_i^+,	$f(K_i^-)$	$f(K_i^+)$	$f(K_i)$	Ranking
Argentina	1,7158	0,6309	0,2688	0,7312	0,5741	14
Australia	2,0742	0,7626	0,2688	0,7312	0,6940	8
Brazil	1,4825	0,5451	0,2688	0,7312	0,4960	19
Canada	2,0346	0,7480	0,2688	0,7312	0,6808	9
China	1,8004	0,6619	0,2688	0,7312	0,6024	12
France	2,4162	0,8884	0,2688	0,7312	0,8084	3
Germany	2,5525	0,9385	0,2688	0,7312	0,8541	1
India	1,6095	0,5918	0,2688	0,7312	0,5386	17
Indonesia	1,8806	0,6914	0,2688	0,7312	0,6292	11

continued on following page

Table 10. Continued

Italy	2,2984	0,8451	0,2688	0,7312	0,7690	6
Japan	2,3725	0,8723	0,2688	0,7312	0,7938	5
Mexico	1,6375	0,6021	0,2688	0,7312	0,5479	15
Russia	1,5951	0,5865	0,2688	0,7312	0,5337	18
Saudi Arabia	1,6114	0,5925	0,2688	0,7312	0,5392	16
South Africa	1,3016	0,4786	0,2688	0,7312	0,4355	20
South Korea	2,2676	0,8337	0,2688	0,7312	0,7587	7
Turkey	1,7727	0,6518	0,2688	0,7312	0,5931	13
United Kingdom	2,4898	0,9154	0,2688	0,7312	0,8331	2
United States	1,9568	0,7194	0,2688	0,7312	0,6547	10
EU 27	2,3905	0,8789	0,2688	0,7312	0,7999	4

Germany has the highest SD performance among G20 countries, as determined by utility function values generated using the MARCOS method. United Kingdom ranks second in terms of SD performance, with France coming in third. According to data from 2022, South Africa has the lowest SD performance among the G20 countries.

4.3. Analysis of G20 Countries' SD Performance with the CoCoSo Method

The initial decision matrix in Table 4, consisting 20 decision alternatives and 4 evaluation criteria, is normalized as the first stage in the CoCoSo method's solution process. Since every criterion is benefit-oriented, Equation (21) is applied in this normalization step. Table 11 depicts the resulting normalized decision matrix.

Table 11. Normalized decision matrix (CoCoSo)**Error! Not a valid link.**The next step involves using Equation (23) to compute the total weighted comparability sequence (S_i) values for the alternatives and Equation (24) to calculate the sum of the power weighted of comparability sequence (P_i) values. Table 12 provides the alternatives' S_i values, whereas Table 13 provides the P_i values.

Table 12. S_i values

	TPI1	TPI2	TPI3	TPI4	S_i
Argentina	0,0598	0,1577	0,1216	0,0754	0,4145
Australia	0,1359	0,2708	0,0083	0,2216	0,6366

continued on following page

Table 12. Continued

Brazil	0,0270	0,1035	0,1285	0,0162	0,2752
Canada	0,1615	0,2663	0,0000	0,1836	0,6114
China	0,1190	0,2160	0,0417	0,0911	0,4678
France	0,1518	0,2883	0,1982	0,1860	0,8243
Germany	0,2087	0,2940	0,1893	0,2133	0,9053
India	0,0000	0,1001	0,1555	0,0976	0,3532
Indonesia	0,0101	0,1730	0,1859	0,1429	0,5120
Italy	0,1412	0,2273	0,2325	0,1513	0,7522
Japan	0,1677	0,2906	0,1589	0,1832	0,8004
Mexico	0,0424	0,1464	0,1732	0,0000	0,3620
Russia	0,0655	0,2080	0,0446	0,0264	0,3446
Saudi Arabia	0,1427	0,0554	0,0476	0,1138	0,3594
South Africa	0,0439	0,0000	0,0981	0,0305	0,1725
South Korea	0,2313	0,2567	0,0549	0,2021	0,7451
Turkey	0,0949	0,1329	0,1432	0,0754	0,4464
United Kingdom	0,1484	0,2663	0,2531	0,1975	0,8653
United States	0,1966	0,1837	0,0476	0,1328	0,5607
EU 27	0,1624	0,2685	0,1893	0,1897	0,8100
				min	0,1725
				max	0,9053

Table 13. P_i values

	TPI1	TPI2	TPI3	TPI4	P_i
Argentina	0,7312	0,8327	0,8307	0,7875	3,1822
Australia	0,8842	0,9761	0,4215	1,0000	3,2819
Brazil	0,6083	0,7356	0,8424	0,5601	2,7464
Canada	0,9202	0,9713	0,0000	0,9592	2,8507
China	0,8575	0,9133	0,6335	0,8213	3,2257
France	0,9072	0,9943	0,9399	0,9619	3,8033
Germany	0,9764	1,0000	0,9292	0,9915	3,8972
India	0,0000	0,7285	0,8840	0,8339	2,4463
Indonesia	0,4848	0,8557	0,9249	0,9074	3,1728
Italy	0,8921	0,9271	0,9787	0,9189	3,7168

continued on following page

Table 13. Continued

Japan	0,9283	0,9966	0,8889	0,9587	3,7725
Mexico	0,6754	0,8147	0,9084	0,0000	2,3985
Russia	0,7470	0,9034	0,6446	0,6240	2,9188
Saudi Arabia	0,8942	0,6123	0,6551	0,8627	3,0242
South Africa	0,6807	0,0000	0,7867	0,6446	2,1119
South Korea	1,0000	0,9609	0,6793	0,9799	3,6201
Turkey	0,8138	0,7918	0,8658	0,7875	3,2589
United Kingdom	0,9024	0,9713	1,0000	0,9749	3,8486
United States	0,9631	0,8710	0,6551	0,8927	3,3818
EU 27	0,9214	0,9737	0,9292	0,9661	3,7905
				min	2,1119
				max	3,8972

After collecting the total weighted comparability sequence (S_i) and the sum of the power weighted of comparability sequence (P_i) values for every alternative, in the following stage, the relative weights of the options are generated using the aggregation algorithms in Equations (25-27). The integrated scores of the alternatives (k_i) are computed by Equation (28). To rank the alternatives according to performance, k_i values are sorted in decreasing order. Table 14 shows relative evaluation scores, integrated score values and final ranking outcomes.

Table 14. (k_{ia}, k_{ib}, k_{ic}), (k_i) values and rankings

	k_{ia}	k_{ib}	k_{ic}	k_i	Ranking
Argentina	0,0475	3,9100	0,7489	2,0871	14
Australia	0,0518	5,2447	0,8160	2,6427	8
Brazil	0,0399	2,8956	0,6292	1,6057	19
Canada	0,0458	4,8942	0,7209	2,4315	10
China	0,0488	4,2395	0,7691	2,2277	12
France	0,0612	6,5795	0,9636	3,2639	3
Germany	0,0635	7,0934	1,0000	3,4854	1
India	0,0370	3,2058	0,5829	1,6857	18
Indonesia	0,0487	4,4703	0,7673	2,3128	11
Italy	0,0591	6,1210	0,9306	3,0657	6
Japan	0,0604	6,4266	0,9522	3,1975	5

continued on following page

Table 14. Continued

Mexico	0,0365	3,2343	0,5748	1,6897	17
Russia	0,0431	3,3798	0,6795	1,8302	16
Saudi Arabia	0,0447	3,5158	0,7046	1,9019	15
South Africa	0,0302	2,0000	0,4757	1,1415	20
South Korea	0,0577	6,0337	0,9090	3,0148	7
Turkey	0,0490	4,1312	0,7716	2,1890	13
United Kingdom	0,0623	6,8391	0,9816	3,3755	2
United States	0,0521	4,8520	0,8209	2,5004	9
EU 27	0,0608	6,4904	0,9579	3,2261	4

Germany has the highest SD performance among G20 countries, as determined by integrated score values generated using the CoCoSo method. United Kingdom ranks second in terms of SD performance, with France coming in third. According to data from 2022, South Africa has the lowest SD performance among the G20 countries.

The performance ranking results obtained using MARCOS and CoCoSo techniques show more than 99% similarity, indicating the consistency of the findings.

5. RESULTS AND CONCLUSION

Sustainability, defined as the most efficient and effective utilization of existing resources to meet the requirements of both present and future generations, is an increasingly hot topic these days. This topic addresses all concerns including natural resource protection, economic development and appropriate social structure management.

The lowest possible level of production impact on society and the natural environment is achievable not only via technology advancement, but also through a managerial approach that incorporates aspects such as environmental impact analysis and improvement. In this context, it is critical to assess to what extent countries seeking to raise their social welfare levels through increased production consider social, environmental and managerial implications. The study investigates this awareness within the context of G20 countries, which account for around 85% of the global economy. It is hoped that it would contribute to the literature by identifying crucial sub-criteria in the SD process and analysing countries' weaknesses and strengths.

Scorecards have proven to be an effective instrument for informing and monitoring the impacts of national policies. In this context, TPI data, which provides global statistics, can serve as a source of inspiration and action in identifying the best performers worldwide.

In this study, the SD performance of G20 countries is evaluated using 29 indicators. The sustainability assessment model has four main dimensions: economic, social, environmental and governance. In addition, the economic dimension is divided into four sub-dimensions, each with nine indicators. The social dimension consists of four sub-dimensions and seven indicators. The environmental dimension likewise consists of four sub-dimensions, each of which has seven indicators. Finally, the governance dimension contains six indicators. Once the weight coefficients of the criteria have been generated using the MEREC procedure, MARCOS and CoCoSo methods are used to evaluate the G20 countries.

In accordance to the MEREC approach results, the most important dimension in analyzing the G20 countries' SD performance is social transformation. This dimension is succeeded by the environmental, economic and governance dimensions. In this context, policy makers can be advised to rapidly create developmental measures on topics such as health, participation in the workforce, working hours and income distribution equality.

According to MARCOS and CoCoSo's ranking results, Germany is the G20 country with the highest SD performance. The United Kingdom and France come in second and third places in the rankings. South Africa and Brazil have been identified as the countries having the lowest SD performances. These countries must focus on their weak components and develop action plans in a timely manner.

In future research, it may be worthwhile to compare the performance ranking results obtained using alternative MCDM approaches to the current study findings. Analyses can be conducted using various scales that can be employed in the SD performance analysis of countries and similarities and differences with TPI evaluation results can be investigated. Again, the study can be repeated longitudinally over multiple years to track the evolution of countries' SD performances.

REFERENCES

Abacıoğlu, S., Ayan, B., & Pamucar, D. (2024). The Race to Sustainability: Decoding Green University Rankings Through a Comparative Analysis (2018–2022). *Innovative Higher Education*, 1–35.

Alkan, G., & Merdivenci, F. (2021). Sürdürülebilir kalkınma açısından lojistik performans endeksine göre seçilen ülkelerin Entropi temeline dayalı EDAS yöntemi ile değerlendirmesi. *Gümüşhane Üniversitesi Sosyal Bilimler Dergisi*, *12*(2), 627–641.

Alpdoğan, H. (2023). OECD ülkelerinde sürdürülebilir kalkınma politikalarının ARAS metodu ile performans analizi. *Business & Management Studies: An International Journal, 11*(3), 1079–1103. DOI: 10.15295/bmij.v11i3.2285

Altıntaş, F. F. (2024). Avrupa Birliği ülkelerin sürdürülebilir kalkınma performanslarının MEREC tabanlı WEDBA yöntemi ile analizi. *Ordu Üniversitesi Sosyal Bilimler Enstitüsü Sosyal Bilimler Araştırmaları Dergisi*, *14*(1), 117–137.

Antanasijević, D., Pocajt, V., Ristić, M., & Perić-Grujić, A. (2017). A differential multi-criteria analysis for the assessment of sustainability performance of European countries: Beyond country ranking. *Journal of Cleaner Production*, *165*, 213–220. DOI: 10.1016/j.jclepro.2017.07.131

Arman, K., & Organ, A. (2023). AB'ye Üye ve Aday Ülkelerin Lojistik Performanslarının MEREC ve CoCoSo Yöntemleri İle Değerlendirilmesi. *Uluslararası Ticaret ve Ekonomi Araştırmaları Dergisi*, *7*(2), 36–46. DOI: 10.30711/utead.1360959

Arsu, Ş. U., & Arsu, T. (2023). Evaluation of the Corporate Sustainability Performance of Manufacturing Companies in the BIST Sustainability Index with Multi-Criteria Decision Making Methods. *Business & Economics Research Journal, 14*(4).

Ateş, S., & Usman, Ö. (2021). Gelişmekte olan ülkelerin sürdürülebilir kalkınma performanslarının gri ilişkisel analiz yöntemiyle değerlendirilmesi. *İktisadi İdari ve Siyasal Araştırmalar Dergisi, 6*(15), 225-248.

Ayçin, E., & Arsu, T. (2021). Sosyal gelişme endeksine göre ülkelerin değerlendirilmesi: MEREC ve MARCOS yöntemleri ile bir uygulama. *İzmir Yönetim Dergisi, 2*(2), 75-88.

Balcerzak, A. P., & Pietrzak, M. B. (2016). *Application of TOPSIS method for analysis of sustainable development in European Union countries* (No. 22/2016). Institute of Economic Research Working Papers.

Barrutia, J. M., Echebarria, C., Paredes, M. R., Hartmann, P., & Apaolaza, V. (2015). From Rio to Rio+ 20: Twenty years of participatory, long term oriented and monitored local planning? *Journal of Cleaner Production, 106*, 594–607. DOI: 10.1016/j.jclepro.2014.12.085

Bektaş, S. (2022). Türk sigorta sektörünün 2002-2021 dönemi için MEREC, LOPCOW, COCOSO, EDAS ÇKKV yöntemleri ile performansının değerlendrilmesi. *BDDK Bankacılık ve Finansal Piyasalar Dergisi, 16*(2), 247–283. DOI: 10.46520/bddkdergisi.1178359

Böhringer, C. (2003). The Kyoto protocol: A review and perspectives. *Oxford Review of Economic Policy, 19*(3), 451–466. DOI: 10.1093/oxrep/19.3.451

Brodny, J., & Tutak, M. (2023). The level of implementing sustainable development goal" Industry, innovation and infrastructure" of Agenda 2030 in the European Union countries: Application of MCDM methods. *Oeconomia Copernicana, 14*(1), 47–102. DOI: 10.24136/oc.2023.002

Chichilnisky, G. (1999). What is sustainable development? In *Man-Made Climate Change: Economic Aspects and Policy Options* (pp. 42–82). Physica-Verlag HD. DOI: 10.1007/978-3-642-47035-6_4

Cundill, G., & Fabricius, C. (2010). Monitoring the governance dimension of natural resource co-management. *Ecology and Society, 15*(1), art15. DOI: 10.5751/ES-03346-150115

Das, M. C., & Sarkar, B. (2024). Exploring incisive decision for performance assessment of materials under utopian environment: A pluri-disciplinary approach.

Duran, Z. (2023). Evaluation of Supply Chain Resilience in N-11 Countries by MEREC Based EDAS, MARCOS, WASPAS Integrated Method. *Yildiz Social Science Review, 9*(1).

Ecer, F., & Aycin, E. (2023). Novel comprehensive MEREC weighting-based score aggregation model for measuring innovation performance: The case of G7 countries. *Informatica (Vilnius), 34*(1), 53–83. DOI: 10.15388/22-INFOR494

Ecer, F., & Güneş, E. (2024). G7 Ülkelerinin Bilgi İletişim Teknoloji Düzeylerini Belirleme: MEREC-CRITIC Entegre Ağırlıklı CoCoSo Metodolojisi. *Journal of Mehmet Akif Ersoy University Economics and Administrative Sciences Faculty, 11*(1), 219–242.

Ecer, F., Pamucar, D., Zolfani, S. H., & Eshkalag, M. K. (2019). Sustainability assessment of OPEC countries: Application of a multiple attribute decision making tool. *Journal of Cleaner Production, 241*, 118324. DOI: 10.1016/j.jclepro.2019.118324

Ecer, F., & Zolfani, S. H. (2022). Evaluating economic freedom via a multi-criteria MEREC-DNMA model-based composite system: Case of OPEC countries. *Technological and Economic Development of Economy*, *28*(4), 1158–1181. DOI: 10.3846/tede.2022.17152

Ersoy, N. (2022). OECD ve AB Üyesi Ülkelerin İnovasyon Performanslarinin Merec-Marcos Bütünleşik Modeli İle Ölçümü. *Dokuz Eylül Üniversitesi Sosyal Bilimler Enstitüsü Dergisi*, *24*(3), 1039–1063. DOI: 10.16953/deusosbil.1106249

European Commission. Transitions Performance Index 2021, https://projects.research-and-innovation.ec.europa.eu/en/knowledge-publications-tools-and-data/interactive-reports/transition-performance-index-2021

Gamal, A., Abdel-Basset, M., Hezam, I. M., Sallam, K. M., & Hameed, I. A. (2023). An Interactive Multi-Criteria Decision-Making Approach for Autonomous Vehicles and Distributed Resources Based on Logistic Systems: Challenges for a Sustainable Future. *Sustainability (Basel)*, *15*(17), 12844. DOI: 10.3390/su151712844

Ghosh, D., Muhuri, B. R., Mahapatra, G. S., & Mahapatra, B. S. (2024). Integrated MEREC-CoCoSo approach using score function of Neutrosophic for location selection of special economic zone. *Neutrosophic Sets and Systems*, *73*, 694–717.

Ghosh, S., & Bhattacharya, M. (2022). Analyzing the impact of COVID-19 on the financial performance of the hospitality and tourism industries: An ensemble MCDM approach in the Indian context. *International Journal of Contemporary Hospitality Management*, *34*(8), 3113–3142. DOI: 10.1108/IJCHM-11-2021-1328

Goker, N., Karsak, E. E., & Dursun, M. (2022). An integrated QFD and common weight DEA-based fuzzy MCDM framework for performance ranking of countries. *Social Indicators Research*, *159*(1), 1–22. DOI: 10.1007/s11205-021-02751-2

Goodland, R. (1995). The concept of environmental sustainability. *Annual Review of Ecology and Systematics*, *26*(1), 1–24. DOI: 10.1146/annurev.es.26.110195.000245

Güney, T. (2016). AB ÜYESİ ÜLKELERDE YÖNETİŞİMİN SÜRDÜRÜLEBİLİR KALKINMA ÜZERİNDEKİ ETKİSİ: PANEL VERİ ANALİZİ. *Süleyman Demirel Üniversitesi İktisadi ve İdari Bilimler Fakültesi Dergisi*, *21*(1), 193–205.

Hall, J. K., Daneke, G. A., & Lenox, M. J. (2010). Sustainable development and entrepreneurship: Past contributions and future directions. *Journal of Business Venturing*, *25*(5), 439–448. DOI: 10.1016/j.jbusvent.2010.01.002

Haq, R. S. U., Saeed, M., Mateen, N., Siddiqui, F., Naqvi, M., Yi, J. B., & Ahmed, S. (2022). Sustainable material selection with crisp and ambiguous data using single-valued neutrosophic-MEREC-MARCOS framework. *Applied Soft Computing*, *128*, 109546. DOI: 10.1016/j.asoc.2022.109546

Heinberg, R., & Lerch, D. (2010). What is sustainability. *The post carbon reader, 11*, 19.

Hong Son, N., & Hieu, T. T. (2023). Selectıon of weldıng robot by multı-crıterıa decısıonmakıng method. *Eastern-European Journal of Enterprise Technologies, 121*(3).

Huang, S., Cheng, H., Tan, M., Tang, Z., & Teng, C. (2024). Evaluating Regional Potentials of Agricultural E-Commerce Development Using a Novel MEREC Heronian-CoCoSo Approach. *Agriculture*, *14*(8), 1338. DOI: 10.3390/agriculture14081338

Huy, T. Q., Liem, N. B., Hau, T. Q., Cuong, D. Q., Danh, T. H., Nga, N. T. T., & Thieu, N. N. (2022, December). Application of MARCOS Method for Selecting the Best Schema of Scissors Mechanism. In *International Conference on Engineering Research and Applications* (pp. 234-243). Cham: Springer International Publishing.

Karaşan, A., & Kahraman, C. (2018). A novel interval-valued neutrosophic EDAS method: Prioritization of the United Nations national sustainable development goals. *Soft Computing*, *22*(15), 4891–4906. DOI: 10.1007/s00500-018-3088-y

Kaya, S. K. (2020). Evaluation of the Effect of COVID-19 on Countries' Sustainable Development Level: A comparative MCDM framework. *Operational Research in Engineering Sciences: Theory and Applications*, *3*(3), 101–122. DOI: 10.31181/oresta20303101k

Kaya, S. K., Ayçin, E., & Pamucar, D. (2023). Evaluation of social factors within the circular economy concept for European countries. *Central European Journal of Operations Research*, *31*(1), 73–108. DOI: 10.1007/s10100-022-00800-w

Keefer, P. (2004). A review of the political economy of governance: From property rights to voice.

Keshavarz-Ghorabaee, M., Amiri, M., Zavadskas, E. K., Turskis, Z., & Antucheviciene, J. (2021). Determination of objective weights using a new method based on the removal effects of criteria (MEREC). *Symmetry*, *13*(4), 525. DOI: 10.3390/sym13040525

Kumar, S., Ahijith Kumar, P. V., Bharati, K., Patnaik, L., Ranjan Maity, S., & Łepicka, M. (2024). Coating material selection for bulk metal forming dies: A MEREC-integrated approach with multiple MCDM methods. [IJIDeM]. *International Journal on Interactive Design and Manufacturing*, 1–16.

Mahmoudian Azar Sharabiani, A., & Mousavi, S. M. (2023). A Web-Based Decision Support System for Project Evaluation with Sustainable Development Considerations Based on Two Developed Pythagorean Fuzzy Decision Methods. *Sustainability (Basel), 15*(23), 16477. DOI: 10.3390/su152316477

Mastilo, Z., Štilić, A., Gligović, D., & Puška, A. (2024). Assessing the Banking Sector of Bosnia and Herzegovina: An Analysis of Financial Indicators through the MEREC and MARCOS Methods. *Journal of Central Banking Theory and Practice, 13*(1), 167–197. DOI: 10.2478/jcbtp-2024-0008

Mateusz, P., Danuta, M., Małgorzata, Ł., Mariusz, B., & Kesra, N. (2018). TOPSIS and VIKOR methods in study of sustainable development in the EU countries. *Procedia Computer Science, 126*, 1683–1692. DOI: 10.1016/j.procs.2018.08.109

Megyesiova, S., & Lieskovska, V. (2018). Analysis of the sustainable development indicators in the OECD countries. *Sustainability (Basel), 10*(12), 4554. DOI: 10.3390/su10124554

Meral, İ. G. (2023). BRICS-T Ülkelerinin İnovasyon Performanslarının MEREC-MARCOS Yöntemi ile Değerlendirilmesi. *Kastamonu Üniversitesi İktisadi ve İdari Bilimler Fakültesi Dergisi, 25*(2), 550–571.

Moldan, B., Janoušková, S., & Hák, T. (2012). How to understand and measure environmental sustainability: Indicators and targets. *Ecological Indicators, 17*, 4–13. DOI: 10.1016/j.ecolind.2011.04.033

Mondal, M. K., Mahapatra, B. S., Bera, M. B., & Mahapatra, G. S. (2024). Sustainable forest resources management model through Pythagorean fuzzy MEREC–MARCOS approach. *Environment, Development and Sustainability*, 1–32. DOI: 10.1007/s10668-024-05164-6

Morelli, J. (2011). Environmental sustainability: A definition for environmental professionals. *Journal of Environmental Sustainability, 1*(1), 2. DOI: 10.14448/jes.01.0002

Noyan, E. (2023). Banka personeli seçiminin çok kriterli karar verme yöntemleri ile ele alınması. *Kapanaltı Dergisi*, (4), 112–121.

Oliveira, A., Calili, R., Almeida, M. F., & Sousa, M. (2019). A systemic and contextual framework to define a country's 2030 agenda from a foresight perspective. *Sustainability (Basel), 11*(22), 6360. DOI: 10.3390/su11226360

Özdağoğlu, A., Işıldak, B., & Keleş, M. K. (2022). MEREC tabanlı COCOSO yöntemiyle uçuş okullarının uçak seçimlerinin değerlendirilmesi. *Gümüşhane Üniversitesi Sosyal Bilimler Dergisi, 13*(2), 708–719.

Özer, M. A. (2006). Yönetişim üzerine notlar. *Sayıştay Dergisi*, (63), 59–89.

Parris, T. M., & Kates, R. W. (2003). Characterizing and measuring sustainable development. *Annual Review of Environment and Resources, 28*(1), 559–586. DOI: 10.1146/annurev.energy.28.050302.105551

Patterson, J., Schulz, K., Vervoort, J., Van Der Hel, S., Widerberg, O., Adler, C., Hurlbert, M., Anderton, K., Sethi, M., & Barau, A. (2017). Exploring the governance and politics of transformations towards sustainability. *Environmental Innovation and Societal Transitions, 24*, 1–16. DOI: 10.1016/j.eist.2016.09.001

Portney, K. E. (2015). *Sustainability*. MIT Press.

Pradhan, P., Costa, L., Rybski, D., Lucht, W., & Kropp, J. P. (2017). A systematic study of sustainable development goal (SDG) interactions. *Earth's Future, 5*(11), 1169–1179. DOI: 10.1002/2017EF000632

Qiyas, M., Naeem, M., Khan, S., Abdullah, S., Botmart, T., & Shah, T. (2022). Decision support system based on CoCoSo method with the picture fuzzy information. *Journal of Mathematics, 2022*(1), 1476233. DOI: 10.1155/2022/1476233

Rao, P. K., & Shukla, A. (2024). Strategic sustainability in Indian banking industry: A performance analysis. *International Journal of Productivity and Performance Management, 73*(6), 2016–2034. DOI: 10.1108/IJPPM-04-2023-0199

Resce, G., & Schiltz, F. (2021). Sustainable development in Europe: A multicriteria decision analysis. *Review of Income and Wealth, 67*(2), 509–529. DOI: 10.1111/roiw.12475

Ristić, B., Bogdanović, V., & Stević, Ž. (2024). Urban evaluation of pedestrian crossings based on Start-Up Time using the MEREC-MARCOS Model. *J. Urban Dev. Manage, 3*(1), 34–42. DOI: 10.56578/judm030103

Ristono, A., Wahyuningsih, T., & Muhsin, A. (2025). Comprehensive Method for Supplier Selection in the Indonesian Leather Industry Considering Sustainable Development Goals Criteria. *Journal of Lifestyle and SDGs Review, 5*(2), e02994–e02994. DOI: 10.47172/2965-730X.SDGsReview.v5.n02.pe02994

Rogers, P. P., Jalal, K. F., & Boyd, J. A. (2012). *An introduction to sustainable development*. Routledge. DOI: 10.4324/9781849770477

Şahin, M. (2023). Ensemble decision making for logistics center location. *Environment, Development and Sustainability*, 1–35.

Sánchez, L. E., & Croal, P. (2012). Environmental impact assessment, from Rio-92 to Rio+ 20 and beyond. *Ambiente & Sociedade*, *15*(3), 41–54. DOI: 10.1590/S1414-753X2012000300004

Santana, N. B., Aparecida do Nascimento Rebelatto, D., Périco, A. E., & Mariano, E. B. (2014). Sustainable development in the BRICS countries: An efficiency analysis by data envelopment. *International Journal of Sustainable Development and World Ecology*, *21*(3), 259–272. DOI: 10.1080/13504509.2014.900831

Seyhan, N. (2023). AB'de Döngüsel Ekonomi Üretim ve Tüketim Göstergelerinin Değerlendirilmesi: MEREC Temelli MARCOS Uygulaması. *Sosyal Mucit Academic Review*, *4*(3), 364–391. DOI: 10.54733/smar.1338423

Sezgin, A., & Aytekin, S. (2024). BİST Balıkesir endeksi firmalarının MEREC tabanlı CoCoSo yöntemiyle finansal performans analizi. *Balıkesir Üniversitesi Sosyal Bilimler Enstitüsü Dergisi*, *27*(51-1-2024 Yılı Özel Sayısı), 63-77.

Sezgin, A., Aytekin, S., & Sakarya, Ş. (2024). Finansal performansın ölçülmesinde Piotroski F-Skoru bileşenleri ve ÇKKV yöntemlerinin bağlantısı: MEREC tabanlı MARCOS uygulaması. *Ekonomi Politika ve Finans Araştırmaları Dergisi*, *9*(2), 367–395. DOI: 10.30784/epfad.1481070

Simic, V., Gokasar, I., Deveci, M., & Švadlenka, L. (2022). Mitigating climate change effects of urban transportation using a type-2 neutrosophic MEREC-MARCOS model. *IEEE Transactions on Engineering Management*, *71*, 3233–3249. DOI: 10.1109/TEM.2022.3207375

Simić, V., Ivanović, I., Đorić, V., & Torkayesh, A. E. (2022). Adapting urban transport planning to the COVID-19 pandemic: An integrated fermatean fuzzy model. *Sustainable Cities and Society*, *79*, 103669. DOI: 10.1016/j.scs.2022.103669 PMID: 35013703

Sönmez, G. Ö., & Toktaş, P. (2024). Supplier selection using the integrated MEREC–CoCoSo methods in a medical device company. *Journal of Scientific Reports-A*, (056), 116–133. DOI: 10.59313/jsr-a.1420728

Stanujkic, D., Popovic, G., Zavadskas, E. K., Karabasevic, D., & Binkyte-Veliene, A. (2020). Assessment of progress towards achieving Sustainable Development Goals of the "Agenda 2030" by using the CoCoSo and the Shannon Entropy methods: The case of the EU Countries. *Sustainability (Basel)*, *12*(14), 5717. DOI: 10.3390/su12145717

Stević, Ž., Pamučar, D., Puška, A., & Chatterjee, P. (2020). Sustainable supplier selection in healthcare industries using a new MCDM method: Measurement of alternatives and ranking according to COmpromise solution (MARCOS). *Computers & Industrial Engineering*, *140*, 106231. DOI: 10.1016/j.cie.2019.106231

Štilić, A., Puška, A., Božanić, D., & Đurić, A. (2024). Ranking European Countries Using Hybrid MEREC-MARCOS MCDA Based on Travel and Tourism Development Index. *Tourism (Zagreb)*, *72*(4), 592–608. DOI: 10.37741/t.72.4.6

Sutton, P. (2004). A perspective on environmental sustainability. *Paper on the Victorian Commissioner for Environmental Sustainability*, *1*, 32.

Tang, C., Xie, X., Wei, G., Pan, L., & Qi, Z. (2024). Exploring the Evolutionary Characteristics of Food Security in China and the United States from a Multidimensional Perspective. *Foods*, *13*(14), 2272. DOI: 10.3390/foods13142272 PMID: 39063356

Tanrıverdi, G., Merkert, R., Karamaşa, Ç., & Asker, V. (2023). Using multi-criteria performance measurement models to evaluate the financial, operational and environmental sustainability of airlines. *Journal of Air Transport Management*, *112*, 102456. DOI: 10.1016/j.jairtraman.2023.102456

Taş, M. A., & Alptekin, S. E. (2023). Evaluation of major cities in terms of smart cities: A developing country perspective. *Procedia Computer Science*, *225*, 1717–1726. DOI: 10.1016/j.procs.2023.10.161

Thinh, H. X., Van Duc, D., & Bao, N. C. (2024). The Effect of CoCoSo Method on the Ranks of Alternatives: A Case Study of Copper Electrical Wire Selection. *Engineering, Technology &. Applied Scientific Research*, *14*(6), 18307–18315.

Ünlü, U., Yalçın, N., & Avşarlıgil, N. (2022). Analysis of efficiency and productivity of commercial banks in turkey pre-and during COVID-19 with an integrated MCDM approach. *Mathematics*, *10*(13), 2300. DOI: 10.3390/math10132300

Van Dua, T. (2023). Forklift selection by multi-criteria decision making methods. *Eastern-European Journal of Enterprise Technologies*, *125*(3).

Wang, K., Li, B., Tian, T., Zakuan, N., & Rani, P. (2023). Evaluate the drivers for digital transformation in higher education institutions in the era of industry 4.0 based on decision-making method. *Journal of Innovation & Knowledge*, *8*(3), 100364. DOI: 10.1016/j.jik.2023.100364

Yalman, İ. N., Koşaro lu, Ş. M., & Işik, Ö. (2023). 2000-2020 Döneminde Türkiye Ekonomisinin Makroekonomik Performansının Merec-Lopcow-Marcos Modeliyle Değerlendirilmesi. *Finans Politik & Ekonomik Yorumlar*, *60*(664), 57–86.

Yaşar, E., & Ünlü, M. (2023). Üniversitelerde Sürdürülebilirliğin İncelenmesi: LOPCOW ve MEREC Tabanlı CoCoSo Yöntemleriyle Çevreci Üniversitelerin Analizi. *İşletme Akademisi Dergisi, 4*(2), 125-142.

Yazdani, M., Zarate, P., Kazimieras Zavadskas, E., & Turskis, Z. (2019). A combined compromise solution (CoCoSo) method for multi-criteria decision-making problems. *Management Decision*, *57*(9), 2501–2519. DOI: 10.1108/MD-05-2017-0458

Yu, Y., Wu, S., Yu, J., Xu, Y., Song, L., & Xu, W. (2022). A hybrid multi-criteria decision-making framework for offshore wind turbine selection: A case study in China. *Applied Energy*, *328*, 120173. DOI: 10.1016/j.apenergy.2022.120173

Yürüyen, A. A., Ulutaş, A., & Özdağoğlu, A. (2023). Lojistik işletmelerinin performansının bir hibrit ÇKKV modeli ile değerlendirilmesi. *Business & Management Studies: An International Journal*, *11*(3), 731–751.

Zhu, Y., Zeng, S., Lin, Z., & Ullah, K. (2023). Comprehensive evaluation and spatial-temporal differences analysis of China's inter-provincial doing business environment based on Entropy-CoCoSo method. *Frontiers in Environmental Science*, *10*, 1088064. DOI: 10.3389/fenvs.2022.1088064

Chapter 12
Integrating Spectroscopic and Isotopic Data with Multi-Criteria Decision Making for Traceability and Fraud Detection in Edible Oils

Widad Ezhani
Faculty of Sciences, Ibn Tofail University, Kenitra, Morocco

Mohamed El Bakkali
Higher Institute of Nursing and Health Techniques, Kenitra, Morocco

Yassine Mouniane
https://orcid.org/0000-0002-6037-5301
Faculty of Sciences, Ibn Tofail University, Kenitra, Morocco

Yassine Kadmi
LASIRE, Equipe Physico-Chimie de l'Environnement, CNRS UMR 8516, Sciences et Technologies, Université de Lille, France

Sofia Zazouli
Faculty of Science and Techniques, University Sultan Moulay Slimane, Beni Mellal, Morocco

Noureddine Amenzou
National Centre for Nuclear Energy, Science and Technology, Morocco

Amar Habsaoui
Faculty of Sciences, Ibn Tofail University, Kenitra, Morocco

DOI: 10.4018/979-8-3693-8789-4.ch012

ABSTRACT

In the context of increasing food fraud risks and the need for sustainable supply chain management, this study explores a novel multi-criteria approach combining spectroscopic (ATR-FTIR) and isotopic ($\delta^{13}C$, $\delta^{15}N$, $\delta^{18}O$) analyses with advanced chemometric models for the authentication and traceability of sesame oils. By applying principal component analysis (PCA), hierarchical clustering, and classification algorithms (PLS-DA, Random Forest), this integrative methodology enables the robust identification of adulteration with other oils (e.g., soybean, sunflower), and discrimination of oils based on their geographical origin. The incorporation of these analytical features into multi-criteria decision-making (MCDM) frameworks allows for a more reliable and transparent system to support food quality control, consumer trust, and regulatory compliance. This chapter emphasizes the potential of coupling analytical chemistry with decision support tools to promote integrity also in the digital era where traceability and data-driven monitoring are essential

1. INTRODUCTION

Oilseeds play an essential role in human nutrition and world trade, alongside cereals. In their various commercial forms, they contribute to a balanced diet, accounting for around a third of nutritional intake, along with carbohydrates and proteins (Oboulbiga et al., 2023). *Sesamum indicum* L. (sesame) is an oilseed plant cultivated in many parts of the world, including China, India, Sudan, Japan, Mexico and many countries in West Africa, Central Africa and Central America (Myint et al., 2020; Ezhani et al., 2025). The nutritional value of sesame is attracting growing interest, leading to a significant increase in its consumption and use in confectionery (Adewuyi & Pereira, 2017). This evolution in eating habits is reflected in the increasing integration of sesame seeds in food products, both domestically and industrially (Gharby et al., 2017; Wan et al., 2023).

Sesame seeds are renowned not only for their use as spices, but also as a valuable source of high-quality vegetable oil. With a lipid content of around 50-60%, they outperform many other oilseeds in terms of oil yield (Mukta & Neeta, 2017; Aslam et al., 2020). This oil is particularly appreciated in the culinary field for its high content of unsaturated fatty acids, notably oleic acid (around 35-54%) and linoleic acid (39-59%), which give it remarkable nutritional and functional properties (Nzikou et al., 2010). In addition to its role in the diet, it is widely studied for its cardiovascular health benefits, by its ability to modulate blood lipid levels (Wikul et al., 2012). Oleic acid, for example, plays a key role in reducing LDL (low-density lipoprotein) cholesterol while increasing HDL (high-density lipoprotein) cholesterol, contributing to better protection against cardiovascular disease (Hama, 2017). Moreover, linoleic acid is essential for human metabolism, as it cannot be synthesized by the body and must be supplied by the diet (Biswas et al., 2018). Sesame oil's balanced lipid composition places it among the so-called oleic-linoleic oils, recognized for their beneficial role in preventing metabolic diseases. In addition to its essential fatty acids, this oil is distinguished by a high concentration of tocopherols, notably γ-tocopherol, a powerful antioxidant that protects lipids against oxidation, thus preserving the stability and quality of the oil while exerting a protective effect against oxidative damage at cellular level (Liu et al., 2021). Compared to other vegetable oils, sesame oil is particularly rich in tocopherols, with a content of around 45 mg per 100 g, surpassing that of olive oil and sunflower oil (Gharby et al., 2011; Zine et al., 2013). This wealth of antioxidants reinforces its protective role against oxidative stress and cellular aging (Morris et al., 2021). Sesame seeds are also an exceptional source of protein, with a content of around 20%, including all the essential amino acids needed for the body to function properly (Fuji et al., 2018). Among the various protein fractions identified are albumin, globulin, prolamine and glutenin, each playing a specific role in human nutrition (Cui et al., 2021). It's also interesting to note that sesame varieties differ in terms of nutritional composition, with black sesame seeds generally being richer in protein and minerals than white varieties. In addition, sesame is a significant source of essential micronutrients such as calcium and iron, which help to strengthen the bone system and prevent anaemia (Rout et al., 2018; Mili et al., 2021). The lignans present in these seeds, notably sesamin and sesamolin, have bioactive properties that help reduce oxidative stress and improve lipid metabolism, reinforcing sesame's interest as a functional food (Woo et al., 2019). Products of oil extraction, such as sesame cake, are widely used in animal feed due to their high digestible protein content. All these elements make sesame seeds and their oil a real nutritional treasure, combining health benefits, high energy value and a composition rich in essential nutrients (Sanni et al., 2024).

The authenticity of agri-food products, particularly vegetable oils, is a growing concern worldwide. Recent studies have revealed an upsurge in fraudulent practices involving the adulteration of oils with cheaper diluents, such as kerosene or table oil, thus compromising their quality, traceability and safety (Spink & Moyer, 2011; Everstine et al., 2013; Ben Ayed et al., 2022). Sesame oil, widely recognized for its richness in unsaturated fatty acids, phenolic compounds and antioxidant properties, is among the oils most targeted by these fraudulent practices (Rajagukguk et al., 2022; Oboulbiga et al., 2023). Over and above their economic impact, these adulterations raise major health concerns and weaken consumer confidence in agri-food products (Galvin-King et al., 2018; Bannor et al., 2023). In this context, fraud detection and oil purity assessment require reliable, rapid and accurate analytical methods. Fourier transform infrared spectroscopy (FTIR) has emerged as the nondestructive technology of choice for analyzing the chemical composition of oils and identifying their alterations (Fadzlillah et al., 2014). By combining this approach with advanced statistical techniques, it is possible to detect specific markers of authentic oils, such as variations in the infrared vibrations of characteristic functional groups (C-H, C=O, C-O) in precise spectral ranges. At the same time, isotope analysis ($\delta^{13}C/^{12}C$) has proven its effectiveness in tracing the geographical origin of oils and detecting adulteration. Isotope ratios, influenced by environmental factors such as climate and agricultural practices, are sensitive to variations in the composition of oils and diluents. Integrating this isotopic data with machine learning algorithms enables us to capture the complex interactions between dilution, isotopic signatures and FTIR spectra.

Approaches based on advanced models, such as Random Forest, Gradient Boosting and Support Vector Machine (SVM), offer enhanced ability to classify samples and model non-linear relationships often overlooked by traditional methods. These techniques enable more accurate fraud detection and improved oil traceability. The main aim of this study is to develop an integrated methodology combining FTIR spectroscopy, isotope analysis and advanced statistical models to meet the growing demands for quality control and traceability in the food industry, while guaranteeing product compliance with international standards.

2. MATERIALS AND METHODS

2.1. Samples and Oil Extraction

Sesame seeds used in this study were obtained from certified markets specializing in authentic seeds in Morocco and Egypt. The seeds were sorted to remove damaged ones and sieved to eliminate foreign matter. The oil was mechanically extracted from sesame seeds using an automatic oil press machine in the laboratory. For each sample, 100 g of seeds were pressed (Savoire et al., 2013), and the extraction yields were recorded (Table 1).

Table 1. Comparative yields of sesame oil extraction from Egypt and Morocco

Sample	Oil Mass (g)	Cake Mass (g)	Total Mass (g)	Oil Yield (%)	Cake Yield (%)
Egypt Oil	36.909	58.632	95.541	36.909	58.632
Morocco Oil	38.5936	58.961	97.554	38.5936	58.961

2.2. Sample Preparation

Two sets of oils for the analyses were prepared:

- Authentic Oils: Sesame oils of Moroccan and Egyptian origin, pure table oil (Cheaper priced oil in the Moroccan market), and pure paraffin oil.
- Mixed Oils: Several dilutions of mixed oils were prepared by blending Egyptian and Moroccan sesame oils with paraffin oil and table oil (cheaper-priced oil from the market). The sesame oils for the adulteration test were mixed in proportions ranging from 10% to 90% with table oil, and the same procedure was applied to paraffin oil for both Egyptian and Moroccan sesame oils (Figure 1).

Figure 1. Preparation of sesame oil mixtures with table and paraffin oils for isotopic analysis.

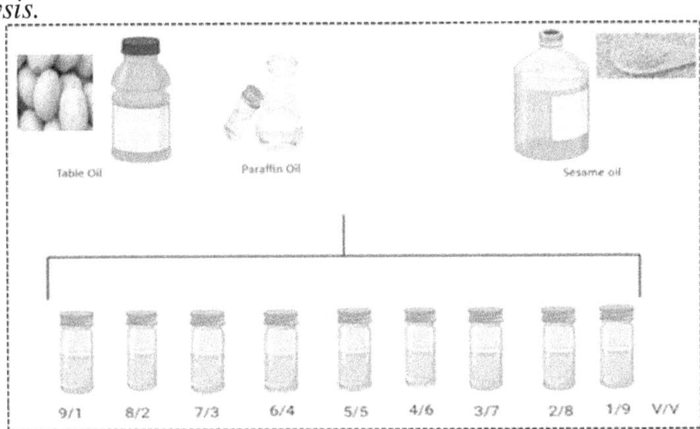

2.3. Isotope Ratio Mass Spectrometry (IRMS) Analysis

To characterize the constituents of sesame oil, an isotope ratio mass spectrometer coupled with gas chromatography (EA-IRMS) was used to analyze the stable carbon-13 isotopes. This method provides information on the authenticity of sesame oil by measuring the total carbon content (Taous et al., 2020).

2.3.1. FTIR Spectroscopy Analysis

Fourier transform infrared (FTIR) spectra of all samples were collected using a Spectrum Two FT-IR spectrometer (Perkin-Elmer, USA) with an attenuated total reflectance (ATR) crystal. Spectra were obtained in the range of 650-4000 cm^{-1} with 32 co-added scans at a spectral resolution of 4 cm^{-1}. Before spectral collection, the adulterated sesame oil samples were shaken to ensure homogeneity (Taous et al., 2022). Approximately 10 ml of oil was placed on the ATR surface, and the air background spectrum was subtracted from each spectrum obtained.

2.3.2. Carbon Isotope Ratio Analysis by Isotope Ratio Mass Spectrometry

Carbon analyses in the samples were conducted using isotope ratio mass spectrometry (IRMS) (Isochrom-EA, VG ISOTECH, UK). The samples were mixed, and 0.15 mg of the oil samples were placed in tin capsules. For carbon isotopic analysis, the separated compounds were converted to CO2 by passing the eluted analyte flow through a ceramic oxidation reactor at a gas temperature of 1030 °C. Carbon dioxide gas standards were injected before and after the species of interest to allow for the calculation of $\delta^{13}C$‰ values. Helium was used as the carrier gas. Results are expressed in the conventional per mille notation relative to the Pee Dee Belemnite (PDB) marine carbonate standard (Brand et al., 2014).

2.3.3. Coding and Meaning of Oil Samples

Table 2 shows a standardized codification and their meaning for different types of oils analyzed. Each code reflects the composition of the samples, notably the proportions of pure sesame oil, table oil, or other types of oil such as kerosene. This nomenclature allows clear and precise identification of blends and geographical origins (Egypt and Morocco) for better interpretation of results.

Table 2. Coding and meaning of oil samples

Code	Significance
Egypt 100%	100% pure Egyptian sesame oil, not mixed with other oils
Egypt 1/9 Table Oil	Egyptian sesame oil diluted 10% with 90% table oil
Egypt 2/8 Table Oil	Egyptian sesame oil diluted 20% with 80% table oil
Egypt 3/7 Table Oil	30% pure sesame oil blended with 70% table oil

continued on following page

Table 2. Continued

Code	Significance
Morocco 100%	100% pure, unblended sesame oil from Morocco
Morocco 1/9 Table Oil	Moroccan sesame oil diluted 10% with 90% table oil
Paraffin 100%	Pure kerosene oil
Table Oil	Table oil used as a diluent
Egypt	Referring to Egypt (origin of sesame oil)
Morocco	Reference in Morocco (origin of sesame oil)

2.4. Statistical Modeling

Spectroscopic analyses were carried out using Fourier Transform Infrared (FTIR) spectroscopy on samples of pure oils (E100%, M100%) and those mixed with various diluents (table oil and kerosene). Spectra were recorded in the 4000-400 cm^{-1} range, enabling identification of the characteristic bands of the compounds present.

For data analysis, heat maps were generated for specific spectral ranges (4000-3000 cm^{-1}, 3000-2800 cm^{-1}, 1800-1500 cm^{-1}, and 1200-1000 cm^{-1}) to visualize intensity variations and discriminate samples according to dilutions and diluents. Hierarchical clustering was applied to study similarities between samples and enhance interpretation of results.

Statistical analyses were performed using Stata 18 (StataCorp LLC, 4905 Lakeway Drive, College Station, TX, USA) and Python (v3.8) with specialized libraries such as numpy, pandas, scikit-learn and matplotlib. A 3rd-order polynomial regression was fitted in Stata 18 to model the relationship between d13C/12C isotope ratio, dilution and oil type (kerosene or table oil). This modeling included linear, quadratic and cubic terms, as well as their interactions with oil type, to capture the complex effects associated with isotopic alterations and high dilutions. Goodness of fit was assessed by coefficient of determination (R^2) and root mean squared error (RMSE).

To explore alternative models, machine learning approaches, including Support Vector Machine (SVM), Gradient Boosting and Random Forest, were developed in Py-thon to classify samples according to oil type and fraud status. SVM, known for its theoretical foundation based on statistical learning theory, was applied as a classification and regression tool. Thanks to the use of kernel functions, SVMs project input vectors into a higher-dimensional space, enabling the construction of a maximum separation boundary between classes. This method is recognized for its robustness against overlearning (overfitting), making it a suitable tool for complex analyses, as shown by the work of Jiménez Carvelo et al. (2017) and Kaneko & Funatsu, (2015). Hyperparameter optimization was carried out via a cross-validation search, and performance was evaluated using standard metrics such as precision, recall, F1 score and area under the ROC curve (AUC).

An additional categorical variable, representing the geographical origin of sesame oils (Morocco or Egypt), was introduced to assess its impact on classification performance and its relevance to sample traceability. Finally, graphical visualizations were generated to illustrate the individual contributions of linear, quadratic and cubic terms, as well as the comparative performance of the models. Isotopic critical thresholds (-30 and -27) were used to identify anomalies and minimum detectable dilutions, reinforcing the practical interpretation of results in an industrial setting.

To determine the minimum detectable levels of adulteration at each wavenumber, we employ a binary classification approach using a Random Forest (RF) ensemble method (Breiman, 2001). Each RF model is trained independently using only one spectral feature (i.e., the absorbance value at a specific wavenumber), allowing for targeted evaluation of its discriminatory power across a range of fraud thresholds. The core prediction function is defined as:

$$\widehat{y}(x) = majority\_vote\left\{ h_t(x) \right\}_{t=1}^{T}$$

where ht(x) ∈ {0,1} represents the prediction of the tth decision tree (0 = pure, 1 = adulterated), and T=200 is the total number of trees in the forest. Each decision tree is trained on a random subset (bootstrap sample) of the training data (Tibshirani & Efron, 1993), and the final predicted label is the class selected by most trees (Breiman, 2001).

For each combination of wavenumber λi and fraud threshold sj, we define the label y ∈ {0,1} such that: y=1 if the adulteration percentage ≥ sj and y=0 for pure sesame oil samples.

The input variable xxx corresponds to the absorbance at the selected wavenumber λi. A Random Forest classifier is trained on this single feature to predict y, and its clas-sification accuracy is evaluated using 3-fold cross-validation (Kohavi, 1995).

The minimum detectable fraud level at a given wavenumber λi is then defined as:

$$s_{min}(\lambda_i) = min\left\{ s_j \mid Accuracy(\lambda_i, s_j) \geq 90\% \right\}$$

This methodology produces a fraud detection matrix that maps the minimum detectable fraud level (above 90% accuracy) for each wavenumber and for each type of adulteration. The matrix is visualized as a heatmap, highlighting the most sensitive spectral regions for early and accurate detection of table oil and paraffin adulterants.

All computations were performed using the Scikit-learn machine learning library in Python (Pedregosa et al., 2011) and heatmaps were generated with Seaborn (Waskom, 2021).

3. RESULTS

Descriptive statistics (Table 3) calculated for variables related to the transmittance of sesame oil blends show consistent results. The wave number (cm^{-1}) shows a mean of 2200 cm^{-1} with a standard deviation of 1039.66 cm^{-1}, covering a range from 400 to 4000 cm^{-1}, reflecting an analysis over a wide spectral range. For pure Egyptian sesame oil (E 100%), mean transmittance is high at 95.61%, with little variation (6.81%), indicating a homogeneous composition. Blends with table oil, such as E 1/9 HT and E 2/8 HT, show similar mean transmittances (95.52% and 95.65%, respectively), confirming that the addition of table oil only slightly affects transmittance values. The quartiles for these blends also remain close to those for the pure oil, reflecting the high contribution of sesame oil to the blend. Moroccan oils (M) show similar trends, suggesting results comparable to those of Egyptian oils. These results highlight the low absorption and high transmittance of both pure and blended oils, establishing a solid basis for qualitative comparisons between the different samples.

Table 3. Descriptive statistics for transmittance values and wavenumbers.

					Quartiles			
	N	**mean**	**std**	**min**	**25%**	**50%**	**75%**	**max**
Wave number (cm-1)	3601	2200	1039,663	400	1300	2200	3100	4000
E 100%	3601	95,611	6,811822	56,52	94,405	99,01	99,615	99,835
Egypt 1/9 Table Oil	3601	95,51606	6,767845	56,435	94,055	98,955	99,55	99,795
Egypt 2/8 Table Oil	3601	95,65274	6,756944	56,39	94,13	99,08	99,695	99,99
Egypt 3/7 Table Oil	3601	95,5939	6,76207	56,275	94,145	99	99,61	99,9
Egypt 4/6 Table Oil	3601	95,61782	6,775934	56,28	94,22	99,03	99,635	99,925
Egypt 5/5 Table Oil	3601	95,61518	6,772431	56,4	94,255	99,025	99,625	99,98
Egypt 6/4 Table Oil	3601	95,62342	6,771238	56,445	94,28	99,03	99,625	99,885
Egypt 7/3 Table Oil	3601	95,55667	6,7597	56,78	94,095	99,015	99,585	99,91
Egypt 8/2 Table Oil	3601	95,55203	6,746784	57,055	94,025	99,015	99,575	99,915

continued on following page

Table 3. Continued

					Quartiles			
	N	mean	std	min	25%	50%	75%	max
Egypt 9/1 Table Oil	3601	95,651	6,733069	56,82	94,44	99,025	99,62	99,925
Table Oil 100%	3601	95,60066	6,81068	55,9	94,07	99,05	99,66	100,015
Morocco 100%	3601	95,71891	6,769855	56,875	94,43	99,105	99,73	99,945
Morocco 1/9 Table Oil	3601	95,60952	6,75833	56,16	94,125	99,025	99,625	99,93
Morocco 2/8 Table Oil	3601	95,55465	6,808474	55,93	94,06	99	99,595	99,885
Morocco 3/7 Table Oil	3601	95,57612	6,824397	56,005	94,11	99,03	99,63	99,91
Morocco /6 Table Oil	3601	95,53255	6,778214	56,29	94,045	98,985	99,575	99,875
Morocco 5/5 Table Oil	3601	95,64831	6,775119	56,44	94,295	99,065	99,67	99,91
Morocco 6/4 Table Oil	3601	95,58943	6,77823	56,47	94,205	99,015	99,605	99,88
Morocco 7/3 Table Oil	3601	95,55279	6,780534	56,745	94,005	99,015	99,59	99,93
Morocco 8/2 Table Oil	3601	95,6606	6,748711	56,785	94,31	99,055	99,65	99,985
Morocco 9/1 Table Oil	3601	95,63778	6,761356	56,835	94,275	99,05	99,645	99,97
Egypt 1/9 Paraffin	3601	97,67701	5,29988	54,43	97,705	99,37	99,725	99,965
Egypt 2/8 Paraffin	3601	97,40493	5,293601	55,015	97,31	99,255	99,68	99,89
Egypt 3/7 Paraffin	3601	97,13801	5,343748	55,9	96,87	99,205	99,675	99,94
Egypt 4/6 Paraffin	3601	97,04451	5,344358	56,92	96,72	99,205	99,705	99,895
Egypt 5/5 Paraffin	3601	96,74294	5,55672	57,215	96,31	99,125	99,645	99,945
Egypt 6/4 Paraffin	3601	96,56435	5,673465	58,195	95,99	99,12	99,645	99,87
Egypt 7/3 Paraffin	3601	96,31903	5,960688	58,63	95,63	99,1	99,66	99,97
Egypt 8/2 Paraffin	3601	96,0481	6,261358	59,655	95,15	99,07	99,655	99,94
Egypt 9/1 Paraffin	3601	95,85073	6,508455	59,45	94,825	99,055	99,64	99,935
Morocco 1/9 Paraffin	3601	97,65916	5,319984	54,225	97,72	99,35	99,71	99,91
Morocco 2/8 Paraffin	3601	97,36978	5,303763	55,115	97,245	99,255	99,69	99,985
Morocco 3/7 Paraffin	3601	97,17092	5,342704	55,77	96,93	99,225	99,675	99,93
Morocco 4/6 Paraffin	3601	96,90074	5,427486	55,88	96,59	99,09	99,56	99,92
Morocco 5/5 Paraffin	3601	96,63286	5,651687	57,055	96,135	99,135	99,645	99,875
Morocco 6/4 Paraffin	3601	96,486	5,69082	57,27	95,66	99,1	99,615	99,895
Morocco 7/3 Paraffin	3601	96,32553	5,949615	58,28	95,65	99,095	99,635	99,91
Morocco 8/2 Paraffin	3601	96,11271	6,188439	59,605	95,225	99,1	99,69	99,905
Morocco 9/1 Paraffin	3601	95,89933	6,492089	59,805	94,88	99,085	99,67	99,905
Paraffin 100%	3601	97,88606	5,42105	53,475	98,2	99,495	99,725	100

3.1. Comparative FTIR Spectra of Pure and Blended Oils: Global Analysis of Spectral Signatures

The FTIR spectra presented (Figure 2) show characteristic variations according to sample type and blend proportions. The main bands, located in specific regions, enable us to differentiate between pure oils and fraudulent blends. In the 3000-2800 cm-^{1} region, peaks associated with elongation vibrations of aliphatic C-H bonds (CH2 and CH3) are present in all samples, but their intensity decreases with increasing proportions of diluents (table oil or kerosene). The band around 1740 cm-^{1}, characteristic of the C=O group of esters present in sesame oil, is also a key marker: it diminishes or gradually disappears in mixtures with kerosene, which does not contain this functional group.

In mixtures with table oil, the spectra show diluent-specific contributions, visible in the 1200-1000 cm-^{1} region (C-O vibrations). Moroccan and Egyptian oils show similar spectra for pure oils (E100% and M100%), but subtle differences in band intensities could be linked to their geographical origin, particularly in the 1160 cm-^{1} region. Diluted samples show a correlation between the loss of intensity of the main bands and the percentage of dilution. This trend could be used to build a quantitative model, based on relative intensities of key bands, to estimate the concentration of pure sesame oil in blends. In conclusion, FTIR spectra offers relevant information for detecting fraud and assessing sample purity. The spectral regions to be favored for detailed analysis are those around 1740 cm-^{1}, 3000-2800 cm-^{1} and 1200-1000 cm-^{1}. A calibration model based on these bands could be developed for accurate quantitative dilution detection.

Figure 2. FTIR transmittance spectra for various dilutions.

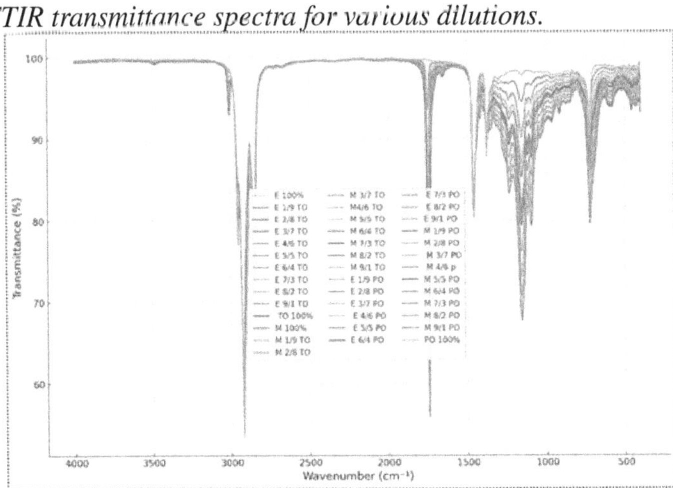

3.2. Spectral analysis by specific ranges

The heat maps obtained for different spectral ranges highlight distinctive spectral variations between pure oils and blends, enabling samples to be differentiated and fraud detected.

3.2.1. 4000-3000 cm^{-1} Range

This range (Figure 3) reveals O-H, N-H and C-H elongation vibrations, characteristic of triglycerides. Pure oils (E100%, M100%) are distinguished by high intensities in the aliphatic C-H bands around 3000 cm^{-1}, marked by solid yellow areas. Samples diluted with table oil (TO) show progressive attenuation, consistent with the dilution of aliphatic chains. In contrast, samples containing kerosene (PO) show low or absent in-tensities, reflecting the absence of polar groups such as O-H and N-H. Key bands around 3400-3200 cm^{-1}, sensitive to the presence of polar impurities, confirm that this range is crucial for differentiating purity and characterizing diluents. Hierarchical clustering shows a clear separation between pure oils and TO and PO mixtures, confirming the discriminating impact of this range.

Figure 3. Heatmap with hierarchical clustering for the 4000–3000 cm^{-1} range: O-H, N-H, and C-H vibrations.

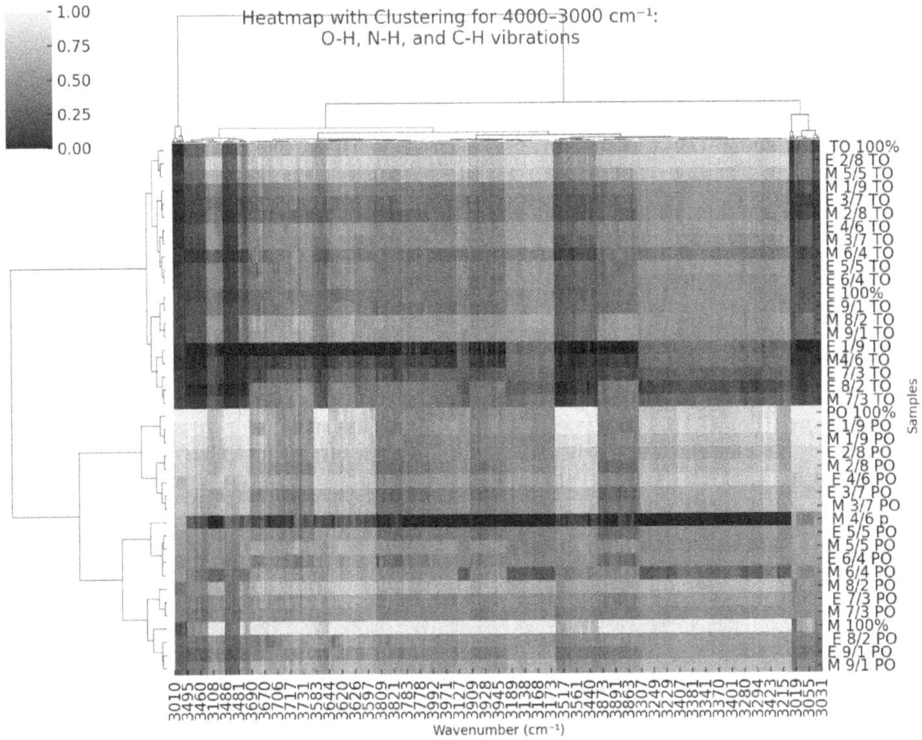

3.2.2. Range 3000-2800 cm-[1]

This range (Figure 4) corresponds to aliphatic CH2 and CH3 elongation vibrations. Pure oils (E100%, M100%) show high, homogeneous intensities (yellow zones), particularly around 2921 cm-[1] and 2854 cm-[1], characteristic of long aliphatic triglyceride chains. Samples diluted with table oil (TO) show a progressive attenuation of intensities, reflecting the proportional reduction of aliphatic chains. Mixtures with kerosene (PO), although also containing aliphatic chains, show lower intensities and increased variability, attributed to the absence of complex triglyceride structures. Bands around 2921 and 2854 cm-[1] are reliable markers for detecting purity or fraud. Hierarchical clustering confirms the relevance of this range for discriminating dilutions.

Figure 4. Heatmap with hierarchical clustering for the 3000–2800 cm^{-1} range: Aliphatic CH2 and CH3 vibrations.

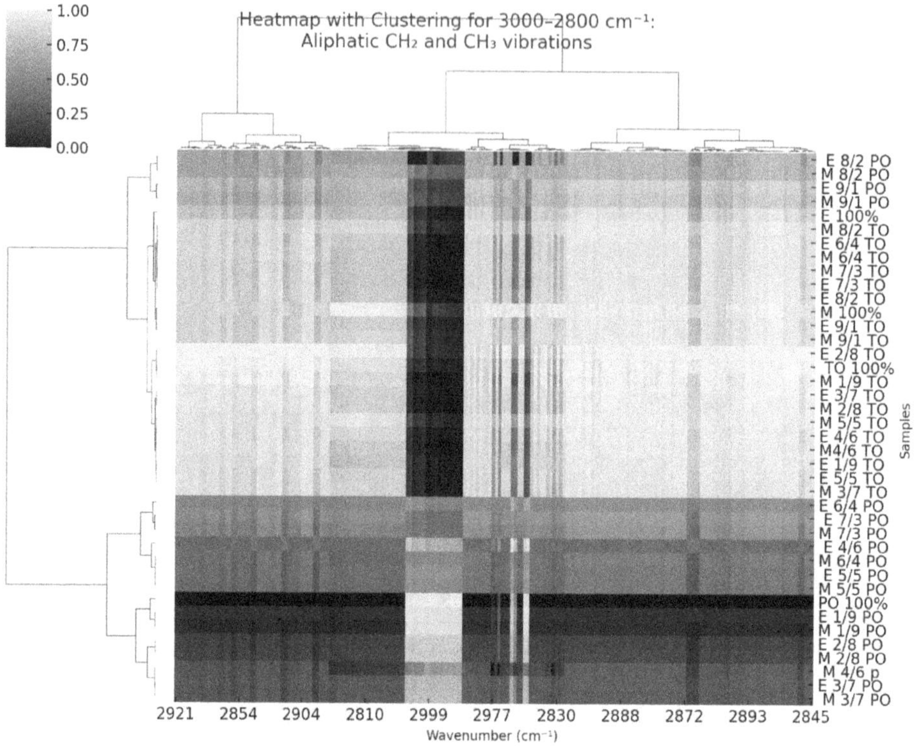

3.2.3. Plage 1800-1500 cm-[1]

This range (Figure 5) covers the vibrations of carbonyl (C=O) and aromatic groups. Pure oils (E100%, M100%) show high intensities around 1743 cm-[1], characteristic of the C=O vibrations of the esters present in triglycerides. In blends containing table oil (TO), a progressive decrease in this band is observed, reflecting the dilution of the triglycerides. Blends with kerosene (PO) show an almost complete absence of this band, confirming the absence of carbonyl groups in the saturated kerosene structures. Hierarchical clustering illustrates a marked separation between pure oils and blends, underlining that C=O vibrations are an essential marker for detecting fraud and quantifying dilution.

Figure 5. Heatmap with hierarchical clustering for the 1800–1500 cm^{-1} range: Carbonyl (C=O) and aromatic group vibrations.

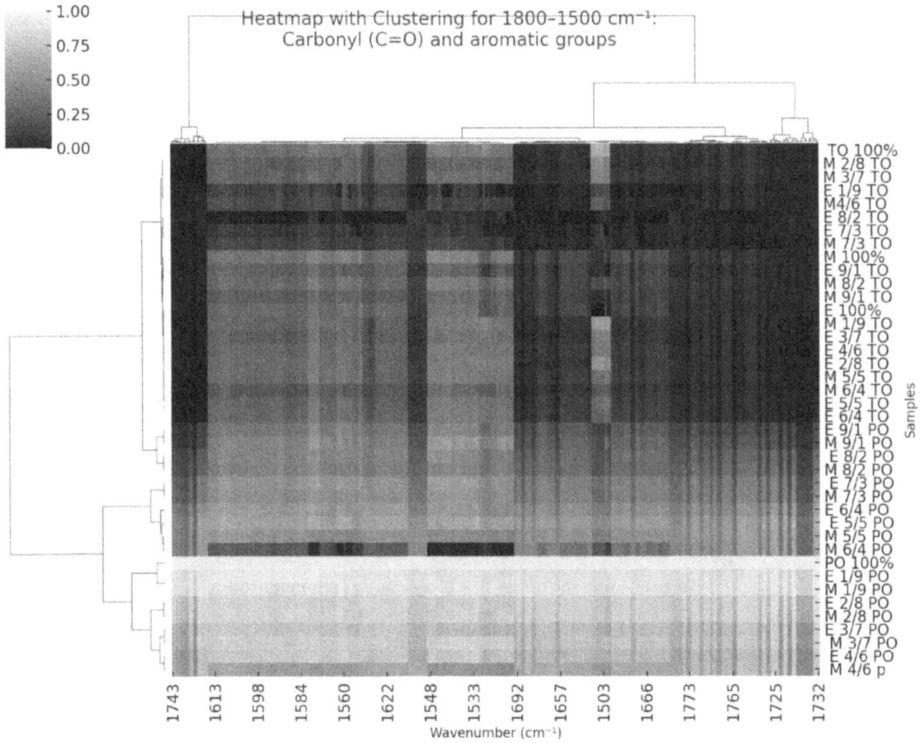

3.2.4. Plage 1200-1000 cm^{-1}

This range (Figure 6) corresponds to C-O vibrations and the fingerprint region, essential for identifying complex triglyceride structures. Pure oils (E100%, M100%) show moderate to high intensities around 1160 cm^{-1}, associated with ester C-O vibrations. Blends with table oil (TO) show slightly reduced intensities, reflecting the contribution of esterified fatty acids in the diluents. In contrast, blends with kerosene (PO) show significantly lower or absent intensities, due to the absence of functional C-O groups in the saturated structures. Hierarchical clustering reveals a clear distinction between pure oils and TO and PO blends according to their fingerprint signatures, reinforcing the relevance of this range for discriminating against fraudulent blends and verifying the authenticity of sesame oils.

Figure 6. Heatmap with hierarchical clustering for the 1200–1000 cm⁻¹ range: C-O vibrations and fingerprint region.

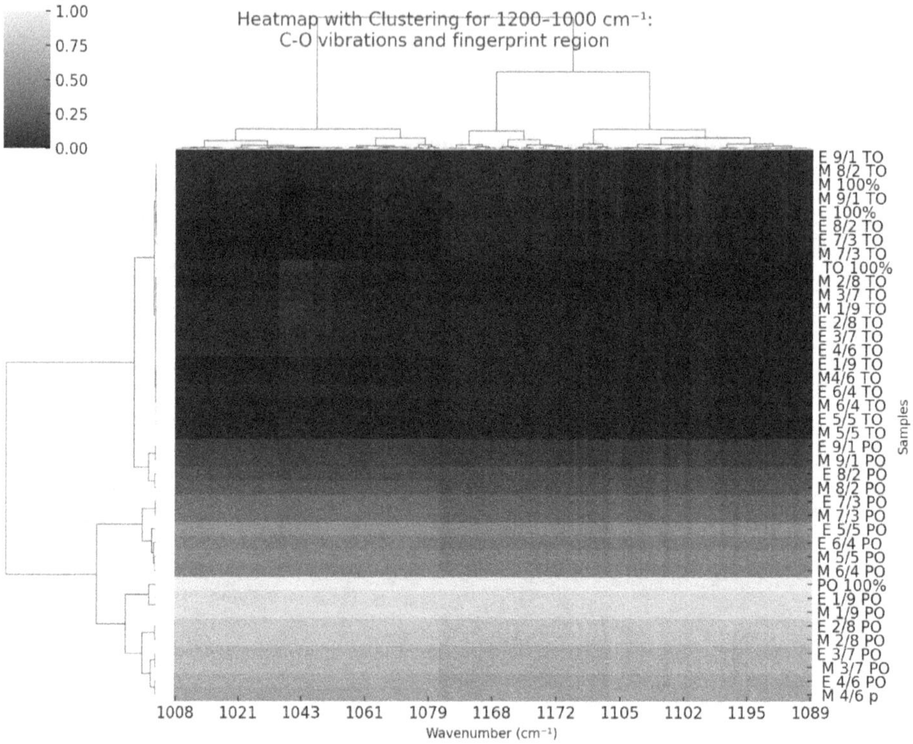

3.3. Spectral Wavenumbers Enabling Ultra-Sensitive Detection of Adulterants in Sesame Oil (≥90% Accuracy) (Random Forest Classification)

Based on the heatmap analysis of minimal detectable adulteration thresholds at a classification accuracy of 90% or more, several key wavenumbers demonstrate exceptional sensitivity to trace levels of adulterants in sesame oil. For table oil adulteration, the lowest possible detection threshold of 0% was achieved at the following wave-numbers: 3030 cm^{-1}, 2520 cm^{-1}, 2080 cm^{-1}, 2040 cm^{-1}, 1630 cm^{-1}, 1590 cm^{-1}, 1570 cm^{-1}, 1530 cm^{-1}, and 550 cm^{-1}. These spectral positions are thus the most responsive to the presence of table oil, allowing its detection even at negligible levels. Similarly, for paraffin adulteration, the following wavenumbers reached a minimum detection threshold of 0%: 3620 cm^{-1}, 2520 cm^{-1}, 2470 cm^{-1}, 2300 cm^{-1}, and 2080 cm^{-1}. These indicate regions of the infrared spectrum where paraffin traces are most discriminative, enabling high-accuracy identification from the earliest signs of contamination. Together, these results highlight the critical spectral fingerprints enabling ultra-sensitive and selective detection of adulteration by either table oil or paraffin.

Figure 7. Minimal Detectable Adulteration Thresholds Using FTIR Spectroscopy Combined with Random Forest Classification (≥90% Accuracy) for Table Oil and Paraffin Detection in Sesame Oil

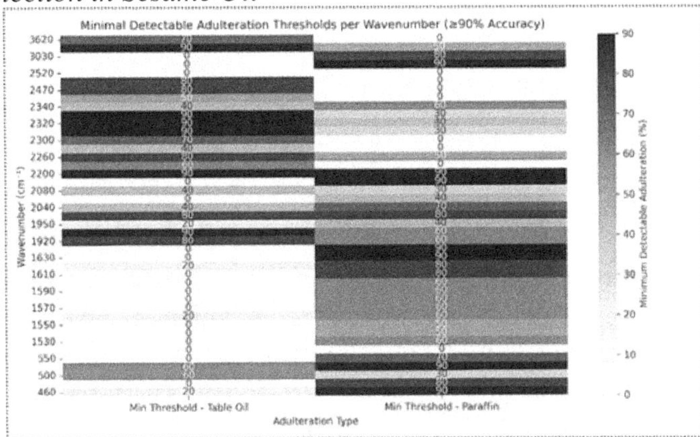

3.4. Integrated Analysis of Isotopic Interactions and Advanced Models for Fraud Detection in Sesame Oils

Figure 8 illustrates the variation in d13C/12C isotope ratios as a function of the proportion of pure oil for different blends involving Moroccan and Egyptian sesame oils, combined with kerosene or table oil. For pure oils, Moroccan sesame oil shows a slightly less negative isotopic ratio (-28.92) compared to Egyptian sesame oil (-29.14), reflecting intrinsic differences probably influenced by environmental or geographical factors. When mixed with kerosene, the isotopic ratio gradually approaches the value of pure kerosene (-27.32) as the proportion of sesame oil decreases. Moroccan and Egyptian oils follow similar trends, with slight but perceptible isotopic differences. On the other hand, blends with table oil show a marked decrease in isotope ratios, due to the very negative value of pure table oil (-38.99). As the proportion of sesame oil decreases, the isotope ratio for Moroccan and Egyptian oils converges towards -31.0, indicating the dominant influence of table oil in these blends. This clear separation of trends between blends with kerosene and those with table oil highlights the potential of isotope ratios to precisely identify the type and extent of sesame oil adulteration, as well as to differentiate geographical origins through their distinct isotope profiles.

Figure 8. Variation of d13C/12C Isotopic Ratios with Oil Purity Levels.

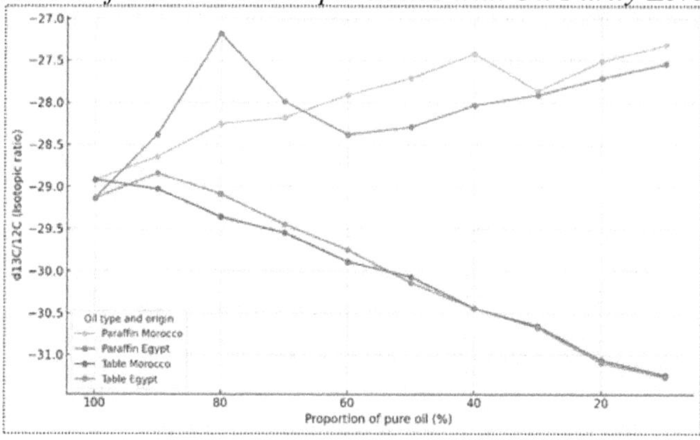

The fitted model, based on polynomial regression with interactions, shows a robust ability to capture the relationship between $\delta^{13}C/^{12}C$, dilution and oil type. With an R^2 of 0.8611 and an Adj. R^2 of 0.8325, it explains over 86% of the variance in the dependent variable, indicating a remarkable overall fit. The Root MSE (0.80499) reflects notable predictive accuracy. The model coefficients, presented in Table 2, highlight a significant decrease in $\delta^{13}C/^{12}C$ with increasing dilution ($\beta = -0.3196$, $p = 0.005$), while the quadratic ($\beta = 0.0087$, $p = 0.002$) and cubic ($\beta = -0.0007$, $p < 0.001$) terms reveal non-linear complex-ity. Although the main effect of oil type was non-significant ($\beta = -0.4910$, $p = 0.499$), its interactions with dilution proved significant, highlighting a more marked isotopic modulation for kerosene. These interactions reflect the complex dynamics of isotopic effects, particularly at high dilutions.

Table 4. Multinomial modeling of parameters influencing the d13c12c isotope ratio.

d13c12c	Coefficient	Std. err.	t	p-value	95% CI	
Dilution: a	-0.3196253	0.105700	-3.02	p < 0.01	-0.5344352	-0.1048153
(Dilution)²: b	0.0086873	0.002596	3.35	p < 0.01	0.0034096	0.0139649
(Dilution)³: c	-0.0000725	0.000017	-4.13	p < 0.001	-0.0001082	-0.0000369
Type de dilution (d)						
Paraffin Oil	-0.4910433	0.718218	-0.68	0.499	-1.950639	0.9685521
Interaction: a x d	0.1889126	0.066851	2.83	p < 0.01	0.0530548	0.3247703
Interaction: b x d	-0.004882	0.001642	-2.97	p < 0.01	-0.0082199	-0.0015441

continued on following page

Table 4. Continued

d13c12c	Coefficient	Std. err.	t	p-value	95% CI	
Interaction: c x d	0.0000396	0.000011	3.57	$p < 0.01$	0.0000171	0.0000622
Constante	-28.44829	0.507857	-56.02	$p < 0.001$	-29.48038	-27.4162

$F(7, 34) = 30.11$; Prob > F= 0.0000; R-squared = 0.8611; Adj R-squared= 0.8325; Root MSE= 0.80499

The model's predictions, illustrated in Figure 9, show distinct isotopic behavior depending on the type of dilution. Table oil shows an isotopic increase at low dilution (<20%), followed by a marked non-linearity, while kerosene shows a constant isotopic decrease. Critical thresholds (-30 and -27) clearly identify anomalies: samples outside this range correspond either to high dilutions or to amplified interaction effects. These results validate the use of the polynomial model to efficiently differentiate oils and detect isotopic anomalies, offering significant potential for industrial and scientific applications.

Figure 9. Predictions of d13c12c with Polynomial Model and Detection of Anomalies.

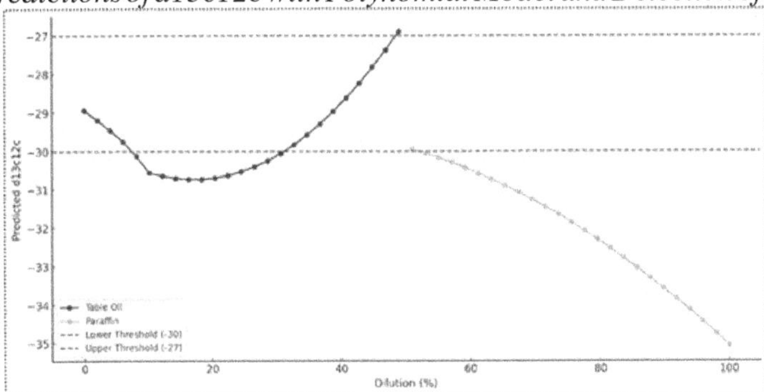

The robustness of the model is reinforced by a combined analysis, presented in Figure 10, highlighting the isotopic behaviors of the samples. Section (a) illustrates the distribution of isotopic values as a function of oil type and fraud status, showing that fraudulent samples approach critical thresholds. Section (b) summarizes these observations through the averages of isotopic values, revealing a clear separation between fraudulent and non-fraudulent samples. Finally, section (c) highlights the minimum detectable dilution: 7.62% for table oil and 12.02% for kerosene, underlining an increased sensitivity to isotopic alteration.

Figure 10. Analysis of Predicted d13c12c, Fraud Detection, and Minimum Detectable Dilution for Oil Types. a. Distribution of d13c12c predictions by oil type and fraud status; b. Average predic-tions by oil type and fraud status; c. Minimum detectable dilution for each oil type.

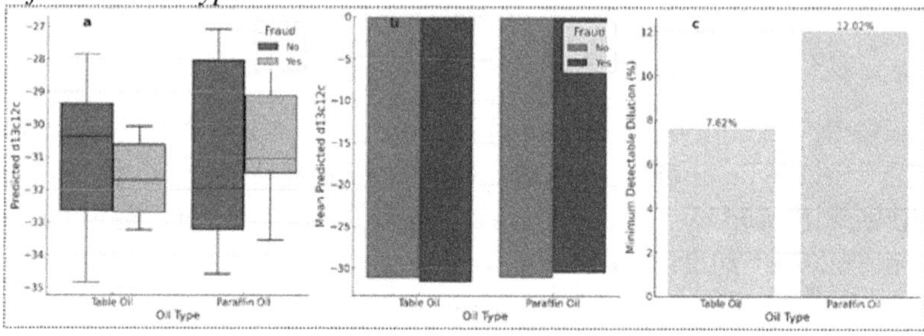

In addition, the associated Receiver Operating Characteristic (ROC) curve, shown in Figure 11, reveals an Area Under the Curve (AUC) of 0.73, attesting to robust performance under realistic conditions. Although slightly lower than a perfect theoretical classification (AUC = 1.00), this curve confirms the practical effectiveness of the polynomial model for detecting isotopic anomalies in industrial scenarios.

Figure 11. ROC curve for fraud detection.

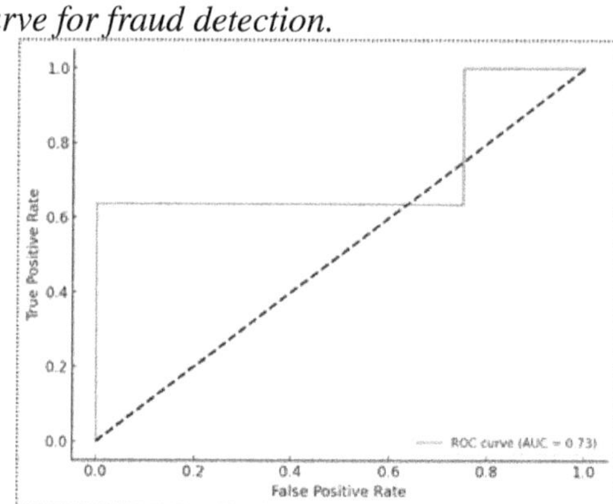

Comparative analyses of the models highlighted the superiority of Gradient Boosting and Random Forest over SVM. With a perfect AUC of 1.00, Random Forest emerged as the best-performing model, particularly after the addition of the "Country" variable, which reflects isotopic or spectral geographical differences between Moroccan and Egyptian oils. This variable proved essential for improving the classification and enhancing the traceability of sesame oils. Gradient Boosting, for its part, demonstrated perfect accuracy thanks to its ability to model the complex relationships identified in the quadratic and cubic terms of the polynomial model. These contributions, visualized in Figure 12 (a), underline the importance of non-linear relationships in capturing the complex isotopic effects associated with dilution.

Comparative ROC curves, presented in Figure 12 (b), confirm these results. With an AUC of 1.00 for Random Forest, classification is perfect, while SVM, with an AUC of 0.57, suffers from inefficient class separation, probably due to limitations in linear modeling or insufficient optimization of hyperparameters. These results justify the use of approaches such as Gradient Boosting and Random Forest for industrial applications, where detection reliability and accuracy are crucial.

Finally, these analyses reveal the importance of non-linear contributions to fraud detection. Quadratic and cubic terms, in addition to linear contributions, show that isotopic effects depend strongly on interactions between variables, notably dilution and oil type. These results position non-linear models and their interactions as reliable and innovative tools for improving quality control, traceability and the fight against fraud in the food industry.

Figure 12. Comparative analysis: a. Feature Contributions; b. Model Performance.

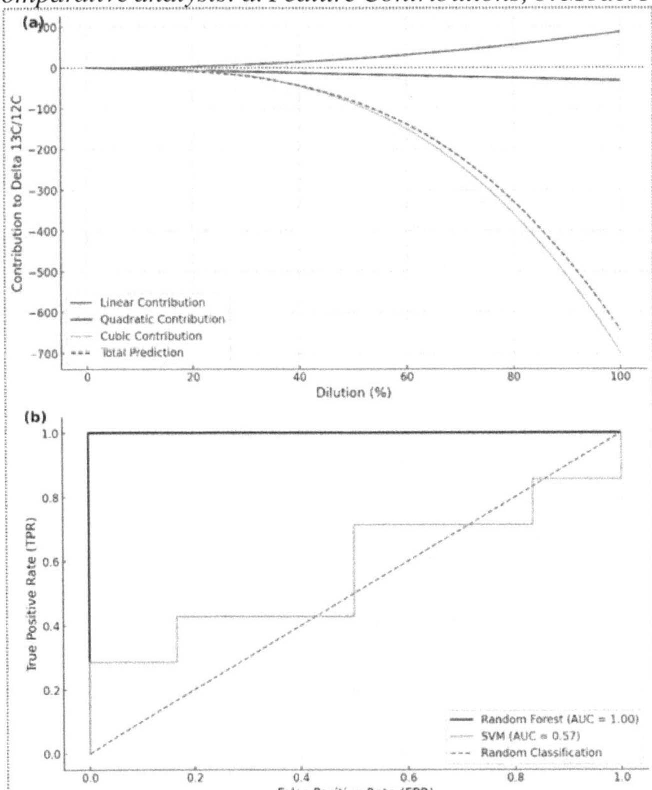

4. DISCUSSION

FTIR analysis of the sesame oils studied revealed significant spectral variations between pure oils (E100%, M100%) and diluted blends (TO: table oil, PO: kerosene). These variations, observed in specific ranges of the infrared spectrum, enable not only the detection of fraud, but also the quantitative assessment of sample purity. The 4000-3000 cm^{-1} range reveals O-H, N-H and C-H vibrations characteristic of triglycerides. Pure oils are characterized by high intensities in the aliphatic C-H bands (~3000 cm^{-1}), with well-defined continuous zones. Dilutions with table oil lead to a progressive decrease in intensities, while mixtures with kerosene show low or absent intensities, reflecting the absence of polar O-H and N-H groups. This range, particularly around 3400-3200 cm^{-1}, is crucial for differentiating pure oils from fraudulent samples, in line with the work of (Vlachos et al., 2006). The 3000-2800 cm^{-1} range, corresponding to aliphatic CH_2 and CH_3 vibrations, is particularly relevant for differentiating pure samples from diluted mixtures. Bands at 2921 cm^{-1} and 2854 cm^{-1} are reliable markers of long aliphatic triglyceride chains. Pure oils show high and homogeneous intensities in these regions. However, dilutions with table oil cause a proportional attenuation of these bands, while mixtures with kerosene show lower intensities and increased variability, due to the absence of complex structures in kerosene. These observations are consistent with studies by Valdés et al. (2015), who highlighted the importance of these bands for monitoring oxidation state.

The 1800-1500 cm^{-1} range includes C=O and aromatic group vibrations. The band at 1743 cm^{-1}, associated with C=O vibrations of triglyceride esters, is a key marker for differentiating samples. Pure oils show high intensities, while blends with table oil show a progressive decrease in this band, reflecting the dilution of triglycerides. Blends with kerosene show an almost total absence of this band, confirming the absence of carbonyl groups in kerosene. These results concur with those of Suri et al. (2019), who showed that the band at 1745 cm^{-1} is associated with vibrations of ester carbonyl functions in triglycerides.

The 1200-1000 cm^{-1} range, corresponding to C-O vibrations and the fingerprint region, is essential for identifying complex triglyceride structures. Pure oils show moderate to high intensities around 1160 cm^{-1}, while blends with table oil show intensity reductions due to the presence of esterified fatty acids. On the other hand, blends show intensity decreases due to the presence of diluting oils, such as table oil, or to the absence of functional C-O groups in kerosene. These observations confirm the results of Liang et al. (2015), who highlighted the sensitivity of C-O vibrations in detecting esterified structures in triglycerides. Additional ranges, such as those between 1267-1209 cm^{-1} and 1121-1045 cm^{-1}, identified in the study by

Fadzlillah et al. (2014), proved particularly effective in discriminating pure oils from fraudulent mixtures.

The FTIR spectra reveal a direct correlation between the decrease in the intensities of the main bands (2921, 2854, 1743, and 1160 cm-[1]) and the percentage dilution of the pure oils. These results suggest the possibility of developing a calibration model based on the relative intensities of these bands to quantitatively estimate sample purity. The use of regression models based on these spectral intensities, as mentioned in the study by Ozulku et al. (2017) showed an excellent correlation between predicted and actual values, with a high R^2 (0.9633 in the case of blends with hazelnut oil). FTIR analysis, combined with cluster heatmaps, is a powerful tool for detecting fraud and assessing the purity of sesame oils. Heatmaps enable spectral variations to be visualized and samples to be classified according to their spectral similarities. Key spectral regions, including those around 1743 cm-[1] (C=O groups), 2921 cm-[1] and 2854 cm-[1] (CH_2 and CH_3 vibrations), and 1160 cm-[1] (C-O vibrations), offer accurate and reliable information for differentiating pure oils from dilute blends. These results highlight the potential of FTIR analysis and visual classification approaches to detect fraudulent blends and strengthen quality control of edible oils.

Isotope analysis of organic elements, such as carbon, is a powerful tool for determining food provenance, as isotopic compositions reflect various factors related to the natural environment (Nakashita et al., 2008). Studies have shown that stable isotope analysis is useful for highlighting a clear disparity between C3 and C4 plants (Rhodes et al., 2010). C3 plants use the Cal-vin-Benson cycle to fix CO_2, resulting in lower $\delta^{13}C$ values compared with C4 plants, which use the Hatch-Slack cycle (Primrose et al., 2010). Clear distinctions between the carbon isotope ratios of photosynthetic cycles make it easy to detect the adulteration of vegetable oils. In the case of sesame oils (from C3 plants), when mixed with kerosene or table oil, significant variations in $\delta^{13}C$ values can be observed. C3 plants, such as sesame, follow the Calvin cycle, leading to generally low $\delta^{13}C$ values. By way of example, Moroccan and Egyptian sesame oils have $\delta^{13}C$ values of -28.92‰ and -29.14‰ respectively. On the other hand, kerosene, derived from fossil sources and presenting a $\delta^{13}C$ value of -27.32‰, progressively modifies isotopic ratios when added to sesame oil. Similarly, table oil, with an even more negative $\delta^{13}C$ isotopic value (around -38.99‰), strongly in-fluences isotopic ratios when fraudulent blends are made. These variations reflect the isotopic origins of the added oils. In line with the work of Kelly et al. (1997), oils from authentic C3 plants, such as sesame, retain $\delta^{13}C$ values between -27.6‰ and -32.1‰. Thus, the addition of kerosene or table oil results in different $\delta^{13}C$ values from pure oils, which can be detected by accurate isotope analysis. This method is therefore proving to be a powerful tool for spotting fraudulent blends and guaranteeing the authenticity of oils (Osorio et al., 2014; Kakouri et al., 2021).

Isotopic analyses of pure sesame oils reveal significant variability linked to geographical origin. Moroccan samples show an average $\delta^{13}C$ value of -28.92, while Egyptian samples show a slightly more negative value of -29.14. This isotopic distinction between the two origins can be attributed to specific environmental factors, such as soil composition, climatic conditions and agricultural practices. These observations are in line with studies showing that environmental factors influence the isotopic signatures of vegetable oils, particularly as a function of rainfall and average temperatures in producing regions (Bontempo et al., 2009; Horacek et al., 2015). Furthermore, isotopic data reported in the literature confirms this variability according to geographical regions: sesame oils from Paraguay display $\delta^{13}C$ values between -28.5‰ and -28.0‰, while those from Kenya vary between -29.0‰ and -28.0‰, and those from Bolivia reach significantly more negative values, between -30.7‰ and -30.0‰ producers (Horacek et al., 2015). These differences can also be explained by the type of plant photosynthesis, particularly the C3 pathways, predominant in sesame crops, which produce typically negative $\delta^{13}C$ values within a narrow range. In contrast, plants using the C4 pathway (plants using the C4 photosynthetic cycle), such as maize, show much higher $\delta^{13}C$ values, making it possible to detect fraudulent blends involving these oils even at low proportions (5% or more), using isotope mass spectrometry (Huang et al., 2017; Lovkis et al., 2019). Furthermore, the isotopic composition of oils can be influenced by the nature of the seeds used. Oils from dark seeds show systematically more negative $\delta^{13}C$ values than those from white seeds, as observed for Egyptian samples, whose dark seeds show values between -29.5‰ and -29.1‰. This parameter may also explain some of the variation observed between Moroccan and Egyptian oils in this study, highlighting the importance of taking into account the varieties used during isotope analysis (Horacek et al., 2015).

These results on pure oils provide a reliable isotopic basis for detecting fraudulent blends. When diluted with oils with different isotopic signatures, such as kerosene ($\delta^{13}C = -27.32$), derived from C4 plants or fossil sources, or table oil ($\delta^{13}C \approx -38.99$), the isotopic ratios of the blends show predictable linear variations as a function of diluent proportions. These isotopic trends are consistent with previous work demonstrating the effectiveness of isotopic models in accurately quantifying dilution levels, even in complex mixtures (Huang et al., 2017). In addition, the integration of oxygen ($\delta^{18}O$) and hydrogen ($\delta^{2}H$) isotopes could reinforce the geographical differentiation of sesame oils, as these parameters are sensitive to the specific climatic conditions of production regions, such as average temperature and precipitation. For example, grapeseed oils produced in Turkey, Armenia and Italy show significant isotopic variations in $\delta^{18}O$ (respectively 19.40‰, 16.55‰, and

23.29‰) and δ^2H (respectively -163.17‰, -189.86‰, and -160.72‰) (Bontempo et al., 2009). These approaches could be considered in future studies to enhance the traceability of edible oils on a regional scale (Nasr et al., 2022).

At the same time, the δ^{13}C values of Moroccan and Egyptian pure oils serve as re-liable references for detecting and quantifying fraudulent blends. The use of isotopes as an advanced analytical tool makes it possible to develop robust predictive models to ensure oil traceability and effectively combat food fraud. The fitted model, based on polynomial regression with interactions, shows a robust ability to capture the relationship between $\delta^{13}C/^{12}C$, dilution and oil type. With an R^2 of 0.8611 and an Adj. R^2 of 0.8325, it explains over 86% of the variance of the dependent variable, indicating a re-markable overall fit. These results validate the use of non-linear models in contexts where complex interactions need to be modeled. This approach is consistent with the work of Zhang et al. (2016), who demonstrated the effectiveness of SVM models in discriminating oils according to their authenticity with an accuracy of up to 94.2%. The model's predictions, illustrated in Figure 1, reveal distinct isotopic behaviors according to oil type and dilu-tion level. Table oil shows an isotopic increase at low dilution (<20%), followed by a marked non-linearity, while kerosene shows a constant isotopic decrease. These observations confirm the relevance of identifying critical isotopic thresholds (-30 and -27) to effectively distinguish fraudulent samples. These results follow a similar logic to the work of Peng et al. (2015) and Xing et al. (2019), who reported respective RMSEs of 1.19-4.29% and 5.0757% for the detection of adulterations in oils using advanced models.

The robustness of the model is reinforced by a combined analysis, which highlights the isotopic behaviour of the samples. Isotopic averages, synthesized reveal a clear separation between genuine and fraudulent samples, while the minimum detectable dilution (7.62% for table oil and 12.02% for kerosene) confirms the increased sensitivity of the model to subtle isotopic alterations. These results are in line with the observations of [33], who also used techniques such as ATR-FTIR to discriminate oils based on their chemical composition, with high accuracy (R = 0.976). In addition, the associated Receiver Operating Characteristic (ROC) curve, shown in Figure 3, reveals an Area Under the Curve (AUC) of 0.73, attesting to robust performance under realistic conditions. Although this performance is slightly lower than perfect classification (AUC = 1.00), it remains consistent with the performance reported by [48], who used SVM models to detect oil adulterations with 100% accuracy, sensitivity and specificity. These results reinforce the practical reliability of nonlinear approaches for detecting isotopic anomalies. Comparative analyses show a clear superiority of the Gradient Boosting and Random Forest models over the SVM. With a perfect AUC of 1.00, Random Forest emerged as the best-performing model, particularly after incorporating the "Country" variable, which reflects isotopic or spectral geographical differences between Moroccan and Egyptian oils.

These results confirm the importance of geographical data, as highlighted in the work of Yuan et al. (2020), for improving traceability and combating fraud in food products. Furthermore, Gradient Boosting has demonstrated its ability to model complex relationships through non-linear interactions, highlighting quadratic and cubic contributions already identified in polynomial models. The findings underline the fact that nonlinear models and their interactions are innovative and reliable tools for improving isotope fraud detection. Established critical thresholds and minimum detectable dilutions give these models operational utility for industrial applications. In the future, combinations with advanced techniques, such as those reported by Ozulku et al. (2017) and Yuan et al. (2020), (matrix fluorescence), could further improve the sensitivity and accuracy of detection systems.

4.1. Limitations and Strengths

The strengths of this study lie in the integration of advanced analytical and algorithmic techniques, enabling precise discrimination of fraudulent blends and geo-graphical origins, as well as in the identification of critical thresholds for quantifying dilution. However, the environmental variability influencing isotopic signatures, the complexity of the analyses requiring sophisticated equipment and technical skills, and the difficulty of generalizing these results to other types of oil without methodological adaptation, represent notable limitations.

4.2. Scientific and Industrial Implications

This study provides a robust framework for improving quality control and traceability in the food industry, offering reliable tools for detecting fraud and guaranteeing product authenticity in line with international standards, while making a significant contribution to scientific research by demonstrating the relevance of combining analytical chemistry and machine learning, with potential for extension to include other isotopes or oil types for advanced traceability purposes.

5. CONCLUSION

This study shows that the combination of FTIR spectroscopy, isotope analysis and advanced models can accurately detect fraud in sesame oils while differentiating their geographical origins. The approaches implemented are both robust and innovative, offering practical solutions for the agri-food industry and solid foundations for future research. These results reinforce the need to adopt advanced analytical tools to improve traceability and guarantee the authenticity of food products worldwide.

REFERENCES

Adewuyi, A., & Pereira, F. (2017). Fatty alkyl tosylate from *Sesamum indicum* seed oil: A potential resource for the oleochemical industry. *La Rivista Italiana delle Sostanze Grasse*, *94*(3), 161–167.

Aslam, M., Shabbir, M. A., Pasha, I., Shukat, R., Siddique, U., Manzoor, M. F., & Ayub, S. (2020). Protective effect of sesame (*Sesamum indicum*) seed oil against hypercholesterolemic in Sprague-Dawley male rats. *Food Science and Technology (Campinas)*, *41*(Suppl 2), 741–745. DOI: 10.1590/fst.35320

Bannor, R. K., Arthur, K. K., Oppong, D., & Oppong-Kyeremeh, H. (2023). A comprehensive systematic review and bibliometric analysis of food fraud from a global perspective. *Journal of Agriculture and Food Research*, *14*, 100686. DOI: 10.1016/j.jafr.2023.100686

Ben Ayed, R., Hanana, M., Ercisli, S., Karunakaran, R., Rebai, A., & Moreau, F. (2022). Integration of innovative technologies in the agri-food sector: The fundamentals and practical case of DNA-based traceability of olives from fruit to oil. *Plants*, *11*(9), 1230. DOI: 10.3390/plants11091230 PMID: 35567232

Biswas, S., Natta, S., Ray, D. P., Mondal, P., & Saha, U. (2018). Til (*Sesamum indicum* L.)—An underexploited but promising oilseed with multifarious applications: A review. *International Journal of Bioresource Science*, *5*(2), 127–139. DOI: 10.30954/2347-9655.02.2018.8

Bontempo, L., Camin, F., Larcher, R., Nicolini, G., Perini, M., & Rossmann, A. (2009). Coast and year effect on H, O and C stable isotope ratios of Tyrrhenian and Adriatic Italian olive oils. *Rapid Communications in Mass Spectrometry*, *23*(7), 1043–1048. DOI: 10.1002/rcm.3968 PMID: 19253913

Brand, W. A., Coplen, T. B., Vogl, J., Rosner, M., & Prohaska, T. (2014). Assessment of international reference materials for isotope-ratio analysis (IUPAC technical report). *Pure and Applied Chemistry*, *86*(3), 425–467. DOI: 10.1515/pac-2013-1023

Breiman, L. (2001). Random forests. *Machine Learning*, *45*(1), 5–32. DOI: 10.1023/A:1010933404324

Cui, C., Liu, Y., Liu, Y., Cui, X., Sun, Z., Du, Z., Wu, K., Jiang, X., Mei, H., & Zheng, Y. (2021). Genome-wide association study of seed coat color in sesame (*Sesamum indicum* L.). *PLoS One*, *16*(5), e0251526. DOI: 10.1371/journal.pone.0251526 PMID: 34019554

Everstine, K., Spink, J., & Kennedy, S. (2013). Economically motivated adulteration (EMA) of food: Common characteristics of EMA incidents. *Journal of Food Protection, 76*(4), 723–735. DOI: 10.4315/0362-028X.JFP-12-399 PMID: 23575142

Ezhani, W., El Bakkali, M., Amenzou, N., Ebn Touhami, M., Taous, F., & Habsaoui, A. (2025). Detection of adulteration in Moroccan and Egyptian sesame oil using Isotopic analysis and Infrared spectroscopy. *Journal of Applied and Natural Science, 17*(1), 186–192. DOI: 10.31018/jans.v17i1.6171

Fadzlillah, M., Che Man, Y. B., & Rohman, A. (2014). FTIR spectroscopy combined with chemometric for analysis of sesame oil adulterated with corn oil. *International Journal of Food Properties, 17*(6), 1275–1282. DOI: 10.1080/10942912.2012.689409

Fuji, Y., Ohtsuki, T., & Matsufuji, H. (2018). Accumulation and subcellular localization of acteoside in sesame plants (*Sesamum indicum* L.). *ACS Omega, 3*(12), 17287–17294. DOI: 10.1021/acsomega.8b02798

Galvin-King, P., Haughey, S. A., & Elliott, C. T. (2018). Herb and spice fraud: The drivers, challenges and detection. *Food Control, 88*, 85–97. DOI: 10.1016/j.foodcont.2017.12.031

Gharby, S., Harhar, H., Bouzoubaa, Z., Asdadi, A., El Yadini, A., & Charrouf, Z. (2017). Chemical characterization and oxidative stability of seeds and oil of sesame grown in Morocco. *Journal of the Saudi Society of Agricultural Sciences, 16*(2), 105–111. DOI: 10.1016/j.jssas.2015.03.004

Gharby, S., Harhar, H., Guillaume, D., Haddad, A., Matthäus, B., & Charrouf, Z. (2011). Oxidative stability of edible argan oil: A two-year study. *Lebensmittel-Wissenschaft + Technologie, 44*(1), 1–8. DOI: 10.1016/j.lwt.2010.07.003

Hama, J. R. (2017). Comparison of fatty acid profile changes between unroasted and roasted brown sesame (*Sesamum indicum* L.) seeds oil. *International Journal of Food Properties, 20*(5), 957–967. DOI: 10.1080/10942912.2016.1190744

Horacek, M., Hansel-Hohl, K., Burg, K., Soja, G., Okello-Anyanga, W., & Fluch, S. (2015). Control of origin of sesame oil from various countries by stable isotope analysis and DNA-based markers—A pilot study. *PLoS One, 10*(4), e0123020. DOI: 10.1371/journal.pone.0123020 PMID: 25831054

Huang, J., Norgbey, E., Nkrumah, P. N., Opoku, P. A., & Apreku, T. O. (2017). Detection of corn oil in adulterated olive and soybean oil by carbon stable isotope analysis. *Journal für Verbraucherschutz und Lebensmittelsicherheit, 12*(3), 201–208. DOI: 10.1007/s00003-017-1097-x

Jiménez Carvelo, A. M., Pérez Castaño, E., González Casado, A., & Cuadros Rodríguez, L. (2017). One-input and two-input-class classifications for differentiating olive oil from other edible vegetable oils by use of the normal-phase liquid chromatography fingerprint of the methyl-transesterified fraction. *Food Chemistry*, *221*, 1784–1791. DOI: 10.1016/j.foodchem.2016.10.103 PMID: 27979162

Kakouri, E., Revelou, P. K., Kanakis, C., Daferera, D., Pappas, C. S., & Tarantilis, P. A. (2021). Authentication of the botanical and geographical origin and detection of adulteration of olive oil using gas chromatography, infrared and Raman spectroscopy techniques: A review. *Foods*, *10*(7), 1565. DOI: 10.3390/foods10071565 PMID: 34359435

Kaneko, H., & Funatsu, K. (2015). Fast optimization of hyperparameters for support vector regression models with highly predictive ability. *Chemometrics and Intelligent Laboratory Systems*, *142*, 64–69. DOI: 10.1016/j.chemolab.2015.01.001

Kelly, S., Parker, I., Sharman, M., Dennis, J., & Goodall, I. (1997). Assessing the authenticity of single seed vegetable oils using fatty acid stable carbon isotope ratios (13C/12C). *Food Chemistry*, *59*(2), 181–186. DOI: 10.1016/S0308-8146(96)00286-5

Kohavi, R. (1995). A study of cross-validation and bootstrap for accuracy estimation and model selection. *IJCAI (United States)*, *14*(2), 1137–1145.

Liang, J., Appukuttan Aachary, A., & Thiyam-Holländer, U. (2015). Hemp seed oil: Minor components and oil quality. *Lipid Technology*, *27*(10), 231–233. DOI: 10.1002/lite.201500050

Liu, H. M., He, M. K., Yao, Y. G., Qin, Z., Cai, X. S., & Wang, X. D. (2021). Pectic polysaccharides extracted from sesame seed hull: Physicochemical and functional properties. *International Journal of Biological Macromolecules*, *192*, 1075–1083. DOI: 10.1016/j.ijbiomac.2021.10.077 PMID: 34673100

Lovkis, Z. V., Pochitskaya, I. M., & Morgunova, E. M. (2019). Research and methodological basis for identification of palm oil in food. *Vescì Nacyânal'naj Akadèmìì Navuk Belarusì. Seryâ Agrarnyh Navuk*, *57*(4), 494–508. DOI: 10.29235/1817-7204-2019-57-4-494-508

Mili, A., Das, S., Nandakumar, K., & Lobo, R. (2021). A comprehensive review on *Sesamum indicum* L.: Botanical, ethnopharmacological, phytochemical, and pharmacological aspects. *Journal of Ethnopharmacology*, *281*, 114503. DOI: 10.1016/j.jep.2021.114503 PMID: 34364969

Morris, J. B., Wang, M. L., & Tonnis, B. D. (2021). Variability for oil, protein, lignan, tocopherol, and fatty acid concentrations in eight sesame (*Sesamum indicum* L.) genotypes. *Industrial Crops and Products, 164*, 113355. DOI: 10.1016/j.indcrop.2021.113355

Mukta, N., & Neeta, P. M. (2017). A review on sesame—An ethno medicinally significant oil crop. *International Journal of Life Science and Pharma Research, 7*(2), L58–L63.

Myint, D., Gilani, S. A., Kawase, M., & Watanabe, K. N. (2020). Sustainable sesame (*Sesamum indicum* L.) production through improved technology: An overview of production, challenges, and opportunities in Myanmar. *Sustainability (Basel), 12*(9), 3515. DOI: 10.3390/su12093515

Nakashita, R., Suzuki, Y., Akamatsu, F., Iizumi, Y., Korenaga, T., & Chikaraishi, Y. (2008). Stable carbon, nitrogen, and oxygen isotope analysis as a potential tool for verifying geographical origin of beef. *Analytica Chimica Acta, 617*(1–2), 148–152. DOI: 10.1016/j.aca.2008.03.048 PMID: 18486650

Nasr, E. G., Epova, E. N., Sebilo, M., Larivière, D., Hammami, M., Souissi, R., Abderrazak, H., & Donard, O. F. X. (2022). Olive oil traceability studies using inorganic and isotopic signatures: A review. *Molecules (Basel, Switzerland), 27*(6), 2014. DOI: 10.3390/molecules27062014 PMID: 35335378

Nzikou, J., Mvoula-Tsiéri, M., Ndangui, C., Pambou-Tobi, N., Kimbonguila, A., Loumouamou, B., Silou, T., & Desobry, S. (2010). Characterization of seeds and oil of sesame (*Sesamum indicum* L.) and the kinetics of degradation of the oil during heating. *Research Journal of Applied Sciences, Engineering and Technology, 2*(3), 227–232.

Oboulbiga, E. B., Douamba, Z., Compaoré-Sérémé, D., Semporé, J. N., Dabo, R., Semde, Z., Tapsoba, F. W. B., Hama-Ba, F., Songré-Ouattara, L. T., Parkouda, C., & Dicko, M. H. (2023). Physicochemical, potential nutritional, antioxidant and health properties of sesame seed oil: A review. *Frontiers in Nutrition, 10*, 1127926. DOI: 10.3389/fnut.2023.1127926 PMID: 37377483

Osorio, M. T., Haughey, S. A., Elliott, C. T., & Koidis, A. (2014). Evaluation of methodologies to determine vegetable oil species present in oil mixtures: Proposition of an approach to meet the EU legislation demands for correct vegetable oils labelling. *Food Research International, 60*, 66–75. DOI: 10.1016/j.foodres.2013.12.013

Ozulku, G., Yildirim, R. M., Toker, O. S., Karasu, S., & Durak, M. Z. (2017). Rapid detection of adulteration of cold pressed sesame oil with hazelnut, canola, and sunflower oils using ATR-FTIR spectroscopy combined with chemometrics. *Food Control, 82*, 212–216. DOI: 10.1016/j.foodcont.2017.06.034

Pedregosa, F., Varoquaux, G., Gramfort, A., Michel, V., Thirion, B., Grisel, O., Blondel, M., Prettenhofer, P., Weiss, R., & Dubourg, V. (2011). Scikit-learn: Machine learning in Python. *Journal of Machine Learning Research, 12*, 2825–2830.

Peng, D., Bi, Y., Ren, X., Yang, G., Sun, S., & Wang, X. (2015). Detection and quantification of adulteration of sesame oils with vegetable oils using gas chromatography and multivariate data analysis. *Food Chemistry, 188*, 415–421. DOI: 10.1016/j.foodchem.2015.05.001 PMID: 26041212

Primrose, S., Woolfe, M., & Rollinson, S. (2010). Food forensics: Methods for determining the authenticity of foodstuffs. *Trends in Food Science & Technology, 21*(12), 582–590. DOI: 10.1016/j.tifs.2010.09.006

Rajagukguk, Y. V., Utcu, M. A., Islam, M., Muzolf-Panek, M., & Tomaszewska-Gras, J. (2022). Authenticity assessment from sesame seeds to oil and sesame products of various origin by differential scanning calorimetry. *Molecules (Basel, Switzerland), 27*(21), 7496. DOI: 10.3390/molecules27217496 PMID: 36364323

Rhodes, C. N., Lofthouse, J. H., Hird, S., Rose, P., Reece, P., Christy, J., Macarthur, R., & Brereton, P. A. (2010). The use of stable carbon isotopes to authenticate claims that poultry have been corn-fed. *Food Chemistry, 118*(4), 927–932. DOI: 10.1016/j.foodchem.2008.05.113

Rout, K., Yadav, B. G., Yadava, S. K., Mukhopadhyay, A., Gupta, V., Pental, D., & Pradhan, A. K. (2018). QTL landscape for oil content in Brassica juncea: Analysis in multiple bi-parental populations in high and "0" erucic background. *Frontiers in Plant Science, 9*, 1448. DOI: 10.3389/fpls.2018.01448 PMID: 30386353

Sanni, G. B. T. A., Ezin, V., Chabi, I. B., Missihoun, A. A., Florent, Q., Hamissou, Z., Niang, M., & Ahanchede, A. (2024). Production and achievements of *Sesamum indicum* industry in the world: Past and current state. *Oil Crop Science, 9*(3), 187–197. DOI: 10.1016/j.ocsci.2024.06.006

Spink, J., & Moyer, D. C. (2011). Defining the public health threat of food fraud. *Journal of Food Science, 76*(9), R157–R163. DOI: 10.1111/j.1750-3841.2011.02417.x PMID: 22416717

Suri, K., Singh, B., Kaur, A., Yadav, M. P., & Singh, N. (2019). Impact of infrared and dry air roasting on the oxidative stability, fatty acid composition, Maillard reaction products and other chemical properties of black cumin (Nigella sativa L.) seed oil. *Food Chemistry*, *295*, 537–547. DOI: 10.1016/j.foodchem.2019.05.140 PMID: 31174793

Taous, F., Amenzou, N., Marah, H., Maia, R., Maguas, C., Bahmad, L., & Kelly, S. (2020). Stable isotope ratio analysis as a new tool to trace the geographical origin of Argan oils in Morocco. *Forensic Chemistry (Amsterdam, Netherlands)*, *17*, 100198. DOI: 10.1016/j.forc.2019.100198

Taous, F., El Ghali, T., Marah, H., Laraki, K., Islam, M., Cannavan, A., & Kelly, S. (2022). Geographical classification of authentic Moroccan argan oils and the rapid detection of soya and sunflower oil adulteration with ATR-FTIR spectroscopy and chemometrics. *Food Analytical Methods*, *15*(11), 3032–3044. DOI: 10.1007/s12161-022-02333-z

Tibshirani, R. J., & Efron, B. (1993). An introduction to the bootstrap. *Monographs on Statistics and Applied Probability*, *57*(1), 1–436.

Valdés, A., Beltrán, A., Karabagias, I., Badeka, A., Kontominas, M. G., & Garrigós, M. C. (2015). Monitoring the oxidative stability and volatiles in blanched, roasted and fried almonds under normal and accelerated storage conditions by DSC, thermogravimetric analysis and ATR-FTIR. *European Journal of Lipid Science and Technology*, *117*(8), 1199–1213. DOI: 10.1002/ejlt.201400384

Vlachos, N., Skopelitis, Y., Psaroudaki, M., Konstantinidou, V., Chatzilazarou, A., & Tegou, E. (2006). Applications of Fourier transform-infrared spectroscopy to edible oils. *Analytica Chimica Acta*, *573*, 459–465. DOI: 10.1016/j.aca.2006.05.034 PMID: 17723561

Wan, Y., Zhou, Q., Zhao, M., & Hou, T. (2023). Byproducts of sesame oil extraction: Composition, function, and comprehensive utilization. *Foods*, *12*(12), 2383. DOI: 10.3390/foods12122383 PMID: 37372594

Waskom, M. L. (2021). Seaborn: Statistical data visualization. *Journal of Open Source Software*, *6*(60), 3021. DOI: 10.21105/joss.03021

Wikul, A., Damsud, T., Kataoka, K., & Phuwapraisirisan, P. (2012). (+)-Pinoresinol is a putative hypoglycemic agent in defatted sesame (*Sesamum indicum*) seeds though inhibiting α-glucosidase. *Bioorganic & Medicinal Chemistry Letters*, *22*(16), 5215–5217. DOI: 10.1016/j.bmcl.2012.06.068 PMID: 22818971

Woo, M., Han, S., & Song, Y. O. (2019). Sesame oil attenuates renal oxidative stress induced by a high fat diet. *Preventive Nutrition and Food Science*, *24*(2), 114–120. DOI: 10.3746/pnf.2019.24.2.114 PMID: 31328114

Xing, C., Yuan, X., Wu, X., Shao, X., Yuan, J., & Yan, W. (2019). Chemometric classification and quantification of sesame oil adulterated with other vegetable oils based on fatty acids composition by gas chromatography. *Lebensmittel-Wissenschaft + Technologie*, *108*, 437–445. DOI: 10.1016/j.lwt.2019.03.085

Yuan, Y. Y., Wang, S. T., Wang, J. Z., Cheng, Q., Wu, X. J., & Kong, D. M. (2020). Rapid detection of the authenticity and adulteration of sesame oil using excitation-emission matrix fluorescence and chemometric methods. *Food Control*, *112*, 107145. DOI: 10.1016/j.foodcont.2020.107145

Zhang, L., Shuai, Q., Li, P., Zhang, Q., Ma, F., Zhang, W., & Ding, X. (2016). Ion mobility spectrometry fingerprints: A rapid detection technology for adulteration of sesame oil. *Food Chemistry*, *192*, 60–66. DOI: 10.1016/j.foodchem.2015.06.096 PMID: 26304320

Zine, S., Gharby, S., & El Hadek, M. (2013). Physicochemical characterization of Opuntia ficus-indica seed oil from Morocco. *Biosciences Biotechnology Research Asia*, *10*(1), 99–105. DOI: 10.13005/bbra/1099

Chapter 13
Industry 4.0 Analysis and Integration of Leading Technology Enterprises in Turkey

Feyza Günbüz
https://orcid.org/0000-0002-6327-8232
Erciyes University, Kayseri, Turkey

Yasemin Nur Karabiyik
Erciyes University, Turkey

Alper Kaan Eraslan
Erciyes University, Turkey

Yasin Çelik
Erciyes University, Turkey

ABSTRACT

Where we have come from the past to the present with the industrial revolutions, manpower is not seen as necessary as before and leaves its place to technology. At this point, Industry 4.0 applications come into play and it is inevitable that human power will be replaced by systems intertwined with technology such as computer applications, artificial intelligence, smart systems and big data. Rapidly growing technology startups in the internet age have had a direct share in the development of countries in line with the principles of innovative and innovative thinking. In this study, the results of the survey conducted on the leading technology initiatives in Turkey were interpreted with the SWOT Analysis method, and current and future

DOI: 10.4018/979-8-3693-8789-4.ch013

scenarios were extracted. According to the results obtained, it has been seen that although the level of awareness of technology companies about Industry 4.0 is high, they prioritize profitability in the current situation, but this situation is likely to change in the future.

1. INTRODUCTION

Today, production systems and technologies are changing rapidly. This change leads to a change in classical production concepts as well as physical change. The most important issue of modern production systems is technology, and in this context, businesses, states and policy makers have major roles in the development or renewal of existing production technologies.

In the globalizing world, especially in recent years, these initiatives, which have created added value for our country, received domestic and foreign investments and opened up new business areas, also contribute to the development and welfare of our country to a great extent. This situation caused developed countries to become information societies and affected their economic structures. (Bulut & Akçacı, 2017).

Industry 4.0 is called smart production, where each part of the supply chain in the production process interacts with each other and forms a whole, and machines communicate with each other (Kabaklarlı, 2016). Defined as a complex and flexible system that includes network communication, digital production, automation and computer technologies, Industry 4.0 (Zhou et al., 2015) is the sum of networked smart systems that organize themselves, perform production, and communicate with each other (Gubán & Kovács, 2017). In other words, Industry 4.0 is the combination of interconnected and innovative technologies.

The concept of Industry 4.0, which is used to define digitalization and production automation as a new trend (Oesterreich & Teuteberg, 2016), is the ability to produce new values and services in an environmentally friendly way in the production center through advanced information technology and automation applications (Khan & Turovski, 2016). In Industry 4.0, the combination of elements such as information, data, process and sensors eliminates unqualified labor and replaces it with stable and error-free processes (Şener & Elevli, 2017).

Industry 4.0 is the desire to bring together informatics and industry. Our main goal can be said to be less cost, less energy use, space saving, high speed production as well as productivity increase and quality improvement. Changing customer needs and habits since the existence of markets always bring change. Just as the transition to industry 1.0 with the invention of the steam engine took its place in the history books, industry 4.0 and even society 5.0 will go through the same paths. As those who cannot keep up with change, it should be our duty to be on the side that is praised as the pioneers of change, rather than finding a place for ourselves in the dusty pages of history.

Industry 4.0 has a content aimed at increasing competitiveness in production (Acet & Koç, 2020) and brings together many different components (dimensions). In today's conditions, the level of competition is increasing and it is becoming difficult to have a good position in the competitive environment. At this point, Industry 4.0 is expected to contribute positively. Industry 4.0 is the step-by-step application of information and internet technologies to factories. With the transition to an information society, industry has also received its share of these transformations. At this point, flexibility in production, resource efficiency, cost savings and new workflow models have emerged. Automation, condition monitoring, planning and information technologies stand out as the main factors in the new business model created by Industry 4.0 (Abersfelder et al., 2016: 467).

Recently, Industry 4.0 has become one of the important problems in Turkey and the paths to be followed for the transition process have begun to be determined (Salik Ata, 2024). The advantages provided by Industry 4.0, known as Manufacturing 4.0, can be listed as follows (Kasa & Arslan, 2020):

- The use of software such as Manufacturing Execution System and Enterprise Resource Planning in businesses accelerates the production process and increases efficiency, while managers can proactively ensure the delivery of cost-effective and quality products.
- It is possible to host micro services such as Customer Relationship Management - CRM, Promotion management, Sales management (Commercial Set), and Export management and Repair service center management in the Management Information Systems subgroup.
- It is easy to establish, activate and change the Industry 4.0 architecture.
- Transparent and observable communication paths in Industry 4.0 facilitate resource management.
- It is easy to add new protocols and processes.
- It is possible to communicate between components in the production department.
- With Industry 4.0; pressures have emerged on companies to adapt to modern technologies and a need for change in education and skills has begun to be felt in the labor market. At the same time, in order to reach the economic growth targets of countries, it has become necessary to use renewable energy resources instead of using coal and other fossil fuels that have served humanity in production since the industrial revolution.

The disadvantages that emerged with Industry 4.0 can be listed as follows (Kasa & Arslan, 2020):

- The importance given to education should be increased in order to train the qualified manpower needed with changing industrial production systems. Otherwise, while the need for qualified manpower increases, the need for unqualified manpower will decrease and the unemployment problem will gradually increase.
- The security of objects (IoT security) becomes an important problem and the analysis of the resulting big data becomes complex and difficult.
- The need for a large number of workers working in the IT departments of institutions will decrease.
- Since the transition to Industry 4.0 will take time and is a costly process, there may be reluctance in institutions.

In addition to all its negative aspects, Industry 4.0 is an inevitable process. Following developing and changing technologies from behind or resisting adaptation means the formation of new traps for economies. Therefore, changing needs should be determined in advance and the necessary structural reforms should be implemented, especially by countries in the middle-income trap.

In this study, Turkey's best initiatives were examined. Do we know Industry 4.0? What applications have we made regarding Industry 4.0, what applications do we plan to make in the future? What industry level are we at? etc. Various questions were answered, such as Leading initiatives were contacted using the survey method. E-mail, telephone conversation and various social networking platforms were used for communication. A total of 26 companies were contacted, open-ended questions and multiple-choice questions were asked and appropriate answers were received. The SWOT factors of 20 companies that gave their answers in accordance with the format were extracted. Determinations were made regarding the current situation of our companies, and recommendations and suggestions were made regarding their future situations. As a result, various results have been reached regarding the integration of these companies into industry 4.0.

In the continuation of the study, a literature study is presented in Chapter 2. In Chapter 3, the definition of the problem is made and the relevant data are presented. In Chapter 4, the solution methods used are explained and the results are analyzed. Chapter 5 summarizes all the results and outlines the roadmap to plan for the future.

1. LITERATURE STUDY

Industry 4.0; internet, automation, digital production, computer etc. is an elastic and complex system in which many technologies are used together. It is still under development and serves as a bridge from the past to the future. Industry 4.0 was first put forward in 2011 in Hannover, a city of Germany, with the idea of industrial renewal and becoming the sole owner of the market (Yildiz, 2018).

Three major industrial revolutions have taken place until the current industrial age. These; The first (18th century) started with steam engines, the second started with mass production (first quarter of the 20th century), the third started with the era of automation and digitalization (last quarter of the 20th century). From past to present, companies have had to change their production styles depending on various factors in the globalizing world. Before the 60's in the world, the customer mass who only bought the existing product started to prefer companies that responded to it in line with their wishes after this date. This has led to a stronger mindset of change. The historical process until Industry 4.0 has had a large share in the formation of industry 4.0, which provides an interdisciplinary working environment and provides the communication of objects with internet connection (Gov & Erdogan, 2020).

In their study, Faulds and Raju (2019) defined industry 4.0 as smart factories, cloud computing, big data, Internet of Things (IoT), cyber-physical systems, system integration, 3D printers, autonomous robots, augmented reality and simulation. The concept of Industry 4.0 appears as a phenomenon in which all these sub-titles work as a whole, rather than a single phenomenon. These are given below:

- **Smart Factories:** The term smart factory is defined as the factory model created by the autonomous operation of all technological components (robots, machines, etc.) (Sozen and Mescioglu, 2019). Similar to the Social Network, there is communication between workers, machines and resources working in smart factories. Products can be uniquely identified, located at any time, and know their history, current time and the goals they will achieve (Ayboğa & Görmüş, 2022). One of the advantages of smart factories is that they can be monitored 24/7 and provide ease of access to the right data at any time (Shekkeli, 2018).
- **Cloud Computing Systems:** It is expressed as the reconfiguration of cloud computing systems and services related to information systems without the need for a third party (Yasim, 2020). Cloud technology, which is also widely used by consumers today, can provide storage of images, audio, text and many other files found on smartphones, tablets and computers. Thanks to this technology, even if the physical storage devices owned by users are damaged or lost, the data in question is instantly stored and updated in the cloud

system, and the users' data continues to be protected. In addition, users can access the most up-to-date data in their cloud accounts on all their devices (Ayboğa & Görmüş, 2022).

- **Big Data:** The bulk of large and complex data coming from data providers is called big data, it cannot be processed with classical data processing methods (Goktas, Berkay, & Aksu, 2021). It refers to huge and non-traditional data sets. Compared to traditional data sets, big data includes unstructured data sets that need much more real-time analysis (Chen et al., 2014). Search engines, banking-related transactions, various sensors, blogs, and shopping sites can be given as examples among the sources where data is collected. When these collected data are analyzed correctly, the roadmap to be followed will provide social and institutional benefits and serve many purposes (Aktan, 2018).
- **Internet of Things (IoT):** It is expressed as a network created for objects to communicate with each other (Ersoz, 2020). It is the connection of the digital devices used with physical objects over the internet or a network. These digital objects are called the (IoT) because they transfer their data over the network infrastructure of the internet (Öztuna, 2017). The internet of things is a network system created by buildings, vehicles, machines, physical devices and objects containing various mechanical or electronic hardware and software to collect, distribute and communicate data (Banger, 2017).
- **Cyber-Physical (Security) Systems:** It is defined as systems that connect our world and cyber systems (Toker, 2018). Cybersecurity is the discipline that covers the measures taken and technological solutions implemented to protect computer systems, networks, software and digital data against unwanted access, attacks and harmful effects. Its main purpose is to ensure critical values such as confidentiality, integrity and accessibility by keeping information and technology assets safe (Akpınar et al, 2024).
- **System Integration:** It is defined as the work that enables all systems to work better and harmoniously by using data integration networks (Ertugrul and Deniz, 2018).
- **3D Printers:** Also known as additive manufacturing, it is the production of a physical product from a virtual software (Aksoy, 2017). 3D printers can be called one of the foundations of the future with the fourth industrial revolution. They produce by using the width, length and height inputs. Parts designed with CAD programs can be easily printed with 3D printers. After this technology becomes capable of mass production, it will carry the production sector to a completely different dimension (Vuran and Yavuz, 2021).
- **Autonomous robots:** Autonomous robots are robots that can perform requested actions with a high level of autonomy skills and have a structure

that can learn to perform programmed actions in new ways by adapting to environmental conditions (Akpınar et al, 2024). Intelligent robots used in smart factories. Robot technology that detects the product on the production line through sensors and processes what needs to be done is called (Davis, Sessions, Check, 2015).

- **Augmented (Virtual) reality:** Virtual reality is the creation of a semblance of the real world using computers, software and other technological tools. Thanks to this technology, users can feel real in virtual environments and have visual and auditory experiences. On the other hand, augmented reality is the addition of virtual content created by computers to objects or events that exist in the real world. In this way, users can have a richer and more interactive experience by adding virtual layers to objects in the real world (Akpınar et al, 2024). It is a set of systems in which the virtual image can be transferred to the real environment. With the virtual image, it enables the real image to be perceived as if it were an image (Devezas and Sarygulov, 2017).
- **Simulation:** It is the representation of the virtual world as close as possible to the real world (Akıncı & Kahraman, 2024). It can be called simulation models in which real logical and mathematical concepts are applied to understand the structure of systems (Aksoy, 2017).

Pamuk and Soysal (2018), in addition to the ten sub-titles mentioned above, also discussed Block chain and Web 3.0 issues in their studies. These are as follows:

- **Blockchain:** Block chain technology ensures that data is transmitted securely in the fastest way so that business processes can function properly and efficiently (Sayar, 2019). This technology is used to create a decentralized trading environment by removing all structures between the buyer and the seller. It can be used regardless of time (Barca, 2005).
- **Web 3.0:** Web 3.0 is a technology based on artificial intelligence, blockchain and machine learning. When it comes to Web 3.0, it is based on creating a peer-to-peer personalized and block chain-supported decentralized internet platform by destroying the authority on the internet platform (Kablan, 2018; Singh and Gulati, 2011).

Industry 4.0 has affected and continues to affect all sectors such as education, health, technology, transportation, and communication (Şen, 2022). The transformations experienced in all sectors with Industry 4.0 are also among the issues that constitute the importance of Industry 4.0 today. Since there are expectations that Industry 4.0 will continue the transformation, it is expected that its importance will continue to increase. This information is important in terms of supporting the fact that the effects of Industry 4.0 are observed in every area of life.

There are many studies published in the literature on Industry 4.0. Some of these, as well as studies on Turkey, are also mentioned in this section.

Khan and Emon (2025) found that the adoption of Industry 4.0 significantly increases digital supply chain integration, supply chain innovation, and supply chain visibility, which collectively improve overall supply chain performance by using a structured survey administered to 570 manufacturing professionals in Bangladesh.

Ghobakhloo el al. (2025), identified 16 functions through which Industry 4.0 enhances supply chain resilience, revealing that these Industry 4.0 supply chain resilience functions are highly interrelated and that supply chain members need to align their digitalization strategies with the order in which Industry 4.0 delivers these functions.

Rath et al., (2024) mentioned the role and impact of IoT in Industry 4.0 in their study, stating that it enables manufacturers to achieve more efficiency, lower costs and improved quality control. They also stated that IoT can help manufacturers reduce waste, minimize downtime, and increase production flexibility, and by providing real-time data and insights into the production process, it can help manufacturers make more informed decisions and improve overall performance.

According to the findings obtained in their study, Al-Khatip et al. (2024) reveal the positive effects of three components, including sensing, capturing and reconstruction, on Industry 4.0 capabilities. They also confirm the positive effect of Industry 4.0 capabilities on technological innovation.

Alhammadi et al. (2024) examined the relationship between Industry 4.0 technologies and Sustainable Development Goals in the United Arab Emirates.

Perera et al. (2025) investigated the implementation, maturity and adoption interest of 14 Industry 4.0 related technologies in Australian construction firms, identifying five key application areas: real-time data capture, digital communication, data analysis, visualization and off-site construction.

In their study, Amrani et al. (2024) proposed a strategic method in which industrial managers who are affected by giant transformations and are trying to initially implement Lean and Industry 4.0 will benefit from a structured roadmap (algorithm-based) that determines the priority of the implemented tools and technologies.

Javaid et al, (2024) in their work have discussed and defined the important requirements of Industry 4.0 which are fulfilled through digital economy.

Zong and Guan (2024) investigated the impact of artificial intelligence-supported smart data analytics and predictive analysis on economic efficiency and management practices within the scope of Industry 4.0.

In their study, Görçün et al. (2024) proposed a methodological framework to determine the best Industry 4.0 strategy for the automotive manufacturing sector, providing an example of a roadmap that will help companies achieve a simpler digital transformation.

Temimhan et al. (2024) presented an analysis of industry 4.0 applications for the Turkish agriculture sector.

Yıldırım et al. (2025) used text mining methods to investigate the similarities and differences between the national digital transformation and Industry 4.0 policies of countries. They also discussed the position of Turkey's digital transformation and Industry 4.0 national policy in the context of a developing country.

Alnıpak and Toraman (2024) measured the intentions of various stakeholders in the industry to adopt blockchain technology in terms of payment transactions across Turkey through Technology Acceptance Model and showed that there are strong positive relationships between the Intention to Use and Perceived Usefulness as well as Perceived Ease of Use of Blockchain Technology-based payment transactions, separately.

Karademir (2024), examined the Industry 4.0 maturity levels of companies operating in the manufacturing sector in Turkey.

Atlı et al. (2024), In order to reveal the perception of Logistics 4.0 among logistics companies in Turkey, the stage it is at, the level of awareness on the subject, the important issues and success factors on this subject, a case study was conducted using exploratory and descriptive methods in a logistics company that manages its business processes with the Logistics 4.0 approach.

In his study, Turgut (2024) discussed the process of using Industry 4.0 technologies in agricultural-food supply chains and logistics activities in order to explain Industry 4.0 technologies in supply chain activities and logistics activities in the agricultural food sector and to introduce them to the local literature.

Eslami et al. (2021), evaluated the relationship between supply chain integration, supply chain agility and financial performance with a dynamic capabilities perspective.

Surmen and Guler (2021) used a method including qualitative research technique in their study on industry 4.0 in the automotive sector. The automotive sector in Bursa industry has been examined. As a result of the SWOT analysis, it was observed that they had knowledge about Industry 4.0, but the level of the companies could not exceed the Industry 3.0 level.

Soylu (2018), mentioned that change is inevitable and it cannot be predicted how long it will take. They also emphasized that there had been no such technological attack before and that some occupational groups would disappear and some new occupations would emerge.

Kaygın, Zengin, and Topcuoglu (2019), mentioned that the academics at the Kafkas University agree that Industry 4.0 is an inevitable and important reality and is also a necessity for companies.

Studies that analyze the obstacles to Industry 4.0 with an empirical approach are important. There are studies in the literature that determine the positive and negative effects of obstacles with SWOT analysis (Calabrese et al., 2021).

Sever (2021), SWOT analysis is a scientific situation analysis method used to understand strengths and weaknesses of the institution, technique, situation or process under consideration, and to realize threats and opportunities. In addition to strategic planning, it is also used as a tool for problem solving and policy making. The basis of this analysis method is to make a comprehensive analysis of the internal and external environment of the institution or business and to design future scenarios accordingly.

2. PROBLEM DEFINITION

Our country's industrial establishments and companies have always been behind the times in industrial revolutions until now. From the first industrial revolution that emerged at the end of the 18th century to Industry 4.0, the fourth industrial revolution we are in, we had to follow many technological innovations from behind due to both our opportunities and our geopolitical position (Yilmaz and Koyuncu, 2020).

The aim of this study; It is to determine how Turkey's leading technology companies are integrated into Industry 4.0, what they do right and wrong as a pioneer in this context, and whether they are ready for the next industrial revolution. However, as a result of the study, it is aimed to give tips and suggestions for the next revolution to the leading technology companies of Turkey, in particular the companies that are the subject of the research.

2.1. Historical Development of Industrial Revolutions

The invention of the steam engine, which James Watt, an inventor, developed and later patented in 1769, played a major role in the start of Industry 1.0, which started in England and later became more and more widespread. With this invention, Watt has masterfully integrated circular energy into mechanical energy (Ozdogan, 2017). In this ongoing process, with the discovery of new machines, the mechanization of production has begun. The second industrial revolution, also called the Technology Revolution, forms the basis of the production techniques used today. Henry Ford, who continued to produce automobiles with an intense labor force in the early 1900s, saw that this method they used cost them much more production. Henry Ford established the mass production line in 1903 to produce cars faster and thus achieved the desired performance (Berber, 2016). The existence of mass production has brought with it many scientific researches. In addition to the studies on productivity, the concept of quality has also emerged and various studies have been carried out on this subject (Aksoy, 2017). The third industrial revolution, also called the information technology era, started after the Second World War and gained momentum especially after the 1970s. Technologies developed during the war led to this revolution, and together with automation, serious progress was made in the field of software, allowing the development and production of existing resources (Gabaclı and Uzunoz, 2017). When we look at the prominent titles of this period, it is seen that computer and the technologies it covers, bio agriculture, renewable energy sources, fiber optic and laser technology. The third industrial revolution can also be called the initiation and implementation of the integration of technology into industry. The fourth industrial revolution (I4.0) was first mentioned at the Hannover Fair in Germany in 2011. In October 2012, the working group formed by Robert Bosch GmbH and Henning Kagermannn submitted the I4.0 proposal file to the German Federal Government. Industry 4.0 is a strategy that aims to combine industry and technology on a common ground (Ocal and Altıntas, 2018). The cycle of production, which is gradually evolving into digitalization, has achieved a significant transformation thanks to this strategy. The first of the main components that unite the industry with information technologies is New Generation Software and Hardware, and the second is the Device-Based IoT (Madakam and Lake, 2015). To explain the concepts covered by Industry 4.0 in detail; the internet of things can be defined as a system that allows the objects we use in our daily lives to exchange data through an internet connection. These objects work in coordination with each other, and this is one of the foundations of this technology that they have created. These devices transmit the data they collect via a WIFI or Bluetooth connection to the gateway and share this data by transferring it to a cloud system to be analyzed. The IoT consists of five main components. These; Smart Devices and Sensors, Gateway, Cloud Technology (Cloud), Analytics, Advanced User Interface.

The internet of services is one of the sectors where the most potential growth is expected in the future. Industry 4.0 has brought a new dimension to the service sector with this technology. With the internet of services, the data coming from various cloud services is developed and implemented by web compatible services and projects. In this process, where business-related services will come to the fore with Web 3.0 technology, it can be said that the target of the internet of things and services is the company and the public.

Cyber-physical systems are systems that connect the virtual world and the physical world. They consist of different constituent components and often use embedded technologies when communicating with the physical world. These technologies can alert cyber-physical systems by detecting changes in their environment. Since cyber-physical systems can control physical actions through their components, they can share data between actions with each other and have the ability to act autonomously.

2.2. SWOT Analysis

SWOT Analysis is a very useful technique that allows to understand the strengths and weaknesses of a business or an individual, and to identify possible or current opportunities and threats (Erol, 2019). The word SWOT is formed by the abbreviation of the initials of four English words; Strengths, Weaknesses, Opportunities, Threats (Mintzberg et al., 1998). SWOT Analysis enables the evaluation of strengths-weaknesses, opportunities or threats together as a whole in the stage of making personal or business decisions and making investments. It acts as a kind of mirror about the company or person in the steps to be taken and the decisions to be made.

In practice, each of the four boxes contains the itemization of factors, usually in the form of a list with supporting documents (Sarsby, 2016). Strengths consist of the internal characteristics of the subject under study, current capabilities, competitive advantages and current assets. Opportunities consist of external environmental conditions reflecting positive factors beyond the control of the organization, positive changes in the market, demand growth and market trends and technological developments. Weaknesses represent internal deficiencies, limited financial resources, lack of skills or inadequate technological infrastructure. Finally, threats represent potential risks arising from external factors, threats beyond control such as market competition, economic fluctuations, changing regulations or natural disasters.

SWOT analysis is often used in business management, marketing strategies, business plans, competitive analysis, and strategic decisions. The main purpose here is to determine the internal and external factors required for the successful progress and completion of the targeted initiative or project (Özcan, 2024).

In addition, SWOT Analysis allows not only the person or the company to analyze itself but also its competitors to see its advantages or disadvantages.

2.3. Industry 4.0 in Turkey and in the World

Along with the technological progress, leading countries, companies and various organizations have entered the infrastructure and strategy race. Infrastructure, training and strategy, etc. in accordance with Industry 4.0 principles. Along with the development, they aimed to take the leadership in various fields. Turkey is also in an effort to be included in this race and to achieve better. In Turkey, there is a digitalization breakthrough that has started to be used by different production and service providers, especially the automotive sector. Sectors such as telecommunications, banking and insurance are at the top in terms of the percentage of digital investments made for Industry 4.0.

In the world, it can be said that Germany and Japan are leading the rest of the world in establishing the needed technologies and organizations. Germany is working in line with its desire to be a pioneer in this field by adding Industry 4.0 on top of the existing engineering school. Founded under the name of 'Plattform Industry 4.0', this organization works to coordinate legal regulations, research and development studies, sector-based training and vision. In this way, they plan to draw their own Industry 4.0 lines and take appropriate maneuvers (Islam, 2019). On the other hand, Japan talks about Society 5.0 with a people-oriented perspective on Industry 4.0. They are in a social development plan by including the human factor in this digital transformation, which started rapidly in the production and service sectors. In this way, they aim to take their existing positions to a higher level (Saracel and Aksoy, 2020).

China is more focused on the automation part of the digitalization process. China, which is currently carrying out the "Smart Factory 1.0" project, has created an initial fund of 230 billion dollars for the "Made in China 2025" strategy. The USA, which established the Industrial Internet Consortium, allocated 2 billion dollars for this fund alone. It also continues to develop its "America Produces" strategy (Ertugrul and Deniz, 2018).

2.4. Application Problem

In this study, where they are in the use of Industry 4.0 regarding certain initiatives in Turkey, how they will proceed in the current and future situation, their approach to Industry 4.0, the technologies used, how they will keep up with the transformation, etc. It is a work on the subject. Leading initiatives were contacted through the surveys. A total of 26 companies were contacted and answers were received by asking open-ended questions and multiple-choice questions. We examined 20 companies that gave their answers in accordance with the format using the SWOT analysis method. Determinations about the current situation of our companies, recommendations and suggestions about their future situations were made. It has been tried to shed light on our companies and Industry 4.0 with the general conclusions in the "Conclusion and Suggestions" section of the study.

3. METHOD AND ANALYSIS

In our research, different forms and questionnaires, including classical and multiple-choice questions, were transmitted to the relevant units of the companies and the data forming the basis of our study were obtained. With the data we obtained as a result of the results we obtained, we created the Strengths, Weaknesses, Opportunities and Threats sub-factors for companies. From this point of view, we created a SWOT Analysis table as a result of both the feedback we received from the companies and the research we made.

The companies that are the subject of our study were taken from the first quarter list of "Turkey's Leading Technology Initiatives 2021" (Egirisim, 2022). 26 companies at the top of the list were interviewed and 20 companies that met our criteria were included in the research. The companies in question were contacted via various social media platforms, e-mails and company websites. As a result of the interviews with the companies in terms of the confidentiality of the data, the companies that are the subject of the research will be mentioned as "C1, C2, C3, ...". You can see the results of our survey study, which we have done below, in Appendix 1 in the form of circular graphs.

According to the graphics obtained in the appendix; While 45.5% of the companies participating in the survey state that they keep their data both physically and in the cloud, half of the remaining companies state that they only keep it physically and half only in the cloud. Although 54.5% stated that they did not receive consultancy within the scope of Industry 4.0 and its integration, "Do you think it is necessary to get consultancy?" The rate of those who gave the answer is 81.8%.

Companies currently invest mostly in the Internet of Services area with 54.5%. This area is followed by the Internet of Things with 27.3% and Cyber-Physical Systems with 18.2%. The most popular technology that Turkey's leading companies are currently investing in is Big Data. Cloud Computing follows it, and a common distribution is seen among other technologies. In the future, while investing in Big Data and Cloud Computing continues to be popular, no new investments are planned in block chain and Smart Robots.

Apart from the survey questions, the other questions we ask classically in order to examine the companies in detail and to make SWOT Analysis are briefly as follows;

- Can you talk a little bit about your company's approach to Industry 4.0 and its integration?
    -What steps are you taking for your business to transition to Industry 4.0? Have you created a roadmap?
- What were the most challenging factors for you as a company in the transition to Industry 4.0? What are you doing to facilitate this transition? Do you organize training, etc.?
    -In which areas do you intend to invest in Industry 4.0? (Big Data, Web3.0, Blockchain, Smart Factory and Intelligent Robots etc.)
    -When you compare your company with other companies within the scope of Industry 4.0, what are the areas that you think you are better or think to improve?

3.1. Results

Table 1-4 shows the comprehensive SWOT Analysis we created based on the answers we received from the classical and multiple choice questions asked to the companies that were the subject of the survey.

As seen in Table 1, the most distinctive common feature of Turkey's 20 leading technology companies is that they have an innovative and visionary perspective. In addition to this, having a talented IT team is seen as a must in order to provide a quality service.

At the same time, having a strong financial structure and a wide customer portfolio is among the main common points of successful companies operating in the technology sector in our country. Another point that draws attention here is that businesses with such potential do not yet have sufficient branding skills and are not conscious enough about Industry 4.0.

As seen in Table 2, the biggest weaknesses of companies are not being conscious enough about Industry 4.0, not creating a roadmap and not allocating enough resources. In addition, the lack of cooperation with universities and industries leads to an inability to train qualified and conscious employees about Industry 4.0.

Looking at Table 3, the country's young population potential and the opportunities to train young-qualified personnel in parallel with it are seen as a great advantage for companies. In addition, it is of great importance for companies to receive investments in foreign currency and to benefit from grant-incentive programs in terms of their rapid growth.

The biggest threat to the companies that are the subject of our research. As seen in Table 4, we can say that the costs of using technology will increase and the costs of foreign operations will increase. However, the increase in global competitors, the uncertainties in the exchange rate and political instability are also seen as the biggest obstacles to the growth of companies.

Table 1. Strengths of the companies

STRENGTHS										
QUESTIONS/COMPANIES	**C1**	**C2**	**C3**	**C4**	**C5**	**C6**	**C7**	**C8**	**C9**	**C10**
Branding Ability	X	X		X		X		X		
Having a Roadmap for Industry 4.0	X						X	X		X
Having Strong Know How	X	X		X						X
Having a Strong Customer Portfolio	X	X	X	X		X		X		
Having a Strong Product/Service Portfolio	X	X		X		X				X
Operating in Multiple Countries	X	X		X	X	X			X	

continued on following page

Table 1. Continued

STRENGTHS										
QUESTIONS/COMPANIES	**C1**	**C2**	**C3**	**C4**	**C5**	**C6**	**C7**	**C8**	**C9**	**C10**
Having a Strong Financial Structure	X	X	X	X		X		X		
Having a Strong Data Infrastructure		X	X						X	
Having a Talented IT Team	X	X		X	X	X			X	
Owning an R&D Center		X								
Successfully Satisfying Customer Expectations	X		X					X	X	
Making Investments Focused on Technology and Industry 4.0		X								
Export Oriented Working		X							X	
Having Sufficient Qualified Employees	X	X		X	X	X			X	
Having an Innovative/Visionary Perspective	X	X	X	X	X		X		X	X

Table 2. Cont.

STRENGTHS										
QUESTIONS/COMPANIES	**C11**	**C12**	**C13**	**C14**	**C15**	**C16**	**C17**	**C18**	**C19**	**C20**
Branding Ability	X						X		X	
Having a Roadmap for Industry 4.0	X		X					X		
Having Strong Know How	X	X		X		X			X	
Having a Strong Customer Portfolio	X			X	X	X	X		X	X
Having a Strong Product/Service Portfolio			X	X		X	X	X		X
Operating in Multiple Countries	X	X								X
Having a Strong Financial Structure	X	X		X	X				X	X
Having a Strong Data Infrastructure	X			X	X	X	X		X	X
Having a Talented IT Team	X	X		X	X	X			X	X
Owning an R&D Center		X		X						
Successfully Satisfying Customer Expectations	X		X		X	X		X	X	
Making Investments Focused on Technology and Industry 4.0		X		X	X			X		
Export Oriented Working	X	X								X
Having Sufficient Qualified Employees	X	X		X	X	X			X	X
Having an Innovative/Visionary Perspective	X	X	X	X	X	X		X	X	X

Table 3. Weaknesses' of the companies

WEAKNESSES										
QUESTIONS/COMPANIES	**C1**	**C2**	**C3**	**C4**	**C5**	**C6**	**C7**	**C8**	**C9**	**C10**
Lack of Branding			X		X		X		X	
Inability to Reach Sufficient Export Capacity			X	X	X		X	X	X	X
Not Being Multinational			X		X		X	X		X
Lack of Marketing							X			
Not Having Adequate Awareness About Industry 4.0	X		X	X	X	X	X	X	X	
Inability to Allocate Enough Budget for Industry 4.0	X	X	X	X	X	X	X	X	X	
Inadequacy in Technology Management										X
Not Having Enough Qualified Personnel	X									X
Not Having a Crisis Management Memory	X		X		X	X			X	
Absence from Global Competition			X		X		X	X		X
Lack of Industry 4.0 Roadmap	X		X	X		X	X	X		
Not Having Enough Physical Space			X							
Having Problems With Removing Quality Products										X
Lack of Strength in Supply/Logistics										
Not Collaborating with Universities and Industries	X	X	X		X	X	X		X	X

Table 4. Weaknesses' of the companies (continued)

WEAKNESSES										
QUESTIONS/COMPANIES	**C11**	**C12**	**C13**	**C14**	**C15**	**C16**	**C17**	**C18**	**C19**	**C20**
Lack of Branding		X	X		X	X				
Inability to Reach Sufficient Export Capacity			X	X	X	X	X		X	
Not Being Multinational			X	X	X		X		X	
Lack of Marketing					X					
Not Having Adequate Awareness About Industry 4.0	X	X	X	X	X		X		X	X
Inability to Allocate Enough Budget for Industry 4.0	X		X	X	X		X		X	X
Inadequacy in Technology Management			X					X		
Not Having Enough Qualified Personnel			X					X		
Not Having a Crisis Management Memory			X			X	X	X		
Absence from Global Competition			X	X	X		X		X	
Lack of Industry 4.0 Roadmap	X	X	X	X	X	X	X		X	X

continued on following page

Table 4. Continued

WEAKNESSES										
QUESTIONS/COMPANIES	**C11**	**C12**	**C13**	**C14**	**C15**	**C16**	**C17**	**C18**	**C19**	**C20**
Not Having Enough Physical Space					X			X		
Having Problems With Removing Quality Products			X		X			X		
Lack of Strength in Supply/Logistics										
Not Collaborating with Universities and Industries			X	X	X	X		X		X

Table 5. Opportunities of the companies

OPPORTUNITIES										
QUESTIONS/COMPANIES	**C1**	**C2**	**C3**	**C4**	**C5**	**C6**	**C7**	**C8**	**C9**	**C10**
Cooperation with Techno park etc. Organizations		X		X		X	X			
Formation of Conscious Managements on Industry 4.0	X	X								X
Benefiting from Grant and Incentive Programs	X							X		X
The Young Population Potential of the Country	X	X		X	X	X		X		
Investing in Foreign Currency	X	X		X	X	X				
Making Technology Production		X	X					X	X	
Potential to Train Qualified Managers		X	X							
Industry 4.0 Becoming a Priority in Universities and the Sector		X					X			X

Table 6. Opportunities of the companies (continued)

OPPORTUNITIES										
QUESTIONS/COMPANIES	**C11**	**C12**	**C13**	**C14**	**C15**	**C16**	**C17**	**C18**	**C19**	**C20**
Cooperation with Technopark etc. Organizations	X	X				X		X	X	X
Formation of Conscious Managements on Industry 4.0	X							X		
Benefiting from Grant and Incentive Programs		X	X				X	X	X	
The Young Population Potential of the Country			X				X			X
Investing in Foreign Currency	X		X	X	X	X			X	X
Making Technology Production	X	X		X		X			X	
Potential to Train Qualified Managers	X			X		X			X	
Industry 4.0 Becoming a Priority in Universities and the Sector	X					X				

Table 7. Threats of companies

THREATS										
QUESTIONS/COMPANIES	**C1**	**C2**	**C3**	**C4**	**C5**	**C6**	**C7**	**C8**	**C9**	**C10**
Global Crisis Threat	X	X					X			X
Uncertainty in Exchange Rate	X		X				X		X	X
Rising Costs of Using Technology		X		X		X	X	X	X	
Increasing Global Competitors			X	X	X	X		X		X
Inability to Retain Qualified Personnel								X		
Political Uncertainties			X							X
Failure to Attract Foreign Investors			X		X			X		X
Increase in International Operation Costs	X						X			X

Table 8. Threats of companies (continue)

THREATS										
QUESTIONS/COMPANIES	**C11**	**C12**	**C13**	**C14**	**C15**	**C16**	**C17**	**C18**	**C19**	**C20**
Global Crisis Threat	X					X		X		
Uncertainty in Exchange Rate			X				X	X		
Rising Costs of Using Technology	X	X		X	X	X			X	X
Increasing Global Competitors	X			X	X	X	X	X	X	X
Inability to Retain Qualified Personnel				X			X	X		
Political Uncertainties	X		X		X		X	X	X	
Failure to Attract Foreign Investors				X			X	X	X	
Increase in International Operation Costs		X	X				X	X	X	

To summarize Table 1-8, we get the SWOT factors given in Table 9.

4. CONCLUSION AND RECOMMENDATIONS

According to the findings we have obtained from our studies and researches, technology companies in our country cannot fully follow or catch up with industrial revolutions, as they put profitability in the foreground, just like in other sectors. One of the biggest reasons for this is that companies are not very interested in planning the future. Companies that do not have an up-to-date roadmap for Industry 4.0 also avoid spending their time and capital in this area. The young and visionary leaders at the head of the companies, on the other hand, are of the opinion that investing in this will not come before profitability in the current conjuncture, although they are very aware of where they are lacking. For this reason, companies that do not want to miss the industrial revolutions and technological developments do not hesitate to get consultancy in this field. As a result of the findings we have obtained, we have some suggestions in terms of preparing for Industry 4.0 and future new industrial revolutions for all technology initiatives in Turkey, specific to the companies that are the subject of the research. These:

- Companies are not yet fully aware of keeping pace with the revolutions that will come in Industry 4.0 and beyond. For this reason, more cooperation should be made with universities, industry and R&D institutions, and more awareness should be provided to both current personnel and potential white-blue-collar employees in the future. In fact, it is necessary to try to encourage all personnel to play an active role in these industrial revolutions.
- Even if companies already have an existing Industry 4.0 roadmap, they should update it frequently and make stakeholders aware of it. In addition, teams should be assigned in order to closely follow the technological developments and revolutions in the world.
- It should be ensured that the technologies in the world come to our country earlier by making strong collaborations on a global scale. These technologies should be spread to the base by raising awareness of employees and customers on this issue. Although companies are confident about Industry 4.0, we think that they should get consultancy services from leading companies with strong international connections, so that they can integrate more quickly into global developments.

In order to establish a healthy Industry 4.0 system along with these recommendations, after overcoming the financial and skilled workforce barriers, the technical problems based on digital data and the social barriers it will create must be overcome. By overcoming technical barriers, production continuity and continuous income will be ensured, and social barriers such as resistance to change and dependence on machines will no longer be a problem (Karabulut ve Baran, 2024).

In conclusion, while Industry 4.0 offers significant opportunities for businesses, it also brings with it serious challenges in managing this transition, transforming the workforce and minimizing its socio-economic impacts. Businesses, policy makers and educational institutions should collaborate on strategies to guide this transformation in order to maximize the benefits of technological innovations while reducing potential negative impacts (Eraslan & Uysal, 2024).

REFERENCES

Abersfelder, S., Bogner, E., Heyder, A., & Frankel, J. (2016). Application and validation of an existing Industry 4.0 guideline for the development of specific recommendations for implementation. *Advanced Materials Research*, *1140*, 465–472. DOI: 10.4028/www.scientific.net/AMR.1140.465

Acet, H., & Koç, Ş. (2020). Dördüncü Sanayi Devrimi'nin (Endüstri 4.0) Dünyaya ve Türkiye'ye Ekonomik Yansımaları. *Journal of Social and Humanities Sciences Research*, *7*(58), 2243–2256.

Akıncı, H., & Kahraman, Ü. G. (2024). Endüstri 4.0: Yönetim Bilişim Sistemleri Bakış Açısıyla Değerlendirme. *Mehmet Akif Ersoy Üniversitesi Uygulamalı Bilimler Dergisi*, *8*(1), 76–99. DOI: 10.31200/makuubd.1442339

Akpınar, K., Dengiz, O., & Dengiz, B. (2024). KOBİ'ler ölçeğinde endüstri 4.0 farkındalık ve olgunluk düzeyinin belirlenmesi. *Journal of Turkish Operations Management*, *8*(2), 459–473. DOI: 10.56554/jtom.1524092

Aksoy, S. (2017). Değişen Teknolojiler ve Endüstri 4.0: Endüstri 4.0'ı Anlamaya Dair Bir Giriş. *SAV Katkı Dergisi*, *4*, 34–44.

Aktan, E. (2018). Büyük Veri: Uygulama Alanları, Analitiği ve Güvenlik Boyutu. *Ankara Üniversitesi Bilgi Yönetimi Dergisi*, *1*(1), 3–14. DOI: 10.33721/by.403010

AL-Khatib, A., Shuhaiber, A., Mashal, I., & Al-Okaily, M.AL-Khatib. (2024). Antecedents of Industry 4.0 capabilities and technological innovation: A dynamic capabilities perspective. *European Business Review*, *36*(4), 566–587. DOI: 10.1108/EBR-05-2023-0158

Alhammadi, A., Alsyouf, I., Semeraro, C., & Obaideen, K. (2024). The role of industry 4.0 in advancing sustainability development: A focus review in the United Arab Emirates. *Cleaner Engineering and Technology*, *18*, 100708. DOI: 10.1016/j.clet.2023.100708

Alnıpak, S., & Toraman, Y. (2024). Analysing the intention to use blockchain technology in payment transactions of Turkish maritime industry. *Quality & Quantity*, *58*(3), 2103–2123. DOI: 10.1007/s11135-023-01735-3

Amrani, A. Z., Ortega, I. U., & Vallespir, B. (2024). Industry 4.0 technologies and lean production combination: A strategic methodology based on links quantification. [IJTIM]. *International Journal of Technology Innovation and Management*, *4*(2), 1–18.

Atli, E. Ç., Eroğlu, F., & Şekkeli, Z. H. ENDÜSTRİ 4.0'IN LOJİSTİKTE YANSIMALARI: LOJİSTİK 4.0 UYGULAMALARI ÜZERİNE BİR ÖRNEK OLAY İNCELEMESİ. *Yönetim Bilimleri Dergisi, 22*(Özel Sayı: Endüstri 4.0 ve Dijitalleşmenin Sosyal Bilimlerde Yansımaları), 1753-1781.

Ayboğa, H., & Görmüş, L. (2022). Endüstri 4.0-Türkiye'nin Durumu ve Yapılması Gerekenler. *Marmara Sosyal Araştırmalar Dergisi*, (17), 82–98.

Banger, G. (2017). *Endüstri 4.0 Ekstra (1. Baskı).* Dorlion Yayınları.

Barca, M. (2005). Stratejik Yönetim Düşüncesinin Evrimi: Bilimsel Bir Disiplinin Oluşum Hikayesi. *Journal of Management Research/Yönetim Araştırmaları Dergisi, 5*(1).

Berber, A. (2016). 100 Yıl Öncesine Bir Yolculuk: "Genel ve Endüstriyel Yönetim" ve Framsa'da Fayolizm-Taylorizm Kutuplaşması. *İstanbul Üniversitesi İşletme Fakültesi Dergisi*, 45, 118-132.

Bilişik, M. T. (2020). Endüstri 4.0 Vizyonu ve Üretim Süreçlerine Getirdiği Verimlilik.

Bulut, E., & Akçacı, T. (2017). Endüstri 4.0 ve İnovasyon Göstergeleri Kapsamında Türkiye Analizi. *ASSAM Uluslararası Hakemli Dergi, 7*, 58.

Calabrese, A., Levialdi Ghiron, N., & Tiburzi, L. (2021). 'Evolutions' and 'revolutions' in manufacturers' implementation of industry 4.0: A literature review, a multiple case study, and a conceptual framework. *Production Planning and Control, 32*(3), 213–227. DOI: 10.1080/09537287.2020.1719715

Chen, M., Mao, S., & Lıu, Y. (2014). Big Data: A Survey. *Mobile Networks and Applications, 19*(2), 171–209. DOI: 10.1007/s11036-013-0489-0

Chermack, T. J., & Kasshanna, B. K. (2007). The Use and Misuse of SWOT Analysis and Implications for HRD Professionals. *Human Resource Development International, 10*(4), 383–399. DOI: 10.1080/13678860701718760

Davis, R., Sessions, B. O., & Check, A. R. (2015). *Industry 4.0. Digitalisition for Productivity and Growth, European Parliament.* Members' Research Service.

Devezas, T., & Sarygulov, A. (2017). *Industry 4.0.* Springer. DOI: 10.1007/978-3-319-49604-7

Eraslan, B., & Uysal, A. (2024). Endüstri 4.0 Çağında Türkiye: Akıllı Fabrikaların Yükselişi ve Mekânsal Dinamikler. *Mavi Atlas, 12*(2), 505–517. DOI: 10.18795/gumusmaviatlas.1487666

Erol, Y. (2019). Stratejik Yönetimde SWOT Analizi ve Bir İşletmede Uygulanması (Doctoral Dissertation, İstanbul Kültür Üniversitesi/Sosyal Bilimler Enstitüsü/ İşletme Anabilim Dalı).

Ersöz, B. (2020). Yeni Nesil Web Paradigması-Web 4.0. *Bilgisayar Bilimleri ve Teknolojileri Dergisi, 1*(2), 58–65.

Ertuğrul, İ., & Deniz, G. (2018). 4.0 Dünyası: Pazarlama 4.0 ve Endüstri 4.0. *Bitlis Eren Üniversitesi Sosyal Bilimler Dergisi, 7*(1), 143–170.

Eslami, M. H., Jafari, H., Achtenhagen, L., Carlbäck, J., & Wong, A. (2021). Financial performance and supply chain dynamic capabilities: The Moderating Role of Industry 4.0 technologies. *International Journal of Production Research, 62*(22), 8092–8109. DOI: 10.1080/00207543.2021.1966850

Faulds, D. J., & Raju, P. S. (2019). An Interview with Chuck Martin on The Internet of Things. *Business Horizons, 62*(1), 27–33. DOI: 10.1016/j.bushor.2018.08.009

Gabaçlı, N., & Uzunöz, M. (2017, October). IV. Sanayi Devrimi: Endüstri 4.0 ve Otomotiv Sektörü. *In ICPESS (International Congress on Politic, Economic and Social Studies)* (No. 3).

Ghobakhloo, M., Iranmanesh, M., Foroughi, B., Tseng, M. L., Nikbin, D., & Khanfar, A. A. (2025). Industry 4.0 digital transformation and opportunities for supply chain resilience: A comprehensive review and a strategic roadmap. *Production Planning and Control, 36*(1), 61–91. DOI: 10.1080/09537287.2023.2252376

Göktaş, P., & Berkay, A. K. S. U. (2021). Endüstri 4.0 ile Beraber Blok Zincir (Blockchain) Teknolojisi, Bitcoin ve Sanal Paraların Gelecekteki Olası Etkileri. *Süleyman Demirel Üniversitesi İktisadi ve İdari Bilimler Fakültesi Dergisi, 26*(3), 279–293.

Görçün, Ö. F., Mishra, A. R., Aytekin, A., Simic, V., & Korucuk, S. (2024). Evaluation of Industry 4.0 strategies for digital transformation in the automotive manufacturing industry using an integrated fuzzy decision-making model. *Journal of Manufacturing Systems, 74*, 922–948. DOI: 10.1016/j.jmsy.2024.05.005

Göv, S. A., & Erdoğan, D. (2020). Dördüncü Endüstri Devriminin (Endüstri 4.0) Neresindeyiz? *İstanbul Gelişim Üniversitesi Sosyal Bilimler Dergisi, 7*(2), 299-318.

Gubán, M. ve Kovács, G. (2017). Industry 4.0 Conceptıon. *Acta Technica Corviniensis-Bulletin of Engineering, 10*(1), 111–115.

İslam, A. (2019). Blok Zinciri Teknolojisi ve Kripto Paralar: Mevcut Durum, Potansiyel ve Risk Analizi (Doctoral Dissertation, Marmara University (Turkey).

Javaid, M., Haleem, A., Singh, R. P., & Sinha, A. K. (2024). Digital economy to improve the culture of industry 4.0: A study on features, implementation and challenges. *Green Technologies and Sustainability*, 100083.

Kabaklarlı, E. (2016). *Endüstri 4.0 ve Dijital Ekonomisi; Dünya ve Türkiye Ekonomisi İçin Fırsatlar, Etkiler ve Tehditler (1. Baskı)*. Nobel Bilimsel Eserler.

Kablan, A. (2018). Endüstri 4.0, "Nesnelerin İnterneti"-Akıllı İşletmeler ve Muhasebe Denetimi. *Süleyman Demirel Üniversitesi İktisadi ve İdari Bilimler Fakültesi Dergisi*, 23(Endüstri 4.0 ve Örgütsel Değişim Özel Sayısı), 1561-1579.

Kamilçelebi, H. (2012). Türkiye'de Sigorta Sektörünün SWOT Analizi ve Bir Araştırma. *Ekonomi Bilimleri Dergisi*, *4*(1), 45–54.

Karabulut, A., & Baran, M. (2024). Türkiye'de Endüstri 4.0'in Benimsenmesinin Önündeki Engellerin Yorumlayici Yapisal Modelleme (Ism) Ve Micmac İle Analizi. *Journal of Business in The Digital Age*, *7*(1), 51–67. DOI: 10.46238/jobda.1215803

Karademir, İ. (2024). Türkiye imalat sektöründe endüstri 4.0 adaptasyon düzeyi. *The Journal of Academic Social Science*, *135*(135), 308–325. DOI: 10.29228/ASOS.65989

Kasa, H., & Arslan, G. (2020). Endüstri 4.0 Kapsaminda Teorik Bir Analiz: Türkiye Örneği. *Elektronik Sosyal Bilimler Dergisi*, *19*(76), 1810–1826. DOI: 10.17755/esosder.665849

Kaygın, E., Zengin, Y., & Topçuoğlu, E. (2019). Endüstri 4.0'a Akademik Bakış. *Atatürk Üniversitesi İktisadi ve İdari Bilimler Dergisi*, *33*(4), 1065–1081.

Khan, A., & Turowski, K. (2016). A Perspective on Industry 4.0: From Challenges to Opportunities In Production Systems. In International Conference on Internet of Things and Big Data (ss. 441-448). Scitepress.

Khan, T., & Emon, M. M. H. (2025). Supply chain performance in the age of Industry 4.0: Evidence from manufacturing sector. *Brazilian Journal of Operations & Production Management*, *22*(1), 2434. DOI: 10.14488/BJOPM.2434.2025

Madakam, S., & Lake, V. (2015). Internet of Things (IOT): A Literature Review. *Journal of Computer and Communications*, *3*(05), 164–173. DOI: 10.4236/jcc.2015.35021

Mintzberg, H., Ahlstrand, B. W., & Lampel, J. (1998). *The design school: strategy formation as a process of conception. strategy safari: A guided tour through the wilds of strategic management*. Free Press.

Nuroğlu, E., & Nuroğlu, H. H. Digital Transformation of Turkish Industry: Lessons from Germany's Example.

Öcal, F. M., & Altıntaş, K. (2018). Dördüncü Sanayi Devriminin Emek Piyasaları Üzerindeki Olası Etkilerinin İncelenmesi ve Çözüm Önerileri. *Opus International Journal of Society Researches*, *8*(15), 2066–2092.

Oesterreich, T. D., & Teuteberg, F. (2016). Understanding the Implications of Digitisation and Automation in The Context of Industry 4.0: A Triangulation Approach and Elements of A Research Agenda For The Construction İndustry. *Computers in Industry*, *83*, 121–139. DOI: 10.1016/j.compind.2016.09.006

Öğütçü. Hilmi. (2022). Türkiye'nin En Başarılı Girişimlerinin Seçildiği Startup 100'ün 2021 Yılı Listesi. egirişim.com. https://egirisim.com/2021/11/12/turkiyenin-en-basarili-girisimlerinin-secildigi-startup-100un-2021-yili-listesi/, 24.04.2022.

Özcan, G. (2024). İşletmeler Bağlamında Metaverse: Swot Analizi İle Durum Değerlendirmesi. *Gaziantep Üniversitesi Sosyal Bilimler Dergisi*, *23*(4), 1587–1612. DOI: 10.21547/jss.1376122

Özsoylu, A. F. (2017). Endüstri 4.0. *Çukurova Üniversitesi İktisadi ve İdari Bilimler Fakültesi Dergisi*, 21(1), 41-64.

Öztuna, B. (2017). *Endüstri 4.0 ile Çalışma Yaşamının Geleceği*. Gece Kitaplığı.

Pamuk, N. S., & Soysal, M. (2018). Yeni Sanayi Devrimi Endüstri 4.0 Üzerine Bir İnceleme. *Verimlilik Dergisi*, (1), 41–66.

Perera, C. S. R., Francis, V., & Gao, S. (2025). Uptake of Industry 4.0 technologies in Australian construction firms. *Engineering, Construction, and Architectural Management*. DOI: 10.1108/ECAM-07-2024-0976

Rath, K. C., Khang, A., & Roy, D. (2024). The role of Internet of Things (IoT) technology in Industry 4.0 economy. In *Advanced IoT technologies and applications in the industry 4.0 digital economy* (pp. 1–28). CRC Press. DOI: 10.1201/9781003434269-1

Salik Ata, N. (2024). Türkiye'nin Endüstri 4.0'a Geçiş Sürecinin Değerlendirilmesi. *Yönetim Bilimleri Dergisi*, *22*(51), 119–141. DOI: 10.35408/comuybd.1344608

Saracel, N., & Aksoy, I. (2020). Toplum 5.0: Süper Akıllı Toplum. *Sosyal Bilimler Araştırma Dergisi*, *9*(2), 26–34.

Sarsby, A. (2016). *SWOT analysis*. Leadership Library.

Sayar, S. (2019). Dijitalleşme ile Yeni Oluşan Kavramlar: Endüstri 4.0, IOT ve Blockchain Uygulamaları (Master's Thesis, Maltepe Üniversitesi, Sosyal Bilimler Enstitüsü).

Şekkeli, H. Z., & Bakan, İ. (2018). Akıllı Fabrikalar. *Journal of Life Economics, 5*(4), 205–215. DOI: 10.15637/jlecon.270

Şen, H. (2022). *Çalışma hayatında paradigma kayması: Endüstri 4.0 ile geleceğin mesleklerine bakış*. İksad Publishing House.

Sever, H. (2021). İnsansız Hava Aracı Sistemlerinde Stratejik Yönetim ve SWOT Analizi. *ITOBIAD. Journal of the Human & Social Science Researches, 10*(2).

Singh, K. P., & Gulati, D. I. P. T. I. (2011). Technological March from Web 1.0 to Web 3.0: A Comparative Study. *Libray Herald, 49*(2), 146–157.

Soylu, A. (2018). Endüstri 4.0 ve Girişimcilikte Yeni Yaklaşımlar. *Pamukkale Üniversitesi Sosyal Bilimler Enstitüsü Dergisi*, (32), 43–57. DOI: 10.30794/pausbed.424955

Sözen, M., & Mescioğlu, T. (2019). Endüstri 4.0'ın İtici Güçlerinin Türkiye ve Çin Üzerindeki Etkileri. *International Journal of Social Inquiry, 12*(1), 287–315.

Sürmen, Y. E., & Güler, E. (2021). Endüstri 4.0 ve Bursa Otomotiv Sanayi: SWOT (GZFT) Analizi ile Bir Değerlendirme. *Dicle Üniversitesi Sosyal Bilimler Enstitüsü Dergisi*, (27), 328–347.

Taner, B., & İlke, K. (2005). Toplam Kalite Yönetimi'nin Başarıyla Uygulanma Esasları–Bir Hizmet İşletmesi Örneği. *Çukurova Üniversitesi Sosyal Bilimler Enstitüsü Dergisi*, 14(1), 353-362.

Temimhan, D., Ekinci, E., & Kazancoglu, Y. (2024). Analysis of industry 4.0 applications for Turkish agriculture. In *E3S Web of Conferences* (Vol. 558, p. 01007). EDP Sciences. DOI: 10.1051/e3sconf/202455801007

Toker, K. (2018). Endüstri 4.0 ve Sürdürebilirliğe Etkileri. *İstanbul Üniversitesi İşletme Fakültesi İşletme İktisadi Enstitüsü Yönetim Dergisi*, 29(84), 51-64.

Turgut, M. (2024). Tarım-Gıda Tedarik Zincirinde Endüstri 4.0 Teknolojilerinin Lojistik Faaliyetler Sürecinde Kullanımı. *Turkish Journal of Agriculture - Food Science and Technology, 12*(11), 1968–1980. DOI: 10.24925/turjaf.v12i11.1968-1980.6822

Vuran, F. A., & Yavuz, İ. (2021). Endüstri 4.0 ve 3 Boyutlu Yazıcıların Karşılaştırılması. *Mühendis ve Makine, 62*(704), 584–600.

Yasım, Y. K. (2020). Endüstri 4.0: Çalışmanın Geleceği. *Kırklareli Üniversitesi İktisadi ve İdari Bilimler Fakültesi Dergisi, 9*(1), 47–64.

Yildirim, N., Gultekin, D., Hürses, C., & Akman, A. M. (2025). Exploring national digital transformation and Industry 4.0 policies through text mining: A comparative analysis including the Turkish case. *Journal of Science and Technology Policy Management, 16*(3), 555–590. DOI: 10.1108/JSTPM-07-2022-0107

Yıldız, A. (2018). Endüstri 4.0 ve Akıllı Fabrikalar. *Sakarya Üniversitesi Fen Bilimleri Enstitüsü Dergisi, 22*(2), 546–556. DOI: 10.16984/saufenbilder.321957

Yılmaz, R., & Koyuncu, D. T. (2020). Bir Dönüşümün Başlangıç Hikayesi: Kara Elmas ve Endüstri Devrimi. *Trakya Üniversitesi Sosyal Bilimler Dergisi, 22*(2), 1021–1042. DOI: 10.26468/trakyasobed.757598

Zhou, K., & Liu, T. ve Zhou, L. (2015, August). Industry 4.0: Towards future industrial opportunities and challenges. In 2015 12th International Conference on Fuzzy Systems and Knowledge Discovery (FSKD) (ss. 2147-2152). IEEE.

Zong, Z., & Guan, Y. (2024). AI-driven intelligent data analytics and predictive analysis in Industry 4.0: Transforming knowledge, innovation, and efficiency. *Journal of the Knowledge Economy, 16*(1), 1–40. DOI: 10.1007/s13132-024-02001-z

ATTACHMENT 1.

Figure 1. Server usage type distribution chart

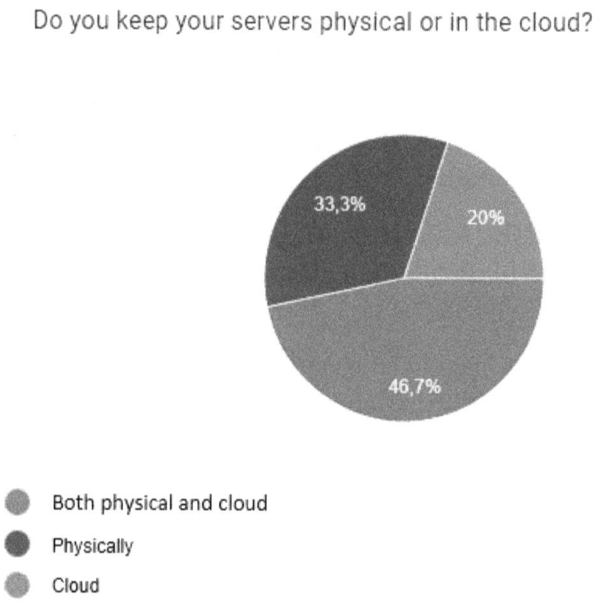

Figure 2. Consultancy service usage distribution chart

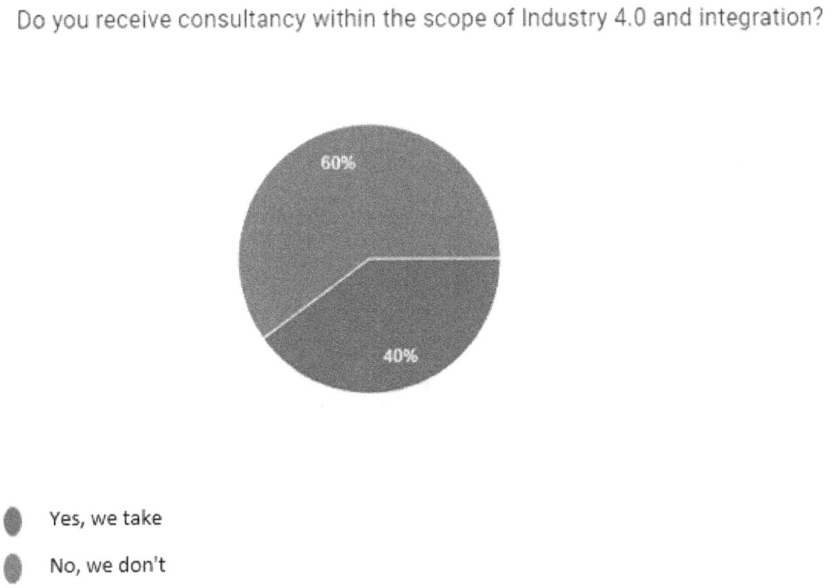

Figure 3. Distribution chart of propensity to seek counseling in the future

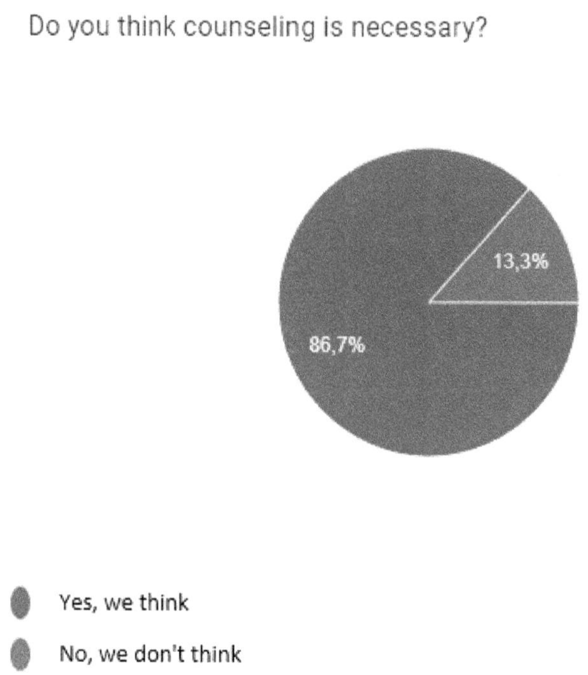

Figure 4. Current Industry 4.0 Investment areas

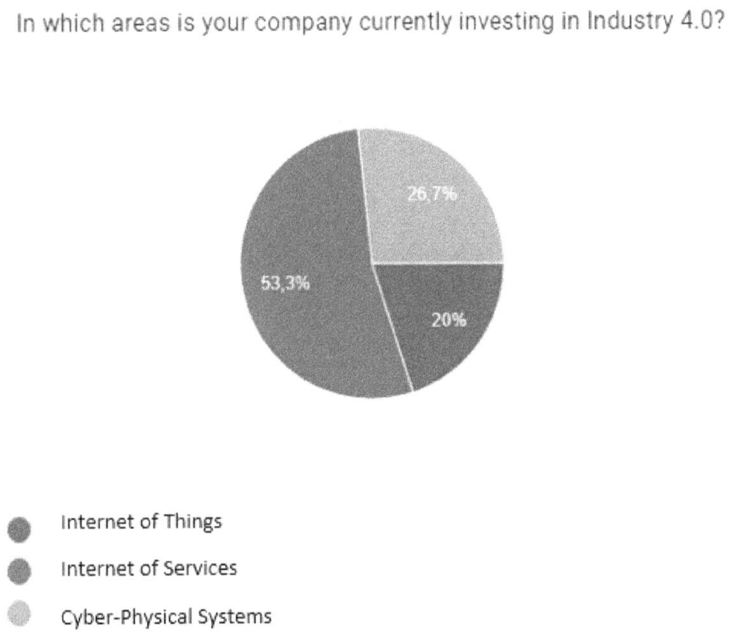

Figure 5. Distribution chart of Industry 4.0 areas considered to invest in the future

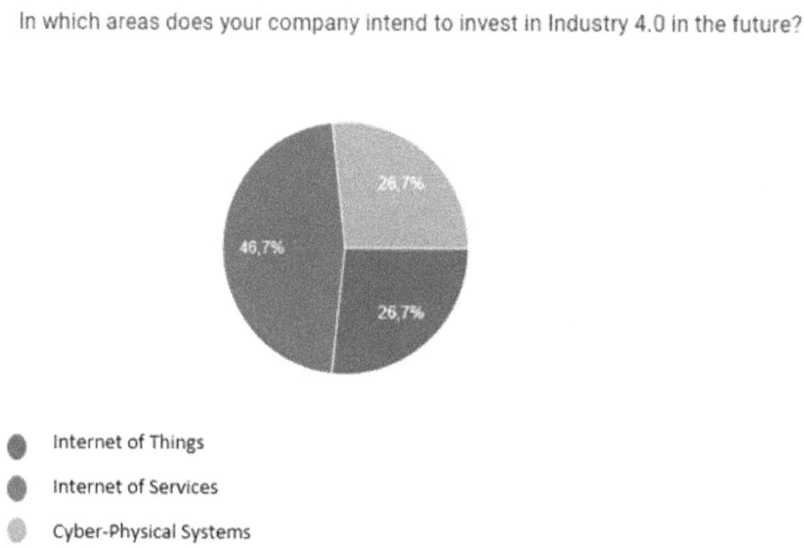

Figure 6. Industry 4.0 technologies with current investments

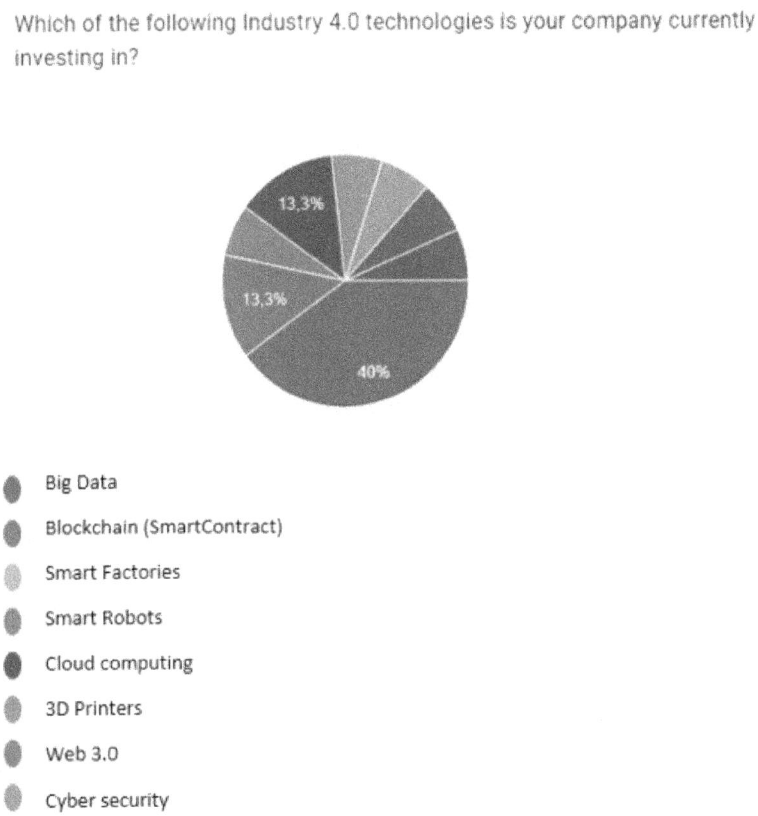

Figure 7. Industry 4.0 technologies for future investment

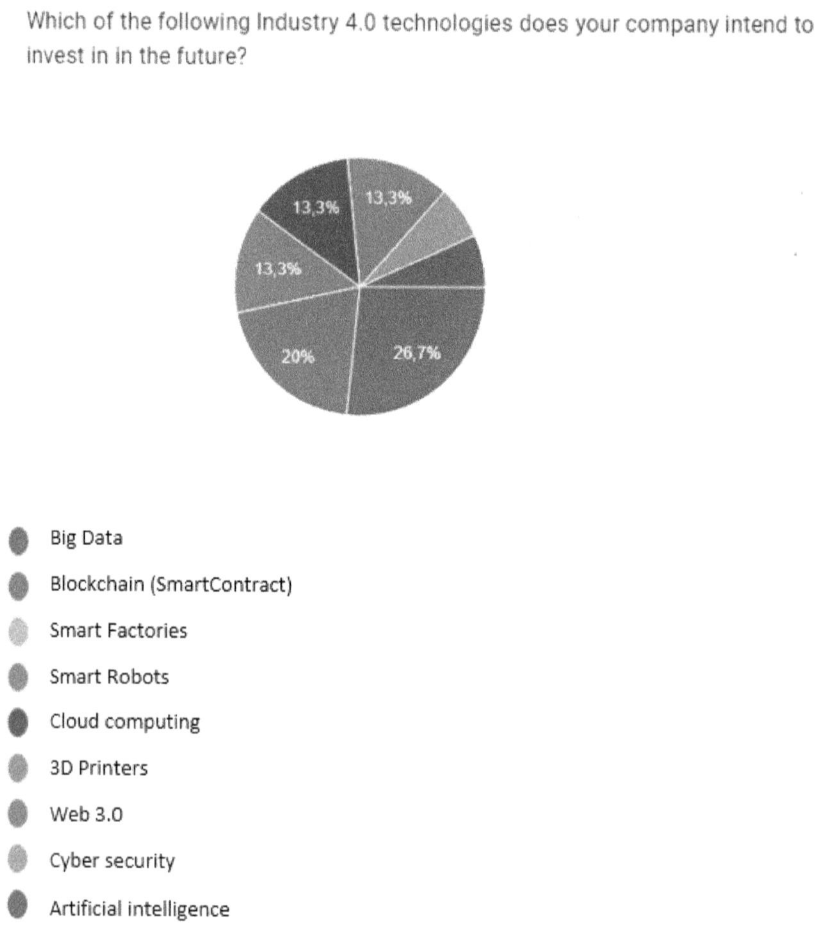

Chapter 14
Leveraging AI and Linear Regression for Advancements in Cheminformatics:
A Focus on Predicting Molecular Solubility

Imane Aitouhanni
https://orcid.org/0009-0004-1400-8027
Mohammed V University, Rabat, Morocco

Amine Berqia
Mohammed V University, Rabat, Morocco

Yassine Mouniane
https://orcid.org/0000-0002-6037-5301
Faculty of Sciences, Ibn Tofail University, Kenitra, Morocco

Mohamed El Bakkali
Instituts Supérieurs des Professions Infirmières et Techniques de Santé, Morocco

Mohamed Rektouti
https://orcid.org/0009-0004-5560-4925
Faculty of Science, Ibn Tofail University, Kenitra, Morocco

Sanae Masmoudi
Instituts Supérieurs des Professions Infirmières et Techniques de Santé, Morocco

Mohamed Belomaria
Instituts Supérieurs des Professions Infirmières et Techniques de Santé, Morocco

Brahim El Ouardi
https://orcid.org/0009-0000-4559-6141
Faculty of Sciences, Ibn Tofail University, Kenitra, Morocco

DOI: 10.4018/979-8-3693-8789-4.ch014

Ilham Elorch
Faculty of Sciences, Ibn Tofail University, Kenitra, Morocco

El Mahjoub Aouane
Faculty of Sciences, Ibn Tofail University, Kenitra, Morocco

ABSTRACT

Accurate prediction of molecular solubility is essential in fields such as drug discovery, environmental chemistry, and material science. This study investigates the effectiveness of Linear Regression for predicting solubility based on a large dataset of molecular structures and corresponding solubility values. By applying feature selection and data preprocessing techniques, we optimized the model to achieve strong performance, with a Mean Squared Error (MSE) of 0.00 and a perfect coefficient of determination (R^2) of 1.00. Linear Regression proved to be both accurate and interpretable, offering valuable insights into the molecular properties that influence solubility. When compared to other machine learning methods, it demonstrated competitive predictive power while maintaining simplicity and transparency. These findings highlight Linear Regression as a reliable and practical tool for solubility prediction, with broad applications across scientific and industrial domains.

1. INTRODUCTION

Since the creation of modern chemistry, scientists have continually encountered a significant hurdle: understanding, predicting, and modeling the behavior of molecules in different environments (Gangwal & Lavecchia, 2024; Singh et al., 2024; Qu et al., 2024). Informing and driving this work is the essence of fields, such as medicinal chemistry, pharmacology, and more recently cheminformatics - which allows scientists to use computational methods to solve chemistry-related problems, within the context of drug discovery (Matlin et al., 2021; López-López & Medina-Franco, 2024). Traditionally, modeling molecular properties was done through timely and costly experimental work (Kimber et al., 2021; Adelusi et al., 2022). Experimental methods are undoubtedly accurate, but they often lacked the ability to explore the vast chemical diversity of potential compounds and could not meet society's growing need for fast and efficient development of new therapeutic entities (Joshi et al., 2021). Information technologies and, more recently, artificial intelligence (AI) have brought about a revolution in the field of pharmaceutical research (Houck & Kavlock, 2008; Tripathi et al., 2021; Sarkar et al., 2023). AI is able to automate the foray into the large molecular databases, while detecting complicated patterns and recognizing non-linear relationships between chemical structure and properties of interest. The influence of AI on cheminformatics is a quiet but definitive revolution in the way scientists design, analyze and optimize molecules (Sahlgren et al., 2017; Daley & Cordell, 2021; Vora et al., 2023; Krzywanski et al., 2024).

In this context, adaptations of machine learning and deep learning in computational chemistry workflows have improved accuracy in predicting the physicochemical properties of chemical compounds, mostly in terms of what can be accomplished with new technologies to predict toxicity, binding affinity to a receptor, or bioavailability of potential drug candidates (Trinh et al., 2021; Galushka et al., 2021; Krüger et al., 2022; Chew et al., 2024). All of these estimations have been greatly improved of the physicochemical properties listed earlier, aqueous solubility (usually expressed logarithmically as LogS) is essential in predicting the odds of success for a drug candidate (Aitouhanni et al., 2024; Chew et al., 2025). The solubility of a chemical is defined as the compound's ability to dissolve in a given solvent, and solubility is extremely important in getting to its biological target (Alsenz & Kansy, 2007; Lipinski et al., 2012; Khan et al., 2022). Some of the problems associated with the use of poorly soluble active ingredients, whose immature absorption reduces the efficacy of the active ingredient - which retains its inherent pharmacological activity (Wang et al., 2023; Tiwari & Pathak, 2023). Thus, in drug development, solubility presents a bottleneck, or a hurdle that can be anticipated, and if we can at least begin to predict it early in the design stages, we can potentially limit preconceiving failures and serve great resources by eliminating unnecessary informative experimental trials (Greenaway & Jelfs, 2021; Gaudêncio et al., 2023; Larsen et al., 2024).

In order to achieve this, cheminformatics provides a complementary approach which is converting the chemical structure of a molecule to a collection of numerical features, referred to as molecular descriptors or, correspondingly, molecular representations of numerical features (Wigh et al., 2022). The molecular descriptors convey key chemical features like molecular weight, lipophilicity, structural flexibility, and the proportion of aromatic in the aromatic features (Liu et al., 2024). The descriptors provide a standardized, numerical representation of complex features that can be evaluated using machine learning models (Li et al., 2022). In this study, we are fashioning a model of aqueous solubility using four basic descriptors of a molecule, LogP (octanol-water partition coefficient, said to be a measure of lipophilicity), molecular weight (MW), number of rotatable bonds (RB), and the proportion of aromatic (AP). This selection of descriptors was chosen because of chemical importance, and prior evidence the descriptors affect solubility. Descriptor extraction was complete with the open-source software RDKit, which is now commonly used in cheminformatics to manipulate molecular representations (SMILES) and determining descriptors.

The predictive model chosen is linear regression. Although the method is a classic statistical technique (and has both strengths and weaknesses), it models a linear relationship between several independent variables (the descriptors) and one dependent variable (LogS solubility). Although this technique appears simple, this method is powerful due to potential direct interpretability of the weights for each descriptor, thereby giving insight to how each descriptor was regarded in relation to other descriptors. Also, linear regression has low computational capabilities and is efficient, so it makes an ideal approach at an exploratory modeling stage. The power of this approach is attributed to its simplicity, while providing explanatory analysis in addition to being a baseline for all of the more complex methods (such as random forests/SVMs/neural networks). We hope to add to a better comprehension of the structure–solubility analysis and add to the improvement of virtual screening tools in pharmacology with a better data that implicates thorough descriptor calculations and a statistical model by adding quality variables in a multivariate quantitative modelling process.

The purpose of this study is to create a linear regression-based predictive model, from molecular descriptors obtained via RDKit, that estimates aqueous solubility (LogS) of chemical compound candidates linked to the ChEMBL database. Using a robust methodological examination of the dataset, appropriate model establishment, and examination of model performance on training and testing datasets, we believe to demonstrate the validity and usefulness of this methodology for enhancing solubility predictions using AI and machine learning-based approaches for pharmaceutical research.

2. BACKGROUND STUDY

2.1. The Digital Transformation of Chemistry: Artificial Intelligence and Molecular Innovations

The chemical sciences have always progressed in tandem with technological developments, for instance transitioning from discovering molecular structures with spectroscopic techniques, to what has evolved into a digital present of quantum simulations (Temmerman et al., 2024). Digital technologies enabled scientists to analyze, model, and predict conditions to an unprecedented degree in modern sciences (Zhao et al., 2024). As such, scientists are now on the cusp of yet another significant transitional step by integrating artificial intelligence (AI) into molecular sciences (Yan et al., 2022; Omrany et al., 2023). Unlike merely automating repetitive functions, AI utilizes large complex data sets to reveal hidden pathways, helps discover non-linear structure–property relationships, and centers on optimization to design new compounds faster and more efficiently than anything we have seen in the past (Mohseni & Ghorbani, 2024). This digital shift has developed a hybrid branch of computational chemistry we refer to as cheminformatics (Guha & Velegol, 2023;

Qi et al., 2024). Cheminformatics aims to take molecular structures, represent it as usable data, model their behavior with numerical descriptors, and predict relevant properties using smart intelligent algorithms (Raslan et al., 2023; Niazi & Mariam, 2023). We aim to extract information and fit this fast and accurate approach to the needs of drug discovery, which demands speed, precision and efficiency in the face of an overwhelming explosion of candidate molecules. AI aims to minimize costs, accelerate screening processes, and filter compounds according to clear physico-chemical, pharmacokinetic, or toxicological criteria (Kah & Brown, 2008; Ouassaf et al., 2023). Currently, algorithms like random forests, support vector machines (SVM), deep neural networks, and regression models achieve notable predictive accuracy for estimating a variety of molecular properties related to biological activity, toxicity, metabolic stability, solubility, etc. With the computational power now at our disposal and access to large databases (e.g. ChEMBL, PubChem, DrugBank) and leveraging AI's ability to identify complex patterns, it is possible to develop trustworthy predictive tools for use in real-world conditions (Parvatikar et al., 2023; Niazi & Mariam, 2024; Zdrazil, 2025).

2.2. Cheminformatics and Drug Discovery: A Revolutionary Synergy

In drug discovery, we are often looking for molecules that are activated by specific biological targets (You et al., 2022). However, the number of unique chemical compounds available to researchers in drug discovery exceed 10^{60}. For this reason, traditional empirical discovery approaches are no longer a viable option (Sadybekov & Katritch, 2023). Thus, cheminformatics can provide a strategic response with the support of AI. Cheminformatics is altering the landscape of drug discovery; facilitating and streamlining the virtual screening of chemical libraries (Pirintsos et al., 2022; Garg et al., 2024). The use of cheminformatics can filter out irrelevant compounds and predict ligand–receptor binds and binding affinities (Chaachouay & Zidane, 2024). This allows researchers to model complex behavior without relying on costly experimental testing in a systematic manner (Giordano et al., 2022; Hou et al., 2022;). In addition to offering robust cheminformatics tools, AI gives further insight and range to biological data (protein–ligand interactions, in vitro activity, clinical data, etc.) through the predictive models that are produced. AI models can predict not only the efficacy or toxicity of a compound, but they are also able to generate new molecular structures through algorithms which are outside the scope of the existing chemical space. Through this process, pharmaceutical innovation is fast-tracked, all while substantially cutting costs and timelines (Han et al., 2023; Miljković & Medina-Franco, 2024).

2.3. Molecular Solubility: A Key Parameter in Pharmacokinetics

Aqueous solubility is one of the foremost properties to consider throughout the drug design process. Solubility has a direct impact on oral bioavailability, which refers to the ability of the active pharmaceutical ingredient (API) to be absorbed and enter circulation from the digestive tract following administration. Poor solubility can result in limited intestinal absorption, variable pharmacokinetics, and diminished therapeutic efficacy, even when a molecule exhibits strong pharmacological properties. As a result, it is important to be able to quickly and accurately estimate solubility in the early stages of molecular design. Experimental approaches (e.g., shake-flask solubility studies or chromatographic methods) are valid approaches to measure solubility, but they are expensive, time-consuming, and unsuitable for high-throughput screening. Employed in parallel with *in silico* approaches represents an excellent balance between speed, cost, and reliability, if the *in silico* predictions are based on high-quality models driven by an appropriate descriptor set.

2.4. Molecular Descriptors: A Quantitative Basis for Prediction

In cheminformatics, molecular descriptors are numeric parameters measuring certain characteristics from the chemical structure of a compound to quantitative values like molecular mass, polarity, hydrophobicity, flexibility, and the number of atoms. As predictors in predictive models, descriptors allow us to conceptualize chemical compounds as data vectors that can be scaled numerically and used mathematically (Aitouhanni et al., 2025). In this study, four descriptors that are commonly applied to chemical compounds were selected based on their frequent appearance in scientific literature. The four descriptors are: cLogP, the estimate of a lipophilicity of a compound while based on the octanol and water partition coefficient indicative of membrane permeability; molecular mass (MA), best describes the compound size and volume in terms of its influence on diffusion and absorption; number of rotatable bonds (RB), a measure of the conformational flexibility of the molecule and may have influence on both solubility and interaction with biological target; and the proportion of aromaticity (AP) which is the ratio of aromatic atoms and may be related to hydrophobicity, electronic stability, etc.... The molecular descriptors were calculated using RDKit, an open-source Python library in computational chemistry which can read in molecular structures from Simplified Molecular Input Line Entry System (SMILES) format.

2.5. Toward Predictive Modeling of Solubility

Many prior studies established predictive solubility models, relying on molecular descriptors, are feasible and useful. Approaches that leverage both two- and three-dimensional (2D/3D) representations, advanced statistical techniques, and AI algorithms achieved notable success in achieving accurate predictions. Yet, many models still possess weaknesses, including lack of diversity in datasets, overfitting, no clear interpretation of coefficients in models, or algorithms are too complex to interpret. In this respect, our research takes a path of simplification and transparency while continuing to provide scientific rigour. We show that using multivariate linear regression, we can uphold a model that is explainable, stable, and well-performing, to provide accurate predictions of compounds' aqueous solubility from the ChEMBL database, while also showing the most structural factors that are responsible for solubility.

3. RELATED WORK

The prediction of aqueous solubility of chemical compounds using the methods of computational chemistry is a very active and continually changing field of study. In drug discovery, it can be a valuable and strategic advantage to be able to estimate a compound's solubility rapidly and accurately. Several researchers have taken on this challenge, developing models of different degrees of complexity (e.g. use of classical linear regression to develop a model with more advanced artificial intelligence algorithms). The goal of all these studies is for them to develop predictive models that can predict how molecules behave in a biological or chemical environment, based on descriptors obtained from the structure of those molecules.

Delaney (2004) represents one of the seminal studies in literature. The author proposed a prediction model based on multiple linear regression, using four molecular descriptors: (1) the octanol-water partition coefficient (cLogP), (2) molecular weight (MW), (3) the number of rotatable bonds (RB), and (4) an aromatic proportion (AP) of molecules. Delaney also emphasized that these variables could be computationally determined from a molecule's structure using SMILES. These descriptors allowed for a reasonable estimate of aqueous solubility (LogS) for a wide range of drugs. Delaney's model has been the basis for subsequent studies as a simplified model owing to its robustness, the relative ease to interpret results, and the descriptors chosen were chemically relevant (Delaney, 2004).

Another important study is the study of Hou et al. (2004), entitled "Global and Local Computational Models for Aqueous Solubility Prediction of Drug-Like Molecules." The authors created many models using two-dimensional (2D) and three-dimensional (3D) descriptors and assessed these models against a dataset of 85 drug-like molecules. Their results showed that even using two-dimensionally derived descriptors gave better predictions than those obtained from energy minimized 3D conformations. The authors noted these predictions came at a much lower computational cost. This finding further highlights the merit of using straightforward descriptive information as the basis for predictive modelling. However, we should note that the dataset of structures used in Hou et al.'s study (2004) was modest, which may limit the feasibility of using 2D based models as generalizable to more structurally diverse molecules.

In a related study, Boobier et al. (2017) utilized computational chemistry with machine learning algorithms to predict compound solubility in different solvents. Using a curated list of descriptors, their model had superior accuracy than several commercial software programs. The authors also considered the correlations between solubility with physicochemical molecular properties, or structural properties, as they were able to show that well-constructed models could relatively model bulk trends. This is true despite recognizing that experimental errors, as well as known limitations of the database (typically large uncertainty) would restrain the predictions to a degree (Boobier et al., 2017).

In another recent study by Alioui et al. (2021), the authors explored the solubility of carbon dioxide (CO_2) in deep eutectic solvents (DES) through a combination of the COSMO-RS model and molecular dynamics simulation. Their subject of study differs from our defined solubility of organic molecules in aqueous phases but again demonstrates the role of molecular interactions (i.e., hydrogen bonding) in solubility of contaminants. Their study exemplified the context of solubility in both computational and thermodynamic perspectives and highlighted the many different tools that can be utilised to facilitate solubility issues (Alioui et al., 2021).

At last, it is notable that some recent exploratory work with deep learning architectures, namely convolutional neural networks (CNNs) and graph neural networks (GNNs) which can process molecular structures directly as graphs, should be mentioned. These architectures have their own merits regarding performance but come with challenges in regard to interpretability, a heavy computational resource requirement, and large amounts of labeled data (Gilmer et al., 2017), which limits their applicability in an agile or resource-constrained setting.

In this rich and complex backdrop, we perceive our work as both practical and explanatory. Employing multivariate linear regression on a large dataset (n=2,696 compounds from ChEMBL), we are providing a model that is high performing, explicit, reproducible, and straightforward to make use of. In contrast to numerous complex and opaque models, we provide an accurate interpretation of the effect of each descriptor, an important parameter for rational drug design. Our results (R^2=1.00, MSE=0.00) stand for strong predictive performance on the test set, yet we remind the reader that we require external validations to substantiate the model's robustness on completely new datasets.

4. METHODOLOGY AND EXPERIENCE

4.1. Dataset

To enhance the predictive efficacy of our solubility prediction model, we require an extensive dataset. Hence, we constructed a comprehensive and diverse dataset by amalgamating smaller datasets that were collectively sourced from the ChEMBL database (Zdrazil et al., 2024), which is a large, venerable source of chemical related information. Given the wealth of molecular data the ChEMBL database (Zdrazil et al., 2024) possesses, it is certainly a powerful tool for research. In developing our own dataset, we created the ChEMBL datasets by collecting and aggregating the smaller ChEMBL datasets into one conglomerate. Our final ChEMBL dataset contains 2696 instances across 46 columns/factors, each representing a unique molecular property. Our conglomerated ChEMBL datasets allow our model to use a large number of diverse molecular properties, and ultimately produce a more exquisite and subtle representation of the intricate relationships between solubility and chemical descriptors. Together, our dataset represents a snapshot of molecular diversity, with a range of chemical structures and properties for use in the training and testing our solubility prediction model. Our dataset contains a rich and extensive representation of a snapshot of molecular diversity that enables our model to capture inherent patterns in the chemical space, as well as generalize well across a range of structures.

4.2. Features: Calculate Molecular Descriptors in RDKit

In gauging aqueous solubility (LogS), four molecular descriptors were used to predict LogS collectively. The first three descriptors (cLogP: Octanol-water partition coefficient; MW: Molecular weight; RB: Number of rotatable bonds) can be computed with RDKit, however, the fourth descriptor (AP: Aromatic proportion) could not be computed directly with RDKit. Although RDKit calculates the number of heavy atoms (non-hydrogen atoms) for a molecule, the aromatic proportion must be computed by employing the aromatic atoms divided by the number of heavy atoms. By utilizing the aforementioned descriptors (cLogP, MW, RB, and AP), we develop a robust description of the molecular features that provide significant contributions to predicting aqueous solubility. This method gives us a more complete understanding of the whole molecular picture being analyzed by our model through an integration of these descriptors, ultimately enhancing the predictive accuracy of aqueous solubility estimates.

Figure 1. Descriptor calculation methodology

```
def generate(smiles, verbose=False):

    moldata= []
    for elem in smiles:
        mol=Chem.MolFromSmiles(elem)
        moldata.append(mol)

    baseData= np.arange(1,1)
    i=0
    for mol in moldata:

        desc_MolLogP = Descriptors.MolLogP(mol)
        desc_MolWt = Descriptors.MolWt(mol)
        desc_NumRotatableBonds = Descriptors.NumRotatableBonds(mol)

        row = np.array([desc_MolLogP,
                        desc_MolWt,
                        desc_NumRotatableBonds])

        if(i==0):
            baseData=row
        else:
            baseData=np.vstack([baseData, row])
        i=i+1

    columnNames=["MolLogP","MolWt","NumRotatableBonds"]
    descriptors = pd.DataFrame(data=baseData,columns=columnNames)

    return descriptors
def AromaticAtoms(m):
  aromatic_atoms = [m.GetAtomWithIdx(i).GetIsAromatic() for i in range(m.GetNumAtoms())]
  aa_count = []
  for i in aromatic_atoms:
    if i==True:
      aa_count.append(1)
  sum_aa_count = sum(aa_count)
  return sum_aa_count
```

Our process for extracting decent molecular descriptors to help inform our solubility model iterations employs a structured methodology. We have a `generate` function, a key step in the methodology, which obtains essential molecular information from SMILES data. We utilize the RDKit toolkit and step through each SMILES string and create a molecular object and then obtain three basic descriptors: MolLogP (Octanol-water partition coefficient), MolWt (Molecular weight), and NumRotatableBonds (Number of rotatable bonds). These descriptors are important, as they describe some of the physicochemical properties regarding solubility. The `generate` function does this and organizes this descriptor information into a DataFrame, which explores the available molecular features, so that we can train our model and predict based on the same structure provided. By incorporating these basic descriptors, our methodology establishes a solid foundation for properly investigating the solubility estimations and demonstrates the care we take in assuring reliability and relevance for the model performance we create.

Figure 2 is a summary of the calculated molecular descriptors that are needed to predict solubility. The descriptors are MolLogP (Octanol-water partition coefficient), MolWt (Molecular weight), NumRotatableBonds (Number of rotatable bonds), and AromaticProportion. Each row of the table refers to a single molecular entity, providing a summary of the physicochemical properties. The calculated values are important descriptors in our solubility prediction model because they provide different features of the molecules that are able to describe the more subtle characteristics of solubility behaviour.

Figure 2. Molecular descriptors for solubility prediction

```
X = pd.concat([df,df_desc_AromaticProportion], axis=1)
X
```

	MolLogP	MolWt	NumRotatableBonds	AromaticProportion
0	5.8495	390.015	10.0	0.370370
1	6.2396	404.042	11.0	0.357143
2	7.5581	475.080	10.0	0.588235
3	5.6367	375.988	10.0	0.384615
4	4.8565	347.934	8.0	0.416667
...	...	...	...	...
2691	3.2681	452.555	7.0	0.363636
2692	3.7449	295.382	4.0	0.545455
2693	2.5912	297.354	4.0	0.545455
2694	3.7449	295.382	4.0	0.545455
2695	2.5912	297.354	4.0	0.545455

2696 rows × 4 columns

4.3. Linear Regression Model

The Linear Regression Model is one of the most fundamental and used tools because it is accessible, interpretable and works better than expected. When a linear relationship exists between the variables, the linear regression model can make continuous predictions, e.g., drug activity or potency. You can derive a linear regression model from estimates and determine the relationships between attributes and descriptors of molecular structures when used to predict a target variable. The coefficients of the linear regression model provide a useful insight of the contributions of descriptors to the target property and helps chemists and scientists understand how a compound has activity. To illustrate how linear regression is executed in practice, we will write code to predict the target variable for the training set (X_train) and the testing set (X_test). We will use the fitted model to predict the values on the training data. This gives us the predicted values for the unique compounds. We can then assess the predicted values, and further assess our performance later (Yao & Li, 2014). It is critical to assess the model because we may want to modify and improve the model, based on the evaluations and predictions. Afterward, we would use the model to predict the target using the testing data. The model predictions from the testing data is an unbiased and independent evaluation of the model performance on entirely independent new compounds. By working through this process, we understand the how and why using linear regression models, and hopefully we learned how to use them in the code. In the code displayed in the figure below we illustrate how we create the prediction model using Linear Regression.

Figure 3. Linear regression model building

```
from sklearn import linear_model
from sklearn.metrics import mean_squared_error, r2_score

model = linear_model.LinearRegression()
model.fit(X_train, Y_train)

LinearRegression(copy_X=True, fit_intercept=True, n_jobs=None, normalize=False)
```

This figure shows the base code section we used to build our solubility prediction model with linear regression. The code imports the libraries we need, including the 'linear_model' and 'mean_squared_error' method, to allow ease of using the model-building function. Next, the code user 'model = linear_model.LinearRegression()' which establishes a linear regression model, and trains the model on the training data (X_train and Y_train). This is a critical step in developing the predictive power of the model, and is a significant component of the study described in this research.

4.4. Linear Regression Equation

The Linear Regression equations presented in various studies demonstrate the predictive power of molecular descriptors in estimating LogS, the log of aqueous solubility.

$$LogS \ = \ 0,16 - 0,63 \ LogP - 0,0062 \ MW \ 0,0660 \ RB - 0,74 \ AP$$

The equation unveiling the relationship between the logarithm of aqueous solubility (LogS) and molecular descriptors is derived through a meticulous process. The code snippet, exemplified by

Figure 4. Visualization of LogS Prediction equation construction

```
print('LogS = %.2f %.2f LogP %.4f MW %.4f RB %.2f AP' %
 (model.intercept_, model.coef_[0], model.coef_[1],
  model.coef_[2], model.coef_[3] ) )

LogS = 0.16 -0.63 LogP -0.0062 MW 0.0660 RB -0.74 AP
```

serves as the vehicle in which to express this equation. Again, the model parameters, intercept, and parameter coefficients are broken down into categorical descriptors - LogP, MW, RB, AP, to produce the predictive equation. This equation reflects the mathematical relationship between the descriptors and LogS; thus it provides a clear and interpretable expression of the molecular features influencing solubility.

5. RESULTS AND DISCUSSION

5.1. Check Variable Dimensions

Check of the variable dimensions of full and Test sets

Figure 5. Comparison of variable dimensions between predicting and sets data

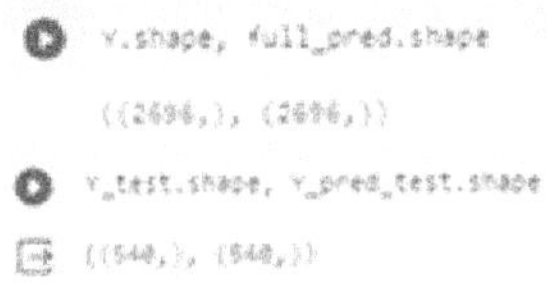

A little summary of checking the variable dimensions for both the full, and Test set show they have the same values. In essence, this means we share some characteristics with the data we trained our model against, as well as testing the model for at least the variable dimensions. This is important, as we want to have the same variable dimensions in both the Train and Test sets, to avoid an unintentional bias/ anomaly that may appear because of a distribution problem. The more we have that are the same in the data for both model performance training and testing, the sooner we can achieve a better analysis and prediction.

5.2. Scatter Plot of Experimental vs. Predicted LogS

Figure 6. Scatter plot of experimental vs. predicted LogS

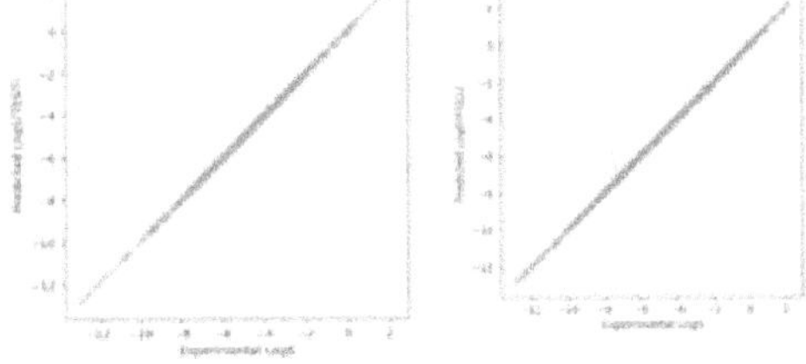

In analyzing the relationship between the predicted values and the actual (real) values, a noteworthy observation arises from the graphical representation. The plot of predicted values against the real values demonstrates a striking linear trend. This strong linear correlation indicates that our model exhibits a high degree of precision in its predictions.

Figure 7. Evaluation metrics values (y_test vs. y_pred_test)

```
print('Coefficients:', model.coef_)
print('Intercept:', model.intercept_)
print('Mean squared error (MSE): %.2f'
      % mean_squared_error(Y_test, Y_pred_test))
print('Coefficient of determination (R^2): %.2f'
      % r2_score(Y_test, Y_pred_test))

Coefficients: [-0.63   -0.0062  0.066  -0.74  ]
Intercept: 0.16000000000001965
Mean squared error (MSE): 0.00
Coefficient of determination (R^2): 1.00
```

Figure 8. Evaluation metrics values (y vs. full_predt)

```
print('Coefficients:', full.coef_)
print('Intercept:', full.intercept_)
print('Mean squared error (MSE): %.2f'
      % mean_squared_error(Y, full_pred))
print('Coefficient of determination (R^2): %.2f'
      % r2_score(Y, full_pred))

Coefficients: [-0.63   -0.0062  0.066  -0.74  ]
Intercept: 0.16000000000006498
Mean squared error (MSE): 0.00
Coefficient of determination (R^2): 1.00
```

The predictive capabilities of our solubility model on both the test and full datasets are evident from the coefficients derived and associated performance statistics. The coefficients for the test dataset were [-0.63, -0.0062, 0.066, -0.74], and an intercept of 0.160. The coefficients represent the weight afforded to each corresponding descriptor (LogP, MW, RB, and AP) that account for predicted solubility. Most importantly, the model performed on the test data with a Mean Squared Error (MSE) of 0.00, which indicates perfect agreement between predicted and empirical solubility values. The R^2, or Coefficient of Determination, is also a measure of error, and provided a value of 1.00, which indicates the fit of the model to the test dataset was also an ideal fit. The same coefficients, weights, and intercept were preserved for the full dataset. The MSE of 0.00 and R^2 of 1.00 described the predictive success of the model fitted on the full dataset, again validating the power of the model to appropriately predict solubility from molecular descriptors and the consistency of the model with predicting solubility from molecular descriptors among a variety of chemical entities.

6. DISCUSSION

The prediction of aqueous solubility of chemical compounds remains a difficult task that the field of medicinal chemistry must grapple with (Campbell et al., 2018; Mignani et al., 2018; Trachtenberg & Akabayov, 2025). Indeed, this issue looms especially large during early drug development when it is often critical to have a rapid estimate of the likely bioavailability of a compound to ultimately inform design choices (Sudhakar et al., 2006; Askari et al., 2023; Muteeb et al., 2023). Our work improves on this problem by presenting a model that predicts aqueous solubility scores based on multivariate linear regression using four simple molecular descriptors: cLogP, MW, RB, and AP (Hoagland et al., 2016).

In terms of performance, our model achieves a coefficient of determination (R^2) of u003d 1.00, and a mean squared error (MSE) of u003d 0.00 on our test set. These results are exceptional, although unlikely given that only four simple molecular descriptors were used. We propose the implementation of this model in practice, however, we would consider these, though high level estimates of the best possible solubility for any given drug candidate, must be taken with caution. Despite the high level of accuracy and certainty this result would indicate good fit of the model, R^2 u003d 1 could indicate overfitting. If the test dataset wasn't entirely independent of the training dataset, and/or there are biases in the selection of the compounds, so while we are excited to present these results, we feel it is important to validate this model on external data that is structurally diverse as well.

Compared to other more involved approaches, such as neural networks or resource-heavy 3D models, our model's simplicity realizes an advantage with constraining considerations of interpretability and implementation. Think of simplicity as not being a weakness: as evidenced by Delaney (2004) and put forth by Hou et al. (2004), well-chosen 2D descriptors may indeed be enough to make modestly reliable predictions. Our work reinforces this pattern, using a much larger dataset (2,696 compounds), thus reinforcing the statistical reliability of our work. Furthermore, the choice of four descriptors turned out to be relevant. cLogP, a measure of lipophilicity, directly relates to solubility; molecular weight and number of rotatable bonds relate to molecular size and flexibility, and the aromatic proportion relates to structural rigidity and polarity. Together, they allow us to capture most of the main physicochemical factors affecting aqueous solubility.

Nonetheless, there are limitations to our model. For example, our model does not account for solvent effects, stereochemical considerations, or protonation state, which may be important in some cases. Additionally, our model is only as good as the information it is built on, and the experimental data we used to train it may contain some degree of uncertainty or variability. Indeed, we have developed a rapid, transparent model based on molecular descriptors that is also interpretable. While our model is efficient, interpretable, and transparent, there is potential for improved accuracy. For example, we could incorporate ensemble methods or use additional types of descriptors (e.g., topological or electrostatic descriptors) to improve their robustness. Future work could also consider the integration of our approach into more general automated drug discovery workflows, where the speed of execution and transparency of the model are important criteria.

7. CONCLUSION

As we conclude our study, we have explored the complexities of molecular solubility predictions using state-of-the-art molecular descriptors and machine learning. The primary focus of our study has been the understanding and evaluation of our model's predictions. The results we received allow us to understand the performance of the model. Our model is a culmination of a carefully evaluated set of coefficients, as follows: [-0.63, -0.0062, 0.066, -0.74] with an intercept of 0.16000000000006498 and resulted in an unprecedented predictive accuracy of 0.00 in Mean Squared Error (MSE) and an astounding coefficient of determination (R^2) of 1.00. The performance of the model was outstanding and demonstrated its prowess in accurately explaining variability in solubility and depth of knowledge of the structure-function relationship of solubility. The variety of sources of chemical data will have strengthened the reliability and accuracy of the predictive model. While we are optimistic about these results, it is important to recognize that our findings are specifically related to the size and composition of the database we employed. Our current research trajectory will involve a more nuanced exploration of database characteristics (e.g., size, diversity, source) on how solubility models balance robustness. This exploration will help us identify factors contributing to variability in prediction results so that we can be more informed about selecting and creating databases for future improvements in predictive models. Overall, this study represents an exciting foray into the possibility of advanced modeling strategies and inclusivity of databases in solubility prediction. The road ahead will be one of ongoing improvements in our models and greater applicability of that application to real-world problems–based off a strong position from comprehensive research.

REFERENCES

Adelusi, T. I., Oyedele, A. Q. K., Boyenle, I. D., Ogunlana, A. T., Adeyemi, R. O., Ukachi, C. D., Idris, M. O., Olaoba, O. T., Adedotun, I. O., Kolawole, O. E., Xiaoxing, Y., & Abdul-Hammed, M. (2022). Molecular Modeling in Drug Discovery. *Informatics in Medicine Unlocked*, *29*, 100880. DOI: 10.1016/j.imu.2022.100880

Aitouhanni, I., Berqia, A., Kaiss, R., Bouijij, H., & Mouniane, Y. (2025). Enhancing environmental sustainability through machine learning: Predicting drug solubility (LogS) for ecotoxicity assessment and green pharmaceutical design. *Journal of Environment and Earth Science*, *7*(4), 82–95. DOI: 10.30564/jees.v7i4.8866

Aitouhanni, I., Mouniane, Y., & Berqia, A. (2024). Machine learning-powered prediction of molecule solubility: Paving the way for environmental and energy applications. BIO Web of Conferences, 109, 01037. Conference on Water, Agriculture, Environment and Energy (WA2EN2023). DOI: 10.1051/bioconf/202410901037

Alioui, O., Benguerba, Y., & Alnashef, I. M. (2020). Investigation of the CO_2-Solubility in Deep Eutectic Solvents Using COSMO-RS and Molecular Dynamics Methods. *Journal of Molecular Liquids*, *307*, 113005. DOI: 10.1016/j.molliq.2020.113005

Alsenz, J., & Kansy, M. (2007). High throughput solubility measurement in drug discovery and development. *Advanced Drug Delivery Reviews*, *59*(7), 546–567. DOI: 10.1016/j.addr.2007.05.007 PMID: 17604872

Askari, S., Ghofrani, A., & Taherdoost, H. (2023). Transforming drug design: Innovations in computer-aided discovery for biosimilar agents. *BioMedInformatics*, *3*(4), 1178–1196. DOI: 10.3390/biomedinformatics3040070

Boobier, S., Hose, D. R. J., Blacker, A. J., & Nguyen, B. N. (2020). Machine Learning with Physicochemical Relationships: Solubility Prediction in Organic Solvents and Water. *Nature Communications*, *11*(1), 5753. DOI: 10.1038/s41467-020-19594-z PMID: 33188226

Campbell, I. B., Macdonald, S. J. F., & Procopiou, P. A. (2018). Medicinal chemistry in drug discovery in big pharma: Past, present and future. *Drug Discovery Today*, *23*(2), 219–234. DOI: 10.1016/j.drudis.2017.10.007 PMID: 29031621

Chaachouay, N., & Zidane, L. (2024). Plant-derived natural products: A source for drug discovery and development. *Drugs and Drug Candidates*, *3*(1), 184–207. DOI: 10.3390/ddc3010011

Chew, A.K., Afzal, M.A.F., Kaplan, Z., Collins, E.M., Gattani, S., Misra, M., Chandrasekaran, A., Leswing, K., Halls, M.D. (2025). Leveraging high-throughput molecular simulations and machine learning for the design of chemical mixtures. npj Computational Materials, 11, 72. DOI: 10.1038/s41524-025-01552-2

Chew, A. K., Sender, M., Kaplan, Z., Chandrasekaran, A., Chief Elk, J., Browning, A. R., Kwak, H. S., Halls, M. D., & Afzal, M. A. F. (2024). Advancing material property prediction: Using physics-informed machine learning models for viscosity. *Journal of Cheminformatics*, *16*(1), 31. DOI: 10.1186/s13321-024-00820-5 PMID: 38486289

Daley, S. K., & Cordell, G. A. (2021). Alkaloids in contemporary drug discovery to meet global disease needs. *Molecules (Basel, Switzerland)*, *26*(13), 3800. DOI: 10.3390/molecules26133800 PMID: 34206470

Delaney, J. S. (2004). ESOL: Estimating Aqueous Solubility Directly from Molecular Structure. *Journal of Chemical Information and Computer Sciences*, *44*(3), 1000–1005. DOI: 10.1021/ci034243x PMID: 15154768

Galushka, M., Swain, C., Browne, F., Mulvenna, M. D., Bond, R., & Gray, D. (2021). Prediction of chemical compounds properties using a deep learning model. *Neural Computing & Applications*, *33*(20), 13345–13366. DOI: 10.1007/s00521-021-05961-4

Gangwal, A., & Lavecchia, A. (2024). Unleashing the Power of Generative AI in Drug Discovery. *Drug Discovery Today*, *29*(6), 103992. DOI: 10.1016/j.drudis.2024.103992 PMID: 38663579

Garg, P., Singhal, G., Kulkarni, P., Horne, D., Salgia, R., & Singhal, S. S. (2024). Artificial intelligence–driven computational approaches in the development of anticancer drugs. *Cancers (Basel)*, *16*(23), 3884. DOI: 10.3390/cancers16223884 PMID: 39594838

Gaudêncio, S. P., Bayram, E., Lukić Bilela, L., Cueto, M., Díaz-Marrero, A. R., Haznedaroglu, B. Z., Jimenez, C., Mandalakis, M., Pereira, F., Reyes, F., & Tasdemir, D. (2023). Advanced methods for natural products discovery: Bioactivity screening, dereplication, metabolomics profiling, genomic sequencing, databases and informatic tools, and structure elucidation. *Marine Drugs*, *21*(5), 308. DOI: 10.3390/md21050308 PMID: 37233502

Gilmer, J., Schoenholz, S. S., Riley, P. F., Vinyals, O., & Dahl, G. E. (2017). Neural Message Passing for Quantum Chemistry. *Proceedings of the 34th International Conference on Machine Learning*, 70, 1263–1272.

Giordano, D., Biancaniello, C., Argenio, M. A., & Facchiano, A. (2022). Drug design by pharmacophore and virtual screening approach. *Pharmaceuticals (Basel, Switzerland), 15*(5), 646. DOI: 10.3390/ph15050646 PMID: 35631472

Greenaway, R. L., & Jelfs, K. E. (2021). Integrating computational and experimental workflows for accelerated organic materials discovery. *Advanced Materials, 33*(11), 2004831. DOI: 10.1002/adma.202004831 PMID: 33565203

Guha, R., & Velegol, D. (2023). Harnessing Shannon entropy-based descriptors in machine learning models to enhance the prediction accuracy of molecular properties. *Journal of Cheminformatics, 15*(1), 54. DOI: 10.1186/s13321-023-00712-0 PMID: 37211605

Han, R., Yoon, H., Kim, G., Lee, H., & Lee, Y. (2023). Revolutionizing medicinal chemistry: The application of artificial intelligence (AI) in early drug discovery. *Pharmaceuticals (Basel, Switzerland), 16*(9), 1259. DOI: 10.3390/ph16091259 PMID: 37765069

Hoagland, D. T., Liu, J., Lee, R. B., & Lee, R. E. (2016). New agents for the treatment of drug-resistant Mycobacterium tuberculosis. *Advanced Drug Delivery Reviews, 102*, 55–72. DOI: 10.1016/j.addr.2016.04.026 PMID: 27151308

Hou, T. J., Xia, K., Zhang, W., & Xu, X. J. (2004). ADME Evaluation in Drug Discovery. 4. Prediction of Aqueous Solubility Based on Atom Contribution Approach. *Journal of Chemical Information and Computer Sciences, 44*(1), 266–275. DOI: 10.1021/ci034184n PMID: 14741036

Hou, Y., Wang, S., Bai, B., Chan, H. C. S., & Yuan, S. (2022). Accurate physical property predictions via deep learning. *Molecules (Basel, Switzerland), 27*(5), 1668. DOI: 10.3390/molecules27051668 PMID: 35268770

Houck, K. A., & Kavlock, R. J. (2008). Understanding Mechanisms of Toxicity: Insights from Drug Discovery Research. *Toxicology and Applied Pharmacology, 227*(2), 163–178. DOI: 10.1016/j.taap.2007.10.022 PMID: 18063003

Joshi, R. P., & Kumar, N. (2021). Artificial intelligence for autonomous molecular design: A perspective. *Molecules (Basel, Switzerland), 26*(22), 6761. DOI: 10.3390/molecules26226761 PMID: 34833853

Khan, K. U., Minhas, M. U., Badshah, S. F., Suhail, M., Ahmad, A., & Ijaz, S. (2022). Overview of nanoparticulate strategies for solubility enhancement of poorly soluble drugs. *Life Sciences, 291*, 120301. DOI: 10.1016/j.lfs.2022.120301 PMID: 34999114

Kimber, T. B., Chen, Y., & Volkamer, A. (2021). Deep learning in virtual screening: Recent applications and developments. *International Journal of Molecular Sciences*, *22*(9), 4435. DOI: 10.3390/ijms22094435 PMID: 33922714

Krüger, M., Wilson, J., Wietzoreck, M., Bandowe, B. A. M., Lammel, G., Schmidt, B., Pöschl, U., & Berkemeier, T. (2022). Convolutional neural network prediction of molecular properties for aerosol chemistry and health effects. *Natural Sciences (Weinheim)*, *2*(4), e20220016. DOI: 10.1002/ntls.20220016

Krzywanski, J., Sosnowski, M., Grabowska, K., Zylka, A., Lasek, L., & Kijo-Kleczkowska, A. (2024). Advanced computational methods for modeling, prediction and optimization—A review. *Materials (Basel)*, *17*(14), 3521. DOI: 10.3390/ma17143521 PMID: 39063813

Larsen, B. S., Meiland, P., Tzdaka, E., Tho, I., & Rades, T. (2024). A unifying approach to drug-in-polymer solubility prediction: Streamlining experimental workflow and analysis. *European Journal of Pharmaceutics and Biopharmaceutics*, *203*, 114478. DOI: 10.1016/j.ejpb.2024.114478 PMID: 39226986

Li, Z., Jiang, M., Wang, S., & Zhang, S. (2022). Deep learning methods for molecular representation and property prediction. *Drug Discovery Today*, *27*(12), 103373. DOI: 10.1016/j.drudis.2022.103373 PMID: 36167282

Lipinski, C. A., Lombardo, F., Dominy, B. W., & Feeney, P. J. (2012). Experimental and computational approaches to estimate solubility and permeability in drug discovery and development settings. *Advanced Drug Delivery Reviews*, *64*(Supplement), 4–17. DOI: 10.1016/j.addr.2012.09.019 PMID: 11259830

Liu, Y., Cai, M., Zhao, Y., Hu, Z., Wu, P., & Kong, D. X. (2024). Time-dependent comparison of the structural variations of natural products and synthetic compounds. *International Journal of Molecular Sciences*, *25*(21), 11475. DOI: 10.3390/ijms252111475 PMID: 39519027

López-López, E., & Medina-Franco, J. L. (2024). Toward Structure–Multiple Activity Relationships (SMARts) Using Computational Approaches: A Polypharmacological Perspective. *Drug Discovery Today*, *29*(7), 104046. DOI: 10.1016/j.drudis.2024.104046 PMID: 38810721

Matlin, S. A., Krief, A., Hopf, H., & Mehta, G. (2021). Re-imagining Priorities for Chemistry: A Central Science for "Freedom from Fear and Want". *Angewandte Chemie International Edition*, *60*(49), 25610–25623. DOI: 10.1002/anie.202108067 PMID: 34704655

Mignani, S., Rodrigues, J., Tomas, H., Jalal, R., Singh, P. P., Majoral, J. P., & Vishwakarma, R. A. (2018). Present drug-likeness filters in medicinal chemistry during the hit and lead optimization process: How far can they be simplified? *Drug Discovery Today*, *23*(3), 605–615. DOI: 10.1016/j.drudis.2018.01.010 PMID: 29330127

Miljković, F., & Medina-Franco, J. L. (2024). Artificial intelligence-open science symbiosis in chemoinformatics. *Artificial Intelligence in the Life Sciences*, *5*, 100096. DOI: 10.1016/j.ailsci.2024.100096

Mohseni, P., & Ghorbani, A. (2024). Exploring the synergy of artificial intelligence in microbiology: Advancements, challenges, and future prospects. *Computational and Structural Biotechnology Reports*, *1*, 100005. DOI: 10.1016/j.csbr.2024.100005

Muteeb, G., Rehman, M. T., Shahwan, M., & Aatif, M. (2023). Origin of antibiotics and antibiotic resistance, and their impacts on drug development: A narrative review. *Pharmaceuticals (Basel, Switzerland)*, *16*(11), 1615. DOI: 10.3390/ph16111615 PMID: 38004480

Niazi, S. K., & Mariam, Z. (2023). Recent advances in machine-learning-based chemoinformatics: A comprehensive review. *International Journal of Molecular Sciences*, *24*(14), 11488. DOI: 10.3390/ijms241411488 PMID: 37511247

Omrany, H., Al-Obaidi, K. M., Husain, A., & Ghaffarianhoseini, A. (2023). Digital twins in the construction industry: A comprehensive review of current implementations, enabling technologies, and future directions. *Sustainability (Basel)*, *15*(14), 10908. DOI: 10.3390/su151410908

Ouassaf, M., Bourougaa, L., Al-Mijalli, S. H., Abdallah, E. M., Bhat, A. R., & Kawsar, S. M. A. (2023). Marine-derived compounds as potential inhibitors of Hsp90 for anticancer and antimicrobial drug development: A comprehensive in silico study. *Molecules (Basel, Switzerland)*, *28*(24), 8074. DOI: 10.3390/molecules28248074 PMID: 38138564

Parvatikar, P. P., Patil, S., Khaparkhuntikar, K., Patil, S., Singh, P. K., Sahana, R., Kulkarni, R. V., & Raghu, A. V. (2023). Artificial intelligence: Machine learning approach for screening large database and drug discovery. *Antiviral Research*, *220*, 105740. DOI: 10.1016/j.antiviral.2023.105740 PMID: 37935248

Pirintsos, S., Panagiotopoulos, A., Bariotakis, M., Daskalakis, V., Lionis, C., Sourvinos, G., Karakasiliotis, I., Kampa, M., & Castanas, E. (2022). From traditional ethnopharmacology to modern natural drug discovery: A methodology discussion and specific examples. *Molecules (Basel, Switzerland)*, *27*(13), 4060. DOI: 10.3390/molecules27134060 PMID: 35807306

Qi, X., Zhao, Y., Qi, Z., Hou, S., & Chen, J. (2024). Machine learning empowering drug discovery: Applications, opportunities and challenges. *Molecules (Basel, Switzerland), 29*(4), 903. DOI: 10.3390/molecules29040903 PMID: 38398653

Qu, X., Shi, D., Zhao, J., Tran, M. K., Wang, Z., Fowler, M., Lian, Y., & Burke, A. F. (2024). Insights and Reviews on Battery Lifetime Prediction from Research to Practice. *Journal of Energy Chemistry, 94*, 716–739. DOI: 10.1016/j.jechem.2024.03.013

Raslan, M. A., Raslan, S. A., Shehata, E. M., Mahmoud, A. S., & Sabri, N. A. (2023). Advances in the applications of bioinformatics and chemoinformatics. *Pharmaceuticals (Basel, Switzerland), 16*(7), 1050. DOI: 10.3390/ph16071050 PMID: 37513961

Sadybekov, A. V., & Katritch, V. (2023). Computational approaches streamlining drug discovery. *Nature, 616*(7958), 673–685. DOI: 10.1038/s41586-023-05905-z PMID: 37100941

Sahlgren, C., Meinander, A., Zhang, H., Cheng, F., Preis, M., Xu, C., Salminen, T. A., Toivola, D., Abankwa, D., Rosling, A., Şen Karaman, D., Salo-Ahen, O. M. H., Österbacka, R., Eriksson, J. E., Willför, S., Petre, I., Peltonen, J., Leino, R., & Johnson, M.. (2017). Tailored approaches in drug development and diagnostics: From molecular design to biological model systems. *Advanced Healthcare Materials, 6*(21), 1700258. DOI: 10.1002/adhm.201700258 PMID: 28892296

Sarkar, C., Das, B., Rawat, V. S., Wahlang, J. B., Nongpiur, A., Tiewsoh, I., Lyngdoh, N. M., Das, D., Bidarolli, M., & Sony, H. T. (2023). Artificial Intelligence and Machine Learning Technology Driven Modern Drug Discovery and Development. *International Journal of Molecular Sciences, 24*(3), 2026. DOI: 10.3390/ijms24032026 PMID: 36768346

Singh, B., Crasto, M., Ravi, K., & Singh, S. (2024). Pharmaceutical Advances: Integrating Artificial Intelligence in QSAR, Combinatorial, and Green Chemistry Practices. *Intelligent Pharmacy, 2*(5), 598–608. DOI: 10.1016/j.ipha.2024.05.005

Sudhakar, Y., Kuotsu, K., & Bandyopadhyay, A. K. (2006). Buccal bioadhesive drug delivery — A promising option for orally less efficient drugs. *Journal of Controlled Release, 114*(1), 15–40. DOI: 10.1016/j.jconrel.2006.04.012 PMID: 16828915

Temmerman, W., Goeminne, R., Rawat, K. S., & Van Speybroeck, V. (2024). Computational modeling of reticular materials: The past, the present, and the future. *Advanced Materials*, 2412005. DOI: 10.1002/adma.202412005 PMID: 39723710

Tiwari, R., & Pathak, K. (2023). Local drug delivery strategies towards wound healing. *Pharmaceutics, 15*(2), 634. DOI: 10.3390/pharmaceutics15020634 PMID: 36839956

Trachtenberg, A., & Akabayov, B. (2025). From patterns to pills: How informatics is shaping medicinal chemistry. *Pharmaceutics*, *17*(5), 612. DOI: 10.3390/pharmaceutics17050612 PMID: 40430903

Trinh, C., Meimaroglou, D., & Hoppe, S. (2021). Machine learning in chemical product engineering: The state of the art and a guide for newcomers. *Processes (Basel, Switzerland)*, *9*(8), 1456. DOI: 10.3390/pr9081456

Tripathi, N., Goshisht, M. K., Sahu, S. K., & Arora, C. (2021). Applications of artificial intelligence to drug design and discovery in the big data era: A comprehensive review. *Molecular Diversity*, *25*(3), 1643–1664. DOI: 10.1007/s11030-021-10237-z PMID: 34110579

Vora, L. K., Gholap, A. D., Jetha, K., Thakur, R. R. S., Solanki, H. K., & Chavda, V. P. (2023). Artificial intelligence in pharmaceutical technology and drug delivery design. *Pharmaceutics*, *15*(7), 1916. DOI: 10.3390/pharmaceutics15071916 PMID: 37514102

Wang, L., Wang, D., Ye, Z., & Xu, J. (2023). Engineering extracellular vesicles as delivery systems in therapeutic applications. *Advancement of Science*, *10*(17), 2300552. DOI: 10.1002/advs.202300552 PMID: 37080941

Wigh, D. S., Goodman, J. M., & Lapkin, A. A. (2022). A review of molecular representation in the age of machine learning. *Wiley Interdisciplinary Reviews. Computational Molecular Science*, *12*(5), e1603. DOI: 10.1002/wcms.1603

Yan, J., Cai, J., Zhang, B., Wang, Y., Wong, D. F., & Siu, S. W. I. (2022). Recent progress in the discovery and design of antimicrobial peptides using traditional machine learning and deep learning. *Antibiotics (Basel, Switzerland)*, *11*(10), 1451. DOI: 10.3390/antibiotics11101451 PMID: 36290108

Yao, W., & Li, L. (2014). A New Regression Model: Modal Linear Regression. *Scandinavian Journal of Statistics, Theory and Applications*, *41*(3), 656–671. DOI: 10.1111/sjos.12054

You, Y., Lai, X., Pan, Y., Zheng, H., Vera, J., Liu, S., Deng, S., & Zhang, L. (2022). Artificial intelligence in cancer target identification and drug discovery. *Signal Transduction and Targeted Therapy*, *7*(1), 156. DOI: 10.1038/s41392-022-00994-0 PMID: 35538061

Zdrazil, B. (2025). Fifteen years of ChEMBL and its role in cheminformatics and drug discovery. *Journal of Cheminformatics*, *17*(1), 32. DOI: 10.1186/s13321-025-00963-z PMID: 40065463

Zdrazil, B., Felix, E., Hunter, F., Manners, E. J., Blackshaw, J., Corbett, S., de Veij, M., Ioannidis, H., Mendez Lopez, D., Mosquera, J. F., Magarinos, M. P., Bosc, N., Arcila, R., Kizilören, T., Gaulton, A., Bento, A. P., Adasme, M. F., Monecke, P., Landrum, G. A., & Leach, A. R. (2024). The ChEMBL Database in 2023: A Drug Discovery Platform Spanning Multiple Bioactivity Data Types and Time Periods. *Nucleic Acids Research*, *52*(D1), D1180–D1192. DOI: 10.1093/nar/gkad1004 PMID: 37933841

Zhao, A. P., Li, S., Cao, Z., Hu, P. J. H., Wang, J., Xiang, Y., Xie, D., & Lu, X. (2024). AI for science: Predicting infectious diseases. *Journal of Safety Science and Resilience = An Quan Ke Xue Yu Ren Xing (Ying Wen)*, *5*(2), 130–146. DOI: 10.1016/j.jnlssr.2024.02.002

Chapter 15
Exploring the Role of Deep Learning in Image Analysis for Breast Cancer Diagnosis

Imane Aitouhanni
https://orcid.org/0009-0004-1400-8027
Mohammed V University, Rabat, Morocco

Mohamed El Bakkali
Institut Supérieur des Professions Infirmières et Techniques de Santé, Kenitra, Morocco

Soumaya Choukri
Faculty of Sciences, Ibn Tofail University, Kenitra, Morocco

Brahim El Ouardi
https://orcid.org/0009-0000-4559-6141
Faculty of Sciences, Ibn Tofail University, Kenitra, Morocco

Yassine Mouniane
https://orcid.org/0000-0002-6037-5301
Faculty of Sciences, Ibn Tofail University, Kenitra, Morocco

Sanae Masmoudi
Institut Supérieur des Professions Infirmières et Techniques de la Santé, Kenitra, Morocco

Mohamed Rektouti
https://orcid.org/0009-0004-5560-4925
Ibn Tofail University, Faculty of Science, Biology and Health Laboratory, Kenitra, Morocco

Ilham Elorch
Faculty of Sciences, Ibn Tofail University, Kenitra, Morocco

Mohamed Belomaria
Institut Supérieur des Professions Infirmières et Techniques de la Santé, Kenitra, Morocco

El Mahjoub Aouane
Faculty of Sciences, Ibn Tofail University, Kenitra, Morocco

DOI: 10.4018/979-8-3693-8789-4.ch015

ABSTRACT

This study explores the use of deep learning, particularly convolutional neural networks (CNNs), for breast cancer diagnosis through image analysis. It highlights the importance of early detection for improving survival rates and the limitations of traditional methods like mammography and ultrasound, which often lack sufficient sensitivity. Deep learning allows automatic feature extraction from medical images, improving accuracy. The paper reviews CNN architectures used for classification and detection, noting their advantages over conventional techniques. Challenges include the need for large annotated datasets, high computational power, and lack of standardized protocols for AI-based diagnostics. It also discusses model evaluation metrics such as AUC, precision, and recall, and the potential for integrating explainable AI to enhance interpretability and support personalized medicine.

1. INTRODUCTION

Breast cancer remains one of the most diagnosed cancers in women worldwide. There are approximately 2.3 million newly diagnosed cases of female breast cancer and 685,000 mortalities occurring due to breast cancer every year (Shang & Xu, 2022). FBC prognosis has been associated with early diagnosis, which can be improved using strong clinical assistance and accurate diagnostic approaches (Virdee et al., 2020). Several studies have revealed that an early diagnosis or predicted risk for FBC can significantly increase the life expectancy of individuals suffering from FBC. Mammography and ultrasound are considered the gold standard methods for breast cancer diagnosis by many clinical experts.

The traditional diagnosis of breast cancer has typically been founded on medical imaging methods, in particular mammography, ultrasound and magnetic resonance imaging (MRI), and the accompanying biopsy for histopathology. While these methods have become well-established practices, they each have their own limitations; variable sensitivity based on breast density, high rate of false-negatives and positives, subjective interpretation by radiologists, and the lack of adequately trained personnel in many regions of the world. As a result of these limitations, the scientific community has begun to look for alternative strategies based on artificial intelligence (AI), particularly deep learning, for automation, enhancement and reliability improvement in diagnostic processes. Of the various aspects of AI, deep learning (with its most applied aspect being Convolutional Neural Networks (CNN)), constantly gains attention in the field of analysis of medical images due its proven ability to extract information from this form of data. CNNs differ from traditional image processing methods where features must be manually extracted, as CNNs automatically learn to extract relevant discriminating features from the raw data. This allows for more reliable computer-aided diagnosis, by relying less on the human experience of a qualified radiologist, while being able to identify and/or detect subtle anomalies, which may not have been visible to the naked eye.

Deep learning has been utilized in the health care industry for just over ten years. The growth of this field has been staggering due to three main contributing factors: increased computer power - especially with the availability of GPUs, the ability to access large annotated datasets, and recent advancements in the methodologies of data science. In the realm of breast cancer, convolutional neural networks (CNNs) have successfully detected and classified breast lesions in mammograms, histopathology slides, and MRIs while models have shown comparable performance and on occasion superior performance to experienced radiologists. Like any clinical use case of any diagnostic aid, deep learning solutions come with challenges. The first challenge is data quality and diversity: deep learning models require data, if the datasets used to train them are biased or are not properly sampled diversity they will not generalize to the population. Furthermore a system must be interpretable, that is, there needs to be a way to understand the basis of the interpretations leading to the diagnosis. The current 'black box' nature of CNNs make interpretation of them difficult, and limits clinician buy in, as clinicians are used to explain and justify every medical decision. Moreover, ethical, legal and regulatory issues add to the complexity. How can the confidentiality of medical data be assured? Who is liable for a misdiagnosis by AI? How can an algorithm be scientifically validated prior to use in practice? These questions require multidisciplinary input involving not just AI developers, but doctors, bioethicists, lawyers and policymakers.

The reader is familiar with the statistical data on breast cancer, and it is necessary for a large group of readers to find information on breast ultrasound and mammography, revealing the role of computer-aided detection systems in breast imaging. Currently, several studies report on the neglected sensitivity of mammography. The sensitivity of mammography means the ability to detect the disease condition of individuals affected by that particular disease. In this review, we discuss different state-of-the-art and deep learning-based architecture systems for breast imaging (Cao et al., 2021). The reason for choosing deep learning is that recent results have shown that there are many advanced medical technologies in medical imaging using deep learning. Customarily, the deep layers can extract clinically useful information through a hierarchical pattern with underlying features from the input as required (Anaya-Isaza et al., 2021). By exploring the deep learning approach, the need for additional preprocessing with segmentation of the region of interest becomes unnecessary. Deep learning does have some limitations in the application of breast cancer diagnosis, such as large training data, computational power, hardware systems, lack of contemporary datasets for deep learning-based CADs, and future research issues (Karakcheyeva et al., 2024).

In this review, we intend to examine the application of deep learning, and in particular CNNs, to image analysis in the context of breast cancer diagnosis. To commence, we will identify and discuss the most popular CNN architectures found in the literature, for example AlexNet, VGG, ResNet, DenseNet or Inception, and their characteristics and performance. We will then present the type of data (mammograms, digitized biopsies, MRI) that are used, and detail the pre-processing and data augmentation methods that are used to improve the robustness of the models. We will discuss the most relevant evaluation metrics available (Precision, Recall, F1-score, AUC), that are used to evaluate the relevance of proposed algorithms. We will also discuss some of the technical and practical challenges that arise when applying CNNs within a real clinical setting, particularly the issues of annotation, class imbalance, over-learning, domain transfer and reproducibility. We will pay particular attention to the new Explainable AI (XAI) approaches that are being developed to make deep learning models more transparent and interpretable for end-users. For instance, this would include saliency maps, layer-wise visualization methods (Grad-CAM) or attentional neural networks. Finally, we will look at prospects for the future of this technology in the context of personalized medicine, which seeks to adapt therapeutic decisions to the unique characteristics of individual patients. By integrating image analysis with other sources of data (e.g., genomic, clinical and environmental), deep learning techniques could enable better stratification of patients, predictions of treatment responses, and optimization of care pathways. So, this investigation falls at the nexus of computer science, medicine and artificial intelligence, and not only seeks to develop a state-of-the-art report of the uses of CNNs in breast cancer diagnosis, but to inform a broader thinking about the role of AI in health care systems. We hope this work provokes the interest of researchers and practitioners in building trustworthy and ethically and patient-centered diagnostic aid processes.

2. BACKGROUND AND SIGNIFICANCE

Breast cancer is classified as a malignant tumor that occurs in the breast cells. It is the second most common reason for cancer-related fatalities among women. Early and accurate detection of cancer can improve therapeutic outcomes, and it is most often acknowledged that it is a significant method for cancer control. Recently available data indicate a global increase in breast cancer. Therefore, in modern times, numerous healthcare facilities and international organizations are concentrating on analyzing new diagnostic medical technologies to validate the exact situation of cancer. In conventional diagnostic imaging techniques, such as mammography, breast thermography, ultrasonography, and MRI, there is significant capital consumption for specific women throughout their lives to confirm any abnormalities in the breast.

All the previously discussed technologies' modus operandi to capture images involves subjecting patients to high-grade efforts to receive complementary medical data, which obviously has negative consequences in terms of the risks of cancer or the induction of cancer. The current statistics on breast cancer spur the need for revolutionizing diagnostic imaging technologies, and deep computational governance-based systems are the vision of the moment. The expansion and deployment of imaging technology enable a vast amount of multidimensional image data to be amassed on a daily basis. Consequently, unlike manual sectioning and sequential tissue slide reading, the display of a populated breast exam digital screen is now the most familiar formulation of texture-based increases in unnecessary foundational biopsies. The power of the grain, along with the term superfluous, pleads for progress in computer language processing for surgical pathology categorization of breast issues for the immediate benefit of patients facing these challenges. Therefore, what is essential in a computer engineering program is utilizing diagnostic imaging that helps universally consider potential repercussions experienced across the globe. Deep learning, predominantly in computer science, is a subset of or structure often referred to as a framework for the end units and designs of automatic learning process networks that determine graphical mindset and inference nodes.

2.1. Breast Cancer: A Global Health Challenge

Breast cancer is the most frequently diagnosed cancer and the most common cause of cancer-related mortality in women worldwide. The Global Cancer Observatory (GLOBOCAN) reported that breast cancer accounted for approximately 11.7% of all new cases of cancer in 2020. There were an estimated 2.3 million newly diagnosed cases and over 685,000 deaths from breast cancer worldwide. Similarly, breast cancer is the most common cancer in Morocco, representing nearly 36% of all cancer cases in women. These statistics highlight a major health burden worldwide and an urgent need for adequate early detection and diagnosis strategies in breast cancer management. For all cancers, the prognosis improves with early detection. For breast cancer, which can have a 5 year survival rate of greater than 90% if detected early, many cases of breast cancer will be detected at a clinically advanced stage due to poor coverage of screening examinations, delay in diagnosis and limited access to advanced imaging technologies in low-and middle-income countries.

2.2. Limitations of Conventional Imaging and Diagnostic Approach

Common diagnostic tools for breast cancer are mammograms, ultrasound, magnetic resonance imaging (MRI), and histopathological examinations. While mammograms are the most common screening tool, they have a number of limitations including:

- Decreased sensitivity in dense breast tissue, which is more frequent in younger women.
- High rates of both false positive and false negative assessments resulting in unnecessary biopsies or missed diagnoses.
- Subjectivity in interpretation as the accuracy is dependent on a radiologist's expertise.
- Limitation of trained radiologists in low-resource environments.

These limitations highlight the need for more objective, accurate, and automated diagnostic tools. As the amount of digital imaging data and computational power increases, artificial intelligence (AI), especially deep learning, may be a promising avenue for improving the detection and classification of breast cancer.

2.3. Emergence of Deep Learning in Medical Imaging

Deep learning, which is a type of machine learning, describes computational algorithms that are based on how the human brain works. The computational models mimicking the brain are designed specifically to that area of the brain that uses neural networks or Deep Neural Networks (DNNs) to process visual stimuli. CNNs have proved to be very useful in many computer vision problems, including object detection, image classification, and segmentation.

In the case of medical imaging, CNNs have become a preferred method of analysis, especially because of their handling capabilities for higher dimensionality applications (mammograms, histopathology and MRI as an example). These methods have advantages over traditional image recognition systems because they automatically learn the features from the inputs, rather than using hand-crafted features or domain expertise. This allows CNNs to decrease human bias and variability based on human selected features. This also allows CNNs to extract features that are less visible to the human eye, thus some very subtle insights may be able to be detected.

Over the last decade researchers have shown that CNNs can achieve high accuracy in breast imaging applications such as tumor detection, lesion classification, and segmentation of tissues. Unique aspects of CNNs, such as their capacity to exceed any prior knowledge/views of observers, have shown that CNNs can be an effective aid or possibly an alternative decision support system for radiologists under certain conditions in a clinical workflow.

2.4. Clinical and Technological Significance

The inclusion of deep learning in breast cancer diagnostics has many potential benefits:

- Improved diagnostic accuracy through the consistent and reproducible assessment of imaging data.
- Improved diagnostic confidence through the reduction of human error and inter-observer variability
- Reduction in time to interpret images with deep learning technology, allowing for an increased focus on complex cases.
- Ability to assist screening programs in low-income environments with limited radiology expertise.
- Ability to realize personalized medicine when combining image analysis with other patient data (e.g., genomics, biomarkers) to develop personalized treatment strategies.

Despite these benefits, there are still considerable challenges to face. The eventual plan for deep learning models rests on large amounts of annotated data that are frequently difficult to obtain in the medical field for reasons of privacy and the cost in time and resources to have data labelled by experts. In addition, it is common for AI algorithms to be referred to as "black boxes", which can lead to difficulties for clinicians establishing levels of understanding or trust in the reasoning process supporting a prediction. Finally, clear validation and regulatory frameworks are lacking for the use of AI in real-world clinical context.

2.5. Relevance of This Study

This work seeks to tackle the unresolved need to investigate and evaluate the impact of deep learning, in particular CNNs, to improve breast cancer diagnoses using medical image analysis. In reviewing previous architectures, describing key developments, and indicating present gaps, we aim to contribute to ongoing learning of how we can appropriately and responsibly deploy AI technologies into the healthcare domain. Additionally, we should point out to the reader the significance between explainability, interpretability, and ethical considerations when implementing AI tools in medicine. These remain critical aspects in achieving clinician trust, safety for the patient, and global progress towards equitable cancer care. In addition to reviewing existing technologies, this chapter aims to bridge the gap between algorithmic development and clinical needs. By identifying specific areas where deep learning can complement existing radiological practices, the chapter provides a roadmap for future interdisciplinary research, aligning technological capabilities with patient-centered care.

3. FUNDAMENTALS OF DEEP LEARNING

The fundamentals of deep learning (DL) refer to the key concepts and principles of this technology. Deep learning (DL) has been developed to learn an effective representation of data. DL-based methods are inspired by the functioning of the human brain. Neural networks (NN) – the fundamental structure of DL – are composed of several layers (Wang et al., 2021). Deep learning can be seen as the next step in advancing a predictive model, like traditional machine learning. There are various architectures of DL models, convolutions, autoencoders, and so forth. In this review, we pay special attention to CNNs. Convolutional NNs are a type of neural network that is naturally suitable for image analysis due to their local connectivity (Alom et al., 2019).

There are a few algorithms that can train a model, and depending on the choice, the performance of the final trained model will change. To help DL architectures learn a better representation of the given dataset, some optimization algorithms are designed (Wei et al., 2021). To enhance the performance of the network, the backpropagation algorithm is used to correct the errors encountered in learning. Apart from the widely used libraries, there are many other frameworks available for you to use when designing your deep neural network (Suganyadevi et al., 2022). DL has been applied across a number of fields, including natural language processing, object detection, and image segmentation, among others. When training a model, the set of all samples is often divided between a training set and a test set. EMC applications run on biomedical images (Chakraborty & Mali, 2020). Two of the main categories of deep learning are archetype neural network (ANN) represented by multi-layer perceptrons (MLP) and CNN. The structure of CNN is based on the organization of the visual cortex (Sharma et al., 2022).

4. IMAGE ANALYSIS TECHNIQUES IN BREAST CANCER DIAGNOSIS

There exist various image analysis techniques that are currently being used or are under development to detect and diagnose breast cancer in the early stage. Digital mammography, synthetic mammography, and full-field digital mammography are among the imaging techniques used for breast tissue density analysis (Polat et al., 2020; Nicosia et al., 2023). Although several imaging modalities, such as mammography and ultrasound, to an extent of Magnetic Resonance Imaging are dominant in patient diagnosis, some of the traditional techniques are not sensitive and specific for small size lesions. Digital mammography, the most effective breast imaging technique in use now, is highly sensitive. In recent years, several researchers have dedicated their efforts to improving the diagnostic capability of MRI images for mammography (Iranmakani et al., 2020; Gerami et al., 2022). Breast tissues are typically classified according to their attenuated features based on the texture of the breasts. Moreover, contrast-enhanced computed tomography and scintimammography, positron emission mammography, and thermography are some of the additional imaging techniques in breast cancer detection that are still in the clinical phase of development (Aruleba et al., 2020).

Image segmentation is useful for cancerous tissue analysis in the breast, and not only segmentation, but feature extraction can help to extract relevant information from mammographic images (Shahidi et al., 2020). Due to complex image texture and external interference of breast tissues, the use of segmentation algorithms for these images is not effective. The main limitations of this classification model are highly categorized features of breast cancer, less accurate initial segmentation of tumor mass, and removal of features to diagnose breast tumors (Mohapatra et al., 2022). Moreover, currently, global and local features of breast mammogram images are not addressed. Automatic or semiautomatic analytic methods are needed to improve the diagnosis process and provide an efficient system for diagnosis and patient management. Therefore, a deep learning network such as convolutional neural networks and pooling techniques shows superiority in the task of breast cancer classification (Litjens et al., 2016; Wani et al., 2024). Each CNN layer contains several filters that work as feature extractors in the CNN system. The extracted features are shown as 'blobs' containing edges, spots, or parts of the mammogram's specific structures (Majanga et al., 2025).

5. TRADITIONAL METHODS VS. DEEP LEARNING APPROACHES

Traditional mammographic diagnostic methods for breast cancer screening might suffer from low specificity, with false-positive rates ranging from 9.8% to 75% due to factors such as high glandular density in younger women and structural similarity between benign and malignant lesions, resulting in unnecessary follow-ups and biopsies. Moreover, these methods are operator-dependent, require a high level of expertise, and can be affected by reader variability, making the assessment of mammograms and the final outcome of the diagnosis a time-consuming task (Giampietro et al., 2020). Currently, the evolution of computational methods has led to a new era, with numerous studies presenting a novel, intelligent breast cancer diagnosis system enhanced by deep learning approaches (Ramadan, 2020; Oza et al., 2021). Nevertheless, the inference behind the promising results of these newly introduced deep learning methods, as well as the great potential demonstrated mainly in CAD systems for breast cancer, is not trivial. The paradigm shift between traditional methods and deep learning techniques can be summarized in terms of feature engineering. Adding to a lack of additional domain knowledge, deep learning strategies are in a better position to learn and build intuitive embeddings for the processable inputs, automatically acting as a diagnostic model by themselves (Sechopoulos et al., 2021).

Deep learning approaches have already shown remarkable performance in feature extraction and pattern recognition, thanks to their data-driven analysis. Moreover, deep learning seems to come with a number of advantages (Houssein et al.,2021; Reshma et al., 2022). The possibility of using big data acquired via different medical devices, high scalability of deep neural networks, and the possibility of an automated and fully digital system make these particular machine learning strategies appealing for the automatic analysis of medical images. Nonetheless, due to specific diagnostic needs in breast cancer, only a handful of studies have proven the effectiveness of deep learning techniques outside of experimental scenarios. Recent works specifically developed for computer-aided diagnosis systems of breast cancer report demonstrable clinical effects while managing the specific case of breast cancer in terms of localized interpretability for diagnostic purposes (Balkenende et al., 2022). In particular, researchers reported the application of deep learning methods to different breast imaging datasets, observing a considerable increase in the diagnostic performance by means of ROC-AUC on all pathological results (Khan et al., 2022). Limited to specific sections of clinical-stage studies, deep learning methods for breast cancer have been applied to early (and at most locally advanced) stages of the disease, continuing to be some steps closer to bedside developments and surgical pathology (Mohi et al., 2022). Only small numbers of cases have been discussed in the prior studies, showing the inherent challenges of this research question. Concerning the generalization of the discussed data within this review, cases are discussed relating to an overall prevalence of malignant lesions (Hosseini et al., 2025). This publication maps the data landscape of alternative diagnostic strategies, revealing the need for a growing pool of possibly multi-institutional datasets as a result of the new gold-standard diagnosis: radiological, post-operative, and possibly radiomorphological (not just considering the update of the radiological biomass and its possible correlation with large-scale pathology). Therefore, we consider new gold standards not only referring to pure breast pathology but also to the new and rapidly evolving field of breast imagery, which we define here as radiomorphology in its current shape.

6. DEEP LEARNING ARCHITECTURES FOR IMAGE ANALYSIS

Conventional Deep Learning Architectures Some popular deep learning architectures applicable in image analysis for breast cancer are as follows: Convolutional Neural Networks, Recurrent Neural Networks and Autoencoders These architectures, being inherently deep, can handle and analyze the complex image data relevant to breast cancer with high sensitivity and specificity (Zhang et al., 2021; Masud et al., 2022). Convolutional Neural Networks Capable of performing imaging tasks and learning specific image patterns from histopathology, molecular images, radiological, and genetic images, the CNN architecture is widely used for applications in breast cancer imaging analysis for diagnostics and research. Architectural Design: The CNN architecture consists of layers such as convolutional, pooling, nonlinearity or activation, fully connected, and output (Oyelade & Ezugwu, 2021). The input layer receives an image in an array of pixels. The first layer processes the input image and starts the feature extraction process using filter depths as learned or man-made in the first-level kernels. The subsampling or down-sampling feature extraction is done in the pooling layer. Further, the CNN consists of more convolutional, subsampling, and fully connected layers. Finally, the fully connected or dense layer is used for classification based on the features learned from the previous layers. CNN Training and Optimization: The CNN architecture is trained using stochastic gradient-based weight updates such as backpropagation and gradient descent optimization techniques. Advancements: Transfer Learning: Transfer learning techniques are more focused on fine-tuning the pretrained model to a specific task based on a given input dataset (Fu et al., 2017; Taye, 2023; Salehi et al., 2023).

7. DATASETS AND PREPROCESSING IN BREAST CANCER IMAGE ANALYSIS

Breast cancer-related deep learning research is dominated by the scarcity and quality of datasets, as well as preprocessing design for model training. Data scarcity influences deep learning model training and interpretation, supervised annotation labeling tasks, and finally model performance evaluation. Diverse, complete, and high-quality data are key to the whole sensitivity and consistency of a large-scale compressive modeling process. In deep learning networks for diagnosable breast cancer, this pattern connects to the whole concept, which deteriorates with data statistics that model precision and recall (Mridha et al., 2021).

Publicly available datasets have significantly contributed to the clinical diagnosis and treatment of breast cancer. These open-access databases facilitate publicly credited algorithm model testing. However, all of the public datasets are pixel values and are restricted because complete information on electrical, biological, and medical treatment is lacking. Ethical issues could arise from the use of proprietary data and emphasize the importance of investigating what is allowed to communicate regarding promotional data usage (Ben Ammar et al., 2024). Standard preprocessing techniques are crucial in the design and preparation of proprietary datasets. Data normalization and z-score standardization operations set a global reference system and give a mid-city value, show the allocation of values, improve kernel intuitions of internal learning strategies for deep convolutional neural networks, and decrease training time; resizing of images makes the dimensions suitable for deep learning models used for tasks; data augmentation methods include over-sampling approaches, synthetic minority over-sampling techniques, and random rotations during training (Sharafaddini et al., 2024).

Creating labeled datasets represents one of the major challenges in supervised learning. Moreover, creating labeled data is extremely time-consuming and expensive. Data imbalances can have a detrimental effect on model training. Systematic detection of imbalanced target variable distribution and imbalanced datasets was comprehensively reviewed for the first time. Hereafter, in presenting medical imbalanced classification in computer-aided diagnosis applications, comprehensive reviews were given. Attempts have been made to mitigate the influence of imbalances using various data cleaning techniques, including data over-sampling and under-sampling techniques, in some cases (Mahmood et al., 2020). The use of available techniques in the identification of model sensitivity and robustness still poses open questions. Apart from the imbalanced data affecting supervised learning, there are additional challenges in manually labeling abnormalities in mammographic images. One of the sensitive issues was human study ethics, the use of image data, and the process of collecting fully informed consent from the patient. Patient consent is useful for identifying potential release and usage of screening images, as patient-facing screening technology (Tran et al., 2021).

8. PERFORMANCE EVALUATION METRICS

Deep learning algorithms are evaluated and compared using several metrics. Accuracy measures the overall agreement between the classification outputs and given class labels and expresses how well a model can accurately identify and classify images (Nabipour et al., 2020). Sensitivity, also known as the true positive rate, indicates the ability of the model to correctly classify patients diagnosed with breast cancer. On the other hand, specificity, or the true negative rate, illustrates the model's capacity to identify individuals free of breast cancer. Precision quantifies the accuracy of the positive predictions and indicates the model's ability to detect real BCS and avoid false examinations (Zhou et al., 2021). Finally, the F1 score, which balances both precision and recall, measures overall model performance with a single value. It is essential to have multiple evaluative metrics, as strong performance in a single metric can be misleading.

Receiver operating characteristic curves are graphs representative of the model's true positive versus false positive rates at varying classification thresholds, presenting the trade-offs between sensitivity and specificity (Brown & Davis, 2006). An area under the curve value of 1.0 indicates perfect classification ability, with a 0.5 value representing the performance of random guess classifiers. Thus, an area under the curve value close to 1.0 indicates a robust and effective classification model. Cross-validation techniques, comprising k-fold, stratified k-fold, and leave-one-out cross-validation, are employed to assess the model's performance across varied datasets and repeatability, randomization, and robustness of model findings (Gamage & Samarabandu, 2020). While various performance evaluation indices have been proposed throughout the literature for deep learning models, they are not simply adapted from traditional learning model metrics (Elmrabit et al., 2020). The clinical application of AI for BCS diagnosis relies on the combination of these computational results with data collected from additional medical exams, symptoms, or other bioinformation to personalize treatment strategies for individual patients (Padilla et al., 2020; Hicks et al., 2022).

9. CHALLENGES AND LIMITATIONS IN DEEP LEARNING FOR BREAST CANCER DIAGNOSIS

While deep learning technologies are advancing rapidly, there is a critical need to address methodological shortcomings and increase transparency to facilitate a wider adoption of these models (Luca et al., 2022). This review identifies nine major challenges and limitations of applications of deep learning in image analysis for breast cancer. Based on this, we identify potential pathways that may help address these challenges to allow for further research and development in deep learning for breast cancer. Challenges and Limitations: Firstly, data quality is a key challenge. The amount of available labeled data for training deep learning models is still limited, especially for rare cancer subgroups. Furthermore, the reported performance of deep learning models is limited by the quality and complexity of the imaging data, as it is typically highly heterogeneous, subjective, and its relation to disease and desired outcomes is potentially spurious. The phenomenon of model overfitting is both a methodological and translational obstacle (Sharafaddini et al.2024). The ultimate clinical setting a trained deep learning model will be applied to at the time of approval is still years away, making it challenging to train deep learning models that will have a wider generalizability to future patients seeing future radiologists with differing levels of training and expertise in various clinical contexts. Another challenge is interpretation: deep learning models are highly complex multilayered algorithms, which makes interpretation of model predictions difficult (Janiesch et al., 2021). This is a particular problem in fields with human involvement such as healthcare. Due to the potentially sensitive nature of their predictions, especially decisions with ethical implications, it is necessary to be able to interpret deep learning models and establish their clinical utility. Furthermore, ethical and practical issues related to clinical implementation exist, including legal implications, potential institutional barriers, patient risk, data safety, and interoperability. These practical challenges require interdisciplinary collaboration and efficient translation to deep learning research in clinical practice (Kurian et al., 2021).

10. FUTURE DIRECTIONS AND EMERGING TRENDS

Explainable AI involves making the decision-making process of deep learning techniques more transparent, so that healthcare professionals can trust the automated diagnostic system. There is potential to combine deep learning with other technologies such as genomics, radiomics, and patient-specific historical data, advancing breast cancer treatment towards personalized medicine (Wang et al., 2022). In the era of precision medicine, healthcare professionals are increasingly moving towards a more patient-centered approach, deeming explainable AI methods essential. Some emerging and promising AI techniques are few-shot learning, which adapts a model trained on a large dataset to a dataset that is data scarce, and self-supervised learning, which extracts information directly from large datasets. The application of these new deep learning techniques in combination with a variety of sources of information is likely to play an emerging role in the diagnosis of breast cancer. Considering that deep learning networks have been implemented in image-based diagnosis for just over ten years, there is much to advance (Jiang et al., 2021). The use of dermatology as a prosperous example, due to the plethora of recent reviews, is valid, but it is also crucial to highlight the importance of the validation of AI networks used. As in the development of any new equipment, tool, or model in breast imaging, any new deep learning model requires thorough validation in order to be robust, reproducible, and potentially useful in moving the field forward. This need stresses the importance of multi-center collaborations between academic centers, industry, and healthcare providers to assure that deep learning significantly benefits patient outcomes in the clinical space. It is important to mention that in light of rapid technological advancements, the computational cost and the time and resources required for developing and applying AI models is also likely to significantly reduce, and the prospect of being able to use sophisticated AI models, such as on-the-fly model personalization, is emerging. Further research will be required to develop unique approaches that can enhance deep learning model interpretation and explain the appearances and behaviors that assist in their prognostic and diagnostic capabilities. Many challenges lie ahead, and as a result, researchers must remain intrepid in their efforts to overcome these obstacles in order to revolutionize healthcare.

Future studies should focus on large-scale, multi-institutional datasets to evaluate the generalizability and robustness of deep learning models in diverse populations. Comparative analyses of CNNs with newer architectures such as vision transformers or hybrid models combining imaging with genomic and clinical data are needed. Additionally, incorporating federated learning methods can address privacy concerns while enabling collaborative training across hospitals. Explainable AI techniques must continue evolving to meet the transparency expectations of clinicians, patients, and regulators.

11. CONCLUSION

In conclusion, this is a comprehensive review to investigate the significant roles of deep learning in the early diagnosis and prognosis of breast cancer. The prominent performance of deep learning in terms of enhancement in computer-aided systems, mainly its accuracy, precision, and sensitivity for the retrieval results, offers the potential of integrating image analysis with current clinical practice of radiological image interpretations, which results in the reduction of missed cancer cases as well as improving patient outcomes. In these systematic review results, deep learning approaches achieved superior results in accordance with most investigations by both human expert radiologists and computer-aided systems using traditional machine learning methodologies, especially regarding high accuracy, sensitivity, specificity, positive prediction, and superior areas under their receiver operating characteristics curve. Deep learning models further outperformed published research in terms of prediction of breast cancer-related prognostic pathological features, disease-free survival, and overall survival in most studies, which could strongly propose their potential role in tumor behavior characterizations as well as patient outcomes. There are several challenges, limitations, and knowledge gaps in the published research discussed in detail, for example, annotation imbalance, small or relatively larger data volume, model architecture design, no direct comparison, feature representation, and diagnostic procedure protocol concerns. An adoption of comprehensive international collaboration for standardization and refining marker evaluation is necessary, as too often potential biomarkers are presented without this standardization. In this regard, we suggest further collaborations involving computer scientists with researchers/pathologists with specialized diagnostic/clinical interests and imaging specialists with an understanding of imaging pitfalls, all working alongside biologists identifying possible targets. The success of such an approach is evident from other disorders, including the burgeoning research into the applications of AI in cancer studies. In summary, while CNN-based deep learning models offer transformative potential for breast cancer diagnosis, their successful clinical translation depends on a careful balance between performance, interpretability, and ethical considerations. Collaborative efforts across disciplines — involving AI developers, radiologists, pathologists, ethicists, and policymakers — are essential to build trustworthy, reproducible, and patient-centered diagnostic tools.

REFERENCES

Alom, M. Z., Taha, T. M., Yakopcic, C., Westberg, S., Sidike, P., Nasrin, M. S., Hasan, M., Van Essen, B. C., Awwal, A. A. S., & Asari, V. K. (2019). A State-of-the-Art Survey on Deep Learning Theory and Architectures. *Electronics (Basel), 8*(3), 292. DOI: 10.3390/electronics8030292

Anaya-Isaza, A., Mera-Jiménez, L., & Zequera-Diaz, M. (2021). An overview of deep learning in medical imaging. *Informatics in Medicine Unlocked, 26*, 100723. DOI: 10.1016/j.imu.2021.100723

Aruleba, K., Obaido, G., Ogbuokiri, B., Fadaka, A. O., Klein, A., Adekiya, T. A., & Aruleba, R. T. (2020). Applications of computational methods in biomedical breast cancer imaging diagnostics: A review. *Journal of Imaging, 6*(10), 105. DOI: 10.3390/jimaging6100105 PMID: 34460546

Balkenende, L., Teuwen, J., & Mann, R. M. (2022). Application of deep learning in breast cancer imaging. *Seminars in Nuclear Medicine, 52*(5), 584–596. DOI: 10.1053/j.semnuclmed.2022.02.003 PMID: 35339259

Ben Ammar, M., Labbene Ayachi, F., Cardoso de Paiva, A., Ksantini, R., & Mahjoubi, H. (2024). Harnessing Deep Learning for Early Breast Cancer Diagnosis: A Review of Datasets, Methods, Challenges, and Future Directions. *International Journal of Computing and Digital Systems, 16*(1), 1643–1661. DOI: 10.12785/ijcds/1601122

Brown, C. D., & Davis, H. T. (2006). Receiver operating characteristics curves and related decision measures: A tutorial. *Chemometrics and Intelligent Laboratory Systems, 80*(1), 24–38. DOI: 10.1016/j.chemolab.2005.05.004

Cao, W., Chen, H. D., Yu, Y. W., Li, N., & Chen, W. Q. (2021). Changing Profiles of Cancer Burden Worldwide and in China: A Secondary Analysis of the Global Cancer Statistics 2020. *Chinese Medical Journal, 134*(7), 783–791. DOI: 10.1097/CM9.0000000000001474 PMID: 33734139

Chakraborty, S., & Mali, K. (2020). In Chakraborty, S., & Mali, K. (Eds.), *An Overview of Biomedical Image Analysis From the Deep Learning Perspective. Applications of Advanced Machine Intelligence in Computer Vision and Object Recognition: Emerging Research and Opportunities* (pp. 197–218). IGI Global., DOI: 10.4018/978-1-7998-2736-8.ch008

Elmrabit, N., Zhou, F., Li, F., & Zhou, H. 2020. Evaluation of machine learning algorithms for anomaly detection. In 2020 International Conference on Cyber Security and Protection of Digital Services (Cyber Security), 1-8. IEEE. DOI: 10.1109/CyberSecurity49315.2020.9138871

Fu, G., Liu, C., Zhou, R., Sun, T., & Zhang, Q. (2017). Classification for High Resolution Remote Sensing Imagery Using a Fully Convolutional Network. *Remote Sensing (Basel)*, *9*(5), 498. DOI: 10.3390/rs9050498

Gamage, S., & Samarabandu, J. (2020). Deep learning methods in network intrusion detection: A survey and an objective comparison. *Journal of Network and Computer Applications*, *169*, 102767. DOI: 10.1016/j.jnca.2020.102767

Gerami, R., Sadeghi Joni, S., Akhondi, N., Etemadi, A., Fosouli, M., Foroughi Eghbal, A., & Souri, Z. (2022). A literature review on the imaging methods for breast cancer. *International Journal of Physiology, Pathophysiology and Pharmacology*, *14*(3), 171. PMID: 35891932

Giampietro, R. R., Cabral, M. V. G., Lima, S. A. M., Weber, S. A. T., & Nunes-Nogueira, V. S. (2020). Accuracy and effectiveness of mammography versus mammography and tomosynthesis for population-based breast cancer screening: A systematic review and meta-analysis. *Scientific Reports*, *10*(1), 7991. DOI: 10.1038/s41598-020-64802-x PMID: 32409756

Hicks, S. A., Strümke, I., Thambawita, V., Hammou, M., Riegler, M. A., Halvorsen, P., & Parasa, S. (2022). On evaluation metrics for medical applications of artificial intelligence. *Scientific Reports*, *12*(1), 5979. DOI: 10.1038/s41598-022-09954-8 PMID: 35395867

Hosseini, H., Heydari, S., Hushmandi, K., Daneshi, S., & Raesi, R. (2025). Bone tumors: A systematic review of prevalence, risk determinants, and survival patterns. *BMC Cancer*, *25*(1), 321. DOI: 10.1186/s12885-025-13720-0 PMID: 39984867

Houssein, E. H., Emam, M. M., Ali, A. A., & Suganthan, P. N. (2021). Deep and machine learning techniques for medical imaging-based breast cancer: A comprehensive review. *Expert Systems with Applications*, *167*, 114161. DOI: 10.1016/j.eswa.2020.114161

Iranmakani, S., Mortezazadeh, T., Sajadian, F., Ghaziani, M. F., Ghafari, A., Khezerloo, D., & Musa, A. E. (2020). A review of various modalities in breast imaging: Technical aspects and clinical outcomes. *The Egyptian Journal of Radiology and Nuclear Medicine*, *51*(1), 1–22. DOI: 10.1186/s43055-020-00175-5

Janiesch, C., Zschech, P., & Heinrich, K. (2021). Machine learning and deep learning fundamentals. *Electronic Markets*, *31*(3), 685–695. DOI: 10.1007/s12525-021-00475-2

Jiang, S., Li, H., & Jin, Z. (2021). A visually interpretable deep learning framework for histopathological image-based skin cancer diagnosis. *IEEE Journal of Biomedical and Health Informatics, 25*(5), 1483–1494. DOI: 10.1109/JBHI.2021.3052044 PMID: 33449890

Karakcheyeva, V., Willis-Johnson, H., Corr, P. G., & Frame, L. A. (2024). The Well-Being of Women in Healthcare Professions: A Comprehensive Review. *Global Advances in Integrative Medicine and Health, 13*, 27536130241232929. DOI: 10.1177/27536130241232929 PMID: 38344248

Khan, N., Adam, R., Huang, P., Maldjian, T., & Duong, T. Q. (2022). Deep learning prediction of pathologic complete response in breast cancer using MRI and other clinical data: A systematic review. *Tomography : a Journal for Imaging Research, 8*(6), 2784–2795. DOI: 10.3390/tomography8060232 PMID: 36412691

Kurian, N. C., Sethi, A., Konduru, A. R., Mahajan, A., & Rane, S. U. (2021). A 2021 update on cancer image analytics with deep learning. *Wiley Interdisciplinary Reviews. Data Mining and Knowledge Discovery, 11*(4), e1410. DOI: 10.1002/widm.1410

Litjens, G., Sánchez, C. I., Timofeeva, N., Hermsen, M., Nagtegaal, I., Kovacs, I., Hulsbergen-van de Kaa, C., Bult, P., van Ginneken, B., & van der Laak, J. (2016). Deep learning as a tool for increased accuracy and efficiency of histopathological diagnosis. *Scientific Reports, 6*(1), 26286. DOI: 10.1038/srep26286 PMID: 27212078

Luca, A. R., Ursuleanu, T. F., Gheorghe, L., Grigorovici, R., Iancu, S., Hlusneac, M., & Grigorovici, A. (2022). Impact of quality, type and volume of data used by deep learning models in the analysis of medical images. *Informatics in Medicine Unlocked, 29*, 100911. DOI: 10.1016/j.imu.2022.100911

Mahmood, T., Li, J., Pei, Y., Akhtar, F., Imran, A., & Rehman, K. U. (2020). A brief survey on breast cancer diagnostic with deep learning schemes using multi-image modalities. *IEEE Access : Practical Innovations, Open Solutions, 8*, 165779–165809. DOI: 10.1109/ACCESS.2020.3021343

Majanga, V., Mnkandla, E., Wang, Z., & Moulla, D. K. (2025). Automatic blob detection method for cancerous lesions in unsupervised breast histology images. *Bioengineering (Basel, Switzerland), 12*(4), 364. DOI: 10.3390/bioengineering12040364 PMID: 40281724

Masud, M., Rashed, A. E. E., & Hossain, M. S. (2022). Convolutional neural network-based models for diagnosis of breast cancer. *Neural Computing & Applications, 34*(14), 11383–11394. DOI: 10.1007/s00521-020-05394-5 PMID: 33052172

Mohapatra, S., Muduly, S., Mohanty, S., Ravindra, J. V. R., & Mohanty, S. N. (2022). Evaluation of deep learning models for detecting breast cancer using histopathological mammograms images. *Sustainable Operations and Computers.*, *3*, 296–302. DOI: 10.1016/j.susoc.2022.06.001

Mohi, N., Ahmad Dar, R., Rasool, M., & Assad, A. (2022). Breast cancer detection using deep learning: Datasets, methods, and challenges ahead. *Computers in Biology and Medicine*, *149*, 106073. DOI: 10.1016/j.compbiomed.2022.106073 PMID: 36103745

Mridha, M. F., Hamid, M. A., Monowar, M. M., Keya, A. J., Ohi, A. Q., Islam, M. R., & Kim, J.-M. (2021). A Comprehensive Survey on Deep-Learning-Based Breast Cancer Diagnosis. *Cancers (Basel)*, *13*(23), 6116. DOI: 10.3390/cancers13236116 PMID: 34885225

Nabipour, M., Nayyeri, P., Jabani, H., Shahab, S., & Mosavi, A. (2020). Predicting stock market trends using machine learning and deep learning algorithms via continuous and binary data; a comparative analysis. *IEEE Access : Practical Innovations, Open Solutions*, *8*, 150199–150212. DOI: 10.1109/ACCESS.2020.3015966

Nicosia, L., Gnocchi, G., Gorini, I., Venturini, M., Fontana, F., Pesapane, F., Abiuso, I., Bozzini, A. C., Pizzamiglio, M., Latronico, A., Abbate, F., Meneghetti, L., Battaglia, O., Pellegrino, G., & Cassano, E. (2023). History of Mammography: Analysis of Breast Imaging Diagnostic Achievements over the Last Century. *Health Care*, *11*(11), 1596. DOI: 10.3390/healthcare11111596 PMID: 37297735

Oyelade, O. N., & Ezugwu, A. E. (2021). A bioinspired neural architecture search based convolutional neural network for breast cancer detection using histopathology images. *Scientific Reports*, *11*(1), 19940. DOI: 10.1038/s41598-021-98978-7 PMID: 34620891

Oza, P., Sharma, P., Patel, S., & Bruno, A. (2021). A bottom-up review of image analysis methods for suspicious region detection in mammograms. *Journal of Imaging*, *7*(9), 190. DOI: 10.3390/jimaging7090190 PMID: 34564116

Padilla, R., Netto, S. L., & Da Silva, E. A. B. (2020). A survey on performance metrics for object-detection algorithms. *International Conference on Systems, Signals and Image Processing (IWSSIP)*, 237-242. IEEE. DOI: 10.1109/IWSSIP48289.2020.9145130

Polat, D. S., Evans, W. P., & Dogan, B. E. (2020). Contrast-enhanced digital mammography: Technique, clinical applications, and pitfalls. *AJR. American Journal of Roentgenology*, *215*(5), 1267–1278. DOI: 10.2214/AJR.19.22412 PMID: 32877247

Ramadan, S.Z. (2020). Methods used in computer-aided diagnosis for breast cancer detection using mammograms: A review. Journal of Healthcare Engineering. Article ID 9162464, 21 pages. DOI: 10.1155/2020/9162464

Reshma, V. K., Arya, N., Ahmad, S. S., Wattar, I., Mekala, S., Joshi, S., & Krah, D. (2022). *Detection of breast cancer using histopathological image classification dataset with deep learning techniques.* BioMed Research International. DOI: 10.1155/2022/8363850

Salehi, A. W., Khan, S., Gupta, G., Alabduallah, B. I., Almjally, A., Alsolai, H., Siddiqui, T., & Mellit, A. (2023). A Study of CNN and Transfer Learning in Medical Imaging: Advantages, Challenges, Future Scope. *Sustainability (Basel)*, *15*(7), 5930. DOI: 10.3390/su15075930

Sechopoulos, I., Teuwen, J., & Mann, R. (2021). Artificial intelligence for breast cancer detection in mammography and digital breast tomosynthesis: State of the art. *Seminars in Cancer Biology*, *72*, 214–225. DOI: 10.1016/j.semcancer.2020.06.002 PMID: 32531273

Shahidi, F., Mohd Daud, S., Abas, H., Ahmad, N. A., & Maarop, N. (2020). Breast cancer classification using deep learning approaches and histopathology image: A comparison study. *IEEE Access : Practical Innovations, Open Solutions*, *8*, 187531–187552. DOI: 10.1109/ACCESS.2020.3029881

Shang, C., & Xu, D. (2022). Epidemiology of Breast Cancer. *Oncologie*, *24*(4), 649–663. DOI: 10.32604/oncologie.2022.027640

Sharafaddini, A. M., Kouhpah Esfahani, K., & Mansouri, N. (2024). Deep learning approaches to detect breast cancer: A comprehensive review. *Multimedia Tools and Applications*, 1–112.

Sharma, R., Kim, M., Gupta, A. 2022. Motor imagery classification in brain–machine interface with machine learning algorithms: Classical approach to multi-layer perceptron model. Biomedical Signal Processing and Control. 71 (A), 103101. DOI: 10.1016/j.bspc.2021.103101

Suganyadevi, S., Seethalakshmi, V., & Balasamy, K. (2022). A review on deep learning in medical image analysis. *International Journal of Multimedia Information Retrieval*, *11*(1), 19–38. DOI: 10.1007/s13735-021-00218-1 PMID: 34513553

Taye, M. M. (2023). Theoretical Understanding of Convolutional Neural Network: Concepts, Architectures, Applications, Future Directions. *Computation (Basel, Switzerland)*, *11*(3), 52. DOI: 10.3390/computation11030052

Tran, K. A., Kondrashova, O., Bradley, A., Williams, E. D., Pearson, J. V., & Waddell, N. (2021). Deep learning in cancer diagnosis, prognosis and treatment selection. *Genome Medicine, 13*(1), 1–17. DOI: 10.1186/s13073-021-00968-x PMID: 34579788

Virdee, P. S., Marian, I. R., Mansouri, A., Elhussein, L., Kirtley, S., Holt, T., & Birks, J. (2020). The full blood count blood test for colorectal cancer detection: A systematic review, meta-analysis, and critical appraisal. *Cancers (Basel), 12*(9), 2348. DOI: 10.3390/cancers12092348 PMID: 32825191

Wang, J., Zhu, H., Wang, S. H., & Zhang, Y. D. (2021). A review of deep learning on medical image analysis. *Mobile Networks and Applications, 26*(6), 2343–2365.

Wang, L., Wang, H., Huang, Y., Yan, B., Chang, Z., Liu, Z., Zhao, M., Cui, L., Song, J., & Li, F. (2022). Trends in the application of deep learning networks in medical image analysis: Evolution between 2012 and 2020. *European Journal of Radiology, 146*, 110069. DOI: 10.1016/j.ejrad.2021.110069 PMID: 34847395

Wani, N. A., Kumar, R., & Bedi, J. (2024). DeepXplainer: An interpretable deep learning based approach for lung cancer detection using explainable artificial intelligence. *Computer Methods and Programs in Biomedicine, 243*, 107879. DOI: 10.1016/j.cmpb.2023.107879 PMID: 37897989

Wei, X., Song, Y. Z., Mac Aodha, O., Wu, J., Peng, Y., Tang, J., Yang, J., & Belongie, S. (2021). Fine-grained image analysis with deep learning: A survey. *IEEE Transactions on Pattern Analysis and Machine Intelligence, 44*(12), 8927–8948. DOI: 10.1109/TPAMI.2021.3126648 PMID: 34752384

Zhang, Y., Chen, J.-H., Lin, Y., Chan, S., Zhou, J., Chow, D., Chang, P., Kwong, T., Yeh, D.-C., Wang, X., Parajuli, R., Mehta, R. S., Wang, M., & Su, M.-Y. (2021). Prediction of breast cancer molecular subtypes on DCE-MRI using convolutional neural network with transfer learning between two centers. *European Radiology, 31*(4), 2559–2567. DOI: 10.1007/s00330-020-07274-x PMID: 33001309

Zhou, J., Gandomi, A. H., Chen, F., & Holzinger, A. (2021). Evaluating the quality of machine learning explanations: A survey on methods and metrics. *Electronics (Basel), 10*(5), 593. DOI: 10.3390/electronics10050593

Compilation of References

Abacıoğlu, S., Ayan, B., & Pamucar, D. (2024). The Race to Sustainability: Decoding Green University Rankings Through a Comparative Analysis (2018–2022). *Innovative Higher Education*, 1–35.

Abdulaal, R. M. S., & Bafail, O. A. (2022). Two New Approaches (RAMS-RATMI) in Multi-Criteria Decision-Making Tactics. *Journal of Mathematics, 2022*(1). DOI: 10.1155/2022/6725318

Abdullah, A., Ahmad, S., Athar, M. A., Rajpoot, N., & Talib, F. (2022). Healthcare performance management using integrated FUCOM-MARCOS approach: The case of India. *The International Journal of Health Planning and Management*, *37*(5), 2635–2668. DOI: 10.1002/hpm.3488 PMID: 35484727

Abersfelder, S., Bogner, E., Heyder, A., & Frankel, J. (2016). Application and validation of an existing Industry 4.0 guideline for the development of specific recommendations for implementation. *Advanced Materials Research*, *1140*, 465–472. DOI: 10.4028/www.scientific.net/AMR.1140.465

Acet, H., & Koç, Ş. (2020). Dördüncü Sanayi Devrimi'nin (Endüstri 4.0) Dünyaya ve Türkiye'ye Ekonomik Yansımaları. *Journal of Social and Humanities Sciences Research*, *7*(58), 2243–2256.

ACI. (2023). *Environment*. https://aci.aero/advocacy/environment/

Acuña-Carvajal, F., Pinto-Tarazona, L., López-Ospina, H., Barros-Castro, R., Quezada, L., & Palacio, K. (2019). An integrated method to plan, structure and validate a business strategy using fuzzy DEMATEL and the balanced scorecard. *Expert Systems with Applications*, *122*, 351–368. DOI: 10.1016/j.eswa.2019.01.030

Adelusi, T. I., Oyedele, A. Q. K., Boyenle, I. D., Ogunlana, A. T., Adeyemi, R. O., Ukachi, C. D., Idris, M. O., Olaoba, O. T., Adedotun, I. O., Kolawole, O. E., Xiaoxing, Y., & Abdul-Hammed, M. (2022). Molecular Modeling in Drug Discovery. *Informatics in Medicine Unlocked*, *29*, 100880. DOI: 10.1016/j.imu.2022.100880

Adewuyi, A., & Pereira, F. (2017). Fatty alkyl tosylate from *Sesamum indicum* seed oil: A potential resource for the oleochemical industry. *La Rivista Italiana delle Sostanze Grasse*, *94*(3), 161–167.

Adrià Menéndez i Molist, Z. K. (2024). Assessing the Downstream and Upstream Preferences of Stakeholders for Sustainability Attributes in the Tomato Value Chain. *Sustainability (Basel)*, *16*(6), 1–24. DOI: 10.3390/su16062505

Afkham, L., Abdi, F., & Komijan, A. R. (2012). Evaluation of service quality by using fuzzy MCDM: A case study in Iranian health-care centers. *Management Science Letters*, *2*(1), 291–300. DOI: 10.5267/j.msl.2011.08.009

Aitouhanni, I., Mouniane, Y., & Berqia, A. (2024). Machine learning-powered prediction of molecule solubility: Paving the way for environmental and energy applications. BIO Web of Conferences, 109, 01037. Conference on Water, Agriculture, Environment and Energy (WA2EN2023). DOI: 10.1051/bioconf/202410901037

Aitouhanni, I., Berqia, A., Kaiss, R., Bouijij, H., & Mouniane, Y. (2025). Enhancing environmental sustainability through machine learning: Predicting drug solubility (LogS) for ecotoxicity assessment and green pharmaceutical design. *Journal of Environment and Earth Science*, *7*(4), 82–95. DOI: 10.30564/jees.v7i4.8866

Akandere, G. (2021). DİJİTALLEŞME DÜZEYİ VE YEŞİL LOJİSTİK UYGULAMALARIN LOJİSTİK PERFORMANSA ETKİSİ. *Nevşehir Hacı Bektaş Veli Üniversitesi SBE Dergisi*, *11*(4), 1979–2000. DOI: 10.30783/nevsosbilen.1022778

Akdag, H., Kalaycı, T., Karagöz, S., Zülfikar, H., & Giz, D. (2014). The evaluation of hospital service quality by fuzzy MCDM. *Applied Soft Computing*, *23*, 239–248. DOI: 10.1016/j.asoc.2014.06.033

Akhtar, S. (2008). Islamic Finance: Sustainability and Challenges. *NBR Anal.*, *18*, 15–24.

Akıncı, H., & Kahraman, Ü. G. (2024). Endüstri 4.0: Yönetim Bilişim Sistemleri Bakış Açısıyla Değerlendirme. *Mehmet Akif Ersoy Üniversitesi Uygulamalı Bilimler Dergisi*, *8*(1), 76–99. DOI: 10.31200/makuubd.1442339

Akintayo, B. D., Babatunde, O. M., & Olanrewaju, O. A. (2024). Comparative Analysis of Cement Production Methods Using a Life Cycle Assessment and a Multicriteria Decision-Making Approach. *Sustainability (Basel)*, *16*(2), 484. DOI: 10.3390/su16020484

Akpınar, K., Dengiz, O., & Dengiz, B. (2024). KOBİ'ler ölçeğinde endüstri 4.0 farkındalık ve olgunluk düzeyinin belirlenmesi. *Journal of Turkish Operations Management*, *8*(2), 459–473. DOI: 10.56554/jtom.1524092

Aksin-Sivrikaya, S., & Bhattacharya, C. B. (2017). Where digitalization meets sustainability: opportunities and challenges. *Sustainability In a Digital World: New Opportunities Through New Technologies*, 37-49. DOI: 10.1007/978-3-319-54603-2_3

Aksoy, S. (2017). Değişen Teknolojiler ve Endüstri 4.0: Endüstri 4.0'ı Anlamaya Dair Bir Giriş. *SAV Katkı Dergisi*, *4*, 34–44.

Aktan, E. (2018). Büyük Veri: Uygulama Alanları, Analitiği ve Güvenlik Boyutu. *Ankara Üniversitesi Bilgi Yönetimi Dergisi*, *1*(1), 3–14. DOI: 10.33721/by.403010

Akundi, A., Euresti, D., Luna, S., Ankobiah, W., Lopes, A., & Edinbarough, I. (2022a). State of Industry 5.0—Analysis and Identification of Current Research Trends. *Applied System Innovation*, *5*(1), 27. DOI: 10.3390/asi5010027

Al-Gerafi, M. A., Goswami, S. S., Khan, M. A., Naveed, Q. N., Lasisi, A., AlMohimeed, A., & Elaraby, A. (2024). Designing of an effective e-learning website using inter-valued fuzzy hybrid MCDM concept: A pedagogical approach. *Alexandria Engineering Journal*, *97*, 61–87. DOI: 10.1016/j.aej.2024.04.012

Alguliyev, R., Aliguliyev, R., & Sukhostat, L. (2025). An approach for assessing the functional vulnerabilities criticality of CPS components. *Cyber Security and Applications*, *3*, 100058. DOI: 10.1016/j.csa.2024.100058

Alhammadi, A., Alsyouf, I., Semeraro, C., & Obaideen, K. (2024). The role of industry 4.0 in advancing sustainability development: A focus review in the United Arab Emirates. *Cleaner Engineering and Technology*, *18*, 100708. DOI: 10.1016/j.clet.2023.100708

Al-Harbi, K. M. A. S. (2001). Application of the AHP in project management. *International Journal of Project Management*, *19*(1), 19–27. DOI: 10.1016/S0263-7863(99)00038-1

Alimohammadzadeh, K., Bahadori, M., & Hassani, F. (2016). Application of analytical hierarchy process approach for service quality evaluation in radiology departments: A cross-sectional study. *Iranian Journal of Radiology : a Quarterly Journal published by the Iranian Radiological Society*, *13*(1). DOI: 10.5812/iranjradiol.29424 PMID: 27127577

Alioui, O., Benguerba, Y., & Alnashef, I. M. (2020). Investigation of the CO_2-Solubility in Deep Eutectic Solvents Using COSMO-RS and Molecular Dynamics Methods. *Journal of Molecular Liquids*, *307*, 113005. DOI: 10.1016/j.molliq.2020.113005

Alizon, F., Shooter, S. B., & Simpson, T. W. (2008, January). Henry Ford and the Model T: lessons for product platforming and mass customization. In International Design Engineering Technical Conferences and Computers and Information in Engineering Conference (Vol. 43291, pp. 59-66).

Alkan, G., & Merdivenci, F. (2021). Sürdürülebilir kalkınma açısından lojistik performans endeksine göre seçilen ülkelerin Entropi temeline dayalı EDAS yöntemi ile değerlendirmesi. *Gümüşhane Üniversitesi Sosyal Bilimler Dergisi*, *12*(2), 627–641.

AL-Khatib, A., Shuhaiber, A., Mashal, I., & Al-Okaily, M.AL-Khatib. (2024). Antecedents of Industry 4.0 capabilities and technological innovation: A dynamic capabilities perspective. *European Business Review*, *36*(4), 566–587. DOI: 10.1108/EBR-05-2023-0158

Alnıpak, S., & Toraman, Y. (2024). Analysing the intention to use blockchain technology in payment transactions of Turkish maritime industry. *Quality & Quantity*, *58*(3), 2103–2123. DOI: 10.1007/s11135-023-01735-3

Alom, M. Z., Taha, T. M., Yakopcic, C., Westberg, S., Sidike, P., Nasrin, M. S., Hasan, M., Van Essen, B. C., Awwal, A. A. S., & Asari, V. K. (2019). A State-of-the-Art Survey on Deep Learning Theory and Architectures. *Electronics (Basel)*, *8*(3), 292. DOI: 10.3390/electronics8030292

Alpdoğan, H. (2023). OECD ülkelerinde sürdürülebilir kalkınma politikalarının ARAS metodu ile performans analizi. *Business & Management Studies: An International Journal*, *11*(3), 1079–1103. DOI: 10.15295/bmij.v11i3.2285

Alsenz, J., & Kansy, M. (2007). High throughput solubility measurement in drug discovery and development. *Advanced Drug Delivery Reviews*, *59*(7), 546–567. DOI: 10.1016/j.addr.2007.05.007 PMID: 17604872

Alshamsi, A. M., El-Kassabi, H., Serhani, M. A., & Bouhaddioui, C. (2023). A multi-criteria decision-making (MCDM) approach for data-driven distance learning recommendations. *Education and Information Technologies*, *28*(8), 10421–10458. DOI: 10.1007/s10639-023-11589-9 PMID: 36718426

Altın, S. (2023). Sürdürülebilir Tüketimi Sağlamak İçin Çevresel Duyarlilik Etkili Bir Faktör Müdür? *Erciyes Akademi*, *37*(3), 1062–1083. DOI: 10.48070/erciyesakademi.1343768

Altıntaş, F. F. (2024). Avrupa Birliği ülkelerin sürdürülebilir kalkınma performanslarının MEREC tabanlı WEDBA yöntemi ile analizi. *Ordu Üniversitesi Sosyal Bilimler Enstitüsü Sosyal Bilimler Araştırmaları Dergisi*, *14*(1), 117–137.

Altuntaş, H. (2019). Biodiversity Management. In *Sustainable Aviation* (pp. 81–95). Springer.

Aly, H. (2020). Digital transformation, development and productivity in developing countries: Is artificial intelligence a curse or a blessing? *Review of Economics and Political Science*, *7*(4), 238–256. DOI: 10.1108/REPS-11-2019-0145

Amrani, A. Z., Ortega, I. U., & Vallespir, B. (2024). Industry 4.0 technologies and lean production combination: A strategic methodology based on links quantification. [IJTIM]. *International Journal of Technology Innovation and Management*, *4*(2), 1–18.

Anaya-Isaza, A., Mera-Jiménez, L., & Zequera-Diaz, M. (2021). An overview of deep learning in medical imaging. *Informatics in Medicine Unlocked*, *26*, 100723. DOI: 10.1016/j.imu.2021.100723

Andrejić, M., & Pajić, V. (2023). Optimizing personnel selection in transportation: An application of the BWM-CoCoSo decision-support model. *Journal of Organizations. Technology and Entrepreneurship*, *1*(1), 35–46. DOI: 10.56578/jote010103

Angelstam, P., Bush, T., & Manton, M. (2023). Challenges and Solutions for Forest Biodiversity Conservation in Sweden: Assessment of Policy, Implementation Outputs, and Consequences. *Land (Basel)*, *12*(5), 1098. DOI: 10.3390/land12051098

Antanasijević, D., Pocajt, V., Ristić, M., & Perić-Grujić, A. (2017). A differential multi-criteria analysis for the assessment of sustainability performance of European countries: Beyond country ranking. *Journal of Cleaner Production*, *165*, 213–220. DOI: 10.1016/j.jclepro.2017.07.131

Antoine, N. E., & Kroo, I. M. (2004). Aircraft optimization for minimal environmental impact. *Journal of Aircraft*, *41*(4), 790–797. DOI: 10.2514/1.71

Antoniuk, I., Svitek, R., Krajcovic, M., & Furmannová, B. (2021). Methodology of design and optimization of internal logistics in the concept of Industry 4.0. *Transportation Research Procedia*, *55*, 503–509. DOI: 10.1016/j.trpro.2021.07.093

Aras, G., Tezcan, N. ve Kutlu Furtuna, Ö. (2018). Çok Boyutlu Kurumsal Sürdürülebilirlik Yaklaşımı ile Türk Bankacılık Sektörünün Değerlemesi: Kamu-Özel Banka Farklılaşması, Ege Akademik Bakış. Cilt 18 · Sayı 1 · SS. 47 / 62.

Aras, G., & Crowther, D. (2009). Corporate Sustainability Reporting: A Study in Disingenuity? *Journal of Business Ethics*, *87*(S1), 279–288. DOI: 10.1007/s10551-008-9806-0

Arbolino, R., Boffardi, R., Ioppolo, G., Lantz, T. L., & Rosa, P. (2022). Evaluating industrial sustainability in OECD countries: A cross-country comparison. *Journal of Cleaner Production, 331*, 129773. DOI: 10.1016/j.jclepro.2021.129773

Arman, K., & Kundakcı, N. (2023). Yeni bütünleşik FUCOM-WEDBA yaklaşımı ile bir işletme için bulut hizmet sağlayıcısı seçimi. *Pamukkale Üniversitesi Sosyal Bilimler Enstitüsü Dergisi*, (56), 281–295. DOI: 10.30794/pausbed.1212975

Arman, K., & Organ, A. (2023). AB'ye üye ve aday ülkelerin lojistik performanslarının MEREC ve COCOSO yöntemleri ile değerlendirilmesi. *Uluslararası Ticaret ve Ekonomi Araştırmaları Dergisi*, *7*(2), 36–46. DOI: 10.30711/utead.1360959

Arsu, Ş. U., & Arsu, T. (2023). Evaluation of the Corporate Sustainability Performance of Manufacturing Companies in the BIST Sustainability Index with Multi-Criteria Decision Making Methods. *Business & Economics Research Journal, 14*(4).

Aruldoss, M., Lakshmi, T. M., & Venkatesan, V. P. (2013). A survey on multi criteria decision making methods and its applications. *American Journal of Information Systems*, *1*(1), 31–43.

Aruleba, K., Obaido, G., Ogbuokiri, B., Fadaka, A. O., Klein, A., Adekiya, T. A., & Aruleba, R. T. (2020). Applications of computational methods in biomedical breast cancer imaging diagnostics: A review. *Journal of Imaging*, *6*(10), 105. DOI: 10.3390/jimaging6100105 PMID: 34460546

Asadabadi, M. R., Chang, E., & Saberi, M. (2019). Are MCDM methods useful? A critical review of analytic hierarchy process (AHP) and analytic network process (ANP). *Cogent Engineering*, *6*(1), 1623153. DOI: 10.1080/23311916.2019.1623153

Ashford, N. J., Stanton, H. P. M., Moore, C. A., Coutu, P., & Beasley, J. R. (2013). *Airport Operations* (3.baskı). McGraw-Hill.

Ashford, N., Mumayiz, S., & Wright, P. (2011). *Airport Engineering: Planning, Design, and Development of 21st Century Airports* (4. baskı). John Wiley & Sons.

Ashton, K. (2010). That "internet of things" Thing. In *RFID Journal*.

Askari, S., Ghofrani, A., & Taherdoost, H. (2023). Transforming drug design: Innovations in computer-aided discovery for biosimilar agents. *BioMedInformatics*, *3*(4), 1178–1196. DOI: 10.3390/biomedinformatics3040070

Aslam, M., Shabbir, M. A., Pasha, I., Shukat, R., Siddique, U., Manzoor, M. F., & Ayub, S. (2020). Protective effect of sesame (*Sesamum indicum*) seed oil against hypercholesterolemic in Sprague-Dawley male rats. *Food Science and Technology (Campinas)*, *41*(Suppl 2), 741–745. DOI: 10.1590/fst.35320

ATAG. (2020). *Aviation: Benefits Beyond Borders*. https://aviationbenefits.org/media/167517/aw-oct-final-atag_abbb-2020-publication-digital.pdf

Ateş, S., & Usman, Ö. (2021). Gelişmekte olan ülkelerin sürdürülebilir kalkınma performanslarının gri ilişkisel analiz yöntemiyle değerlendirilmesi. *İktisadi İdari ve Siyasal Araştırmalar Dergisi, 6*(15), 225-248.

Atli, E. Ç., Eroğlu, F., & Şekkeli, Z. H. ENDÜSTRİ 4.0'IN LOJİSTİKTE YANSIMALARI: LOJİSTİK 4.0 UYGULAMALARI ÜZERİNE BİR ÖRNEK OLAY İNCELEMESİ. *Yönetim Bilimleri Dergisi, 22*(Özel Sayı: Endüstri 4.0 ve Dijitalleşmenin Sosyal Bilimlerde Yansımaları), 1753-1781.

Ayboğa, H., & Görmüş, L. (2022). Endüstri 4.0-Türkiye'nin Durumu ve Yapılması Gerekenler. *Marmara Sosyal Araştırmalar Dergisi*, (17), 82–98.

Ayçin, E., & Arsu, T. (2021). Sosyal gelişme endeksine göre ülkelerin değerlendirilmesi: MEREC ve MARCOS yöntemleri ile bir uygulama. *İzmir Yönetim Dergisi, 2*(2), 75-88.

Ayçin, E., & Aşan, H. (2021). İş zekası uygulamaları seçimindeki kriterlerin önem ağırlıklarının FUCOM yöntemi ile belirlenmesi. *KOCATEPEİİBFD, 23*(2), 195–208. DOI: 10.33707/akuiibfd.903563

Aytekin, S., ve Sakarya, Ş. (2013). Bist de işlem gören gıda işletmelerinin topsis yöntemi ile finansal performanslarının değerlendirilmesi,1. *Yönetim ve Ekonomi Araştırmaları Dergisi*, (21), 30–47.

Babiak, K., & Trendafilova, S. (2011). CSR and environmental responsibility: Motives and pressures to adopt green management practices. *Corporate Social Responsibility and Environmental Management, 18*(1), 11–24. DOI: 10.1002/csr.229

Badi, I., Bouraima, M. B., Qiu, Y., & Stević, Ž. (2024). Optimizing priority sequencing rules in parallel machine scheduling: An evaluation and selection approach using hybrid MCDM techniques. *Decision Making Advances, 2*(1), 22–31. DOI: 10.31181/dma21202422

Badi, I., Muhammad, L. J., Abubakar, M., & Bakır, M. (2022). Measuring sustainability performance indicators using FUCOM-MARCOS methods. *Operational Research in Engineering Sciences: Theory and Applications, 5*(2), 99–116. DOI: 10.31181/oresta040722060b

Bai, Y. (2011), Financing A Green Future An Examination Of China's Banking Sector For Green Finance, Master Thesis, Beijing, Lund University, Master of Science in Environmental Sciences Policy & Management.

Baker, D., & Evans, W. (2015). *Digital information strategies: From applications and content to libraries and people.* Chandos Publishing.

Balcerzak, A. P., & Pietrzak, M. B. (2016). *Application of TOPSIS method for analysis of sustainable development in European Union countries* (No. 22/2016). Institute of Economic Research Working Papers.

Balkenende, L., Teuwen, J., & Mann, R. M. (2022). Application of deep learning in breast cancer imaging. *Seminars in Nuclear Medicine, 52*(5), 584–596. DOI: 10.1053/j.semnuclmed.2022.02.003 PMID: 35339259

Banger, G. (2017). *Endüstri 4.0 Ekstra (1. Baskı).* Dorlion Yayınları.

Bannor, R. K., Arthur, K. K., Oppong, D., & Oppong-Kyeremeh, H. (2023). A comprehensive systematic review and bibliometric analysis of food fraud from a global perspective. *Journal of Agriculture and Food Research, 14*, 100686. DOI: 10.1016/j.jafr.2023.100686

Barca, M. (2005). Stratejik Yönetim Düşüncesinin Evrimi: Bilimsel Bir Disiplinin Oluşum Hikayesi. *Journal of Management Research/Yönetim Araştırmaları Dergisi, 5*(1).

Bardakçı, S. (2020). SWARA Yöntemi. In Bircan, H. (Ed.), *Çok kriterli karar verme problemlerinde kriter ağırlıklandırma yöntemleri* (1st ed.). Nobel Akademik Yayıncılık.

Barreto, L., Amaral, A., & Pereira, T. (2017). Industry 4.0 implications in logistics: An overview. *Procedia Manufacturing, 13*, 1245–1252. DOI: 10.1016/j.promfg.2017.09.045

Barrutia, J. M., Echebarria, C., Paredes, M. R., Hartmann, P., & Apaolaza, V. (2015). From Rio to Rio+ 20: Twenty years of participatory, long term oriented and monitored local planning? *Journal of Cleaner Production, 106*, 594–607. DOI: 10.1016/j.jclepro.2014.12.085

Basiago, A. D. (1998). Economic, social, and environmental sustainability in development theory and urban planning practice. *The Environmentalist, 19*(2), 145–161. DOI: 10.1023/A:1006697118620

Baxter, G. (2022). An assessment of water management at a major global hub airport: A case study of Frankfurt Airport. *International Journal of Environment, Agriculture and Biotechnology, 7*(1), 1–13. DOI: 10.22161/ijeab.71.1

Baxter, G., Wild, G., & Sabatini, R. (2014). A sustainable approach to airport design and operations: Case study of Munich airport. In Arora, M. (Ed.), *Proceedings of Practical Responses to Climate Change 2014*.

Baydaş, M., & Pamučar, D. (2022). Determining objective characteristics of MCDM methods under uncertainty: An exploration study with financial data. *Mathematics, 10*(7), 1115. DOI: 10.3390/math10071115

Bayraktutan, Y., & Özbilgin, M. (2015). Lojistik Maliyetler ve Lojistik Performans Ölçütleri. *Maliye Araştırmaları Dergisi, 1*(2), 95–112.

Bektaş, S. (2022). Türk sigorta sektörünün 2002-2021 dönemi için MEREC, LOP-COW, COCOSO, EDAS ÇKKV yöntemleri ile performansının değerlendrilmesi. *BDDK Bankacılık ve Finansal Piyasalar Dergisi, 16*(2), 247–283. DOI: 10.46520/bddkdergisi.1178359

Belas, J., Çera, G., Dvorský, J., & Čepel, M. (2021). Corporate social responsibility and sustainability issues of small-and medium-sized enterprises. *Corporate Social Responsibility and Environmental Management, 28*(2), 721–730. DOI: 10.1002/csr.2083

Ben Ammar, M., Labbene Ayachi, F., Cardoso de Paiva, A., Ksantini, R., & Mahjoubi, H. (2024). Harnessing Deep Learning for Early Breast Cancer Diagnosis: A Review of Datasets, Methods, Challenges, and Future Directions. *International Journal of Computing and Digital Systems, 16*(1), 1643–1661. DOI: 10.12785/ijcds/1601122

Ben Ayed, R., Hanana, M., Ercisli, S., Karunakaran, R., Rebai, A., & Moreau, F. (2022). Integration of innovative technologies in the agri-food sector: The fundamentals and practical case of DNA-based traceability of olives from fruit to oil. *Plants, 11*(9), 1230. DOI: 10.3390/plants11091230 PMID: 35567232

Berber, A. (2016). 100 Yıl Öncesine Bir Yolculuk: "Genel ve Endüstriyel Yönetim" ve Framsa'da Fayolizm-Taylorizm Kutuplaşması. *İstanbul Üniversitesi İşletme Fakültesi Dergisi*, 45, 118-132.

Bertoni, M. (2019). Multi-criteria decision making for sustainability and value assessment in early PSS design. *Sustainability (Basel), 11*(7), 1952. DOI: 10.3390/su11071952

Bhatia, A., & Tuli, S. (2018). Sustainability reporting practices in US and UK: An empirical comparison. *International Journal of Law and Management, 60*(4), 1034–1056. DOI: 10.1108/IJLMA-04-2017-0102

Bhushan, N., & Rai, K. (2004). The analytic hierarchy process. In *Strategic decision making: applying the analytic hierarchy process* (pp. 11–21). Springer London. DOI: 10.1007/978-1-85233-864-0_2

Bilişik, M. T. (2020). Endüstri 4.0 Vizyonu ve Üretim Süreçlerine Getirdiği Verimlilik.

Bin, A. (2023). Assessing the Role of Sustainable Construction Practices in the One Belt One Road Initiative: A Comparative Analysis of China and Southeast Asian Countries. *Journal of Digitainability* [DREAM]. *Realism & Mastery*, *2*(02), 39–44. DOI: 10.56982/dream.v2i02.86

Binder, S., Holdahl, E., Trinh, L., & Smith, J. H. (2020). Humanity's Fundamental Environmental Limits. *Human Ecology: an Interdisciplinary Journal*, *48*(2), 235–244. DOI: 10.1007/s10745-020-00140-w

Biswas, S., Natta, S., Ray, D. P., Mondal, P., & Saha, U. (2018). Til (*Sesamum indicum* L.)—An underexploited but promising oilseed with multifarious applications: A review. *International Journal of Bioresource Science*, *5*(2), 127–139. DOI: 10.30954/2347-9655.02.2018.8

Blackwell, B. F., DeVault, T. L., Fernández-Juricic, E., & Dolbeer, R. A. (2009). Wildlife collisions with aircraft: A missing component of land-use planning for airports. *Landscape and Urban Planning*, *93*(1), 1–9. DOI: 10.1016/j.landurbplan.2009.07.005

Böhringer, C. (2003). The Kyoto protocol: A review and perspectives. *Oxford Review of Economic Policy*, *19*(3), 451–466. DOI: 10.1093/oxrep/19.3.451

Bontempo, L., Camin, F., Larcher, R., Nicolini, G., Perini, M., & Rossmann, A. (2009). Coast and year effect on H, O and C stable isotope ratios of Tyrrhenian and Adriatic Italian olive oils. *Rapid Communications in Mass Spectrometry*, *23*(7), 1043–1048. DOI: 10.1002/rcm.3968 PMID: 19253913

Boobier, S., Hose, D. R. J., Blacker, A. J., & Nguyen, B. N. (2020). Machine Learning with Physicochemical Relationships: Solubility Prediction in Organic Solvents and Water. *Nature Communications*, *11*(1), 5753. DOI: 10.1038/s41467-020-19594-z PMID: 33188226

Börü, E. (2022). *Sürdürülebilirlik en iyi yatırım aracı. Fast Company, 13*. Şubat-Mart.

Brand, W. A., Coplen, T. B., Vogl, J., Rosner, M., & Prohaska, T. (2014). Assessment of international reference materials for isotope-ratio analysis (IUPAC technical report). *Pure and Applied Chemistry*, *86*(3), 425–467. DOI: 10.1515/pac-2013-1023

Breiman, L. (2001). Random forests. *Machine Learning*, *45*(1), 5–32. DOI: 10.1023/A:1010933404324

Breque, M., De Nul, L., & Petridis, A. (2021). *Industry 5.0: towards a sustainable, human-centric and resilient European industry.*

Bressanelli, G., Saccani, N., Pigosso, D. C. A., & Perona, M. (2020). Circular Economy in the WEEE industry : A systematic literature review and a research agenda. *Sustainable Production and Consumption*, *23*, 174–188. DOI: 10.1016/j.spc.2020.05.007

Breuer, H., Fichter, K., Lüdeke-Freund, F., & Tiemann, I. (2018). Sustainability-oriented business model development: Principles, criteria and tools. *International Journal of Entrepreneurial Venturing*, *10*(2), 256–286. DOI: 10.1504/IJEV.2018.092715

Brodny, J., & Tutak, M. (2021). Assessing the level of digital maturity of enterprises in the Central and Eastern European countries using the MCDM and Shannon's entropy methods. *PLoS One*, *16*(7), e0253965. DOI: 10.1371/journal.pone.0253965 PMID: 34228755

Brodny, J., & Tutak, M. (2023). The level of implementing sustainable development goal" Industry, innovation and infrastructure" of Agenda 2030 in the European Union countries: Application of MCDM methods. *Oeconomia Copernicana*, *14*(1), 47–102. DOI: 10.24136/oc.2023.002

Brodovskaya, E. V., Dombrovskaya, A. Y., Pyrma, R. V., & Azarov, A. A. (2020). Criteria for rating the level and quality of digitalization of the educational process in universities of the Russian Federation. *Vestnik Volgogradskogo Gosudarstvennogo Universiteta. Serii a 4, Istorii a , Regionovedenie, Mezhdunarodnye Otnoshenii a ,* *25*(2), 268-283.

Brotons, J. M., & Sansalvador, M. E. (2020). The relation between corporate social responsibility certification and financial performance: An empirical study in Spain. *Corporate Social Responsibility and Environmental Management*, *27*(3), 1465–1477. DOI: 10.1002/csr.1899

Brown, C. D., & Davis, H. T. (2006). Receiver operating characteristics curves and related decision measures: A tutorial. *Chemometrics and Intelligent Laboratory Systems*, *80*(1), 24–38. DOI: 10.1016/j.chemolab.2005.05.004

Brtnický, M., Pecina, V., Baltazár, T., Vašinová Galiová, M., Baláková, L., Bęś, A., & Radziemska, M. (2020). Environmental Impact Assessment of Potentially Toxic Elements in Soils Near the Runway at the International Airport in Central Europe. *Sustainability (Basel), 12*(17), 7224. DOI: 10.3390/su12177224

Budd, T. (2017). Environmental impacts and mitigation. In L. Budd & S. Ison (Eds.), *Air transport management: an international perspective* (1. baskı). Routledge.

Bulut, E., & Akçacı, T. (2017). Endüstri 4.0 ve İnovasyon Göstergeleri Kapsamında Türkiye Analizi. *ASSAM Uluslararası Hakemli Dergi, 7*, 58.

Büyüközkan, G., & Çifçi, G. (2012). A combined fuzzy AHP and fuzzy TOPSIS based strategic analysis of electronic service quality in healthcare industry. *Expert Systems with Applications, 39*(3), 2341–2354. DOI: 10.1016/j.eswa.2011.08.061

Büyüközkan, G., Çifçi, G., & Güleryüz, S. (2011). Strategic analysis of healthcare service quality using fuzzy AHP methodology. *Expert Systems with Applications, 38*(8), 9407–9424. DOI: 10.1016/j.eswa.2011.01.103

Calabrese, A., Levialdi Ghiron, N., & Tiburzi, L. (2021). 'Evolutions' and 'revolutions' in manufacturers' implementation of industry 4.0: A literature review, a multiple case study, and a conceptual framework. *Production Planning and Control, 32*(3), 213–227. DOI: 10.1080/09537287.2020.1719715

Campbell, I. B., Macdonald, S. J. F., & Procopiou, P. A. (2018). Medicinal chemistry in drug discovery in big pharma: Past, present and future. *Drug Discovery Today, 23*(2), 219–234. DOI: 10.1016/j.drudis.2017.10.007 PMID: 29031621

Cao, W., Chen, H. D., Yu, Y. W., Li, N., & Chen, W. Q. (2021). Changing Profiles of Cancer Burden Worldwide and in China: A Secondary Analysis of the Global Cancer Statistics 2020. *Chinese Medical Journal, 134*(7), 783–791. DOI: 10.1097/CM9.0000000000001474 PMID: 33734139

Carayannis, E. G., & Morawska-Jancelewicz, J. (2022). The Futures of Europe: Society 5.0 and Industry 5.0 as Driving Forces of Future Universities. *Journal of the Knowledge Economy, 13*(4), 3445–3471. DOI: 10.1007/s13132-021-00854-2 PMID: 40477679

Carli, R., Dotoli, M., & Pellegrino, R. (2018). Multi-criteria decision-making for sustainable metropolitan cities assessment. *Journal of Environmental Management, 226*, 46–61. DOI: 10.1016/j.jenvman.2018.07.075 PMID: 30107310

Carlucci, D., Ferreira, F. A. F., Schiuma, G., Jalali, M. S., & António, N. J. S. (2018). A Holistic Conception of Sustainable Banking: Adding Value with Fuzzy Cognitive Mapping. *Technological and Economic Development of Economy*, *24*(4), 1303–1322. DOI: 10.3846/20294913.2016.1266412

Ceballos, B., Lamata, M. T., & Pelta, D. A. (2016). A comparative analysis of multi-criteria decision-making methods. *Progress in Artificial Intelligence*, *5*(4), 315–322. DOI: 10.1007/s13748-016-0093-1

Cerin, P., & Scholtens, B. (2011). Linking responsible investments to societal influence: Motives, assessments and risks. *Sustainable Development (Bradford)*, *19*(2), 71–76. DOI: 10.1002/sd.508

Chaachouay, N., & Zidane, L. (2024). Plant-derived natural products: A source for drug discovery and development. *Drugs and Drug Candidates*, *3*(1), 184–207. DOI: 10.3390/ddc3010011

Chakraborty, S., & Mali, K. (2020). In Chakraborty, S., & Mali, K. (Eds.), *An Overview of Biomedical Image Analysis From the Deep Learning Perspective. Applications of Advanced Machine Intelligence in Computer Vision and Object Recognition: Emerging Research and Opportunities* (pp. 197–218). IGI Global., DOI: 10.4018/978-1-7998-2736-8.ch008

Chang, B., Chang, C. W., & Wu, C. H. (2011). Fuzzy DEMATEL method for developing supplier selection criteria. *Expert Systems with Applications*, *38*(3), 1850–1858. DOI: 10.1016/j.eswa.2010.07.114

Chang, T. H. (2014). Fuzzy VIKOR method: A case study of the hospital service evaluation in Taiwan. *Information Sciences*, *271*, 196–212. DOI: 10.1016/j.ins.2014.02.118

Chao, C. C., Lirn, T. C., & Lin, H. C. (2017). Indicators and evaluation model for analyzing environmental protection performance of airports. *Journal of Air Transport Management*, *63*, 61–70. DOI: 10.1016/j.jairtraman.2017.05.007

Chen, C. Y., & Huang, J. J. (2022). A novel DEMATEL approach by considering normalization and invertibility. *Symmetry*, *14*(6), 1109. DOI: 10.3390/sym14061109

Chen, F. H. (2021). Sustainable education through e-learning: The case study of ilearn2. 0. *Sustainability (Basel)*, *13*(18), 10186. DOI: 10.3390/su131810186

Chen, M., Mao, S., & Lıu, Y. (2014). Big Data: A Survey. *Mobile Networks and Applications*, *19*(2), 171–209. DOI: 10.1007/s11036-013-0489-0

Chermack, T. J., & Kasshanna, B. K. (2007). The Use and Misuse of SWOT Analysis and Implications for HRD Professionals. *Human Resource Development International, 10*(4), 383–399. DOI: 10.1080/13678860701718760

Chew, A.K., Afzal, M.A.F., Kaplan, Z., Collins, E.M., Gattani, S., Misra, M., Chandrasekaran, A., Leswing, K., Halls, M.D. (2025). Leveraging high-throughput molecular simulations and machine learning for the design of chemical mixtures. npj Computational Materials, 11, 72. DOI: 10.1038/s41524-025-01552-2

Chew, A. K., Sender, M., Kaplan, Z., Chandrasekaran, A., Chief Elk, J., Browning, A. R., Kwak, H. S., Halls, M. D., & Afzal, M. A. F. (2024). Advancing material property prediction: Using physics-informed machine learning models for viscosity. *Journal of Cheminformatics, 16*(1), 31. DOI: 10.1186/s13321-024-00820-5 PMID: 38486289

Chichilnisky, G. (1999). What is sustainable development? In *Man-Made Climate Change: Economic Aspects and Policy Options* (pp. 42–82). Physica-Verlag HD. DOI: 10.1007/978-3-642-47035-6_4

Chong, A. Y. L., Li, B., Ngai, E. W. T., Ch'ng, E., & Lee, F. (2016). Predicting online product sales via online reviews, sentiments, and promotion strategies. *International Journal of Operations & Production Management, 36*(4), 358–383. DOI: 10.1108/IJOPM-03-2015-0151

Chowdhury, P., & Paul, S. K. (2020). Applications of MCDM methods in research on corporate sustainability: A systematic literature review. *Management of Environmental Quality, 31*(2), 385–405. DOI: 10.1108/MEQ-12-2019-0284

Çilek, A., & Şeyranlıoğlu, O. (2023). Mobil bankacılık kullanımını etkileyen faktörlerin BWM ve FUCOM yöntemiyle analizi. Bal, H., Kandır, S. Y., & Ülbeği, İ. D. (Ed.), *Ekonomi ve Yönetim Bilimlerinde Güncel Akademik Araştırmalar II* (pp. 131-155). Ankara: Akademisyen Publishing.

Cinelli, M., Coles, S. R., & Kirwan, K. (2014). Analysis of the potentials of multi criteria decision analysis methods to conduct sustainability assessment. *Ecological Indicators, 46*, 138–148. DOI: 10.1016/j.ecolind.2014.06.011

Cismaru, D. M., Gazzola, P., Ciochina, R. S., & Leovaridis, C. (2018). The rise of digital intelligence: Challenges for public relations education and practices. *Kybernetes, 47*(10), 1924–1940. DOI: 10.1108/K-03-2018-0145

Cohen, J. (2017). How many people can the Earth support? *The Journal of Population and Sustainability, 2*(1). DOI: 10.3197/jps.2017.2.1.37

Collins, B. C. (2022). *Game Theory, Multiple-Criteria Decision Making, and Sustainability Focused Decisions for Mineral Development*. McGill University.

Comendador, V. F. G., Valdés, R. M. A., & Lisker, B. (2019). A holistic approach to the environmental certification of green airports. *Sustainability (Basel), 11*(15), 4043. DOI: 10.3390/su11154043

Cooper, M. (2024). Understanding Supplier Selection Criteria: Perspectives from Procurement Professionals in Diverse Industries.

Creswell, J. W. (2013). *Research Design: Qualitative, Quantitative and Mixed Method Approaches* (4th Editio). *Sage (Atlanta, Ga.)*.

Cui, C., Liu, Y., Liu, Y., Cui, X., Sun, Z., Du, Z., Wu, K., Jiang, X., Mei, H., & Zheng, Y. (2021). Genome-wide association study of seed coat color in sesame (*Sesamum indicum* L.). *PLoS One*, *16*(5), e0251526. DOI: 10.1371/journal.pone.0251526 PMID: 34019554

Cundill, G., & Fabricius, C. (2010). Monitoring the governance dimension of natural resource co-management. *Ecology and Society*, *15*(1), art15. DOI: 10.5751/ES-03346-150115

Dağdeviren, M., Eraslan, E., Kurt, M., & Dizdar, E. N. (2005). Tedarikçi seçimi problemine analitik ağ süreci ile alternatif bir yaklaşım. *Teknoloji, 8*(2), 115-122. https://eds.p.ebscohost.com/eds/pdfviewer/pdfviewer?vid=0&sid=9071ff55-b7c3-41a3-8be6-7e9fa7c72714%40redis

Daley, B. (2010). *Air Transport and the Environment* (1. baskı). Ashgate.

Daley, B., Dimitriou, D., & Thomas, C. (2008). The environmental sustainability of aviation and tourism. In Anne Graham & P. Forsyth (Eds.), *Aviation and Tourism* (1. baskı, pp. 239–253). Routledge.

Daley, S. K., & Cordell, G. A. (2021). Alkaloids in contemporary drug discovery to meet global disease needs. *Molecules (Basel, Switzerland), 26*(13), 3800. DOI: 10.3390/molecules26133800 PMID: 34206470

Danang Kumara Hadi, A. P. (2023). Evaluation of Sustainability Supply Chain Performance in the Food Industry: A Case Study. *Journal Teknik Industri*, 1-11.

Darms, I. (2023). Fuzzy Analytic Hierarchy Process Utilization in Government Projects: A Systematic Review of Implementation Processes.

Das, M. C., & Sarkar, B. (2024). Exploring incisive decision for performance assessment of materials under utopian environment: A pluri-disciplinary approach.

Davis, R., Sessions, B. O., & Check, A. R. (2015). *Industry 4.0. Digitalisition for Productivity and Growth, European Parliament*. Members' Research Service.

De Vries, J. (1994). The industrial revolution and the industrious revolution. *The Journal of Economic History*, *54*(2), 249–270. DOI: 10.1017/S0022050700014467

Deepu, T. S., & Ravi, V. (2021). Supply chain digitalization: An integrated MCDM approach for inter-organizational information systems selection in an electronic supply chain. *International Journal of Information Management Data Insights*, *1*(2), 100038. DOI: 10.1016/j.jjimei.2021.100038

Delaney, J. S. (2004). ESOL: Estimating Aqueous Solubility Directly from Molecular Structure. *Journal of Chemical Information and Computer Sciences*, *44*(3), 1000–1005. DOI: 10.1021/ci034243x PMID: 15154768

Derici, S. (2024). Digitalization Concept and the Historical Evolution of Digitalization. Ahmed, E. M. (Ed.), *Developing Digital Inclusion Through Globalization and Digitalization* (pp. 93-110). USA: IGI Global. DOI: 10.4018/979-8-3693-4111-7.ch006

Derici, S., & Doğan, N. Ö. (2021). Hasta perspektifinden hastanelerde hizmet kalitesi: Bulanık AHP ile bir uygulama. *Nevşehir Hacı Bektaş Veli Üniversitesi SBE Dergisi*, *11*(3), 1155–1177. DOI: 10.30783/nevsosbilen.994496

Devezas, T., & Sarygulov, A. (2017). *Industry 4.0*. Springer. DOI: 10.1007/978-3-319-49604-7

Dewi, S. K., & Utama, D. M. (2021). A New Hybrid Whale Optimization Algorithm for Green Vehicle Routing Problem. *Systems Science & Control Engineering*, *9*(1), 61–72. DOI: 10.1080/21642583.2020.1863276

Dhurkari, R. K. (2022). MCDM methods: Practical difficulties and future directions for improvement. *Operations Research*, *56*(4), 2221–2233. DOI: 10.1051/ro/2022060

Diakoulaki, D., Mavrotas, G., & Papayannakis, L. (1995). Determining Objective Weights in Multiple Criteria Problems: The CRITIC Method. *Computers & Operations Research*, *22*(7), 763–770. DOI: 10.1016/0305-0548(94)00059-H

Digital Intelligenge Index. (2020). Digital in the time of covid trust in the digital economy and Its evolution across 90 economies as the planet paused for a pandemic, https://digitalplanet.tufts.edu/wp-content/uploads/2022/09/digital-intelligence-index .pdf, (accessed on 01 September 2024).

Dimitriou, D., Voskaki, A., & Sartzetaki, M. (2014). Airports environmental management: Results from the evaluation of European airports environmental plans. [IJISSCM]. *International Journal of Information Systems and Supply Chain Management*, *7*(1), 1–14. DOI: 10.4018/IJISSCM.2014010101

Dinica, V., Lund-Durlachery, D., & Reiser, D. (2019). *Challenges for tourism-transitioning to corporate sustainability and responsibility*. Springer International Publishing.

Doane, D., & MacGillivray, A. (2001). Economic sustainability: The business of staying in business. *New Economics Foundation*, *1*, 52.

dos Santos, A. J., Mancini, S. D., Frutuoso Roveda, J. A., Ewbank, H., & Roveda, S. R. M. M. (2020). A fuzzy assessment method to airport waste management: A case study of Congonhas Airport, Brazil. *Journal of Air Transport Management*, *87*(January), 101838. DOI: 10.1016/j.jairtraman.2020.101838

Dos Santos, P. H., Neves, S. M., Sant'Anna, D. O., De Oliveira, C. H., & Carvalho, H. D. (2019). The analytic hierarchy process supporting decision making for sustainable development: An overview of applications. *Journal of Cleaner Production*, *212*, 119–138. DOI: 10.1016/j.jclepro.2018.11.270

Duan, Y., Edwards, J. S., & Dwivedi, Y. K. (2019). Artificial intelligence for decision making in the era of Big Data–evolution, challenges and research agenda. *International Journal of Information Management*, *48*, 63–71. DOI: 10.1016/j.ijinfomgt.2019.01.021

Dubey, A., & Lal, R. (2009). Carbon footprint and sustainability of agricultural production systems in Punjab, India, and Ohio, USA. *Journal of Crop Improvement*, *23*(4), 332–350. DOI: 10.1080/15427520902969906

Duong, T. T. T., & Thao, N. X. (2021). TOPSIS model based on entropy and similarity measure for market segment selection and evaluation. *Asian Journal of Economics and Banking*, *5*(2), 194–203. DOI: 10.1108/AJEB-12-2020-0106

Durak, İ., Arslan, H. M., & Özdemir, Y. (2022). Application of AHP–TOPSIS methods in technopark selection of technology companies: Turkish case. *Technology Analysis and Strategic Management*, *34*(10), 1109–1123. DOI: 10.1080/09537325.2021.1925242

Duran, Z. (2023). Evaluation of Supply Chain Resilience in N-11 Countries by MEREC Based EDAS, MARCOS, WASPAS Integrated Method. *Yildiz Social Science Review*, *9*(1).

Durmaz, V. (2018). Havaalanı Çevre Etkileşimi. In Oktal, H. (Ed.), *Havaalanı Sistemi*. Anadolu Üniversitesi Açıköğretim Yayınları.

Durmić, E. (2019). The evaluation of the criteria for sustainable supplier selection by using the FUCOM method. *Operational Research in Engineering Sciences: Theory and Applications*, *2*(1), 91–107. DOI: 10.31181/oresta1901085d

Durmić, E., Stević, Ž., Chatterjee, P., Vasiljević, M., & Tomašević, M. (2020). Sustainable supplier selection using combined FUCOM–Rough SAW model. *Reports in Mechanical Engineering*, *1*(1), 34–43. DOI: 10.31181/rme200101034c

Duško, T., & Bozanic, D. (2023). Optimizing military decision-making: Application of the FUCOM–EWAA–COPRAS-G MCDM model. *Acadlore Transactions on Applied Mathematics and Statistics*, *1*(3), 148–160. DOI: 10.56578/atams010303

Dwivedi, P. P., & Sharma, D. K. (2022). Application of Shannon entropy and CoCoSo methods in selection of the most appropriate engineering sustainability components. *Cleaner Materials*, *5*, 100118. DOI: 10.1016/j.clema.2022.100118

Ecer, F. (2021a). Sürdürülebilir tedarikçi seçimi: FUCOM sübjektif ağırlıklandırma yöntemi temelli MAIRCA yaklaşımı. *Mehmet Akif Ersoy Üniversitesi İktisadi ve İdari Bilimler Fakültesi Dergisi*, *8*(1), 26–48. DOI: 10.30798/makuiibf.691693

Ecer, F. (2021b). FUCOM sübjektif ağırlıklandırma yöntemi ile rüzgâr çiftliği yer seçimini etkileyen faktörlerin analizi. *Pamukkale Üniversitesi Mühendislik Bilimleri Dergisi*, *27*(1), 24–34. DOI: 10.5505/pajes.2020.93271

Ecer, F., & Aycin, E. (2023). Novel comprehensive MEREC weighting-based score aggregation model for measuring innovation performance: The case of G7 countries. *Informatica (Vilnius)*, *34*(1), 53–83. DOI: 10.15388/22-INFOR494

Ecer, F., & Güneş, E. (2024). G7 Ülkelerinin Bilgi İletişim Teknoloji Düzeylerini Belirleme: MEREC-CRITIC Entegre Ağırlıklı CoCoSo Metodolojisi. *Journal of Mehmet Akif Ersoy University Economics and Administrative Sciences Faculty*, *11*(1), 219–242.

Ecer, F., Pamucar, D., Zolfani, S. H., & Eshkalag, M. K. (2019). Sustainability assessment of OPEC countries: Application of a multiple attribute decision making tool. *Journal of Cleaner Production*, *241*, 118324. DOI: 10.1016/j.jclepro.2019.118324

Ecer, F., & Zolfani, S. H. (2022). Evaluating economic freedom via a multi-criteria MEREC-DNMA model-based composite system: Case of OPEC countries. *Technological and Economic Development of Economy*, *28*(4), 1158–1181. DOI: 10.3846/tede.2022.17152

Eğilmez, Ö, Savaş, B . (2021). İş Etiği Dinamiklerinin Dematel Yöntemi ile İncelenmesi . İnsan ve Toplum Bilimleri Araştırmaları Dergisi, 10 (2), 1580-1600 .

El-kassar, A., & Kumar, S. (2019). Social Change Green innovation and organizational performance : The in fl uence of big data and the moderating role of management commitment and HR practices. *Technological Forecasting and Social Change, 144*, 483–498. DOI: 10.1016/j.techfore.2017.12.016

Elmrabit, N., Zhou, F., Li, F., & Zhou, H. 2020. Evaluation of machine learning algorithms for anomaly detection. In 2020 International Conference on Cyber Security and Protection of Digital Services (Cyber Security), 1-8. IEEE. DOI: 10.1109/CyberSecurity49315.2020.9138871

Eraslan, B., & Uysal, A. (2024). Endüstri 4.0 Çağında Türkiye: Akıllı Fabrikaların Yükselişi ve Mekânsal Dinamikler. *Mavi Atlas, 12*(2), 505–517. DOI: 10.18795/gumusmaviatlas.1487666

Erol, Y. (2019). Stratejik Yönetimde SWOT Analizi ve Bir İşletmede Uygulanması (Doctoral Dissertation, İstanbul Kültür Üniversitesi/Sosyal Bilimler Enstitüsü/İşletme Anabilim Dalı).

Erol, H. M. (2006). *Dünyada ve Türkiye'de bankacılık sektörünün gelişimi ve Türkiye'de kamu bankalarının yeniden yapılandırılması*. Marmara Üniversitesi Sosyal Bilimler Enstitüsü.

Ersoy, N. (2022). OECD ve AB Üyesi Ülkelerin İnovasyon Performanslarinin Merec-Marcos Bütünleşik Modeli İle Ölçümü. *Dokuz Eylül Üniversitesi Sosyal Bilimler Enstitüsü Dergisi, 24*(3), 1039–1063. DOI: 10.16953/deusosbil.1106249

Ersöz, B. (2020). Yeni Nesil Web Paradigması-Web 4.0. *Bilgisayar Bilimleri ve Teknolojileri Dergisi, 1*(2), 58–65.

Ertuğrul, İ., & Deniz, G. (2018). 4.0 Dünyası: Pazarlama 4.0 ve Endüstri 4.0. *Bitlis Eren Üniversitesi Sosyal Bilimler Dergisi, 7*(1), 143–170.

Eskandarpour, M., Masehian, E., Soltani, R., & Khosrojerdi, A. (2014). A reverse logistics network for recovery systems and a robust metaheuristic solution approach. *International Journal of Advanced Manufacturing Technology, 74*(9–12), 1393–1406. DOI: 10.1007/s00170-014-6045-7

Eslami, M. H., Jafari, H., Achtenhagen, L., Carlbäck, J., & Wong, A. (2021). Financial performance and supply chain dynamic capabilities: The Moderating Role of Industry 4.0 technologies. *International Journal of Production Research, 62*(22), 8092–8109. DOI: 10.1080/00207543.2021.1966850

EUROCONTROL. (2021). *EUROCONTROL Comprehensive Assessment for Thursday, 25 November 2021*. https://www.eurocontrol.int/sites/default/files/2021-11/covid19-eurocontrol-comprehensive-air-traffic-assessment-25112021.pdf

European Commission. Transitions Performance Index 2021, https://projects.research-and-innovation.ec.europa.eu/en/knowledge-publications-tools-and-data/interactive-reports/transition-performance-index-2021

Everest, T., Savaşkan, G. S., Or, A., & Özcan, H. (2022). Suitable site selection by using full consistency method (FUCOM): A case study for maize cultivation in northwest Turkey. *Environment, Development and Sustainability*, *26*(1), 1831–1850. DOI: 10.1007/s10668-022-02787-5 PMID: 36506642

Everstine, K., Spink, J., & Kennedy, S. (2013). Economically motivated adulteration (EMA) of food: Common characteristics of EMA incidents. *Journal of Food Protection*, *76*(4), 723–735. DOI: 10.4315/0362-028X.JFP-12-399 PMID: 23575142

Ezhani, W., El Bakkali, M., Amenzou, N., Ebn Touhami, M., Taous, F., & Habsaoui, A. (2025). Detection of adulteration in Moroccan and Egyptian sesame oil using Isotopic analysis and Infrared spectroscopy. *Journal of Applied and Natural Science*, *17*(1), 186–192. DOI: 10.31018/jans.v17i1.6171

Fadzlillah, M., Che Man, Y. B., & Rohman, A. (2014). FTIR spectroscopy combined with chemometric for analysis of sesame oil adulterated with corn oil. *International Journal of Food Properties*, *17*(6), 1275–1282. DOI: 10.1080/10942912.2012.689409

Faulds, D. J., & Raju, P. S. (2019). An Interview with Chuck Martin on The Internet of Things. *Business Horizons*, *62*(1), 27–33. DOI: 10.1016/j.bushor.2018.08.009

Fazlollahtabar, H., Smailbašić, A., & Stević, Ž. (2019). FUCOM method in group decision-making: Selection of forklift in a warehouse. *Decision Making: Applications in Management and Engineering*, *2*(1), 49–65. DOI: 10.31181/dmame1901065f

Fetting, C. (2020). The European green deal. ESDN Report, December, 2(9), 53.

Filatovas, E., Marcozzi, M., Mostarda, L., & Paulavičius, R. (2022). A MCDM-based framework for blockchain consensus protocol selection. *Expert Systems with Applications*, *204*, 117609. DOI: 10.1016/j.eswa.2022.117609

Fontela, E. ve Gabus, A., (1974). "DEMATEL, innovative methods, Technical Report no. 2, Structural analysis of the world problematique". Battelle Geneva Research Institute

Foster, T., Pérez-Blanco, C. D., & Schmidt, G. (2024). *Monitoring agricultural water use: challenges and solutions for sustainable water management.*, DOI: 10.19103/AS.2023.0123.26

Franchuk, G. M., Antonov, A. M., Madzhd, S. M., & Zagoruy, Y. V. (2005). Analysis of pollution of ground waters in the airport zone. *Proceedings of the National Aviation University*. DOI: 10.18372/2306-1472.24.1159

Fu, G., Liu, C., Zhou, R., Sun, T., & Zhang, Q. (2017). Classification for High Resolution Remote Sensing Imagery Using a Fully Convolutional Network. *Remote Sensing (Basel)*, *9*(5), 498. DOI: 10.3390/rs9050498

Fuji, Y., Ohtsuki, T., & Matsufuji, H. (2018). Accumulation and subcellular localization of acteoside in sesame plants (*Sesamum indicum* L.). *ACS Omega*, *3*(12), 17287–17294. DOI: 10.1021/acsomega.8b02798

Fu, Y., & Zhu, J. (2019). Operation Mechanisms for Intelligent Logistics System: A Blockchain Perspective. *IEEE Access : Practical Innovations, Open Solutions*, *7*, 144202–144213. DOI: 10.1109/ACCESS.2019.2945078

Gabaçlı, N., & Uzunöz, M. (2017, October). IV. Sanayi Devrimi: Endüstri 4.0 ve Otomotiv Sektörü. *In ICPESS (International Congress on Politic, Economic and Social Studies)* (No. 3).

Gabus, A. ve Fontela, E., (1973). "Perceptions of the world problematique: Communication procedure, communicating with those bearing collective responsibility (DEMATEL Report no. 1)". Battelle Geneva Research Centre.

Gachnang, P., Ehrenthal, J. C. F., Hanne, T., & Dornberger, R. (2022). Quantum Computing in Supply Chain Management State of the Art and Research Directions. *Asian Journal of Logistics Management*, *1*(1), 57–73. DOI: 10.14710/ajlm.2022.14325

Galushka, M., Swain, C., Browne, F., Mulvenna, M. D., Bond, R., & Gray, D. (2021). Prediction of chemical compounds properties using a deep learning model. *Neural Computing & Applications*, *33*(20), 13345–13366. DOI: 10.1007/s00521-021-05961-4

Galvin-King, P., Haughey, S. A., & Elliott, C. T. (2018). Herb and spice fraud: The drivers, challenges and detection. *Food Control*, *88*, 85–97. DOI: 10.1016/j.foodcont.2017.12.031

Gamage, S., & Samarabandu, J. (2020). Deep learning methods in network intrusion detection: A survey and an objective comparison. *Journal of Network and Computer Applications*, *169*, 102767. DOI: 10.1016/j.jnca.2020.102767

Gamal, A., Abdel-Basset, M., Hezam, I. M., Sallam, K. M., & Hameed, I. A. (2023). An Interactive Multi-Criteria Decision-Making Approach for Autonomous Vehicles and Distributed Resources Based on Logistic Systems: Challenges for a Sustainable Future. *Sustainability (Basel), 15*(17), 12844. DOI: 10.3390/su151712844

Gangwal, A., & Lavecchia, A. (2024). Unleashing the Power of Generative AI in Drug Discovery. *Drug Discovery Today, 29*(6), 103992. DOI: 10.1016/j.drudis.2024.103992 PMID: 38663579

Garg, P., Singhal, G., Kulkarni, P., Horne, D., Salgia, R., & Singhal, S. S. (2024). Artificial intelligence–driven computational approaches in the development of anticancer drugs. *Cancers (Basel), 16*(23), 3884. DOI: 10.3390/cancers16223884 PMID: 39594838

Gasco, L., Asensio, C., & de Arcas, G. (2017). Communicating airport noise emission data to the general public. *The Science of the Total Environment, 586*, 836–848. DOI: 10.1016/j.scitotenv.2017.02.063 PMID: 28214112

Gaudêncio, S. P., Bayram, E., Lukić Bilela, L., Cueto, M., Díaz-Marrero, A. R., Haznedaroglu, B. Z., Jimenez, C., Mandalakis, M., Pereira, F., Reyes, F., & Tasdemir, D. (2023). Advanced methods for natural products discovery: Bioactivity screening, dereplication, metabolomics profiling, genomic sequencing, databases and informatic tools, and structure elucidation. *Marine Drugs, 21*(5), 308. DOI: 10.3390/md21050308 PMID: 37233502

Gavade, R. K. (2014). Multi-Criteria Decision Making: An overview of different selection problems and methods. *International Journal of Computer Science and Information Technologies, 5*(4), 5643–5646.

Gawer, A. (2022). Digital platforms and ecosystems: Remarks on the dominant organizational forms of the digital age. *Innovation (North Sydney, N.S.W.), 24*(1), 110–124. DOI: 10.1080/14479338.2021.1965888

General Directorate of Health Services. (2016). *Healthcare quality standards-hospital (version-5, revision-01)*. Ankara: Ministry of Health of the Republic of Turkey, General Directorate of Health Services, Department of Quality and Accreditation in Health. Accessed at: https://dosyamerkez.saglik.gov.tr/Eklenti/3460/0/skshastanesetiv5r1pdf.pdf Access Date: 12.04.2024.

General Directorate of Health Services. (2020). *Healthcare quality standards-hospital (version 6.1)*. Ankara: Ministry of Health of the Republic of Turkey, General Directorate of Health Services, Department of Quality and Accreditation in Health. Accessed at: https://www.saglikpersoneli.com.tr/images/upload/Ek-2._SKS_Hastane_Surum_6_pdf_tYklayYnYz.pdf Access Date: 12.04.2024.

General Directorate of Health Services. (n.d.). *SKS kospitals (versions)*. Ministry of Health of the Republic of Turkey, General Directorate of Health Services, Department of Quality and Accreditation in Health and Employee Rights. Accessed at: https://shgmkalitedb.saglik.gov.tr/TR,9064/sks-hastaneversiyonlar.html Access Date: 12.04.2024.

Gerami, R., Sadeghi Joni, S., Akhondi, N., Etemadi, A., Fosouli, M., Foroughi Eghbal, A., & Souri, Z. (2022). A literature review on the imaging methods for breast cancer. *International Journal of Physiology, Pathophysiology and Pharmacology, 14*(3), 171. PMID: 35891932

Gervasi, R., Mastrogiacomo, L., & Franceschini, F. (2020). A conceptual framework to evaluate human-robot collaboration. *International Journal of Advanced Manufacturing Technology, 108*(3), 841–865. DOI: 10.1007/s00170-020-05363-1

Gharby, S., Harhar, H., Bouzoubaa, Z., Asdadi, A., El Yadini, A., & Charrouf, Z. (2017). Chemical characterization and oxidative stability of seeds and oil of sesame grown in Morocco. *Journal of the Saudi Society of Agricultural Sciences, 16*(2), 105–111. DOI: 10.1016/j.jssas.2015.03.004

Gharby, S., Harhar, H., Guillaume, D., Haddad, A., Matthäus, B., & Charrouf, Z. (2011). Oxidative stability of edible argan oil: A two-year study. *Lebensmittel-Wissenschaft + Technologie, 44*(1), 1–8. DOI: 10.1016/j.lwt.2010.07.003

Ghobakhloo, M., Iranmanesh, M., Foroughi, B., Tseng, M. L., Nikbin, D., & Khanfar, A. A. (2025). Industry 4.0 digital transformation and opportunities for supply chain resilience: A comprehensive review and a strategic roadmap. *Production Planning and Control, 36*(1), 61–91. DOI: 10.1080/09537287.2023.2252376

Ghorabaee, M. K., Zavadskas, E. K., Amiri, M., & Turskis, Z. (2016). Extended EDAS method for fuzzy multi-criteria decision-making: An application to supplier selection. *International Journal of Computers, Communications & Control, 11*(3), 358–371. DOI: 10.15837/ijccc.2016.3.2557

Ghosh, D., Muhuri, B. R., Mahapatra, G. S., & Mahapatra, B. S. (2024). Integrated MEREC-CoCoSo approach using score function of Neutrosophic for location selection of special economic zone. *Neutrosophic Sets and Systems, 73*, 694–717.

Ghosh, S., & Bhattacharya, M. (2022). Analyzing the impact of COVID-19 on the financial performance of the hospitality and tourism industries: An ensemble MCDM approach in the Indian context. *International Journal of Contemporary Hospitality Management, 34*(8), 3113–3142. DOI: 10.1108/IJCHM-11-2021-1328

Giampietro, R. R., Cabral, M. V. G., Lima, S. A. M., Weber, S. A. T., & Nunes-Nogueira, V. S. (2020). Accuracy and effectiveness of mammography versus mammography and tomosynthesis for population-based breast cancer screening: A systematic review and meta-analysis. *Scientific Reports, 10*(1), 7991. DOI: 10.1038/s41598-020-64802-x PMID: 32409756

Gilmer, J., Schoenholz, S. S., Riley, P. F., Vinyals, O., & Dahl, G. E. (2017). Neural Message Passing for Quantum Chemistry. *Proceedings of the 34th International Conference on Machine Learning*, 70, 1263–1272.

Giordano, D., Biancaniello, C., Argenio, M. A., & Facchiano, A. (2022). Drug design by pharmacophore and virtual screening approach. *Pharmaceuticals (Basel, Switzerland), 15*(5), 646. DOI: 10.3390/ph15050646 PMID: 35631472

Gobble, M. M. (2018). Digitalization, digitization, and innovation. *Research Technology Management, 61*(4), 56–59. DOI: 10.1080/08956308.2018.1471280

Goker, N., Karsak, E. E., & Dursun, M. (2022). An integrated QFD and common weight DEA-based fuzzy MCDM framework for performance ranking of countries. *Social Indicators Research, 159*(1), 1–22. DOI: 10.1007/s11205-021-02751-2

Göktaş, P., & Berkay, A. K. S. U. (2021). Endüstri 4.0 ile Beraber Blok Zincir (Blockchain) Teknolojisi, Bitcoin ve Sanal Paraların Gelecekteki Olası Etkileri. *Süleyman Demirel Üniversitesi İktisadi ve İdari Bilimler Fakültesi Dergisi, 26*(3), 279–293.

Goodland, R. (1995). The concept of environmental sustainability. *Annual Review of Ecology and Systematics, 26*(1), 1–24. DOI: 10.1146/annurev.es.26.110195.000245

Görçün, Ö. F., Mishra, A. R., Aytekin, A., Simic, V., & Korucuk, S. (2024). Evaluation of Industry 4.0 strategies for digital transformation in the automotive manufacturing industry using an integrated fuzzy decision-making model. *Journal of Manufacturing Systems, 74*, 922–948. DOI: 10.1016/j.jmsy.2024.05.005

Gössling, S., & Upham, P. (2009). Introduction: Aviation and Climate Change in Context. In Gössling, S., & Upham, P. (Eds.), *Climate Change and Aviation: Issues, Challenges and Solutions*. Springer.

Göv, S. A., & Erdoğan, D. (2020). Dördüncü Endüstri Devriminin (Endüstri 4.0) Neresindeyiz? *İstanbul Gelişim Üniversitesi Sosyal Bilimler Dergisi, 7*(2), 299-318.

Graham, A. (2023). *Managing Airports: An International Perspective* (6th ed.). Routledge.

Gray, J., & Rumpe, B. (2015). Models for digitalization. *Software & Systems Modeling, 14*(4), 1319–1320. DOI: 10.1007/s10270-015-0494-9

Greenaway, R. L., & Jelfs, K. E. (2021). Integrating computational and experimental workflows for accelerated organic materials discovery. *Advanced Materials*, *33*(11), 2004831. DOI: 10.1002/adma.202004831 PMID: 33565203

Greer, F., Rakas, J., & Horvath, A. (2020a). Airports and environmental sustainability: A comprehensive review. *Environmental Research Letters*, *15*(10), 103007. DOI: 10.1088/1748-9326/abb42a

Grosse, E. H., Sgarbossa, F., Berlin, C., & Neumann, W. P. (2023). Human-centric production and logistics system design and management: transitioning from Industry 4.0 to Industry 5.0. In *International Journal of Production Research* (Vol. 61, Issue 22, pp. 7749–7759). Taylor and Francis Ltd. DOI: 10.1080/00207543.2023.2246783

Grover, V., & Malhotra, M. K. (1997). Business process reengineering: A tutorial on the concept, evolution, method, technology and application. *Journal of Operations Management*, *15*(3), 193–213. DOI: 10.1016/S0272-6963(96)00104-0

Gubán, M. ve Kovács, G. (2017). Industry 4.0 Conceptıon. *Acta Technica Corviniensis-Bulletin of Engineering*, *10*(1), 111–115.

Gubbi, J., Buyya, R., Marusic, S., & Palaniswami, M. (2013). Internet of Things (IoT): A vision, architectural elements, and future directions. *Future Generation Computer Systems*, *29*(7), 1645–1660. DOI: 10.1016/j.future.2013.01.010

Gudehus, T., & Kotzab, H. (2012). *Comprehensive Logistics* (2nd ed.). Springer. DOI: 10.1007/978-3-642-24367-7

Guha, R., & Velegol, D. (2023). Harnessing Shannon entropy-based descriptors in machine learning models to enhance the prediction accuracy of molecular properties. *Journal of Cheminformatics*, *15*(1), 54. DOI: 10.1186/s13321-023-00712-0 PMID: 37211605

Gulledge, T., & Chavusholu, T. (2008). Automating the construction of supply chain key performance indicators. *Industrial Management & Data Systems*, *108*(6), 750–774. DOI: 10.1108/02635570810883996

Gümüş, Y. (2009). Lojistik Faaliyetlerin Rekabet Stratejileri ve İşletme Kârı İle Olan İlişkisi. *Muhasebe ve Finansman Dergisi*, 97–114.

Güney, T. (2016). AB ÜYESİ ÜLKELERDE YÖNETİŞİMİN SÜRDÜRÜLEBİLİR KALKINMA ÜZERİNDEKİ ETKİSİ: PANEL VERİ ANALİZİ. *Süleyman Demirel Üniversitesi İktisadi ve İdari Bilimler Fakültesi Dergisi*, *21*(1), 193–205.

Gür, E. D., Canan, G. O., Hamutoğlu, N. B., Kaya, U. G., & Demirtaş, T. T. (2019). The relation of lifelong learning trends, digital literacy levels and usage of web 2.0 tools, with social entrepreneurship characteristics. *Croation Journal of Education, 21*(1), 45–76. DOI: 10.15516/cje.v21i1.2989

Gyani, J., Ahmed, A., & Haq, M. A. (2022). MCDM and various prioritization methods in AHP for CSS: A comprehensive review. *IEEE Access : Practical Innovations, Open Solutions, 10*, 33492–33511. DOI: 10.1109/ACCESS.2022.3161742

Hadizadeh, M., Khodaparast, P., Ghasemi, A., & Fakhrzad, M. B. (2023). Analysis of supply chain anti-fragility in the textile industry using the Best-Worst method and CoCoSo. *Journal of Advertising and Sales Management, 4*(3), 426-440. DOI: JABM.3.2.15564.0954

Hall, J. K., Daneke, G. A., & Lenox, M. J. (2010). Sustainable development and entrepreneurship: Past contributions and future directions. *Journal of Business Venturing, 25*(5), 439–448. DOI: 10.1016/j.jbusvent.2010.01.002

Hallstedt, S. I. (2017). Sustainability criteria and sustainability compliance index for decision support in product development. *Journal of Cleaner Production, 140*, 251–266. DOI: 10.1016/j.jclepro.2015.06.068

Hama, J. R. (2017). Comparison of fatty acid profile changes between unroasted and roasted brown sesame (*Sesamum indicum* L.) seeds oil. *International Journal of Food Properties, 20*(5), 957–967. DOI: 10.1080/10942912.2016.1190744

Han, R., Yoon, H., Kim, G., Lee, H., & Lee, Y. (2023). Revolutionizing medicinal chemistry: The application of artificial intelligence (AI) in early drug discovery. *Pharmaceuticals (Basel, Switzerland), 16*(9), 1259. DOI: 10.3390/ph16091259 PMID: 37765069

Haq, R. S. U., Saeed, M., Mateen, N., Siddiqui, F., Naqvi, M., Yi, J. B., & Ahmed, S. (2022). Sustainable material selection with crisp and ambiguous data using single-valued neutrosophic-MEREC-MARCOS framework. *Applied Soft Computing, 128*, 109546. DOI: 10.1016/j.asoc.2022.109546

Hasan, A. M., & Trianni, A. (2023). Boosting the adoption of industrial energy efficiency measures through Industry 4.0 technologies to improve operational performance. *Journal of Cleaner Production, 425*, 138597. DOI: 10.1016/j.jclepro.2023.138597

Heinberg, R., & Lerch, D. (2010). What is sustainability. *The post carbon reader, 11*, 19.

Helleiner, E., & Thistlethwaite, J. (2009). The greening of international financial regulation. In Clapp, J. (Ed.), *Environmental Sustainability and the Financial Crisis: Linkages and Policy Recommendations* (pp. 10–12). CIGI Working Group on Environment and Resources.

Henning Kagermann. (2015). Change Through Digitization - Value Creation in the Age of Industry 4.0. In Albach, H., Pinkwart, A., Meffert, H., & Reichwald, R. (Eds.), *Management of Permanent Change* (1st ed., pp. 23–45). Springer Gabler. DOI: 10.1007/978-3-658-05014-6_2

Herrera, A. O., González, R. C., & Abu-Muhor, E. B. (2008). Multi-criteria decision model for assessing health service information technology network support using the analytic hierarchy process. *Computación y Sistemas*, *12*(2), 173–182. https://www.redalyc.org/articulo.oa?id=61513251003

Hicks, S. A., Strümke, I., Thambawita, V., Hammou, M., Riegler, M. A., Halvorsen, P., & Parasa, S. (2022). On evaluation metrics for medical applications of artificial intelligence. *Scientific Reports*, *12*(1), 5979. DOI: 10.1038/s41598-022-09954-8 PMID: 35395867

Hillman, J., & Keim, G. (2001). Shareholder value, stakeholder management, and social issues: What's the bottom line? *Strategic Management Journal*, *22*(2), 125–139. DOI: 10.1002/1097-0266(200101)22:2<125::AID-SMJ150>3.0.CO;2-H

Hjort, J., & De Souza Nazareth Giorgi, R. (2024). Multi-Criteria Decision Analysis as a Supporting Tool for Decision-Making in Construction Projects.

Hoagland, D. T., Liu, J., Lee, R. B., & Lee, R. E. (2016). New agents for the treatment of drug-resistant Mycobacterium tuberculosis. *Advanced Drug Delivery Reviews*, *102*, 55–72. DOI: 10.1016/j.addr.2016.04.026 PMID: 27151308

Hodosi, G., Sule, E., & Bodis, T. (2023, November). MULTI-CRITERIA DECISION MAKING: A COMPARATIVE ANALYSIS. In Economic and Social Development (Book of Proceedings), 103rd International Scientific Conference on Economic and Social Development (p. 81).

Hofmann, E., & Rüsch, M. (2017). Industry 4.0 and the current status as well as future prospects on logistics. *Computers in Industry*, *89*, 23–34. DOI: 10.1016/j.compind.2017.04.002

Hong Son, N., & Hieu, T. T. (2023). Selectıon of weldıng robot by multı-crıterıa decısıonmakıng method. *Eastern-European Journal of Enterprise Technologies*, *121*(3).

Hopkinson, P., Zils, M., Hawkins, P., & Roper, S. (2018). Managing a complex global circular economy business model: Opportunities and challenges. *California Management Review*, *60*(3), 71–94. DOI: 10.1177/0008125618764692

Horacek, M., Hansel-Hohl, K., Burg, K., Soja, G., Okello-Anyanga, W., & Fluch, S. (2015). Control of origin of sesame oil from various countries by stable isotope analysis and DNA-based markers—A pilot study. *PLoS One*, *10*(4), e0123020. DOI: 10.1371/journal.pone.0123020 PMID: 25831054

Horonjeff, R., McKelvey, F. X., Sproule, W. J., & Young, S. B. (2010). *Planning and Design of Airports* (5th ed.). McGraw-Hill.

Hossein Motlagh, N., Mohammadrezaei, M., Hunt, J., & Zakeri, B. (2020). Internet of Things (IoT) and the energy sector. *Energies*, *13*(2), 494. DOI: 10.3390/en13020494

Hosseini, H., Heydari, S., Hushmandi, K., Daneshi, S., & Raesi, R. (2025). Bone tumors: A systematic review of prevalence, risk determinants, and survival patterns. *BMC Cancer*, *25*(1), 321. DOI: 10.1186/s12885-025-13720-0 PMID: 39984867

Houck, K. A., & Kavlock, R. J. (2008). Understanding Mechanisms of Toxicity: Insights from Drug Discovery Research. *Toxicology and Applied Pharmacology*, *227*(2), 163–178. DOI: 10.1016/j.taap.2007.10.022 PMID: 18063003

Houssein, E. H., Emam, M. M., Ali, A. A., & Suganthan, P. N. (2021). Deep and machine learning techniques for medical imaging-based breast cancer: A comprehensive review. *Expert Systems with Applications*, *167*, 114161. DOI: 10.1016/j.eswa.2020.114161

Hou, T. J., Xia, K., Zhang, W., & Xu, X. J. (2004). ADME Evaluation in Drug Discovery. 4. Prediction of Aqueous Solubility Based on Atom Contribution Approach. *Journal of Chemical Information and Computer Sciences*, *44*(1), 266–275. DOI: 10.1021/ci034184n PMID: 14741036

Hou, Y., Wang, S., Bai, B., Chan, H. C. S., & Yuan, S. (2022). Accurate physical property predictions via deep learning. *Molecules (Basel, Switzerland)*, *27*(5), 1668. DOI: 10.3390/molecules27051668 PMID: 35268770

Hsu, C. H., Chen, S. J., Huang, M. Q., & Le, Q. (2024). Industry 5.0 Drivers Analysis Using Grey-DEMATEL: A Logistics Case in Emerging Economies. *Mathematics*, *12*(22), 3588. DOI: 10.3390/math12223588

Hsu, C. H., Wu, J. Z., Zhang, T. Y., & Chen, J. Y. (2024). Deploying Industry 5.0 drivers to enhance sustainable supply chain risk resilience. *International Journal of Sustainable Engineering*, *17*(1), 1–28. DOI: 10.1080/19397038.2024.2327381

Huang, J., Norgbey, E., Nkrumah, P. N., Opoku, P. A., & Apreku, T. O. (2017). Detection of corn oil in adulterated olive and soybean oil by carbon stable isotope analysis. *Journal für Verbraucherschutz und Lebensmittelsicherheit, 12*(3), 201–208. DOI: 10.1007/s00003-017-1097-x

Huang, S., Cheng, H., Tan, M., Tang, Z., & Teng, C. (2024). Evaluating Regional Potentials of Agricultural E-Commerce Development Using a Novel MEREC Heronian-CoCoSo Approach. *Agriculture, 14*(8), 1338. DOI: 10.3390/agriculture14081338

Hu, J., Miao, L., Han, J., Zhou, W., & Qian, X. (2024). Waste separation behavior with a new plastic category for the plastic resource circulation: Survey in Kansai, Japan. *Journal of Environmental Management, 349*, 119370. DOI: 10.1016/j.jenvman.2023.119370 PMID: 37879224

Hussain, N, Ugo R ve Rene´ P. Orij. (2016). Corporate Governance and Sustainability Performance: Analysis of Triple Bottom Line Performance. *Journal of Business Ethics, 25*, 1–22.

Huy, T. Q., Liem, N. B., Hau, T. Q., Cuong, D. Q., Danh, T. H., Nga, N. T. T., & Thieu, N. N. (2022, December). Application of MARCOS Method for Selecting the Best Schema of Scissors Mechanism. In *International Conference on Engineering Research and Applications* (pp. 234-243). Cham: Springer International Publishing.

Hwang, C. L., & Yoon, K. (1981). Methods for multiple attribute decision making. In *Multiple attribute decision making: methods and applications a state-of-the-art survey* (pp. 58-191). Springer Berlin Heidelberg.

IATA. (2021). *Net-Zero Carbon Emissions by 2050*. https://www.iata.org/en/pressroom/pressroom-archive/2021-releases/2021-10-04-03/

ICAO. (2015). *Airport Local Air Quality Guidance Manual Doc 9889*.

ICAO. (2017). *Waste Management at Airports*. https://www.icao.int/environmental-protection/Documents/ecoairports/Final Waste_Management_Case_Studies.pdf

ICAO. (2018). *Airport Planning Manual 9184 Part 2 - Land use and environmental management*.

ICAO. (2019). *Consolidated statement of continuing ICAO policies and practices related to environmental protection - Climate change*. https://www.icao.int/environmental-protection/Documents/Assembly/Resolution_A40-18_Climate_Change.pdf

ICAO. (2022). *A Focus on the Production of Renewable Energy at the Airport Site*.

ICAO. (2023). *Aircraft Noise*. https://www.icao.int/environmental-protection/Pages/noise.aspx

İGA. (2023). *İGA Sustainability Report 2021-2022*. https://www.igairport.aero/umbraco/surface/download/DownloadReport?filePath=/media/ioze1im2/2021-22-sustainability-report-1.pdf&fileName=2021 22 Sustainability Report (1)&type=pdf

Iranmakani, S., Mortezazadeh, T., Sajadian, F., Ghaziani, M. F., Ghafari, A., Khezerloo, D., & Musa, A. E. (2020). A review of various modalities in breast imaging: Technical aspects and clinical outcomes. *The Egyptian Journal of Radiology and Nuclear Medicine*, *51*(1), 1–22. DOI: 10.1186/s43055-020-00175-5

İslam, A. (2019). Blok Zinciri Teknolojisi ve Kripto Paralar: Mevcut Durum, Potansiyel ve Risk Analizi (Doctoral Dissertation, Marmara University (Turkey).

Islam, D. M. Z., Fabian Meier, J., Aditjandra, P. T., Zunder, T. H., & Pace, G. (2013). Logistics and supply chain management. *Research in Transportation Economics*, *41*(1), 3–16. DOI: 10.1016/j.retrec.2012.10.006

Islam, L. M. (2021). A Hybrid Traceability Technology Selection Approach for Sustainable Food Supply Chains. *Sustainability*, 1–23.

Ismail, J. N., Rodzi, Z., Al-Sharqi, F., Hashim, H., & Sulaiman, N. H. (2023). The Integrated Novel Framework: Linguistic Variables in Pythagorean Neutrosophic Set with DEMATEL for Enhanced Decision Support. [IJNS]. *International Journal of Neutrosophic Science*, *21*(2), 129–141. DOI: 10.54216/IJNS.210212

Jafari, M., & Khanachah, S. N. (2024). Integrated knowledge management in the supply chain: Assessment of knowledge adoption solutions through a comprehensive CoCoSo method under uncertainty. *Journal of Industrial Information Integration*, *39*, 100581. DOI: 10.1016/j.jii.2024.100581

Jamwal, A., Agrawal, R., Sharma, M., & Kumar, V. (2021). Review on multi-criteria decision analysis in sustainable manufacturing decision making. *International Journal of Sustainable Engineering*, *14*(3), 202–225. DOI: 10.1080/19397038.2020.1866708

Janić, M. (2011). *Greening airports: Advanced technology and operations*. Springer Science & Business Media. DOI: 10.1007/978-0-85729-658-0

Janiesch, C., Zschech, P., & Heinrich, K. (2021). Machine learning and deep learning fundamentals. *Electronic Markets*, *31*(3), 685–695. DOI: 10.1007/s12525-021-00475-2

Jassbi, J., Mohamadnejad, F., & Nasrollahzadeh, H. (2011). A Fuzzy DEMATEL framework for modeling cause and effect relationships of strategy map. *Expert Systems with Applications*, *38*(5), 5967–5973. DOI: 10.1016/j.eswa.2010.11.026

Javaid, M., Haleem, A., Singh, R. P., & Sinha, A. K. (2024). Digital economy to improve the culture of industry 4.0: A study on features, implementation and challenges. *Green Technologies and Sustainability*, 100083.

Javaid, M., Khan, S., Haleem, A., & Rab, S. (2023). Adoption of modern technologies for implementing industry 4.0: An integrated MCDM approach. *Benchmarking*, *30*(10), 3753–3790. DOI: 10.1108/BIJ-01-2021-0017

Jeucken, M.H.A. & Bouma, J. J. (1999). The Changing Environment of Banks, GMI Theme Issue: Sustainable Banking: The Greening of Finance, 21-35.

Jeucken, M. (2001). *Sustainable Finance And Banking, The Finance Sector And The Future Of The Planet, (1.Baskı)*. Earthscan.

Jeucken, M. H. A., & Bouma, J. J. (1999). The Changing Environment of Banks. *Greener Manag. Int.*, *27*, 21–35.

Jiang, H., Shen, Z. J. M., & Liu, J. (2022). Quantum Computing Methods for Supply Chain Management. *Proceedings - 2022 IEEE/ACM 7th Symposium on Edge Computing, SEC 2022*, 400–405. DOI: 10.1109/SEC54971.2022.00059

Jiang, S., Li, H., & Jin, Z. (2021). A visually interpretable deep learning framework for histopathological image-based skin cancer diagnosis. *IEEE Journal of Biomedical and Health Informatics*, *25*(5), 1483–1494. DOI: 10.1109/JBHI.2021.3052044 PMID: 33449890

Jiang, S., Li, Y., Jiang, P., & Gan, L. (2017). Evaluating the quality performance of reconstructive community public health service based on weighted TOPSIS method. *Proceedings of the Tenth International Conference on Management Science and Engineering Management* (pp. 113-123). Singapore: Springer. DOI: 10.1007/978-981-10-1837-4_10

Jiang, Y., Yin, S., Li, K., Luo, H., & Kaynak, O. (2021). Industrial applications of digital twins. *Philosophical Transactions. Series A, Mathematical, Physical, and Engineering Sciences*, *379*(2207), 20200360. DOI: 10.1098/rsta.2020.0360 PMID: 34398651

Jiménez Carvelo, A. M., Pérez Castaño, E., González Casado, A., & Cuadros Rodríguez, L. (2017). One-input and two-input-class classifications for differentiating olive oil from other edible vegetable oils by use of the normal-phase liquid chromatography fingerprint of the methyl-transesterified fraction. *Food Chemistry*, *221*, 1784–1791. DOI: 10.1016/j.foodchem.2016.10.103 PMID: 27979162

Jo, H., Kim, H., & Park, K. (2014). Corporate Environmental Responsibility And Firm Performance İn The Financial Services Sector. *SSRN, 131*, 1–28. DOI: 10.2139/ssrn.2470872

Jorgenson, D. W. (2001). Information technology and the US economy. *The American Economic Review, 91*(1), 1–32. DOI: 10.1257/aer.91.1.1

Joshi, R. P., & Kumar, N. (2021). Artificial intelligence for autonomous molecular design: A perspective. *Molecules (Basel, Switzerland), 26*(22), 6761. DOI: 10.3390/molecules26226761 PMID: 34833853

Josimović, B., Krunić, N., & Nenković-Riznić, M. (2016). The impact of airport noise as part of a Strategic Environmental Assessment, case study: The Tivat (Montenegro) Airport expansion plan. *Transportation Research Part D, Transport and Environment, 49*, 271–279. DOI: 10.1016/j.trd.2016.10.005

Kabaklarlı, E. (2016). *Endüstri 4.0 ve Dijital Ekonomisi; Dünya ve Türkiye Ekonomisi İçin Fırsatlar, Etkiler ve Tehditler (1. Baskı)*. Nobel Bilimsel Eserler.

Kablan, A. (2018). Endüstri 4.0, "Nesnelerin İnterneti"-Akıllı İşletmeler ve Muhasebe Denetimi. *Süleyman Demirel Üniversitesi İktisadi ve İdari Bilimler Fakültesi Dergisi*, 23(Endüstri 4.0 ve Örgütsel Değişim Özel Sayısı), 1561-1579.

Kaivo-Oja, J. R. L., & Lauraeus, I. T. (2018). The VUCA approach as a solution concept to corporate foresight challenges and global technological disruption. foresight, 20(1), 27-49.

Kakouri, E., Revelou, P. K., Kanakis, C., Daferera, D., Pappas, C. S., & Tarantilis, P. A. (2021). Authentication of the botanical and geographical origin and detection of adulteration of olive oil using gas chromatography, infrared and Raman spectroscopy techniques: A review. *Foods, 10*(7), 1565. DOI: 10.3390/foods10071565 PMID: 34359435

Kamilçelebi, H. (2012). Türkiye'de Sigorta Sektörünün SWOT Analizi ve Bir Araştırma. *Ekonomi Bilimleri Dergisi, 4*(1), 45–54.

Kaneko, H., & Funatsu, K. (2015). Fast optimization of hyperparameters for support vector regression models with highly predictive ability. *Chemometrics and Intelligent Laboratory Systems, 142*, 64–69. DOI: 10.1016/j.chemolab.2015.01.001

Kar, A., & Özer, Ö. (2020). Türkiye'de sağlık hizmetleri altyapı kaynaklarının, hizmet kullanım düzeylerinin ve sağlık sonuçlarının bölgesel düzeyde karşılaştırılması. *Dicle Üniversitesi İktisadi ve İdari Bilimler Fakültesi Dergisi, 10*(20), 331–350.

Karabulut, A., & Baran, M. (2024). Türkiye'de Endüstri 4.0'in Benimsenmesinin Önündeki Engellerin Yorumlayici Yapisal Modelleme (Ism) Ve Micmac İle Analizi. *Journal of Business in The Digital Age*, *7*(1), 51–67. DOI: 10.46238/jobda.1215803

Karademir, İ. (2024). Türkiye imalat sektöründe endüstri 4.0 adaptasyon düzeyi. *The Journal of Academic Social Science*, *135*(135), 308–325. DOI: 10.29228/ASOS.65989

Karakcheyeva, V., Willis-Johnson, H., Corr, P. G., & Frame, L. A. (2024). The Well-Being of Women in Healthcare Professions: A Comprehensive Review. *Global Advances in Integrative Medicine and Health*, *13*, 27536130241232929. DOI: 10.1177/27536130241232929 PMID: 38344248

Karaşan, A., & Kahraman, C. (2018). A novel interval-valued neutrosophic EDAS method: Prioritization of the United Nations national sustainable development goals. *Soft Computing*, *22*(15), 4891–4906. DOI: 10.1007/s00500-018-3088-y

Kasa, H., & Arslan, G. (2020). Endüstri 4.0 Kapsaminda Teorik Bir Analiz: Türkiye Örneği. *Elektronik Sosyal Bilimler Dergisi*, *19*(76), 1810–1826. DOI: 10.17755/esosder.665849

Katrakazas, C., Quddus, M., Chen, W. H., & Deka, L. (2015). Real-time motion planning methods for autonomous on-road driving: State-of-the-art and future research directions. *Transportation Research Part C, Emerging Technologies*, *60*, 416–442. DOI: 10.1016/j.trc.2015.09.011

Kaya, A., Pamucar, D., Gürler, H. E., & Ozcalici, M. (2024). Determining the financial performance of the firms in the Borsa Istanbul sustainability index: Integrating multi criteria decision making methods with simulation. *Financial Innovation*, *10*(1), 21. DOI: 10.1186/s40854-023-00512-3

Kaya, S. K. (2020). Evaluation of the Effect of COVID-19 on Countries' Sustainable Development Level: A comparative MCDM framework. *Operational Research in Engineering Sciences: Theory and Applications*, *3*(3), 101–122. DOI: 10.31181/oresta20303101k

Kaya, S. K., Ayçin, E., & Pamucar, D. (2023). Evaluation of social factors within the circular economy concept for European countries. *Central European Journal of Operations Research*, *31*(1), 73–108. DOI: 10.1007/s10100-022-00800-w

Kaygın, E., Zengin, Y., & Topçuoğlu, E. (2019). Endüstri 4.0'a Akademik Bakış. *Atatürk Üniversitesi İktisadi ve İdari Bilimler Dergisi*, *33*(4), 1065–1081.

Kayikci, Y. (2018). Sustainability impact of digitization in logistics. *Procedia Manufacturing*, *21*, 782–789. DOI: 10.1016/j.promfg.2018.02.184

Kazda, A., & Caves, R. E. (2015). *Airport Design and Operation* (3rd ed.). Emerald.

Keefer, P. (2004). A review of the political economy of governance: From property rights to voice.

Kelly, S., Parker, I., Sharman, M., Dennis, J., & Goodall, I. (1997). Assessing the authenticity of single seed vegetable oils using fatty acid stable carbon isotope ratios (13C/12C). *Food Chemistry, 59*(2), 181–186. DOI: 10.1016/S0308-8146(96)00286-5

Keršuliene, V., Zavadskas, E. K., & Turskis, Z. (2010). Selection of rational dispute resolution method by applying new step-wise weight assessment ratio analysis (Swara). *Journal of Business Economics and Management, 11*(2), 243–258. DOI: 10.3846/jbem.2010.12

Keshavarz-Ghorabaee, M., Amiri, M., Zavadskas, E. K., Turskis, Z., & Antucheviciene, J. (2021). Determination of objective weights using a new method based on the removal effects of criteria (MEREC). *Symmetry, 13*(4), 525. DOI: 10.3390/sym13040525

Khalili, N. R., & Duecker, S. (2013). Application of multi-criteria decision analysis in design of sustainable environmental management system framework. *Journal of Cleaner Production, 47*, 188–198. DOI: 10.1016/j.jclepro.2012.10.044

Khan, A., & Turowski, K. (2016). A Perspective on Industry 4.0: From Challenges to Opportunities In Production Systems. In International Conference on Internet of Things and Big Data (ss. 441-448). Scitepress.

Khan, A. M. R., Prasad, P. N., & Rajamanoharane, S. (2012). Service quality performance measurement management in corporate hospitals using analytical hierarchy process. *International Journal of Manufacturing Technology and Management, 26*(1-4), 196–212. DOI: 10.1504/IJMTM.2012.051434

Khan, K. U., Minhas, M. U., Badshah, S. F., Suhail, M., Ahmad, A., & Ijaz, S. (2022). Overview of nanoparticulate strategies for solubility enhancement of poorly soluble drugs. *Life Sciences, 291*, 120301. DOI: 10.1016/j.lfs.2022.120301 PMID: 34999114

Khan, M., Azizul Islam, M., Kayeser Fatima, J., & Ahmed, K. (2011). Corporate Sustainability Reporting of Major Commercial Banks in line with GRI: Bangladesh Evidence. *Social Responsibility Journal, 7*(3), 347–352. DOI: 10.1108/17471111111154509

Khan, N., Adam, R., Huang, P., Maldjian, T., & Duong, T. Q. (2022). Deep learning prediction of pathologic complete response in breast cancer using MRI and other clinical data: A systematic review. *Tomography : a Journal for Imaging Research, 8*(6), 2784–2795. DOI: 10.3390/tomography8060232 PMID: 36412691

Khan, S., & Haleem, A. (2021). Investigation of circular economy practices in the context of emerging economies: A CoCoSo approach. *International Journal of Sustainable Engineering*, *14*(3), 357–367. DOI: 10.1080/19397038.2020.1871442

Khan, T., & Emon, M. M. H. (2025). Supply chain performance in the age of Industry 4.0: Evidence from manufacturing sector. *Brazilian Journal of Operations & Production Management*, *22*(1), 2434. DOI: 10.14488/BJOPM.2434.2025

Kılkış, Ş., & Kılkış, Ş. (2016). Benchmarking airports based on a sustainability ranking index. *Journal of Cleaner Production*, *130*, 248–259. DOI: 10.1016/j.jclepro.2015.09.031

Kimber, T. B., Chen, Y., & Volkamer, A. (2021). Deep learning in virtual screening: Recent applications and developments. *International Journal of Molecular Sciences*, *22*(9), 4435. DOI: 10.3390/ijms22094435 PMID: 33922714

Kobryń, A. (2017). DEMATEL as a weighting method in multi-criteria decision analysis. *Multiple Criteria Decision Making*, *12*(12), 153–167. DOI: 10.22367/mcdm.2017.12.11

Kohavi, R. (1995). A study of cross-validation and bootstrap for accuracy estimation and model selection. *IJCAI (United States)*, *14*(2), 1137–1145.

Köhler, J., De Haan, F., Holtz, G., Kubeczko, K., Moallemi, E. A., Papachristos, G., & Chappin, E. (2018). Modelling sustainability transitions: an assessment of approaches and challenges.

Korhonen, J., Honkasalo, A., & Seppälä, J. (2018). Circular Economy : The Concept and its Limitations. *Ecological Economics*, *143*, 37–46. DOI: 10.1016/j.ecolecon.2017.06.041

Kou, G., Ergu, D., Lin, C., & Chen, Y. (2016). Pairwise comparison matrix in multiple criteria decision making. *Technological and Economic Development of Economy*, *22*(5), 738–765. DOI: 10.3846/20294913.2016.1210694

Kravchenko, O., Leshchenko, M., Marushchak, D., Vdovychenko, Y., & Boguslavska, S. (2019). The digitalization as a global trend and growth factor of the modern economy. In SHS Web of Conferences (Vol. 65, p. 07004). EDP Sciences. DOI: 10.1051/shsconf/20196507004

Kreeb, M., & Haasis, H. D. (2017). Sustainable cooperate information portals: Digital knowledge communities for SME. *Sustainability in a digital world: New opportunities through new technologies,* 145-158.

Kreiss, D., & Brennen, J. S. (2016). Normative models of digital journalism. *The Sage Handbook of Digital Journalism*, 299-314.

Krüger, M., Wilson, J., Wietzoreck, M., Bandowe, B. A. M., Lammel, G., Schmidt, B., Pöschl, U., & Berkemeier, T. (2022). Convolutional neural network prediction of molecular properties for aerosol chemistry and health effects. *Natural Sciences (Weinheim)*, *2*(4), e20220016. DOI: 10.1002/ntls.20220016

Krzywanski, J., Sosnowski, M., Grabowska, K., Zylka, A., Lasek, L., & Kijo-Kleczkowska, A. (2024). Advanced computational methods for modeling, prediction and optimization—A review. *Materials (Basel)*, *17*(14), 3521. DOI: 10.3390/ma17143521 PMID: 39063813

Kuhn, T., & Deetz, S. (2009). Critical theory and corporate social responsibility: Can/Should we get beyond cynical reasoning? In Crane, A., McWilliams, A., Matten, D., Moon, J., & Siegel, D. S. (Eds.), *The Oxford handbook of social responsibility, (ss* (pp. 1–29). Oxford University Press. DOI: 10.1093/oxfordhb/9780199211593.003.0008

Kumar, A., Aswin, A., & Gupta, H. (2020). Evaluating green performance of the airports using hybrid BWM and VIKOR methodology. *Tourism Management*, *76*(July 2019), 103941. DOI: 10.1016/j.tourman.2019.06.016

Kumar, V., Vrat, P., & Shankar, R. (2021). *Prioritization of strategies to overcome the barriers in Industry 4.0: a hybrid MCDM approach*. Opsearch, 1-40.

Kumar, A., & A, R. (2020). An MCDM framework for assessment of social sustainability indicators of the freight transport industry under uncertainty. A multi-company perspective. *Journal of Enterprise Information Management*, *33*(5), 1023–1058. DOI: 10.1108/JEIM-09-2019-0272

Kumar, S., Ahijith Kumar, P. V., Bharati, K., Patnaik, L., Ranjan Maity, S., & Łepicka, M. (2024). Coating material selection for bulk metal forming dies: A MEREC-integrated approach with multiple MCDM methods. [IJIDeM]. *International Journal on Interactive Design and Manufacturing*, 1–16.

Kumar, V., Kalita, K., Chatterjee, P., Zavadskas, E. K., & Chakraborty, S. (2022). A SWARA-CoCoSo-based approach for spray painting robot selection. *Informatica (Vilnius)*, *33*(1), 35–54. DOI: 10.15388/21-INFOR466

Kurian, N. C., Sethi, A., Konduru, A. R., Mahajan, A., & Rane, S. U. (2021). A 2021 update on cancer image analytics with deep learning. *Wiley Interdisciplinary Reviews. Data Mining and Knowledge Discovery*, *11*(4), e1410. DOI: 10.1002/widm.1410

Lai, H., Liao, H., Wen, Z., Zavadskas, E. K., & Al-Barakati, A. (2020). An improved CoCoSo method with a maximum variance optimization model for cloud service provider selection. *The Engineering Economist*, *31*(4), 411–424. DOI: 10.5755/j01.ee.31.4.24990

Larsen, B. S., Meiland, P., Tzdaka, E., Tho, I., & Rades, T. (2024). A unifying approach to drug-in-polymer solubility prediction: Streamlining experimental workflow and analysis. *European Journal of Pharmaceutics and Biopharmaceutics*, *203*, 114478. DOI: 10.1016/j.ejpb.2024.114478 PMID: 39226986

Lasi, H., Fettke, P., Kemper, H. G., Feld, T., & Hoffmann, M. (2014). Industry 4.0. *Business & Information Systems Engineering*, *6*(4), 239–242. DOI: 10.1007/s12599-014-0334-4

Lee, E. A. (2008). Cyber Physical Systems: Design Challenges. *11th IEEE Symposium on Object/Component/Service-Oriented Real-Time Distributed Computing, ISORC*, 363–369. DOI: 10.1109/ISORC.2008.25

Lee, I., & Lee, K. (2015). The Internet of Things (IoT): Applications, investments, and challenges for enterprises. *Business Horizons*, *58*(4), 431–440. DOI: 10.1016/j.bushor.2015.03.008

Leng, J., Sha, W., Wang, B., Zheng, P., Zhuang, C., Liu, Q., Wuest, T., Mourtzis, D., & Wang, L. (2022). Industry 5.0: Prospect and retrospect. *Journal of Manufacturing Systems*, *65*, 279–295. DOI: 10.1016/j.jmsy.2022.09.017

Liang, J., Appukuttan Aachary, A., & Thiyam-Holländer, U. (2015). Hemp seed oil: Minor components and oil quality. *Lipid Technology*, *27*(10), 231–233. DOI: 10.1002/lite.201500050

Li, C. W., & Tzeng, G. H. (2009). Identification of a threshold value for the DEMATEL method using the maximum mean de-entropy algorithm to find critical services provided by a semiconductor intellectual property mall. *Expert Systems with Applications*, *36*(6), 9891–9898. DOI: 10.1016/j.eswa.2009.01.073

Lidiia Savchenko, S. S. (2021). *ENVIRONMENTAL AND SOCIAL RESPONSIBILITY IN SUPPLY CHAINS*. Izdevniecība “Baltija Publishing”.

Lijesen, M., van der Straaten, W., Dekkers, J., van Elk, R., & Blokdijk, J. (2010). How much noise reduction at airports? *Transportation Research Part D, Transport and Environment*, *15*(1), 51–59. DOI: 10.1016/j.trd.2009.07.006

Li, L., & Loo, B. P. Y. (2016). Impact analysis of airport infrastructure within a sustainability framework: Case studies on Hong Kong International Airport. *International Journal of Sustainable Transportation, 10*(9), 781–793. DOI: 10.1080/15568318.2016.1149647

Lim, M. W., Von Lau, E., & Poh, P. E. (2016). A comprehensive guide of remediation technologies for oil contaminated soil — Present works and future directions. *Marine Pollution Bulletin, 109*(1), 14–45. DOI: 10.1016/j.marpolbul.2016.04.023 PMID: 27267117

Lin, B., & Jones, C. (2008). Digital Supply Chain Management and Implementation: A Research Review. *Southwest Decision Sciences Institute*, 589–592. http://swdsi.org/swdsi2009/Papers/9Q02.pdf

Lin, A. J., & Chang, H. Y. (2019). Business Sustainability Performance Evaluation For Taiwanese Banks—A Hybrid Multiple-Criteria Decision-Making Approach. *Sustainability (Basel), 11*(8), 2236. DOI: 10.3390/su11082236

Lipinski, C. A., Lombardo, F., Dominy, B. W., & Feeney, P. J. (2012). Experimental and computational approaches to estimate solubility and permeability in drug discovery and development settings. *Advanced Drug Delivery Reviews, 64*(Supplement), 4–17. DOI: 10.1016/j.addr.2012.09.019 PMID: 11259830

Litjens, G., Sánchez, C. I., Timofeeva, N., Hermsen, M., Nagtegaal, I., Kovacs, I., Hulsbergen-van de Kaa, C., Bult, P., van Ginneken, B., & van der Laak, J. (2016). Deep learning as a tool for increased accuracy and efficiency of histopathological diagnosis. *Scientific Reports, 6*(1), 26286. DOI: 10.1038/srep26286 PMID: 27212078

Liu, H. M., He, M. K., Yao, Y. G., Qin, Z., Cai, X. S., & Wang, X. D. (2021). Pectic polysaccharides extracted from sesame seed hull: Physicochemical and functional properties. *International Journal of Biological Macromolecules, 192*, 1075–1083. DOI: 10.1016/j.ijbiomac.2021.10.077 PMID: 34673100

Liu, W., Zhang, J., Shi, Y., Lee, P. T. W., & Liang, Y. (2022). Intelligent logistics transformation problems in efficient commodity distribution. *Transportation Research Part E, Logistics and Transportation Review, 163*, 102735. DOI: 10.1016/j.tre.2022.102735

Liu, Y., Cai, M., Zhao, Y., Hu, Z., Wu, P., & Kong, D. X. (2024). Time-dependent comparison of the structural variations of natural products and synthetic compounds. *International Journal of Molecular Sciences, 25*(21), 11475. DOI: 10.3390/ijms252111475 PMID: 39519027

Li, Y., Hu, Y., Zhang, X., Deng, Y., & Mahadevan, S. (2014). An Evidential DEMATEL Method to Identify Critical Success Factors in Emergency Management. *Applied Soft Computing*, *22*, 504–510. DOI: 10.1016/j.asoc.2014.03.042

Li, Z., Jiang, M., Wang, S., & Zhang, S. (2022). Deep learning methods for molecular representation and property prediction. *Drug Discovery Today*, *27*(12), 103373. DOI: 10.1016/j.drudis.2022.103373 PMID: 36167282

López-López, E., & Medina-Franco, J. L. (2024). Toward Structure–Multiple Activity Relationships (SMARts) Using Computational Approaches: A Polypharmacological Perspective. *Drug Discovery Today*, *29*(7), 104046. DOI: 10.1016/j.drudis.2024.104046 PMID: 38810721

Lovkis, Z. V., Pochitskaya, I. M., & Morgunova, E. M. (2019). Research and methodological basis for identification of palm oil in food. *Vescì Nacyânal'naj Akadèmìì Navuk Belarusì. Seryâ Agrarnyh Navuk*, *57*(4), 494–508. DOI: 10.29235/1817-7204-2019-57-4-494-508

Luca, A. R., Ursuleanu, T. F., Gheorghe, L., Grigorovici, R., Iancu, S., Hlusneac, M., & Grigorovici, A. (2022). Impact of quality, type and volume of data used by deep learning models in the analysis of medical images. *Informatics in Medicine Unlocked*, *29*, 100911. DOI: 10.1016/j.imu.2022.100911

Lu, M., Hsu, C., Liou, J. J. H., & Lo, H. (2018). A hybrid MCDM and sustainability-balanced scorecard model to establish sustainable performance evaluation for international airports. *Journal of Air Transport Management*, *71*, 9–19. DOI: 10.1016/j.jairtraman.2018.05.008

Luo, J., Yi, J., Zhu, X., & Xu, J. (2016). A Smart Sensors-based real-time decision making system for the Cold Supply Chain. In Yarlagadda, P. (Ed.), *Proceedings of the 2016 3rd International Conference on Mechatronics and Information Technology* (pp. 714–719). ICMIT., DOI: 10.2991/icmit-16.2016.128

Lu, Y. (2017a). Cyber Physical System (CPS)-Based Industry 4.0: A Survey. *Journal of Industrial Integration and Management*, *02*(03), 1750014. DOI: 10.1142/S2424862217500142

Lu, Y. (2017b). Industry 4.0: A survey on technologies, applications and open research issues. *Journal of Industrial Information Integration*, *6*, 1–10. DOI: 10.1016/j.jii.2017.04.005

Madakam, S., & Lake, V. (2015). Internet of Things (IOT): A Literature Review. *Journal of Computer and Communications*, *3*(05), 164–173. DOI: 10.4236/jcc.2015.35021

Maddikunta, P. K. R., Pham, Q. V., B, P., Deepa, N., Dev, K., Gadekallu, T. R., Ruby, R., & Liyanage, M. (2022). Industry 5.0: A survey on enabling technologies and potential applications. *Journal of Industrial Information Integration*, *26*, 100257. DOI: 10.1016/j.jii.2021.100257

Mahashabde, A., Wolfe, P., Ashok, A., Dorbian, C., He, Q., Fan, A., Lukachko, S., Mozdzanowska, A., Wollersheim, C., Barrett, S. R. H., Locke, M., & Waitz, I. A. (2011). Assessing the environmental impacts of aircraft noise and emissions. *Progress in Aerospace Sciences*, *47*(1), 15–52. DOI: 10.1016/j.paerosci.2010.04.003

Mahmood, T., Li, J., Pei, Y., Akhtar, F., Imran, A., & Rehman, K. U. (2020). A brief survey on breast cancer diagnostic with deep learning schemes using multi-image modalities. *IEEE Access : Practical Innovations, Open Solutions*, *8*, 165779–165809. DOI: 10.1109/ACCESS.2020.3021343

Mahmoudian Azar Sharabiani, A., & Mousavi, S. M. (2023). A Web-Based Decision Support System for Project Evaluation with Sustainable Development Considerations Based on Two Developed Pythagorean Fuzzy Decision Methods. *Sustainability (Basel)*, *15*(23), 16477. DOI: 10.3390/su152316477

Majanga, V., Mnkandla, E., Wang, Z., & Moulla, D. K. (2025). Automatic blob detection method for cancerous lesions in unsupervised breast histology images. *Bioengineering (Basel, Switzerland)*, *12*(4), 364. DOI: 10.3390/bioengineering12040364 PMID: 40281724

Malik, R. S. (2018). Educational challenges in 21st century and sustainable development. *Journal of Sustainable Development Education and Research*, *2*(1), 9–20. DOI: 10.17509/jsder.v2i1.12266

Malterud, K., Siersma, V. D., & Guassora, A. D. (2016). Sample Size in Qualitative Interview Studies: Guided by Information Power. *Qualitative Health Research*, *26*(13), 1753–1760. DOI: 10.1177/1049732315617444 PMID: 26613970

Manoharan, N. S. (2023). Trust Model to Identify Reputed Miners in Blockchain Pool Mining. *International Conference on Signal Processing, Computation, Electronics, Power and Telecommunication (IConSCEPT), Karaikal, India, 2023* (pp. 1-6). Karikal: IEEE.

Manoharan, N. S. (2023). Cluster-based Trust Evaluation of Blockchain Miners in Pool Mining. *2023 Second International Conference on Advances in Computational Intelligence and Communication (ICACIC),* Puducherry, India, 2023 (pp. 1-6). Puducherry: IEEE Publisher.

Marais, K., Wolfe, P. J., & Waitz, I. A. (2016). Air Transport and the Environment. In Belobaba, P., Odoni, A., & Barnhart, C. (Eds.), *The Global Airline Industry*. Wiley.

Mardani, A., Zavadskas, E. K., Khalifah, Z., Zakuan, N., Jusoh, A., Nor, K. M., & Khoshnoudi, M. (2017). A review of multi-criteria decision-making applications to solve energy management problems: Two decades from 1995 to 2015. *Renewable & Sustainable Energy Reviews*, *71*, 216–256. DOI: 10.1016/j.rser.2016.12.053

Maretto, L., Faccio, M., & Battini, D. (2022). A multi-criteria decision-making model based on fuzzy logic and AHP for the selection of digital technologies. *IFAC-PapersOnLine*, *55*(2), 319–324. DOI: 10.1016/j.ifacol.2022.04.213

Marija Jeremić, B. M. (n.d.). The Green Food Supply Chain Concept. *29th International Scientific Conference Strategic Management and Decision Support Systems in Strategic Management.*

Mariyappan, S. S., Penthala, H. R., Nagaram, A., & Arisham, D. (2024, July). *Retina fundus disease gray scale image perception using semantic segmentation model.* In AIP Conference Proceedings (Vol. 3028, No. 1). AIP Publishing. DOI: 10.1063/5.0212988

Markevičius, A., Katinas, V., Perednis, E., & Tamašauskienė, M. (2010). Trends and sustainability criteria of the production and use of liquid biofuels. *Renewable & Sustainable Energy Reviews*, *14*(9), 3226–3231. DOI: 10.1016/j.rser.2010.07.015

Marmara, A. (2006). *Sürdürülebilir Kalkınma Çerçevesinde İşletmelerin Sosyal Sorumluluğu* (Master's thesis, Sakarya Universitesi (Turkey)).

Martin, J. A., Conkling, T. J., Belant, J. L., Biondi, K. M., Blackwell, B. F., DeVault, T. L., Fernández-Juricic, E., Schmidt, P. M., & Seamans, T. W. (2013). Wildlife conservation and alternative land uses at airports. In DeVault, T. L., Blackwell, B. F., & Belant, J. L. (Eds.), *Wildlife in airport environments: preventing animal-aircraft collisions through science-based management*. Johns Hopkins University Press.

Masiol, M., & Harrison, R. M. (2014). Aircraft engine exhaust emissions and other airport-related contributions to ambient air pollution: A review. *Atmospheric Environment*, *95*, 409–455. DOI: 10.1016/j.atmosenv.2014.05.070 PMID: 32288558

Mastilo, Z., Štilić, A., Gligović, D., & Puška, A. (2024). Assessing the Banking Sector of Bosnia and Herzegovina: An Analysis of Financial Indicators through the MEREC and MARCOS Methods. *Journal of Central Banking Theory and Practice*, *13*(1), 167–197. DOI: 10.2478/jcbtp-2024-0008

Masuda, K., Tsuyumine, Y., Kitada, T., Hachikawa, T., & Haga, T. (2023). Optimization of Delivery Plan by Quantum Computing. *SEI Technical Review*, *96*, 85–88.

Masud, M., Rashed, A. E. E., & Hossain, M. S. (2022). Convolutional neural network-based models for diagnosis of breast cancer. *Neural Computing & Applications, 34*(14), 11383–11394. DOI: 10.1007/s00521-020-05394-5 PMID: 33052172

Mateusz, P., Danuta, M., Małgorzata, Ł., Mariusz, B., & Kesra, N. (2018). TOPSIS and VIKOR methods in study of sustainable development in the EU countries. *Procedia Computer Science, 126*, 1683–1692. DOI: 10.1016/j.procs.2018.08.109

Matlin, S. A., Krief, A., Hopf, H., & Mehta, G. (2021). Re-imagining Priorities for Chemistry: A Central Science for "Freedom from Fear and Want". *Angewandte Chemie International Edition, 60*(49), 25610–25623. DOI: 10.1002/anie.202108067 PMID: 34704655

McFarlane, D., Giannikas, V., & Lu, W. (2016). Intelligent logistics: Involving the customer. *Computers in Industry, 81*, 105–115. DOI: 10.1016/j.compind.2015.10.002

Mckinnon, A., Cullinane, S., Browne, M., & Whiteing, A. (2010). Greenn Logistics: Improving the environmental sustaintability of logistics. In *The Chartered Institute of Logistics and Transport (UK)*. Kogan Page.

McKinnon, A., Browne, M., Whiteing, A., & Piecyk, M. (2015). *Green Logistics: Improving The Environmental Sustainability of Logistics* (3rd ed.). KoganPage.

Megyesiova, S., & Lieskovska, V. (2018). Analysis of the sustainable development indicators in the OECD countries. *Sustainability (Basel), 10*(12), 4554. DOI: 10.3390/su10124554

Mensour, O. N., El Ghazzani, B., Hlimi, B., & Ihlal, A. (2019). A geographical information system-based multi-criteria method for the evaluation of solar farms locations: A case study in Souss-Massa area, southern Morocco. *Energy, 182*, 900–919. DOI: 10.1016/j.energy.2019.06.063

Meral, İ. G. (2023). BRICS-T Ülkelerinin İnovasyon Performanslarının MEREC-MARCOS Yöntemi ile Değerlendirilmesi. *Kastamonu Üniversitesi İktisadi ve İdari Bilimler Fakültesi Dergisi, 25*(2), 550–571.

Mercan, T., & Can, A. (2023). İşgören seçiminde etkili olan faktörlerin FUCOM yöntemi ile değerlendirilmesi: Bir havayolu işletmesinde uygulama. *Süleyman Demirel Üniversitesi Vizyoner Dergisi, 14*(40), 1311–1329. DOI: 10.21076/vizyoner.1271318

Mian, S. H., & Al-Ahmari, A. (2019). Comparative analysis of different digitization systems and selection of best alternative. *Journal of Intelligent Manufacturing, 30*(5), 2039–2067. DOI: 10.1007/s10845-017-1371-x

Mignani, S., Rodrigues, J., Tomas, H., Jalal, R., Singh, P. P., Majoral, J. P., & Vishwakarma, R. A. (2018). Present drug-likeness filters in medicinal chemistry during the hit and lead optimization process: How far can they be simplified? *Drug Discovery Today*, *23*(3), 605–615. DOI: 10.1016/j.drudis.2018.01.010 PMID: 29330127

Mili, A., Das, S., Nandakumar, K., & Lobo, R. (2021). A comprehensive review on *Sesamum indicum* L.: Botanical, ethnopharmacological, phytochemical, and pharmacological aspects. *Journal of Ethnopharmacology*, *281*, 114503. DOI: 10.1016/j.jep.2021.114503 PMID: 34364969

Miljković, F., & Medina-Franco, J. L. (2024). Artificial intelligence-open science symbiosis in chemoinformatics. *Artificial Intelligence in the Life Sciences*, *5*, 100096. DOI: 10.1016/j.ailsci.2024.100096

Mintzberg, H., Ahlstrand, B. W., & Lampel, J. (1998). *The design school: strategy formation as a process of conception. strategy safari: A guided tour through the wilds of strategic management*. Free Press.

Mittal, P. (2020, November). A multi-criterion decision analysis based on PCA for analyzing the digital technology skills in the effectiveness of government services. In *2020 International Conference on Decision Aid Sciences and Application (DASA)* (pp. 490-494). IEEE. DOI: DOI: 10.1109/DASA51403.2020.9317241

Mohapatra, S., Muduly, S., Mohanty, S., Ravindra, J. V. R., & Mohanty, S. N. (2022). Evaluation of deep learning models for detecting breast cancer using histopathological mammograms images. *Sustainable Operations and Computers.*, *3*, 296–302. DOI: 10.1016/j.susoc.2022.06.001

Mohi, N., Ahmad Dar, R., Rasool, M., & Assad, A. (2022). Breast cancer detection using deep learning: Datasets, methods, and challenges ahead. *Computers in Biology and Medicine*, *149*, 106073. DOI: 10.1016/j.compbiomed.2022.106073 PMID: 36103745

Mohseni, P., & Ghorbani, A. (2024). Exploring the synergy of artificial intelligence in microbiology: Advancements, challenges, and future prospects. *Computational and Structural Biotechnology Reports*, *1*, 100005. DOI: 10.1016/j.csbr.2024.100005

Moldan, B., Janoušková, S., & Hák, T. (2012). How to understand and measure environmental sustainability: Indicators and targets. *Ecological Indicators*, *17*, 4–13. DOI: 10.1016/j.ecolind.2011.04.033

Mondal, M. K., Mahapatra, B. S., Bera, M. B., & Mahapatra, G. S. (2024). Sustainable forest resources management model through Pythagorean fuzzy MEREC–MARCOS approach. *Environment, Development and Sustainability*, 1–32. DOI: 10.1007/s10668-024-05164-6

Mondejar, M. E., Avtar, R., Diaz, H. L. B., Dubey, R. K., Esteban, J., Gómez-Morales, A., Hallam, B., Mbungu, N. T., Okolo, C. C., Prasad, K. A., She, Q., & Garcia-Segura, S. (2021). Digitalization to achieve sustainable development goals: Steps towards a Smart Green Planet. *The Science of the Total Environment*, *794*, 148539. DOI: 10.1016/j.scitotenv.2021.148539 PMID: 34323742

Monsalud, A., Ho, D., & Rakas, J. (2015). Greenhouse gas emissions mitigation strategies within the airport sustainability evaluation process. *Sustainable Cities and Society*, *14*, 414–424. DOI: 10.1016/j.scs.2014.08.003

Morelli, J. (2011). Environmental sustainability: A definition for environmental professionals. *Journal of Environmental Sustainability*, *1*(1), 2. DOI: 10.14448/jes.01.0002

Morris, J. B., Wang, M. L., & Tonnis, B. D. (2021). Variability for oil, protein, lignan, tocopherol, and fatty acid concentrations in eight sesame (*Sesamum indicum* L.) genotypes. *Industrial Crops and Products*, *164*, 113355. DOI: 10.1016/j.indcrop.2021.113355

Mridha, M. F., Hamid, M. A., Monowar, M. M., Keya, A. J., Ohi, A. Q., Islam, M. R., & Kim, J.-M. (2021). A Comprehensive Survey on Deep-Learning-Based Breast Cancer Diagnosis. *Cancers (Basel)*, *13*(23), 6116. DOI: 10.3390/cancers13236116 PMID: 34885225

Müezzinoğlu, A. (2000). *Hava Kirliliği ve Kontrolünün Esasları*. Dokuz Eylül Yayınları.

Mukta, N., & Neeta, P. M. (2017). A review on sesame—An ethno medicinally significant oil crop. *International Journal of Life Science and Pharma Research*, *7*(2), L58–L63.

Munier, N., & Hontoria, E. (2021). *Uses and Limitations of the AHP Method*. Springer International Publishing. DOI: 10.1007/978-3-030-60392-2

Munirathinam, S. (2020). Industry 4.0: Industrial internet of things (IIOT). [). Elsevier.]. *Advances in Computers*, *117*(1), 129–164. DOI: 10.1016/bs.adcom.2019.10.010

Murphy, P. R., & Poist, R. F. (2000). Green Logistics Strategies: An Analysis of Usage Patterns. *Transportation Journal*, *40*(2), .

Muteeb, G., Rehman, M. T., Shahwan, M., & Aatif, M. (2023). Origin of antibiotics and antibiotic resistance, and their impacts on drug development: A narrative review. *Pharmaceuticals (Basel, Switzerland), 16*(11), 1615. DOI: 10.3390/ph16111615 PMID: 38004480

Myint, D., Gilani, S. A., Kawase, M., & Watanabe, K. N. (2020). Sustainable sesame (*Sesamum indicum* L.) production through improved technology: An overview of production, challenges, and opportunities in Myanmar. *Sustainability (Basel), 12*(9), 3515. DOI: 10.3390/su12093515

Nabeeh, N. A., & Sallam, K. M. (2024). A Combined Compromise Solution (CoCo-So) of MCDM Problems for Selection of Medical Best Bearing Ring. *Neutrosophic Optimization and Intelligent Systems, 1*, 1-13. https://orcid.org/0000-0003-3214-1556

Nabipour, M., Nayyeri, P., Jabani, H., Shahab, S., & Mosavi, A. (2020). Predicting stock market trends using machine learning and deep learning algorithms via continuous and binary data; a comparative analysis. *IEEE Access : Practical Innovations, Open Solutions, 8*, 150199–150212. DOI: 10.1109/ACCESS.2020.3015966

Naga Sravanthi Puppala, R. M. (2023). "Cluster-based Trust Evaluation of Blockchain Miners in Pool Mining". *Second International Conference on Advances in Computational Intelligence and Communication (ICACIC),* 1-6.

Naidoo, M., & Gasparatos, A. (2018). Corporate environmental sustainability in the retail sector: Drivers, strategies and performance measurement. *Journal of Cleaner Production, 203*, 125–142. DOI: 10.1016/j.jclepro.2018.08.253

Nakashita, R., Suzuki, Y., Akamatsu, F., Iizumi, Y., Korenaga, T., & Chikaraishi, Y. (2008). Stable carbon, nitrogen, and oxygen isotope analysis as a potential tool for verifying geographical origin of beef. *Analytica Chimica Acta, 617*(1–2), 148–152. DOI: 10.1016/j.aca.2008.03.048 PMID: 18486650

Nalbant, K. G. (2024). The interaction of fuzzy logic with machine learning and artificial intelligence in decision-making models. In *Decision-Making Models* (pp. 563–571). Academic Press. DOI: 10.1016/B978-0-443-16147-6.00006-2

Nasr, E. G., Epova, E. N., Sebilo, M., Larivière, D., Hammami, M., Souissi, R., Abderrazak, H., & Donard, O. F. X. (2022). Olive oil traceability studies using inorganic and isotopic signatures: A review. *Molecules (Basel, Switzerland), 27*(6), 2014. DOI: 10.3390/molecules27062014 PMID: 35335378

Ndiango, S., Mwagike, L. R., & Changalima, I. A. (2025). Mapping the conceptual structure of green and sustainable human resource management in supply chain management research. *Discover Sustainability*, *6*(1), 348. DOI: 10.1007/s43621-025-00952-0

Nguyen, T. M. H., Nguyen, V. P., & Nguyen, D. T. (2024). A new hybrid Pythagorean fuzzy AHP and COCOSO MCDM based approach by adopting artificial intelligence technologies. *Journal of Experimental & Theoretical Artificial Intelligence*, *36*(7), 1279–1305. DOI: 10.1080/0952813X.2022.2143908

Niazi, S. K., & Mariam, Z. (2023). Recent advances in machine-learning-based chemoinformatics: A comprehensive review. *International Journal of Molecular Sciences*, *24*(14), 11488. DOI: 10.3390/ijms241411488 PMID: 37511247

Nicosia, L., Gnocchi, G., Gorini, I., Venturini, M., Fontana, F., Pesapane, F., Abiuso, I., Bozzini, A. C., Pizzamiglio, M., Latronico, A., Abbate, F., Meneghetti, L., Battaglia, O., Pellegrino, G., & Cassano, E. (2023). History of Mammography: Analysis of Breast Imaging Diagnostic Achievements over the Last Century. *Health Care*, *11*(11), 1596. DOI: 10.3390/healthcare11111596 PMID: 37297735

Nilashi, M., Zakaria, R., Ibrahim, O., Majid, M., Zin, R., & Farahmand, M. (2015). MCPCM: A DEMATEL-ANPBased Multi-Criteria Decision-Making Approach to Evaluate the Critical Success Factors in Construction Projects. *Arabian Journal for Science and Engineering*, *40*(2), 343–361. DOI: 10.1007/s13369-014-1529-1

Nişel, R., & Nişel, S. (2024). Advancing Global Innovation Metrics: A Comprehensive Country Ranking Using the Novel LOPCOW-CoCoSo Model. In *Ethics and Sustainability in Accounting and Finance* (Vol. IV, pp. 99–118). Springer Nature Singapore.

Niu, B., Zhang, J., & Xie, F. (2024). Drone logistics' resilient development: Impacts of consumer choice, competition, and regulation. *Transportation Research Part A, Policy and Practice*, *185*, 104126. DOI: 10.1016/j.tra.2024.104126

Niu, Y., Xie, G., Xiao, Y., Qin, K., Gan, S., & Liu, J. (2021). Spatial and temporal changes of ecosystem service value in airport economic zones in China. *Land (Basel)*, *10*(1054), 1–16. DOI: 10.3390/land10101054

Nobanee, H., & Ellili, N. (2016). Corporate Sustainability Disclosure in Annual Reports: Evidence from UAE Banks: Islamic versus Conventional. *Renewable & Sustainable Energy Reviews*, *55*, 1336–1341. DOI: 10.1016/j.rser.2015.07.084

Nordelöf, A., Messagie, M., Tillman, A. M., Ljunggren Söderman, M., & Van Mierlo, J. (2014). Environmental impacts of hybrid, plug-in hybrid, and battery electric vehicles—What can we learn from life cycle assessment? *The International Journal of Life Cycle Assessment, 19*(11), 1866–1890. DOI: 10.1007/s11367-014-0788-0

Noyan, E. (2023). Banka personeli seçiminin çok kriterli karar verme yöntemleri ile ele alınması. *Kapanaltı Dergisi*, (4), 112–121.

Nuroğlu, E., & Nuroğlu, H. H. Digital Transformation of Turkish Industry: Lessons from Germany's Example.

Nyambuu, U., & Semmler, W. (2023). *Fossil Fuel Resources.* Environment, and Climate Change., DOI: 10.1007/978-3-031-27982-9_4

Nzikou, J., Mvoula-Tsiéri, M., Ndangui, C., Pambou-Tobi, N., Kimbonguila, A., Loumouamou, B., Silou, T., & Desobry, S. (2010). Characterization of seeds and oil of sesame (*Sesamum indicum* L.) and the kinetics of degradation of the oil during heating. *Research Journal of Applied Sciences, Engineering and Technology*, *2*(3), 227–232.

Oboulbiga, E. B., Douamba, Z., Compaoré-Sérémé, D., Semporé, J. N., Dabo, R., Semde, Z., Tapsoba, F. W. B., Hama-Ba, F., Songré-Ouattara, L. T., Parkouda, C., & Dicko, M. H. (2023). Physicochemical, potential nutritional, antioxidant and health properties of sesame seed oil: A review. *Frontiers in Nutrition, 10*, 1127926. DOI: 10.3389/fnut.2023.1127926 PMID: 37377483

Öcal, F. M., & Altıntaş, K. (2018). Dördüncü Sanayi Devriminin Emek Piyasaları Üzerindeki Olası Etkilerinin İncelenmesi ve Çözüm Önerileri. *Opus International Journal of Society Researches*, *8*(15), 2066–2092.

Oesterreich, T. D., & Teuteberg, F. (2016). Understanding the Implications of Digitisation and Automation in The Context of Industry 4.0: A Triangulation Approach and Elements of A Research Agenda For The Construction İndustry. *Computers in Industry, 83*, 121–139. DOI: 10.1016/j.compind.2016.09.006

Öğütçü. Hilmi. (2022). Türkiye'nin En Başarılı Girişimlerinin Seçildiği Startup 100'ün 2021 Yılı Listesi. egirişim.com. https://egirisim.com/2021/11/12/turkiyenin-en-basarili-girisimlerinin-secildigi-startup-100un-2021-yili-listesi/, 24.04.2022.

Oliveira, A., Calili, R., Almeida, M. F., & Sousa, M. (2019). A systemic and contextual framework to define a country's 2030 agenda from a foresight perspective. *Sustainability (Basel), 11*(22), 6360. DOI: 10.3390/su11226360

Omrany, H., Al-Obaidi, K. M., Husain, A., & Ghaffarianhoseini, A. (2023). Digital twins in the construction industry: A comprehensive review of current implementations, enabling technologies, and future directions. *Sustainability (Basel), 15*(14), 10908. DOI: 10.3390/su151410908

Ömürbek, N., & Tunca, M. Z. (2013). ANALİTİK HİYERARŞİ SÜRECİ VE ANALİTİK AĞ SÜRECİ YÖNTEMLERİNDE GRUP KARARI VERİLMESİ AŞAMASINA İLİŞKİN BİR ÖRNEK UYGULAMA. *Süleyman Demirel Üniversitesi İktisadi ve İdari Bilimler Fakültesi Dergisi, 18*(3), 47–70. https://dergipark.org.tr/tr/pub/sduiibfd/issue/20817/222729

ONAY, A. (2015). Sürdürülebilir Kalkınma, Kurumsal Sürdürülebilirlik ve Sürdürülebilirlik Raporlaması. *Elektronik Mesleki Gelişim ve Araştırma Dergisi, 3*, 104–118.

Opricovic, S., & Tzeng, G. H. (2004). Compromise solution by MCDM methods: A comparative analysis of VIKOR and TOPSIS. *European Journal of Operational Research, 156*(2), 445–455. DOI: 10.1016/S0377-2217(03)00020-1

Osato Itohan Oriekhoe, B. A. (2023). Review of technological advancement in food supply chain management: Comparison between USA and Africa. *World Journal of Advanced Research and Reviews*, 1681-1693.

Osburg, T. (2017). Sustainability in a digital world. T. Osburg & C. Lohrmann (Eds.), *Sustainability in a Digital World Needs Trust* (pp. 3-19). Springer International Publishing.

Osorio, M. T., Haughey, S. A., Elliott, C. T., & Koidis, A. (2014). Evaluation of methodologies to determine vegetable oil species present in oil mixtures: Proposition of an approach to meet the EU legislation demands for correct vegetable oils labelling. *Food Research International, 60*, 66–75. DOI: 10.1016/j.foodres.2013.12.013

Ouassaf, M., Bourougaa, L., Al-Mijalli, S. H., Abdallah, E. M., Bhat, A. R., & Kawsar, S. M. A. (2023). Marine-derived compounds as potential inhibitors of Hsp90 for anticancer and antimicrobial drug development: A comprehensive in silico study. *Molecules (Basel, Switzerland), 28*(24), 8074. DOI: 10.3390/molecules28248074 PMID: 38138564

Oyegunle, A. (2016), An Assessment of Sustainable Banking Regulations in Emerging Economies, Watrerloo, Yüksek Lisans Tezi, University of Waterloo, Sustainability Management.

Oyelade, O. N., & Ezugwu, A. E. (2021). A bioinspired neural architecture search based convolutional neural network for breast cancer detection using histopathology images. *Scientific Reports*, *11*(1), 19940. DOI: 10.1038/s41598-021-98978-7 PMID: 34620891

Oza, P., Sharma, P., Patel, S., & Bruno, A. (2021). A bottom-up review of image analysis methods for suspicious region detection in mammograms. *Journal of Imaging*, *7*(9), 190. DOI: 10.3390/jimaging7090190 PMID: 34564116

Özbek, A. (2019). *Çok Kriterli Karar Verme Yöntemleri ve Excel İle Problem Çözümü: Kavram - Teori - Uygulama* (2nd ed.). Seçkin Yayıncılık.

Özcan, G. (2024). İşletmeler Bağlamında Metaverse: Swot Analizi İle Durum Değerlendirmesi. *Gaziantep Üniversitesi Sosyal Bilimler Dergisi*, *23*(4), 1587–1612. DOI: 10.21547/jss.1376122

Özdağoğlu, A., Keleş, M. K., & Genç, V. (2021). FUCOM ve PROMETHEE yöntemleri ile ticari araç seçimi: Peyzaj firmasında bir uygulama. *Atatürk Üniversitesi Sosyal Bilimler Enstitüsü Dergisi, 25*(Özel Sayı), 231-253. DOI: 10.53487/ataunisosbil.825910

Özdağoğlu, A., Işıldak, B., & Keleş, M. K. (2022). MEREC tabanlı COCOSO yöntemiyle uçuş okullarının uçak seçimlerinin değerlendirilmesi. *Gümüşhane Üniversitesi Sosyal Bilimler Dergisi*, *13*(2), 708–719.

Özdağoğlu, A., & Özdağoğlu, G. (2007). Comparison of AHP and fuzzy AHP for the multi-criteria decision making processes with linguistic evaluations. İstanbul Ticaret Üniversitesi. *Fen Bilimleri Dergisi*, *6*(11), 65–85.

Ozdagoglu, A., Ulutas, A., & Keles, M. K. (2020). The ranking of Turkish universities with COCOSO and MARCOS. *Journal of Economic Behavior & Organization*, •••, 374–392.

Özdemir, A., & Özgüner, M. (2018). Endüstri 4.0 ve Lojistik Sektörüne Etkileri: Lojistik 4.0. *İsletme Ve İktisat Çalışmaları Dergisi, 6*(4), 39–47. https://dergipark.org.tr/en/pub/iicder/issue/49884/639432

Özer, M. A. (2006). Yönetişim üzerine notlar. *Sayıştay Dergisi*, (63), 59–89.

Ozkaya, G., & Erdin, C. (2020). Evaluation of smart and sustainable cities through a hybrid MCDM approach based on ANP and TOPSIS technique. *Heliyon*, *6*(10), e05052. DOI: 10.1016/j.heliyon.2020.e05052 PMID: 33117896

Ozkurt, N. (2014). Current assessment and future projections of noise pollution at Ankara Esenbo a Airport, Turkey. *Transportation Research Part D, Transport and Environment*, *32*, 120–128. DOI: 10.1016/j.trd.2014.07.011

Özsoylu, A. F. (2017). Endüstri 4.0. *Çukurova Üniversitesi İktisadi ve İdari Bilimler Fakültesi Dergisi*, 21(1), 41-64.

Öztuna, B. (2017). *Endüstri 4.0 ile Çalışma Yaşamının Geleceği*. Gece Kitaplığı.

Ozulku, G., Yildirim, R. M., Toker, O. S., Karasu, S., & Durak, M. Z. (2017). Rapid detection of adulteration of cold pressed sesame oil with hazelnut, canola, and sunflower oils using ATR-FTIR spectroscopy combined with chemometrics. *Food Control*, *82*, 212–216. DOI: 10.1016/j.foodcont.2017.06.034

Padilla, R., Netto, S. L., & Da Silva, E. A. B. (2020). A survey on performance metrics for object-detection algorithms. *International Conference on Systems, Signals and Image Processing (IWSSIP)*, 237-242. IEEE. DOI: 10.1109/IWSSIP48289.2020.9145130

Pagano, A. M., & Liotine, M. (2020). *Technology in Supply Chain Management and Logistics: Current Practice and Future Applications*. Elsevier.

Paling, C., & Thomas, C. (2018). Airport sustainability and corporate social responsibility. In Halpern, N., & Graham, A. (Eds.), *The Routledge Companion to Air Transport Management*. Routledge. DOI: 10.4324/9781315630540-19

Pamucar, D., Deveci, M., Canıtez, F., & Bozanic, D. (2020). A fuzzy full consistency method-Dombi-Bonferroni model for prioritizing transportation demand management measures. *Applied Soft Computing*, *87*, 105952. DOI: 10.1016/j.asoc.2019.105952

Pamucar, D., Stević, Ž., & Sremac, S. (2018). A new model for determining weight coefficients of criteria in MCDM models: Full consistency method (FUCOM). *Symmetry*, *10*(9), 393. DOI: 10.3390/sym10090393

Pamuk, N. S., & Soysal, M. (2018). Yeni Sanayi Devrimi Endüstri 4.0 Üzerine Bir İnceleme. *Verimlilik Dergisi*, (1), 41–66.

Parris, T. M., & Kates, R. W. (2003). Characterizing and measuring sustainable development. *Annual Review of Environment and Resources*, *28*(1), 559–586. DOI: 10.1146/annurev.energy.28.050302.105551

Parvatikar, P. P., Patil, S., Khaparkhuntikar, K., Patil, S., Singh, P. K., Sahana, R., Kulkarni, R. V., & Raghu, A. V. (2023). Artificial intelligence: Machine learning approach for screening large database and drug discovery. *Antiviral Research*, *220*, 105740. DOI: 10.1016/j.antiviral.2023.105740 PMID: 37935248

Parviainen, P., Tihinen, M., Kääriäinen, J., & Teppola, S. (2017). Tackling the digitalization challenge: how to benefit from digitalization in practice. International journal of information systems and project management, 5(1), 63-77.

Patterson, J., Schulz, K., Vervoort, J., Van Der Hel, S., Widerberg, O., Adler, C., Hurlbert, M., Anderton, K., Sethi, M., & Barau, A. (2017). Exploring the governance and politics of transformations towards sustainability. *Environmental Innovation and Societal Transitions*, *24*, 1–16. DOI: 10.1016/j.eist.2016.09.001

Patton, M. Q. (2002). Qualitative research and evaluation methods. In *Sage* (3rd ed.). Sage., DOI: 10.2307/330063

Pawlak, K., & Kołodziejczak, M. (2020). The role of agriculture in ensuring food security in developing countries: Considerations in the context of the problem of sustainable food production. *Sustainability (Basel)*, *12*(13), 5488. DOI: 10.3390/su12135488

Pearce, B. (2012). The state of air transport markets and the airline industry after the great recession. *Journal of Air Transport Management*, *21*, 3–9. DOI: 10.1016/j.jairtraman.2011.12.011

Pedregosa, F., Varoquaux, G., Gramfort, A., Michel, V., Thirion, B., Grisel, O., Blondel, M., Prettenhofer, P., Weiss, R., & Dubourg, V. (2011). Scikit-learn: Machine learning in Python. *Journal of Machine Learning Research*, *12*, 2825–2830.

Peng, D., Bi, Y., Ren, X., Yang, G., Sun, S., & Wang, X. (2015). Detection and quantification of adulteration of sesame oils with vegetable oils using gas chromatography and multivariate data analysis. *Food Chemistry*, *188*, 415–421. DOI: 10.1016/j.foodchem.2015.05.001 PMID: 26041212

Pereira, A. C., & Romero, F. (2017). A review of the meanings and the implications of the Industry 4.0 concept. *Procedia Manufacturing*, *13*, 1206–1214. DOI: 10.1016/j.promfg.2017.09.032

Perera, C. S. R., Francis, V., & Gao, S. (2025). Uptake of Industry 4.0 technologies in Australian construction firms. *Engineering, Construction, and Architectural Management*. DOI: 10.1108/ECAM-07-2024-0976

Petruni, A., Giagloglou, E., Douglas, E., Geng, J., Leva, M. C., & Demichela, M. (2019). Applying Analytic Hierarchy Process (AHP) to choose a human factors technique: Choosing the suitable Human Reliability Analysis technique for the automotive industry. *Safety Science*, *119*, 229–239. DOI: 10.1016/j.ssci.2017.05.007

Pinter, É., Nikolett, D., & Zoltán, O. 2006. New Direction Line of Sustainable Development and Marketing in Green Banking. 22nd IMP-Conference in Milan. Italy.

Pirintsos, S., Panagiotopoulos, A., Bariotakis, M., Daskalakis, V., Lionis, C., Sourvinos, G., Karakasiliotis, I., Kampa, M., & Castanas, E. (2022). From traditional ethnopharmacology to modern natural drug discovery: A methodology discussion and specific examples. *Molecules (Basel, Switzerland)*, *27*(13), 4060. DOI: 10.3390/molecules27134060 PMID: 35807306

Pitt, M., Brown, A., & Smith, A. (2002). Waste management at airports. *Facilities*, *20*(5/6), 198–207. DOI: 10.1108/02632770210426684

Pitt, M., & Smith, A. (2003). Waste management efficiency at UK airports. *Journal of Air Transport Management*, *9*(2), 103–111. DOI: 10.1016/S0969-6997(02)00063-7

Polat, D. S., Evans, W. P., & Dogan, B. E. (2020). Contrast-enhanced digital mammography: Technique, clinical applications, and pitfalls. *AJR. American Journal of Roentgenology*, *215*(5), 1267–1278. DOI: 10.2214/AJR.19.22412 PMID: 32877247

Popović, M. (2021). An MCDM approach for personnel selection using the CoCoSo method. *Journal of process management and new technologies, 9*(3-4), 78-88. DOI:DOI: 10.5937/jouproman2103078P

Postorino, M. N., & Mantecchini, L. (2014). A transport carbon footprint methodology to assess airport carbon emissions. *Journal of Air Transport Management*, *37*, 76–86. DOI: 10.1016/j.jairtraman.2014.03.001

Pradhan, P., Costa, L., Rybski, D., Lucht, W., & Kropp, J. P. (2017). A systematic study of sustainable development goal (SDG) interactions. *Earth's Future*, *5*(11), 1169–1179. DOI: 10.1002/2017EF000632

Primrose, S., Woolfe, M., & Rollinson, S. (2010). Food forensics: Methods for determining the authenticity of foodstuffs. *Trends in Food Science & Technology*, *21*(12), 582–590. DOI: 10.1016/j.tifs.2010.09.006

Puppala, N. S., & Manoharan, R. (2024). Optimizing pool mining performance: A VIKOR-based model for identifying reputed miners in blockchain networks. *Concurrency and Computation*, *36*(21), 1–30. DOI: 10.1002/cpe.8211

Qi, X., Zhao, Y., Qi, Z., Hou, S., & Chen, J. (2024). Machine learning empowering drug discovery: Applications, opportunities and challenges. *Molecules (Basel, Switzerland)*, *29*(4), 903. DOI: 10.3390/molecules29040903 PMID: 38398653

Qiyas, M., Naeem, M., Khan, S., Abdullah, S., Botmart, T., & Shah, T. (2022). Decision support system based on CoCoSo method with the picture fuzzy information. *Journal of Mathematics*, *2022*(1), 1476233. DOI: 10.1155/2022/1476233

Quaschning, V. V. (2019). *Renewable energy and climate change*. John Wiley & Sons.

Quintana-García, C., Benavides-Chicón, C. G., & Marchante-Lara, M. (2021). Does a green supply chain improve corporate reputation? Empirical evidence from European manufacturing sectors. *Industrial Marketing Management*, *92*, 344–353. DOI: 10.1016/j.indmarman.2019.12.011

Qu, X., Shi, D., Zhao, J., Tran, M. K., Wang, Z., Fowler, M., Lian, Y., & Burke, A. F. (2024). Insights and Reviews on Battery Lifetime Prediction from Research to Practice. *Journal of Energy Chemistry*, *94*, 716–739. DOI: 10.1016/j.jechem.2024.03.013

Rachmad, Y. E. (2003). *Digital Ecological Transformation Philosophy Theory*. Education Training Centre.

Radenović, M., Tenodi, S., Krčmar, D., Zrnić Tenodi, K., Rončević, S., Radjenovic, D., & Dalmacija, B. (2024). Navigating the transition: An in-depth analysis of a non-sanitary landfill and a novel approach to selecting future sanitary landfill sites. *SSRN*. DOI: 10.2139/ssrn.4719592

Radomska, M., Cherniak, L., Madzhd, S., & Mikhyeyev, O. (2020). Environmental pollution in the airport impact area–case study of the Boryspil. *Environmental Problems*, *5*(2), 76–82. DOI: 10.23939/ep2020.02.076

Ragazzini, A. (2021). R&D Project Selection Problem: An analysis and application of AHP and PROMETHEE (Doctoral dissertation, Politecnico di Torino).

Raja Santhi, A., & Muthuswamy, P. (2023). Industry 5.0 or industry 4.0S? Introduction to industry 4.0 and a peek into the prospective industry 5.0 technologies. *International Journal on Interactive Design and Manufacturing*, *17*(2), 947–979. DOI: 10.1007/s12008-023-01217-8 PMID: 40478102

Rajagukguk, Y. V., Utcu, M. A., Islam, M., Muzolf-Panek, M., & Tomaszewska-Gras, J. (2022). Authenticity assessment from sesame seeds to oil and sesame products of various origin by differential scanning calorimetry. *Molecules (Basel, Switzerland)*, *27*(21), 7496. DOI: 10.3390/molecules27217496 PMID: 36364323

Rajan, S. C. (2006). Climate change dilemma: technology, social change or both?: An examination of long-term transport policy choices in the United States. *Energy Policy*, *34*(6), 664–679. DOI: 10.1016/j.enpol.2004.07.002

Rajeev Bhat, I. J. (2019). *Emerging issues and challenges in agri-food supply chain*. Academic Press.

Rajkumar, R., Lee, I., Sha, L., & Stankovic, J. (2010). Cyber-physical systems: The next computing revolution. *Design Automation Conference*, 731–736. DOI: 10.1145/1837274.1837461

Rakhmangulov, A., Burmistrov, K., & Osintsev, N. (2024). Multi-criteria system's design methodology for selecting open pits dump trucks. *Sustainability (Basel), 16*(2), 863. DOI: 10.3390/su16020863

Ramadan, S.Z. (2020). Methods used in computer-aided diagnosis for breast cancer detection using mammograms: A review. Journal of Healthcare Engineering. Article ID 9162464, 21 pages. DOI: 10.1155/2020/9162464

Rane, N., Achari, A., & Choudhary, S. (2023). Multi-Criteria Decision-Making (MCDM) as a powerful tool for sustainable development: Effective applications of AHP, FAHP, TOPSIS, ELECTRE, and VIKOR in sustainability. *International Research Journal of Modernization in Engineering Technology and Science, 5*(4), 2654–2670.

Rao, P. K., & Shukla, A. (2024). Strategic sustainability in Indian banking industry: A performance analysis. *International Journal of Productivity and Performance Management, 73*(6), 2016–2034. DOI: 10.1108/IJPPM-04-2023-0199

Raslan, M. A., Raslan, S. A., Shehata, E. M., Mahmoud, A. S., & Sabri, N. A. (2023). Advances in the applications of bioinformatics and chemoinformatics. *Pharmaceuticals (Basel, Switzerland), 16*(7), 1050. DOI: 10.3390/ph16071050 PMID: 37513961

Rath, K. C., Khang, A., & Roy, D. (2024). The role of Internet of Things (IoT) technology in Industry 4.0 economy. In *Advanced IoT technologies and applications in the industry 4.0 digital economy* (pp. 1–28). CRC Press. DOI: 10.1201/9781003434269-1

Raut, R., Naoufel, C., & Kharat, M. (2017). Sustainability in The Banking Industry: A Strategic Multi-Criteria Analysis. *Business Strategy and the Environment, 26*(4), 550–568. DOI: 10.1002/bse.1946

Ravan Ramzani, S., Konhaeusner, P., Olaniregun, O. A., Abu-Alkheil, A., & Alsharari, N. (2024). Integrating AI-Driven Green Finance Strategies for Sustainable Development: A Comparative Analysis of Renewable Energy Investments in Germany and Denmark. *European Journal of Business and Management Research, 9*(2), 43–55. DOI: 10.24018/ejbmr.2024.9.2.2277

Rebai, S., Azaiez, M., & Saidane, D. (2012). Sustainable Performance Evaluation of Banks Using A Multi-Attribute Utility Model: An Application to French Banks. *Procedia Economics and Finance, 2*, 363–372. DOI: 10.1016/S2212-5671(12)00098-6

Redman, A. (2018). Harnessing the Sustainable Development Goals for businesses: A progressive framework for action. *Business Strategy & Development, 1*(4), 230–243. DOI: 10.1002/bsd2.33

Remondino, M., & Zanin, A. (2022). Logistics and Agri-Food: Digitization to Increase Competitive Advantage and Sustainability. Literature Review and the Case of Italy. *Sustainability (Basel), 14*(2), 787. DOI: 10.3390/su14020787

Resce, G., & Schiltz, F. (2021). Sustainable development in Europe: A multicriteria decision analysis. *Review of Income and Wealth, 67*(2), 509–529. DOI: 10.1111/roiw.12475

Reshma, V. K., Arya, N., Ahmad, S. S., Wattar, I., Mekala, S., Joshi, S., & Krah, D. (2022). *Detection of breast cancer using histopathological image classification dataset with deep learning techniques.* BioMed Research International. DOI: 10.1155/2022/8363850

Reynolds, S. (2024). Exploring Sustainable Procurement Practices: A Qualitative Study of Supplier Selection Criteria.

Rezvani, S. M., Falcão, M. J., Komljenovic, D., & de Almeida, N. M. (2023). A systematic literature review on urban resilience enabled with asset and disaster risk management approaches and GIS-based decision support tools. *Applied Sciences (Basel, Switzerland), 13*(4), 2223. DOI: 10.3390/app13042223

Rhodes, C. N., Lofthouse, J. H., Hird, S., Rose, P., Reece, P., Christy, J., Macarthur, R., & Brereton, P. A. (2010). The use of stable carbon isotopes to authenticate claims that poultry have been corn-fed. *Food Chemistry, 118*(4), 927–932. DOI: 10.1016/j.foodchem.2008.05.113

Ristić, B., Bogdanović, V., & Stević, Ž. (2024). Urban evaluation of pedestrian crossings based on Start-Up Time using the MEREC-MARCOS Model. *J. Urban Dev. Manage, 3*(1), 34–42. DOI: 10.56578/judm030103

Ristono, A., Wahyuningsih, T., & Muhsin, A. (2025). Comprehensive Method for Supplier Selection in the Indonesian Leather Industry Considering Sustainable Development Goals Criteria. *Journal of Lifestyle and SDGs Review, 5*(2), e02994–e02994. DOI: 10.47172/2965-730X.SDGsReview.v5.n02.pe02994

Rogers, P. P., Jalal, K. F., & Boyd, J. A. (2012). *An introduction to sustainable development.* Routledge. DOI: 10.4324/9781849770477

Rondinelli, D. A., & Berry, M. A. (2000). Environmental citizenship in multinational corporations: Social responsibility and sustainable development. *European Management Journal, 18*(1), 70–84. DOI: 10.1016/S0263-2373(99)00070-5

Roosta, M., Javadpoor, M., & Ebadi, M. (2024). Operationalizing urban cooling; a framework for heat-resilient spaces in Iran's dry climates. *SSRN.* DOI: 10.2139/ssrn.4733169

Rout, K., Yadav, B. G., Yadava, S. K., Mukhopadhyay, A., Gupta, V., Pental, D., & Pradhan, A. K. (2018). QTL landscape for oil content in Brassica juncea: Analysis in multiple bi-parental populations in high and "0" erucic background. *Frontiers in Plant Science*, *9*, 1448. DOI: 10.3389/fpls.2018.01448 PMID: 30386353

Ryley, T., Elmirghani, J., Budd, T., Miyoshi, C., Mason, K., Moxon, R., Ahmed, I., Qazi, B., & Zanni, A. (2013). Sustainable development and airport surface access: The role of technological innovation and behavioral change. *Sustainability (Basel)*, *5*(4), 1617–1631. DOI: 10.3390/su5041617

Saaty, T. (1980, November). The analytic hierarchy process (AHP) for decision making. In Kobe, Japan (Vol. 1, p. 69).

Saaty, T. L. (1996). *Decision making with dependence and feedback: The analytic network process*. RWS Publications. https://scholar.archive.org/work/bmi3dl3urnhn3kx6x5cauuyyz4/access/wayback/http://www.cs.put.poznan.pl/ewgmcda/pdf/SaatyBook.pdf

Saaty, T. L. (2001). Fundamentals of the analytic hierarchy process. The analytic hierarchy process in natural resource and environmental decision making, 15-35.

Saaty, T. L. (2004). Decision making—The analytic hierarchy and network processes (AHP/ANP). *Journal of Systems Science and Systems Engineering*, *13*(1), 1–35. DOI: 10.1007/s11518-006-0151-5

Saaty, T. L. (2008). Relative measurement and its generalization in decision making why pairwise comparisons are central in mathematics for the measurement of intangible factors the analytic hierarchy/network process. *RACSAM-Revista de la Real Academia de Ciencias Exactas Fisicas y Naturales. Serie A. Revista de la Real Academia de Ciencias Exactas, Físicas y Naturales. Serie A, Matemáticas*, *102*(2), 251–318. DOI: 10.1007/BF03191825

Saaty, T. L. (2008). Relative measurement and its generalization in decision making why pairwise comparisons are central in mathematics for the measurement of intangible factors the analytic hierarchy/network process. RACSAM-Revista de la Real Academia de Ciencias Exactas, Fisicas y Naturales. Serie A. *Matematicas*, *102*, 251–318.

Saaty, T. L. (2013). Analytic hierarchy process. In *Encyclopedia of operations research and management science* (pp. 52–64). Springer. DOI: 10.1007/978-1-4419-1153-7_31

Saaty, T. L., & Vargas, L. G. (2006). *DECISION MAKING WITH THE ANALYTIC NETWORK PROCESS Economic, Political, Social and Technological Applications with Benefits, Opportunities, Costs and Risks*. Springer.

Saaty, T. L., & Vargas, L. G. (2012). *Models, methods, concepts & applications of the analytic hierarchy process* (Vol. 175). Springer Science & Business Media. DOI: 10.1007/978-1-4614-3597-6

Sadybekov, A. V., & Katritch, V. (2023). Computational approaches streamlining drug discovery. *Nature*, *616*(7958), 673–685. DOI: 10.1038/s41586-023-05905-z PMID: 37100941

Şahin, M. (2023). Ensemble decision making for logistics center location. *Environment, Development and Sustainability*, 1–35.

Sahlgren, C., Meinander, A., Zhang, H., Cheng, F., Preis, M., Xu, C., Salminen, T. A., Toivola, D., Abankwa, D., Rosling, A., Şen Karaman, D., Salo-Ahen, O. M. H., Österbacka, R., Eriksson, J. E., Willför, S., Petre, I., Peltonen, J., Leino, R., & Johnson, M.. (2017). Tailored approaches in drug development and diagnostics: From molecular design to biological model systems. *Advanced Healthcare Materials*, *6*(21), 1700258. DOI: 10.1002/adhm.201700258 PMID: 28892296

Sahoo, S. K., Choudhury, B. B., & Dhal, P. R. (2024). A bibliometric analysis of material selection using MCDM methods: Trends and insights. *Spectrum of Mechanical Engineering and Operational Research*, *1*(1), 189–205. DOI: 10.31181/smeor11202417

Sahoo, S. K., & Goswami, S. S. (2023). A comprehensive review of multiple criteria decision-making (MCDM) Methods: Advancements, applications, and future directions. *Decision Making Advances*, *1*(1), 25–48. DOI: 10.31181/dma1120237

Sahoo, S. K., & Goswami, S. S. (2024). Green supplier selection using MCDM: A comprehensive review of recent studies. *Spectrum of Engineering and Management Sciences*, *2*(1), 1–16. DOI: 10.31181/sems1120241a

Sahoo, S. K., Goswami, S. S., & Halder, R. (2024). Supplier selection in the age of industry 4.0: A review on MCDM applications and trends. *Decision Making Advances*, *2*(1), 32–47. DOI: 10.31181/dma21202420

Sain, Z. H., Nurtina, S., Agoi, M. A., & Thelma, C. C. (2024). Sustainable Development. *Journal of Information Systems and Technology Research*, *3*(2), 80–85. DOI: 10.55537/jistr.v3i2.830

Salehi, A. W., Khan, S., Gupta, G., Alabduallah, B. I., Almjally, A., Alsolai, H., Siddiqui, T., & Mellit, A. (2023). A Study of CNN and Transfer Learning in Medical Imaging: Advantages, Challenges, Future Scope. *Sustainability (Basel), 15*(7), 5930. DOI: 10.3390/su15075930

Salik Ata, N. (2024). Türkiye'nin Endüstri 4.0'a Geçiş Sürecinin Değerlendirilmesi. *Yönetim Bilimleri Dergisi, 22*(51), 119–141. DOI: 10.35408/comuybd.1344608

Salimian, S., & Mousavi, S. M. (2023). A multi-criteria decision-making model with interval-valued intuitionistic fuzzy sets for evaluating digital technology strategies in COVID-19 pandemic under uncertainty. *Arabian Journal for Science and Engineering, 48*(5), 7005–7017. DOI: 10.1007/s13369-022-07168-8 PMID: 36090763

Sánchez, L. E., & Croal, P. (2012). Environmental impact assessment, from Rio-92 to Rio+ 20 and beyond. *Ambiente & Sociedade, 15*(3), 41–54. DOI: 10.1590/S1414-753X2012000300004

Sanjay Narang, D., Monika Panchani, D., Kiran Chauhan, D., Manoj Thakur, D., & Radhika Jamwal, D. (2024). ENVIRONMENTAL INNOVATION AND SUSTAINABLE DEVELOPMENT THROUGH GREEN TECHNOLOGYs. In *Futuristic Trends in Renewable & Sustainable Energy Volume 3 Book 3* (pp. 285–291). Iterative International Publishers, Selfypage Developers Pvt Ltd. DOI: 10.58532/V3BIRS3P12CH1

Sanni, G. B. T. A., Ezin, V., Chabi, I. B., Missihoun, A. A., Florent, Q., Hamissou, Z., Niang, M., & Ahanchede, A. (2024). Production and achievements of *Sesamum indicum* industry in the world: Past and current state. *Oil Crop Science, 9*(3), 187–197. DOI: 10.1016/j.ocsci.2024.06.006

Santana, N. B., Aparecida do Nascimento Rebelatto, D., Périco, A. E., & Mariano, E. B. (2014). Sustainable development in the BRICS countries: An efficiency analysis by data envelopment. *International Journal of Sustainable Development and World Ecology, 21*(3), 259–272. DOI: 10.1080/13504509.2014.900831

Saracel, N., & Aksoy, I. (2020). Toplum 5.0: Süper Akıllı Toplum. *Sosyal Bilimler Araştırma Dergisi, 9*(2), 26–34.

Sarkar, C., Das, B., Rawat, V. S., Wahlang, J. B., Nongpiur, A., Tiewsoh, I., Lyngdoh, N. M., Das, D., Bidarolli, M., & Sony, H. T. (2023). Artificial Intelligence and Machine Learning Technology Driven Modern Drug Discovery and Development. *International Journal of Molecular Sciences, 24*(3), 2026. DOI: 10.3390/ijms24032026 PMID: 36768346

Sarsby, A. (2016). *SWOT analysis*. Leadership Library.

Savaresi, A. (2016). The Paris Agreement: A new beginning? *Journal of Energy & Natural Resources Law*, *34*(1), 16–26. DOI: 10.1080/02646811.2016.1133983

SAVRAM. M. ve KARAKOÇ, A. (2012). Bankacılık Sektöründe İtibar Riskinin Önemi. International Conference on Euroasian Economies (ss. 328-332). Almaata: Kazakistan.

Sayar, S. (2019). Dijitalleşme ile Yeni Oluşan Kavramlar: Endüstri 4.0, IOT ve Blockchain Uygulamaları (Master's Thesis, Maltepe Üniversitesi, Sosyal Bilimler Enstitüsü).

Sbihi, A., & Eglese, R. W. (2010). Combinatorial optimization and Green Logistics. *Annals of Operations Research*, *175*(1), 159–175. DOI: 10.1007/s10479-009-0651-z

Schmidt, R., Möhring, M., Härting, R. C., Reichstein, C., Neumaier, P., & Jozinović, P. (2015). Industry 4.0 - Potentials for Creating Smart Products: Empirical Research Results. *18th International Conference on Business Information Systems, LNBIP*, 16–27. DOI: 10.1007/978-3-319-19027-3_2

Scholtens, B. (2008). Corporate social responsibility in the international banking industry. *Journal of Business Ethics*, *86*(2), 159–175. DOI: 10.1007/s10551-008-9841-x

Scholtens, B., & Van't Klooster, S. (2019). Sustainability and Bank Risk. *Palgrave Communications*, *5*(1), 1–8. DOI: 10.1057/s41599-019-0315-9

Sebastian, R. M., & Louis, J. (2021). Understanding waste management at airports: A study on current practices and challenges based on literature review. *Renewable & Sustainable Energy Reviews*, *147*(May), 111229. DOI: 10.1016/j.rser.2021.111229

Sechopoulos, I., Teuwen, J., & Mann, R. (2021). Artificial intelligence for breast cancer detection in mammography and digital breast tomosynthesis: State of the art. *Seminars in Cancer Biology*, *72*, 214–225. DOI: 10.1016/j.semcancer.2020.06.002 PMID: 32531273

Seidel, S., Recker, J., & Vom Brocke, J. (2013). Sensemaking and sustainable practicing: Functional affordances of information systems in green transformations. *Management Information Systems Quarterly*, *37*(4), 1275–1299. DOI: 10.25300/MISQ/2013/37.4.13

Şekkeli, H. Z., & Bakan, İ. (2018). Akıllı Fabrikalar. *Journal of Life Economics*, *5*(4), 205–215. DOI: 10.15637/jlecon.270

Semeraro, F., Griffiths, A., & Cangelosi, A. (2023). Human–robot collaboration and machine learning: A systematic review of recent research. *Robotics and Computer-integrated Manufacturing*, *79*, 102432. DOI: 10.1016/j.rcim.2022.102432

Şendurur, U., & Temelli, F. (2018). Türkiye'de Faaliyet Gösteren Geleneksel Bankalar ve Katılım Bankalarının Sürdürülebilirlik Açısından Karşılaştırılması. *Muhasebe Bilim Dünyası Dergisi*, *20*(2), 330–346. DOI: 10.31460/mbdd.344785

Şen, H. (2022). *Çalışma hayatında paradigma kayması: Endüstri 4.0 ile geleceğin mesleklerine bakış*. İksad Publishing House.

Sergi, D., & Ucal Sari, I. (2021). Prioritization of public services for digitalization using fuzzy Z-AHP and fuzzy Z-WASPAS. *Complex & Intelligent Systems*, *7*(2), 841–856. DOI: 10.1007/s40747-020-00239-z

Sever, H. (2021). İnsansız Hava Aracı Sistemlerinde Stratejik Yönetim ve SWOT Analizi. *ITOBIAD. Journal of the Human & Social Science Researches*, *10*(2).

Seyedmohammadi, J., Sarmadian, F., Jafarzadeh, A. A., Ghorbani, M. A., & Shahbazi, F. (2018). Application of SAW, TOPSIS and fuzzy TOPSIS models in cultivation priority planning for maize, rapeseed and soybean crops. *Geoderma*, *310*, 178–190. DOI: 10.1016/j.geoderma.2017.09.012

Seyhan, N. (2023). AB'de Döngüsel Ekonomi Üretim ve Tüketim Göstergelerinin Değerlendirilmesi: MEREC Temelli MARCOS Uygulaması. *Sosyal Mucit Academic Review*, *4*(3), 364–391. DOI: 10.54733/smar.1338423

Sezgin, A., & Aytekin, S. (2024). BİST Balıkesir endeksi firmalarının MEREC tabanlı CoCoSo yöntemiyle finansal performans analizi. *Balıkesir Üniversitesi Sosyal Bilimler Enstitüsü Dergisi, 27*(51-1-2024 Yılı Özel Sayısı), 63-77.

Sezgin, A., Aytekin, S., & Sakarya, Ş. (2024). Finansal performansın ölçülmesinde Piotroski F-Skoru bileşenleri ve ÇKKV yöntemlerinin bağlantısı: MEREC tabanlı MARCOS uygulaması. *Ekonomi Politika ve Finans Araştırmaları Dergisi*, *9*(2), 367–395. DOI: 10.30784/epfad.1481070

Shahidi, F., Mohd Daud, S., Abas, H., Ahmad, N. A., & Maarop, N. (2020). Breast cancer classification using deep learning approaches and histopathology image: A comparison study. *IEEE Access : Practical Innovations, Open Solutions*, *8*, 187531–187552. DOI: 10.1109/ACCESS.2020.3029881

Shah, N. (2023). Technology Adoption in Food Supply Chain Management in Developing Countries: A Review. *International Journal of Engineering and Advanced Technology*, *12*(3), 11–18. DOI: 10.35940/ijeat.C3961.0212323

Shang, C., & Xu, D. (2022). Epidemiology of Breast Cancer. *Oncologie*, *24*(4), 649–663. DOI: 10.32604/oncologie.2022.027640

Shanmuga Sundari, M., Sudha Rani, M., & Kranthi, A. (2022). *Detect traffic lane image using geospatial LiDAR data point clouds with machine learning analysis.* In Intelligent System Design [Singapore: Springer Nature Singapore.]. *Proceedings of INDIA, 2022*, 217–225.

Shanmuganathan, M. P. (2024). A Strategic Decision Analysis Framework for Software-as-a-Service Selection: A Systematic Data-Driven Approach (Master's thesis, University of Twente).

Sharafaddini, A. M., Kouhpah Esfahani, K., & Mansouri, N. (2024). Deep learning approaches to detect breast cancer: A comprehensive review. *Multimedia Tools and Applications*, 1–112.

Sharma, R., Kim, M., Gupta, A. 2022. Motor imagery classification in brain–machine interface with machine learning algorithms: Classical approach to multi-layer perceptron model. Biomedical Signal Processing and Control. 71 (A), 103101. DOI: 10.1016/j.bspc.2021.103101

Sharma, R. C., & Kohli, D. (2024). Embracing digital transformation for sustainable development: The synergy between learning organizations, human resource management, and service quality. *Journal of Chinese Human Resource Management*, *14*(3), 3–17. DOI: 10.47297/wspchrmWSP2040-800501.20231403

Sharma, Y., Yadav, A. K., Mangla, S. K., & Patil, P. P. (2018). Ranking the Success Factors to Improve Safety and Security in Sustainable Food Supply Chain Management Using Fuzzy AHP. *Materials Today: Proceedings*, *5*(5), 12187–12196. DOI: 10.1016/j.matpr.2018.02.196

Sheehy, B., & Farneti, F. (2021). Corporate social responsibility, sustainability, sustainable development and corporate sustainability: What is the difference, and does it matter? *Sustainability (Basel)*, *13*(11), 5965. DOI: 10.3390/su13115965

Shieh, J. I., Wu, H. H., & Huang, K. K. (2010). A DEMATEL method in identifying key success factors of hospital service quality. *Knowledge-Based Systems*, *23*(3), 277–282. DOI: 10.1016/j.knosys.2010.01.013

Shrivastava, P. (2018). Environmental technologies and competitive advantage. In *Business Ethics and Strategy* (Vol. I and II, pp. 317–334). Routledge.

Signitzer, B., & Prexl, A. (2007). Corporate sustainability communications: Aspects of theory and professionalization. *Journal of Public Relations Research*, *20*(1), 1–19. DOI: 10.1080/10627260701726996

Simão, L. E., Gonc, M. B., Manuel, C., & Rodriguez, T. (2016). *An approach to assess logistics and ecological supply chain performance using postponement strategies. 63*, 398–408. DOI: 10.1016/j.ecolind.2015.10.048

Simic, V., Gokasar, I., Deveci, M., & Švadlenka, L. (2022). Mitigating climate change effects of urban transportation using a type-2 neutrosophic MEREC-MARCOS model. *IEEE Transactions on Engineering Management*, *71*, 3233–3249. DOI: 10.1109/TEM.2022.3207375

Simić, V., Ivanović, I., Đorić, V., & Torkayesh, A. E. (2022). Adapting urban transport planning to the COVID-19 pandemic: An integrated fermatean fuzzy model. *Sustainable Cities and Society*, *79*, 103669. DOI: 10.1016/j.scs.2022.103669 PMID: 35013703

Singh, B., Crasto, M., Ravi, K., & Singh, S. (2024). Pharmaceutical Advances: Integrating Artificial Intelligence in QSAR, Combinatorial, and Green Chemistry Practices. *Intelligent Pharmacy*, *2*(5), 598–608. DOI: 10.1016/j.ipha.2024.05.005

Singh, K. P., & Gulati, D. I. P. T. I. (2011). Technological March from Web 1.0 to Web 3.0: A Comparative Study. *Libray Herald*, *49*(2), 146–157.

Singh, S., Agrawal, V., & Mohanty, R. P. (2022). Multi-criteria decision analysis of significant enablers for a competitive supply chain. *Journal of Advances in Management Research*, *19*(3), 414–442. DOI: 10.1108/JAMR-09-2021-0322

Sinh, U. (2024). IDENTIFICATION AND EVALUATION OF DISTRIBUTION RISK IN FOOD SUPPLY CHAIN USING AHP METHOD. *INTERANTIONAL JOURNAL OF SCIENTIFIC RESEARCH IN ENGINEERING AND MANAGEMENT*, 1-5.

Sipahi, S., & Timor, M. (2010). The analytic hierarchy process and analytic network process: An overview of applications. *Management Decision*, *48*(5), 775–808. DOI: 10.1108/00251741011043920

Si, S. L., You, X. Y., Liu, H. C., & Zhang, P. (2018). DEMATEL technique: A systematic review of the state-of-the-art literature on methodologies and applications. *Mathematical Problems in Engineering*, *2018*(1), 3696457. DOI: 10.1155/2018/3696457

Sobhani, F. A., Amran, A., & Zainuddin, Y. (2009). Revisiting the Practices of Corporate Social and Environmental Disclosure in Bangladesh. *Corporate Social Responsibility and Environmental Management*, *16*(3), 167–183. DOI: 10.1002/csr.193

Sobhani, F. A., Amran, A., & Zainuddin, Y. (2012). Sustainability Disclosure in Annual Reports and Websites: A Study of Banking Industry in Bangladesh. *Journal of Cleaner Production*, *23*(1), 75–85. DOI: 10.1016/j.jclepro.2011.09.023

Sönmez, G. Ö., & Toktaş, P. (2024). Supplier selection using the integrated MEREC–CoCoSo methods in a medical device company. *Journal of Scientific Reports-A*, (056), 116–133. DOI: 10.59313/jsr-a.1420728

Sousa, M., Almeida, M. F., & Calili, R. (2021). Multiple criteria decision making for the achievement of the UN sustainable development goals: A systematic literature review and a research agenda. *Sustainability (Basel)*, *13*(8), 4129. DOI: 10.3390/su13084129

Soydaş, Ş. S. (2024). Portfolio selection with AHP and TOPSIS methods: An application in BIST. *Trends in Business and Economics*, *39*(2), 181–194. DOI: 10.16951/trendbusecon.1580489

Soylu, A. (2018). Endüstri 4.0 ve Girişimcilikte Yeni Yaklaşımlar. *Pamukkale Üniversitesi Sosyal Bilimler Enstitüsü Dergisi*, (32), 43–57. DOI: 10.30794/pausbed.424955

Sözen, M., & Mescioğlu, T. (2019). Endüstri 4.0'ın İtici Güçlerinin Türkiye ve Çin Üzerindeki Etkileri. *International Journal of Social Inquiry*, *12*(1), 287–315.

Sparviero, S., & Ragnedda, M. (2021). Towards digital sustainability: The long journey to the sustainable development goals 2030. Digital Policy. *Regulation & Governance*, *23*(3), 216–228. DOI: 10.1108/DPRG-01-2021-0015

Spink, J., & Moyer, D. C. (2011). Defining the public health threat of food fraud. *Journal of Food Science*, *76*(9), R157–R163. DOI: 10.1111/j.1750-3841.2011.02417.x PMID: 22416717

SPK. (2005). *Kurumsal Yönetim İlkeleri.*

Srdjevic, B. (2005). Combining different prioritization methods in the analytic hierarchy process synthesis. *Computers & Operations Research*, *32*(7), 1897–1919. DOI: 10.1016/j.cor.2003.12.005

Sreenath, S., Sudhakar, K., & Yusop, A. F. (2021). Sustainability at airports: Technologies and best practices from ASEAN countries. *Journal of Environmental Management*, *299*(August), 113639. DOI: 10.1016/j.jenvman.2021.113639 PMID: 34479146

Sriram, S., Ramachandran, M., Chinnasamy, S., & Mathivanan, G. (2022). A review on multi-criteria decision-making and its application. REST Journal on Emerging trends in Modelling and Manufacturing, 7(4), 101-107.

Stankovic, M., Neftenov, N., & Gupta, R. (2022). Use of Digital Tools in Fighting Climate Change: A Review of Best Practices. Availabe online: https://bit. ly/3Gxodt6 (accessed on 21 October).

Stankovic, J. J., Marjanovic, I., Drezgic, S., & Popovic, Z. (2021). The digital competitiveness of European countries: A multiple-criteria approach. *Journal of Competitiveness*, *13*(2), 117–134. DOI: 10.7441/joc.2021.02.07

Stanujkic, D., Popovic, G., Zavadskas, E. K., Karabasevic, D., & Binkyte-Veliene, A. (2020). Assessment of progress towards achieving Sustainable Development Goals of the "Agenda 2030" by using the CoCoSo and the Shannon Entropy methods: The case of the EU Countries. *Sustainability (Basel)*, *12*(14), 5717. DOI: 10.3390/su12145717

Stearns, P. N. (2020). *The industrial revolution in world history*. Routledge. DOI: 10.4324/9781003050186

Stephens, C., Skinner, C. (2013), " Banks For A Better PLlanet? The Challenge of Sustainable Social and Environmental Development and the Emerging Response of the Banking Sector" Environmental Development, 5-1, 175-179, DOI: 10.1016/j.envdev.2012.11.011

Stević, Ž., & Brković, N. (2020). A novel integrated FUCOM-MARCOS model for evaluation of human resources in a transport company. *Logistics (Basel)*, *4*(1), 4–14. DOI: 10.3390/logistics4010004

Stević, Ž., Pamučar, D., Puška, A., & Chatterjee, P. (2020). Sustainable supplier selection in healthcare industries using a new MCDM method: Measurement of alternatives and ranking according to COmpromise solution (MARCOS). *Computers & Industrial Engineering*, *140*, 106231. DOI: 10.1016/j.cie.2019.106231

Štilić, A., Puška, A., Božanić, D., & Đurić, A. (2024). Ranking European Countries Using Hybrid MEREC-MARCOS MCDA Based on Travel and Tourism Development Index. *Tourism (Zagreb)*, *72*(4), 592–608. DOI: 10.37741/t.72.4.6

Stojčić, M., Zavadskas, E. K., Pamučar, D., Stević, Ž., & Mardani, A. (2019). *Application of MCDM methods in sustainability engineering: A literature review* 2008–2018. *Symmetry*, *11*(3), 350. DOI: 10.3390/sym11030350

Strandhagen, J. O., Vallandingham, L. R., Fragapane, G., Strandhagen, J. W., Stangeland, A. B. H., & Sharma, N. (2017). Logistics 4.0 and emerging sustainable business models. *Advances in Manufacturing*, *5*(4), 359–369. DOI: 10.1007/s40436-017-0198-1

Styvén, M. E., & Wallström, Å. (2019). Benefits and barriers for the use of digital channels among small tourism companies. *Scandinavian Journal of Hospitality and Tourism, 19*(1), 27–46. DOI: 10.1080/15022250.2017.1379434

Subramanian, N., & Abdulrahman, M. D. (2017). Logistics and cloud computing service providers' cooperation: A resilience perspective. *Production Planning and Control, 28*(11–12), 919–928. DOI: 10.1080/09537287.2017.1336793

Sudhakar, Y., Kuotsu, K., & Bandyopadhyay, A. K. (2006). Buccal bioadhesive drug delivery — A promising option for orally less efficient drugs. *Journal of Controlled Release, 114*(1), 15–40. DOI: 10.1016/j.jconrel.2006.04.012 PMID: 16828915

Suganyadevi, S., Seethalakshmi, V., & Balasamy, K. (2022). A review on deep learning in medical image analysis. *International Journal of Multimedia Information Retrieval, 11*(1), 19–38. DOI: 10.1007/s13735-021-00218-1 PMID: 34513553

Suri, K., Singh, B., Kaur, A., Yadav, M. P., & Singh, N. (2019). Impact of infrared and dry air roasting on the oxidative stability, fatty acid composition, Maillard reaction products and other chemical properties of black cumin (Nigella sativa L.) seed oil. *Food Chemistry, 295*, 537–547. DOI: 10.1016/j.foodchem.2019.05.140 PMID: 31174793

Sürmen, Y. E., & Güler, E. (2021). Endüstri 4.0 ve Bursa Otomotiv Sanayi: SWOT (GZFT) Analizi ile Bir Değerlendirme. *Dicle Üniversitesi Sosyal Bilimler Enstitüsü Dergisi*, (27), 328–347.

Sutton, P. (2004). A perspective on environmental sustainability. *Paper on the Victorian Commissioner for Environmental Sustainability, 1*, 32.

Tandoğan, D., & Özyurt, H. (2013). Bankacılık sektörünün ekonomik büyüme ve sürdürülebilir ekonomik kalkınma üzerine etkisi: Türkiye ekonomisi üzerine nedensellik testleri (1981-2009). *Marmara Üniversitesi İktisadi İdari Bilimler Dergisi, 35*(2), 49–80. DOI: 10.14780/iibdergi.201324459

Taner, B., & İlke, K. (2005). Toplam Kalite Yönetimi'nin Başarıyla Uygulanma Esasları–Bir Hizmet İşletmesi Örneği. *Çukurova Üniversitesi Sosyal Bilimler Enstitüsü Dergisi*, 14(1), 353-362.

Tang, C., Xie, X., Wei, G., Pan, L., & Qi, Z. (2024). Exploring the Evolutionary Characteristics of Food Security in China and the United States from a Multidimensional Perspective. *Foods, 13*(14), 2272. DOI: 10.3390/foods13142272 PMID: 39063356

Tanrıverdi, G., Bakır, M., & Merkert, R. (2020). What can we learn from the JATM literature for the future of aviation post Covid-19? - A bibliometric and visualization analysis. *Journal of Air Transport Management, 89*(June), 101916. DOI: 10.1016/j.jairtraman.2020.101916 PMID: 32901183

Tanrıverdi, G., Merkert, R., Karamaşa, Ç., & Asker, V. (2023). Using multi-criteria performance measurement models to evaluate the financial, operational and environmental sustainability of airlines. *Journal of Air Transport Management, 112*, 102456. DOI: 10.1016/j.jairtraman.2023.102456

Tanyaş, M. (2015). *İstanbul Loji sti k Sektör Anali zi Raporu.* Mavi Ofset. www .musiad.org.tr

Taous, F., Amenzou, N., Marah, H., Maia, R., Maguas, C., Bahmad, L., & Kelly, S. (2020). Stable isotope ratio analysis as a new tool to trace the geographical origin of Argan oils in Morocco. *Forensic Chemistry (Amsterdam, Netherlands), 17*, 100198. DOI: 10.1016/j.forc.2019.100198

Taous, F., El Ghali, T., Marah, H., Laraki, K., Islam, M., Cannavan, A., & Kelly, S. (2022). Geographical classification of authentic Moroccan argan oils and the rapid detection of soya and sunflower oil adulteration with ATR-FTIR spectroscopy and chemometrics. *Food Analytical Methods, 15*(11), 3032–3044. DOI: 10.1007/s12161-022-02333-z

Taş, M. A., & Alptekin, S. E. (2023). Evaluation of major cities in terms of smart cities: A developing country perspective. *Procedia Computer Science, 225*, 1717–1726. DOI: 10.1016/j.procs.2023.10.161

Taye, M. M. (2023). Theoretical Understanding of Convolutional Neural Network: Concepts, Architectures, Applications, Future Directions. *Computation (Basel, Switzerland), 11*(3), 52. DOI: 10.3390/computation11030052

Temimhan, D., Ekinci, E., & Kazancoglu, Y. (2024). Analysis of industry 4.0 applications for Turkish agriculture. In *E3S Web of Conferences* (Vol. 558, p. 01007). EDP Sciences. DOI: 10.1051/e3sconf/202455801007

Temmerman, W., Goeminne, R., Rawat, K. S., & Van Speybroeck, V. (2024). Computational modeling of reticular materials: The past, the present, and the future. *Advanced Materials*, 2412005. DOI: 10.1002/adma.202412005 PMID: 39723710

Thakkar, J. J. (2021). *Multi-criteria decision making* (Vol. 336). Springer. DOI: 10.1007/978-981-33-4745-8

Theodorakopoulos, L., Theodoropoulou, A., & Halkiopoulos, C. (2024). Enhancing Decentralized Decision-Making with Big Data and Blockchain Technology: A Comprehensive Review. *Applied Sciences (Basel, Switzerland)*, *14*(16), 7007. DOI: 10.3390/app14167007

Thiele, L. P. (2024). *Sustainability*. John Wiley & Sons.

Thinh, H. X., Van Duc, D., & Bao, N. C. (2024). The Effect of CoCoSo Method on the Ranks of Alternatives: A Case Study of Copper Electrical Wire Selection. *Engineering, Technology &. Applied Scientific Research*, *14*(6), 18307–18315.

Thomas, C. S., Maughan, J. A., Hooper, P. D., & Hume, K. I. (2010). Aircraft noise and community impacts. In R. Blockley & W. Shyy (Eds.), *Encyclopaedia of Aerospace Engineering: Volume 6 Environmental Impact, Manufacturing and Operations*. John Wiley & Sons. DOI: 10.1002/9780470686652.eae343

Tibshirani, R. J., & Efron, B. (1993). An introduction to the bootstrap. *Monographs on Statistics and Applied Probability*, *57*(1), 1–436.

Timm, I. J., & Lorig, F. (2015). Logistics 4.0 - A challenge for simulattion. *Winter Simulation Conference*, 3118–3119. DOI: 10.1109/WSC.2015.7408428

Tıraş, H. H. (2012). Sürdürülebilir kalkınma ve çevre: Teorik bir inceleme. *Kahramanmaraş Sütçü İmam Üniversitesi İktisadi ve İdari Bilimler Fakültesi Dergisi*, *2*(2), 57–73.

Tiwari, R., & Pathak, K. (2023). Local drug delivery strategies towards wound healing. *Pharmaceutics*, *15*(2), 634. DOI: 10.3390/pharmaceutics15020634 PMID: 36839956

Toker, K. (2018). Endüstri 4.0 ve Sürdürebilirliğe Etkileri. *İstanbul Üniversitesi İşletme Fakültesi İşletme İktisadi Enstitüsü Yönetim Dergisi*, 29(84), 51-64.

Toktaş, P., & Can, G. (2020). Görev Temelli Yeni Bir Stokastik Çok Kriterli Karar Verme Yaklaşımı Önerisi. *Avrupa Bilim ve Teknoloji Dergisi*, (18), 61–75. DOI: 10.31590/ejosat.657719

Tolliver, C., Keeley, A. R., & Managi, S. (2020). Drivers of green bond market growth: The importance of Nationally Determined Contributions to the Paris Agreement and implications for sustainability. *Journal of Cleaner Production*, *244*, 118643. DOI: 10.1016/j.jclepro.2019.118643

Torkayesh, A. E., Pamucar, D., Ecer, F., & Chatterjee, P. (2021). An integrated BWM-LBWA-CoCoSo framework for evaluation of healthcare sectors in Eastern Europe. *Socio-Economic Planning Sciences*, *78*, 101052. DOI: 10.1016/j.seps.2021.101052

Torkayesh, A. E., & Torkayesh, S. E. (2021). *Evaluation of information and communication technology development in G7 countries:* An integrated MCDM approach. *Technology in Society*, *66*, 101670. DOI: 10.1016/j.techsoc.2021.101670

Trachtenberg, A., & Akabayov, B. (2025). From patterns to pills: How informatics is shaping medicinal chemistry. *Pharmaceutics*, *17*(5), 612. DOI: 10.3390/pharmaceutics17050612 PMID: 40430903

Tran-Dang, H., Nicolas, K., Patrick, C., & Kim, D.-S. (2022). The Internet of Things for Logistics: Perspectives, Application Review, and Challenges. *IETE Technical Review*, *39*(1), 93–121. DOI: 10.1080/02564602.2020.1827308

Tran, K. A., Kondrashova, O., Bradley, A., Williams, E. D., Pearson, J. V., & Waddell, N. (2021). Deep learning in cancer diagnosis, prognosis and treatment selection. *Genome Medicine*, *13*(1), 1–17. DOI: 10.1186/s13073-021-00968-x PMID: 34579788

Trinh, C., Meimaroglou, D., & Hoppe, S. (2021). Machine learning in chemical product engineering: The state of the art and a guide for newcomers. *Processes (Basel, Switzerland)*, *9*(8), 1456. DOI: 10.3390/pr9081456

Tripathi, N., Goshisht, M. K., Sahu, S. K., & Arora, C. (2021). Applications of artificial intelligence to drug design and discovery in the big data era: A comprehensive review. *Molecular Diversity*, *25*(3), 1643–1664. DOI: 10.1007/s11030-021-10237-z PMID: 34110579

Tseng, M. L., & Lin, Y. H. (2009). Application of fuzzy DEMATEL to develop a cause and effect model of municipal solid waste management in Metro Manila. *Environmental Monitoring and Assessment*, *158*(1-4), 519–533. DOI: 10.1007/s10661-008-0601-2 PMID: 18951134

Tucker, C. (2020). We know how many people the earth can support. *The Journal of Population and Sustainability*, *5*(1). DOI: 10.3197/jps.2020.5.1.77

Turgut, M. (2024). Tarım-Gıda Tedarik Zincirinde Endüstri 4.0 Teknolojilerinin Lojistik Faaliyetler Sürecinde Kullanımı. *Turkish Journal of Agriculture - Food Science and Technology*, *12*(11), 1968–1980. DOI: 10.24925/turjaf.v12i11.1968-1980.6822

Türkoğlu, S. P., & Tuzcu, S. E. (2021). Assessing country performances during the COVID-19 pandemic: A standard deviation based range of value method. *Operational Research in Engineering Sciences: Theory and Applications*, *4*(3), 59–81. DOI: 10.31181/oresta081221059t

Tzeng, G. H., & Huang, J. J. (2011). *Multiple attribute decision making: methods and applications*. Chapman and Hall/CRC. DOI: 10.1201/b11032

UNEP FI. 2008 Overview, https://www.unepfi.org/fileadmin/documents/unepfi_overview_2008.pdf

United Nations Environment Programme. (2024). *Emissions Gap Report 2024: No more hot air ... please! With a massive gap between rhetoric and reality, countries draft new climate commitments*. United Nations Environment Programme., DOI: 10.59117/20.500.11822/46404

Ünlü, U., Yalçın, N., & Avşarlıgil, N. (2022). Analysis of efficiency and productivity of commercial banks in turkey pre-and during COVID-19 with an integrated MCDM approach. *Mathematics, 10*(13), 2300. DOI: 10.3390/math10132300

Upham, P. J., & Mills, J. N. (2005). Environmental and operational sustainability of airports: Core indicators and stakeholder communication. *Benchmarking, 12*(2), 166–179. DOI: 10.1108/14635770510593103

Uzgör, M. (2024). *Evaluation of airport environmental management performance with multi criteria decision making methods: An application at five major airports in Türkiye.* (Publication No. 843343) [Doctoral dissertation, Anadolu University] YÖK Ulusal Tez Merkezi.

Uzgör, M., Selahattin Ateş, S., & Kafalı, H. (2024). Bibliometric Analysis of Environmental Management Literature in Aviation. *Transportation Research Record, 2678*(8), 374-395. DOI: 10.1177/03611981231216981

Valdés, A., Beltrán, A., Karabagias, I., Badeka, A., Kontominas, M. G., & Garrigós, M. C. (2015). Monitoring the oxidative stability and volatiles in blanched, roasted and fried almonds under normal and accelerated storage conditions by DSC, thermogravimetric analysis and ATR-FTIR. *European Journal of Lipid Science and Technology, 117*(8), 1199–1213. DOI: 10.1002/ejlt.201400384

Valentina, D. S., Di Pasquale, V., Giubileo, V., & Miranda, S. (2022). Human-Robot Collaboration: An analysis of worker's performance. *Procedia Computer Science, 200*, 1540–1549. DOI: 10.1016/j.procs.2022.01.355

Van Dua, T. (2023). Forklift selection by multi-criteria decision making methods. *Eastern-European Journal of Enterprise Technologies, 125*(3).

Vargas, L. G. (1990). An overview of the analytic hierarchy process and its applications. *European Journal of Operational Research, 48*(1), 2–8. DOI: 10.1016/0377-2217(90)90056-H

Vartolomei, V. C., & Avasilcai, S. (2019, August). Challenges of digitalization process in different industries. Before and after. In *IOP Conference Series: Materials Science and Engineering, 568* (Vol. 1). IOP Publishing.

Vinay Surendra Yadav, B. E. (2022). A systematic literature review of the agro-food supply chain: Challenges, network design, and performance measurement perspectives. *Sustainable Production and Consumption*, *29*, 685–704. DOI: 10.1016/j.spc.2021.11.019

Virdee, P. S., Marian, I. R., Mansouri, A., Elhussein, L., Kirtley, S., Holt, T., & Birks, J. (2020). The full blood count blood test for colorectal cancer detection: A systematic review, meta-analysis, and critical appraisal. *Cancers (Basel)*, *12*(9), 2348. DOI: 10.3390/cancers12092348 PMID: 32825191

Vlachos, N., Skopelitis, Y., Psaroudaki, M., Konstantinidou, V., Chatzilazarou, A., & Tegou, E. (2006). Applications of Fourier transform-infrared spectroscopy to edible oils. *Analytica Chimica Acta*, *573*, 459–465. DOI: 10.1016/j.aca.2006.05.034 PMID: 17723561

Vora, L. K., Gholap, A. D., Jetha, K., Thakur, R. R. S., Solanki, H. K., & Chavda, V. P. (2023). Artificial intelligence in pharmaceutical technology and drug delivery design. *Pharmaceutics*, *15*(7), 1916. DOI: 10.3390/pharmaceutics15071916 PMID: 37514102

Vuran, F. A., & Yavuz, İ. (2021). Endüstri 4.0 ve 3 Boyutlu Yazıcıların Karşılaştırılması. *Mühendis ve Makine*, *62*(704), 584–600.

Wang, J. J., Jing, Y. Y., Zhang, C. F., & Zhao, J. H. (2009). Review on multi-criteria decision analysis aid in sustainable energy decision-making. *Renewable & Sustainable Energy Reviews*, *13*(9), 2263–2278. DOI: 10.1016/j.rser.2009.06.021

Wang, J., Zhu, H., Wang, S. H., & Zhang, Y. D. (2021). A review of deep learning on medical image analysis. *Mobile Networks and Applications*, *26*(6), 2343–2365.

Wang, K., Li, B., Tian, T., Zakuan, N., & Rani, P. (2023). Evaluate the drivers for digital transformation in higher education institutions in the era of industry 4.0 based on decision-making method. *Journal of Innovation & Knowledge*, *8*(3), 100364. DOI: 10.1016/j.jik.2023.100364

Wang, L., Wang, D., Ye, Z., & Xu, J. (2023). Engineering extracellular vesicles as delivery systems in therapeutic applications. *Advancement of Science*, *10*(17), 2300552. DOI: 10.1002/advs.202300552 PMID: 37080941

Wang, L., Wang, H., Huang, Y., Yan, B., Chang, Z., Liu, Z., Zhao, M., Cui, L., Song, J., & Li, F. (2022). Trends in the application of deep learning networks in medical image analysis: Evolution between 2012 and 2020. *European Journal of Radiology*, *146*, 110069. DOI: 10.1016/j.ejrad.2021.110069 PMID: 34847395

Wang, S., Wan, J., Li, D., & Zhang, C. (2016). Implementing Smart Factory of Industrie 4.0: An Outlook. *International Journal of Distributed Sensor Networks, 2016*(1), 3159805. DOI: 10.1155/2016/3159805

Wani, N. A., Kumar, R., & Bedi, J. (2024). DeepXplainer: An interpretable deep learning based approach for lung cancer detection using explainable artificial intelligence. *Computer Methods and Programs in Biomedicine, 243*, 107879. DOI: 10.1016/j.cmpb.2023.107879 PMID: 37897989

Wan, Y., Zhou, Q., Zhao, M., & Hou, T. (2023). Byproducts of sesame oil extraction: Composition, function, and comprehensive utilization. *Foods, 12*(12), 2383. DOI: 10.3390/foods12122383 PMID: 37372594

Waskom, M. L. (2021). Seaborn: Statistical data visualization. *Journal of Open Source Software, 6*(60), 3021. DOI: 10.21105/joss.03021

Weber, O. (2012). Environmental credit risk management in banks and financial service institutions. *Business Strategy and the Environment, 21*(4), 248–263. DOI: 10.1002/bse.737

Weber, O., Diaz, M., & Schwegler, R. (2014). Corporate social responsibility of the financial sector – strengths, weaknesses and the impact on sustainable development. *Sustainable Development (Bradford), 22*(5), 321–335. DOI: 10.1002/sd.1543

Weber, O., Scholz, R. W., & Michalik, G. (2010). Incorporating sustainability criteria into credit risk management. *Business Strategy and the Environment, 19*(1), 39–50. DOI: 10.1002/bse.636

Weber, R. P. (1990). *Basic Content Analysis*. Sage. DOI: 10.4135/9781412983488

Wei, X., Song, Y. Z., Mac Aodha, O., Wu, J., Peng, Y., Tang, J., Yang, J., & Belongie, S. (2021). Fine-grained image analysis with deep learning: A survey. *IEEE Transactions on Pattern Analysis and Machine Intelligence, 44*(12), 8927–8948. DOI: 10.1109/TPAMI.2021.3126648 PMID: 34752384

Wigh, D. S., Goodman, J. M., & Lapkin, A. A. (2022). A review of molecular representation in the age of machine learning. *Wiley Interdisciplinary Reviews. Computational Molecular Science, 12*(5), e1603. DOI: 10.1002/wcms.1603

Wikul, A., Damsud, T., Kataoka, K., & Phuwapraisirisan, P. (2012). (+)-Pinoresinol is a putative hypoglycemic agent in defatted sesame (*Sesamum indicum*) seeds though inhibiting α-glucosidase. *Bioorganic & Medicinal Chemistry Letters, 22*(16), 5215–5217. DOI: 10.1016/j.bmcl.2012.06.068 PMID: 22818971

Williams, A., & Cai, Y. (2024). Insights into Weighted Sum Sampling Approaches for Multi-Criteria Decision Making Problems. arXiv preprint arXiv:2410.03931.

Wilson, M. (2003). Corporate sustainability: what is it and where does it come from? *Ivey Business Journal*, *1*(2), 1–5.

Windt, K., Böse, F., & Philipp, T. (2008). Autonomy in production logistics: Identification, characterisation and application. *Robotics and Computer-integrated Manufacturing*, *24*(4), 572–578. DOI: 10.1016/j.rcim.2007.07.008

Winkelhaus, S., & Grosse, E. H. (2020a). Logistics 4.0: A systematic review towards a new logistics system. *International Journal of Production Research*, *58*(1), 18–43. DOI: 10.1080/00207543.2019.1612964

Winkelhaus, S., & Grosse, E. H. (2020b). Work characteristics in logistics 4.0: Conceptualization of a qualitative assessment in order picking. *IFAC-PapersOnLine*, *53*(2), 10609–10614. DOI: 10.1016/j.ifacol.2020.12.2816

Winter, S. R., Crouse, S. R., & Rice, S. (2021). The development of 'green' airports: Which factors influence willingness to pay for sustainability and intention to act? A structural and mediation model analysis. *Technology in Society*, *65*(March), 101576. DOI: 10.1016/j.techsoc.2021.101576

Woo, M., Han, S., & Song, Y. O. (2019). Sesame oil attenuates renal oxidative stress induced by a high fat diet. *Preventive Nutrition and Food Science*, *24*(2), 114–120. DOI: 10.3746/pnf.2019.24.2.114 PMID: 31328114

Wråke, M., Karlsson, K., Kofoed-Wiuff, A., Folsland Bolkesjø, T., Lindroos, T. J., Hagberg, M., ... & Koljonen, T. (2021). Nordic clean energy scenarios: Solutions for carbon neutrality.

Wu, W. W. (2008). Choosing Knowledge Management Strategies By Using A Combined ANP and DEMATEL Approach. *Expert Systems with Applications*, *35*(3), 828–835. DOI: 10.1016/j.eswa.2007.07.025

Xie, F., & Liang, C. Z. (2014). Research of internet of things based on cloud computing. *Applied Mechanics and Materials*, *443*, 589–593. . DOI: 10.4028/www.scientific.net/AMM.443.589

Xing, C., Yuan, X., Wu, X., Shao, X., Yuan, J., & Yan, W. (2019). Chemometric classification and quantification of sesame oil adulterated with other vegetable oils based on fatty acids composition by gas chromatography. *Lebensmittel-Wissenschaft + Technologie*, *108*, 437–445. DOI: 10.1016/j.lwt.2019.03.085

Xiong, X., Song, X., Kaygorodova, A., Ding, X., Guo, L., & Huang, J. (2023). Aviation and carbon emissions: Evidence from airport operations. *Journal of Air Transport Management, 109*(August 2022), 102383. DOI: 10.1016/j.jairtraman.2023.102383

Xu, M., David, J. M., & Kim, S. H. (2018). The fourth industrial revolution: Opportunities and challenges. International journal of financial research, 9(2), 90-95.

Xu, X., Lu, Y., Vogel-Heuser, B., & Wang, L. (2021). Industry 4.0 and Industry 5.0—Inception, conception and perception. *Journal of Manufacturing Systems*, *61*, 530–535. DOI: 10.1016/j.jmsy.2021.10.006

Yalman, İ. N., Koşaro lu, Ş. M., & Işik, Ö. (2023). 2000-2020 Döneminde Türkiye Ekonomisinin Makroekonomik Performansının Merec-Lopcow-Marcos Modeliyle Değerlendirilmesi. *Finans Politik & Ekonomik Yorumlar*, *60*(664), 57–86.

Yang, J. L., & Tzeng, G. H. (2011). An integrated MCDM technique combined with DEMATEL for a novel cluster-weighted with ANP method. *Expert Systems with Applications*, *38*(3), 1417–1424. DOI: 10.1016/j.eswa.2010.07.048

Yang, Y., & Stohl, C. (2020). The (in) congruence of measures of corporate social responsibility performance and stakeholder measures of corporate social responsibility reputation. *Corporate Social Responsibility and Environmental Management*, *27*(2), 969–981. DOI: 10.1002/csr.1859

Yan, J., Cai, J., Zhang, B., Wang, Y., Wong, D. F., & Siu, S. W. I. (2022). Recent progress in the discovery and design of antimicrobial peptides using traditional machine learning and deep learning. *Antibiotics (Basel, Switzerland)*, *11*(10), 1451. DOI: 10.3390/antibiotics11101451 PMID: 36290108

Yao, W., & Li, L. (2014). A New Regression Model: Modal Linear Regression. *Scandinavian Journal of Statistics, Theory and Applications*, *41*(3), 656–671. DOI: 10.1111/sjos.12054

Yapraklı, T. Ş., & Ünalan, M. (2017). Küresel lojistik performans endeksi ve Türkiye'deki son 10 yıllık lojistik performans analizi. *Atatürk Üniversitesi İktisadi ve İdari Bilimler Dergisi*, *31*(3), 589–606.

Yarlıkaş, S., & Öztürk, C. (2021). Bankacılık sektöründe kurumsal sürdürülebilirlik performansının Critic-Moora önem katsayısı yaklaşımı ile değerlendirilmesi. *Journal of Social and Humanities Sciences Research*, *8*(77), 3124–3136.

Yaşar, E., & Ünlü, M. (2023). Üniversitelerde Sürdürülebilirliğin İncelenmesi: LOPCOW ve MEREC Tabanlı CoCoSo Yöntemleriyle Çevreci Üniversitelerin Analizi. *İşletme Akademisi Dergisi, 4*(2), 125-142.

Yasım, Y. K. (2020). Endüstri 4.0: Çalışmanın Geleceği. *Kırklareli Üniversitesi İktisadi ve İdari Bilimler Fakültesi Dergisi, 9*(1), 47–64.

Yazdani, M., Wen, Z., Liao, H., Banaitis, A., & Turskis, Z. (2019). A grey combined compromise solution (CoCoSo-G) method for supplier selection in construction management. *Journal of Civil Engineering and Management, 25*(8), 858–874. DOI: 10.3846/jcem.2019.11309

Yazdani, M., Zarate, P., Kazimieras Zavadskas, E., & Turskis, Z. (2019). A combined compromise solution (CoCoSo) method for multi-criteria decision-making problems. *Management Decision, 57*(9), 2501–2519. DOI: 10.1108/MD-05-2017-0458

Yildirim, N., Gultekin, D., Hürses, C., & Akman, A. M. (2025). Exploring national digital transformation and Industry 4.0 policies through text mining: A comparative analysis including the Turkish case. *Journal of Science and Technology Policy Management, 16*(3), 555–590. DOI: 10.1108/JSTPM-07-2022-0107

Yıldız, A. (2018). Endüstri 4.0 ve Akıllı Fabrikalar. *Sakarya Üniversitesi Fen Bilimleri Enstitüsü Dergisi, 22*(2), 546–556. DOI: 10.16984/saufenbilder.321957

Yılmaz, Ü., & Duman, B. (2019). Lojistik 4.0 Kavramına Genel Bir Bakış: Geçmişten Bugüne Gelişim ve Değişimi. *Bilecik Şeyh Edebali Üniversitesi Sosyal Bilimler Enstitüsü Dergisi*, 186–200. DOI: 10.33905/bseusbed.465962

Yılmaz, R., & Koyuncu, D. T. (2020). Bir Dönüşümün Başlangıç Hikayesi: Kara Elmas ve Endüstri Devrimi. *Trakya Üniversitesi Sosyal Bilimler Dergisi, 22*(2), 1021–1042. DOI: 10.26468/trakyasobed.757598

Yong, Z. J., Bashir, M. J., Ng, C. A., Sethupathi, S., Lim, J. W., & Show, P. L. (2019). Sustainable waste-to-energy development in Malaysia: Appraisal of environmental, financial, and public issues related with energy recovery from municipal solid waste. *Processes (Basel, Switzerland), 7*(10), 676. DOI: 10.3390/pr7100676

You, Y., Lai, X., Pan, Y., Zheng, H., Vera, J., Liu, S., Deng, S., & Zhang, L. (2022). Artificial intelligence in cancer target identification and drug discovery. *Signal Transduction and Targeted Therapy, 7*(1), 156. DOI: 10.1038/s41392-022-00994-0 PMID: 35538061

Yuan, Y. Y., Wang, S. T., Wang, J. Z., Cheng, Q., Wu, X. J., & Kong, D. M. (2020). Rapid detection of the authenticity and adulteration of sesame oil using excitation-emission matrix fluorescence and chemometric methods. *Food Control, 112*, 107145. DOI: 10.1016/j.foodcont.2020.107145

Yucesan, M., & Gul, M. (2020). Hospital service quality evaluation: An integrated model based on pythagorean fuzzy AHP and fuzzy TOPSIS. *Soft Computing*, *24*(5), 3237–3255. DOI: 10.1007/s00500-019-04084-2

Yukihide, H. (2019). Japanese Science and Technology Basic Plan: A Perspective of Policy Process. *Xinli Kexue Jinzhan*, *1*(1), 24. DOI: 10.3724/SP.J.2096-5141.2019.0003

Yüksel, L. İ. Ç., & Arıkan, M. (2019). Sağlık sektöründe hizmet kalitesinin çok ölçütlü karar verme yöntemleri ile değerlendirilmesi: Ankara'da bir uygulama. *Uludağ Üniversitesi Mühendislik Fakültesi Dergisi*, *24*(3), 13–30. DOI: 10.17482/uumfd.450667

Yürüyen, A. A., Ulutaş, A., & Özdağoğlu, A. (2023). Lojistik işletmelerinin performansının bir hibrit ÇKKV modeli ile değerlendirilmesi. *Business & Management Studies: An International Journal*, *11*(3), 731–751.

Yu, Y., & Jiang, Y. (2024). *Understanding the Digital Revolution and Its Influences*. Springer Books. DOI: 10.1007/978-981-97-4939-3

Yu, Y., Wu, S., Yu, J., Xu, Y., Song, L., & Xu, W. (2022). A hybrid multi-criteria decision-making framework for offshore wind turbine selection: A case study in China. *Applied Energy*, *328*, 120173. DOI: 10.1016/j.apenergy.2022.120173

Zdrazil, B. (2025). Fifteen years of ChEMBL and its role in cheminformatics and drug discovery. *Journal of Cheminformatics*, *17*(1), 32. DOI: 10.1186/s13321-025-00963-z PMID: 40065463

Zdrazil, B., Felix, E., Hunter, F., Manners, E. J., Blackshaw, J., Corbett, S., de Veij, M., Ioannidis, H., Mendez Lopez, D., Mosquera, J. F., Magarinos, M. P., Bosc, N., Arcila, R., Kizilören, T., Gaulton, A., Bento, A. P., Adasme, M. F., Monecke, P., Landrum, G. A., & Leach, A. R. (2024). The ChEMBL Database in 2023: A Drug Discovery Platform Spanning Multiple Bioactivity Data Types and Time Periods. *Nucleic Acids Research*, *52*(D1), D1180–D1192. DOI: 10.1093/nar/gkad1004 PMID: 37933841

Zenat Mohamed, M. I.-G. (2024). Sustainable Supplier Selection using Neutrosophic Multi-Criteria Decision Making Methodology. *Sustainable Machine Intelligence Journal*.

Zeshui, X., & Cuiping, W. (1999). A consistency improving method in the analytic hierarchy process. *European Journal of Operational Research*, *116*(2), 443–449. DOI: 10.1016/S0377-2217(98)00109-X

Zhang, B., & Dafoe, A. (2019, January 9). Artificial intelligence: American attitudes and trends. *SSRN*. DOI: 10.2139/ssrn.3312874

Zhang, L., Shuai, Q., Li, P., Zhang, Q., Ma, F., Zhang, W., & Ding, X. (2016). Ion mobility spectrometry fingerprints: A rapid detection technology for adulteration of sesame oil. *Food Chemistry*, *192*, 60–66. DOI: 10.1016/j.foodchem.2015.06.096 PMID: 26304320

Zhang, N. (2018). Smart Logistics Path for Cyber-Physical Systems With Internet of Things. *IEEE Access: Practical Innovations, Open Solutions*, *6*, 70808–70819. DOI: 10.1109/ACCESS.2018.2879966

Zhang, S., Lee, C. K. M., Chan, H. K., Choy, K. L., & Wu, Z. (2015). Swarm intelligence applied in green logistics: A literature review. *Engineering Applications of Artificial Intelligence*, *37*, 154–169. DOI: 10.1016/j.engappai.2014.09.007

Zhang, Y., Chen, J.-H., Lin, Y., Chan, S., Zhou, J., Chow, D., Chang, P., Kwong, T., Yeh, D.-C., Wang, X., Parajuli, R., Mehta, R. S., Wang, M., & Su, M.-Y. (2021). Prediction of breast cancer molecular subtypes on DCE-MRI using convolutional neural network with transfer learning between two centers. *European Radiology*, *31*(4), 2559–2567. DOI: 10.1007/s00330-020-07274-x PMID: 33001309

Zhang, Z., Chen, Z., Zhang, J., Liu, Y., Chen, L., Yang, M., Osman, A. I., Farghali, M., Liu, E., Hassan, D., Ihara, I., Lu, K., Rooney, D. W., & Yap, P. S. (2024). Municipal solid waste management challenges in developing regions: A comprehensive review and future perspectives for Asia and Africa. *The Science of the Total Environment*, *930*, 172794. DOI: 10.1016/j.scitotenv.2024.172794 PMID: 38677421

Zhao, A. P., Li, S., Cao, Z., Hu, P. J. H., Wang, J., Xiang, Y., Xie, D., & Lu, X. (2024). AI for science: Predicting infectious diseases. *Journal of Safety Science and Resilience = An Quan Ke Xue Yu Ren Xing (Ying Wen)*, *5*(2), 130–146. DOI: 10.1016/j.jnlssr.2024.02.002

Zhao, B., Wang, N., Fu, Q., Yan, H. K., & Wu, N. (2019). Searching a site for a civil airport based on bird ecological conservation: An expert-based selection (Dalian, China). *Global Ecology and Conservation*, *20*, e00729. DOI: 10.1016/j.gecco.2019.e00729

Zhao, N., Hong, J., & Lau, K. H. (2023). Impact of supply chain digitalization on supply chain resilience and performance: A multi-mediation model. *International Journal of Production Economics*, *259*, 108817. DOI: 10.1016/j.ijpe.2023.108817 PMID: 36852136

Zhou, K., & Liu, T. ve Zhou, L. (2015, August). Industry 4.0: Towards future industrial opportunities and challenges. In 2015 12th International Conference on Fuzzy Systems and Knowledge Discovery (FSKD) (ss. 2147-2152). IEEE.

Zhou, F., Yu, K., Xie, W., Lyu, J., Zheng, Z., & Zhou, S. (2024). Digital Twin-Enabled Smart Maritime Logistics Management in the Context of Industry 5.0. *IEEE Access: Practical Innovations, Open Solutions*, *12*, 10920–10931. DOI: 10.1109/ACCESS.2024.3354838

Zhou, J., Gandomi, A. H., Chen, F., & Holzinger, A. (2021). Evaluating the quality of machine learning explanations: A survey on methods and metrics. *Electronics (Basel)*, *10*(5), 593. DOI: 10.3390/electronics10050593

Zhou, K., Liu, T., & Zhou, L. (2015). Industry 4.0: Towards Future Industrial Opportunities and Challenges. *12th International Conference on Fuzzy Systems and Knowledge Discovery (FSKD)*, 2147–2152. DOI: 10.1109/FSKD.2015.7382284

Zhou, Q., Huang, W., & Zhang, Y. (2011). Identifying Critical Success Factors in Emergency Management Using A Fuzzy DEMATEL method. *Safety Science*, *49*(2), 243–252. DOI: 10.1016/j.ssci.2010.08.005

Zhu, Y., Zeng, S., Lin, Z., & Ullah, K. (2023). Comprehensive evaluation and spatial-temporal differences analysis of China's inter-provincial doing business environment based on Entropy-CoCoSo method. *Frontiers in Environmental Science*, *10*, 1088064. DOI: 10.3389/fenvs.2022.1088064

Zine, S., Gharby, S., & El Hadek, M. (2013). Physicochemical characterization of Opuntia ficus-indica seed oil from Morocco. *Biosciences Biotechnology Research Asia*, *10*(1), 99–105. DOI: 10.13005/bbra/1099

Zong, Z., & Guan, Y. (2024). AI-driven intelligent data analytics and predictive analysis in Industry 4.0: Transforming knowledge, innovation, and efficiency. *Journal of the Knowledge Economy*, *16*(1), 1–40. DOI: 10.1007/s13132-024-02001-z

About the Contributors

Serkan Derici, who works at Nevşehir Hacı Bektaş Veli University, has scientific studies on digitalization, big data, machine learning, multi-criteria decision making and supply chain management. Currently working as Assistant Professor and Associate Dean at the same institution, Derici wrote his master's thesis on Service Quality with Fuzzy AHP and his PhD thesis on Supply Chain Management with Big Data and Machine Learning Algorithms. He teaches undergraduate and graduate courses on Operations Research, Production Management, Supply Chain Management, Statistics, Decision Making and Multi-Criteria Decision Making. Additionally, he serves as a journal editor and quality manager. In addition to his published works, he has published books on digital supply chain management and big data, digital transformations.

***

Hande EREN was born in Ankara in 1990. She completed her undergraduate studies at Süleyman Demirel University, Department of Business Administration in 2012. She graduated from Süleyman Demirel University, Department of Business Administration in 2016. She completed her PhD in Süleyman Demirel University, Department of Business Administration in 2020. EREN, who started working as a Dr. Lecturer at Cappadocia University in 2021, continues to work at Cappadocia University, Department of Management Information Systems. She has studies in various fields such as Multi-Criteria Decision Making Methods, Cluster Analysis, Logistics.

Emel Gelmez Ph.D., currently works as an Associate Professor in the Department of Business Administration, Faculty of Economics and Administrative Science, Selçuk University, Türkiye. Her areas of interest include production management, innovation management, technology management and supply chain management.

Mustafa Kayyali, an ardent advocate for excellence in higher education, driven by a relentless pursuit of quality, recognition, and innovation. My journey in academia started with a Master's in Quality Management and Evaluation in Higher Education from Universitat Oberta de Catalunya, followed by a Ph.D. in Quality Management from Azteca University. These academic pursuits have laid a strong foundation for my expertise in Accreditation, Quality Assurance, and Higher Education Rankings. As an entrepreneur, researcher, translator, and publisher, I am deeply involved in various facets of the academic world. My diverse interests encompass Management, Translation, Interpretation, and Academic consulting, contributing to a well-rounded understanding of the industry. Throughout my career, I have made significant contributions to academic literature, with more than 20 published papers and 7 book chapters to my name. Additionally, I take pride in having translated 5 books, bridging language gaps, and promoting knowledge exchange on a global scale. I am committed to fostering positive change in higher education and contributing to its continuous improvement.

Ahmet Bahadır Şimşek received his Ph.D. in 2019 from the Hacettepe University Department of Business Administration. He has been working as a lecturer/researcher at the Faculty of Health Sciences at Gumushane University since 2019. He gives lectures within the scope of operations research and conducts thesis consultancy in various undergraduate and graduate programs such as Health Management, Disaster Management and Business Administration. His research interest focuses on mathematical modeling applications in managerial decision-making and includes interdisciplinary collaboration.

Aybala Şimşek is an industrial engineer. Her PhD education is ongoing and she is also working as a researcher at Burdur Mehmet Akif Ersoy University. Her research interests are Optimisation, Operations Research, Multi-Criteria Decision Making, and Ergonomics and Human Factors Management.

Naga Sravanthi Puppala currently serves as an Assistant Professor at Vignan Deemed University in Guntur, bringing with her a decade of valuable teaching experience. Simultaneously, she is immersed in her Ph.D. pursuits at Puducherry Technological University since April 2021, with a specific focus on Blockchain and the Mining Pool Consensus. In her research, Naga Sravanthi underscores the critical need to enhance the security measures governing blockchain pool mining consensus for maintaining network integrity. Her approach involves implementing advanced cryptographic techniques, secure communication protocols, and robust authentication mechanisms. Emphasizing the ongoing importance of vigilance, she stresses the necessity of continuous monitoring and threat detection to promptly identify and address potential vulnerabilities. Additionally, Naga Sravanthi advocates for collaborative efforts among miners within the pool as a means to collectively strengthen overall security, thereby increasing the resilience of the consensus mechanism. Furthermore, she highlights the significance of regular updates and strict adherence to security best practices as integral components in creating a safer blockchain environment. By doing so, she aims to fortify defenses against potential threats, ensuring the reliability of the consensus process within the mining pool. Naga Sravanthi's research contributes to the broader goal of advancing secure and dependable Blockchain technologies.

Mustafa Uzgör is currently working at Muğla Sıtkı Koçman University as Assistant Professor. He has completed his bachelor's degree in aviation management at Erciyes University and his master's and doctoral degrees in aviation management at Anadolu University. He also has industry experience in the operational department at HAVAŞ Ground Handling Company. His research areas include airport and airline management, aviation policies, environmental management in aviation, and multi-criteria decision-making. His research interests focus on unmanned aerial vehicle transportation, urban air mobility, airport capacity, and operational management.

Index

A

B

C

D

E

F

G

H

www.ingramcontent.com/pod-product-compliance
Lightning Source LLC
LaVergne TN
LVHW080615300926
849162LV00005B/1162
* 9 7 9 8 3 6 9 3 8 7 8 9 4 *